SYSTEMATIC THEOLOGY

T0385631

Systematic Theology

Anthony C. Thiselton

Published in the United States of America in 2015 by
Wm. B. Eerdmans Publishing Co., Grand Rapids, Michigan

First published in Great Britain in 2015

Society for Promoting Christian Knowledge
36 Causton Street
London SW1P 4ST
www.spck.org.uk

British Library Cataloguing-in-Publication Data
A catalogue record for this book is available from the British Library

ISBN 978–0–281–07330–6
eBook ISBN 978–0–281–07331–3

First printed in Great Britain by Ashford Colour Press
Subsequently digitally printed in Great Britain

eBook by Graphicraft Limited, Hong Kong

Produced on paper from sustainable forests

Contents

Contents

Preface

I am grateful for the invitation from the publishers to write a systematic theology that would be "affordable" for students and ministers, as well as others, and would easily fit into a single volume. Financial resources especially for students and ministers are seldom plentiful, and there is a firm limit to what we can reasonably ask of them.

In addition to this, the best systematic theology to date is probably that of Wolfhart Pannenberg, but it is a three-volume work, and often requires rigorous, demanding, and detailed reading. John Webster's projected systematic theology is said to extend over five volumes; Sarah Coakley's projected work is said to extend to three or four volumes; and Robert Jenson's work extends to two volumes. At the opposite end of the spectrum, several one-volume works, useful as they are, have now become a little dated, and are in places too brief or overselective to comprehensively cover the subject.

The compromise for me has been the requirement to write in less detail than I should have chosen. This is why I have had to call the chapter on Christology, for example, "A Concise Christology," and several other chapters have been shortened to make room for necessary philosophical, exegetical, and linguistic concerns. Nevertheless, others have encouraged me to include several issues that might normally be included in a philosophy of religion, and to integrate these concerns fully with Christian theology. I have attempted to do this unreservedly and gladly.

I began university teaching fifty years ago, and this work has grown out of many years of teaching systematic theology (alongside New Testament, hermeneutics, and formerly philosophy of religion), and also from conversations and discussions with university colleagues and seminary and university students. To facilitate this volume as a teaching tool, I have divided it into fifteen chapters of relatively equal length, to match weekly sessions in an average-length semester. Major universities in the USA and UK seem to vary between fourteen- and sixteen-week semesters. Each chapter, in turn, contains five subsections of roughly equal length. Only chapter 5 is a little longer than the others, since it covers three very different areas.

One of the most distinctive contributions of this volume is perhaps that it offers as broad an interdisciplinary perspective as has been possible. Within this framework, I have included the traditional elements expected of any systematic theology: a theological understanding of God and creation; issues about the existence of God and atheism; a theology of humankind and misdirected desire and alienation; the work and person of Christ; the person and work of the Holy Spirit; the church, ministry, and sacraments; and two chapters on the last things. All these have careful foundations in biblical exegesis, and also interaction with major thinkers through the centuries and today. The latter is not simply for the purpose of recording a chronicle of what has occurred in history, but more especially to illustrate hermeneutical bridges and possibilities. I have tried to include personal assessments.

I am very grateful for an almost casual but crucial warning from Dr. Peter Forster, bishop of Chester, that too often systematic theologies are found to yield disappointingly few practical lessons for Christian discipleship, or to provide too little practical inspiration for Christian devotion. I have tried my utmost, while retaining academic integrity, also to be fully mindful of these utterly right Christian and practical concerns. I have punctuated theological discussions with practical observations about their relevance to the Christian life, while also seeking firmly to avoid any hint of a pious or homiletic tone.

Finally, I am extremely grateful to Miss Rowan Gillam-Hull for her careful and meticulous typing, and to Dr. Tim Hull for some fruitful theological conversations in recent years. As always, my wife, Rosemary, has given generously of her time and her support, including typing and suggestions for clarifications, without which this work could not have been written.

May 2015   ANTHONY C. THISELTON, Ph.D., D.D., F.B.A.
Emeritus Professor of Christian Theology,
University of Nottingham, UK

Abbreviations

AB	Anchor Bible
ANF	*Ante-Nicene Fathers.* Edited by A. Roberts and J. Donaldson. 10 vols. Grand Rapids: Eerdmans, 1993
BDAG	W. Bauer, F. W. Danker, A. F. Arndt, and F. W. Gingrich. *A Greek-English Lexicon of the New Testament and Other Early Christian Literature.* 3rd ed. Chicago: University of Chicago Press, 2000
BDB	F. Brown, S. R. Driver, and C. A. Briggs. *The New Hebrew and English Lexicon.* Lafayette, Ind.: Associated Publishers, 1980
BQT	*Basic Questions in Theology.* By W. Pannenberg. 3 vols. London: SCM, 1970-1973
CD	*Church Dogmatics.* By Karl Barth. Edited by G. W. Bromiley and T. F. Torrance. 14 vols. Edinburgh: T. & T. Clark, 1957-1975
CGTC	Cambridge Greek Testament Commentary
ConBNT	Coniectanea biblica: New Testament Series
ConBOT	Coniectanea biblica: Old Testament Series
CUP	Cambridge University Press
Grimm-Thayer	C. L. W. Grimm and J. H. Thayer. *A Greek-English Lexicon of the New Testament.* Edinburgh: T. & T. Clark, 1901
Hatch-Redpath	Edwin Hatch and Henry A. Redpath. *A Concordance to the Septuagint and Other Greek Versions of the Old Testament.* 2 vols. Athens: Beneficial Books, 1897
ICC	International Critical Commentary
IJSST	*International Journal for the Study of Systematic Theology*
JETS	*Journal of the Evangelical Theology Society*

Abbreviations

JGM	*Jesus — God and Man.* By W. Pannenberg. Philadelphia: Westminster; London: SCM, 1968
JPT	*Journal of Pentecostal Theology*
JPTSS	Journal of Pentecostal Theology Supplement Series
JR	*Journal of Religion*
JSNT	*Journal for the Study of the New Testament*
JSNTSup	Journal for the Study of the New Testament: Supplement Series
JTS	*Journal of Theological Studies*
Lampe	G. W. H. Lampe. *A Patristic Greek Lexicon.* Oxford: OUP, 1961
LCC	Library of Christian Classics
Moulton-Geden	W. F. Moulton and A. S. Geden. *A Concordance to the Greek Testament.* Edinburgh: T. & T. Clark, 1899
NCB	New Century Bible
NICNT	New International Commentary on the New Testament
NIDOTTE	*New International Dictionary of Old Testament Theology and Exegesis.* Edited by Willem A. VanGemeren. 5 vols. Carlisle: Paternoster, 1996
NIGTC	New International Greek Testament Commentary
NovTSupp	Supplements to Novum Testamentum
NPNF	*Nicene and Post-Nicene Fathers.* Series 1, 14 vols. Series 2, 14 vols.
NTS	*New Testament Studies*
OUP	Oxford University Press
PG	Patrologia Graeca. Edited by J.-P. Migne
PL	Patrologia Latina. Edited by J.-P. Migne
SBT	Studies in Biblical Theology
SJT	*Scottish Journal of Theology*
SNTSM	Studiorum Novi Testamenti Societas Monograph series
SNTSMS	Society for New Testament Studies Monograph Series
ST	*Systematic Theology.* By W. Pannenberg. 3 vols. Grand Rapids: Eerdmans, 1992-1998
Summa	*Summa Theologiae.* By Thomas Aquinas. 60 vols. Blackfriars ed. New York: McGraw-Hill; London: Blackfriars, 1964-1973
TDNT	*Theological Dictionary of the New Testament.* Edited by G. Kittel and G. Friedrich. 10 vols. Grand Rapids: Eerdmans, 1964-1976
TDOT	*Theological Dictionary of the Old Testament.* Edited by G. J. Botterweck, H. Ringgren, and H.-J. Fabry. 15 vols. Grand Rapids: Eerdmans, 1974-
WBC	Word Biblical Commentary
WUNT	Wissenschaftliche Untersuchungen zum Neuen Testament

CHAPTER I

Method and Truth

In many ways it is a pity to begin a volume with an introduction that largely concerns method. Many lecture series put people off because "introductions" seldom reach the heart of the subject in lively and practical ways. This volume aims at including practical and devotional material, while discussions of "method" do not usually encourage this. Indeed, Jeffrey Stout and Sarah Coakley have warned us about introductions that amount to mere "throat clearing."[1] Some readers may prefer to postpone this chapter until later, but the logical place for an introduction on method and truth is here at the beginning, and with good reason, especially for anyone who is skeptical about the value of the subject.

1. The Need for Coherence and Objections to "System"

Many seem to express reservations about the term "systematic theology." It has come to replace "dogmatic theology," which denotes Christian doctrine "received" (from Gk. *dechomai*) as "dogma" by the church. "Systematic theology" has become the conventional term for "doctrine" as used in universities and academia, as Webster notes.[2] It embraces material from biblical,

---

1. Sarah Coakley, *God, Sexuality, and the Self: An Essay "On the Trinity"* (Cambridge: CUP, 2013), 33.
2. John Webster, "Systematic Theology," in *The Oxford Handbook of Systematic Theology*, ed. John Webster, Kathryn Tanner, and Iain Torrance (Oxford: OUP, 2007), 1-15, especially 1-3.

historical, and philosophical sources. It further stresses a need for coherence or consistency.

It is this last point that gives rise to most criticism. First, "system" may suggest a static "freezing" of theology, whereas most theologians today would recognize its living, organic character. Second, "system" may suggest a finished and closed arrangement of doctrine, as if new insights from the Bible and experiences of God were excluded, let alone changes in the concepts used by a given culture. But theology is a living and growing subject. Webster and Coakley note this conventional objection, although Webster also mentions Colin Gunton's rejoinder that this simply anticipates provisionally an eschatological vision of the whole.[3] To suggest a practical point, there is something wrong if our belief system has remained exactly the same over long years. The work of the Holy Spirit, an increased understanding of Scripture, and sometimes even experiences of doubt, critical reflection, and refinement all contribute to growth.

One of the most famous (or notorious) attacks against system was mounted by Søren Kierkegaard (1813-1855), who is often called the father of existentialism. As a Christian he was deeply committed to truth as *lived* truth, not merely as an *abstract* system of thought. His concern was not simply for "*what* is said" but for "*how* it is said."[4] Christian truth is not simply *about* God, but is an address *from* God. Both Karl Barth and Rudolf Bultmann have stressed this from very different angles. Truth often emerges in a specific situation. It evokes obedience, not simply assent. Kierkegaard thought the classic advocate of abstract *system* in his lifetime was G. W. F. Hegel (1770-1831). Hegel attempted to capture "the Whole" of Reality in his philosophy. This "reality," which Kierkegaard dubbed "the System," seemed to him to be divorced from everyday life. He wrote with irony, "I should be as willing as the next man to fall down in worship before the System, if only I could manage to set eyes on it."[5] But, he reflects, in the end it is not quite finished. Thinkers who build great systems often only speculate about them. Human beings, even philosophers, are finite and even sinful, and they cannot grasp the whole of the infinite. They cannot view reality "eternally or theocentrically," even granted revelation from God. Kierkegaard concludes,

3. Webster, "Systematic Theology," 13, and Colin Gunton, *Intellect and Action: Elucidations on Christian Theology and the Life of Faith* (Edinburgh: T. & T. Clark, 2000), 36.

4. Søren Kierkegaard, *Concluding Unscientific Postscript to the Philosophical Fragments* (Princeton: Princeton University Press, 1941), 181.

5. Kierkegaard, *Concluding Unscientific Postscript,* 97.

"A logical system is possible. . . . An existential system (i.e., a real-life one) is impossible."[6]

Kierkegaard made a classic case for attacking system, and was not alone in expressing skepticism about attempts to embrace infinite truth within a closed system of propositions. As early as the fifth and sixth centuries Dionysius (known as Pseudo-Dionysius) argued the case for a theology of *negation*, in which God is said to surpass all human concepts and language. This is also known as apophatic theology. Since God is transcendent, he argued, God surpasses all analogies and human speech. This approach has regularly had a place in the mystical tradition.

In contemporary thinking Vladimir Lossky represents this partially in the Russian Orthodox tradition. Paul Tillich represents it partially in the Protestant tradition. Tillich argued that unless we use *symbols,* which transcend descriptive concepts, superlatives that we use to describe God can actually become diminutives when we place him within the horizons of human language.

A further turn in this debate was introduced by the dialectical theology of the early Barth and early Bultmann, and by the literary claims of Mikhail Bakhtin (1895-1975) about "polyphonic" discourse. Bakhtin argued, like Kierkegaard, that reality is too complex to be described in terms of a packaged "monologic" truth. He urged that Dostoevsky had shown that truth can be expressed only "by people collectively searching for the truth" in ongoing dialogue, or in a narrative in which several "voices" contributed different perspectives.[7] Dostoevsky's *The Brothers Karamazov* and the different speeches of the book of Job provide examples. The best example of all is the variety of books or "voices" that make up our Bible, or the biblical canon.

On the other hand, this represents only one side of the case. First of all, it does not seem entirely fair for Kierkegaard to call Hegel's system "a sort of world-historical absent-mindedness." Hegel takes history and human finitude seriously. In Hegel, system does not exclude radical historical finitude.

Second, as the modern theologian Eberhard Jüngel (b. 1934) points out, since Christ is the *Logos* or Word of God, it would seem odd to exclude words or speech from theology. Speech becomes possible through Jesus Christ. Admittedly, Jüngel advocates the importance of the use of metaphor.

6. Kierkegaard, *Concluding Unscientific Postscript,* 99 and 107.
7. M. Bakhtin, *Problems of Dostoevsky's Poetics* (Minneapolis: University of Minnesota Press, 1984), 110.

But he also argues that the incarnation of Jesus Christ makes God "thinkable" and "conceivable."[8]

Third, another modern theologian, Wolfhart Pannenberg (1928-2014), argues convincingly and forcefully for the importance of *coherence and system* in theology. The first of his arguments, especially in his *Theology and the Philosophy of Science,* is that truth must be "testable" according to the criteria used in the university and elsewhere.[9] With the possible exception of Tertullian, the overwhelming majority of Church Fathers from the second-century apologists onward were keen to show that Christian faith was rational, coherent, and defensible against unbelief and counterclaims. This does not blur the distinction between theology as based on the self-revelation of God and naturalistic thought.

A second argument, which Pannenberg endorses, concerns the compatibility of coherence and system with *historical* contexts of truth. Pannenberg uses the philosophical term "contingent" for our experience of the truth of God. In an admittedly complex statement, he observes, "The presence of the all-determining reality in a historical phenomenon can be investigated only through an analysis of the totality of meaning implicit in the phenomenon."[10] In other words, God manifested his acts in the history of Israel, and in the life, death, and resurrection of Jesus Christ.

These are *"contingent"* events in the sense that they can be understood in terms of historical context, as well as the sovereign revelation of God. Elsewhere Pannenberg comments, "History is the most comprehensive horizon of Christian theology."[11] Hence to interpret a historical event entails understanding it within the framework of God's purposes and saving acts throughout history. History is reality in its totality. It is not surprising, then, that Pannenberg speaks of "the anthropocentricity of the historical-critical procedure" when this seeks to exclude all references to a transcendent reality and theological purpose.[12]

A third argument, also endorsed by Pannenberg, is the role of *rational argumentation* in the quest for coherence and truth. He states with the utmost clarity: *"Argumentation and the operation of the Spirit are not in compe-*

---

8. Eberhard Jüngel, *God as the Mystery of the World* (Edinburgh: T. & T. Clark, 1983), 111, 220-21, 229.

9. Wolfhart Pannenberg, *Theology and the Philosophy of Science* (Philadelphia: Westminster, 1976), 7-14.

10. Pannenberg, *Theology,* 338.

11. Pannenberg, *BQT* 1:15.

12. Pannenberg, *BQT* 1:39.

tition with each other. In trusting in the Spirit, Paul in no way spared himself thinking and arguing."[13] Eminent Pauline scholars also underline that faith and reason are not in competition in Paul. Günther Bornkamm, for example, argues that Paul allots to reason and rationality "an exceedingly important role," and avoids such "revelation-speech" as "Thus says the Lord."[14] Stanley K. Stowers argues the same case more recently and in greater detail, as we shall note again.[15]

With the partial demise in philosophy of the oversimple "correspondence theory" of truth, the "coherence" approach has perhaps even greater force. This is even more the case in the light of criticisms of pragmatic theories of truth. What may appear "successful" in one period of history may be deemed a failure in another historical era. More than coherence may well be required. But coherence of some kind may be a *minimum requirement for truth.*

"Systematic theology," then, need not denote an abstract, static system divorced from life. The Old Testament stressed, and Gregory of Nyssa among others reemphasized, that God is primarily revealed through a continuous pattern of *acts* in the world. God's truth is not simply disclosed in terms of his "timeless" Being. The protests of Kierkegaard, Dionysius, Bakhtin, and others do not eliminate the need for systematic theology. They simply *qualify and shape* what would otherwise be too static and abstract a formulation of a system.

Finally and most importantly, the overriding reason why a complete system is impossible lies in our *eschatological* situation. We still await the final revelation of God's glory in Christ. Colin Gunton's allusion, noted above, does not overlook this. Only after the return or parousia of Christ, together with the Last Judgment, and the resurrection of the dead, will our knowledge and understanding become complete. As Paul states so clearly: "Now we see in a mirror, dimly, but then we shall see face to face. Now I know only in part; then I will know fully, even as I have been fully known" (1 Cor. 13:12).[16]

From the point of view of Christian discipleship, this means that Chris-

---

13. Pannenberg, *BQT* 2:35, italics mine.

14. Günther Bornkamm, "Faith and Reason in Paul," in *Early Christian Experience* (London: SCM, 1968), 35 and 36; cf. 29-46.

15. Stanley K. Stowers, "Paul on the Use and Abuse of Reason," in *Greeks, Romans, Christians,* ed. D. L. Balch and others (Minneapolis: Fortress, 1990), 253-86.

16. Direct quotations of the Bible in this book come from the New Revised Standard Version, unless otherwise noted.

tian faith demands a rational, faithful, and growing understanding of truth. This does not mean that we know the answer to every question, any more than the Bible is meant to be a comprehensive encyclopedia of all arts and sciences, or of all human knowledge. But this does *not* prevent us from asserting many truths with confidence, while we simultaneously suspend judgment on others. Our growth may even include times when we doubt certain claims. But further study and experience may later confirm them, and expand our horizons. We may have assurance of faith, while regarding Christian faith as a pilgrimage and adventure in which we constantly seek further understanding. This comes through prayer, study, Bible reading, and the fellowship of the whole wider church in time and place, as well as our local Christian community. Sarah Coakley is one of a number who have called for prayer, contemplation, participation in God, and discipline in any creative work of systematic theology.[17] We shall return to this point.

2. Truth, Theology, and Philosophy:
The New Testament and Earlier Church Fathers

Whether it immediately appeals to us or not, we cannot doubt that philosophical inquiry has played an important part in shaping Christian theology over the centuries. Some would say for better, others for worse; but it remains a fact. Even within the New Testament, Paul "argued" (Gk. *dielegeto*, Acts 17:17) with people at Athens, where "Epicurean and Stoic philosophers debated with him" (Gk. *syneballon autō*, 17:18). One clear example of the use of philosophical *terminology* and *concepts* in the New Testament comes from Hebrews. Hebrews 9:24 refers to "a sanctuary made by human hands, a mere copy of the true" (Gk. *antitypa tōn alēthinōn*). "Copy" would at once be understood by readers in the light of philosophical influences of the time. If they came from Alexandria, Plato's philosophical distinction between the true in the heavenly realm and its "copy" in the material realm would be in the air (Plato, *Republic* 7). Platonic thought was largely diffused even among those who did not know of Plato.

A close parallel occurs in Hebrews 8:5. Aaronic priests offer worship in a sanctuary that is a shadow (Gk. *hypodeigmati kai skiā*) of heavenly realities. But New Testament ideas are not philosophical alone. Alongside this philosophical terminology in Hebrews is *the eschatological and christological*

---

17. Coakley, *God, Sexuality, and the Self,* 13-27 and throughout.

content of the message. Numerous NT studies offer convincing *terminological* comparisons between Paul and Seneca, between Paul and Epictetus, and between Paul and the Stoics. But they also show radical differences of *substance.*

Admittedly Colossians 2:8 does seem to warn readers against "philosophy" (Gk. *philosophia*) and "human tradition." But the term "philosophy" here indicates the *kind* of philosophy that is addressed. According to J. D. G. Dunn and others, "It is in no way disparaging."[18] In fact, as Pogoloff indicates, ancient rhetoricians seem to receive greater criticism than serious-minded philosophers.[19]

Immediately after the New Testament period, the early Christian apologists composed *apologia,* which defended the *reasonableness* of the Christian faith for secular thinkers. They first presented petitions to the emperor Hadrian when he visited Athens in 124. Probably Quadratus and certainly Aristides used philosophical definitions of God. One such is: "He who made all things and sustains them, without beginning, eternal, immortal, without needs."[20]

One of the most widely known early apologists is Justin Martyr (c. 100– c. 165). He wrote his *First Apology* to the emperor Antoninus Pius (c. 155), and his *Second Apology* (c. 161) to the Roman Senate. His *Dialogue with Trypho* described his studies in philosophy. In this work Justin debated the charge of atheism brought against Christians (1.5.6). He argued that idolatry from a rational viewpoint is folly (1.9), as the book of Wisdom also stresses. He claimed that "We reasonably worship him (Christ)" as Son of the true God (1.13). In 1.69.1 Justin claimed that Plato borrowed from Moses the notion that God shaped shapeless matter to make the world. In 1.60 he engaged with Plato on the *Logos,* who is with God (*ANF* 1:182-83). In 1.13 he returned to the theme that service to God must be rational, for God is "eternal God, the Creator of all" (*ANF* 1:167). In the *Second Apology* Justin rejected the Stoic teaching on fate (2.7), but compared Christ with Socrates (2.10; *ANF* 1:191).

Theophilus, bishop of Antioch (late second century), addressed his apologetic to the emperor Commodus. He expounded the Christian doctrine of God as Creator, regarding the Spirit as life-giving power.[21] Book 1.13-26

18. James D. G. Dunn, *The Epistles to the Colossians and to Philemon,* NIGTC (Grand Rapids: Eerdmans, 1996), 147.

19. Stephen M. Pogoloff, *Logos and Sophia: The Rhetorical Situation in 1 Corinthians* (Atlanta: Scholars Press, 1992), 7-172.

20. Robert M. Grant, *Greek Apologists of the Second Century* (London: SCM, 1988), 37.

21. Theophilus, *To Autolycus* 2.13.

attacked the errors of philosophers who fail to understand the workings of providence, and the nature of the "soul." In 72-83 he expounded a doctrine of the true and invisible God. It used the language of Judaism and of Middle Platonism, as well as biblical passages.[22] Theophilus argued that belief in creation is more rational than the immoral myths of Greco-Roman polytheism.

In the writings of the Church Fathers, it is well known that Clement of Alexandria (c. 150–c. 215) regularly discussed philosophy and *gnōsis*. He argued that "Even if philosophy were useless . . . it is yet useful [in a different sense]."[23] He urged that we cannot condemn or criticize those of whom we have a mere hearsay acquaintance. But more than this, good philosophy can be "preparatory training" for faith. "Philosophy was a preparation, paving the way for him who is perfected in Christ."[24] It may be part of the path to truth. He cited Paul's debate in Acts 17 at the Areopagus, and argued that such philosophy as Plato's *Republic* reflected some part of the truth. "Philosophy, being the search for the truth, contributes to the comprehension of truth."[25] Yet he also warned readers that philosophy can lead to pride.[26] Christians need faith. Philosophy, he argued, contains a germ of truth, but usually it is only a half-truth. Plato taught that the chief good is assimilation to God; but the highest source of wisdom is the Bible.[27] Philosophy conveys only imperfect knowledge of God.[28]

The testimony of the Church Fathers, however, is not universally the same. It is well known that Tertullian (c. 150–c. 225), who was converted in middle life, attacked Greek philosophy, although he also borrowed from Stoic philosophy for his work on the human "soul." He famously asked, "What has Jerusalem to do with Athens, the Church with the Academy? . . . I have no use for a Stoic or a Platonic . . . dialectic Christianity."[29] Irenaeus (c. 130–c. 200) is often viewed as the earliest systematic theologian of the church. He regarded the role of philosophy as minimal in comparison with the apostolic tradition and the rule of faith.

By contrast, Origen (c. 185–c. 254) investigated the role of philosophical

22. See Grant, *Greek Apologists*, 165-74.

23. Clement of Alexandria, *Stromata* 1.2.1.

24. Clement of Alexandria, *Stromata* 1.5.1 and 7.

25. Clement of Alexandria, *Stromata* 1.19-20; *ANF* 2:323.

26. Clement of Alexandria, *Stromata* 2.2.

27. Clement of Alexandria, *Stromata* 2.22; *ANF* 2:375.

28. Clement of Alexandria, *Stromata* 6.17; *ANF* 2:515.

29. Tertullian, *Prescription against Heretics* 7; S. L. Greenslade, ed., *Early Latin Theology*, LCC (London: SCM, 1956), 36.

inquiry for Christians thoroughly, and understood the complexity of the problem. Philosophy, he wrote, cannot be indispensable, or Jesus would not have chosen simple fishermen.[30] But it can be valuable (i) as a tool for understanding the self, as Socrates had maintained; (ii) as a preparation for understanding Scripture; (iii) for defending and testing the faith; and (iv) for creation and ethics. To counter criticisms from nonintellectuals, Origen created an aphorism almost as famous as Tertullian's: it is "spoiling the Egyptians" of their gold and precious stones (Exod. 12:36), that is, making use of the best in pagan culture.[31]

Origen advocated a middle course between enthusiasm for philosophy and wise caution. If the philosophy is broadly "theistic," he emphasized its agreement about God as Creator and that God creates all things through the *Logos;* he also emphasized overlapping ethical principles and content. But he disagreed with those philosophies that deny the providence of God in daily affairs, substitute "the movements of the stars" or astrology for God's providence, and claim that "the world is eternal and will never have an end."[32] He rejected Epicurean logical atomism and Stoic materialism, but he found some value in Stoic teleology and notions of good and evil. He regarded some philosophical inquiries as helpful to Christians, but others as misleading. At its broadest, philosophy is the exercise of rational inquiry inherent in all humankind. This was most explicit in his counterarguments against Celsus. Like Clement, he encouraged the study of philosophy "as a preparation for the investigation of the deeper mysteries of the Bible."[33]

Adolf von Harnack (1851-1930) grossly exaggerated the outcome of the first four centuries when he described that period as "the union between Hellenism . . . and Christian teaching."[34] A cautious use of philosophy does not entail "hellenization," as a host of more recent scholars have shown. As Edwards writes in his more recent work, *Origen against Plato,* Origen and others remained faithful to the apostolic gospel but resorted to philosophy for particular purposes, such as the battle against Gnosticism.[35] The problem for Harnack was his suspicion of "doctrine" as Hellenistic, as well as his

30. Origen, *Against Celsus* 1.62.

31. Origen, *Philocalia* 13; cf. J. W. Trigg, *Origen: The Bible and Philosophy* (Atlanta: John Knox, 1983), 172.

32. Origen, *Homily on Genesis* 14.3.

33. Origen, *Against Celsus* 3.58.

34. Adolf von Harnack, *What Is Christianity?* (London: Benn, 1958), 159.

35. M. J. Edwards, *Origen against Plato* (Aldershot, UK, and Burlington, Vt.: Ashgate, 2002), 1-86 and 159-61.

trimming down the gospel of Jesus to the central principles of nineteenth-century liberalism.

This is not the place to examine each of the Church Fathers in turn. They often used philosophy with extreme caution. But Gregory of Nyssa (c. 330-395) and Augustine deserve mention here. Gregory preferred to speak of "the *activity* of the Father, the Son, and the Holy Spirit," rather than of their *"being."*[36] This represents a preference for biblical rather than philosophical concepts. Yet Gregory also used what might today be called a philosophical analysis of concepts to stress that "three," when used of the Holy Trinity, is in no way "numerical"; numbers apply to created objects or people, not to God.[37]

Augustine of Hippo (354-430) bequeathed a huge quantity of writings to the church. In his early life, before his conversion, he recalls that studies in philosophy helped him to discard "the tedious fables of the Manicheans."[38] Philosophy also helped him to begin to understand God's work as Creator.[39] Following Socrates, he even half-believed those philosophers who teach us to doubt everything. This certainly includes false doctrine.[40] On the other hand, he rejected the philosophy of Neoplatonism.[41] In his mature thought, many of the anti-Pelagian writings turn on the sovereignty of God and the nature of human freedom, which are perennial philosophical subjects. His work *City of God* is often described as a philosophy of history. Part of its purpose is to address the problem of evil and suffering in the wake of the Goths' sack of Rome, in 410.

On this subject, Augustine frequently defined evil as "privation of good" *(privatio boni,* or *deprivatio, defectus,* or *negatio):* "What is anything we call evil except the privation of good?"[42] His *Enchiridion* sets out the problem of evil (chaps. 3–4). Augustine argued, "There can be no evil where there is no good."[43] He asked, "Whence earthquakes?" He concluded that God is not the author of evil. Expounding what philosophers call "the principle of plenitude," he also addressed the variety and complexity of the world and human life, as Aquinas did after him. He admitted that this carries with it the by-product of "inequality." Yet Augustine affirmed, "All creation together

36. Gregory of Nyssa, *On the Trinity* 6.
37. Gregory of Nyssa, *On the Holy Spirit* 18 and 19, and *On "Not Three Gods."*
38. Augustine, *Confessions* 5.3.3.
39. Augustine, *Confessions* 5.3.5.
40. Augustine, *Confessions* 5.10.19.
41. Augustine, *Confessions* 7.1.1.
42. Augustine, *Enchiridion* 3.11.
43. Augustine, *Enchiridion* 4.13.

was better than the higher things alone."[44] He considered also the problem of animal pain.

These are all issues that likely would be classified today as philosophy of religion or philosophical theology, although earlier they might have come under systematic theology. Thomas Aquinas (1225-1274) certainly explored these problems in his *Summa Theologiae*. He was heavily reliant on Augustine, although also on Aristotle.[45]

Although the Enlightenment shifted much of the ground in theological inquiry, the questions that are usually discussed in the philosophy of religion continued to have a rightful place in systematic theology. Friedrich Schleiermacher (1768-1834) discussed freedom, the problem of evil, divine causality, and other such issues. In a very different tradition, Charles Hodge (1797-1878) discussed rationalism, knowledge of God, arguments for the existence of God, atheism and materialism, pantheism, and almost all of what today would come under philosophy of religion.[46]

In the late twentieth century and early twenty-first, these questions are often discussed by philosophers in separate volumes, even if systematic theologians may also consider these problems. Four Christian philosophers spring to mind. Theology would be infinitely impoverished if we lost the magnificent discussions by Alvin Plantinga (b. 1932), Nicholas Wolterstorff (also b. 1932), Richard Swinburne (b. 1934), and Vincent Brümmer (b. 1932). A number of systematic theologians tackle these philosophical problems head-on. Two key examples are Hans Küng (b. 1928), from the Catholic Church, and Wolfhart Pannenberg (1928-2014) from the Protestant Lutheran church. We could also add Karl Rahner (1904-1984) and many others.

There is a lesson for Christian discipleship in this otherwise apparently intellectualist perspective, as some may imagine it to be. It is usual for committed Christians to pray, meditate, and seek God's presence during study of the Bible. But usually the Church Fathers and thinkers such as the devout Anselm would not have been any more reluctant to bring their philosophical reading and inquiries before God in prayer and meditation. Nor would Luther have drawn a sharp dividing line between the sacred and what we nowadays regard as "secular." Theological inquiry is a mind-expanding activity. Even philosophical reflection within theology can honor God no less

---

44. Augustine, *Confessions* 7.13.

45. Aquinas, *Summa* I, qu. 48-49.

46. Charles Hodge, *Systematic Theology*, 3 vols. (Grand Rapids: Eerdmans, 1946), 1:34-60, 204-40, 241-334, and elsewhere.

than biblical studies in the quest for truth and hermeneutical resources. Although Sarah Coakley forms one notable exception, many have complained that systematic theology is not in every case notable for inspiring valuable devotional or prayer-related thoughts; rather, it appears dry and academic.

3. Truth, Theology, and the Bible in Historical Context

When we surveyed all too briefly the approach to truth and theology in the early Church Fathers, we noted a two-sided attitude to philosophy. Even Origen, one of the most hospitable to certain philosophical inquiries, insisted that the apostolic witness and the biblical writings embodied a "higher" and more fundamental truth. Justin valued Plato because he regarded him as compatible with Moses. Clement regarded philosophy as paving the way to an authentic gospel and truth-revealed theism. Philosophy, he said, is "a half-truth," which conveys only imperfect knowledge of God. Origen, too, compiled a careful list of positive and negative features, but saw it as no more than "a preparation for . . . the deeper mysteries of the Bible."[47]

Irenaeus based the "rule of faith" on biblical and apostolic tradition. The two Testaments, he insisted, provide a common foundation for the church in both East and West. Origen asserted, "The sacred books were not [merely] the compositions of men. . . . They were composed by inspiration of the Holy Spirit."[48] This is not the place to offer a full-scale comment on the authority of the Bible. We may, however, note that the earlier and supposedly "Catholic" notion of the Bible and tradition as two rival sources of authority has become thoroughly discredited, and is certainly not Catholic doctrine today. "Tradition" includes the biblical writings.[49]

Given that the Bible constitutes the primary source of Christian theology, the biblical material must be used and applied as it emerges from its specific historical context. Not every systematic theology has done this. In the nineteenth and first half of the twentieth century, some treated the Bible as a monochrome landscape. But *coherence and system did not exclude history and contingency.* From many examples of this argument, we may cite J. C. Beker's work *Paul the Apostle.* Beker argues that Paul "did not dash off casual and incidental observations to his various churches. . . . His letters are

---

47. Origen, *Against Celsus* 3.58.
48. Origen, *De principiis* 4.1.9.
49. Yves Congar, *The Meaning of Tradition* (San Francisco: Ignatius, 1964), 1-8, 9-33.

occasional, but not casual."[50] Yet they have a "coherent centre" and "doctrinal unity."[51] This is not an "abstraction" divorced from various specific audiences; Paul's message has a coherent center and message, but it is not a "frozen" system of concepts.

Even a few NT scholars and historians may seem to suggest this unwittingly. Thus F. C. Baur saw Paul wholly in terms of the anti-Judaistic debate, and dismissed as "un-Pauline" any letter that did not have this as a central theme. Albert Schweitzer selected "eschatological mysticism" as Paul's central theme. Nowadays a more constructive trend is to stress the diversity of Paul and the NT, but not to miss its unity altogether. Beker admits that each side should be modified in the light of the other.

Nowhere does this become more apparent than in the tragic gulf that divides many biblical specialists from many systematic theologians. I recall preparing a course in hermeneutics for an American seminary and receiving the following communication from the dean's office: "We are puzzled. Is this a course in New Testament, or in Systematic Theology, or in Philosophy? Which Department should announce it, enroll for it, and fund it?" In the event, it was the smallest class I have ever taught in America. A student explained, "We like to stick to our subject. It is scary to put down for an 'interdisciplinary' subject!"

The divide grows worse, at various levels. Many biblical scholars think in terms only of a historical particularity, and historically conditioned biblical passages. Many theologians, especially more than fifty years ago, tended to think in terms of a hierarchical or monochrome system. Philosophy and linguistics tended to become separate subjects, except in such cases as we have noted above.

Systematic theology, however, cannot be true to its biblical foundations unless it takes with utter seriousness *both exegesis of specific passages and the historical context and conditioning* of most biblical utterances. Biblical material has usually been spoken by a *particular biblical author* and directed to a *particular audience.* When A. H. Strong, for example, wrote on the humanity of Jesus Christ in his *Systematic Theology* of 1907, his first citation was John 8:40: "You are trying to kill me, a man *(anthrōpos)* who has told you the truth."[52] But this topic is not the immediate concern of this verse. F. Danker provides twenty-two nuances of the meaning of *anthrōpos* in English, and

50. J. Christiaan Beker, *Paul the Apostle: The Triumph of God in Life and Thought* (Edinburgh: T. & T. Clark, 1980), 23.

51. Beker, *Paul the Apostle,* 24 and 27.

52. A. H. Strong, *Systematic Theology,* 3 vols. in one (London: Pickering and Inglis, 1907, 1965), 673.

R. E. Brown and many commentators entitle this passage "Abraham and the Jews," not Christology.[53]

Today, however, there are overtures from both sides of the modern divide of disciplines. The Roman Catholic Church's Pontifical Biblical Commission, for example, produced the document *The Interpretation of the Bible in the Church,* in which it commends almost every kind of approach used in NT Protestant thought, including historical-critical and hermeneutical methods.[54] From the *biblical* side, Christopher Seitz in North America and Walter Moberly in England are both primarily OT scholars, and yet both show a lively interest in systematic theology for today. From the side of systematic theology, W. Pannenberg remained scrupulous in observing the particularities of virtually every biblical text he examined. Preachers will find this *liberating.* If theologians appear to treat the Bible as a monochrome source, preachers will soon exhaust each biblical doctrine as a "finished" reservoir of thought. Conversely, if biblical specialists remain locked into the ancient world alone, preachers may be tempted to find far-fetched "bridges" of their own making for today.

Part of the reason for Pannenberg's success was his enormous respect for *history* as the primary vehicle of God's self-revelation, including the historical nature of the Bible and revelation. He was influenced by Gerhard von Rad, and recognized that history "deals with once-occurring matters."[55] The biblical writings, he commented, do not deal with general truths but with "particular events, which they attest to be acts of God." He rejected the neo-Kantian and Bultmannian disjunction between fact and value.[56] Theology has to be universal, he argued, because it is "unavoidably bound up with the fact that it speaks of God . . . the creator of all things."[57] Yet universality does not exclude historical contingency. Israel experienced God in historical change itself, and "drew the whole of creation into history. History is reality in its totality."[58]

In terms of Christian discipleship, it may be unwise to specialize in one narrow area too early. I have never accepted a candidate for an M.A. or Ph.D. program who has not first completed a thorough and broad degree in biblical

53. BDAG 81-82; Raymond E. Brown, *The Gospel according to St. John,* 2 vols. (London: Chapman; New York: Doubleday, 1966), 361-63.

54. Joseph A. Fitzmyer, ed., *The Biblical Commission's Document "The Interpretation of the Bible in the Church"* (Rome: Pontifical Biblical Institute, 1994), 26.

55. Pannenberg, *BQT* 1:83.

56. Pannenberg, *BQT* 1:86.

57. Pannenberg, *BQT* 1:1.

58. Pannenberg, *BQT* 1:21.

studies and theology. The further danger is that of too prematurely affiliating oneself with conferences or "guilds" that reflect too narrow a mind-set. Undoubtedly this has to be offset against the pressures of passing time, if one hopes for an academic career or academic advancement. I well remember that my early lecturing duties involved both lecturing in New Testament and tutoring in philosophy of religion. The latter ignited a lifelong enthusiasm for Wittgenstein. Yet I also recall a colleague warning me against becoming a jack-of-all-trades. The price at the time was risking becoming a "slow developer," as in earlier years contemporaries seemed to be publishing far more than I. Yet in retrospect, I am glad that I had this discipline. Two requirements of Christian scholarship are patience and broad interests, as well as the more obvious ones of humility, self-involvement, and prayer. Judgments about truth require seeing the big picture from as many angles as possible.

4. A Further Aspect of Philosophy: Conceptual "Grammar"

Modern philosophy took a decisive turn with the later philosophy of Ludwig Wittgenstein (1889-1951) and his demand for *precision and particularity.* Even if such philosophers as G. W. F. Hegel and F. H. Bradley had been concerned with "the whole," Wittgenstein regarded "our craving for generality" as a mistaken "pre-occupation with the method of science." He called it "the contemptuous attitude towards the particular case."[59] We are seduced, he argued, by asking such general questions as "What is language?" and "*What is* a proposition?"[60] Rather, we should inquire about specific uses of language or propositions in the settings-in-life (or "language-games," to use his term) in which they occur.

These different settings, Wittgenstein pointed out, could radically change the concepts to which language and its use give currency. "What determines . . . our concepts . . . is the whole hurly-burly of human actions, the background against which we see any action."[61] He greatly illuminated such concepts as love, fear, expectation, and belief, many of which are basic to the language of faith (as well as providing cautionary words for our use of the Bible).

To select one example, Wittgenstein imagined a specific setting in life

59. Ludwig Wittgenstein, *The Blue and the Brown Books,* 2nd ed. (Oxford: Blackwell, 1969), 18.
60. Ludwig Wittgenstein, *Philosophical Investigations,* 2nd ed. (Oxford: Blackwell, 1958), sect. 92.
61. Ludwig Wittgenstein, *Zettel* (Oxford: Blackwell, 1967), sect. 567.

in which someone says, "I love you forever"; but then he adds: "Oh, it's all right; it's gone off now!" This might well happen in the case of *pain,* he urged, but *not love.* "Love is not a feeling. Love is put to the test, pain not. One does not say, 'That was true pain, or it would not have gone off so quickly.' "[62] We may have concluded that love is not an emotion also on the grounds of biblical exegesis, since love is commanded. But Wittgenstein brings out the further everyday significance of these concepts.

We should not minimize the significance of all this for the debates about religious language in the 1960s and 1970s. This approach released theists from the supposed problem suggested by A. J. Ayer (1910-1989) and logical positivism. This approach was seen to be no more than old-fashioned positivism or materialism, disguised as a new linguistic or logical theory. By sheer accident, not by design, Wittgenstein and Gilbert Ryle (1900-1976) showed that what had sometimes been regarded as conceptual conflicts in theology were in fact due to confusing different concepts from different settings in life, as if they were the same, or even gave rise to contradiction.

Ryle begins his set of essays entitled *Dilemmas* (1954) by pointing out: "There often arise quarrels between theories . . . which . . . seem to be irreconcilable with one another."[63] But often each line of thought or theory has arisen from a different setting-in-life and type of inquiry. "Sometimes thinkers are at loggerheads with one another, not because their propositions do conflict, but because . . . they are talking at cross-purposes with one another" (1). He proceeds to discuss some six examples of this (11).

The most famous of these concerns Zeno's paradox about Achilles and the tortoise. Achilles begins a race against a tortoise well behind the tortoise. But because he is faster, common sense dictates that Achilles will easily overtake the tortoise. But if a mathematician or logician were to measure the progress of each runner by separate stages one-at-a-time, it may seem as if Achilles can never catch up to the tortoise. This is because Achilles has to reach "the tortoise's starting-line, — by which time the tortoise has advanced *a little way ahead of this line. . . .* Ahead of each lead that Achilles makes up, *there always remains a further . . . lead* for him still to make up" (36). In terms of *this* division of the running track, Achilles *can never* overtake the tortoise. In terms of a division *dictated by common sense,* Achilles will *certainly overtake* the tortoise (38-52, italics mine).

62. Wittgenstein, *Zettel,* sect. 504.
63. Gilbert Ryle, *Dilemmas* (Cambridge: CUP, 1954), 1. The page numbers placed in the text refer to this work.

In my book *Life after Death,* I drew on Ryle's logical clarification of concepts to show, for example, that Paul could teach, *without contradiction, both* immediate entry into the presence of Christ at death *and* a waiting period until Christ's return, or his parousia. I compared this noncontradiction with two consistent ways of approaching Christmas. First, we could tell a child, "The sooner you fall asleep, the sooner Christmas will come." Second, we could make room simultaneously for a period in which adults prepare for Christmas morning, and even go to a church service.[64] Neither approach would constitute a lie, or contradict the other.

Wittgenstein's legacy also paved the way for an important *dispositional* account of belief, as classically expressed in H. H. Price, *Belief.*[65] Wittgenstein observes, "Believing . . . is a kind of disposition of the believing person. This is shown to me . . . by (someone's) behaviour."[66] Does a believer cease to believe when he or she falls asleep? Clearly belief is not just a conscious "mental state." Wittgenstein asserts, "One hardly ever says that one has believed . . . uninterruptedly since yesterday."[67] Wittgenstein and Price agree that *belief* is bound up with *action* and regular *behavior.* It is logically impossible to declare, "I believe it, but it is false," because "I believe" is what philosophers since Austin have called "a performative": it is commissive; it *acts* when it *is spoken as a pledge.* Price explains this in terms of belief: "He (the believer) is taking a stand. . . . 'I believe' has what J. L. Austin calls a performatory character."[68]

To declare "I believe," Price urges, is "equivalent to a series of conditional statements describing what he (the believer) *would* be likely to say or do or feel if such and such circumstance were to arise."[69] Belief *commits* the believer to *act* in certain ways. He would have a disposition to affirm the belief if it was denied, and to respond with thanksgiving if the believer was restored to health after illness. This has profound consequences for the nature of belief in Christian theology.

Price's chapter on *half-belief* prompted me to preach a particular sermon on Jonah. Price defines half-belief as *acting as* a believer "on some occasions" but as an unbeliever "on other occasions."[70] That is what Jonah did. Facing an

---

64. Anthony C. Thiselton, *Life after Death: A New Approach to the Last Things* (Grand Rapids: Eerdmans, 2012); otherwise entitled *The Last Things* (London: SPCK, 2012), 68-88.

65. H. H. Price, *Belief* (New York: Humanities Press; London: Allen and Unwin, 1969).

66. Wittgenstein, *Investigations* II. x, 191.

67. Wittgenstein, *Zettel*, sect. 85.

68. Price, *Belief,* 30.

69. Price, *Belief,* 20.

70. Price, *Belief,* 305.

audience of unbelieving sailors, he exclaims, "I am a Hebrew. . . . I worship the LORD, the God of heaven, who made the sea and the dry land" (Jon. 1:9). But faced with a commission from God, he "set out to flee to Tarshish from the presence of the LORD" (1:3). From the stomach of the fish, he confessed his faith in a style reminiscent of the rhythmic Hebrew poetry of the Psalms:

> "I called to the LORD out of my distress,
>   and he answered me. . . .
> How shall I look again
>   upon your holy temple?" (Jon. 2:2, 4)

Faced with the repentance of Nineveh and its king, Jonah sulked, "sat in ashes," and said, "That is why I fled to Tarshish . . . , for I knew that you are a gracious God" (3:6; 4:2). Confronted with the destruction of his protective bush, he declared, "It is better for me to die than to live" (4:8). The book ends with God's question: "You are concerned about the bush . . . should I not be concerned about Nineveh, that great city, in which there are more than a hundred and twenty thousand persons . . . and also many animals?" (4:10-11). Belief that operates only in some circumstances and not in others proves to be no more than "half-belief." It does not share the concern of God for his creation. Belief proves that it is genuine by *consistent action,* as James insists in his epistle.

I have tried on several occasions to show that conceptual elucidation remains of fundamental importance to the doctrines of the Christian faith. I have applied this, for example, to justification by grace through faith in *The Two Horizons* (1980).[71] To be righteous and still a sinner is no contradiction. We are sinners as God sees us within the framework of *cause-effect history and the Law;* God judges us righteous within the framework of *future eschatology,* to which judgment belongs, and our life "in Christ" by grace.

5. Speech-Acts, Hermeneutics, Sociology, and Literary Theory

(i) *Speech Acts.* John L. Austin (1911-1960), together with John R. Searle and F. Recanati, brought forward a new stage in the philosophy of language, which has proved to be fruitful for theology. It concerns performative utter-

---

71. Anthony C. Thiselton, *The Two Horizons: New Testament Hermeneutics and Philosophical Description* (Grand Rapids: Eerdmans; Carlisle: Paternoster, 1980), 415-27.

ances in Austin and eventually *speech-act theory* in Searle and others. Austin defined an "illocutionary act" as "the performance of an act *in* saying something" (i.e., in the very saying of the utterance), in contrast to an act *of* saying something.[72] Classic examples include "I do" in a marriage service, where the words constitute an *act* of marrying, in appropriate circumstances. Similarly "I appoint" *performs an action* that changes the status of the addressee, again in appropriate circumstances. The verb does not have to be a first-person indicative; it may be replaced by one-word utterances, such as "Guilty!" when spoken on behalf of a jury.

It is incorrect to claim, as some theologians do, that the utterance and its context are noncognitive. Austin writes, "For a certain performative utterance to be happy, certain statements have *to be true.*"[73] Continental theologians have in many cases called language "performative" when no illocutions, conventions, or regularities are involved. The equivalent in theology to conventions in secular society may well be the covenant.

Austin gives a number of examples of conditions for operative performatives that have been incomplete or broken. He imagines an appointed person (in his example, an archbishop) declaring, "I open this library," just when "the key snaps in the lock."[74] "I will," he suggests, in the context of marriage, is abortive if the speaker is already married.

We can see the seriousness of this issue for theology especially if we recall William Tyndale's anticipation of speech acts at the Reformation. Tyndale was greatly influenced by his near contemporary, Luther, and shared his belief that the Word of God in the Bible made *promises*. Barth also rightly promotes this view. *A promise is a paradigm case of a speech act.* It *commits* the speaker to act in certain ways.

Tyndale argued that many such speech acts are performed by the Word of God: it "conveys promises . . . it makes a man's heart glad . . . it proclaims joyful tidings."[75] In the dozen or so pages that follow this, he cited some eighteen speech acts: promising, naming, appointing, giving, condemning, cursing, killing, wounding, blessing, healing, curing, awaking, and so on. All these are actions expressed in speech, usually as illocutions. This performative dimension plays a positive part in the context of the authority and function of the Bible in life.

72. John L. Austin, *How to Do Things with Words* (Oxford: Clarendon, 1962), 99.

73. Austin, *How to Do Things,* 45.

74. Austin, *How to Do Things,* 37.

75. William Tyndale, *A Pathway into the Holy Scripture* (Cambridge: CUP/Parker Society, 1848), 8-9; cf. 7-29.

19

Austin's work has been developed, modified, and overtaken by John R. Searle, first in *Speech Acts* (1969), and then in *Expression and Meaning: Studies in the Theory of Speech Acts* (1979). He explains that actions involved in speech acts may "get the world to match the words" of the performative utterance. This contrasts with descriptive propositions that "get the words . . . to match the world," by seeking to represent or reflect reality or the world.[76]

To explain this, Searle borrows an analogy, which apparently came from the philosopher G. E. M. Anscombe. This suggests that a shopping list can *actively cause* "the world" of the *kitchen* to *match* that of *the store*. It is like a performative *"directive"* (Searle's term). On the other hand, if a store detective has only to give a *report* about the conduct of a shopper, his report simply reflects the world by stating facts. He uses *words* to *match* the *"world"* *of the store* as it is.

The theological applications of this principle are numerous. My first attempt to point out some of these focused on *Jesus' pronouncement of forgiveness of sins.* In Matthew 9:2, when Jesus pronounces "Your sins are forgiven," the operative validity of the absolution depends on the *status and authority of the speaker.* Hence to recognize Jesus' use of a speech act implies a *christological status,* as even his Pharisaic critics observed. He is acting in the place of God.[77]

When he makes a *covenant promise,* God chooses to limit his own freedom. He is *committed* to what he has promised, and cannot and will not go back on his promise. The speech act reveals how the sovereign God may be "limited" or constrained by his own speech acts, without compromising his sovereignty. I have considered the varied implications of speech acts for theology in *Thiselton on Hermeneutics* (2006), and Richard Briggs has also done this in his *Words in Action.*[78] The work of expounding the impact of speech-act theory for theology continues, with fruitful results for systematic theology as well as biblical studies.[79]

---

76. John R. Searle, *Expression and Meaning: Studies in the Theory of Speech Acts* (Cambridge: CUP, 1979), 3.

77. Anthony C. Thiselton, *New Horizons in Hermeneutics* (Grand Rapids: Zondervan, 1992, 2012), 295-300 and 597-600; reprinted in part in *Thiselton on Hermeneutics* (Grand Rapids: Eerdmans; Aldershot, UK: Ashgate, 2006), 75-98.

78. *Thiselton on Hermeneutics,* 51-150; and Richard S. Briggs, *Words in Action: Speech Act Theory and Biblical Interpretation* (Edinburgh and New York: T. & T. Clark, 2001), 147-298.

79. See further, Roger Lundin, Clarence Walhout, and Anthony C. Thiselton, *The Promise of Hermeneutics* (Grand Rapids: Eerdmans, 1999); Nicholas Wolterstorff, *Divine Discourse: Philosophical Reflections on the Claim That God Speaks* (Cambridge: CUP, 1995);

(ii) *Hermeneutics.* Even more important than speech-act theory, *hermeneutics constitutes a key part of systematic theology.* Indeed, it is vital not only for *biblical* interpretation in the light of today; it also rescues *historical* theology from becoming a tedious record of past successes and failures, or even mere facts of the past. We have already noted that *hermeneutics* also constitutes an *interdisciplinary* study.

The recovery of this discipline from the mid–twentieth century onward was partly due to an increased awareness of *"preunderstanding"* and the *hermeneutical circle.* All the major writers on the subject have stressed this, including Friedrich Schleiermacher, Martin Heidegger, Rudolf Bultmann, Hans-Georg Gadamer, and Paul Ricoeur.

The notion of the interpreter's preliminary understanding was at first severely neglected or underrated in biblical scholarship. But recently it has become exaggerated and overpressed, especially in reader-response theory, liberation theology, and feminist hermeneutics. It is sometimes almost as if the prior interests of interpreters and readers began to eclipse the immediate contextual concerns of the biblical writers. My first major work, *The Two Horizons,* was intended to show that the *communicative action* of biblical texts engaged *the horizons of the reader as well as those of the text.* But sometimes this lesson has been overlearned. Extreme examples of reader-response theory illustrate this. In many nontheological or "literary" theorists, such as Stanley Fish and David Bleich, the text of an author has been regarded as less authoritative or definitive than that of the present community of readers.

Preunderstanding, however, amounts to only *one* of many important emphases. Listening with sensitivity to the *"other"* is vital, whether this be the text or another reader, such as one whom a pastor or preacher addresses. W. Dilthey called this bond of mutual understanding *(Einverständnis)* "empathy." In *New Horizons in Hermeneutics* (1992) I entitled the last two chapters "The Hermeneutics of Pastoral Theology." In this book as a whole, I tried

---

Donald D. Evans, *The Logic of Self-Involvement* (London: SCM, 1963); Kevin Vanhoozer, *Is There a Meaning in This Text? The Bible, the Reader, and the Morality of Literary Knowledge* (Grand Rapids: Zondervan, 1998), 208-14; Kevin Vanhoozer, *The Drama of Doctrine: A Canonical-Linguistic Approach to Christian Theology* (Louisville: Westminster John Knox, 2005); Terence W. Tilley, *The Evils of Theodicy* (Washington, D.C.: Georgetown University Press, 1991); Dieter Neufeld, *Re-conceiving Texts as Speech-Acts: An Analysis of 1 John* (Leiden: Brill, 1994); Alexandra R. Brown, *The Cross and Human Transformation: Paul's Apocalyptic Word in 1 Corinthians* (Minneapolis: Fortress, 1995); and Jim W. Adams, *The Performative Nature and Function of Isaiah 40–55* (New York and London: T. & T. Clark, 2006).

to match specific and varied hermeneutical procedures to specific types of texts and audiences. *New Horizons in Hermeneutics,* however, concerned only *biblical* texts. I had not yet examined the role of *doctrine and tradition* in hermeneutics. Hence later I produced *The Hermeneutics of Doctrine* (2007) to try to address this problem.[80] It sought to bring together the two dimensions that we have considered, *coherence* and historical *contingency.* I began with an exploration of Gadamer's contrast between "questions" and free-floating "problems." *Questions* arise from specific *historical and pastoral contexts. Problems* readily became *free-flowing fixed problems.* This is one reason why so many find a gap between systematic theology, biblical studies, and everyday pastoral problems.

None of the biblical writings, or perhaps very few, are free-floating treatises. To select an example from one area, namely, the Holy Trinity, A. W. Wainwright, *The Trinity in the New Testament* (1962), has relatively little pastoral material; whereas Paul S. Fiddes, *Participating in God: A Pastoral Doctrine of the Trinity* (2000), offers some rare examples of making pastoral connections with doctrine.[81] Gadamer is not the only exponent of the value of context-related *questions:* R. G. Collingwood, F. Waismann, and M. Bakhtin also deserve note.

I also argued that a hermeneutical approach must involve *conversation or dialogue,* in contrast to a monologic declaration of one person's opinion, and also be related to settings in human life. Our three ecumenical creeds are not monologic, because they were formulated by communities (often of bishops), and were formulated to meet specific situations. Both the lived-out ministry of the incarnation and a dispositional account of belief are relevant. If a doctrine is to be believed, it must have *consequences in conduct and life,* or else it amounts to little more than theoretical assertion, as James insists in his epistle.

(iii) *Sociology.* The important relation of belief to *human life and society* suggests that *sociology* cannot or should not be ignored. First, this area naturally arises from within hermeneutics in two ways. One is from a study of how people have interpreted and used biblical and theological texts down the centuries. This is usually called "reception history," with its theoretical basis in reception theory. Hans Robert Jauss was one pioneer in his literary

80. Anthony C. Thiselton, *The Hermeneutics of Doctrine* (Grand Rapids: Eerdmans, 2007).

81. Paul S. Fiddes, *Participating in God: A Pastoral Doctrine of the Trinity* (Louisville: Westminster John Knox, 2000).

theory, but in biblical studies Brevard Childs and Ulrich Luz, among others, have become noted practitioners. Wiley-Blackwell's series of commentaries "through the centuries," edited by Chris Rowland and Judith Kovacs (on the NT) and John Sawyer and David Gunn (on the OT), provide a number of examples. (I contributed the commentary on 1 and 2 Thessalonians in this series in 2011.) A second direction arose from what I termed "sociocritical" hermeneutics when I discussed the interaction between hermeneutics and sociology in Jürgen Habermas and Karl-Otto Apel. They lead an established school of sociological thought, and Habermas explores the basic hermeneutical factor of "human interests" that the interpreter brings to the text.[82] On top of this, active responses to the biblical text are also explored in what is called "reader-response" hermeneutics, to which we referred under hermeneutics above.

A second, quite different direction of relevance is passionately advocated by Sarah Coakley. She writes: "I first came to understand the under-appreciated *theological* acuity of his (Troeltsch's) *The Social Teaching of the Christian Churches*."[83] She regularly pleads also for a broader integration with sociological aspects of human life as a whole. Theology should never be shut off from life.

(iv) *Literary Theory.* In recent years, as hermeneutics has developed, two further areas have emerged increasingly. These relate to *linguistics* and *literary theory.* Linguistics does not simply concern lexicography and grammar. Creative hermeneutics has appropriated the two areas of *narrative* and *metaphor* or symbol, which feature in *literary theory* as well as in linguistics.

Narrative has too often been treated as a simple *descriptive* or historical *report.* This has often had disastrous consequences. To be sure, *some* narratives are descriptive reports, although even these carry with them interpretations of a theological nature. In much Pentecostal theology, for example, it is usually simply *assumed, not argued,* whatever biblical scholars have said, that the narrative of Acts provides a straightforward report that serves as a model to be replicated today. But alternative understandings are possible. Might not Luke have wished to show that within the NT era, the church developed *beyond* its earliest beginnings? As many have urged, Luke may have portrayed an early, unrepeatable era. Only a small and special class of narratives fall under the heading of "descriptive report." Paul Ricoeur underlines

82. Thiselton, *New Horizons in Hermeneutics,* 379-410; Jürgen Habermas, *Knowledge and Human Interests* (London: Heinemann, 1978) and *The Theory of Communicative Action,* 2 vols. (Cambridge: Polity Press, 1984, 1987); and Karl-Otto Apel, *Understanding and Explanation: A Transcendental-Pragmatic Perspective* (Cambridge: MIT Press, 1984).

83. Coakley, *God, Sexuality, and the Self,* 186; more broadly, cf. 1-2 and 186-88.

this.[84] Clearly such features as speed of narration, flashbacks, characters, and plot serve to make additional points, which (to use Ricoeur's term) refigure narrative so that it is no longer a mere chronological description.

Flashbacks have been used for several centuries. If Charles Dickens had not hidden the identity of Pip's benefactor until the end of the story, the tension and plot of *Great Expectations* would have disintegrated. Clearly Mark, to cite a *biblical* example, uses three types of tempo in his narrative.[85] Until Mark 8:29 the narrative moves ahead at breakneck speed, often using the Greek *euthys,* usually meaning "at once." It occurs at least thirty-two times before Peter's confession. Then the narrative slows to medium pace. Finally, the events of the passion are portrayed in slow motion. Is this to falsify the report? Not at all! It is to show that the cross and passion are what give meaning to the entire narrative. Several biblical scholars have made this point.

Much anxiety might have been saved if we discerned purposes other than those we assumed unthinkingly in the Gospels. We might cite the sequence of the messianic temptations, or that of the cleansing of the temple. On the OT, Robert Alter has traced the different purposes entailed in the two narratives of God's anointing of David. He compares the short narrative of 1 Samuel 16:4-13, which focuses on God's decree, with the longer narrative of 1 Samuel 16:14–2 Samuel 5:5. He dismisses the notion of a clumsy editor putting together two incompatible sources, in favor of the well-known narrative and literary resource of "point of view." The shorter narrative, he concludes, recounts David's anointing from the point of view of God's purpose; the longer narrative recounts it from the point of view of the "brawling chaos" of human life and situations, such as David's battle with Goliath.[86]

Recently Walter Moberly, a significant and respected OT scholar who also has a concern for current Christian theology, has criticized John Carroll, another respected OT scholar, for exaggerating polemically "contradictions" within the Bible.[87] On the other hand, he warns us not to expect smooth "explanations" of all tensions among our many biblical witnesses within the canon. Some, for example, may use paradox. He rightly discusses faith and perplexity, in which the many "voices" in the OT may not always seem

84. Paul Ricoeur, *Time and Narrative,* 3 vols. (Chicago: University of Chicago Press, 1984-1988).

85. Wesley A. Kort, *Story, Text, and Scripture: Literary Interests in Biblical Narrative* (University Park: Pennsylvania State University Press, 1988), 44 and throughout.

86. Robert Alter, *The Art of Biblical Narrative* (New York: Basic Books, 1981), 147-53.

87. R. W. L. Moberly, *Old Testament Theology* (Grand Rapids: Baker Academic, 2013), 111-16.

"sweetly reasonable."[88] Doubt and perplexity can sometimes stimulate fresh inquiry and growth. In our opening section on coherence we referred to the important work of Bakhtin on polyphonic voices.

All these features are familiar in narrative theory and literary criticism. Another important resource in narrative theory is *"defamiliarization."* This is employed to present the apparently overfamiliar story in fresh or surprising ways. Many preachers would long to use such resources for a regular Bible-reading congregation, and this is part of what can be learned from hermeneutics and narrative theory.

Reader-response theory also presents a narrative or event in such a way as to provoke readers into *active* response. This is another tool that many preachers need, and that we cited under hermeneutics. A narrative or parable may be left deliberately "incomplete," so that the reader is provoked, enticed, or simply invited to fill in "gaps" from what the reader already knows. One of the first major theorists was Wolfgang Iser. His approach may be well known to some ministers and pastors. He writes, "The text represents a potential effect that is realized in the reading process."[89] In other words, it may do only half the job if we provide a Bible in every pew, unless readers *actualize* the potential communication of biblical material for themselves. Robert Fowler suggested the possible example from two feeding miracles in the Gospel of Mark.[90] In Mark 6 Jesus feeds five thousand. Two chapters later, Jesus is confronted with a crowd of four thousand. Yet the disciples apparently ask, "How can one feed these people with bread here in the desert?" (Mark 8:4). Fowler suggests that the aim of the two narratives for Mark is to distance the readers' Christology from that of the disciples. It provokes the question: "Could they really be *that* devoid of understanding who Jesus is?"

Another feature in narrative theory is *narrative world.* Millions are drawn into the "world" of the serial story or soap opera every evening. They see as the *participants* see, and feel what they feel. Thus readers may enter the "world" of the workers in the parable of the laborers in the vineyard (Matt. 20:1-16). They share the reaction of the majority: "That's not fair!" Hence they are shocked by the employer's response: Is it really not fair? Everyone has a full day's wage. In theological terms, *grace and generosity eclipse justice.* The teaching of Jesus is close to that of Paul. The NT scholar

88. Moberly, *Old Testament Theology,* 211-42.

89. Wolfgang Iser, *The Act of Reading: A Theory of Aesthetic Response* (Baltimore: Johns Hopkins University Press, 1978, 1980).

90. Robert Fowler, *Loaves and Fishes: The Function of the Feeding Stories in the Gospel of Mark* (Chico, Calif.: Scholars Press, 1975).

Ernst Fuchs commented that Jesus here achieved far more than "a pallid sermon on grace." The point enters into the very bones of the readers, and provides a place of meeting where otherwise there may have been mere indifference or hostility.

The parable of the rich man and the poor man that Nathan told King David offers an OT example. It would have been dangerous to confront an Oriental king with a direct accusation of adultery. But David became so engrossed in the story of the rich man who stole the poor man's sheep that he reacted with anger: such a man ought to be horsewhipped! Nathan could then dare to say, "You are the man" (2 Sam. 12:1-7).

The narrative world is a philosophical category as well as a literary one. Martin Heidegger and Hans-Georg Gadamer use it prominently. These philosophers regard it not as a fictional device, but as a genuine path to knowledge. Heidegger sees this as integral with the world of art, and Gadamer illustrates it from the "world" of play or the game. He comments, "The player loses himself in the play. . . . Here *the primacy of the play over the consciousness of the player* is fundamentally acknowledged. . . . Every game presents the man who plays it with a task . . . transforming the aims of his . . . behavior."[91] Like Habermas, Gadamer is aware that *simple reflection can be deceptive,* and that is one reason why he attacks the Enlightenment. He writes, "The focus of subjectivity is a distorting mirror"; preunderstanding and rootedness in history and tradition can be more fruitful for apprehending truth.[92]

A further area that has begun to loom large in hermeneutics is the role of *metaphor and symbol.* This, too, is a huge subject. Some earlier studies have called attention to the creative power of metaphor. Max Black edited *The Importance of Language* (1963), in which C. S. Lewis and Owen Barfield participated. Metaphors, it was repeatedly argued, are not simply substitutes for what could be expressed in propositions, nor are they mere illustrations or embellishments. As W. Pannenberg regularly reminds us, we need ways of *expanding our horizons,* and metaphor can achieve this. Metaphors make genuinely cognitive truth claims, as J. Martin Soskice argues in *Metaphor and Religious Language* (1985).

Paul Ricoeur is a key exponent of both metaphor and symbol, as well as narrative, in hermeneutics. Ricoeur adopts a positive view of all three topics, but metaphor has also become a key issue for claims about truth. On

91. Hans-Georg Gadamer, *Truth and Method,* 2nd ed. (London: Sheed and Ward, 1989), 102, 104, 107.

92. Gadamer, *Truth and Method,* 276.

one side, F. Nietzsche argues that "truth" was "a mobile army of metaphors, metonyms and anthropomorphisms," while Jacques Derrida argues that we can be seduced by so-called philosophical metaphors.[93] On the other side, E. Jüngel argues, "Metaphors are the articulations of discoveries," and insists that Nietzsche's language can be interpreted more positively.[94] Metaphor, Jüngel declares, brings together not only two semantic or linguistic domains, but also "two horizons." Above all, "The horizon of this world is expanded."[95] Paul Avis takes this exploration further.[96]

Jüngel argues that metaphor is crucial for systematic theology, not least to release us from self-preoccupation, narcissism, and the limits of prior, preexisting horizons. Clearly, metaphors also embrace biblical *poetry.* John Goldingay comments, "The genius of prose is a capacity to make things clear. The genius of poetry is a capacity to obscure them. . . . Poetic utterances . . . make people think. . . . Poetry attacks the mind . . . indirectly and subversively."[97] Biblical poetry, symbol, and metaphor all need special treatment. Often this impinges on doctrine in particular ways. For example, to interpret the symbols and poetry of the book of Revelation as a sequential description of heavenly events would normally constitute a mistake. As G. R. Beasley-Murray observes, "heavenly horses" are not stabled in heavenly stables, and "streets of gold" are not thoroughfares in a city that is several miles in height, length, and width, and shaped like a cube (Rev. 6:2-8; 21:15-21). G. B. Caird also rescues Mark 13 from being regarded as a discourse primarily about the end of the world by seeing the language as "a curious interplay between the metaphorical and the literal."[98]

In addition to narrative and metaphor, we have noted Bakhtin's concern for *polyphonic discourse* and corporate conversation. This needs to be developed and taken into full account in both hermeneutics and systematic theology. I attempted this all too briefly in *The Hermeneutics of Doctrine.*[99]

93. Jacques Derrida, *Margins of Philosophy* (London: Harvester, 1982), 213.

94. Eberhard Jüngel, *Theological Essays,* 2 vols. (Edinburgh: T. & T. Clark, 1989), 1:51 and 28.

95. Jüngel, *Essays,* 1:60 and 71.

96. Paul Avis, *God and the Creative Imagination: Metaphor, Symbol, and Myth in Religion and Theology* (New York: Routledge, 1999).

97. John Goldingay, "Poetry and Theology in Isaiah 56–66," in *Horizons in Hermeneutics: A Festschrift in Honor of A. C. Thiselton,* ed. S. E. Porter and M. R. Malcolm (Grand Rapids: Eerdmans, 2013), 29.

98. George B. Caird, *The Language and Imagery of the Bible* (London: Duckworth, 1980), 246.

99. Thiselton, *The Hermeneutics of Doctrine,* 43-80, 98-118, and 119-44.

Yet another development concerns H. R. Jauss (1921-1997) and *reception history* or *reception theory,* to which we have referred. It is valuable to know not only how various interpreters have understood authors and texts, but also how a succession of communities have "received" and interpreted the texts. At worst this may simply suggest a random variety of understandings, but at its best it demonstrates the continuity of major understandings of texts, including biblical texts. Jauss also emphasizes the role of *provocation* in interpretation, and "horizons of *expectation.*"[100] He shows how a work "satisfies, surpasses, disappoints, or refutes, the expectation of the first audience."[101]

All these literary resources have become part of *contemporary hermeneutics.* They serve not only biblical studies, but also systematic theology, even if especially its biblical foundations. This concludes our methodological discussion of the role of method, truth, and philosophical inquiry. We have considered especially coherence and system, philosophical inquiry, biblical material in its contingency and context, conceptual clarification, hermeneutics, sociology, and literary theology. All these areas remain indispensable for systematic theology today, and should be used to inform our pursuit of theology and truth. All can be regarded in turn as serving the aims of Christian discipleship, and can facilitate, through reflection, prayer, and the Holy Spirit, our growing understanding of, and relationship with, God.

---

100. H. R. Jauss, *Towards an Aesthetics of Reception* (Minneapolis: University of Minnesota Press, 1982). See also A. C. Thiselton, "Reception Theory, Jauss, and the Formative Power of Scripture," *SJT* 65 (2012): 289-308.

101. Jauss, *Aesthetics of Reception,* 25.

CHAPTER II

God: Personhood, Trinity, Holy Love, and Grace

1. God: Impersonal, Personal, or Suprapersonal?

To the philosophical inquirer, the question, "Is God personal?" may often
be of acute concern. To the Christian, Jewish, or Islamic believer, it appears
almost a ridiculous question, comparable with Kierkegaard's view of traditional arguments for the existence of God, which he regarded as a "shame-
less affront." As Barth commented, if God speaks, this implies the Word's
personal quality: "God's Word means the speaking God."[1] Moreover, Barth
adds, this is bound up with the belief in the Trinity. John says of Christ, "In
the beginning was the *Logos (speech* or *articulate language),* and the Word
was with (Gk. *pros*) God, and the Word was God" (John 1:1). A "thing" can
scarcely speak, except in a highly metaphorical sense. Barth explains, we
cannot avoid "the personifying of . . . the Word of God, when we remember
that Jesus Christ is the Word of God."[2] This "Word" has a purposive character. Only a person can determine purpose or directed intention, especially
if this is spoken in love. Barth regards the speech of God as his loving *act:*
"The Word of God is itself the act of God," and "The Holy Spirit . . . cannot
be separated from the Word."[3]

This approach may seem obvious to the Christian, but it perhaps cuts
little ice with those who do not share these beliefs about God's speech. Both
Rahner and Pannenberg admit that "*God* . . . has become as enigmatic for

1. Barth, *CD* I/1, 136.
2. Barth, *CD* I/1, 138.
3. Barth, *CD* I/1, 143 and 150.

us today as a blank face."[4] Many, however, are prepared to acknowledge some transcendent "Being" above and beyond human life. A subpersonal being, on the other hand, who does not or cannot intervene in human affairs, matches the outlook of Deism, which we consider more fully below. At the other end of the spectrum stands the "All" of pantheism, which understands the presence and action of *God* to be diffused throughout all reality, and not focused in a particular "person." This, too, we have yet to consider.

Many have concerns that in a universe that scientists reveal to be vast in space and time, we can no longer reduce "God" to the status of person. Perhaps much of the fault here lies with theologians who call God "personal." It would be wiser and more accurate to use the term "suprapersonal." For God is *more* than a person but *not less* than a person. It would be talking at cross-purposes (see above on Ryle) to insist simply that God is *either* personal *or* impersonal. There is a third alternative. Because God is suprapersonal, the entire tradition of a theology of negation from Dionysius onward has had profound influence on Christian theology and mysticism. Admittedly Paul Tillich is accused of diminishing the personhood of God, but this was not his intention. Most impartial readers will acknowledge that he made a valid point when he declared that we must search for God, the ultimate, beyond the cozy, domesticated concepts of God in childhood or children's church. Tillich explained, "When applied to God superlatives become diminutives. They place him on the level of other beings, while elevating him above all of them."[5] For this reason he would not call God "a being" or even "the highest being," but "Being-itself." This may go too far in the direction of pantheism (see below), but the general point is correct. The philosopher C. A. Campbell considered that the abandonment of "the subject-object distinction is . . . an overstatement of the truth," but he insisted on the term "suprapersonal."[6]

Many objections to the notion of God being a person are based on the concept of what it is for a *human being to be a person*. The thought of a single mind being fully aware both of galaxies and stars and of men and women all over the world through all times gives some people a mental cramp. We seem to have run up against the limits of human thought. Kant had argued that the limits of human reason prevent us from considering even "the edge of space."

4. Karl Rahner, *Foundations of Christian Faith: An Introduction to the Idea of Christianity* (New York: Crossroad, 1978, 2004), 46; Pannenberg, *ST* 1:64.

5. Paul Tillich, *Systematic Theology*, 3 vols. (London: Nisbet, 1953, 1959, 1964), 1:261.

6. C. A. Campbell, *On Selfhood and Godhood* (New York: Macmillan; London: Allen and Unwin, 1957), 312, 411.

If we try to conceive of space extending *ad infinitum,* we cannot conceive of any boundary of space. If we could do so, we then have to conceive of "more space" on the other side of this boundary. Similarly, we cannot conceive of "the beginning of time." For as soon as we try to conceive of it, our minds suggest a period of time on the yonder side of "the beginning." Kant called these difficulties *antinomies,* and argued from these that the human mind imposes limits to our thinking. But a moment's reflection will show us that these "limits" concern an anthropocentric or "human" notion of time and space. "God" cannot be located within human concepts of what it would be like, or amount to, to know the *entire* universe.

For Christians, indeed for all theists, including Jews and Muslims, although we must show extreme caution in using such words as "greater," in principle the greater the Mind, *the greater the Mind's knowledge and understanding of detail.* In the teaching of Jesus, "Not one [sparrow] will fall to the ground apart from your Father. And even the hairs of your head are all counted" (Matt. 10:29-30).

We have now introduced the notion of "mind." Personhood entails "mind," and suprapersonhood entails supramind. Mind, in turn, implies self-awareness, self-consciousness, knowledge, and will. The quest for a meaningful universe would reach a dead end if its first cause and Creator were merely an impersonal "thing." We should have relapsed from purpose to accident. As we shall see, God went, as it were, "out of himself" to choose to create the universe, and his motive was not to make a spectacle for enjoyment or a plaything, but *God created us entirely out of love.* He wants humankind to be his companion in a meaningful *relationship.* This brings us to a further aspect of "mind." Mind may enjoy communication and active relationship with others. Hence to conceive of God as a person will say something about humankind, made in God's image. God created humankind to share and *represent* to the world his self-awareness, self-consciousness, knowledge, will, purpose, and the capacity to enter into, and enjoy, a relationship (as well as his love and other qualities of character; see discussion on the image of God, below). We shall return to the question of whether all this could be "accidental" when we consider creation and the teleological argument for the being of God. God's self-revelation and his incarnation in Christ are the major arguments for understanding him as suprapersonal, or as "not less" than a person.

It is worth recalling our earlier discussion of the theology of negation. Many Christian believers have rightly hesitated to rush into anthropomorphic language about God, and that is a real danger. According to James,

Abraham "was called the friend of God" (James 2:23). But when overdevout people sometimes speak of "friend" in ways that are blasé or careless, we may be concerned about whether overfamiliarity may seem to reduce God's unique otherness. God may indeed become a "friend," but most Christians use such terms with reverence and caution, fearing undue presumption. There is a distance between God and the world, as well as love and the possibility of reconciliation in the event of estrangement. The world is *not an emanation of God.* Nor is reality a dualism of a two-story reality in which "body" is regarded as inferior to spirit. God has chosen to create humankind as an embodied being. Ernst Käsemann points out, in the conditions of the everyday world, that this gives us the gift of visibility, recognition, and communication in the public world.[7] Once again, *communication, identity, and relationship* bring us to the heart of personhood; even this also entails self-awareness, self-consciousness, thought, and will.

2. God as Holy Trinity: Complication or Confirmation?

To Christians, the Trinitarian nature of God is of central concern. But does this complicate our argument about the personhood of God? Although this may appear as a prima facie complication, it nevertheless confirms that the personhood of God is beyond what we mean when we call human beings *persons.* God as Holy Trinity is *suprapersonal,* not three human-like persons.

We may begin with some very fundamental conceptual analyses that date from Gregory of Nyssa (c. 330-395) and Gregory of Nazianzus (c. 330-390) in the fourth century. This distinctly addresses all those talks or sermons that try to offer analogies that explain how "one" can also be "three," including clover leaves, shamrocks, and so on. This is *not* the best way to approach the subject. Gregory of Nazianzus insisted that "three" has nothing to do with numbers. He wrote that God is one (*On the Holy Spirit* 14); but he also asserted, "'Three' (Gk. *treis*) does not denote numerals, like 'three Peters' or 'three Johns'" (19). Gregory of Nyssa also stressed this specifically in *On "Not Three Gods."* He declared, "The operation of the Father, the Son, and the Holy Spirit, differing or varying in nothing, the oneness of their nature must be inferred from the identity of their operation" (*On the Trinity* 6). Gregory of Nyssa argued in *On "Not Three Gods"* that the use of numerals

7. Ernst Käsemann, *New Testament Questions of Today* (London: SCM, 1969), 135.

to denote "Peter, James, and John" is quite different from "'three' Persons of the Holy Trinity," or three objects or things.[8] He concluded, "The Father does not do anything by himself in which the Son does not work co-jointly, or again the Son has no special operation apart from the Holy Spirit. . . . Every operation . . . has its origin from the Father, and proceeds through the Son, and is perfected in the Holy Spirit."[9] The persons of the Godhead are "three," but not in the sense that may be "enumerated" or "contemplated in multiple," he wrote, like pieces of gold or "coins." In philosophical terms, numerals may be applied only to contingent objects, not to the category of *"necessary Being."*

What does this suggest for our discussion about the personhood of God? It underlines that the nature of God is not "personal" in the same sense as *human* persons, but, as we have argued, that God is "suprapersonal." Just as "three" or any numeral cannot be applied in a mathematical or numerical way, so *gender* is equally an inappropriate category. There is a well-worn argument that the Son as *Logos* is masculine, while the Holy Spirit as Hebrew *ruach* is feminine. But Greek *pneuma* is neuter. Jesus Christ is certainly masculine in his incarnate condition, and God is indeed "Father" (masculine) in prayerful address, as Jesus taught. As Pannenberg insists, this title for God is nonnegotiable. "On the lips of Jesus, 'Father' became a proper name for God. It thus ceased to be one designation among others."[10] He adds, "The words 'God' and 'Father' are not just time-bound concepts, from which we can detach the true content of the message."[11] To be sure, the biblical material also uses similes and metaphors involving *both* genders. Matthew 6:7-11 speaks of God's fatherly care to provide for his children who seek bread (vv. 9-11). Psalm 103:13 uses the simile

> As a father has compassion for his children,
>   so the LORD has compassion for those who fear him.

But Isaiah 66:13 states,

> As a mother comforts her child,
>   so I will comfort you.

8. Gregory of Nyssa, *On "Not Three Gods"* 3; *NPNF*, ser. 2, 5:331.
9. Gregory of Nyssa, *On "Not Three Gods"* 3; *NPNF*, ser. 2, 5:334.
10. Pannenberg, *ST* 1:262.
11. Pannenberg, *ST* 1:263.

James Barr has also convincingly demonstrated that the *grammatical* gender ascribed to a word is almost entirely a matter of *linguistic convention.* The plentiful ascription of gender to words by the French no more provides a commentary on their supposedly erotic obsessions than the absence of such ascription in Turkish suggests the opposite for Turks.[12] To the Greeks a child is not without gender simply because *teknon* is neuter. While spirit or Spirit is feminine in Hebrew, the Spirit *(pneuma)* in Greek is neuter, while the Spirit is also referred to as *ekeinos* and *paraklētos* (masculine in grammar) in John (John 16:7-8, both terms).

It does not underplay the maleness of the incarnate Jesus as representing all humankind, to claim that strictly God is *beyond* gender, just as God is beyond being "counted" in numbers. Indeed, the confession "there is one God" (1 Cor. 8:6) has more to do with the unity of God and God's character and integrity than with arithmetical calculation. To worship one God is to be united in heart and mind with a single focus.

The second way of approach to the doctrine of the Holy Trinity is more positive: it concerns both *relationships,* or better, *relationality,* and *narrative.* This approach has been expounded most distinctively by J. Moltmann, W. Pannenberg, and Eugene F. Rogers. In his book *The Trinity and the Kingdom of God,* Moltmann unfolds "Trinitarian hermeneutics" in a way that reaches the following conclusion: *"The NT talks about God by proclaiming in narrative the relationships of the Father, the Son, and the Holy Spirit, which are relationships of fellowship."*[13]

It is impossible to understand the messianic mission of Jesus Christ in abstraction from his awareness of "being sent" by God *the Father.* This is evident not only from well-known passages such as John 3:16, but also especially from the baptism of Jesus recounted in all four Gospels (Mark 1:9-11; Matt. 3:13-17; Luke 3:21-22; John 1:32-34). In turn, this baptism cannot be understood without the descent of the *Holy Spirit* and the Father's words in Mark 1:11, "You are my *Son,* the Beloved; with you I am well pleased." Matthew, Mark, and Luke see the consequences of the messianic anointing in baptism in terms of the Holy Spirit's "driving" Jesus (Mark 1:12, *ekballei*), or "leading him" (Matt. 4:1, *anēchthē*), to the wilderness to undergo the messianic temptation or testing *(peirazō).* In other words, as the narrative unfolds, the *identity of Jesus is bound up with a Trinitarian framework.* When

12. James Barr, *The Semantics of Biblical Language* (Oxford: OUP, 1961), 39-40.
13. Jürgen Moltmann, *The Trinity and the Kingdom of God: The Doctrine of God* (London: SCM, 1981), 64.

Jesus proclaims the kingdom, this is the kingdom of *God*. In spite of John's special emphasis on Christology, in the Synoptic Gospels Jesus primarily proclaims God rather than himself. He leaves it to God to vindicate his mission and person, and trusts in the power of the Holy Spirit for his ministry (also Heb. 2:4, 13).

Moltmann adds such passages in the NT epistles as "God's sending" in Romans 8:3-4 and Galatians 4:4, as well as such passages in the Gospels as Matthew 11:27. He concludes, "The Father sends the Son through the Spirit; the Son comes from the Father in the power of the Spirit. The Spirit brings people into the fellowship of the Son with the Father."[14] He argues that patient, careful reading of NT narrative will constitute a less complex way of understanding the Holy Trinity than beginning with the post-Nicene Fathers.

Pannenberg adopts a similar way forward. Jesus is "seen as a *recipient* of the Spirit," both in his baptism and in his resurrection (Rom. 1:4 and 8:11).[15] We cannot fully understand Jesus Christ without also appreciating his Trinitarian frame. But Eugene Rogers provides the longest and most detailed exposition of a narrative approach to the Trinity.[16] First, like many other writers, he argues that *narrative* distinctively reveals a person as a person, not as an abstract concept or category. He appeals to Gregory of Nazianzus, Basil, and Augustine. Then, like Moltmann, he appeals to the agency of the Holy Spirit and God the Father in the narrative of the baptism of Jesus. He declares: "NT narratives featuring Father, Son, and Spirit, give us a glimpse into the intra-Trinitarian life . . . the most important is the resurrection of Jesus in Romans 8."[17] Here Paul speaks of the Spirit of him who raised Jesus (v. 11). Not only the identity of Jesus Christ, but also the very idea of resurrection, depends on the notion of the Spirit's power, the action of the Father, and "Christ in us."[18] His narrative and reading of the annunciation and the transfiguration may admittedly be more controversial or speculative, but in these the case for the Trinitarian event of the annunciation is stronger and deserves respect.

These NT narratives also show the *relational* nature of the work of Jesus Christ, in relation to God the Father and the Holy Spirit. As Gregory and other

14. Moltmann, *Trinity and the Kingdom,* 75.

15. Pannenberg, *ST* 1:5.

16. Eugene F. Rogers Jr., *After the Spirit: A Constructive Pneumatology from Resources outside the Modern West* (London: SCM, 2005; Grand Rapids: Eerdmans, 2006), 52-175.

17. Rogers, *After the Spirit,* 75.

18. Rogers, *After the Spirit,* 82.

Church Fathers insist, this is not a lone operation exclusive to the incarnate Lord Jesus Christ. Indeed, when we consider the atonement below, we shall argue that the grace and love of God provide its origin, as in Paul's words, "In Christ God was reconciling the world to himself" (2 Cor. 5:19). Paul Fiddes argues that this is a primary pastoral lesson of the doctrine of the Trinity.[19] The Trinity has immediate pastoral relevance because in God the self is *not an isolated self-centered being* but a *self-in-relation to others.* Augustine gave expression to this in the role he assigned to love as the bond that holds together the Holy Trinity or one Godhead. The "persons" of the Trinity *interact as personal Beings* who are constantly *open to one another,* and not self-enclosed or self-contained. The Greek Orthodox theologian John Zizioulas (b. 1931) expresses this admirably. He writes, "God is a relational being: without the concept of communion it would not be possible to speak of the being of God. . . . 'God' has no ontological content, no true being apart from communion."[20] Hence a Christian, or what Zizioulas calls "ecclesial being," is bound to "the very being of God. . . . He takes on God's 'way of being.' "[21] Later in this work we shall argue that this approach is crucial for the doctrine of the church.

Paul Ricoeur provides a close study of the implications of relatedness to the human self in his magisterial book *Oneself as Another.* He argues that the stability, identity, continuity, and accountability of the self rest on our relationship to the other. In a complex argument of 350 pages, he shows that Descartes, Locke, Hume, and even Strawson provide inadequate accounts of selfhood. Descartes is ultimately narcissistic, and Locke and Hume astonishingly individualistic. A human being is a "who," not a "what." Ricoeur approves of Dilthey's notion of the *"interconnectedness" (Zusammenhang)* of life, which Gadamer and Pannenberg take up and develop.[22] Hume's notion of a succession of perceptions leads nowhere. But the speech act of promising does. We make promises to *others* as well as to the self, which promises are actualized over a period of time. Like practical wisdom *(phronēsis)* and virtue, they entail others or "The Other." *Otherness,* Ricoeur concludes, "is inherent in the notion of *intersubjectivity.*"[23]

19. Paul S. Fiddes, *Participating in God: A Pastoral Doctrine of the Trinity* (Louisville: Westminster John Knox, 2000), 15-28.

20. John D. Zizioulas, *Being as Communion: Studies in Personhood and the Church* (New York: St. Vladimir's Seminary Press, 1985), 17.

21. Zizioulas, *Being as Communion,* 15.

22. Paul Ricoeur, *Oneself as Another* (Chicago: University of Chicago Press, 1992), 115-16.

23. Ricoeur, *Oneself as Another,* 318, italics mine.

He writes, "Otherness is not added on to selfhood from outside," and "the other is presupposed."[24]

Fiddes stresses "being in relation" and "openness to the other," which provide the first of several pastoral applications of the doctrine of the Trinity. A well-known secular shortcoming is the same as that of Stoics in NT times: the aim of "independence" and "self-sufficiency." Even God allows himself to become interdependent within his intra-Trinitarian life. Fiddes discusses the opposite errors of indulgence and overdependence, which may become overintense. Some, he argues, reflect overdependence on pastors, to the detriment of both people and ministers. He also explores the balance between the integrity of the self and openness to others, diversity and unity, and "person" and the less personal "personage." Our lives, he argues, "should be shaped by a vision of the triune God."[25] Yet, as our comments above about God as "suprapersonal" suggest, Fiddes warns us not to press analogies between God and human life too far. Barth and others have reservations about the use of analogy, and even the word "person." But the fact that, as Gregory expressed it, all persons of the Trinity are involved in every redemptive act tells us something about the all-too-familiar stance of "going it alone." Moltmann has convincingly argued that in the Father's "sending" of the Son, God is no mere bystander at Calvary: he is deeply involved in its pain and heartache. No human parent could "feel for" his or her son *any more* than God participated in the sufferings of the cross, and it was the Holy Spirit who led Jesus there, and gave him strength to bear his suffering.

A further pastoral application arises from the experience of prayer. If the mass of humanity really doubted that God is "personal," why do so many in practice resort to prayer in moments of crisis or desperation? Yet the doctrine of the Trinity takes us further. Jesus taught us that prayer is typically addressed to God as Father, as the Lord's Prayer ("Our Father") testifies (Matt. 6:9-13; Luke 11:2-4). Paul makes it clear that prayer is prompted within us by the Holy Spirit. He writes, "The Spirit helps us in our weakness; for we do not know how to pray as we ought, but that very Spirit intercedes with sighs too deep for words. And God . . . knows what is the mind of the Spirit, because the Spirit intercedes for the saints according to the will of God" (Rom. 8:26-27; cf. 8:9, 15). Finally, every prayer, the NT teaches, is "through Jesus our Lord" or "for his name's sake," because he is our Mediator

24. Ricoeur, *Oneself as Another,* 317, 332.
25. Fiddes, *Participating in God,* 28.

and Advocate. In other words, *prayer is to the Father, through the Son, by the Spirit*. Prayer is utterly Trinitarian.[26]

We have endeavored to show that Trinitarian theology is full of practical pastoral significance. If we adhere to the NT, Trinitarian theology is also relatively easy to explain, as long as we follow the material set out above. In the fourth century, the doctrine became complex, often helpful, but sometimes potentially misleading. From Arius (c. 250-336) onward, thinkers outside the mainstream church constructed mistaken systems, against which the Fathers defended orthodox faith. As Rowan Williams has shown, Arius was probably not as radically mistaken as he has often been painted.[27] He perhaps aimed at showing the uniqueness and transcendence of God as an "Origin and Source" (Gk. *agenētos archē*). Hence he made the genuine mistake of bracketing Christ *with creation* as "having a beginning," rather than *with God*. Hence the orthodox began to use a greater array of philosophical terms such as "coeternal," of Jesus Christ and God the Father. Eusebius of Nicodemia and the emperor Constantius (c. 337-361) supported a "subordinationist" Christology, namely, the belief that Christ is inferior or subordinate to the Father. After Arius, there emerged the "Tropici" or "Pneumatomachians," who reduced the personhood of the Holy Spirit to an "it" or a "thing" (as some still do even today). Hence Athanasius and Gregory of Nazianzus laid the foundation for the Council of Constantinople (381), which promoted many formulations that appear in our creeds; the Council of Chalcedon (c. 451) followed later.

The key orthodox term was the Greek *homoousios*, "of the same being," often translated by the Latinized "consubstantial." Such terms as *ousia* ("being" or "substance"), *hypostasis* ("person," as denoting distinctions within being), and *perichōrēsis* (interpenetration) were perhaps explications of the less overt philosophical NT teaching. Even subsequent formulations such as "economic Trinity" (God in terms of his activity in the world), "immanent Trinity" (God as he is in himself *apart* from his operation in the world), and "social Trinity" (the relations between Father, Son, and Spirit) are on the whole *later explications, which do not need fully to be understood to understand the Trinity*. They are useful as secondary theological reflection.

For theological discussion and explication, the terms are indeed widely

---

26. See also Sarah Coakley, *God, Sexuality, and the Self: An Essay "On the Trinity"* (Cambridge: CUP, 2013), 130-31.

27. Rowan D. Williams, *Arius: Heresy and Tradition* (Grand Rapids: Eerdmans, 2001), 95-116, 247-68.

used, and meet certain purposes. For example, the term "social Trinity" has both advantages and disadvantages. Moltmann employs the term positively to make two points. First, he argues, it underlines the *coequality* of the Father, the Son, and the Holy Spirit; second, it calls attention to the prime importance of *relationality* between them. Those who criticize the label "social Trinity" stress that, first, *God the Father* is accorded origination and initiative in creation and redemption, and in 1 Corinthians Paul set out two "subordination" passages: 11:2-3 and 15:24-28. To this there is the counterreply that "subordination" verses in 1 Corinthians arose only because of certain distinctive conditions at Corinth. Moffatt and others argue that at Corinth the cult "Lord" might have attracted more emphasis than a supposedly more remote God. Second, critics of "social Trinity" also argue that humankind has been in an *"egalitarian" era from the 1970s to the early twenty-first century,* and is prone to create "God" too readily *in its own image,* as Feuerbach had argued. This is perhaps given added plausibility by Moltmann's sympathy with liberation theology. Such questions, however, would scarcely have troubled NT writers.

The terms "economic Trinity" and "immanent Trinity" also have both advantages and limitations. Many of the Church Fathers indicated that the Holy Trinity *conjointly operates as one will* in operations of creation and redemption. Nevertheless, over the centuries the distinctive operations of God the Father, God the Son, and God the Holy Spirit have been distinguished. Jesus Christ uniquely underwent suffering and death in the incarnation and the cross. Yet at the same time, as Moltmann argues, God the Father and the Holy Spirit also shared in his suffering. The Holy Spirit uniquely sanctifies all God's people. Yet he makes them *Christlike,* to accord with *the will of God the Father.* Paul exposes this tension admirably in 1 Corinthians 12:4-7: "There are varieties of gifts, but the same Spirit; and there are varieties of services, but the same Lord; and there are varieties of activities, but it is the same God who activates all of them in everyone. To each is given the manifestation of the Spirit for the common good." We have set out the narrative approach and that of the patristic conceptual analysis as basic. Other models and terms, in effect, constitute second-stage developments in understanding the Holy Trinity.

3. The Living God or "Theism"?

When pastors and students complain that systematic theology is often irrelevant to pastoral ministry, the suspicion arises that their teachers have replaced the living, acting God of the OT and the Bible with the God of "theism." The term "theism" is not to be despised when used in contrast to Deism and pantheism, or to atheism and agnosticism. In this context it denotes a firm belief in one God, who relates to the world in personal or suprapersonal ways. But "theism" can also be more abstract, static, and theoretical than belief in the living God of the Bible, and especially the God of the OT. As a crude summary of the difference, it may sometimes be said that theism seeks to know God through his *being,* while faith in the living God knows God from his *activity.*

One starting point in the OT is God's self-revelation to Moses in Exodus 3:13-15. This is not the only starting point: we could also begin with the doctrine of creation in Genesis, Psalms, and elsewhere. Moses' question, "What is his (God's) name?" (v. 13), invites the answer from God: "I am who I am" (v. 14). This is amplified by his continuity and activity as "the God of Abraham, the God of Isaac, and the God of Jacob" (v. 15), and the added comment,

> "This is my name forever,
> and this is my title for all generations." (v. 15b)

This is one of the rare occasions, however, when the NRSV may not have conveyed the exact meaning of the Hebrew, when we translate it as "I AM." The Hebrew words are *'eh^{e}yeh '^{a}sher 'eh^{e}yeh.* B. S. Childs comments in his excellent commentary: "Few verses in the entire OT have evoked such heated controversy and such widely divergent opinions."[28] He cites more than twenty books or articles on Hebrew *'eh^{e}yeh* and other aspects of verse 14. It is possible, some argue, that *'eh^{e}yeh* is a play on the word "YHWH" for God. But Childs and others interpret the imperfect as a *future* imperfect: "God said to Moses, 'I will be who I will be.'"[29]

This may amount to a refusal to give a specific answer in purely human language, as if to say: "You will find out who I am or will be." But probably, as Childs suggests, it means: "The people will *experience God's purpose by what he does in their future.*"[30] The NT writers cite this verse in Mark 12:26, Matthew 22:32, and parallels, with special reference to "the God of Abraham, the God of Isaac, and the God of Jacob." Although the immediate reference is

---

28. Brevard S. Childs, *Exodus: A Commentary* (London: SCM, 1974), 61.
29. Childs, *Exodus,* 76.
30. Childs, *Exodus,* 76.

to the living God of the resurrection, the phrase also stresses the *continuity of action* by which God is identified. He is God of the living, whom humankind experiences through his acts in history. It anticipates the God "who is and who was and who is to come" (Rev. 1:8). Much of the misunderstanding of this verse is due to the hellenized translation in the LXX, which rendered it "I am who I am," which in turn invited more philosophical and static speculation about "being" and "essence," or in Latin, "substance," which is yet further away from the Hebrew. Luther interpreted the verse as "I am the God on whom you must fully rely." The thrust of the whole passage stresses God's self-revelation in contrast to human discovery. To quote Childs once more, "God's nature is neither static being, nor eternal presence. The God of Israel makes known his being in specific historical moments."[31]

Childs is far from alone in stressing the futurity of God's self-disclosure in Exodus 3:14. M. A. Grisanti discusses thoroughly the Hebrew verb *h-y-h* in *NIDOTTE,* and concludes that in this verse "I will be" is parallel with frequent covenantal promises, for example, "I will be with you." Moses is concerned not simply with God's identity, but primarily with his *character.*[32] Grisanti, like Childs, reaches his conclusion in the light of a substantial bibliography.

The phrase "the living God" occurs frequently in the OT. First Samuel 17:26 speaks of "the armies of the living God" (repeated in v. 36); in 2 Kings 19:4 the king of Assyria mocks "the living God"; Joshua tells Israel, "By this shall you know that among you is the living God" (Josh. 3:10); and Jeremiah declares,

> The Lord is the true God;
> he is the living God and the everlasting King. (Jer. 10:10)

"Living God" (Heb. *'ēl chay*) stands not simply in contrast to dead idols or human constructions. "Living water" throughout Scripture is water that moves, is fresh, and flows from springs, as against stagnant water from cisterns or jugs. Typically the tabernacle was reverenced as representing God's moving, ongoing presence with his people. Israel had "the tent of testimony in the wilderness, as God directed. . . . But it was Solomon who built a house for him. Yet the Most High does not dwell in houses made with human hands" (Acts 7:44-48). Most Greek-speaking Jews of the Dias-

---

31. Childs, *Exodus,* 88.
32. M. A. Grisanti, *"h-y-h,"* in *NIDOTTE* 1:1023-25.

pora would echo Stephen's words. The cloud and the pillar of fire symbolized God's moving presence with Israel in the wilderness. God could not, and cannot, be domesticated into the God who is confined to a particular place.

This reveals one of the numerous differences from the more philosophical notion of *theism*. As a provisional generalization, we might suggest that "theism" is often timeless, abstract, and static, at least in comparison with the OT concept of the living God. Gerhard von Rad writes, "Israel was not capable of thinking of time in the abstract, time divorced from specific events. She found the idea of a time without a particular event quite inconceivable."[33] In Israel's experience of God, von Rad continues, events move toward some ultimate experience. But in theism, he implies, "an eviscerated eschatological concept of time still lives on."[34] Edmond Jacob is no less emphatic than von Rad. He writes, "Life is what differentiates Yahweh from other gods."[35] But, according to Vriezen, "The historicizing process has, unfortunately, often been ignored by the theologians."[36]

Today there are notable exceptions among systematic theologians. Pannenberg fully acknowledges his indebtedness to von Rad's notion of history. He writes, "The historical consciousness of Israel was always eschatologically oriented. . . . On the basis of the promise and beyond all historical fulfilments, Israel expected further fulfilment."[37] He adds, "It is of great theological significance that the confession of Israel . . . consistently holds fast to the one history of God which binds them [i.e., promise and fulfillment, and Israel and the Christian community] together."[38]

Moltmann speaks of "theism" as a very different approach from that of biblical faith. However, Pannenberg adds the warning that "God's redemptive deed took place within the universal correlative connections of human history, and not in a ghetto of redemptive history."[39] To put it another way, "the biblical writings . . . do not deal with general religious truths."[40] The

33. Gerhard von Rad, *Old Testament Theology,* 2 vols. (Edinburgh: Oliver and Boyd, 1962, 1965), 2:100.

34. Von Rad, *Old Testament Theology,* 2:101.

35. Edmond Jacob, *Theology of the Old Testament* (London: Hodder and Stoughton, 1958), 39.

36. Th. C. Vriezen, *An Outline of Old Testament Theology* (Oxford: Blackwell, 1962), 13.

37. Pannenberg, *BQT* 1:23.

38. Pannenberg, *BQT* 1:25.

39. Pannenberg, *BQT* 1:41.

40. Pannenberg, *BQT* 1:83.

biblical God is completely without analogy. Both Testaments of the Bible provide us with eyewitness testimonies to the activity of God.

In pastoral terms, this suggests that the role of testimony and witness, so widespread in many black and Pentecostal churches, is entirely valid as a way of pointing to the reality of God. Nevertheless, we should not forget that *biblical writings also provide direct, firsthand testimonies* to the activity of God. Recently Richard Bauckham has underlined the firsthand role of witness in the Synoptic Gospels.[41] He builds up a careful case, examining Peter's role in relationship to Mark, and considering Papias on eyewitnesses. To anticipate our later arguments about the sacraments, the Passover was instituted to keep living and contemporary the saving events of the exodus; the Lord's Supper was instituted to keep living and contemporary the events of the Passover of Christ.

4. God as Holy Life-Giver and Loving Creator

In the Christian doctrine of God, the holiness of God, the love of God, and his character as the source of grace are virtually inseparable. To some extent this is partly true of the wrath of God. One of my former students wrote to ask how we can "balance" the holiness and wrath of God with his love and grace. But God is holy love, who wills the best for us. But even his wrath against humankind when it is bent on self-destruction or self-defeating goals shows above all how much he cares for us and loves humankind. This is discussed further in chapter 14. The one major difference between love and holiness or wrath is that, according to John, "God is love" without condition or qualification. This includes *eternal* love, whereas wrath and holiness are "dispositions," which become manifest or active *on particular occasions.* As O. R. Jones rightly argues, holiness is not a quality; it is a "disposition to behave in a certain way," when certain circumstances arise.[42]

Just as "the Living God" becomes virtually a title for God in the OT, so also "the Holy One" is virtually a title ascribed to God regularly. In Hosea 11:9 the prophet indicates God's speech:

> I am God, and no mortal,
>   the Holy One in your midst.

---

41. Richard Bauckham, *Jesus and the Eyewitnesses: The Gospels as Eyewitness Testimony* (Grand Rapids: Eerdmans, 2006).

42. O. R. Jones, *The Concept of Holiness* (London: Allen and Unwin, 1961), 41.

In the NT Peter applies this term to Christ: "You are the Holy One of God" (John 6:69). The Hebrew words for holiness and holy are *qādōsh* and *qādesh*, for which Greek is *hagios* and (verb) *hagiazō*. They stand in contrast to what is common or in everyday use (Heb. *chōl*; Gk. *koinos*). Thus BDB (1980) underlines the themes of being separate, apart, or sacred.[43] Vriezen proposes the *"Wholly Other One."*[44] Isaiah's vision of his call in the temple underlines the unapproachableness of the holy God: "I saw the Lord sitting on a throne, high and lofty. . . . Seraphs were in attendance . . . they covered their faces. . . . And one called to another, and said, 'Holy, holy, holy, is the LORD of hosts; / the whole earth is full of his glory.' The pivots of the thresholds shook at the voices of those who called" (Isa. 6:1-4). Vriezen comments that this passage shows clearly the content of *qādōsh*. He adds that the primary focus here is on a *majestas* or *gravitas,* although other passages will develop the moral or ethical aspect. In Exodus 15:11 God is "majestic in holiness." In terms of "separateness," the Holy of Holies is the hindmost part of the temple, from which even the priests are excluded. The whole temple, with its five courts, indicates simultaneous access and exclusion.

Jacob in some respects confirms Jones's dispositional analysis of "holy." He writes, "Holiness is not one divine quality among others . . . for it expresses what is characteristic of God."[45] In Isaiah 40:25, "the Holy One" is synonymous with the divine. But, Jacob adds, God's holiness is also linked with salvation and deliverance, and especially in the context of the covenant. Certainly in Isaiah 10:7 it is associated with God's wrath. But, as we have noted, wrath may be manifested as a by-product of love, as when a parent or grandparent becomes exasperated if a child is continually bent on self-harm and self-centeredness. Above all, to speak of the *holy God* reminds us that God is beyond ready or easy comparison with humankind. It is not for nothing that the biblical writers emphasize his "separateness" from the commonplace.

Holy love wants the best from us. It seeks not primarily our happiness and pleasure as such, but our holiness and our capacity to be in a saving relationship with God. John Hick shows how relevant this is to the problem of evil and suffering. "The *telos* of man's nature consists in a relationship to God. . . . Conversely, the deepest misery possible to our human nature would be to forfeit that happiness, and to plunge instead into irrevocable

---

43. BDB 871-74.
44. Vriezen, *Old Testament Theology,* 149.
45. Jacob, *Theology of the Old Testament,* 86.

and ever-increasing alienation from the source of our being."[46] God wants us even more to be holy than temporarily happy.

"Love" (Heb. *'āhēb*, verb, and *'ah ăbāh*, noun; Gk. *agapaō* and *agapē*) is defined by G. Quell as "a spontaneous feeling which impels to self-giving."[47] But we may question the first part of this definition. As Wittgenstein observes regularly, no one can command a "spontaneous feeling." This would be as absurd as to command, "Laugh at this joke." But there are biblical *commands to love*. Love constitutes an *act of will and settled habit*. Wittgenstein comments, "Love is not a feeling. Love is put to the test, pain not. One does not say, 'That was not true pain, or it would not have gone off so quickly.'"[48] We could, however, say it of love. Biblical commands to love range from Hosea 3:1, "Go, love a woman," to Deuteronomy 6:5, "You shall love the LORD your God with all your heart, and with all your soul, and with all your might." In the NT Jesus urges us to love the Lord our God and love our neighbor as ourselves (Mark 12:30-31; Matt. 22:37-39). The second part of Quell's definition is valid: it implies self-giving.

When we consider the love of God, this also involves God's giving of himself. Moltmann reminds us that the Genesis account uses *bārā'*, "to create," for the uniquely divine act, and that the world and universe are "created through God's free will," not as an "emanation from God's essential nature . . . [but] based on a divine resolve of the will to create."[49] But he adds at once that this was "out of love. . . . It is love, which means self-communication of the good."[50] From the first, he argues, following Barth, the covenant, not glory, was the basis of creation.[51] *Creatio ex nihilo* implies that "the omnipotent and omnipresent God withdraws his presence and restricts his power."[52] For God has "made room" for a reality that is not-God. He is not simply the "Unmoved Mover," as Aquinas argues, but creates with deep "self-involvement." Moltmann traces the theological tradition of the self-limitation of God to Nicholas of Cusa, J. G. Hamann, F. Oetinger, Barth, and Brunner. It is God's first act of "self-humiliation," which culminated in the cross of Christ. Thus he declares, "God makes room for his creation by

---

46. John Hick, *Evil and the God of Love* (London: Macmillan, 1966), 16.

47. G. Quell, *"Agapē,"* in *TDNT* 1:22.

48. Ludwig Wittgenstein, *Zettel* (Oxford: Blackwell, 1967), sect. 504.

49. Jürgen Moltmann, *God in Creation: A New Theology of Creation and the Spirit of God* (London: SCM, 1985), 75.

50. Moltmann, *God in Creation*, 77.

51. Moltmann, *God in Creation*, 81.

52. Moltmann, *God in Creation*, 87.

withdrawing his presence. What comes into being is a *nihil*," which prepares the space for redemption.[53] We consider creation further in chapter 5.

In this light it becomes doubly clear that *God creates humankind out of love.* There is a close parallel between God's act of *self-giving in creation* and his act of *self-giving in the cross.* I recall an elderly church member who was crippled with arthritis saying that in the "General Thanksgiving" in the Book of Common Prayer, she did thank God for her "preservation," but remained silent when we thanked God for our creation. However, she had clearly misunderstood that these were *both* precious gifts, given "because God loves us." Our existence and birth in the first place, and then every breath that we take, are equally gifts of God's love.

Creation demonstrates that such love cannot be "earned" or merited, for we have done nothing before existence and life, to earn any favor. The famous passage, Deuteronomy 7:7-8, makes this clear in the case of God's love for his people: "It was not because you were more numerous than any other people that the LORD set his heart on you and chose you — for you were the fewest of all peoples. It was because the LORD loved you." The prophet Amos reminded his hearers: "You only have I known of all the families of the earth" (Amos 3:2). The reason for God's love lies solely in the inscrutable will of God. This is the starting point and end point of any doctrine of election: we cannot go further back than the decision of a sovereign and loving God. Similarly, even in marriage most people would decline a list of their "reasons" for loving their partner. Often they would simply reply, "Because I do."

This is often clothed in lofty theological jargon. Anders Nygren in his classic volume *Agape and Eros* argues that the love of God is "unmotivated, spontaneous, and indifferent to [prior] value." Indeed, God's love is "creative of value," in the sense that God's love *gives* value to a person or to humankind.[54] In general terms Nygren's arguments are correct, with the exception that it is not the *words agapē* and *erōs* that carry the load that he places on them, but the *uses* of these words in the NT.

We should also not underestimate the many concrete and particular forms in which love becomes manifest. C. Spicq in his three-volume work on love lists over a hundred "effects" or "activities" that love sets in train.[55] Paul lists the many effects of love in 1 Corinthians 13:4-7. These have an un-

53. Moltmann, *God in Creation,* 87.

54. Anders Nygren, *Agape and Eros* (London: SPCK, 1957), 75-81.

55. C. Spicq, *Agape in the New Testament,* 3 vols. (London and St. Louis: Herder, 1963), 2:139-81.

derlying allusion in the opposite attitudes of Paul's opponents at Corinth. Granted that the passage is composed in rhythmic style in language usually unfamiliar in Paul, Paul may well have borrowed it from a Corinthian friend, or composed it separately, because, as J. Moffatt rightly argues, it springs out of so much that is wrong in Corinth.[56] Paul writes, "Love is not envious or boastful or arrogant" (v. 4). We may contrast this with 3:4 and 8:1, where many at Corinth are said to be jealous, boastful, and arrogant or rude (cf. 11:21-22; 14:26-27). "[Love] does not insist on its own way; it is not irritable or resentful" (13:5; contrast 1:12-13; 3:3-4, where the Corinthians are self-centered and divisive). Paul leaves his readers with a positive definition, however: *love does not give up* (13:7); *love never ends* (13:8); love is the indelible mark of maturity and heavenly existence (13:11-13). In Nygren's words, it comes to us as *new creation*.

5. God as the Giver of Grace

All that has been said about the love of God as spontaneous, unmotivated, and creative finds expression in the word "grace" (Heb. *chēn,* noun; *chānan,* verb; and *chesed,* especially in covenant contexts; Gk. *charis*). In Exodus 34:6-7,

> The LORD passed before him (Moses), and proclaimed,
> "The LORD, the LORD,
> a God merciful and gracious,
> slow to anger,
> and abounding in steadfast love and faithfulness,
> keeping steadfast love for the thousandth generation,
> forgiving iniquity."

The close connection with undeserved love and election is clear in Exodus 33:19, "I will be gracious to whom I will be gracious, and will show mercy on whom I will show mercy." In both passages Hebrew *chānan* and *chesed* are used. Some sixty-seven occurrences of Hebrew *chēn* in the OT mean "grace" or "favor."[57] But *chesed,* often translated "loving-kindness," can merge with

---

56. James Moffatt, *Love in the New Testament* (London: Hodder and Stoughton, 1929; New York: Richard Smith, 1930), 182.
57. D. N. Freedman and J. R. Lundbom, *"Chēn,"* in *TDOT* 5:24.

the same meaning as *chēn,* especially in covenantal contexts. In the Psalms it is even more frequent than *chēn,* amounting to 127 times. The psalmist prays, "Save me according to your steadfast love *(chesed)*" (Ps. 109:26).

The NT uses *charis* often. Jesus Christ as the Word *(Logos)* in John is "full of grace and truth" (John 1:14). John comments, "From his fullness we have all received, grace upon grace (Gk. *charin anti charitos;* i.e., grace piled on grace, or inexhaustible grace)" (John 1:16). Grace constitutes the theme of these parables in the first three Gospels: the laborers in the vineyard (Matt. 20:1-16), the Pharisee and the tax collector (Luke 18:9-14), and the prodigal son (Luke 15:11-32). In the first parable, the crowds are indignant because the employer is perceived as "unjust" or "unfair," to give the agreed day's wage both to those who worked all day in the sun and to those taken on at the eleventh hour in the cool of the evening. The crowd feels this unfairness in their bones. Ernst Fuchs argued that the method of Jesus is thus far more effective than a "pallid sermon on grace." In the narrative world of the parable, *grace and generosity eclipse "fairness"* and human expectations. The word of Jesus "singles out the individual and grasps him deep down."[58] In Luke 18:9-14 *grace* turns audience expectations upside down. The audience would have expected the piety of the Pharisee to be rewarded. But in the event, the tax collector's "God, be merciful to me, a sinner" invites grace rather than supposed justice. One of my former students was nearly lynched when he used the figures of a Catholic priest and an Orangeman to adopt these respective roles before an Irish congregation![59] The parable of the prodigal son compares the elder son's expectations of his "rights" and supposed justice with the father's grace and generosity to the younger son.

Grace is seen especially in God's commission to Paul. He remained aware that, in his words, "[I am] unfit to be called an apostle, because I persecuted the church of God. But by the grace of God I am what I am" (1 Cor. 15:9-10). Hence, again, grace constitutes the *purely undeserved, unmerited, free love that comes from God's sovereign will.* This is why Paul stressed that he was called "before I was born . . . through his grace" (Gal. 1:15). Similarly Paul asked the Christians at Corinth: "What do you have that you did not receive? And if you received it, why do you boast as if it were not a gift?" (1 Cor. 4:7). In Romans 4:16, "The promise [rests] on grace." The *charisma* of God, translated as "free gift" (NRSV), stands in contrast to "wages" *(opsōnia)*

---

58. Ernst Fuchs, *Studies of the Historical Jesus* (London: SCM, 1964), 33-37.

59. Further, Anthony C. Thiselton, *The Two Horizons: New Testament Hermeneutics and Philosophical Description* (Grand Rapids: Eerdmans; Carlisle: Paternoster, 1980), 12-17.

of sin. Paul ironically speaks of "the wages of sin" as a due reward for work done (Rom. 6:23). Finally in Ephesians 2:8-9: "By grace you have been saved . . . this is not your own doing; it is the gift of God — not the result of works, so that no one may boast."

It is unfortunate that the warmth and personal nature of the *love* of God seem to become more "theological" in the sense of more abstract, in the case of *grace*. Oliver Davies expounds the concept of love by examining God's compassion (Heb. *r-ch-m* and Gk. *splanchna*).[60] Love and grace merge. Vincent Brümmer concludes: "I identify with you by seeing your interests as being my own. The devotion to your good is unconditional, in the sense that I do not serve your interests on condition that you serve mine in return."[61] Hans Küng argues that the love of God appears in a new light in the suffering of Jesus, when God encounters me "as redeeming love, a God who has identified himself with me in Jesus, who does not demand, but bestows love: *who is himself wholly love.*"[62] It is precisely here, in our last three quotations, that grace merges with love, and is in no way colder or more remote. Grace initiates God's loving purposes for humankind.

To be sure, the doctrinal history of grace becomes complex and at times tortuous. Augustine was provoked by Pelagius into writing on "irresistible" grace, and Thomas Aquinas speaks of "infused" grace. On the other hand, "grace" is a word that should be more widely used. Miroslav Volf entitled his book that relates to grace *Free of Charge: Giving and Forgiving in a Culture Stripped of Grace.*[63] Nevertheless, Augustine's aim was to show that God is all, that is, that everything comes from God, from the beginning to the end of the Christian life. What provoked him about Pelagius was that somehow Pelagius expected a human "contribution" to everything's being put right. Sin, Augustine urged, cannot adequately be dealt with by simply doing one's best; he did, however, acknowledge Pelagius's piety, moral purity, and sincerity.

The famous quotation from Augustine, which has puzzled many, is: "God, give me what Thou commandest, and command what Thou wilt."[64]

60. Oliver Davies, *The Theology of Compassion: Metaphysics of Difference and the Renewal of Tradition* (London: SCM, 2001), 240-49.

61. Vincent Brümmer, *The Model of Love: A Study in Philosophical Theology* (Cambridge: CUP, 1993), 239.

62. Hans Küng, *Does God Exist? An Answer for Today* (New York and London: Collins, 1980), 695.

63. Miroslav Volf, *Free of Charge: Giving and Forgiving in a Culture Stripped of Grace* (Grand Rapids: Zondervan, 2005).

64. Augustine, *On the Spirit and the Letter* 22.13; *NPNF*, ser. 1, 5:92.

But this does not run counter to the main view of grace in the Greek or Latin Church. John Chrysostom saw everything in the Christian life as a work of grace, even God's law. He wrote, "For what belongs to the law was itself the work of grace, as well as our very creation out of nothing. . . . The beneficence of God is everywhere beforehand."[65] Augustine and others used "grace beforehand," the theological name for which is "prevenient grace." According to Gregory of Nyssa (c. 330-395), the grace of God is the source "of everything good and fair" (*On the Holy Spirit* 23). Grace is virtually equivalent to the work of the Holy Spirit.[66] Basil (c. 330-379) also writes that "All is through the Spirit," restoring "the grace that came of the inbreathing of God."[67]

In the light of such sayings from the Fathers, it is not surprising that Thomas Aquinas (1225-1274) spoke of "infused grace." But one problem with this is that John, Paul, and Augustine often conceived of grace as a single initiatory act, although also with ever-new renewal. Bultmann regarded grace in the NT as an "event," which is also equivalent to God's love in Christ.[68] Even though he sometimes speaks of grace in terms of *knowledge* or revelation, Aquinas also quotes Paul in Romans 9:16: "It is not of him that willeth . . . but of God that showeth mercy."[69] He also quotes Augustine, "Without grace men can do nothing good when they either think or wish or love or act." In the same article he speaks of "infused virtue," claiming that "human nature is not altogether corrupted by sin." This comment differs from Calvin, and partly from Augustine. But he further quotes Augustine as saying, "It is necessary that the will of man should be prepared by the grace of God."[70] He cites Augustine further as stating that one cannot escape the slavery of sin without God's grace.

Luther realized that "grace" was a term increasingly removed from popular understanding. Hence he often replaced it with "God's favor," "God's kindness," "God's free kindness" or "God's gracious power." But he also saw it as identical with God's gift of the righteousness of Christ through faith. He insisted, "God cannot accept a man unless the grace of God is there justifying him."[71] Grace remains fundamental to the possibility of pleasing God: "With-

65. Chrysostom, *Homily on John; NPNF,* ser. 1, 14:49.

66. Gregory of Nyssa, *On the Holy Trinity; NPNF,* ser. 2, 5:328.

67. Basil, *On the Spirit* 16.39; *NPNF,* ser. 2, 8:25.

68. Rudolf Bultmann, *Theology of the New Testament,* vol. 1 (London: SCM, 1952), 288-92.

69. Aquinas, *Summa* II/I, qu. 109, art. 2.

70. Aquinas, *Summa* II/I, qu. 109, art. 5, reply.

71. Luther, *Disputation against Scholastic Theology* 56.

out the grace of God the will produces of necessity an action which is wicked and wrong."[72] In his explicit polemic he stressed that grace is "the favor of God," against Duns Scotus and William of Ockham, whom he perceived as transforming it into "a quality of the soul." Grace enables the once-for-all turning to God. He rejected the notion of partial "installments" of grace.[73]

Calvin is even more emphatic than Luther. He quotes Ephesians 2:10, and asserts, "Everything good in the will is entirely the result of grace."[74] Conversely, "When the will is enchained as the slave of sin, it cannot make a movement towards goodness."[75] Nothing can remain as a ground of boasting. Calvin gives special attention to the grace of perseverance. "As to perseverance, it would undoubtedly have been regarded as the gratuitous gift of God."[76] He adds in this section, "Nothing is left for the will to arrogate as its own." Calvin shares Augustine's concern to recognize that "All is of God," and pays special attention to "the infirmity of the human will."[77] Perhaps the one ambiguity in Calvin is that on the one hand he speaks of "common grace" in God's sustaining all, yet he also writes, "Divine grace is not given to all men." Probably the latter refers to "special" or "saving" grace. Certainly E. Choisy distinguished carefully between "general grace" in the world and "special grace" among believers.[78]

In the Eastern Orthodox Church grace is seen especially in the operation of the sacraments. It is claimed that this stands in the tradition of the Eastern Church Fathers, including John Chrysostom, Basil, Gregory of Nyssa, and Cyril of Alexandria. This may seem to be less "personal" than language about love. But in Methodist thought the two come more closely together. When he preached on free grace, John Wesley based his thought on Romans 8:32: "He who did not withhold his own Son, but gave him up for all of us, will he not with him also give us everything else?" The grace and love of God, Wesley declared, "give us everything." Admittedly, in the nineteenth century Schleiermacher moves away from more personal language about grace, perhaps partly through fear of using anthropomorphic language. Liberalism

---

72. Luther, *Disputation against Scholastic Theology* 7.

73. Heinrich Hermelink, "Grace in the Theology of the Reformers," in *The Doctrine of Grace,* ed. William Thomas Whitley (Edinburgh and London: Oliver and Boyd, 1948), 180; cf. 176-227.

74. Calvin, *Institutes* 2.3.6.

75. Calvin, *Institutes* 2.3.5.

76. Calvin, *Institutes* 2.3.11.

77. Calvin, *Institutes* 2.3.13.

78. Eugène Choisy, "Calvin's Conception of Grace," in *The Doctrine of Grace,* 228-34.

offered a weaker doctrine of grace, because it assumed a weaker doctrine of sin. But this moves us away from Paul, Augustine, Luther, and indeed the Synoptic Gospels. We have only to recall some of the parables of Jesus, especially the laborers in the vineyard, the Pharisee and the tax collector, and the prodigal son, to see that love springs from grace, and grace from love. Every good gift comes from God, because he loves us; his purposes are love, because they are initiated and sustained by divine grace.

CHAPTER III

God and the World

1. The God of Love and the Problem of Evil

Few pastoral problems are as acute as the problem of evil and suffering. If God is both sovereign and loving, why does he permit evil and suffering to occur in the world? It appears to be part of human nature to cry out, "Why has this happened to me?" when tragedy or suffering hits life, but hardly ever to ask, "What have we done to deserve this?" when life is blessed with health or prosperity. Some suggest that the problem of evil can be addressed only when we ask about the problem of good. We discussed much of this under "grace" and "love" in the previous chapter. From a Christian pastoral point of view, one "answer" to experiences of evil and good is sometimes offered. Some insist that evil is a personal punishment and that good is a personal reward. But this would undermine what we have noted about God's love and sheer grace. This answer contradicts the reply of Jesus about those who were killed when the tower of Siloam fell on them (Luke 13:2-5); it also encourages an unchristian "boasting." The book of Job dismisses the suggestion that Job's suffering is proportionate to his guilt or even unknown sin.

The biblical material gives us several examples of deep experiences of suffering, ranging from Job, Ecclesiastes, and the Psalms to the suffering and death of Jesus. Job reflects ironically on the gift of life "to one in misery . . . to the bitter in soul, who [longs] for death" (Job 3:20-21). The writer of Ecclesiastes concedes, "I hated life" (Eccles. 2:17). The psalmist declares, "The snares of death encompassed me . . . I suffered distress and anguish" (Ps. 116:3). Jesus cried, "My God, my God, why have you forsaken me?" (Mark 15:34). In such circumstances, Vincent Brümmer remarks, it is "pastorally insensitive" simply to wade in with traditional academic "replies" to the problem of evil.

Nevertheless, Christian theologians have always been concerned to show that this problem, in all its reality, does not detract either from the love and goodness of God or from God's sovereignty and almighty-ness. Yet here is the dilemma: the ancient Greek philosopher Epicurus (341-271) was among the first to formulate it, although it is usually expressed in the form borrowed by David Hume (1711-1776), who asks, "Is (God) willing to prevent evil, but not able? Then he is impotent. Is he able, but not willing? Then he is malevolent. Is he both able and willing? Whence, then, is evil?"[1] Scripture may argue that we have to erode away, or radically qualify, what we mean by the omnipotence and love of God, or else qualify the tragic nature of evil. Certainly the Christian religion, like Islam and Judaism, cannot relegate the problem to a dualistic worldview, as if all evil came from a rival power, equivalent to the Gnostic "Demiurge," or a second God. Pastorally, it does not solve the problem to ascribe evil to Satan, as if to suggest that Satan is not under the control of God. Otherwise "monotheism" would not mean monotheism. Nor is there any hint, as there is perhaps in Plato and Neoplatonism, that evil is somehow caused by matter or the material world as such.

It is important, however, to define what "the sovereignty of God" entails. Clearly, as Richard Swinburne (b. 1934) insists, God's sovereignty cannot facilitate acts that are *logically* self-contradictory. God "cannot" (*logically,* not empirically) create a square circle, cannot tell lies, or cannot change the past.[2] I have attended prayer meetings in which devout believers have prayed that an event "may have happened." God "cannot" lie, because this would contradict the constraints imposed by his own character as faithful and true. From the point of view of the Deists (defined below), God "cannot" intervene in "laws" or regularities that relate to medical conditions in the natural world. But there are events, such as the resurrection of Christ, which appear on special occasions to modify generally predicted laws. So the majority of informed Christians would suggest not that God *cannot* modify such regularities of nature, but that he chooses *normally* not to do so. The debate about miracles is a separate topic, but is largely related to the fulfillment or nonfulfillment of the kingdom of God, that is, in what sense it is present or

---

1. David Hume, *Dialogue concerning Natural Religion* (New York: Harper, 1948; orig. 1779), part 10, 66.

2. Richard Swinburne, *The Coherence of Theism* (Oxford: Clarendon, 1977), 149-58.

future. If, in the message of Jesus, it is still in *process* of being fulfilled, then at present, as Oscar Cullmann argued, "Christians . . . still die."[3]

This medical or therapeutic example reminds us of the major distinction between natural and moral evil. Natural evils arise from the natural processes of the world; moral evils arise from a decision to embark on a course of action by an act of human will. J. S. Mill writes, "Nearly all the things for which men are hanged or imprisoned for doing to one another are Nature's everyday performances."[4] This may or may not be an exaggeration, but fifty years ago the "Fact and Faith" films were regularly shown with a detailed message of divine purpose in nature (such as *City of the Bees*) while today such films as those by David Attenborough equally show birds, beasts, and insects preying on one another for food. Alfred Lord Tennyson (1809-1892) wrote that while man trusted God as love, "nature, red in tooth and claw . . . shrieked against his creed."

Several "replies" have been made to this. The Catholic mystic Simone Weil (1909-1943) gloried in the wild and dark beauty of a storm at sea, but acknowledged that this may bring shipwrecks. In a more classic philosophical mode, both Augustine and Thomas Aquinas appealed to what Arthur Lovejoy called "The Principle of Plenitude."[5]

Lovejoy argued that the created universe contains the fullest variety of creatures from the highest to the lowest, and that this is a richer and better universe than one consisting only of the higher creatures. Augustine asked, "What is more beautiful than a fire? What is more useful than the heat and comfort? . . . Yet nothing can cause more distress than the burns inflicted by fire."[6] In this sense "difference" can potentially become a root of evil. Similarly Thomas Aquinas declared, "The wisdom of God is the cause of the distinction of things . . . the cause of their inequality. . . . Species seem to be arranged by degrees."[7] This is reflected, he urged, when God "separated" light from darkness in Genesis 1:4, 7.

Aquinas continued, "One opposite is known through the other."[8] Darkness is known through light, and evil is known from good. The sun shines

3. Oscar Cullmann, *Christ and Time: The Primitive Christian Conception of Time and History* (London: SCM, 1951), 69-93.

4. John Stuart Mill, *Three Essays on Religion* (London: Longman Green, 1875), 28.

5. Arthur Lovejoy, *The Great Chain of Being: A Study of the History of an Idea* (Cambridge: Harvard University Press, 1936).

6. Augustine, *City of God* 12.4.

7. Aquinas, *Summa* I, qu. 47, art. 2, reply.

8. Aquinas, *Summa* I, qu. 48, art. 1.

on bright hilltops and dark valleys. He then quoted Augustine, "Evil exists only in good."[9] Evil cannot wholly consume the good, but serves the good of the whole. Again he quoted Augustine, "There is no possible source of evil except good."[10] Our universe enjoys light and shade, and life and death.[11] In turn, this is related to the claim of Gottfried Leibniz (1646-1716), who produced a theodicy in terms of a series of logical syllogisms.[12] He concluded that God had created "the best possible world."

This is sometimes related to an argument that may seem needlessly to inhibit God's almighty-ness. J. S. Mill had written, "The author of the cosmos worked under limitations . . . obliged to adapt himself to conditions independent of his will."[13] He is followed by Edgar S. Brightman (1884-1953), who spoke of a "finite God."[14] In the twentieth century William H. Vanstone (1923-1999) compared God with an artist who must "go with the grain and limitations" of his materials.[15] Augustine and Calvin would never have held this view of the sovereignty of God. Nevertheless, this approach, especially in Vanstone, has helped many to cope with the problem of evil and suffering, not least because of its insights into the "costly" nature of the love of God.

Augustine, Aquinas, and Calvin boldly addressed the problem of *moral* evil, stressing especially the bondage of sin and the human plight, which relates to it. Augustine and Aquinas deployed what philosophers call "the free-will defense argument," in which the possibility of evil is bound up with the human will to choose. Evil, Augustine believed, arose "from a wilful turning of the self in desire from the highest good. The defection of the will is evil."[16] In the *Confessions* he gave a strong autobiographical account of this. "Self-will," he said, generates evil, which is "borne of self-interest, which generates conflict and competitiveness"; even a child has "a wish to be obeyed."[17] Granted that God's gifts are good, evil comes when we misuse them. Certainly evil is not, as the Manichaeans claimed, a positive force or

9. Aquinas, *Summa* I, qu. 48, art. 3, reply, quoting Augustine, *Enchiridion* 14.

10. Aquinas, *Summa* I, qu. 49, art. 1, quoting Augustine, *Against Julian* 1.9.

11. Aquinas, *Summa* I, qu. 49, art. 2.

12. Gottfried W. Leibniz, *Theodicy: Essays on the Goodness of God, the Freedom of Man, and the Origin of Evil* (London: Routledge, Kegan Paul, 1952).

13. Mill, *Three Essays on Religion*.

14. Edgar Brightman, *A Philosophy of Religion* (New York: Skeffington and Prentice-Hall, 1940), 157-58.

15. W. H. Vanstone, *Love's Endeavour, Love's Expense: The Response of Being to the Love of God* (London: DLT, 2007; orig. 1977).

16. Augustine, *City of God* 12.7.

17. Augustine, *Confessions* 1.6.8.

entity in its own right. The whole creation is good, but humankind can abuse it, and misunderstand its function and purpose. Augustine wrote, "An evil will (Lat. *improba voluntas*) is the cause of all evils."[18] In the *Confessions* he declared, "Free will is the cause of our doing evil, and ... thy [God's] just judgment is the cause of having to suffer from its consequences."[19] He also recalled, "I had gone astray of (my) own free will and fallen into error."[20] Humankind substitutes its own private good for the highest good of the will of God.

Clearly this does not imply that human freedom is the cause of evil, but only of *potential* evil. If humankind is free to sin, moral evil is *potentially* inevitable. Otherwise God would (in theory) need to program robot-like humans who would *always* choose *only* the right or good. Aquinas endorsed this argument. Evil has no causal efficacy of its own. In his discussion of the necessity of the incarnation, Aquinas wrote, "God allows evils to happen in order to bring a greater good therefrom: hence it is written (Rom. 5:20); 'Where sin abounded, grace did much more abound.'"[21] He even quoted Augustine, "O happy fault, that merited such and so great a Redeemer."[22]

In modern philosophy, however, this "free-will defense" argument has been questioned. For example, J. L. Mackie insists, "All forms of the free-will defence fail."[23] He claims that God could supposedly have created human beings who *always freely choose* to do the right. Much of this argument depends on analogies with freedom and predictability. We may construct the following hypothetical situation: Tom lives in a fairly dreary town, where most young people of his age have left school at the first opportunity, and speak of nothing but TV soaps, sport, holidays, and clothes. However, next door lives Mary. Like Tom, she enjoys higher education, classical music, and politics. Gradually their common interests bring them together. One day Tom freely chooses to propose marriage, and Mary freely chooses to accept. Everyone, including both sets of parents, say: "We knew it would happen." Mackie and others argue that what was inevitable was freely chosen.

18. Augustine, *On Free Will* 3.17.48.

19. Augustine, *Confessions* 7.3.5; in *Confessions and Enchiridion,* ed. Albert Cook Outler, LCC 7 (Philadelphia: Westminster, 1955), 137.

20. Augustine, *Confessions* 4.15.26; in Outler, 91.

21. Aquinas, *Summa* III, qu. 1, art. 3, reply to obj. 3.

22. Aquinas, *Summa* III, qu. 1, art. 3, reply to obj. 3; Lat. "O Felix culpa, quae talem ac tantum meruit habere redemptorem."

23. J. L. Mackie, *The Miracle of Theism: Arguments for and against the Existence of God* (Oxford: Clarendon, 1982), 176.

The most successful "reply" to Mackie is generally recognized to have come from the Christian philosopher Alvin Plantinga. Plantinga formulates an argument that at first both is negative and concerns *logical,* not empirical or actual, *necessity.* He argues, "It is possible that God, even being omnipotent, could not [logical 'could not'] create a world with free creatures who never choose evil."[24] It is *logically possible,* however, for an "omnibenevolent" God to create a world that contains evil, "if moral goodness requires free moral creatures." Plantinga is not so much concerned with what is true as with what is *logically possible* or *logically impossible.* He argues that a world in which people perform actions freely is a more valuable world than one in which there is no freedom. Their freedom is a *presupposition* of their capacity to perform moral good. This remains the case even if some human beings choose wrongly. To create moral good without the *possibility* of moral evil is *not logically possible* even for an omnipotent God.

Even if God could (logically) create a possible world where people would always freely choose the right, this is not the case where a possible world suffers from what Plantinga calls "transworld depravity." In such a world God cannot "strongly actualize" freedom that would always choose the right or good. The term "depravity" comes from the Reformed tradition of theology, to which Plantinga also belongs.

Chad Meister considers that most, or at least many, philosophers accept Plantinga's logical version of the free-will defense argument.[25] Robert Adams is quoted as saying that "Plantinga has solved the problem."[26] William Alston also offers a positive verdict. On the other hand, some argue that Plantinga is successful *only against Mackie's argument.* Indeed, Mackie himself and Antony Flew argue that he succeeds only if we hold an "incompatibilist" view of freedom. But incompatibilism normally is the doctrine that freedom and determinism cannot both be true. Yet it seems unlikely that Plantinga could be called neither "a hard determinist" nor "a libertarian," although in a modified sense Plantinga does attack "compatibilism."

24. Chad Meister, *Introducing Philosophy of Religion* (New York and London: Routledge, 2009), 133; cf. Alvin Plantinga, *God, Freedom, and Evil* (Grand Rapids: Eerdmans, 1977), 29-55; Alvin Plantinga, "Free Will Defence," in *Philosophy in America,* ed. Max Black (Ithaca, N.Y.: Cornell University Press; London: Allen and Unwin, 1965); and Alvin Plantinga, *The Nature of Necessity* (Oxford: Clarendon, 1974), 165-90.

25. Meister, *Introducing Philosophy of Religion,* 134.

26. Daniel Howard-Snyder and John O'Leary-Hawthorne, "Transworld Sanctity and Plantinga's Free Will Defense," *International Journal for Philosophy of Religion* 44 (1998): 1-28.

Indeed, he spends considerable time elucidating the ideas of freedom and the sovereignty of God.

To return to Brümmer's point about "pastoral sensitivity," these arguments may be too logically complex to help those who suffer from evil at the present moment. Nevertheless, they provide good preparation for later affliction, and good grounds for reflection when such an event no longer colors the present moment so harshly or decisively. Each of the three supposedly incompatible realities, namely, the sovereignty of God, the love of God, and the presence of evil in the world, has been qualified logically in such a way as to minimize a stark paradox. Evil is still real, but is seen as part of a bigger picture. Divine goodness and love are real, but have undergone *logical* constraints. Plantinga argues that just because we do not *know* of a *ready* "answer" to the problem of evil, this does not imply that there is none, *in the inscrutable counsel of God*. Why should we assume that God's self-revelation tells us *everything* about God and the universe?

Because of the supposed harshness of "logical" explanations, some have restricted their approaches to existential or practical considerations. Terrence Tilley attempts to argue that theodicies, or justifications of the ways of God, are positively unhelpful, in his book *The Evils of Theodicy*.[27] Surprisingly, he even denies that Augustine offers a formal theodicy, since almost all of Augustine's writings, with the almost single exception of the *Enchiridion,* or *Handbook,* were written to combat particular errors. These include Manichaeanism (works on dualism), Donatism (works on the purity of the church), Pelagianism (works on grace), and other "heresies," even though it would be hard to avoid seeing *The City of God* as a philosophy of history, which surely includes theodicy. Tilley helpfully regards many Christian confessions in the face of suffering not as "propositions," but as *"speech acts,"* as utterances that commit the speaker to certain attitudes, beliefs, and practices. Indeed, his main thesis is: "Theodicy is a *practice within Christian theology*."[28] To understand God, he argues, we must enter into Job's plight and share his world.[29]

As we have noted above, Simone Weil's witness was primarily one of sheer acceptance of God's ways, even if she also spoke out against "humiliation" by human oppression.[30] Other writers who adopt this more existential

27. Terrence W. Tilley, *The Evils of Theodicy* (Washington, D.C.: Georgetown University Press, 1991).

28. Tilley, *The Evils of Theodicy,* 85, italics mine.

29. Tilley, *The Evils of Theodicy,* 94 and 105.

30. Simone Weil, *Waiting for God* (London: Routledge, 1974; orig. 1939).

approach include F. Dostoevsky and Elie Wiesel in his autobiographical experiences of the Holocaust, recounted in *Night* (1969). Moltmann recounts part of Wiesel's experience, citing the question of a youth in his death throes: "Where is God?" The answer, "He is hanging on the gallows," is seen by Moltmann as a rabbinic equivalent to the Christian response, "God is hanging on the cross."[31]

Somewhere on a spectrum between the "logical" and the "existential" approaches, we may perhaps cite John Hick's book *Evil and the God of Love,* although he discusses in full the logical arguments of the main tradition through Augustine, Aquinas, and others, alongside criticisms of it by Mackie, Flew, and Hume. He describes his approach as the "minority report" in Christian theology. His own reflections have persuaded him of the approach of Irenaeus and Schleiermacher. Rather than looking *back* to the Fall with Augustine and Aquinas, Hick looks *forward* to the End, or eschaton, with its goal of maturity and holiness. He declares, "The *telos* [end or goal] of man's nature consists in a relationship to God."[32] Evil has a part to play in achieving maturity of character. Hick borrows the term "soul-making" theodicy from Keats.

Irenaeus (c. 130–c. 200) distinguished between the image (Gk. *eikōn*) of God and the likeness (Gk. *homoiōsis*) of God in humankind.[33] Although most Hebrew specialists regard these two terms as examples of Hebrew poetic parallelism, and therefore as synonymous, Irenaeus saw the "image" as representing such qualities as rationality, which humankind possesses, and the "likeness" as the spiritual and moral goal that has yet to be fulfilled.[34] We pass through stages or processes of learning and discipline in which we may need to struggle against evils. In a following chapter Hick finds elements of this "Irenaean" theodicy in F. Schleiermacher (1768-1834). Schleiermacher's key term was "God-consciousness," and this may be stimulated in us by "life-hindrance" and pain.[35] Schleiermacher's approach was largely *developmental* in accordance with nineteenth-century evolutionary theories. He regarded "evil" (Ger. *Übel*) as obstructing needed developments. These may be social

31. Jürgen Moltmann, *The Crucified God: The Cross as the Foundation and Criticism of Christian Theology* (London: SCM, 1974), 273-74; cf. Elie Wiesel, *Night* (New York: Hill and Wang, 1960, 1969), 75-76.

32. John Hick, *Evil and the God of Love* (London: Macmillan, 1966; 2nd ed. 1977), 16.

33. Irenaeus, *Against Heresies* 5.6.1; *ANF* 1:532.

34. Hick, *Evil,* 217-21.

35. Friedrich Schleiermacher, *The Christian Faith* (Edinburgh: T. & T. Clark, 1989; Ger. 2nd ed. 1830), sect. 59, 240; Hick, *Evil,* 226-41.

or natural. Hence evil can give us "consciousness of sin," which also consti-tuted part of grace.[36] Evil, Hick argues, becomes "instrumental."[37]

Hick provides other examples of this approach, including evolutionary nineteenth-century approaches, as well as that of F. R. Tennant. For ordi-nary Christians, this means that evil and suffering may be endured as *an opportunity for growth and holiness.* In some Catholic theology this principle leads to the function of purgatory. Within Anglicanism, Hick points to the High Church Anglican Austin Farrer, especially in his *Love Almighty and Ills Unlimited.*[38] Farrer stresses the redemptive and eschatological nature of God's providence and grace. Hick does adhere, however, to his "Vale of Soul-Making Theodicy."[39] On top of this, his eschatology involves universal salvation, and "progressive sanctification after death."[40]

Whether we should drive such a sharp wedge between the so-called Au-gustinian and Irenaean approaches may perhaps be doubted. Pastorally each approach discussed above offers something constructive to say to those who pass, or have passed, through suffering or conflict with evil. At all events, such writers as Plantinga and Swinburne show that the problem of evil does not run counter to what Swinburne calls "the coherence of theism." The confines of space prevent us from considering every aspect of this problem. The subject remains a problem, but there are also hints of a solution. We have tried to focus on those approaches that offer potential or actual help to those who are in pastoral situations of evil or suffering. Perhaps the well-known comments of the logician and mathematician G. W. Leibniz are not as unduly optimistic as is often claimed.

2. Can We Argue from "Cause" to God's Existence? God's Transcendence

People often assume that the most popular argument for the existence of God is probably that which infers that *the world needs a "cause," who is God.* For many centuries this reasoning has been known generally as the *cosmolog-ical argument* for the existence of God. At a commonsense level, it may seem

36. Schleiermacher, *The Christian Faith,* sect. 84, 347.

37. Hick, *Evil,* 237-40.

38. Austin Farrer, *Love Almighty and Ills Unlimited* (New York: Doubleday; London: Collins, 1962), especially chap. 7.

39. Hick, *Evil,* 289-97 and 328-400.

40. Hick, *Evil,* 383.

to work effectively, but on closer examination it breaks down, because the "causes" with which we are familiar in everyday life are all "*caused* causes," that is, they function *within a causal chain.* By contrast, *God as transcendent is uniquely first cause or uncaused cause.* The child who immediately reacts to the cosmological argument by asking, "Then who caused God?" has in fact spotted the flaw. Every "cause" that we experience in daily life has been *caused,* in turn, by some other object or agency. Hence the child is perplexed: Is God part of an infinite chain of cause and effect? If so, who caused God?

We can apply *cause* to God only if we then *qualify* the model of cause by describing God as "*uncaused* cause" or as "*first* cause." This is one of Ian Ramsey's major examples of how models demand "qualifiers" when used of God. Thus God is not simply "wise" *(simple anthropomorphic* or *human-like model),* but "infinitely wise" *(qualified model).*[41] God transcends human qualities.

Alvin Plantinga expounds this contrast between *"commonsense"* arguments and those that are *logically watertight* with reference to the related teleological argument for the existence of God. At a *commonsense* level, arguments from purpose or design in the world may seem to work, even if logical scrutiny might suggest otherwise. But, he points out, they are actually no weaker than our assumptions that "other minds" exist, even if by strict logic alone "solipsism" (the view that only "I" exist) may seem to have logical force and validity.[42]

This qualification that God is *first* cause or *uncaused* cause logically removes the concept of God from our earthly or empirical *chain of cause and effect.* Thereby, in theological terms, this points to the *transcendence* of God as One who is *beyond* or "above" the world.

We have not yet begun to explain the basic theological and philosophical term "transcendent," as well as its converse, "immanent." The term "suprapersonal" certainly implies transcendence. "Transcendence" denotes that which surpasses or goes beyond (Lat. *transcendere*) human thought and human historical finitude. In nontheological language it denotes God's *otherness* from humankind and the world.

Usually, however, Christians immediately *qualify* this, once again, without reducing it, by saying God is *also* active *within* the world. His presence

41. Ian T. Ramsey, *Religious Language: An Empirical Placing of Theological Phrases* (London: SCM, 1957), 49-89.

42. Alvin Plantinga, *God and Other Minds: A Study of the Rational Justification of Belief in God* (Ithaca, N.Y.: Cornell University Press, 1967, 1991), 245-72.

sustains all life. In Acts Paul and the Stoics are at one in declaring: "In him (God) we live and move and have our being" (Acts 17:28; even if a few dispute that this verse genuinely reflects Paul). Paul speaks of the immanence of Christ in other passages. In Colossians 1:17 he asserts, "He (Christ) is before all things, and in him all things hold together" (Gk. *sunestēken*). Paul safeguards the *transcendence* of God the Holy Spirit when he rejects the Stoic understanding of spirit *(pneuma)* as the "world-soul," declaring, "We have received not the spirit of the world, but the Spirit that is from God" (1 Cor. 2:12). The emphatic Greek for this is *to pneuma to ek tou Theou,* which we could well translate "the Spirit who comes forth (or proceeds) from God."

A variety of theologians have emphasized the transcendence of God in different ways. Rudolf Otto expounded this in terms of phenomenology in his book *The Idea of the Holy* (1917). He used the word "numinous" to expound the experience of God as *mysterium tremendum,* but also as *fascinans,* that is, enchanting. God is fathomless, holy, and a mystery. Kierkegaard expounded God's contrast with human finitude. Karl Barth insisted that "God is known through God, and through God alone."[43] God, he declared, "is incomprehensible and inexpressible . . . not defined."[44] But this is not the entire story. E. Jüngel affirmed that God became "thinkable," "conceivable," and "speakable" in Jesus Christ and the cross.[45] In Isaiah the seraphim cover their faces and feet, and God is enthroned "high and lofty" (Isa. 6:1-2). But the reason why God proclaims, "My thoughts are not your thoughts" and "my ways [are] higher than your ways," is that he is willing for Israel, in spite of its sin, *to return,* and to "call upon him while he is near" (Isa. 55:8-9, 6). His grace and *immanent action* are explained in terms of his sheer *transcendence.*

We can now *revisit* the *cosmological argument* with greater *understanding.* Strictly, as a logical syllogism, the argument fails. For in a syllogism it is vital that each term is used with the same meaning in each proposition. But in fact the major premise, "Every event has a *cause,*" uses "cause" to denote *"caused cause";* while the conclusion, "Therefore the world has a *cause,*" uses "cause" in *a different sense* to denote *"uncaused cause."* Otherwise it would merely postulate an infinite chain of cause and effect.

Thomas Aquinas provides a classic account of this argument. He sees

43. Barth, *CD* II/1, 179.

44. Barth, *CD* II/1, 186-87.

45. Eberhard Jüngel, *God as the Mystery of the World* (Edinburgh: T. & T. Clark, 1983), 220-21, 229.

the difficulty at once. He writes, "Now we must stop somewhere, otherwise there will be no first cause of the change, and as a result, no subsequent causes. . . . In the observable world causes are found to be ordered in series[;] we never observe, nor ever could, something causing itself, for this would mean it preceded itself. . . . Such a series of causes must however stop somewhere."[46] But we see at once that this has shifted the ground of the argument. In philosophical and Aristotelian terms, this has shifted arguments from *contingent cause* (or *caused* cause) to *necessary cause* (or *uncaused* cause). Aquinas shows the difference between them. This is no longer a "commonsense" argument about causes *within* the world; it postulates at the beginning the need for a logically *necessary* cause on the part of the God who is transcendent. In practice Aquinas's "five ways" of arguing for God's existence give three versions of "causality" in the first three of his five ways. Technically, the first concerns *movement;* the second, *potentiality* and efficient cause; and the third, *logical necessity* or *"aseity,"* that is, being one's own ground of existence.

This is in line with the editors' introduction and appendix to the standard sixty-volume Blackfriars edition.[47] They suggest that Aquinas does not regard the argument as a "proof," but as a way of "being convinced," that God exists, and that such belief is *not contrary to reason.* They also suggest that all of Aquinas's "five ways" (which amount to the three traditional arguments for the existence of God) point in the same direction. Pastorally and theologically they direct our gaze *from the everyday world to a reality in which the world is grounded.* The editors' third suggestion is that Aquinas's use of Aristotle's conceptuality is a brilliant utilization of the thought of his day. The use of Aristotle shows where knockdown "demonstration" runs out, but nevertheless shows also that the drive toward an infinite chain of causes is no more rational than belief in a final cause. Aquinas maximizes what can be gleaned from argument from the empirical world (i.e., what philosophers call a posteriori argument), even if in the end he resorts to using a priori (i.e., purely logical or rational) assumptions. Although he cannot regard "God" as simply "efficient" cause of the world, Aristotle appears to hold that the supreme God operates as "final" cause of it.

Other thinkers in theist religions have held this position. The Islamic philosophers al-Kindi (c. 813–c. 871) and al-Ghazali (c. 1058-1111) also believed that an infinite chain of caused causes is impossible, as Aristotle and

46. Aquinas, *Summa* I, qu. 2, art. 3, reply (Blackfriars ed., 2:14-15).
47. Aquinas, *Summa,* Blackfriars ed., 2:xx-xxvii and 188-390.

Aquinas did. This is sometimes called the *kalam* tradition of Islam. The Spanish Jewish philosopher Maimonides (1135-1204) also broadly endorsed the cosmological argument, and the finite status of the world. In his "third way" Aquinas wrote that we are forced "to postulate something which is of itself necessary."[48]

Historically Samuel Clarke (1675-1729), John Locke (1632-1704), Sir Isaac Newton (1642-1727), and G. W. Leibniz (1646-1716) all affirmed the *reasonableness* of the argument. On the other hand, David Hume (1711-1776) challenged the notion that observation of the world (and empirical, a posteriori inference) could ever arrive at belief in God. In a masterly examination of *cause,* he argued that cause and effect are never in fact actually *observed.* All that we can empirically *observe* is "constant conjunction," "contiguity," or regularity. Connecting cause and effect, he reflected, is due to mere habit or *convention.* He concluded, "Upon examination . . . the necessity of a cause is fallacious and sophistical."[49] Immanuel Kant (1724-1804) pressed this further, arguing that notions of causality and time were imposed on reality by the mind. They are merely "regulative" principles used by the mind to interpret order and purpose within the world. Yet, again, Aquinas did not regard this as *"proof,"* only as *reasonable.* In this respect, Plantinga's comments about common sense and the basis of solipsism, or the existence of other minds, seem apposite.

The positions of modern or contemporary philosophers can almost be predicted. For example, J. L. Mackie attacks several aspects of the cosmological argument, whereas W. L. Craig revives the *kalam* tradition in *The Cosmological Argument from Plato to Leibniz* (1980). The Catholic philosopher G. E. M. Anscombe presents a positive, sophisticated discussion, which includes the article "Hume's Argument Exposed" in *Analysis* 34 (1974).[50] The nineteenth-century conservative Protestant theologian Charles Hodge concludes that this argument cannot prove the truth of all that theists claim about God, but "It is enough that . . . we must admit the existence of an eternal and necessary Being."[51]

Two of the more recent defenses of the cosmological argument come from William Rowe (b. 1931), of Purdue University, and from Richard Taylor (1919-2003), of Rochester University. Rowe establishes the logical syllogism

48. Aquinas, *Summa* I, qu. 3, art. 3, reply.

49. David Hume, *A Treatise of Human Nature* (Oxford: OUP, 1978; orig. 1739), 79-94.

50. G. E. M. Anscombe, "Hume's Argument Exposed," in her *Collected Philosophical Papers,* 3 vols. (Oxford: Blackwell, 1981).

51. Charles Hodge, *Systematic Theology,* 3 vols. (New York: Scribner, 1871), 1:215.

by substituting the words "dependent" for cause and "self-existent" for first cause. He argues: "Not every being is a dependent being: therefore there exists a self-existent being."[52] He also invokes "the principle of sufficient reason," that is, that everything must have an explanation. Taylor also appeals to the principle of sufficient reason, and begins with the experience of finding a mysterious object that requires an explanation. His next argument is that everything in the world is of finite duration, and everything, including the world, has a beginning. Only a being that depends on nothing outside itself (i.e., a being that is self-caused) can have caused the world.[53] Some writers attempt to argue from the principle of entropy (or running down of the universe) in modern physics. But this is less fundamental to the argument.

From the point of view of biblical and Christian discipleship, it is not unreasonable, for example, that the psalmist exclaims,

> The LORD is my rock, my fortress . . .
> my God, my rock in whom I take refuge,
> my shield . . . my stronghold (Ps. 18:2),

or that a congregation may sing, "Rock of Ages, cleft for me . . ." It reminds us of our constant dependence on God, and of God's self-existence and aseity. Such an uncaused cause or self-existent God (to use Rowe's word) merits absolute trust, and demonstrates absolute faithfulness. To be "caused" makes us dependent beings (Rowe's word again). Christians relish what Schleiermacher called absolute dependence on God. But God is both immanent and transcendent. He is holy and "Other"; he is also love, who invites us to trust him and to commune with him. *God is "all in all"* (1 Cor. 15:28).

3. The Argument from Design, and Modern Science

Kant respected the argument from design at the level of common sense, as the oldest and clearest of the arguments for the existence of God. But he did not think it was philosophically watertight and deductively valid, because he believed that the human sense of purpose, design, and order in the world was

52. William Rowe, "An Examination of the Cosmological Argument," in *Philosophy of Religion: An Anthology,* ed. Louis Pojman (Belmont, Calif.: Wadsworth, 1994), 16-25.

53. Richard Taylor, "The Cosmological Argument: A Defence," in Taylor, *Metaphysics* (Englewood Cliffs, N.J.: Prentice-Hall, 1983), 91-99.

imposed by the human mind, in order to make sense of the world.[54] Some ascribe this argument to Anaxagoras in fifth century B.C. Greece, and probably to Plato, Aristotle, and Augustine. It is the fifth way of Aquinas's "Five Ways." Aquinas wrote, "The fifth way is based on the guidedness of nature *(ex gubernatione rerum)."* He added: "An orderedness of actions to (towards) an end *(finem)* . . . tend(s) to a goal"; it is not accidental. But nothing can do this "except under the direction of someone with awareness and with understanding; the arrow, for example, requires an archer. Everything in nature, therefore, is directed to its goal by someone with understanding and this we call 'God.' "[55] On the basis of the Greek *telos,* "end" or "goal," this approach is commonly called *the teleological argument.*

The most famous formulation of this argument was by William Paley (1743-1805), archdeacon of Carlisle. His *Evidences of the Existence and Attributes of the Deity,* also known as his *Natural Theology* (1802), formulates the argument from design in its first chapter.[56] It begins with an anecdote. He imagines crossing a heath and stumbling over a *stone.* No serious question can be raised about the origins and purpose of a stone. He continues: "But suppose I found a *watch* upon the ground." He might seek a very different answer, he says, from that of finding the stone: "Several parts are framed and put together for a purpose, e.g. they are so formed and adjusted as to produce motion . . . to point out the hour of the day." Its spring, chain, and cogs make this purpose possible. Hence, Paley argues, "The watch must have had a maker . . . an artificer or artificers who formed it for a purpose." This conclusion, he points out, would not become invalidated (i) if we had never known the watchmaker; nor (ii) if the watch went wrong; nor (iii) if we did not understand every part of the watch; and so on. Such mechanisms, Paley concluded, abound in creation, including, for example, the mechanism of the human or animal eye. Hence we must postulate or infer *God as Designer.*

Hume died before Paley wrote his treatise. Yet many of Hume's arguments, even if not original, did in part anticipate Paley's arguments. In his *Dialogues,* while the fictional Cleanthes argues for natural theology, Philo (a thinly disguised Hume) opposes it. First, Philo argues, a design might suggest a plurality of designers. Second, more seriously, the design argument ultimately rests on the validity of the cosmological argument: a designed

54. Immanuel Kant, *Critique of Pure Reason* (London: Macmillan, 1933; 2nd ed. 1787), chap. 3, sect. 6.

55. Aquinas, *Summa* I, qu. 2, art. 3, reply (Blackfriars ed., 2:17).

56. William Paley, *Natural Theology; or, Evidences of the Existence and Attributes of the Deity* (London: Rivington, 1802), chap. 1, sect. 2.

effect implies a designing cause. But Hume has argued that cause and effect *cannot strictly be observed as an empirical phenomenon.* Constant conjunction, he urges, rests only on habit and convention to construe it as "cause." Kant, a near contemporary of Paley and Hume, disagreed with Hume about most things, but agreed with him that causal connections are imposed by the *human mind* in its desire to make sense and order of things.

Even if there is force in the objections of Hume and Kant, we should still be left with the point made by Plantinga about the existence of "other minds," namely, that common sense may suggest what pure logic cannot demonstrate conclusively. Thus Kant expressed respect for the argument, even if it transcended strict logic. However, the greatest challenge to the argument from design came with the evolutionary theories of Charles Darwin (1809-1882), Herbert Spencer (1820-1903), and other nineteenth-century evolutionary thinkers. Darwin's *Origin of Species* appeared in 1859. Spencer called this argument "the survival of the fittest," and suggested that, far from the eye being "designed" to give sight, it was as organisms developed that those who had *developed eyes* could see *to survive.* Skeptics argued that the psalmist could credit God with "filling all things with plenteousness" (Ps. 144:15, Prayer Book translation) only because those who were not so filled died.

Biological processes seemed to substitute competitive survival for individual design. Genetic mutation, rather than design, seemed to ensure adaptation to what was needed to survive. Even in the case of humankind, anthropologists tended to regard tools, weapons, and language as decisive resources for human survival, rather than God's decree to give to humankind "dominion" over the works of their hands (Ps. 8:6).

More than his later book *The Descent of Man* (1871), Darwin's *Origin of Species* made a huge popular impact. It popularized the view that all creatures had evolved by natural, random processes. It provoked massive controversy. But the genuinely scientific question of *how* creatures evolved was not to be confused with the larger theological question of *why* creation and often evolution itself occurred. F. R. Tennant argued, "Gradualness of construction is itself no proof of the absence of . . . design."[57] Purpose, they argued, is more *reasonable* than "groundless contingency" or chance.[58] Darwin himself denied that he was an explicit atheist, and held a view midway between theism and Deism. Augustine and Calvin had never regarded Genesis 1 as

---

57. F. R. Tennant, *Philosophical Theology,* 2 vols. (Cambridge: CUP, 1930), 2:84.
58. Tennant, *Philosophical Theology,* 2:79: cf. 92-93.

a *chronological* or *biological* account of creation. David Livingstone carefully charts the varied reaction of Christians, especially nineteenth-century and early-twentieth-century evangelicals, to Darwin's theory.[59] Thus A. A. Hodge, he comments, insisted on order within the universe but regarded "evolution . . . as a plan of an infinitely wise Person . . . executed under the control of his everywhere-present energies."[60] B. B. Warfield and P. T. Forsyth, Livingstone claims, endorsed this. It was only later, around 1925, that an all-out attack on Darwin was launched. Livingstone comments, "Within . . . about two decades, the old cultured evangelicalism had given way to the bitter polemics of a rampant fundamentalism."[61]

More than fifty years later and on into the twenty-first century, such writers as Richard Swinburne, A. R. Peacocke, John Polkinghorne, Ian Barbour, Malcolm Jeeves, and R. J. Berry argued that whatever we conclude about *individual* organisms, "There has been and will continue to be, in nature *an order recognizable* and describable by men certainly, but *one which exists independently of men.*"[62] Swinburne adds, "The universe is characterized by vast, all-pervasive temporal order."[63] Ian Barbour sums up the general change today with the words, "In a reformulated version, *purposeful design was seen in the laws and structures* through which life and mind emerged and in *the directionality of the total process.*"[64]

Polkinghorne, Barbour, and others go further, insisting that *duration and time* are positively *required* for the creation of carbon-based life and humankind. The odds that this long process can arrive at the creation of humankind by chance or accident are rated by Polkinghorne as "one in a trillion."[65] In an earlier book he wrote, "The actual balance between chance and necessity, contingency and potentiality, which we perceive, seems to me to be consistent with the will of a patient and subtle Creator, content to achieve his purposes through the unfolding of long processes, and accept-

---

59. David N. Livingstone, *Darwin's Forgotten Defenders: The Encounter between Evangelical Theology and Evolutionary Thought* (Grand Rapids: Eerdmans, 1987).

60. Cited by Livingstone, *Darwin's Forgotten Defenders,* 114.

61. Livingstone, *Darwin's Forgotten Defenders,* 165-66.

62. Richard Swinburne, *The Existence of God* (Oxford: Clarendon, 1979), 137, italics mine.

63. Swinburne, *The Existence of God,* 138.

64. Ian G. Barbour, *Religion and Science: Historical and Contemporary Issues* (London: SCM, 1998), 73, italics mine.

65. John Polkinghorne, *Quarks, Chaos, and Christianity: Questions to Science and Religion* (London: SPCK, 2005), 27.

ing thereby a measure of the vulnerability and precariousness which always characterize the gift of freedom by love."[66]

Polkinghorne also discusses Schrödinger's equation on quantum theory, and Maxwell's equations on electromagnetism. These concern the replication of molecules and eventually life. He comments that these are "like a rehabilitation of the argument from design — not as a knockdown argument for the existence of God . . . but as an insight into the way the world is."[67] Similarly, Ian Barbour writes, "God's purposes are expressed not only in the unchanging structural conditions of life, but more specifically in relation to changing situations and patterns. Continuing creation, in this view, is a trial-and-error 'experiment,' always building on what is already there."[68]

This not only helps us to see some of the value and limitations of the argument from design, but elucidates what it might mean to conceive of "God's purpose for our lives," as many Christians express it. God does not ask Christians to respond to some "timeless" blueprint for life. As Christians are often obedient, but sometimes make mistakes, purposes of God "build on what is already there." Some have needless depression about "missing God's will." But God uses natural processes of reflection and decision. This in no way shortcuts the real experience of the Holy Spirit, as Pannenberg also insists. Indeed, it is precisely the creative Spirit of God who constantly brings life out of chaos, and resurrection out of death. God's purposes for us and for the world are loving, and sovereign, and he works for our good with great patience, using what is *there,* or taking us up from the point that we have reached. As Polkinghorne, Barbour, and many others maintain, it was ever thus, from long ago.

We must also note what these thinkers say about "levels of explanation." This can apply to the world, or to individual human life. It is possible to "explain" a glorious symphony as a matter of acoustic wavelengths, or vibrations that we can observe on an oscilloscope. This would be one explanation, on the level of physics. Or we could "explain" it on the level adopted by musicologists. This might involve the key signature, the melody and harmonies, time, crescendo, and so on. Similarly, for the universe we can use reductionist explanations, beginning with the particles of physics; but we can also employ "explanations" of a higher level, including artistic, musical, moral, or theological approaches. Polkinghorne quotes Eric Mascall

66. John Polkinghorne, *One World: The Interaction of Science and Theology* (Princeton: Princeton University Press, 1987), 69.

67. John Polkinghorne, *The Way the World Is: The Christian Perspective of a Scientist* (London: SPCK/Triangle, 1992), 12.

68. Barbour, *Religion and Science,* 240.

as saying, "Though a physicist knows the objective world only through the mediation of sensation, the essential character of the objective world is not sensibility but intelligibility."[69] It requires *understanding* at a higher level, as Bernard Lonergan also argues. In the words of Barbour, "God creates 'in and through' processes of the natural world that science unveils."[70]

For the Christian, this vindicates many approaches in contemporary science, and we are challenged to give thanks for, and to pray for, Christians engaged creatively in the sciences and medical research. More personally, we may be assured that God has major purposes in nature (see chap. 5, sect. 3) and in history, but also has purposes for specific communities and individual lives. We may celebrate the God of both transcendent mystery and immanent, intelligible providence.

4. The Argument from Necessity: The Ontological Argument

This "argument" for the existence of God is important for believers in God because it claims to point not only to God's existence, but also to his character or "Being" as omnipotent, omniscient, and omnibenevolent, as well as transcendent. The ontological argument was first explicitly formulated by Anselm, archbishop of Canterbury, in his *Proslogion* (c. 1077-1078), and represents his theme of "faith seeking understanding." It first emerged in the context of *prayer and contemplation of God.*[71] As Karl Barth insists with emphasis, it was not first intended as a "philosophical proof," but in the context of Anselm's prayer: " 'Seek his face!' Your face, LORD, do I seek" (Ps. 27:8).[72] Yet, over the years it has become the argument that invites the most sophisticated philosophical debate, and is frequently selected for problems of modal logic (i.e., the logic of *possibility,* rather than of *propositions* or "facts"). Even after the most sophisticated philosophical examination, Alvin Plantinga concludes, "It (the argument) establishes not the truth of theism, but its *rational acceptability.*"[73]

69. Polkinghorne, *The Way the World Is,* 10-11.

70. Barbour, *Religion and Science,* 101.

71. Anselm, "An Address (Proslogion)," in *A Scholastic Miscellany: Anselm to Ockham,* ed. Eugene R. Fairweather, LCC (London: SCM; Philadelphia: Westminster, 1956), 69-93.

72. See Karl Barth, *Anselm: Fides Quaerens Intellectum* (London: SCM, 1931; Richmond, Va.: John Knox, 1960), 35-40.

73. Cited by Louis Pojman, "The Ontological Argument," in his *Philosophy of Religion,* 3rd ed. (Belmont, Calif.: Wadsworth, 1998), 55, italics mine.

Anselm formulated the argument in two stages or forms. In *Proslogion* chapters 1–26, he confesses that God truly "is," in a way distinctive to him. In chapter 2 he declares, "We believe that thou art a being than which none greater can be thought."[74] Perhaps only "the fool" of Psalm 14:1 would dare to say "There is no God." Anselm continues: "That than which a greater cannot be thought to exist in the understanding alone. For if it is actually in the understanding alone, it can be thought of as existing also in *reality,* and *this is greater.*"[75] If God did not exist in reality, God would not be "greater than" what I can *think,* or the contents of my mind. Anselm goes on to understand "greater than" to include compassion, immutability, righteousness, mercy, truth, and eternity (chaps. 7–13).

A monk, Gaunilo, a contemporary of Anselm, rejected this argument. He cited the example of an island that had inestimable wealth, an abundance of delicacies, and all that made it the "greatest" conceivable island. But, he argued, the excellence of the island does not provide a basis for its existence in *reality:* only in *thought.*

Anselm therefore reformulated his argument.[76] He withdrew the analogy of an island, and recognized that his argument was "peculiar to God." In fact, he had implied this in *Proslogion,* chapter 4. As Alvin Plantinga expresses the matter, some qualities are *uniquely unsurpassable maximums.* Today he speaks of "maximal greatness."

Much more serious is Kant's criticism of the argument. Ironically the clue to the problem arose from an attempt to defend and to reformulate the argument in a philosophical way by René Descartes (1596-1650). As a mathematician and rationalist, Descartes sought certainty, or *certain knowledge.* He discarded *empirical* or a posteriori arguments as offering no more than probability. A priori truths are logically certain, especially if they are analytical, or true-by-definition. The propositions "2 + 2 = 4" and "All bachelors are unmarried" fall into this category. In the same way, Descartes claimed that "Eternal existence pertains to his (God's) nature." He stated, "Existence can no more be separated from the essence of God" than can the fact that three angles of a triangle must equal two right angles "be separated from the essence of a triangle."[77]

74. Anselm, "An Address (Proslogion)," 73.

75. Anselm, "An Address (Proslogion)," 74, italics mine.

76. Anselm, "An Excerpt from the Author's Reply to the Criticisms of Gaunilo," in *A Scholastic Miscellany,* 94-96.

77. René Descartes, *Meditations* 5 (1641), in *The Philosophical Works of Descartes,* ed. E. S. Haldane and G. R. T. Ross (Cambridge: CUP, 1911).

In spite of his positive intentions, Descartes had given the game away for Kant. If a logically necessary proposition is simply *true by definition* (like the angles of a triangle), does this convey anything of substance? In Kant's distinctive argument, the a priori approach *confuses "existence" with a predicate,* such as "blue" or "heavy." We do not say, "The tea-pot is brown, and it exists," as if these were both equally informative statements. The first proposition *presupposes* the second. Kant declared, "Being is evidently not a real predicate . . . something that can be added to the conception of a thing."[78] One cannot deduce existence from the mere analysis of a formal concept.

Does it make any difference when the concept is the unique concept of God? Hegel attempted to defend this idea. But thinkers since Hegel have been sharply divided. Bertrand Russell (1872-1970) developed Kant's critique further by his notion of an *existential quantifier.* He translated the well-worn philosophical example, "The King of France is bald," into the proposition: "For at least one x, there is an x such that x (the King of France) is bald," or in *logical notation,* (∃x) (Fx): *in effect* "for one king, the king is bald." In other words *"existence" becomes bracketed out* as a different order of proposition.

Richard Swinburne carefully elucidates the cosmological and teleological arguments, but not only largely ignores the ontological argument but also expresses concern that it may end with a "timeless," unbiblical God.[79] Most thinkers reject the *logic* of the argument, even if they acknowledge its "informal" or intuitive "inference" of God's unique greatness.

Notable exceptions include Norman Malcolm and especially Alvin Plantinga on modal logic, and in another direction, Hans Küng, who traces defenses of the argument in Spinoza, Leibniz, Wolff, Fichte, and Hegel. It also features prominently in neo-Thomism or neo-scholasticism. Both Küng and Plantinga disclaim that this argument is a "proof," but defend its capacity to show that theistic belief is not unreasonable.[80]

Leibniz attempted to advance Descartes's argument by arguing that only in God can every kind of "perfection" exist. Both Charles Hartshorne (1897-2000) and Norman Malcolm drew upon modal logic. Malcolm rejected Anselm's first formulation, but argued that "necessary existence" is a form of perfection.[81] Plantinga restates Malcolm's argument in terms of God's "max-

78. Kant, *Critique of Pure Reason,* especially on transcendental dialectic.

79. Swinburne, *The Coherence of Theism,* 210-80.

80. Hans Küng, *Does God Exist? An Answer for Today* (New York and London: Collins, 1980), 529 and 535-51.

81. Norman Malcolm, "Anselm's Ontological Arguments," *Philosophical Review* 69 (1960): 41-62.

imal greatness."[82] He postulates logically a Being of maximal greatness, who exists *in all possible worlds,* and who therefore logically has maximal greatness in *at least one possible world.* From the major premise that this is logically possible, he adds the minor premise that it is practically a necessary truth that an omniscient, omnipotent, and perfectly good Being exists. In other words, such a Being is one of maximal greatness. He does not argue that these premises can be *proved;* merely that they are *not contrary to reason.* To try to express a complex argument simply, Plantinga appears to replace Anselm's concept "conceivable" by what is "logically possible" within modal logic.

Hans Küng (b. 1928), the Catholic theologian, agrees in general with Plantinga in evaluating the argument as a whole. He writes, "It cannot be proved that such a Being actually exists. . . . Nevertheless, here, too, there is food for thought."[83] He rightly urges that the argument implies knowledge of God as "wholly other," which contributes to the fascinating power of the idea of God. Like Anselm, he regards the argument as implying "an *a priori* of trust." The argument is "an expression of trusting faith, as Anselm himself expressed it."[84] If we reject the rationality of the three main arguments, we are left with "the groundlessness, unsupportedness, aimlessness, of everything."[85] This is usually called nihilism.

A second distinguished Catholic theologian, Hans Urs von Balthasar (1905-1988), also argues that in the ontological argument "God can be attained by no concept drawn from the world . . . because God is essentially what cannot be conceived. . . . It is the presupposition for any formation of concepts . . . the presupposition for all being . . . and all thought."[86] In the end, the three main arguments (in their varied forms) all point to the utter transcendence and uniqueness of God. God is *not* merely an entity within the world, whether as a caused cause, an instrumental purpose, or a concept of the human mind. To ascribe this unique transcendence to him is not simply irrational. But as Kierkegaard declared, a God who could be "proved" would not really be *God.* As Barth insists, we cannot "climb up" to God: we need his revelation and grace.

---

82. Alvin Plantinga, *The Ontological Argument* (New York: Doubleday, 1965); Plantinga, *God, Freedom, and Evil;* and James E. Sennett, ed., *The Analytic Theist: An Alvin Plantinga Reader* (Grand Rapids: Eerdmans, 1998).

83. Küng, *Does God Exist?* 535.

84. Küng, *Does God Exist?* 535.

85. Küng, *Does God Exist?* 536.

86. Hans Urs von Balthasar, *The Glory of the Lord: A Theological Aesthetics,* vol. 2 (Edinburgh: T. & T. Clark, 1984), 231.

For Christian discipleship the lesson is transparent. The God whom Christians worship is the basis and presupposition of all that is, whether within or beyond the world. He is our transcendent Creator, who evokes wonder, worship, and awe. But this does not mean that belief in God is unreasonable, even if this lies beyond the proofs of logic. To know such a God requires revelation and grace, to which rational reflection, worship, and obedience are appropriate responses.

5. Almighty, Omniscient, and Omnipresent: Their Meaning

The Nicene Creed begins, "I believe in one God the Father Almighty," and the Apostles' Creed, "I believe in God the Father Almighty." Traditionally God is the God of *power*. In recent years, however, the word "power" may have been eclipsed in many quarters, because of reactions against authoritarian dictators and even absolute monarchs, who supposedly maintain their position by force. On the other hand, from a wholly different angle, because God is powerful, *God may also be and do for the worshiper what the worshiper cannot be and do for himself or herself,* and this is precisely the theme that dominates *the work of Christ in the atonement.* In the atonement we see the entire Godhead "doing for us what we cannot achieve in our own strength." Hence we must resist the unfashionable motion of downplaying "the God of power," even if C. S. Lewis and others rightly claim that God is not simply like a more powerful "bully." This also applies even if some religious people sometimes indulge wickedly in "power plays."

When we discussed the problem of evil, we noted that to be almighty does not entail the ability to do anything, including the ability to make round squares or to tell lies. "Omnipotence," if we use this word, does not entail the ability to overcome *logical contradictions* (e.g., to make a round square) or *internal constraints* of character (e.g., to tell a lie or to break a promise). Nothing would be gained by attributing to God the power to contradict logic, unless we regard God as creating an irrational universe.

"Almighty," rather than the Latinized word "omnipotent," is the regular biblical word for God's sovereign power. The Greek *pantokratōr* is used in 2 Corinthians 6:18; Revelation 1:8; 4:8; 11:17; 15:3; 19:6, 15; and 21:22. G. van den Brink has convincingly argued that this biblical Greek term has several advantages over "omnipotent," as derived from Latin. He also insists that in the case of God, this regularly denotes *"power for,"* in the sense of *enabling,* rather than *"power over"* in the sense of using *brute force.* This still retains the purely logical constraints that we have noted. For example, Augustine stressed that God "cannot die," or "cannot" make what has been done, undone. Peter Geach similarly distinguishes between almighty-ness and omnipotence: "ability to do anything," he argues, must take account of constraints that relate to omnipotence in popular thought.

Nevertheless, Pannenberg writes, "The word 'God' is used meaningfully only if one means by it the power that determines everything that exists."[87] Aquinas quotes the book of Wisdom, "How could anything endure, if you do not will it?" (Wis. 11:25). He also underlines that God's sovereign will often includes "intermediate causes."[88] Thus, for example, "natural healing" as such reflects God's almighty will as special intervention. *Pantokratōr,* meaning all-sovereign, occurs not only in the NT, but also in the Church Fathers with frequency.[89] Clement, Justin, Irenaeus, Origen, and many post-Nicene Fathers use the term.

The sovereignty of God is affirmed not only in the OT, but especially in the term "the kingdom of God," which usually has the sense of God's *kingly rule.* The OT emphasizes God's transcendent sovereignty by such phrases as "Lord of hosts," the One who deploys celestial armies, which occurs 279 times in the OT. The kingdom of God occupies a key position in the teaching of Jesus. It implies complete human obedience, which marks it off from the fallible, even sinful, church. The Christian may rejoice that nothing is outside God's sovereign domain, whatever secondary means God uses to express his will.

The *omniscience* of God is perhaps more difficult to conceive, especially since human beings "know only in part" (1 Cor. 13:9). From the thought of Kierkegaard, through Gadamer, to many postmodernists, it is generally agreed that humans know only "from a given point of view," or in Heidegger's terms, they are *conditioned by their radical historical finitude,* "historicality," or "situatedness."

The most difficult problem of all is raised by asking whether, or in what sense, God knows *the future.* There may seem to be little problem for those who believe that all events in the world are predetermined, and that human freedom is merely illusory. The moral questions such a view would raise are enormous, let alone the numerous "choices" God appears to present to human beings.

87. Pannenberg, *BQT* 1:1.
88. Aquinas, *Summa* I, qu. 19, art. 8, reply.
89. Lampe 1005.

Most thinkers reject such rigid determinism. Yet on the other side, many think that God's perfection and "completeness" demand the future knowledge of every situation, even if this is hypothetical. He would be like a heavenly chess player, who takes account of every possible move that an "opponent" may make, and his hypothetical response to it. It is also the case that God would not "reason" in exactly the same way as humans or even computers, taking time, however brief, to reach a "solution." In this case, God's thought is without analogy.

Most thinkers see insurmountable objections to this claim that God knows the future, simply because the *future has not yet happened,* and is therefore *not part of reality.* It seems to defy logic to suggest that God knows a multitude of *unfulfilled* hypotheses, precisely because most of these would never be fulfilled. R. Swinburne asks how we can apply the terms "true" or "false" to things yet to happen.[90] Indeed, he claims, "Divine foreknowledge [if it includes nonevents] seems incompatible with human free will."[91]

Thomas Aquinas rejects divine foreknowledge for a further and different reason. He argues that the concept of *fore*knowledge *imposes on God a chronological or human notion of time,* whereas God is *outside* time as we know it. If the supposed future becomes a present reality, however, he knows "simultaneously" all reality, whether from a human point of view, past, present, or future. He knows everything as it happens. Aquinas writes, God "must know what is *operable* by Him," that is, that with which he can engage and which he can activate.[92] Yet somehow God knows "not only things actual, but also things possible. . . . God knows future contingent things."[93]

Against the contention that God's omniscience and purposes are somehow "fixed," Swinburne appeals to a number of examples in the OT. One is Abraham's intercession for Sodom, in which God "changes" his plan to destroy Sodom for fifty righteous men (Gen. 18:24) or for thirty (18:30), or even for ten (18:32). A second is the intercession of Moses for Israel (Exod. 32:7-10, 12-14). A third is God's judgment on Nineveh and Jonah's indignation about God sparing the city (Jon. 4:1-11). *God makes conditional promises.* How could this be possible if God knew the outcome?[94] Swinburne's lesson for the Christian is God's willingness to choose to constrain himself, either

90. Swinburne, *The Coherence of Theism,* 173.
91. Swinburne, *The Coherence of Theism,* 173.
92. Aquinas, *Summa* I, qu. 14, art. 16, reply.
93. Aquinas, *Summa* I, qu. 14, art. 13, reply.
94. Swinburne, *The Coherence of Theism,* 177.

by his character or by the rationality of the world, which excludes logical contradiction.

The most practical application of God's omniscience and almighty power concerns especially his declaration of his Word as *promise,* in which he pledges and commits himself to perform what he has promised. Thereby *he limits the options of what he still can do.* The Christian may confidently appropriate these promises in trust. Speech-act theory casts further light upon promises, and we shall explore promise further when we consider the sacraments.

God's omnipresence receives several expositions in the Bible. Probably the best known is in Psalm 139. It includes the verses,

> Where can I go from your spirit?
>   Or where can I flee from your presence?
> If I ascend to heaven, you are there;
>   if I make my bed in Sheol, you are there. . . .
>   At the furthest limits of the sea,
> even there your hand shall lead me. (Ps. 139:7-10)

Barth writes, "Omnipresence is certainly a determination of the freedom of God. It is the sovereignty in which, as the One He is, existing and acting in the way that corresponds to His essence, He is present to everything else."[95] Jeremiah recounts God as saying, "Do not I fill heaven and earth?" (23:24). The religious significance of this is clear.

The philosophical principle that emerges is that God is the very *condition of space,* the *ground* of it. Hence, to think of him as spatially located or limited would be irrational. In the OT, this is one factor that separates God from *idols.* In the NT it separates him, in effect, from the local deities of Greece or Rome. Moltmann recounts his experience of God's presence in the utter hell of despair, when even all his earlier mainstays had collapsed.[96] In his book *The Crucified God,* as we noted in our discussion of the problem of evil, Moltmann cites Wiesel, a survivor of Auschwitz, as writing, "Where is he (God)? He is here, hanging there on the gallows."[97] We may put the matter more bluntly. Whether an individual or the community of God's people are

95. Barth, *CD* II/1, 461.

96. Jürgen Moltmann, *A Broad Place: An Autobiography* (London: SCM, 2007), 29-31; and "My Theological Career," in *History and the Triune God: Contributions to Trinitarian Theology* (London: SCM, 1991), 166-67.

97. Moltmann, *The Crucified God,* 274; from Wiesel, *Night,* 76.

passing through times of delight and plenty, or times of darkness, despair, and persecution, nothing can separate them from the love and presence of God. In Romans 8:39 God's inseparable presence is prompted by his inseparable love: nothing "will be able to separate us from the love of God in Christ Jesus our Lord." Once again, theological reflection gives rise to the most *practical concerns and assurances* that relate to *practical life.*

CHAPTER IV

The Challenge of Atheism: Lessons for Christians

1. The Origins of Atheism: A Simple, Materialist View of Humankind

From the ancient world up until the post-Reformation era, belief in God or the gods was deemed to be relatively "normal." *Explicit* atheism was largely an exception. Admittedly, Democritus (mid-fifth to fourth century B.C.) appeared to teach an *implied* atheism as a part of his theory of atoms. Epicurus (341-270 B.C.) shared a similar viewpoint. Although their philosophies were influential, these views were not the norm.

Even Thomas Hobbes (1588-1679), in spite of his criticism of popular religion, did not commit himself to explicit atheism. He did, however, promote a materialist view of the world. Everything, he urged, is generated by causal forces or human appetites and passions. "Religion" is largely due to ignorance of second causes. In his political treatise *Leviathan* (1651), the supreme power is the state, especially the monarch. A social contract, primarily built on self-interest, prevents civilization sliding back into the remote past, when, as is often quoted, life was "solitary, poor, nasty, brutish, and short."

As David Berman shows in his history of atheism, British government legislation in 1677-1678 and in 1697 tended to drive explicit atheism underground. Nevertheless, without doubt many in England, at least in the upper classes, regarded Hobbes's philosophy as *implying* atheism, which they adopted.[1] Berman cites a number of "free thinkers," including John Wilmot, earl of Rochester, who even believed in a Supreme Being, and could not

---

1. David Berman, *A History of Atheism in Britain from Hobbes to Russell* (London and New York: Routledge, 1990), 48-69.

think that the world came into being through mere chance. He characterized such a being as "a vast power," even if not "personal." Hobbes himself was ambiguous. Much more explicit in his earlier atheism was Daniel Scargill in his work *Recantation* (1669). In this work he recants his previous denial of God as "dangerous and malicious." He explained that, in the past, he "gloried to be . . . an Atheist." Berman described this as "avowed atheism" in contrast to the "speculative atheism" of Hobbes. Whether Hobbes's cautious ambiguity was sincere or diplomatic we cannot be certain, but he had at least provided a theoretical basis for atheism. It is simply a fact that in the seventeenth century *avowed* atheism was generally regarded with horror as subversive.

Anthony Collins (1676-1729) is almost universally identified as a Deist (discussed below). He was well known for his *Essay concerning the Use of Reason* (1707) and for *A Discourse of Freethinking* (1713). Henning Graf Reventlow associates him with "the heyday of Deism," as do most writers, but Berman rejects the term "Deist" for him, calling him "a speculative atheist."[2] He argues, "For prudential reasons Collins held back from . . . publishing his atheism."[3] Berman's next major milestone is probably David Hume (1711-1776). Hume is on record as denying "atheism" twice, and clearly his philosophy points in the direction of skepticism and probably atheism. But his "atheism" is not as clearly explicit or avowed as that of Baron d'Holbach (1723-1789) or Denis Diderot (1713-1784). Both writers were *avowed* atheists, representing the spirit of the French Enlightenment, especially in d'Holbach's *System of Nature* (1770).

In Britain, avowed or explicit atheism emerged in the last decade of the eighteenth century. The Romantic poet Percy Shelley (1792-1822) represents an early-nineteenth-century example. Shelley's system of atheism has been called "Hume made explicit." Like Hume, he concentrated on sense experience, and argued that the world can be explained in a nontheistic, naturalistic way. Like some of the French atheists, he argued that the world did not "need" what he called the hypothesis of God.

Materialism is best seen in the writers of the French Enlightenment. Julien de La Mettrie (1709-1751) wrote *Man the Machine* in 1747. Human beings, he argued, merely reflect physiological processes; speech is no more than physical sound; the human mind is reduced to neurons in the brain. Similarly, d'Holbach saw the whole world as a machine, a huge system of

2. Henning Graf Reventlow, *The Authority of the Bible and the Rise of the Modern World* (London: SCM, 1984), 354; Berman, *History of Atheism,* 70-92.

3. Berman, *History of Atheism,* 75.

material particles. Again, as in Hume, knowledge is derived from sensation or sense experience. The mind is explained as an "epiphenomenon," a by-product of the increasing complexity of physical organisms. In many ways this is the simplest kind of atheism. It relies on a mechanistic account of everything, and stands in contrast with the more sophisticated atheism of Feuerbach, Marx, and Freud. It relies not on Hegel or social theory, but upon a reductive version of empiricism.

Lessons for Christian believers will become more sophisticated when we observe the forms of atheism that follow Feuerbach. Meanwhile, Christians need to value more highly the significance of *God's gift to humankind of reason* (see chap. 6, on humanity). *If* this form of atheism were true, atheists would then have *no grounds whatever for claiming that their own argument was rational,* or even *reasonable.* For presumably their argument arose simply from a *random pattern* of physical atoms, molecules, or neurons in the brain. An atheist would also strain to account for, or to explain, *art or music,* except as sound patterns of wavelengths that could be observed on an oscilloscope. We discussed this in chapter 3, under the argument from design. Christians may find that they have to think twice before sharing the tendency *to disparage and underrate human reason.* It is no accident that the largely secular world of reporting in media today has replaced the traditional question, "What do you *think* about this?" with "How do you *feel* about this?" As we shall note below, rationality is part of "the image of God." In countries where there may be wealth, security, and education, many Christians seem often passively to accept the values of largely materialist societies.

2. "God" as a Human Projection: Feuerbach and Freud

In the wake of Hegel's pupil Ludwig Feuerbach (1804-1872), a far more insidious form of atheism emerged than reductionism or materialism as such. In his youth Feuerbach studied theology in Heidelberg, and philosophy in Berlin. He became disenchanted with Hegel's thought, along with other "young left-wing Hegelians," who included David F. Strauss and Bruno Bauer. Feuerbach sums up the development of his earlier thought in the well-known quasi-chronological aphorism: "God was my first thought; reason, my second; humankind, my third and last thought." We can see this threefold transition by noting his disillusion first with theology and then with Hegel. He believed that theology masked the true *human* origin of religion, while Hegel's philosophy, he claimed, deified reason at the expense of humanity and life. Thus in his major work, *The Essence of Christianity,* he wrote: "The divine is nothing else than the human being, or rather human nature purified, freed from the limits of the individual man, i.e. real, bodily man, made objective — i.e., contemplated and revered as *another, a distinct being.*"[4] Religion, he urged, "is consciousness of the infinite"; but this is directed to some supposed object, when it is really humankind who is "not finite," but has an "infinite nature."[5] He concluded that the aim in religion is "That God may be all, man must be nothing."[6]

This can be viewed in two ways. From Feuerbach's viewpoint, in order to create "God," humankind must be diminished. From the Christian point of view, Feuerbach deifies and elevates humankind into the infinite; humankind will not accept the constraints of being *creatures.* In this second light, his thinking represents *hubris* and idolatry, by putting humankind in the place of God. *Theology becomes anthropology.* This becomes even clearer in Feuerbach's other major work, *The Essence of Religion* (1845). Humankind "projects" or imposes images of its own nature onto "God." It would be left partly to Nietzsche, but mainly to Freud, to develop this notion of *projection* further.

Feuerbach had begun his critique of idealism in his work *Thoughts on Death and Immortality* (1830), even before Hegel's death. Anticipating Nietzsche's "aphorisms," he produced a number of insightful but bitingly cynical "epigrams." Many were satirical, for, he wrote, "Satire — it is a microscope — greatly magnified things."[7] He wrote ironically, "What distinguishes the Christian from other honourable people? At most, a pious face and parted hair."[8] In the same vein he declared: "I admit it: the Christianity you proclaim is pure: but for this very reason it is colourless, odourless, and tasteless."[9] Feuerbach saw Christianity only as a *human phenomenon,* much like certain courses in sociology of religion or even "religious studies." There is a lesson here, not only for Christians, but specifically for Christian theologians. Too often *theology* is reduced to descriptions of *human phenomena.* People often say, "My faith was my anchor," which seems less blunt than "*Christ* was my anchor," which may have been the truth. From his point of

4. Ludwig Feuerbach, *The Essence of Christianity* (New York: Harper, 1957), 14, italics mine.

5. Feuerbach, *The Essence of Christianity,* 2.

6. Feuerbach, *The Essence of Christianity,* 26.

7. Ludwig Feuerbach, *Thoughts on Death and Immortality: From the Papers of a Thinker* (Berkeley: University of California Press, 1980), 175, epigram 1.

8. Feuerbach, *Death and Immortality,* 205.

9. Feuerbach, *Death and Immortality,* 234.

view, Feuerbach dignified humanity; from the opposite viewpoint, he reduced "God" to a human projection of the infinite into a constructed object "out there."

From his point of view, Feuerbach taught a philosophy of liberation; from the Christian viewpoint, he taught human self-sufficiency and thereby idolatry. His materialism is seen clearly in his aphorism "Man is what he eats." Does this really dignify humanity?

Christians are not immune from shaping God in their own image. Catholic theologian Karen Kilby has claimed that an overegalitarian concept of the "social Trinity" too readily follows Feuerbach in imposing late-twentieth-century egalitarian democracy onto a theology of the Trinity. Similar caveats about our concept of God can be made. Does our doctrine of God too easily reflect the particular culture of our church or of society?

Another Catholic theologian, Walter Kasper, makes some illuminating comments on Feuerbach's link with Hegel. He comments, "The religious projection thus leads to alienation and estrangement, to the negation of man. In this perspective atheism is the negation of negation, and thus . . . a 'No' to God and a 'Yes' to man. . . . Faith in God becomes faith in man himself. . . . Religion and the church are replaced by politics, prayer by work."[10]

Further, Feuerbach's assertion of atheism remains simply *assertion* rather than careful critical *argument*. Hans Küng comments, "Must reason and Bible, politics and religion, work and prayer, earth and heaven, necessarily exclude one another?"[11] Whether we might wish for God or not, *wish does not determine reality.* Nothing exists or fails to exist merely because we may wish it.

Sigmund Freud (1856-1939) was an atheist from the beginning of his life, and he regarded conscious states as the "interplay of *forces* which assist or inhibit one another." As Hans Küng observed, "The human *psychē* [was] understood as a kind of machine."[12] Both Küng and Paul Ricoeur note that most of Freud's terms for neurological or mental activity constituted metaphors drawn from the semantic domain of either *physiology* or *economics*. His most distinctive concern was to explore the unconscious. Often he viewed this as a reservoir of repressed wishes and also repressed prohibitions and guilt. Acute conflict within the unconscious can be a source of *neurosis*. A clinician may attempt to bring those conflicts to conscious awareness.

10. Walter Kasper, *The God of Jesus Christ* (New York: Crossroad, 1991; orig. 1982), 29.
11. Hans Küng, *Does God Exist? An Answer for Today* (New York and London: Collins, 1980), 208.
12. Küng, *Does God Exist?* 268.

Freud focused especially on the figure of the father as a source of simultaneous judgment and love, of prohibition and forgiveness, or of protection and kindness. This double impact of the father figure made a strong impact especially on the infantile stage of human development. Freud was influenced by E. B. Tylor's theory that animism constituted the threshold of emerging religion, together with R. R. Marett's theory of a "pre-animistic" stage. Freud saw parallels between human childhood and a supposed totemist stage in the history of humankind. When the totem ceased to serve as a substitute for the father figure, he wrote, "The primal father, at once feared and hated, revered and envied, became the prototype of God himself."[13] Religion, he believed, arose from "a longing for a father . . . as a defence against childhood helplessness." Such an "illusion" is not sheer "error," but a "wish-fulfilment as a prominent factor in its [religion's] motivation."[14] Religion, Freud asserted, is "a universal obsessional neurosis" of humankind.[15]

In Freud's theory, this becomes compounded with his use of "the Oedipus complex." In the Oedipus legend, the protagonist kills his father and marries his mother. In his *Totem and Taboo* (1913), Freud wrote, "Psychoanalysis has taught us that a boy's earliest choice of objects for his love is incestuous, and that those objects are forbidden ones — his mother and his sister."[16] In the same book he declared, "At bottom God is nothing more than an exalted father."

Freud's specific work on "projection" arises from his consideration of *paranoia*. Paranoia, he explains, entails "delusions of persecution," in which a mechanism of "projection" operates. He writes, "An internal perception is suppressed and . . . enters consciousness in the form of an external perception. In delusions of persecution . . . what should have been felt internally as love is perceived externally as hate."[17] Paul Ricoeur, however, comments, "The mechanism of projection is singularly more obscure than its role."[18] Hence to the infant, the face that gazes into the cradle is "magnified into

13. Sigmund Freud, "An Autobiographical Study," in *Complete Psychological Works of Sigmund Freud,* ed. James Strachey (1959; reprint, London and Toronto: Hogarth Press, 1989), 20:94.

14. Sigmund Freud, *The Future of an Illusion* (New York: Norton, 1961), 40.

15. Freud, *Future of an Illusion,* 55.

16. Sigmund Freud, *Totem and Taboo: Points of Agreement in Mental Life between Savages and Neurotics* (London and New York: Routledge, 2004; orig. 1913), 7-20.

17. *Complete Psychological Works of Sigmund Freud,* 12:66.

18. Paul Ricoeur, *Freud and Philosophy: An Essay in Interpretation* (New Haven: Yale University Press, 1970), 239.

infinity." In Ricoeur's language, the omnipotence of thoughts of the self generated in narcissism "projects this omnipotence into reality."[19] Freud's use of the Oedipus legend then suggests "the son's efforts to put himself in the place of the father-god." Repentance and reconciliation then enter in. Freud traces the emergence of Judaism and Christianity in a volume full of historical fantasy, namely, *Moses and Monotheism*. This depicts Moses as an aristocratic Egyptian who worshiped Aten, followed by prophets who call for a return to a monotheistic god. This in turn is followed by acts of repression by the law, sacrifice, and redemption. God is both judge, projected by the *superego* of human beings, and love, projected by the human *id* or *libido*. At this point we may offer the following comments on Freud.

(i) *Religion as "Patently Infantile."* Freud concluded that religion is "patently infantile," especially in his work *The Future of an Illusion* (1927). Religion promotes a sense of guilt and longing for help and comfort. It externalizes this longing into an illusory figure. Religion implies childish *over-dependency*. Bonhoeffer, among others, took up this point in lessons for believing *Christians*. Too often, he wrote in his *Letters and Papers from Prison*, we seek to make mature adults *regress* into childhood, by magnifying feelings of guilt, shame, and dependence, and by promoting infantile attitudes, even including a "projection" of "God." There is some truth in this censure, even if Bonhoeffer tended to exaggerate it.

(ii) *Rejection of the Mechanistic Worldview.* On the other hand, Küng and Ricoeur, while accepting a number of Freud's insights, thoroughly reject the *mechanistic worldview* on which Freud based his work. Volney Gay has set out a good selection of clinical cases on the basis of which Freud reached many of his conclusions.[20] Gay refers to Freud's search for truth as "a eulogy to the claims of science," as if *hypotheses* from clinical evidence could really guarantee *truth*.[21] Küng concludes, "Freud took over from Feuerbach and his successors the essential arguments for his personal atheism."[22] Further, he writes, "We have long ceased to take every advance in science . . . as contradictory of belief in God."[23] Christians need constantly to distinguish between the achievements of scientific *method* and the pretensions of a scientific *worldview*.

19. Ricoeur, *Freud and Philosophy*, 241.
20. Volney P. Gay, *Reading Freud: Psychology, Neurosis, and Religion* (Chico, Calif.: Scholars Press, 1983).
21. Gay, *Reading Freud*, 101.
22. Küng, *Does God Exist?* 299.
23. Küng, *Does God Exist?* 303.

(iii) *The Need for Hermeneutics.* Ricoeur has brilliantly shown, especially from Freud's *Interpretation of Dreams,* the need for *hermeneutics,* both of texts and of human life. Although many of Freud's claims about the unconscious remain open to question, undoubtedly there are *ambiguities* in human life and communication that point to the need for hermeneutics. In spite of the need for healthy caution, it seems that "Freudian slips," "free association," and unconscious "giveaways" point often to a "text" below the surface of conscious thoughts. As Donald E. Capps has shown in *Pastoral Care and Hermeneutics,* pastoral counseling needs less to be dominated by "therapeutic" and clinical models, and more to draw on hermeneutics for in-depth understanding and communication.[24] Charles V. Gerkin, in *The Living Human Document,* convincingly makes the same point.[25] The relation between Freud and hermeneutics has been immortalized by Paul Ricoeur.

At a homely level, I have often suggested to students that a sudden flare-up between family members may be caused not by some trivial, apparent crisis of the moment, but by some deep-seated, long-enduring resentment about something different, which has built up over the months or years. All Christians need to understand conflicts as arising not necessarily from what has last been said, but often from prior attitudes, from histories, or from deeply buried assumptions. This does not provide any defense of Freud's theories about *religion,* but heeds one or two of his insights.

3. "God" and Social Manipulation: Nietzsche and Marx

Friedrich Nietzsche (1844-1900) was in some ways the philosophical successor to Feuerbach. He was a nihilist and an avowed atheist. He became professor at Basel in 1870, but resigned in 1879 because of poor health. During the 1880s he produced several well-known works, including *The Gay Science* (1882), *Thus Spoke Zarathustra* (1883-1885), *Beyond Good and Evil* (1886), and *The Twilight of the Idols* (1889). His most aggressively antitheist book, *The Antichrist,* appeared in 1895. Between 1889 and his death in 1900 his mental health collapsed.

Nietzsche's first book, *The Birth of Tragedy* (1872), glorified the driving

---

24. Donald E. Capps, *Pastoral Care and Hermeneutics* (Philadelphia: Fortress, 1984; Eugene, Ore.: Wipf and Stock, 2012).

25. Charles V. Gerkin, *The Living Human Document: Re-visioning Pastoral Counseling in a Hermeneutical Mode* (Nashville: Abingdon, 1984).

force and raw energy depicted in Euripides' tragedy *The Bacchae*. From the first he represented the "Dionysian" principle of life-affirming force and will, as represented by the Bacchae, as opposed to the "Apollonian" principle of restraint, harmony, and order, represented by Pentheus. His life-affirming principle found common cause, at least in the earlier years, with Richard Wagner, although he later broke with him.

Nietzsche stressed sheer *will* over all *rational* systems. In *The Gay Science* he declares that both Western philosophy and religion are "fictions" and "lies." Also in *The Gay Science,* his "madman" proclaims that God is dead. He adds that there will perhaps be caves in which God's "shadow" will be shown. Elsewhere in the same book the madman cries, "Whither God? . . . I will tell you. *We have killed him* — you and I. All of us are his murderers."[26] Since supposedly "God is dead," everything is permitted. *There is no longer any foundation for truth, ethics, or rationality.*

Thus in his *Notebooks* of 1873, Nietzsche writes, "What is truth? — A mobile army of metaphors, metonyms, and anthropomorphisms."[27] In *The Will to Power,* which Frederick Copleston calls "his real thought," Nietzsche writes, "*Truth is that kind of error* without which a certain species . . . cannot exist."[28] "All that exists consists of *interpretations.*" He also writes, "Truths are illusions we have forgotten are illusions."[29] Nietzsche's atheism is partly connected with his suspicion of language in religion. He declares, "I fear we shall never be rid of God, so long as we still believe in grammar."[30] He repeats his criticism in *Human, All-Too-Human:* "We are constantly led astray by words . . . a hidden philosophical mythology."[31] His suspicion of language follows the tradition of Hobbes, and was later developed by Fritz Mauthner, and in another direction by Wittgenstein and Ryle.

Nietzsche saw religion and knowledge as an *instrument of power and manipulation.* A typical ironic example might be: " 'God forgiveth him that

---

26. Friedrich Nietzsche, *The Gay Science* (London: Vintage, 1974), sect. 125; cf. sect. 108 (Ger. *Die Fröhliche Wissenschaft*). Also in *The Complete Works of Friedrich Nietzsche,* 18 vols. (London: Allen and Unwin, 1909-1913).

27. Friedrich Nietzsche, "On Truth and Lie," in *The Portable Nietzsche,* ed. W. Kaufmann (New York: Viking, 1968; orig. 1954), 46.

28. Friedrich Nietzsche, *The Will to Power,* vol. 2; also in *The Complete Works,* vol. 12, aphorism 481; cf. F. Copleston, *A History of Philosophy,* vol. 7 (London: Burns and Oates, 1968), 395.

29. Nietzsche, in *The Portable Nietzsche,* 46.

30. Friedrich Nietzsche, *The Twilight of the Idols,* in *The Complete Works,* 12:22.

31. Friedrich Nietzsche, *Human, All-Too-Human,* in *The Complete Works,* 7:ii, 192, aphorism 5.

repenteth' — in plain English: him that submitteth himself to the priest."[32] Or, even more bitterly, Nietzsche asserts, "'the salvation of the soul' — in plain English 'The world revolves around me.'"[33] Language can *disguise* the manipulative power of religion.

For Christians the lesson is clear. Most of us have read about, or even witnessed, the abuse of Christian doctrine or Scripture as an instrument of power to manipulate others, or to impose personal will and control over them. Ever since the "splits" (Gk. *schismata*) in ancient Corinth (1 Cor. 1:10), churches have used apparently Christian values to gain ascendancy in power struggles.[34] Paul made it clear that the splits at Corinth were in no way due to doctrinal principles, but reflected a power play to impose personal preferences onto others in the church.[35] Many in the past have appealed to "the will of God" to manipulate another into following their wishes. Dietrich Bonhoeffer gave warning about this, especially in his *Letters and Papers from Prison*.

Nietzsche's program includes "the transvaluation of all values," as he calls it in *The Will to Power*. In this sense he is a nihilist, but in a different sense he points beyond this to something new, although he does not know what this "new" world order will be. All he will say is that "Life is will to power."[36] E. Jüngel thinks that Nietzsche's view of metaphor may more positively point to some reality beyond the "nothing," and Küng seems to hint at this possibility.[37] As with Feuerbach, his atheism was *asserted* rather than *proved*. He believed that Christianity served to render humankind weak, mediocre, and submissive. It is against this background that Jürgen Moltmann calls the Holy Spirit "Yes to Life" or "A Universal Affirmation."[38] He comments, "The liberation of life from the iron grip of morality, and the intensification of life in 'the will to power' was the message of Nietzsche's *Zarathustra*. The moral instrumentalization of life was to be replaced by life's free intensification by way of its creative expression."[39] But, for Moltmann,

---

32. Friedrich Nietzsche, *The Antichrist*, in *The Complete Works*, 16:131, aphorism 26.

33. Nietzsche, *The Antichrist*, 16:186, aphorism 43.

34. Anthony C. Thiselton, *The First Epistle to the Corinthians: A Commentary on the Greek Text*, NIGTC (Grand Rapids: Eerdmans, 2000), 120-33.

35. L. L. Welborn, "On Discord in Corinth: 1 Cor. 1–4 and Ancient Politics," *JBL* 106 (1987): 85-111; also in Welborn, *Politics and Rhetoric in the Corinthian Epistles* (Macon, Ga.: Mercer University Press, 1997), 1-42.

36. Nietzsche, *The Will to Power*, 254.

37. Küng, *Does God Exist?* 394-403; and Eberhard Jüngel, *Theological Essays*, vol. 1 (Edinburgh: T. & T. Clark, 1989).

38. Jürgen Moltmann, *The Spirit of Life: A Universal Affirmation* (London: SCM, 1992).

39. Moltmann, *The Spirit of Life*, 85.

what liberates us is neither the death of God nor narcissistic Dionysian ecstasy, but the Spirit of Life who comes from God.

Karl Marx (1818-1883), partly like Nietzsche, saw religion as a tool for keeping the masses content, weak, and docile. In his view the ruling classes deployed it to promote submission of the proletariat. In this sense, he called religion "the opium of the people," which is well known, although the phrase may not have been original to Marx.[40] In the same work Marx wrote, "The abolition of religion as the illusory happiness of the people is required for their real happiness." Religion functions to create illusory fantasies for the poor, to keep them submissive and content with their lot. Thus it is socially manipulative.

There can be no question that Marx was a materialist. For him, economic forces of labor and production were more fundamental than "ideas." He observed, "The philosophers have only *interpreted* the world in various ways; the point is to *change* it."[41] Admittedly in early years, in the period of the Paris Manuscripts, he regarded himself as a humanist. He wrote, "Atheism is humanism mediated . . . through the suppression of private property."[42] The so-called *Praxis* School of Yugoslavia in the 1960s stressed this *earlier* aspect, and with the exception of its atheism, so did many Latin American liberation theologians. Mainstream Marxists, however, concentrate on the "scientific" and "historical" aspects of later Marxism after 1844.

In 1847 Marx produced the short work *Communist Manifesto*. At the beginning of the *Manifesto* he and Engels asserted, "The history of all hitherto existing society is the history of class struggles: freeman and slave, patrician and plebeian, lord and serf, guild-master and journeyman, in a word, oppressor and oppressed, stood in constant opposition to one another."[43] In the following pages, Marx argued that in history the feudal society gave way to capitalism, and it is predicted that property-owning bourgeoisie will be challenged by the oppressed proletariat. Marx and Engels used the term "dialectical materialism." Some understand Marx as reacting against Hegel and against his stress on ideas; others regard him as reacting primarily against

40. Karl Marx, *Critique of Hegel's Philosophy of the Right* (Cambridge: CUP, 1970; orig. 1843), introduction.

41. Karl Marx, "Eleventh Thesis on Feuerbach" (1845), in *Marx: Early Writings* (London: Pelican, 1975), 423.

42. Karl Marx, *Economic and Philosophical Manuscripts* (Moscow: Progress Publisher, 1959; orig. 1832; Ger. 1844), and *Critique of Hegel's Philosophy of the Right*.

43. Karl Marx and Friedrich Engels, *Communist Manifesto* (London: Pluto Press, 2008), 79.

capitalism. Probably both are true, but Marx did draw upon Hegel's historical reason and dialectic.

The result of revolution was the introduction of state socialism, and Marxist eschatology looked forward to this, in turn, being overtaken by communism, when labor and production would receive from each "according to his ability," and give to each "according to his needs." At the stage of revolution, however, the last king and the last priest would be destroyed. Earlier Marx wrote, "Man makes religion; religion does not make man."[44]

After the revolution of 1919, Russian Marxism flourished under Vladimir Lenin (1870-1924) and under Joseph Stalin (1879-1953). Lenin increased Marx's antipathy toward religion, reemphasizing its supposed role as a tool of establishment class struggle. Under Khrushchev, especially after 1956, this rigidly dogmatic approach began to ease. In China, Marxism underwent a variant form under Mao Tse-tung (1893-1976). Meanwhile in Germany, Georg Lukács (1885-1971) maintained a Marxist profile, especially in *History and Class-Consciousness* (1923). In France, Jean-Paul Sartre (1905-1980) and Louis Althusser (1918-1990) developed variant forms.

The theologian Helmut Gollwitzer criticized Marxist atheism for attempting to treat *all* types of religion as if they were one thing.[45] Further, a human being constitutes *more than a unit of production*. The so-called paradox of materialism remains; if a human being is merely a mechanistic being, why should the arguments of atheism be regarded as *rational*? Feuerbach, Nietzsche, and Marx all suffer from this problem. As Hans Küng concludes, a materialist worldview "cannot be demonstrated."[46] This does not make the question of social justice any less urgent for Christians, nor the need to recognize that Christianity and the Bible *can* be used for manipulative purposes or mere power play.

4. The Attack on Revelation

Karl Barth, among others, has stressed that Christianity stands or falls with belief in God's self-revelation. Divine revelation is not human discovery. Humankind does not construct "God" by thinking "upward" from humanity;

44. *Marx: Early Writings*, 244.
45. Helmut Gollwitzer, *The Existence of God as Confessed by Faith* (London: SCM, 1965), 82-87.
46. Küng, *Does God Exist?* 244.

91

this is idolatry. Faith or belief is a response to the self-revelation and grace of God. This is metaphorically "downward" to humanity. It involves being addressed by God, called by God, and redeemed by God. Hence attacks on revelation cut the ground from beneath the feet of the responsive, listening, and obedient Christians.

Revelation, Barth stresses, is "an act of God."[47] It addresses us as "a promise, a judgment, a claim."[48] It is therefore dynamic, and takes the form of an event. Barth comments, "For me, the Word of God is a *happening,* not a thing . . . an event . . . a living reality."[49] He adds, "God is known through God, and through God alone."[50] God's "knowability" is not a natural capacity or natural right, but depends on God's "good pleasure." As many Christian theologians have urged, there remains a sense in which God is "hidden." "The hiddenness of God is the inconceivability of the Father, the Son, and the Holy Spirit."[51] He discloses or reveals himself, because he is love. In E. Jüngel's phrase, it is through Christ that God becomes *"conceivable" or "thinkable."*[52]

It is not simply the tradition of Luther and Barth that speaks in this way. Karl Rahner, eminent Catholic theologian, writes, "Being is luminous, it is *Logos* [Word or Speech]; it may be revealed in the word." Humankind needs "an open ear for every word that may proceed from the mouth of the eternal."[53] His Catholic collaborator Yves Congar similarly expounds "the self-revealing God," who brings about "revelation in history" and "speaks."[54] Together they prepared the section of Vatican II documents entitled *Dei Verbum,* on the doctrine of revelation. Denis Farkasfalvy comments, "The climate which followed the Council made most Catholic exegetes merge with their Protestant colleagues" on this subject.[55] Vatican II speaks of "hearing the Word of God with reverence," and appeals to biblical concepts of revelation in Romans and in Hebrews 1:1-2, "God has spoken to us by the Son."[56]

---

47. Barth, *CD* I/1, 143.

48. Barth, *CD* I/1, 150.

49. Barth, *CD* I/2, 26 and 42.

50. Barth, *CD* I/2, 179.

51. Barth, *CD* I/2, 197.

52. Eberhard Jüngel, *God as the Mystery of the World* (Edinburgh: T. & T. Clark, 1983), 111; cf. 229 and 226-98.

53. Karl Rahner, *Hearer of the Word* (London: Bloomsbury, 1994), chap. 5.

54. Aidan Nichols, *Yves Congar* (London: Chapman, 1989), 14-15.

55. Denis O. Farkasfalvy, *Inspiration and Interpretation: A Theological Introduction to Sacred Scripture* (Washington, D.C.: Catholic University of America Press, 2010), 5.

56. Austin P. Flannery, ed., *Documents of Vatican II* (Grand Rapids: Eerdmans, 1975), 750-51.

Pannenberg devotes some seventy pages to a discussion of revelation in his *Systematic Theology.* Following Barth, he comments: "God can be known only if he gives himself to be known. The loftiness of divine reality makes it inaccessible to us unless it makes itself known."[57] He also endorses what Luther and Barth say about the hiddenness of God. In the biblical accounts, Pannenberg underlines the special revelation of God to Noah (Gen. 6:13), Abraham, Moses, and the covenant people of Israel. In linguistic terms revelation becomes associated with God's action. He concludes, "It is incontestable that even if in varying words and thought-forms the biblical witnesses do speak expressly of divine revelation."[58] He concedes that the vehicles of revelation take many forms, even in Scripture. One is the revelation of "mystery" in an apocalyptic sense (1 Cor. 2:7-9). Perhaps most of all, self-disclosure through Christ occurs in the Johannine prologue (John 1:14) and in the opening verses of Hebrews (Heb. 1:1-2).

Some relatively minor attacks on the notion come from a minority of Christian thinkers. James Barr argued that the term "communication" more accurately reflects biblical thought than "revelation." He calls the terms that correspond to "revelation" both "limited and specialized."[59] But this still admits the importance of God's communicative action. More serious may be F. Gerald Downing's argument that terms for "revelation" are relatively few, and often bear a performative force expressing simply commitment.[60] But the introduction of a self-involving dimension does not invalidate revelation. Performatives always *presuppose* statements of truth, as J. L. Austin and others firmly make clear.[61] Gerhard Ebeling, Eberhard Jüngel, and a host of modern theologians examine the concept with care, and expound it positively. Ebeling insists that we should not play off the terms "Word of God" and "revelation" against each other.

In his book *Holy Scripture,* John Webster specifically argues that Scripture is the central source of all Christian thinking.[62] More recently in his book *The Domain of the Word,* Webster argues that the medium of human words does not undermine "God's providential ordering of all things," while sanctifi-

57. Pannenberg, *ST* 1:189.

58. Pannenberg, *ST* 1:195.

59. James Barr, *Old and New in Interpretation: A Study of the Two Testaments* (London: SCM, 1966), 88.

60. F. G. Downing, *Has Christianity a Revelation?* (London: SCM, 1964), 179 and 20-125.

61. John L. Austin, *How to Do Things with Words* (Oxford: Clarendon, 1962), 45-56.

62. John Webster, *Holy Scripture: A Dogmatic Sketch* (Cambridge: CUP, 2003).

cation by the Holy Spirit ensures that Scripture is properly "Holy Scripture."[63] He observes, "To acknowledge the authority of Scripture is . . . to confess a norm and place oneself beneath its judgement. But it is also to pledge one-self to a basic act of redeemed intelligence: hearing the text, following its sequence, waiting upon the words of the glorious company of the apostles, and the goodly fellowship of the prophets so that we can do what Scripture instructs us to do."[64] On this basis, "Christian theology is biblical reasoning."[65]

For N. T. Wright, the place of revelation and the Bible enjoyed a firm consensus in the Christian church from the beginning until the Reformation and post-Reformation era. A genuine challenge to the concept of revelation came only with the era ushered in by the rationalism of the Enlightenment.[66] Because Enlightenment thought regarded "reason" as the central capacity of human beings, it came to see "reason" as the arbiter of revelation. Kant's work *Religion within the Limits of Reason Alone* sums up the point.[67] Many such thinkers opted for atheism or for Deism, with its concept of a distant, remote God. In Karl Rahner's thought, revelation is the presupposition for belief in a personal God, with whom we can enter into a relationship. In Scripture itself the resources of *wisdom* are far more fruitful than any consideration of "knowledge" or "reason."

Wisdom enables us to face and to negotiate the complex and practical questions of daily life. In the OT it is associated with *education, training,* and *community.* The Hebrew word *chokmāh* occurs 200 times in the OT, and is used especially in Proverbs, Job, and Ecclesiastes. In the postcanonical books wisdom occurs frequently in Ben Sirach (Ecclesiasticus) and Wisdom of Solomon. In postbiblical thought Vico and Gadamer contrast its communal basis with the narrow individualism of reason.[68] Wisdom often uses indirect communication to address subtle and complex issues of daily life. In the NT, Wisdom Sayings are ascribed to Jesus, Paul, and James.[69]

63. John Webster, *The Domain of the Word: Scripture and Theological Reason* (London and New York: Bloomsbury, 2012), 14-17.

64. Webster, *Domain of the Word,* 19.

65. Webster, *Domain of the Word,* 115.

66. N. T. Wright, *The Last Word: Scripture and the Authority of God — Getting beyond the Bible Wars* (New York: Harper One, 2005), 3-105.

67. Wright, *The Last Word,* 83.

68. Hans-Georg Gadamer, *Truth and Method,* 2nd ed. (London: Sheed and Ward, 1989), 19-30, and G. B. Vico, *On the Study Methods of Our Time* (Indianapolis: Bobbs-Merrill, 1965).

69. Anthony C. Thiselton, "Wisdom in the Jewish and Christian Scriptures," *Theology*

Henning Graf Reventlow traces this in more detail. He surveys Deist doctrine in John Toland, especially in his *Christianity Not Mysterious* (1696 and 1702), and in Anthony Collins in his *Essay concerning the Use of Reason* (1707).[70] Humankind, these writers argued, had all it needed in "reason," even if in theory they also granted the existence of Christian revelation. Each pointed in the same direction. But Reventlow reaches a subtle and masterly conclusion, after much study of their works. They tried, he concludes, to demonstrate the parallel between the "natural" religion of reason and Christian revelation; but they "in fact demonstrated precisely the opposite."[71] They concluded, "Revealed religion is superfluous."[72]

It is impossible to sum up the vicissitudes in the development of the concept of revelation in theology between the eighteenth century and today. This would require not a single-volume systematic theology, but a specialist book on the subject. H. D. McDonald has traced theories of revelation from 1700 to 1960 in two sequential volumes.[73] In his second book McDonald notes the impact of materialism, Darwinism, and radical biblical criticism. But some attacks on the unique authority of the Bible concerned the *mode* of revelation rather than its necessity as such. Even Barth, who majors on revelation as the act and self-disclosure of God, expressed reservations about "the freezing of the connection between Scripture and revelation"; Brunner asserts, "Divine revelation is not a book or a doctrine."[74] On the other hand, James Orr argues, "It is reasonable to expect that provision will be made for the *preservation* of the knowledge of revelation *in some permanent and authoritative form*."[75] Orr adds that revelation includes "the whole divinely guided history of the people of Israel, and . . . the apostolic action in the founding of the Church."[76] John Webster convincingly offers a similar argument today.

On the *modes* of revelation, within the church and theology, debate has

---

114 (2011): 163-72; and vol. 115 (2011): 1-9; cf. Ben Witherington III, *Jesus the Sage: The Pilgrimage of Wisdom* (Edinburgh: T. & T. Clark, 1994), especially 155-208.

70. Reventlow, *Authority,* 294-308 and 354-69.

71. Reventlow, *Authority,* 388.

72. Reventlow, *Authority,* 383.

73. H. D. McDonald, *Ideas of Revelation, 1700-1860* (New York and London: Macmillan, 1959), and *Theories of Revelation, 1860-1960* (London: Allen and Unwin, 1963).

74. McDonald, *Theories of Revelation,* 168; Emil Brunner, *Revelation and Reason: The Christian Doctrine of Faith and Knowledge* (Philadelphia: Westminster, 1946), 8.

75. James Orr, *Revelation and Inspiration* (London: Duckworth, 1910), 155.

76. Orr, *Revelation and Inspiration,* 157.

continued. Some theologians in the tradition of Hodge and Warfield insist that it is universally "propositional." Many others place more emphasis on the Word of God as *promise,* such as Luther, Tyndale, and Barth. In contemporary theology this merges with the emphasis on *speech acts.*[77] Yet, speech acts may *presuppose* propositions.[78] Fundamentally the Roman Catholic Church has asserted officially (1995) that the Bible is "the written testimony to a series of interventions in which God has revealed himself in history."[79]

5. Between Atheism and Theism:
Deism, Pantheism, and Agnosticism

(i) *Deism.* In general, Deists believe that God exists, but also that God has *no personal* dealings with the world. Revelation does not take place in a series of divine acts in history. God did create the world, it is affirmed, but, like a self-regulating machine, the world goes on its way independently of God. God may be transcendent, but God is in no way immanent in the world. Some use clearly impersonal terms for God, like F. H. Bradley's term "the Absolute." The belief in divine interventions such as miracles would seem to imply that God's creation was imperfect, and in need of regular repair. Prayer and worship are unnecessary and inappropriate, other than to benefit a person's mind. Some argue that Aristotle foreshadowed Deism in his *Metaphysics,* book 12, in which God is forever separated from material and changeable things.

More accurately, there are many different versions of Deism. In general terms, however, it is essentially *rationalist.* It springs from the age of reason in the late seventeenth and early eighteenth centuries in England. Thomas Carlyle (1795-1881), in *Sartor Resartus* ("The Tailor Re-tailored" [1836]), an allegorical and satirical novel, caricatures the Deist "God" as "an absentee God, sitting idle ever since the first Sabbath, at the outside of the universe, and seeing it go."[80] His title satirizes the notion of language as the garment

---

77. E.g., Kevin Vanhoozer, *Is There a Meaning in This Text? The Bible, the Reader, and the Morality of Literary Knowledge* (Grand Rapids: Zondervan, 1998), 197-280.

78. Anthony C. Thiselton, *Thiselton on Hermeneutics* (Grand Rapids: Eerdmans; Aldershot, UK: Ashgate, 2006), 51-150.

79. J. A. Fitzmyer, ed., *The Biblical Commission's Document "The Interpretation of the Bible in the Church"* (Rome: Pontifical Biblical Institute, 1995), 191.

80. Thomas Carlyle, *Sartor Resartus: The Life and Opinions of Herr Teufelsdrockh* (Project Gutenberg e-book, #1051), bk. 2, chap. 7.

of thought. The Deists regarded revelation as superfluous, since humankind could use *reason* to fathom all the truths of "natural religion."

Deism is broadly associated with the so-called scientific revolution that began with Isaac Newton (1642-1727) and others. Theists of the day often called them "atheists." God was typically thought of as "the Higher Power." Anticipations of Deism came with Robert Burton in 1621, while "the father of English Deism" is generally agreed to have been Lord Edward Herbert of Cherbury (1583-1648), who made an explicit statement of Deism in *On the Truth* (1624). From England Deism spread to France, and later to the United States. Reventlow refers to Edward Herbert as "a first representative (of Deism) on English soil."[81] But at this very early stage in the development of Deism, he remains "a lonely figure." His basic philosophical stance was that of Aristotle, Cicero, and the Stoics. Fundamentally, he believed that all people can arrive at the truth on the basis of reason. But he is not always consistent, and his literary remains included prayer and signs of religious devotion. His central theme was that of "natural religion" and morality. For the most part, he was ahead of Deism's time.

A more characteristic period for Deism was 1690-1740. Matthew Tindal's *Christianity as Old as Creation* (1730) was often referred to as "the Deists' Bible." Before him came Charles Blount (1654-1693), who championed natural religion in several publications. Blount had a direct link with Herbert, and at the time caused a considerable public uproar. For example, he fulminated against the prophet Elisha as "that hot, angry prophet, who cursed the poor children, and made them be destroyed with bears, only for calling him Bald-pate" (2 Kings 2:23-24).[82]

John Toland (1670-1722) was more significant, especially for his *Christianity Not Mysterious* (1696). Toland was an admirer of John Locke's work on reason, although it is doubtful whether Locke reciprocated this admiration. Even so, G. Gawlick argued that Toland presupposed Christian revelation, and that he was more positive toward theism than many other Deists. Nevertheless, Toland wrote: "Nothing can be said to be a Mystery, because we have not an adequate Idea of it."[83] Reason, he argued, is the critical standard of judgment about all things, and conveys clear and distinct ideas. No Christian doctrine, he urged, can be reputed to be a mystery.

Matthew Tindal (1657-1733) wrote several important books: *The Liberty*

---

81. Reventlow, *Authority,* 186.

82. Charles Blount, *Philostratus* (1680), 37.

83. John Toland, *Christianity Not Mysterious* (New York: Garland, 1702), 75.

of the Press (1698); *The Rights of the Christian Church* (1706-1709); and toward the end of his life, *Christianity as Old as Creation* (1730; 4th ed. 1733). Like other Deist writers, his major themes were human reason and natural religion. The last work was translated into German in 1741. Tindal claimed that Christianity was identical with the *timeless religion of nature.* This book became the focal center of the controversy between Deism and Christian theism. Like Toland, Tindal claimed an affinity with Locke's empiricism. As the second title indicates, Tindal also attacked the established church and its religion, especially "High Church" and "Popish" priests. Yet he followed Locke in advocating tolerance toward Dissenters. He especially attacked "priestcraft" and "superstition."

If Tindal had provided "the Bible of Deism," Anthony C. Collins (1676-1729) represented, according to Reventlow, Deism's peak and heyday. In his *Discourse in Free Thinking* (1713) he stressed the use of *reason and evidence.* His critics accused him of stating the obvious. His aim, however, was to undermine appeals to authority, and this included special revelation. His rejection of theism at times anticipated Nietzsche, as when he claimed, "All priests . . . are hired to lead man into Mistakes."[84] Collins also wrote about prophecy (1724), and this provoked controversy especially with W. Whiston, A. A. Sykes, and E. Chandler. Indeed, there arose a significant anti-Deist polemic. One of many examples is that of John Conybeare's *A Defence of Revealed Religion.* Conybeare argued that natural and revealed religion differ only in their extent.

(ii) *Pantheism.* Pantheism stands at the opposite end of the spectrum to Deism, in that it stresses divine *immanence* rather than divine transcendence. The great problem with it is that if God comes to be identified with the world or with the "All," it is difficult to see how God can remain fully *personal or suprapersonal.* In the Greco-Roman world, Stoicism represented pantheism, with its notion of the world-soul, and cosmic *Logos.* Paul very probably rejected the notion of the Stoic world-soul when he declared, "We have received not the spirit of the world, but the Spirit that is from God" (Gk. *to pneuma to ek tou Theou,* 1 Cor. 2:12).

In the modern period of philosophy, however, most thinkers point to Baruch Spinoza (1632-1677) as the supreme exponent of pantheism or of monist philosophy. He was expelled from the Jewish synagogue in Amsterdam for his unorthodox views of God in 1656. He had changed his Jewish

---

84. Anthony Collins, *Discourse in Free Thinking* (London, 1713; also New York: Garland, 1978), 109.

name "Baruch" to the Latin form "Benedict." His major studies focused on Descartes, but he repudiated Descartes's dualism of mind and body in favor of monism: the belief that all reality is one. In terms of his pantheism, his most famous aphorism is "God or Nature" *("Deus sive Natura"),* which appeared to *identify each with the other.*[85] God has no "personal" will or desire. Spinoza wrote: God is "a being absolutely infinite, i.e. a 'substance' consisting of an infinity of attributes, of which each expresses an eternal and infinite essence." His philosophy was indeed much more complex than this, and some have claimed that he is more theist than naturalist. But the mainstream view of Spinoza is that he identified "God" with the "All" (Gk. *pan*), including the world and nature. Ethics derives not from "God" but from the use of human reason. Spinoza insisted that he was true to his Hebrew roots: "God is one."

Many argue that religious *mysticism* is pantheistic, entailing a sense of being merged into the All. A number of Hindu thinkers have formulated a sophisticated form of pantheism. This usually comes from the nondualist tradition in the Upanishads. The Supreme Being is often called the Brahman. But most *Christian* mysticism holds a more deeply personal view of God, and it is usually anchored especially in the historical events of the passion and cross. In the West, some cite Hegel as a pantheist, although others appeal to the distinctive complexity of Hegel's thought. Christian theism is passionately opposed to identifying God with the world. The Christian doctrine of *creatio ex nihilo* rejects any Gnostic idea of emanations of God. Theists believe that God is *personal* or *suprapersonal,* and that God is simultaneously *transcendent and immanent,* that is, different from, or "above," the world, and simultaneously at work within it.

(iii) *Agnosticism.* Agnostics believe that it is impossible to know whether belief in God is true or false. At first sight agnosticism appears to be open and modest, and must not be identified with *avowed, explicit, or dogmatic atheism.* It derives from the Greek *a-gnosis,* "no knowledge." But it does invite the response that has been called "the paradox of skepticism," namely, how do we *know* that we *cannot* know?

On the other side, agnosticism must not be confused with *doubt.* Many Christian believers pass through periods of doubt, which may lead to constructive questions, reformation, and growth. Paul Tillich encourages doubt about some traditional formulations to entice us to find a more authentic God behind the "God" of early childhood teaching: to find "the God be-

---

85. Benedict de Spinoza, *Theological-Political Treatise* (Leiden: Brill, 1991), 71-79.

yond god."[86] Kierkegaard's life as a Christian involved constant wrestling with doubt. At one end of a spectrum doubt can legitimately question complacent, simplistic, or unexamined beliefs. It may lead to something better. At the other end of the spectrum, some theologians and other people can come to relish doubt, to turn it into an idol, and can almost turn attempting to disturb others into a supposed calling.

Yet, *static* agnosticism may also be the fruit of pride. A perspectival view of belief as a mere noncognitive "point of view" tends to undervalue the testimony of millions, not least of historic eyewitnesses, to insist that belief and unbelief are *equally* "rational." The history of theology and apologetics tends to gather a series of cumulative arguments on the rationality of belief. Philosophers like Alvin Plantinga set out such arguments brilliantly on the Internet and in their books. In a different tradition, Schleiermacher, in *On Religion: Speeches to Its Cultured Despisers,* lamented that many people too often listen to the voice of popular myths, rather than to the voice of those who have expertise and experience in matters of belief. Even if an atheist or agnostic holds religions in contempt, he wrote, "I will ask you . . . just to be well-informed and thorough-going in this contempt."[87] He asserted: "Millions . . . have been satisfied to juggle with its (faith's) trappings. . . . No room remains for the eternal and holy Being that lies beyond the world."[88] Schleiermacher concludes that people need to be "taught by those who have devoted to it (religion) their lives."[89]

As Christian theists, we may be grateful to God both for the anchor of the Bible, the sacraments, and the cross, and for what Irenaeus called "the rule of faith," or the tradition of the apostles. But these things do not simply look to the past. As Barth and others stress, the witness of the Holy Spirit actualizes the Bible, apostolic tradition, and the message of the cross day by day. In Pannenberg's words, these "prove the truth of God anew."[90] As the next chapter will confirm, rational reflection is also a gift of God, as we test this truth for ourselves and in public. The early Church Fathers, we have seen, provided a model *of rational belief,* based on *Scripture,* in the face of varied problems. Ultimately God himself is the guarantor of his truth and his

---

86. Paul Tillich, *The Shaking of the Foundations* (New York: Scribner, 1948, 1962), 49-50.

87. Friedrich Schleiermacher, *On Religion: Speeches to Its Cultured Despisers* (London: Kegan Paul, Trench and Trübner, 1893), 12.

88. Schleiermacher, *On Religion,* 1.

89. Schleiermacher, *On Religion,* 2.

90. Pannenberg, *BQT* 2:8.

promises. Meanwhile, this does not exclude the need for faith, obedience, and trust, especially in times of strain and testing. It is not simply "our faith," but the Trinitarian God, who is the source of all our confidence during our pilgrimage.

CHAPTER V

The Nonhuman Creation, and Ordinances for Human Welfare

1. The Creation and Work of Angels, Mainly in the Biblical Canon

We have stressed several times that God created humankind because God loves us and chose to reach forth, as it were, out of himself, to create beings "other" than himself, to commune with them and enjoy fellowship with them. In the next two chapters we shall see how humankind chose to become alienated from God, and to renounce this fellowship. After that we shall trace God's initiative in restoring this fellowship through Christ.

Meanwhile, it is utterly anthropocentric to assume that God created only humankind. This chapter discusses God's creation of other kinds of beings: angels and animals, but also galaxies, stars, trees, plants, and much else. But there *is no hint of dualism* in the Bible or in the major Christian theologians. Angels are God's *creatures,* just as dependent on God for their creation and continued existence as humankind. This is clear in all primary Christian sources.

Doubtless God created angels to take pleasure in them for their own sake. However, *in the creation accounts* of Genesis 1 and 2, *there is no account of the creation of angels,* although many ancient writers included angels in the creation of "heaven and earth," and cherubim with a flaming sword appear in Genesis 3:24. The biblical writings, including especially the Revelation of John, give us a number of glimpses of the heavenly court, in which angels and heavenly beings are absorbed *in the worship of God and in praise of Christ the Lamb.*

Nevertheless, it is not anthropocentric to insist that angels (and perhaps animals) have a further function of *ministering to, protecting, and preserving human beings.* Indeed, the primary meaning of the Hebrew *(mal'āk)* and

Greek *(aggelos* or *angelos)* words for angel is "messenger." Hebrews 1:14 gives a clear definition of angels: "Are not all angels spirits in the *divine service,* sent to serve for *the sake of those who are to inherit salvation?"* Psalm 34:7 says,

> The angel of the LORD encamps
> around those who fear him, and delivers them.

And Psalm 91:11-12, partly quoted in Matthew 4:6, states:

> He will command his angels concerning you
> to guard you in all your ways.
> On their hands they will bear you up,
> so that you will not dash your foot against a stone.

But the biblical passages *also* show the role of angels at worship: "Let all God's angels *worship* him" (Heb. 1:6); and "I heard the voice of many angels . . . singing with full voice, '*Worthy is the Lamb* that was slaughtered to receive power and . . . honor and glory'" (Rev. 5:11-12).

These three types of passages sum up the three major functions and purposes of angels, as these are perceived in the Christian church. (i) *The Eastern Orthodox Church* accepts all three, but majors on the notion of angels as constantly giving to God *their heavenly worship,* of which earthly human worship is a genuine, but pale, reflection. (ii) *The Roman Catholic Church* accepts all three functions, and ministry, like that in the Orthodox Church, emphasizes the *reality of the heavenly realm.* However, especially in popular piety, it also emphasizes their role as *guardians* or *guardian angels.* This draws on a prominent biblical tradition, including Matthew 18:10: "Their angels continually see the face of my Father in heaven." Indeed, popular Catholic myth ascribes an *individual* "guardian angel" to each baptized Christian, although Calvin and Barth insist that "guarding" is a corporate responsibility of all angels together. (iii) All traditions agree that angels are *messengers* and "ministering spirits," and *Protestant churches* place special emphasis upon this as their primary task. As "messengers," they may sometimes assume human form.

Once we embark upon this subject, numerous questions arise: for example, the names and numbers of angels and evil angels. Many writers, including Andrew Angel, speculate about the names of angels.[1] But Calvin and

---

1. Andrew Angel, *Angels: Ancient Whispers of Another World* (Eugene, Ore.: Wipf and Stock, Cascade Books, 2012), 30-34.

Barth strongly discourage too much study of "marginal" issues. The names Uriel and Raphael come from *1 Enoch* 9–10 and 20:1-8, although Michael and Gabriel also come from canonical biblical passages. Karl Barth, for whom angels are sufficiently important to devote over 150 pages to them in his *Church Dogmatics,* argues that we should "steer a way between" undue detail in *saying too much* about angels and equally undue denial or *saying too little.*[2] Angels, Barth declared, "denote a reality which is distinct both from God and man," and have "the being and activity of heavenly messengers of God."[3] Because in one sense they are "only the servants of God and man . . . (and) essentially marginal figures," and are given a subordinate role in God's purposes, we should speak about them only "incidentally," and "very softly." He applies the term "whisperer," to use Kierkegaard's word, and one alluded to recently by Andrew Angel.[4] Yet they feature not only in numerous biblical passages, but also in the work of Origen, Gregory of Nazianzus, Augustine, Pseudo-Dionysius, Aquinas, also less so in Luther and Calvin.

Calvin, for example, commented, "Angels being the ministers appointed to execute the commands of God must of course be admitted to his creatures."[5] They are clearly *created* beings. Yet Calvin added, anticipating Barth, we should not indulge our curiosity beyond what Scripture clearly says about them. He urged that we should heed "teaching that is true, certain, and useful," while avoiding "curiosity [and] frivolous questions . . . vain babblings."[6] In addition to their being messengers, "they are called hosts, because they surround the Prince as his court, — [to] adorn and display his majesty."[7] Nevertheless, we may confidently assert that *all three major or certain themes can be found in biblical passages.*

(i) *Worship by Angels.* In Revelation 4:8-11 the "four living creatures" (who are winged and all-seeing) and the "twenty-four elders" fall before "the one who is seated on the throne and *worship* the one who lives forever. . . . 'You are worthy, our Lord our God, to receive glory and honor and power.' " More explicitly in Revelation 5:11-13, "I heard the voice of many angels surrounding the throne and the living creatures and the elders . . . singing with full voice, 'Worthy is the Lamb that was slaughtered to receive power and

2. Barth, *CD* III/3, 418-531.

3. Barth, *CD* III/3, 370.

4. Barth, *CD* III/3, 371; cf. Andrew Angel's subtitle.

5. Calvin, *Institutes* 1.14.4; in *The Institutes of the Christian Religion,* 2 vols. (London: James Clarke, 1957), 1:144.

6. Calvin, *Institutes* 1.14.4; 1:144.

7. Calvin, *Institutes* 1.14.4; 1:145.

wealth and wisdom and might and honor and glory and blessing!' Then I heard every creature in heaven and earth . . . singing, 'To the one seated on the throne and to the Lamb be blessing and glory and might forever.'" The Orthodox Church and all Christian traditions hold this theme in common: *"on earth as it is in heaven"* (Matt. 6:10), or more explicitly: "There was with the angel a multitude of the heavenly host, praising God and saying, 'Glory to God in the highest heaven'" (Luke 2:13-14).

(ii) *Guardian Angels.* This theme is common to all Christian traditions, even if it is emphasized especially in Catholic traditions. Matthew 18:10 constitutes a key verse: "Take care that you do not despise one of these little ones; for, I tell you, in heaven their angels (Gk. *hoi angeloi autōn en ouranois*) continually see the face of my Father in heaven." Calvin and Barth, however, insist (in Barth's words): "The expression does not say, as even Calvin maintained, that each of them has his own angel charged to be a guardian angel."[8] Nevertheless, Calvin is prepared to think of angels *corporately* as "guardians." Although there are few or no other explicit references to "guardian" angels in the NT, this may be implied in Exodus 14:19; 23:20, 23; and 33:2 (see below).

Popular Catholicism strays into more fanciful notions of individual assignments of angels. Yet Karl Rahner retains the basic idea. In a sermon on angels, he declares, "When a person makes his way through life . . . two are always walking along the same street: the guardian angel and the human person, and both look on their own toward God."[9] This is part of a very brief comment on Matthew 18:10. He quickly moves to "ministering spirits" in Hebrews, and even argues, "Every person should be a guardian angel for the other." Rahner writes elsewhere that the work of Aquinas is "an opinion which one is free to hold or not."[10]

(iii) *Angels as Messengers.* The tradition that angels constitute *messengers from God* is common to all Christian theology, but especially to Protestants. This aspect recurs constantly in the earliest and latest biblical writings. In Genesis 18 a message from God comes to Abraham, who, when he looks up, sees "three men standing near him" (Gen. 18:2). In Genesis 19:1 two of these are identified as "angels." Then he "took a calf, tender and good, and gave it to the servant, who hastened to prepare it" (18:7). After they had eaten, the angels delivered their message: "Sarah shall have a son" (v. 10).

8. Barth, *CD* III/3, 518.
9. Karl Rahner, "The Angels: A Homily," at www.thevalueofsparrows.com.
10. Karl Rahner, *Encyclopedia of Theology: A Concise Sacramentum Mundi* (London: Burns and Oates, 1975), 11-12.

And the Lord said, "Shall I hide from Abraham what I am about to do . . . ?" (v. 17). Hebrews 13:2 comments, "Show hospitality to strangers, for by doing that some have entertained angels without knowing it." Clearly "angels" can choose to look like human beings.

Such angelic visitations as messengers occur at least seven times in Genesis. The angel of God called to Hagar (Gen. 16:7-8); called urgently to Abraham on Mount Moriah (22:11 and 15); appeared to the servant of Abraham to help him (24:40); was the subject of Jacob's vision (28:12), and his dream (31:11); met or encountered Jacob on his journey (32:1); and, according to Jacob's account to Joseph, "redeemed him from all harm" (48:16). In Exodus the angel of the Lord appeared to Moses out of the burning bush (Exod. 3:2).

Clearly the role of *messenger* occurs in the birth narratives in Matthew and Luke. The angel of the Lord appeared to Joseph in a dream (Matt. 1:20) with a message of confidence to take Mary as wife. In Matthew 2:13 the angel appeared again to Joseph to warn him to flee to Egypt. In 2:19 an angel appeared to tell Joseph that he could return to Israel. In Luke 1:11-13 "an angel of the Lord" appeared to Zechariah, who was terrified, and gave him a message about Elizabeth's pregnancy. In Luke 1:19 the angel says, "I am Gabriel. I stand in the presence of God, and I have been sent to speak to you (Zechariah) and to bring you this good news." Gabriel then appeared to Mary, and brought the message: "Greetings, favored one! The Lord is with you. . . . You will conceive . . . and bear a son, and you will name him Jesus. . . . The Holy Spirit will come upon you" (Luke 1:26-37). An angel then appeared to the shepherds, with "good news of great joy" (Luke 2:9-12). This passage concludes: "Suddenly there was with the angel a multitude of heavenly host, praising God and saying, *'Glory to God in the highest heaven.'*" (2:13-14). The role of the angels was *first as messengers,* and *then as givers of heavenly worship.*

(iv) *Angels as Guards or Warriors.* A subdivision of angelic functions comes from the guardian theme, namely, angels as guards or warriors. In Exodus 14:19 the function of the angel of God is *to keep guard* before and behind the Israelite army, which is also explicit in Exodus 23:20: "I am going to send an angel in front of you, *to guard you*" (cf. 23:23; 32:34). In 33:2 the angel of God is both a *guardian and a warrior:* "I will send an angel before you, and I will drive out the Canaanites, the Amorites, the Hittites . . ." From being messengers in Genesis, they became guardians in the second part of Exodus. This function is repeated in Numbers 20:16.

In the account of Balaam the angel appears as both *guardian* and *messenger* in Numbers 22:23-24, 26, 31; cf. 34-35. Similarly in Judges 2:1 the angel of the Lord is both messenger and warrior-guardian, as in Judges 2:4, 5:23, and 6:11. Judges 6:20-22 repeats the hospitality theme. Judges 13:3 prefigures the news of pregnancy that later comes to Mary. His appearance was "awe-inspiring" (13:6). In 13:16-17 Manoah does not recognize the angel, as he prepares hospitality for him. The angel of God also appears in 1 and 2 Samuel, 1 and 2 Kings, and Chronicles, Job, Psalms, Isaiah, Daniel, and Zechariah.

The OT does, however, portray some other aspects. There are enigmatic allusions to the "sons of God" (Heb. *bᵉnê hāʾᵉlōhîm*) in Genesis 6:1-4, and perhaps Psalm 82:1 and 6. In Genesis 6:1-4 they marry "the daughters of humans," and as a secondary version of the Fall, probably provide the basis for speculation in Enoch, as Williams argued.[11]

(v) *Angels in Various Overlapping Tasks.* The Gospels recount various episodes relating to angels in the ministry of Jesus. John 1:51 recounts the angels of "Jacob's ladder" in Genesis 28:12. They are reapers in the parable of the sower (Matt. 13:39, 41), and instruments of *judgment* in the parable of the good and the bad fish (Matt. 13:49). They witness the acknowledgment of the Son of Man (Luke 12:8-9), and of repentant sinners (15:10). In Matthew 22:30 and Mark 12:25 we learn almost incidentally that they do not marry.

In Matthew 24:31 and Mark 13:26-27 angels perform another well-known task: they appear with the Son of Man at the last trumpet call of the parousia, or return of Christ, when "they will *gather his elect* from the far winds" (also in Matt. 25:31). Angels have no knowledge of the precise date of the return of Christ in Matthew 24:36 and Mark 13:32. Matthew 25:41 is one of the few references to "the eternal fire prepared for the devil and his angels." An angel strengthens Jesus in Gethsemane (Luke 22:43), while in Matthew 26:53 Jesus can call on legions of angels to aid him. Angels feature in the resurrection narratives (Matt. 28:2-3; Luke 24:23; John 20:12).

Although the Gospels portray them mainly as *messengers,* angels also have other tasks. The Greek *angelos* (and the AV/KJV "angel") occurs some twenty-one times in Acts, a dozen times both in Paul and in Hebrews, and some sixty times in the book of Revelation. In Acts, an angel opens a prison gate for Peter (Acts 5:19), features in Stephen's speech (7:30, 35, 38), speaks to Philip (8:26), speaks to Cornelius (10:7), and is said to appear a second time to Peter in prison (12:7, 9-11). In Romans 8:38 angels and powers cannot separate us from the love of God in Christ, while in 1 Corinthians 4:9 Paul speaks of a spectacle to angels, and in 1 Corinthians 13:1, of "tongues"

---

11. Norman P. Williams, *The Ideas of the Fall and of Original Sin* (London: Longmans, Green, 1929), 20-29.

of angels. In 2 Corinthians 11:14 Satan can disguise himself as an angel. In Galatians 3:19, the law "was ordained through angels." In Colossians 2:18, *Paul disapproves of the worship of angels,* as if they were not God's *creatures.*

We return to the other two main traditions, before we leave the canonical writings. Gerhard Kittel writes concerning the NT: "the idea of *guardian,* or better, the directing and ministering angel, is taken over from Judaism."[12] He cites Acts 12:15, when the angel leads Peter out of prison, as an implicit example. The angels of the seven churches in Revelation 1:20 could, he argues, be guardians, although some suggest bishops of the seven churches. He favors the former, especially since Revelation elsewhere uses "angel" of supernatural or nonhuman figures. Gerhard von Rad cites not only many examples of their function as messengers, but also as those who guard Israel by smiting their foes (2 Kings 19:35), protect Israel at the Red Sea (Exod. 14:19), and guide the people (Exod. 23:20).[13] Indeed, "Michael is *the guardian angel of Israel,* and there are references also to the *guardian angels* from heaven (Dan. 4:13, 17, 23) and to . . . hundreds of thousands of angelic servants surrounding the throne."[14] The remaining theme is *worship,* which has a prominent place in Revelation. In Revelation 7:11-12, "The angels stood around the throne . . . and worshiped God, singing, 'Amen! Blessing and glory and wisdom . . . be to our God forever and ever!'"

Nevertheless, in Revelation angels can perform several other roles. These roles include being instruments of *cosmic judgment* (Rev. 8:7-8); causing stars to fall and strike the sun (8:10, 12); and holding the key to the bottomless pit (9:1). Angels also fight against the dragon: "Michael and his angels fought against the dragon," and "that ancient serpent" is thrown down (Rev. 12:7, 9). They act in judgment (14:19), cause plagues (15:6-8), and pour out God's wrath (16:1, 3). All this is admittedly part of John's imagery and symbolism, but these functions also reflect other biblical passages. Biblical passages also refer to seraphim (Isa. 6:2, 6-7) and cherubim (Exod. 25:20; 26:1, 31; 36:8, 35; Ezek. 10:2, 15), who are awesome, fiery, winged creatures. In Romans 8:38 Paul lumps together "angels" with "powers," to which Ephesians 6:12 may refer when it speaks of "cosmic powers" and "spiritual forces." Clearly these verses refer to powers stronger than weak humans. But Caird, Cullmann, and Wink regard these as oppressive structures in the state or society that may overwhelm us, and angels may form a subcategory of these

---

12. Gerhard Kittel, *"Angelos,"* in *TDNT* 1:86, italics mine.
13. Gerhard von Rad, *"Mal'āk* in the OT," in *TDNT* 1:77.
14. Von Rad, *"Mal'āk* in the OT," 1:79, italics mine.

forces. Similarly "Satan" occurs in the NT, although infrequently in the OT. He is the "ruler of the demons" in Mark 3:22, and "the ruler of this world" in John 12:31. But the NT writers are at one in asserting Christ's sovereignty and victory over such forces (cf. 1 Cor. 8:4-8; Col. 1:15-20; 2:8-15, 20-23). The powers may *include* evil spirits, who are behind the oppressive structures, but Christ has won the decisive victory over them.

2. Angels in Postcanonical Judaism and in Historical Christian Thought

(i) *Judaism.* After the close of the OT canon, Greek-speaking Judaism developed OT themes into a fully fledged angelology. Angels played little or no part among the Sadducees, but apocalyptic writers developed much from scattered allusions in Genesis 6 and Daniel. There are over twenty references to angels in Tobit, but only four in Bel and the Dragon, four in 1 Maccabees, and two in 4 Maccabees.[15] In Tobit 5:4-8, 15-16 the angel Raphael guided Tobit on his journey, but also took the form of a man. In 6:1 "a young man" (Gk. *paidarion*) went with him, together with his dog. In 6:4-5 the NRSV translates the word as "angel," and resumes translating it "young man" in 6:6. In 8:3 Raphael bound a demon, who hindered him. In 12:6 Raphael called Tobit to worship God, while in 12:15 he described himself as "one of the seven angels who stand ready and enter before the glory of the Lord." Roman Catholic and Orthodox include the Apocrypha in their canon, which *explains much of the difference from Protestant angelology.*

As we noted earlier, this also accounts for the early mention of names of angels by Andrew Angel. He liberally uses *1 Enoch* 1–36, in which *1 Enoch* 9:1–11:2 allude to the four archangels, *Michael, Sariel, Raphael,* and *Gabriel,* and the angels enact the judgment in *1 Enoch* 88:1-3.[16] *First Enoch* 6–11 develops the account of the enigmatic "Watchers" in Genesis 6:1-4. Their leader was called *Shemihazah,* and they taught their brides sorcery and magic. But the children of these marriages became "giants" (Heb. *gibbōrîm,* "mighty warriors"), and wrought havoc on the earth. The four archangels brought news of this chaos to the Almighty (as if he did not know it!), and God commissioned them to prepare Noah for the flood, and to bind up *Shemihazah*

15. Hatch-Redpath 1:8.
16. Angel, *Angels,* 24, 60, 64-65, 99, and other pages; and Williams, *Ideas of the Fall,* 24-26.

for punishment in the abyss. *First Enoch* 86:1–89:1 (perhaps c. 160 B.C.) has a variant version of this narrative.

Jubilees 5:1-11, 7:21-24, and 10:5-14 (late second century B.C.) recount a similar narrative.[17] The fallen angels are also "sons of the gods," or divine beings, in the original Genesis 6 account. Williams calls *1 Enoch* "the most interesting of all the pseudepigraphic works."[18] He traces fragments from six separate documents on this theme, dating from the third to the first century B.C. They include *1 Enoch* 12–36 (c. 200 B.C.); fragments of the *Book of Noah;* the *Visions of Enoch* (c. 165 B.C. in the Maccabean struggle against Antiochus Epiphanes); and the *Similitudes of Enoch* (c. 94-64 B.C.). The four archangels are also to punish the fallen angels in *1 Enoch* 9–10.

Like the speculations of Aquinas about fallen angels and the origins of evil, this speculative narrative of angels accounts for the antediluvian wickedness of the earth before Noah, and why all creatures, except those saved in the ark, perished in the flood.

The *Prayer of Joseph* identifies the chief angel as *Uriel* of Israel (1:7-8), while the *Apocalypse of Abraham* identifies him as *Iaoel* (10:1-17). On the other hand, as in the canonical biblical writings, the Dead Sea Scrolls, *Baruch,* and *2 Enoch* identify him as *Michael* (1QM 17:6-8; 2 En. 22:6, 3; 3 Bar. 11:4; T. Ab. 14:5).[19] *Jubilees* also depicts angels as being created for particular tasks in organizing the universe: "angels of the presence, angels of sanctification, and angels of the spirit of fire, and angels of the spirit of the winds, and angels of the clouds and darkness and snow and hail and frost . . . thunder and lightning . . . cold and heat" (*Jub.* 2:2; cf. 15:27). Such references also abound in the Dead Sea Scrolls (1QS 1:1-15; 8:5-16; CD 3:14; 6:2-11; 1QM 12:1-2; 1QH 1:21).[20]

Rabbinic thought, Kittel maintains, recognized a doctrine of angels as a legitimate development of the OT, because "it never entails the independent divinization of angels."[21] Angels serve and represent the Word and will of Yahweh, the God of Israel. Michael represents the *Shekīnāh* glory (Exod. 3:2; Exod. Rab. 3:2). Even the angels who are enemies of Israel must bow to his will. The rabbis emphasized, like the OT, that they are created beings. "Guardian angels" are "representations and executors of the divine care and

---

17. Williams, *Ideas of the Fall,* 28, argues that *Jubilees* also draws on Gen. 3:1-24.

18. Williams, *Ideas of the Fall,* 23-24.

19. Angel, *Angels,* 31.

20. Cf. Angel, *Angels,* 32-34.

21. Kittel, "Angels in Judaism," in *TDNT* 1:81.

protection."[22] But today many Protestants would regard many of these references as little more than idle speculations. *The different scope of the Protestant biblical canon must be kept in mind,* although not all of this intertestamental literature is "canonical" for Catholics and Orthodox.

(ii) *Historical Christianity.* Angels were often regarded as intermediaries between God and humankind, especially before the giving of the Mosaic Law. (1) *Augustine* argued that the creation of angels was implied in the Genesis creation account, because "God created *the heavens*" (Gen. 1:1). He wrote, "That the creation of angels was wholly omitted, I am unable to believe."[23] He appealed to the clause in the creed: "Maker of all things visible and invisible," as well as the Song of Three Children or *Benedicite,* which includes, "Praise him, all his angels, praise him all his hosts."[24] Nevertheless, like modern Protestants, he insisted that only Christ was mediator between God and humankind, and never angels.[25] They desire us *not* to worship them, but only to worship *God.*[26] Good angels find the cause of this goodness in "cleaving to God," while bad angels "have forsaken him."[27] Fallen angels and all who are of the devil will perish.[28] However, Augustine stopped short of suggesting "hierarchies" of angels.[29]

(2) *Pseudo-Dionysius,* or Dionysius the Areopagite, was a late-fifth-century or early-sixth-century Syrian monk who heavily influenced the mystical tradition. His work on angels was entitled *The Celestial Hierarchy.* This hierarchy consists of "super-celestial intelligences" (chap. 1). Dionysius alluded to the "fiery wheels," "many coloured horses, and commanders of armies," from Ezekiel and Revelation. Symbolically angels can be "shining men, flashing like lightning." They can be the object of "holy contemplation." *This marks a departure from biblical doctrine to medieval speculation.* Dionysius stated, "Hierarchy is, in my opinion, a holy order and knowledge and activity, which, so far as is attainable, participates in the Divine."[30] He added, "The aim of Hierarchy is the greatest possible assimilation to union

---

22. Kittel, "Angels in Judaism," 1:82.
23. Augustine, *City of God* 11.9; *NPNF,* ser. 1, 2:209.
24. Augustine, *City of God* 11.9; *NPNF,* ser. 1, 2:210.
25. Augustine, *City of God* 9.15; *NPNF,* ser. 1, 2:173-74.
26. Augustine, *City of God* 10.7 and 10.16; *NPNF,* ser. 1, 2:184 and 190.
27. Augustine, *City of God* 12.6; *NPNF,* ser. 1, 2:229.
28. Augustine, *Enchiridion* 29; *NPNF,* ser. 1, 3:247.
29. Augustine, *Enchiridion* 58; *NPNF,* ser. 1, 3:256.
30. Pseudo-Dionysius, *Celestial Hierarchy* 2.1-2. References to this work are placed in the text.

with God" (3.2). Further, he wrote, "We must proceed to honour the Angelic Hierarchy."

Dionysius returned to Galatians by speaking of angels as givers of the divine law, and to the Gospels by referring to the visit of Gabriel to Zechariah and to Mary (4.4). He then wrote of a threefold order of heavenly beings, of whom there were nine orders of angels, including "the many-eyed and many-winged hosts, named in the Hebrew tongue *cherubim* and *seraphim* . . . immediately around God" (6.1 and 7.1). The seraphim who have six "wings" come from Isaiah 6:2, 6-7. Cherubim (Exod. 25:20; Ezek. 10:2, 15) appear ninety times in the OT, and denote awesome winged creatures who adorn the Holy of Holies (Exod. 26:1, 31; 36:8, 35). Dionysius wrote, the "first rank of heavenly beings . . . stands immediately around God, and without symbol . . . dance round his eternal knowledge in the most exulted ever-moving stability" (7.4; cf. 8.1). He concluded, "They (angels) are thousand thousands, myriad myriads, accumulating and multiplying . . . (and) cannot be numbered by us" (14.1). In chapter 15 Dionysius went even further, speculating about angel anatomy: their eyes, noses, ears, mouths, eyelids, eyebrows, and so on. It is largely he who bequeaths this medieval angelology that has inspired so much popular Catholic mythology.

(3) *Thomas Aquinas* (1225-1274) offered a more rational approach than Dionysius, but it is also firmly embedded in medieval scholasticism. He treated the subject at length in *Summa Theologiae* I, questions 50-64. He first quoted "who makes his angels spirits" (Ps. 104:4) to insist that all angels are spiritual or *intellectual* beings, without material body.[31] Angels are not only immaterial, but "exceedingly great in number" (qu. 50, art. 3). In Daniel 7:10, he argued, "Thousands of thousands ministered to him, and ten thousand times a hundred stood before him." In question 54 Aquinas cited Dionysius several times under "objections," that is, as representing the opposite side of the scholastic debate.

On the question of the "will" of angels, Aquinas seemed to indicate that in angels "the will has a natural tendency towards good," although "there is also free will in angels" (qu. 59, arts. 2 and 3). At this point he endorsed Dionysius on angels' will to love, and to seek union with God (qu. 60, art. 3). Indeed, they love God more than self (qu. 60, art. 5). He reaffirmed that angels were made by God: "The angels, of necessity were made by God" (qu. 61, art. 1). He followed Augustine in regarding their creation as implied by

---

31. Aquinas, *Summa Theologiae* I, qu. 50, arts. 1 and 2. References to this work are placed in the text.

Genesis 1:1: "In the beginning God created heaven and earth" (qu. 61, art. 3). Nevertheless, fallen angels and demons can be guilty of "envy and pride" (qu. 63, art. 2). The devil envied God: "The devil has a perverse and obstinate will; he is not sorry for the evil of sin" (qu. 64, art. 4). Aquinas was generally more restrained than Dionysius.

(4) *John Calvin* (1509-1564) rightly placed the subject of angels under "The Creator of the World and All Things" (*Institutes* 1.14). God created angels, Calvin begins, "as ministers appointed to execute the commands of God" (1.14.4). But we should resist undue curiosity about them. They are sometimes called heavenly hosts, and "adorn and display his (God's) majesty" (1.14.5). Like soldiers, they are ready and prompt to obey his command. He cited Daniel 7:10 on their numbers: "ten thousand times ten thousand." They are also "ministers and dispensers of the divine bounty towards us," which tends "most to our comfort" (1.14.6).

Anticipating Caird today, Calvin argues, "Certain angels are appointed as a kind of president over kingdoms and provinces" (Dan. 10:13, 20; 12:1; Matt. 18:10; Luke 15:7; 16:22; Acts 12:15; *Institutes* 1.14.7). The reference of Jesus to the angels of the "little ones" indicates that their safety has been entrusted to them. Similarly Peter appears to have a "guardian angel," who releases him from prison, and *Michael* is described in Scripture as an archangel or mighty prince (Dan. 12:1; Jude 9; 1 Thess. 4:16; Matt. 26:53), but we must not "presume to dogmatise on the ranks and numbers of angels" (1.14.8). It is an "accommodation to us" to describe winged cherubim and seraphim. Although "Stephen and Paul say that the Law was enacted in the hands of angels," *Christ is preeminently the Mediator* (1.14.9). This subject easily gives rise to superstition, but as Revelation 19:10 and 22:8-9 indicate, humans are not to give them worship (1.14.10).

On "devils," Calvin wrote, the purpose of such teaching is "to put us on our guard against their wiles and machinations" (1.14.13). When biblical writers, he says, use such language as "the god and ruler of the world," "the strong man armed," "the prince of the power of the air," and the roaring lion, "the object of all these descriptions is to make us more cautious and vigilant" (2 Cor. 4:4; John 12:31; Matt. 12:29; Eph. 2:2). Calvin refers to "the seven devils" who possess Mary Magdalene. The devil, like the angels, was created by God, but "Satan cannot possibly do anything against the will and consent of God" (1.14.16-17).

(5) *Karl Barth* (1886-1968) begins section 51 of his *Church Dogmatics* by calling angels God's messengers under God's Lordship. But, as we noted, Barth warned against idle speculation, as Calvin did. Yet we must heed an-

gelic "whispers" (III/3, 369-78). He aims at being wholly "biblical," in contrast to Church Fathers who "plainly deviate from the Bible" and draw on "another source" (381). *He especially criticizes Dionysius's notion of "hierarchy"* (385-90; cf. 390-401). He then critically examines various nineteenth-century writers, including J. A. Dorner, Adolf Schlatter, and Ernst Troeltsch. The clear distinction between God and his creation must be maintained (421).

As in the case of human ministers, it is wisest to stress the role of angels as ambassadors of God. This constitutes the theme of section 51:3. It is "centrally a divine happening, and only secondarily . . . a heavenly" (477). Overconcern about "a special experience of angels" can distract us from God, who may use them as his ambassadors. Sometimes "figments of imagination" can become "the opponents of genuine angels." Barth declared, "Where an angel appears . . . speaks, and works, God himself appears . . . speaks and works" (480).

Barth's theology is motivated by a biblical and pastoral concern. As in all his works, he wants nothing to detract from the glory, majesty, and accessibility of God through *Christ.* Although he acknowledges angels' ministry and support, he is aware that some popular forms of the Christian religion actually have the unintended effect of clouding, not facilitating, our vision of God and the all-sufficing of Christ as Mediator.

3. The Creation and Status of Animals: Is Creation Centered on Humankind?

(i) *A Controversial Issue.* Few subjects raise as much passion and controversy as the debate about the place of animals in God's creation. Yet on two starting points virtually everyone agrees. First, we need to pay attention to God's nonhuman creation, including "spiritual" or heavenly beings, and animals, *to avoid an anthropocentric perspective on creation.* Humankind is not alone in being the object of God's love, care, and creative and sustaining power. Animals in the OT are "living beings" (in Hebrew they have *nepesh chayyāh;* Gen. 1:30). Second, Christian theology has very recently given special attention to this subject, partly at least because *environmental pollution, global warming,* and the function of *ecosystems and ecology* have featured increasingly in global thought, as well as a widespread recognition that neither the "image of God" nor "having dominion over" fish and animals (Gen. 1:27-28) implies, still less justifies, *exploitation* of any living species. These factors should rightly direct our attention to what it means to be created in the image of God, which we consider fully in chapter 6. It does not provide excuses for the exploitation of animals or the earth. To bear the image of God, we shall later argue, is to bear the vocation of *representing the love, sovereignty, care, and character of God to the world.*

Robert Wennberg shows us the ambiguity and complexity of the subject, by tracing passionately opposed attitudes to animals since the late eighteenth century. He outlines the preaching of the parish priest James Grainger in 1772, which censured the abuse of animals, including the whipping and starving of horses, and the practice of bear baiting and bull baiting. Grainger appealed to Proverbs 12:10,

> The righteous know the needs of their animals,
> but the mercy of the wicked is cruel.[32]

Yet Wennberg cites the simultaneous urging of a second parish priest, Thomas Newton, to *promote* bear baiting. They inhabited, Wennberg says, "different moral universes." Almost until the twentieth century it was assumed that animals were created primarily for the benefit of humankind. In spite of Copernicus's earlier demonstration that the earth was not the center of the solar system, only with the modern appreciation of the vast size of the universe, and of the place of our galaxy and planet within it, did it gradually dawn on Christian theologians to abandon an anthropocentric idea of the universe. On the other hand, there were exceptions to the trend. A closer study of celestial beings underlined that we could no longer assume that everything in the universe was "for the sake of humankind."

In the second half of the nineteenth century, the RSPCA (Royal Society for the Prevention of Cruelty to Animals) was founded in England, and the SPCA in America. From the mid–twentieth century, ecological concerns became more fashionable. Then in 1975 Peter Singer published his *Animal Liberation*.[33] Singer marked the beginning of modern concerns about "animal rights," which began a large-scale opposition to use of animals for testing for medical research; the spread of vegetarianism on moral grounds; opposition to "factory," or intensive, farming; and opposition to the killing of animals

32. Robert N. Wennberg, *God, Humans, and Animals: An Invitation to Enlarge Our Moral Universe* (Grand Rapids: Eerdmans, 2003), 1-3.

33. Peter Singer, *Animal Liberation* (Berkeley and Los Angeles: University of California Press, 1978); cf. Peter Singer, ed., *In Defence of Animals* (New York: Blackwell, 1985).

for the fur trade or for cosmetic purposes. Individuals had earlier opposed such practices, but now they formed part of a larger, growing movement. Wennberg estimates between half a million and a million members in the USA of such organizations as People for the Ethical Treatment of Animals.[34]

(ii) *Image of God, and Continuities between Animals and Humans.* Blame for the maltreatment of animals was often ascribed to the Christian church, especially to its traditional appeal to God's gift to humans of "dominion" over the earth (Gen. 1:26-28; Ps. 8:6-7). Yet, as we show in chapter 6, these passages are misunderstood if they are interpreted as implying exploitation or mastery. Reinhold Niebuhr, Jürgen Moltmann, and many biblical specialists make this point. The image of God is to represent the caring kingship or sovereignty of God himself, which is certainly not that of brute force and exploitation or mastery.

Further developments in the biological sciences and genetics have revealed a closer kinship between humans and higher animals than might at first have appeared. This fact does not compromise the uniqueness of humankind. A recent volume of essays edited by Malcolm Jeeves under the title *The Emergence of Personhood* convincingly demonstrates this.[35] A dozen neuroscientists, psychologists, and geneticists, in conjunction with two or three theologians, wrote essays for this volume. Some of the scientists stressed, for example, the communicative and "cognitive" skills of chimpanzees and dolphins. Nevertheless, these capacities should not be overstated.

At first it may seem disappointing that *relatively few biblical texts* seem to bear on the matter in hand. However, Genesis 1:26-30 is regularly compared with Genesis 9:1-3, and Psalm 8:6-9 and Isaiah 11:1-9 often feature, together with Matthew 6:26-30, 1 Corinthians 9:9-10, and a few others.[36] The biblical passages may seem few in number, but large volumes have been written on the basis of *expiation/propitiation/mercy-seat* on the basis of Romans 3:25, and other scattered biblical passages.

The traditional function of Genesis 1:26-30 and Psalm 8:6-9 has been to provide a starting point for debates about the respective status of humans and animals. The key phrase is "image of God," which in Augustine, Aquinas,

34. Wennberg, *God, Humans, and Animals*, 7.

35. Malcolm Jeeves, ed., *The Emergence of Personhood: A Quantum Leap* (Grand Rapids: Eerdmans, 2014).

36. Ryan Patrick McLaughlin, *Christian Theology and the Status of Animals: The Dominant Tradition and Its Alternatives* (New York: Macmillan/Palgrave, 2014), 87-113, and David L. Clough, *On Animals*, vol. 1, *Systematic Theology* (London and New York: Bloomsbury, 2012), 15, 18-25, and elsewhere.

and others seemed to denote the uniqueness of humankind and their "dominion" over animals. Clough concludes, "Biblical texts are reticent about the purpose of creation."[37] But the dominant tradition, he argues, began with passages about "the image of God" in Genesis 1:26-27 and Psalm 8:1 and 5-8. He regards the beginning of this tradition as stemming from Plato and Philo. In the postbiblical Christian tradition, this becomes most explicit in Origen.

In his treatise *Against Celsus,* Origen portrayed Celsus as saying, "All things came into existence not more for the sake of man than of the irrational animals," whereas in fact "Providence provides in a special manner for rational creatures; while . . . irrational creatures likewise enjoy the benefit of what is done for the sake of man."[38] He then compared the foolishness of the market-stall holder who provides for dogs as readily as for rational human beings. However, Origen continued, "God created these things . . . not only for us, but also for the animals which are subject to us."[39] He concluded: "The human race . . . perceives their own superiority, which far exceeds that of the irrational animals."[40]

Andrew Linzey attacks especially Augustine and Aquinas for representing "the dominant view." In *Summa Theologiae* Aquinas quoted Augustine on the right to kill animals for food. "Augustine says, 'When we hear it said "Thou shalt not kill"; we do not take it as referring to trees . . . nor to irrational animals.' "[41] Aquinas argued and commented, "There is no sin in using a thing for the purpose for which it is. . . . Hence . . . plants (are) for the use of animals; and animals . . . for the use of men."[42] He continued, "The life of animals and plants is preserved not for themselves but for man. . . . They are naturally enslaved and accommodated to the uses of others."[43] Together with this, most of the Church Fathers and traditional theologians saw human rationality and intellect as a major human characteristic that set humans apart from animals as dominant or superior. In recent thought, however, this "classical" assumption has been challenged on two fronts. By far the more important and more decisive challenge has been a clear understanding of what "image of God" entails. Again, we discuss this in detail

---

37. Clough, *On Animals,* 4.

38. Origen, *Against Celsus* 4.74; *ANF* 4:530.

39. Origen, *Against Celsus* 4.75; *ANF* 4:531.

40. Origen, *Against Celsus* 4.79; *ANF* 4:532.

41. Aquinas, *Summa* II/II, qu. 64, art. 1, quoting Augustine, *City of God* 1.20.

42. Aquinas, *Summa* II/II, qu. 64, art. 1; Andrew Linzey, *Animal Theology* (Urbana and Chicago: University of Illinois Press, 1995), 13.

43. Aquinas, *Summa* II/II, qu. 64, art. 1, reply to obj. 1 and 2.

in the next chapter. To bear the image of God is a calling to humankind to *represent God* to the world, especially in his sovereign grace, care, and love. It is also to enjoy and nurture an *intimate relation* with God and with the rest of creation.

David Clough, from the Protestant side, and Ryan McLaughlin from the Catholic side trace what they term "the dominant tradition" in Christian theology, which maintains that God created the world *for the sake of man;* both condemn this view as *"anthropocentric."* They argue that it assigns to animals *a merely instrumental role* of providing food and welfare for humankind.[44] At best, Clough comments on Philo and Calvin, "Humanity was placed in creation 'as in a theatre of God's works, where everything is ordained for human use.'"[45] Andrew Linzey also takes an emphatically polemical position on this side of the debate.[46]

Clough, McLaughlin, and Wennberg are less harsh on Aquinas than Linzey, because they also recognize (even if on the basis of an inaccurate wording of the Hebrew in the Vulgate) that Aquinas cited, "The Lord has made all things for himself" (Prov. 16:4, Vulgate version). Bonaventure also cites this verse to assert that the final end of creation "cannot be anything outside God."[47] In the end, Clough argues, Aquinas holds "an anthropocentric view" within the frame of a "theocentric" one. Celia Deane-Drummond, however, doubts Linzey's interpretation of Aquinas, calling it overnarrow and one-sided.[48] McLaughlin attempts a balanced, two-sided view.[49]

Clough considers the work of Calvin, while McLaughlin examines Vatican II, Pope John Paul II, Pope Benedict XVI, statements of the Catholic bishops, and the Catholic catechism. Linzey even accuses this catechism of "perpetuating cruelty."[50] However, one of the most thoughtful and sensitive contributions to the debate comes from Wennberg, who invites us to consider the probable moral standing of animals with sensitivity and balance.

44. Clough, *On Animals,* xvi-xxiv, 9-19, 22-24 and 44; McLaughlin, *Christian Theology,* 5-6 and 77-95.

45. Clough, *On Animals,* 9; cf. John Calvin, *Genesis* (Edinburgh: Banner of Truth Trust, 1965), 64.

46. Linzey, *Animal Theology,* 17-155.

47. Clough, *On Animals,* 19.

48. Celia Deane-Drummond, *Eco-Theology* (Winona, Minn.: Anselm Academic, 2008), 103-4 and 213-14 n. 23.

49. McLaughlin, *Christian Theology,* 10-20.

50. Andrew Linzey, *Animal Gospel* (Louisville: Westminster John Knox, 1998), 57.

He, like others, considers the history of ethical concern for animals in theology, church history, and Christian philosophy, but leaves the reader some discretion rather than propagating one-sided propaganda.

Clough cites the work of Francis Bacon for giving "fulsome endorsement to the ambition of advancing human mastery over nature."[51] He reiterates, "The weight of theoretical *opinion* that human beings are God's aim in creation, therefore, is not matched by a similar weight of theological *argument*."[52] He also cites the philosopher René Descartes for denying "souls" to nonhuman animals.

Clough also thinks that Calvin's notion of the world as the "theater" of redemption tends to regard animals as no more than the "scenery" of humankind's creation, and also dissents from Barth's endorsement of Calvin's approach in calling the world "the stage for the story of the covenant of grace." Yet Barth adds: "Of the totality of earthly and heavenly things as they are to be comprehended in Christ (Eph. 1:10) . . . everything is of God."[53]

Meanwhile, McLaughlin dissents from Vatican II, especially for stating: "God intended the earth with everything contained in it for the use of all human beings and peoples" (*Gaudium et Spes,* 1965).[54] He also dissents from Pope John Paul II in his *Peace with God the Creator* (1990), which distinguished between human beings made in the image of God and creation as such, which is "subjected to futility and waits for redemption."[55] Further, he criticizes Pope Benedict XVI for saying that nonhuman creation is derivative of human well-being. The statements of the Catholic bishops and the Catholic catechism fare little better. McLaughlin admits that Linzey's attack on the "cruelty" of the catechism is "a bit strong," but shares Linzey's accusation that it is "guilty of anthropocentrism and an instrumentalist view of animals."[56]

(iii) *The Protest against Anthropocentric, Human-Centered Concepts of Creation.* Pannenberg, for one, *rejects any merely "anthropocentric" perspective on creation.* In his *Systematic Theology,* volume 2, he devotes more than forty pages to "God's creation, preservation and rule of the world," and to

---

51. Clough, *On Animals,* xxi; see xx-xxiii and 14-15.

52. Clough, *On Animals,* 15, italics mine.

53. Barth, *CD* III/1, 44.

54. Vatican II, *Gaudium et Spes* 69; reprinted in Austin P. Flannery, ed., *Documents of Vatican II* (Grand Rapids: Eerdmans, 1975), 975; and McLaughlin, *Christian Theology,* 25.

55. McLaughlin, *Christian Theology,* 26.

56. McLaughlin, *Christian Theology,* 36.

"the world of the creatures."[57] Moltmann similarly addresses "the ecological crisis," "creation," and "God the Creator" in his book *God in Creation*. Their argument carries far more weight than scattered appeals to biblical passages, which too often merely rest on metaphors or analogies, or largely poetic visions of the future, such as that of Isaiah 11:1-9, especially 6-9. This begins:

> The wolf shall live with the lamb,
>> the leopard shall lie down with the kid;
>> the calf and the lion and the fatling together. (11:6)[58]

Pannenberg insists, "God wills to *preserve* the world," and he states, "God cares for *each individual creature,* providing it with food and water at the right time (Deut. 11:12-15; Jer. 5:24; Pss. 104:13ff., 27; 145:15f.)."[59] He cites Matthew 6:25-29 and Luke 12:24-27, in which Jesus speaks of God's care for the birds of heaven and the lilies of the field, as God sees to the needs of each. He even cites animal and cosmic preservation in Augustine and Aquinas.[60] He continues, "Rest from creation does not mean the end of preservation and governing the world. . . . The existence of creatures has its beginning in the act of their creation. . . . The faithfulness of God guarantees . . . the emergence and persistence of continuous existing forms of creaturely reality, and their ongoing identity and independence."[61] Pannenberg concludes that God's creation of humankind "is an expression of his love" (2:57).

Finally, "creaturely reality," Pannenberg declares, "is a plurality of creatures, making up the world" (2:61). Each creature is distinctive in relation to other finite things. God's *logos* creates a "productive principle of diversity . . . (while) order and unity are not just external to the creatures" (2:62). This regularity and order are "a condition of creaturely independence" (2:72). Anyone who lives with animals knows that they can at times show "independence." In terms of self-motivation, this allows for new and more complex forms of the world of creatures. Pannenberg then turns to eschatology. The

57. Pannenberg, *ST* 2:35-76; see also 77-136.
58. McLaughlin, *Christian Theology,* 96-113; Clough, *On Animals,* 155-57; Linzey, *Animal Theology,* 128-31.
59. Pannenberg, *ST* 2:35, italics mine.
60. Aquinas, *Summa* I, qu. 104, art. 1.
61. Pannenberg, *ST* 2:38 and 40. References to this work have been placed in the immediately following text.

goal of God's purpose through Christ was "that all might be reconciled in him (Col. 1:20; Eph. 1:10). . . . The destiny of all creation is at stake (Rom. 8:19-23). . . . The relation of non-human creatures to their Creator thereby also comes to fulfilment" (2:73). Taking it one step further, he asks, "Does the redemption which is bound up with the incarnation relate only to the earthly humanity?" (2:75).

Moltmann, similarly, cannot be accused of anthropocentricism, most notably in *God in Creation*. He relates the ecological crisis to the misunderstanding of "dominion" as "domination."[62] He also dissents from the metaphor of creation "as a theatre for God's history with men."[63] He has reservations about a sharp distinction between "natural theology" and "revealed theology" in a way that could lead to the devaluation of either.[64] In spite of Barth's "brilliant" work, "in his doctrine of creation he did not always do this justice, because he did not take over the Reformed *ordo decretorum*."[65] In the next section we shall note Brunner's difference from Barth in this respect, especially in the debate about *Natural Theology*. In a profound, if controversial, statement, Moltmann declares, "God's creative love is grounded in his humble, self-humiliating love. . . . God does not create merely by calling something into existence. . . . In a more profound sense he 'creates' by letting-be, by making room, and by withdrawing himself."[66]

(iv) *Cruelty to Animals and Moral Vegetarianism.* We noted widespread protests about such practices as factory farming and the use of animals for fur trade, medical research, and even cosmetics, many of which began in response to Singer on animal "rights." This protest would not collapse even though many, following Oliver O'Donovan, think the term "rights" has become overextended today. Vegetarianism relates to several exegetical and hermeneutical issues in Genesis. Gordon Wenham points out that God "blesses" animals (Gen. 1:22) with a possible wordplay on *b-r-k* (bless), *p-r-h* (be fruitful), *r-b-h* (multiply), and *b-r-'* (create).[67] Wennberg writes, "Before the fall, humans ate grass and fruit, and animals ate grass. This is what a world is like without sin . . . in which humans are at peace with God, with animals, and with the world of nature. . . . Here there is

62. Jürgen Moltmann, *God in Creation: A New Theology of Creation and the Spirit of God* (London: SCM, 1985), 23-40.

63. Moltmann, *God in Creation*, 56; cf. 61.

64. Moltmann, *God in Creation*, 59.

65. Moltmann, *God in Creation*, 81.

66. Moltmann, *God in Creation*, 88.

67. Gordon Wenham, *Genesis 1–15* (Waco: Word, 1987), 24-25.

no killing, no eating of flesh."[68] He cites Claus Westermann as saying that Genesis gives "an awareness that the killing of living beings for food is not right, and so is not in accordance with the will of the creator at the beginning."[69]

McLaughlin and others make much of the difference between Genesis 1:28-29 and Genesis 9:1-3. Genesis 9, he argues, leads to dominion and dread, while Genesis 1 led to peace and harmony. Genesis 9:1-3 explicitly declares, "Every moving thing that lives shall be food for you; and just as I gave you the green plants, I [now] give you everything. Only, you shall not eat flesh with its life, that is, its blood" (vv. 3-4). McLaughlin argues that when the image of God was intact in Genesis 1:28-29, humankind's "dominion" was entirely one of peace and nonviolence; after this image was damaged, humankind was given permission to inflict violent death on animals for food. He quotes Gerhard von Rad: "The relationship of man to animals no longer resembles that which was decreed in chapter 1. The animal world lives in fear and terror of man."[70]

Recently R. R. Reno has developed this comment more fully. According to Reno, "The scope and conditions of human dominion over animals change. In the first creation, God gives animals into the care of human beings, and plants as food. Now, God gives the animals as well for food. . . . There is both a price and a condition for this new bequest. The animals will fear humans, and thus they will now be very difficult to find, domesticate, and put into the service of humanity."[71] Similarly Bruce Waltke comments that as "all flesh" became corrupted before the flood, animals "got out of control" and no longer feared human beings, in contrast to earlier peaceful rule.[72] By contrast with the "corruption" period, it is suggested that the ark of Noah represented "a kind of floating Garden of Eden where animals and human beings live together in harmony."[73]

This contrast between Genesis 9:1-3 and Genesis 1:28-30 has often provided grounds for an argument in favor of moral or theological vegetarian-

68. Wennberg, *God, Humans, and Animals*, 292.

69. Claus Westermann, *Genesis 1–11: A Commentary* (Minneapolis: Augsburg, 1984), 164.

70. Gerhard von Rad, *Genesis: A Commentary* (Philadelphia: Westminster, 1961), 127; similarly, D. W. Cotter, *Genesis* (Collegeville, Minn.: Liturgical Press, 2003), 59-60.

71. R. R. Reno, *Genesis* (Grand Rapids: Brazos, 2010), 124.

72. Bruce K. Waltke, with C. J. Fredericks, *Genesis: A Commentary* (Grand Rapids: Zondervan, 2001), 144.

73. W. S. Towner, *Genesis* (Louisville: Westminster John Knox, 2001), 85.

ism. One example among several is Linzey's chapter, "Vegetarianism as a Biblical Ideal," in which he claims that Genesis 9 "reverses" Genesis 1.[74] In Genesis 1:31 God pronounces everything "very good" after he prescribed a vegetarian diet.[75] Admittedly he is fair enough to quote Calvin: "It is an insupportable tyranny, when God . . . has laid open to us the earth and air, in order that we may thence take food as from his storehouse, for these to be shut up from us."[76] But Linzey again stresses the conditions of Genesis 9:1-3. He sees Isaiah 11:6-9 as not a mere poetic vision, but as a description of the eschatological age of peace, which constitutes a fulfillment of Genesis 9.[77] It is part of a case for nonviolence as illustrated from Albert Schweitzer. Further, Jesus Christ is the Prince of Peace, who was "with the wild beasts" (Mark 1:13). Clough agrees with Linzey in this respect.[78]

Other biblical passages have been pressed into the service of those who defend the status of animals. One such is Jonah 4:11, where God's compassion for Nineveh extends to "many animals." In Exodus 20:10 the provision of the Sabbath rest is not just for humans, but includes "your livestock." In Psalm 50:10,

> Every wild animal of the forest is mine (God's),
>   the cattle on a thousand hills.

Lambs were as intimate companions for ancient Jews, as dogs might be for humans in the West today (2 Sam. 12:3). Moderate versions of this argument insist on the minimal use of slaughter or pain in modern economic programs. More polemic versions insist on strict vegetarianism.

On the other hand, we cannot ignore God's institution of sacrifice (for example, Lev. 16:2-34; Heb. 9:6–10:4). Nor can we brush aside Jesus' involvement in the catching and eating of fish (Mark 6:38-41; 8:7-8; and especially John 21:6-13). A counterargument might be that sacrifice was a temporary institution, but it was ordained, and Jesus invited the disciples to continue their diet of fish after the resurrection.

(v) *Claims about Animals and Future Life or Future Salvation.* Clough includes in the effects of incarnation and the atonement the "restoration of

74. Linzey, *Animal Theology,* 125-37.

75. Linzey, *Animal Theology,* 126.

76. John Calvin, *Commentaries on the First Book of Moses,* vol. 1 (Edinburgh: Calvin Translation Society, 1847), 291.

77. Linzey, *Animal Theology,* 129.

78. Clough, *On Animals,* 55 and 155.

all things," including animals, who will be restored.[79] To cite one random example, "The Augustinian characterisation of sin as distorted desire and the feminist image of sin as the breakdown of relationship are both clearly apt representations of the chimpanzee infanticides. . . . Sinful creatures stand in need of reconciliation with God" (116, 119). Jesus took on *"fleshy creatureliness"* (cf. John 1:14; cf. John 3:16-17). "In Christ all things are held together" (130). Clough appeals to God's purpose of redemption for all, and to his providing for all things (Pss. 104; 145; 147; Clough, 133-37). Restoration, Clough argues, will be *universal* (Eph. 1:10), as Irenaeus, Origen, Gregory of Nyssa, and Barth had seemed to imply (149-53). There will be peace between creatures (158-62).

We discuss "the restoration of all things" further in chapter 15. An impressive array of Christian thinkers who believed in the involvement of animals in future salvation or future life may be cited. Wennberg cites Richard Dean's *Essay on the Future Life of Brutes* (1767); the expositor Matthew Henry (1662-1714); Bishop Joseph Butler (1692-1752); the hymn writer Augustus Toplady (1740-1778); John Wesley (1703-1791); Samuel Taylor Coleridge (1772-1834); and more recently C. S. Lewis and Keith Ward. Wesley regarded this as "plainly" implied by Romans 8:21.[80]

Clough's position deserves respect, but his belief that the atonement involves all fleshly existence rather than humankind may seem to be speculative. Many exegetes are cautious about any *dogmatic* conclusion. As we noted, C. F. D. Moule wrote, "The idea of reconciling to God everything — the animate and the inanimate — is a difficult one for the modern reader," although Moule also points to the harmony of nature in Isaiah 11:6-9 and Romans 8:19-21.[81] Calvin advocated caution in avoiding undue speculation on one side, while avoiding undue dogmatism on the other.

4. Human Ordering: Political Communities, Marriage, and Justice

Most writers allude to what we have called *"political communities"* simply as *the state.* However, Oliver O'Donovan argues, "The word 'state' has been a constant seduction to theologians who believe that they could use it of

79. Clough, *On Animals,* 81-176. References to this work have been placed in the immediately following text.

80. Wennberg, *God, Humans, and Animals,* 319-20.

81. C. F. D. Moule, *The Epistles to the Colossians and to Philemon,* CGTC (Cambridge: CUP, 1962), 71.

all political communities in history."[82] He alludes, as an example, to Oscar Cullmann's *The State in the New Testament,* which we shall discuss later. He contends that for the ancient world a better word than "state" is the Latin *civitas,* for which the accurate translation would be "political community." It constitutes, in effect, what Emil Brunner rightly regards as a creation "ordinance" of God. O'Donovan writes, "the essential *esse* of human society is political authority."[83] He agrees with Calvin that ideally this presupposes in Christendom the law of the ascended Christ. Helmut Thielicke declares, "The State is simply the institutionalised form of *God's call to order* . . . a remedy required by our corrupted nature . . . which puts a stop to the self-destruction of the fallen world" for the purpose of creation's preservation.[84]

This explains two words in our heading. The state, or its equivalent, constitutes a divine ordinance for the preservation of the human creation. But why do we add "marriage"? Brunner rightly insists that *two* "ordinances" demonstrate God's "preserving grace." "Both matrimony and the state are instituted by God."[85] Without marriage and the state, "no communal life is conceivable that could in any way be termed human."[86] Brunner went further, commenting, "Monogamous marriage . . . is of higher dignity than the State because, as an institution, as an ordinance, it is . . . unrelated to sin."[87] He added, "Matrimony is a 'natural' ordinance of the Creator because the possibility of, and the desire for, its realisation lies within human nature."[88] People do not have to become believing Christians to become married. It remains a *divine ordinance* for the preservation of *creation,* and Barth's objections to Brunner's understanding of "natural theology" cannot undo this.

In the Sayings of Jesus, the ordinance of marriage features in Mark 10:11-12 (on marriage and divorce), Matthew 5:32, 19:9, and Luke 16:18. Paul refers to a saying of our Lord in 1 Corinthians 7:10, and less directly in 7:1-7 (where 7:1b is clearly a quotation from "matters about which you wrote"), in Colossians 3:18-19, and in Ephesians 5:21-33 (whether or not these are related to

82. Oliver O'Donovan, *The Desire of Nations: Rediscovering the Roots of Political Theology* (Cambridge: CUP, 1996).

83. O'Donovan, *The Desire of Nations,* 233.

84. Helmut Thielicke, *Theological Ethics,* vol. 2, *Politics* (Grand Rapids: Eerdmans, 1979), 17.

85. Emil Brunner, in dialogue with Karl Barth, *Natural Theology* (Eugene, Ore.: Wipf and Stock, 2002; orig. 1948), 45.

86. Brunner, *Natural Theology,* 29.

87. Brunner, *Natural Theology,* 29.

88. Brunner, *Natural Theology,* 30.

supposed "household codes"). Hebrews embodies the positive affirmation, "Let marriage be held in honor by all" (Heb. 13:4). Any mythology about Christian or biblical denigration of "bodily" relations as such is entirely misplaced in the light of clearly positive evaluations.

This brings us to our third term, "justice." Virtually every writer agrees that this is a particular mandate of the state, when it serves the purpose for which God has ordained it. To cite O'Donovan again, "The authority of government resides essentially in the act of judgement . . . to reward the just and punish the evil" (Rom. 13:4).[89] Judgment is "an act of moral discrimination, dividing right from wrong."[90] This is inherently bound up with "order," "the political community," and "creation." In an earlier book O'Donovan wrote, "We must understand 'creation' not merely as the raw material out of which the world as we know it is composed, but as the *order* and coherence *in* which it is composed."[91] Justice ultimately comes from God through Christ at Calvary.[92] It cannot come from totalitarianism, whether state totalitarianism or cultural totalitarianism. It is derived from God's act of justice (*dikaiōma*, Rom. 5:18), and from Hebrew *mishpāt* in the OT.

O'Donovan examines several "human" self-contained systems. These include market theory, reciprocal giving and receiving, and alternative models. Aristotle attempted to add "distributive" justice to "retributive" justice, O'Donovan comments, but this proved to be self-defeating.[93] He traces the Franciscan concern for the "poor," Hugo Grotius's revision of Aristotle, and endless talk about "equality"; but none of these reaches the heart of "justice."

One of the insights of liberation theology is José P. Miranda's emphasis of the social implications of justification by faith. In his book *Marx and the Bible*, Miranda shows carefully how there is a close connection between Paul on justification and justice, righteousness, and freedom from oppression. The Hebrew term *mishpāt*, he argues, signifies "the defence of the weak, the liberation of the oppressed, doing justice to the poor" (cf. Exod. 21:1; 15:25).[94] On Romans 1:18–3:20 Miranda contends that the justice God revealed points

89. Oliver O'Donovan, *The Ways of Judgment* (Grand Rapids: Eerdmans, 2005), 4.
90. O'Donovan, *The Ways of Judgment*, 7.
91. Oliver O'Donovan, *Resurrection and Moral Order: An Outline for Evangelical Ethics* (Grand Rapids: Eerdmans; Leicester: IVP, 1986), 31, first italics mine; second his.
92. O'Donovan, *Resurrection and Moral Order*, 74.
93. O'Donovan, *The Ways of Judgment*, 37.
94. José P. Miranda, *Marx and the Bible: A Critique of the Philosophy of Oppression* (London: SCM, 1977), 137; cf. 109-92.

to the punishment of injustice, and at the same time judicial sentence and eschatological salvation.[95] The revelation of the "righteousness of God" (Gk. *dikaiosynē ek theou,* Phil. 3:9) is no longer a *private, "inner"* affair *only.* He agrees with the work of Bultmann, Otto Michel, and Eberhard Jüngel. It is not our concern here to defend his use of the earlier Marx, nor to defend his use at times of selective biblical texts. We are concerned to trace only the close relation of *justice* to the central concerns of the gospel.

In a very different direction, Sarah Coakley offers a new, more careful, and more critical approach to feminist theology. On one side, she totally affirms and defends the basic concern of feminist writers to establish justice. She is fully aware of the oppression of women, especially in non-Western parts of the world. She writes, "Appeals to human 'rights,' 'justice,' and 'equality' must go on *strategically*."[96] Nevertheless, she also insists, "Authentic feminist freedom must be undergirded by divine grace and power rather than set in competitive opposition to it."[97] She has strong reservations about the earlier feminism that tried to reject "Fatherhood," and misconceived some theological truths in the name of justice.[98] The primary concern of her book is "participation in God," with prayer and contemplation, and the importance of "desire," as well as justice.

In the remainder of this section 4 we shall consider the main view in the Bible, Church Fathers, and the medieval period up to Calvin, which simply *asserts God's ordinance and the need for Christian submission to it.* In section 5 we consider the other side of the debate.

Romans 13:1-7 is the classic citation in this context: "Let every person be subject to the governing authorities; for there is no authority except from God, and those authorities that exist have been instituted by God.... Rulers are not a terror to good conduct, but to bad.... [The authority] is God's servant for your good.... The authorities are God's servants.... Pay to all what is due." Similarly 1 Peter corroborates Paul: "For the Lord's sake accept the authority of every human institution, whether the emperor as supreme, or of governors, as sent by him to punish those who do wrong and to praise those who do right.... Fear God. Honor the emperor" (1 Pet. 2:13-17).

This may seem straightforward. The two passages refer to the authority

---

95. Miranda, *Marx and the Bible,* 172-73.
96. Sarah Coakley, *God, Sexuality, and the Self: An Essay "On the Trinity"* (Cambridge: CUP, 2013), 80; cf. Sarah Coakley, *Powers and Submissions: Philosophy, Spirituality, and Gender* (Cambridge: CUP, 2002).
97. Coakley, *God, Sexuality, and the Self,* 98.
98. Coakley, *God, Sexuality, and the Self,* 74 and 75.

of the Roman Empire. They seem to harmonize with the saying of Jesus: "Give to the emperor the things that are the emperor's, and to God the things that are God's" (Mark 12:17; Matt. 22:21; Luke 20:25). Yet, from time to time NT writers see state authorities as oppressive. For example, "Peter and the apostles answered, 'We must obey God rather than any human authority'" (Acts 5:29). In Revelation 13:5-18 the idolatrous and blasphemous beast "was given authority over every tribe and people . . . and all the inhabitants of the earth will worship it. . . . Here is a call for the endurance and faith of the saints" (vv. 7, 8, 10). Clearly in Romans 13 and 1 Peter 2 the state has authority to curb anarchy and impose justice and order, but Revelation 13 warns against totalitarian oppression and unlimited power.

It should not surprise us that Christian thinkers have sometimes one-sidedly offered an uncritically positive or negative view of the state, often depending on what danger they fear more. Most of the Church Fathers tend to follow the positive assertions of Romans 13:1-7 and 1 Peter 2:13-17. Origen writes to Celsus, "We are not so mad as to stir up the wrath of kings and princes. . . . For we read, 'Let every soul be subject to the higher powers. There is no power, but of God'" (Rom. 13:1-2).[99]

One of the clearest and most emphatic is John Chrysostom, who devotes seven columns in English to Romans 13:1-7.[100] First he quotes Paul in full, and advocates subjection to rulers: "that all things should not just be carried on in confusion." Like Brunner, he compares God's "ordaining" of marriage (Prov. 19:14 LXX); "God made marriage" (Matt. 19:4-5; Gen. 2:24). He comments, "For anarchy . . . is an evil, the cause of confusion." On Romans 13:3 he asks, "Why be afraid?" Will authorities "punish a person that is doing well"? The state is "on guard, like a soldier." On verses 6-8, taxes are to be paid, for rulers ensure "good order and peace."

Lactantius similarly declares, "Render to all (authorities) the fear that is due to them, all offerings, all customs, all honour, gifts, and taxes."[101] Eusebius even credits Polycarp with saying, "We have been taught to render to princes and authorities ordained by God the honour that is due, so long as it does not injure us."[102] Athanasius cites the verse "Render all their dues" from Romans 13:7 twice.[103] Basil assesses his obligations to the magistrate in

---

99. Origen, *Against Celsus* 8.14; *ANF* 4:664.

100. Chrysostom, *Homilies on the Epistle to the Romans,* Homily 23; *NPNF,* ser. 1, 11:511-14.

101. Lactantius, *Constitutions of the Holy Apostles* 2.13; *ANF* 7:436.

102. Eusebius, *Ecclesiastical History* 4.15.22; *NPNF,* ser. 2, 1:190.

103. Athanasius, *Letter* 6.5 and *Letter* 10.1.

the light of Romans 13:4.[104] Augustine writes that the Donatists should not "resist the ordinance of God," and quotes Romans 13:2 and 4.[105] Ambrose declares, "I will pay the deference due to authority, as it is written, 'Honour to whom honour is due, tribute to whom tribute'" (Rom. 13:7).[106] A search of the Fathers has produced eight who took Romans 13:1-7 seriously, with virtually no reservations.

The medieval period reflected the Church Fathers. From the time of Gregory of Rome up to the beginning of the Reformation period, the church and the state were virtually a single authority. The relation between the church and state did not effectively raise urgent questions. Aquinas appeared to consider the issue only in passing. In *Summa Theologiae* he wrote, "As one man is part of the household, as a household is part of the state, and the state is the perfect community. . . . [It] is ordained for the common good."[107] In discussing a parent's right to strike a child, he quoted Proverbs 13:24 and 23:13, and compared the right of the state to impose obedience.[108] In the same passage Aquinas admitted to deriving his thought not only from Romans 13:1-7 but also from Aristotelian politics. He also appealed to Romans 13:1 on several occasions.[109]

In Reformation times the relation between church and state often became urgent. Calvin was very positive about the role of the state, but some argue that Luther's approach was more ambiguous or "softer." Thielicke considered the popular aphorism that "Lutheranism is politically passive. . . . Calvinism shows an incomparably greater and more active interest in politics."[110] Oliver O'Donovan comments, "Luther [is] so often blamed for weakness in political theology."[111] Luther admittedly spoke of "a Two-Kingdoms Christendom, and a Two-Governments Christian doctrine," in which the "twin peaks of authority" were the church and the state.[112] O'Donovan writes: "Both Luther and the Anglican reformers founded their view of church-state relations on this distinction of authority into two disparate

104. Basil, *Letter* 289; *NPNF*, ser. 2, 8:314.
105. Augustine, *The Letter of Petilian the Donatist* 2.45; *NPNF*, ser. 1, 4:540.
106. Ambrose, *Letter* 40.12; *NPNF*, ser. 2, 10:454.
107. Aquinas, *Summa* II/I, qu. 90, art. 3, reply to obj. 3.
108. Aquinas, *Summa* II/II, qu. 65, art. 2.
109. Aquinas, *Summa* II/I, qu. 96, art. 5; II/II, qu. 88, art. 10; II/I, qu. 96, art. 4, reply to obj. 1.
110. Thielicke, *Theological Ethics*, 2:565.
111. O'Donovan, *The Desire of Nations*, 165.
112. O'Donovan, *The Desire of Nations*, 196.

kinds. . . . [The] two kingdoms revives the Augustinian division between opposed, co-existing social relations," that is, the two cities.[113] Yet it is difficult
to call Luther's attitude to the state "negative" when he appealed to "godly
princes" and played a major part in putting down the Peasants' Revolt, in
contrast to the "Radical" Reformers.

Yet a different voice in the Western churches was beginning to emerge.
*When the state does not go beyond its ordained limits, it is easy to affirm the
teaching of Romans 13:1-7 and 1 Peter 2:13-17. But when the state oversteps the
mark, protest against the state's power becomes a moral imperative.* In very
general terms the former view predominated until the Reformation, while
the latter view has become an increasingly sensitive one in modern times.
This was especially the case in the face of Nazism, communism, and totalitarianism. Thielicke argues that in resisting National Socialism the Confessing
Church in Germany owed more to Reformed theology and to Karl Barth
than it did in general terms to Lutheranism.

5. Modern Concerns for the Limitation of the State, and Justice for All

Calvin wrote "of Civil Government" in the *Institutes* 4.20. Like Luther, he attacked the attitude of "the fanatics" or Anabaptists to the state (4.20.1-3). He
not only stated that "The Lord . . . approves and is pleased with" the function
of magistrates, but he also recommended their "very honourable titles," for
"they have a commission from God, that they are invested with divine authority, and in fact represent the person of God" (4.20.4). He cited Proverbs
8:15-16: "By me princes rule, and nobles, even all the judges of the earth."
Supreme power on earth, he continued, "is lodged in kings and governors . . .
by Divine Providence." In this same section he also called them *kybernēseis,*
"governments" (1 Cor. 12:28). He wrote, "Rulers are the ministers of God"
(Rom. 13:1, 3). He then cited God's commission to the offices of king in the
case of "David, Josiah, and Hezekiah, and the governors, Joseph and Daniel
. . . Moses, Joshua, and the Judges" (4.20.4).

Some may seek to disrupt rulers, Calvin wrote, "to introduce anarchy";
but this is "devilish pride" and ignorance (4.20.5). He cited Isaiah 49:23 and
1 Timothy 2:2, which enjoin prayers for kings, "that we may lead a quiet and
peaceable life." As long as magistrates understand that they are appointed

113. O'Donovan, *The Desire of Nations,* 209.

by God, and are his vice-regents, they could not overstep the limits of their power; they "may be animated to duty when they hear that they are the ambassadors of God" (4.20.6). But Jesus rebuked the "kings of the Gentiles [who] lord it over them" (Luke 22:25-26). God limits "vain ambition" and "despotism" (4.20.7).

Although he began to affirm an entirely positive view of the state in accordance with Romans 13:1-7 and 1 Peter 2:13-17, Origen, and Chrysostom, Calvin struck a judicious balance, and in *Institutes* 20.8-25 argued *against* the excessive abuse of power by the state. Thereby Calvin constituted a *"hinge" or transition between the pre-Reformation, largely uncritical, positive view of the state and the modern suspicions of the state.* Calvin was moderate in his view of specific politics. "Monarchy is prone to tyranny [Fr. *la domination*] . . . popular ascendancy [Fr. *démocratie*] [has] the tendency to sedition [Fr. *une domination populaire, en laquelle chacun du peuple a puissance*]" (4.20.8). He declared, "Different countries should be governed by different politics . . . for it has pleased him [God] to appoint kings over kingdoms, and senates . . . over free states, whatever be the form which he has appointed in the places where we live"; but nevertheless he thought that the happiest people live "where liberty is framed with . . . moderation" (4.20.8). Calvin cited David as an example of an anointed king, who aimed at goodness. Today he would perhaps be as sympathetic with the personal conviction of Elizabeth II of the UK that God has called and anointed her to this office, as he would be with American senators and Congress. In each case, "It is righteousness (justice) to take charge of the innocent, to defend and avenge them, and set them free; it is judgement [Heb. *mishpāt*] to withstand the audacity of the wicked, to repress their violence and to punish them their faults" (4.20.9).

Laws, said Calvin, are "the strongest sinews of government" (4.20.14). He cited Romans 13:4 with the proviso that all laws are *just* (4.20.16). He condemned those who refuse to take judicial proceedings, quoting Paul's appeal to Caesar, and thereby dissenting from the Anabaptist tradition (4.20.19, with a balancing comment in 4.20.21). Again, Calvin called for submission to authorities but recognized that tyrants may not pillage or violate (4.20.23-25). He also regarded *marriage* "as an institution of God," although, he added, it was never seen as "a sacrament until the time of Gregory" (4.19.34). Further, he clearly saw *justice* as an ordinance implied by the authority given to rulers.

Several landmark studies appeared in the twentieth century, which bring the tradition of limiting state power to a climax. Two deserve note in particular. Oscar Cullmann published *The State in the New Testament* (1955; Eng. 1956 and 1963), and George B. Caird published *Principalities and Powers* in 1956.[114] Both identified the forces behind an evil state that exceeded God-given boundaries as evil "spiritual" forces. Cullmann specifically identified these evil forces with satanic powers. Of the book of Revelation he wrote, "The beast from the abyss (Revelation 13) is the Roman Empire in so far as it requires the worship of the emperor."[115] This, he wrote, applies to "every empire in any age" that is totalitarian. Satan's temptation in the messianic temptations of Matthew 4 and Luke 4 was to seize power over all the kingdoms of the earth.[116]

Caird and Schlier similarly identify angels as guardians of the nations, of which evil angels inspire and maintain evil regimes.[117] Admittedly, Wesley Carr argued against Caird, Schlier, and others, in his *Angels and Principalities* (1981).[118] But, as Dunn observes, "His thesis has won very little support."[119] Many writers remain divided on Caird's and Schlier's thesis, although they appeal to such passages as 1 Corinthians 2:8 ("the rulers of this age") and Romans 8:38 ("nor angels, nor rulers"). Walter Wink has also argued that "power structures" in the NT today represent such oppressive forces as "tyrants": the market, race, the nation, and even the school.[120] A modern "Anabaptist" view can be found in John Yoder, *The Politics of Jesus*.[121]

No one dissents from the view that the state is ordained by God, provided that it maintains justice and promotes welfare. But, as O'Donovan has shown, there are various concepts of justice, and even "equality" does not

114. Oscar Cullmann, *The State in the New Testament* (London: SCM, 1963), and George B. Caird, *Principalities and Powers: A Study in Pauline Theology* (Oxford: Clarendon, 1956).

115. Cullmann, *The State in the New Testament,* 73.

116. Cullmann, *The State in the New Testament,* 71-74 and 86-87.

117. Heinrich Schlier, *Principalities and Powers in the New Testament* (New York: Herder and Herder, 1961).

118. Wesley Carr, *Angels and Principalities: The Background and Meaning and Development of the Pauline Phrase* hai archai kai hai exousiai, SNTSMS 42 (Cambridge: CUP, 1981).

119. James D. G. Dunn, *The Theology of Paul the Apostle* (Edinburgh: T. & T. Clark, 1998), 106 n. 15.

120. Walter Wink, *Naming the Powers: The Language of Power in the New Testament* (Philadelphia: Fortress, 1984); Walter Wink, *Unmasking the Powers: The Invisible Forces That Determine Human Existence* (Philadelphia: Fortress, 1986); and Walter Wink, *Engaging the Powers: Discernment and Resistance in a World of Domination* (Philadelphia: Fortress, 1992).

121. John Howard Yoder, *The Politics of Jesus* (Grand Rapids: Eerdmans, 1972; 2nd ed. 1994), esp. 104-7.

reach the heart of the problem of justice. Even the Hebrew terms *mishpāt,* "justice," and *dîn,* "judgment," are multifarious in meaning. *Mishpāt* shades off into "vindication," "rights," "norm," or "custom." Only when God is perceived to act in righteousness do multiple criteria seem satisfied. It is almost tautological when the psalmist exclaims,

> He [God] judges the world with righteousness;
> he judges the peoples with equity. (Ps. 9:8)

Yet in concrete terms, especially in the eighth-century prophets, the following verse states: "The LORD is a stronghold for the oppressed" (Ps. 9:9). In Exodus 18:21-22 God appoints judges or magistrates who are "trustworthy and hate dishonest gain." This quality is also demanded of judges in Deuteronomy 1:16-17.

Since God has a special concern for justice to the poor, oppressed, marginalized, and the orphan (Pss. 10:17-18; 82:3-4; Amos 2:6-8), it is perhaps natural to turn to liberation theology and to feminist theology to discover new insights for solving the problem of the state and justice. In both traditions, however, we often find a predictable reliance on a few selected biblical texts, and sometimes even a biased agenda, under the pretext of "hermeneutical preunderstanding." Here Sarah Coakley's insights into theology and history of feminism remain of first importance.

As we have noted, Coakley utterly affirms the basic aim of feminism to find God's justice for those who have been marginalized or oppressed. But she pleads for a more *"creative and critical* relation of theology to the social sciences" than was apparent in the earlier feminist writings of the 1970s and 1980s.[122] We can almost take for granted, she writes, "the form of liberal theology which has survived the various mutations of feminist fashion in the later twentieth century . . . in the (admittedly shrinking) liberal Protestant denominations of North America" (74). But these theologies are severely one-sided and limited. They often ban or suppress "Fatherhood," replacing the biblical concept with "anodyne descriptions" of God as lover or friend; they are spearheaded by or limited to a "middle-aged clerisy of the established churches"; they focus too narrowly on "the rights and dignity of women and other marginalised people." Coakley asserts, " 'God' is freely reconceived to fit with pragmatist feminist goals. . . . [This approach] seems to

---

122. Coakley, *God, Sexuality, and the Self,* 76, italics mine. References to this work have been placed in the immediately following text.

present no lasting way out of feminist anger and stuckness, except by making God *in its own image again*" (75-76).

By contrast, Coakley urges, we need a way in which God can change *us*. Not least does this involve prayer and contemplation and the abandonment of what is "narcissistic and inward-looking" as well as "the traps of unresolved personal resentment and hatred" (80-81). We need "contemplative 'effacement.' To accept and even court such effacement, to seek to enter into such divine participation is not only to embrace change . . . but to learn . . . how to speak a new language" (23). This is *not* to brush aside "women's flourishing," which "remains an urgent theological concern in a world of profound inequalities of wealth and privilege" (82). We must unmask every factor that causes "deprivation, marginalisation, and oppression."

In an earlier study I examined feminist hermeneutics in the writings of Phyllis Trible, Rosemary Radford Ruether, Mary Daly, and Elizabeth Schüssler-Fiorenza.[123] At the time (1992) I used the term "socio-pragmatic hermeneutic" of these writers in explicit contrast to the "socio-critical" in many others, including Habermas and Apel.[124] It anticipated Coakley's use of the term "pragmatic" in this context. Schüssler-Fiorenza contrasts the resurrection appearances of Jesus to the *women,* with the appearances to *Peter.* I queried whether the key difference, as she claimed, was really that of *"gender":* Did it not concern the more profound *transformation* that Peter underwent, but that was hardly urgent for Mary, on the basis of her portrait by Schüssler-Fiorenza?[125]

We return, then, to our primary concern about the causal link between the state or political community and justice. Paul Marshall declares, "The state is what God through Jesus Christ has set up to maintain justice."[126]

In the Catholic tradition social justice indeed has a place, as Vatican II

123. Phyllis Trible, *God and the Rhetoric of Sexuality* (Philadelphia: Fortress, 1978), and Phyllis Trible, *Texts of Terror: Literary-Feminist Readings of Biblical Narratives* (Philadelphia: Fortress, 1984); Rosemary Radford Ruether, *Sexism and God-Talk: Toward a Feminist Theology* (London: SCM, 1983); Elizabeth Schüssler-Fiorenza, *In Memory of Her: A Feminist Theological Reconstruction of Christian Origins* (New York: Crossroad; London: SCM, 1983); and Mary Daly, *Beyond God the Father: Toward a Philosophy of Women's Liberation* (Boston: Beacon Press, 1974).

124. Anthony C. Thiselton, *New Horizons in Hermeneutics: The Theory and Practice of Transforming Biblical Reading* (London: Harper-Collins, 1992; Grand Rapids: Zondervan, 1992, 2012), 379-470.

125. Thiselton, *New Horizons in Hermeneutics,* 445-48.

126. Paul Marshall, *Thine Is the Kingdom* (London: Marshall, Morgan and Scott, 1984), 47.

acknowledges, expounding "works of mercy, assistance and social justice."[127] It alludes to marriage as "the foundation of human society."[128] Yet Calvin was one of the most seminal thinkers on the political community and justice. So it is no surprise that a number of writers have elaborated the Reformed tradition. These include Nicholas Wolterstorff, Richard Mouw, and Jeong Kii Mir, among others.[129] The three books by O'Donovan discussed above stand broadly in a Reformed Anglican tradition. Political theology from Calvin, through Brunner, to O'Donovan establishes that political communities, marriage, and justice constitute a controversial but necessary dimension of theological reflection.

127. Flannery, *Documents of Vatican II.*
128. Flannery, *Documents of Vatican II,* 778.
129. Nicholas Wolterstorff, "Contemporary Views of the State," *Christian Scholar's Review* 3 (1974), and Nicholas Wolterstorff, *Justice, Rights, and Wrongs* (Princeton: Princeton University Press, 2008); Richard Mouw, *Politics and the Biblical Drama* (Grand Rapids: Baker, 1983); and Jeong Kii Mir, *Sin and Politics: Issues in Reformed Theology* (New York: Peter Lang, 2009).

CHAPTER VI

Human Potentiality and the Image of God

1. The Image of God: Human Beings Becoming "Persons"

God created humankind in his own image, both men and women (Gen. 1:26; Ps. 8:6-8). Popular folk religion applies this to newborn babies, as if to bear the image of God is a natural God-given quality or right. But popular religion deviates radically from the biblical accounts. The Russian Orthodox theologian Vladimir Lossky (1903-1958), for example, argues that because humankind damaged the image of God through alienation and self-will, the image of God can be restored only *by grace.*[1]

According to biblical accounts, *Jesus Christ alone* is the perfect image of God (Col. 1:15; cf. Heb. 1:3). For Christ alone perfectly fulfills the *vocation* originally intended for humankind to fulfill. Even in pagan temples, images of deity are meant to reflect the character *of the deity* in visible form. But if God's character is perfectly righteous, holy, kingly, gracious, and loving, who can say that he or she, or even a newborn child, fully reflects this as God's visible image? Hence Lossky rightly insists that the image of God has to be "attained" by grace. On the other hand, he writes, Jesus Christ "the Son is ... a concise declaration of the nature of the Father."[2]

Lossky argues that without the image of God the human self constitutes nothing more than "an individual." He or she belongs to the order of *nature.*

1. Vladimir Lossky, *The Mystical Theology of the Eastern Church* (New York: St. Vladimir's Seminary Press, 1976; Cambridge: Clarke, 1991), 117.

2. Vladimir Lossky, *The Image and Likeness of God* (London and Oxford: Mowbray, 1974), 155.

He comments, "Individual and person mean opposite things. . . . Person . . . distinguishes it (the self) from nature."[3] "Person" is a *relational* term. "Personal existence supposes a relation to the other. . . . A person can be fully personal only insofar as he has nothing that he seeks to possess . . . to the exclusion of others. . . . Otherwise we are in the presence of individuals."[4] The central point about God, especially as *love,* is his entering into an unbroken *relationship* with others, including human beings. To have the image of God restored in humans involves the capacity to enter into relationships with God and with others. When restoration of this image occurs by grace, we may *represent* God and his self-giving love to others.

It was for this purpose that God first created humankind in his own image. In fact, as D. J. A. Clines has convincingly shown, the Hebrew of Genesis 1:26 is more accurately translated "created *as* his image" (Heb. b^e) than "*in* his image." Clines writes, "b^e*tsalmēnû* should be translated '*as* his image' on the ground that b^e is the *beth* of essence."[5] God purposed first Adam, and then Israel, to *represent him,* just as pagan deities were represented in wood and stone by their images or idols. God prohibited "images" not only because they are false, static, inadequate, or idolatrous, but because the *holy, living people of God* were called to be his image. Israel was forbidden to make a false substitute in the form of some artifice or construction of wood or stone.

The term "image of God," then, shows humankind as God *had intended and called* humans to be. It signifies the *potential of human beings for the future. Its measure is Jesus Christ,* the person who actually bears God's image, as Hebrews declares: "the reflection of God's glory and the exact imprint of God's very being" (Heb. 1:3).

On the other hand, the vast majority of theologians argue that the image of God in humankind was *not wholly* destroyed when human beings became alienated and estranged from God. Some distinguish the loss of the "material" image from the retention of "formal" elements. Irenaeus distinguished the "image" (Heb. *tselem*) of God from the "likeness" *(d^emûth)* of God (Gen. 1:26), concluding that humankind lost its likeness to God but not the image of God.[6] Most modern exegetes, however, regard the two words as mutually explanatory, reflecting Hebrew synonymous parallelism. Charles Hodge in the nineteenth century regarded the two terms as "ex-

3. Lossky, *Mystical Theology,* 121.
4. Lossky, *Image and Likeness,* 106.
5. D. J. A. Clines, "The Image of God," *Tyndale Bulletin* 19 (1968): 75; cf. 53-103.
6. Irenaeus, *Against Heresies* 5.15.4.

plaining one of the other," and even called the distinction "Romish."[7] But Thomas Aquinas seems also to have regarded image and likeness in some respects as identical, although in other respects different. Aquinas asserted, " 'Likeness' is not distinct from 'image' in the general notion of 'likeness' "; but also " 'likeness' . . . perfects the idea of 'image.' "[8] He devoted a number of pages to the image of God, including its relation to "likeness."[9] Taken as a whole, "image of God" in Aquinas is seen primarily as humanity's rational capacities. He quotes Augustine: "Man's excellence consists in the fact that God made him in his image by giving him an intellectual soul."[10]

Already by his time, Calvin said, this distinction between "image" and "likeness" "has given rise to no small discussion."[11] He wrote, "The primary seat of the divine image was in the mind and the heart," although it "shone" to other parts of humans. However, he added at once, "When Adam lost his first estate, he became alienated from God. . . . We grant that the image of God was not utterly defaced and destroyed. . . . It was, however . . . corrupted . . . [in] deformity."[12] He continued, "The image of God constitutes the entire excellence of human nature . . . before his fall, but was afterwards vitiated and almost destroyed, nothing remaining but a ruin, confused, mutilated and tainted with impurity," but also "regenerated by the Spirit" in the people of God.[13]

In the twenty-first century, many Christians seem in danger of devaluing God's gift of *reason and rationality*. They tend to forget that the second-century Christian apologists, virtually all the Church Fathers, Aquinas, Calvin, and others rated this highly. If Luther had reservations specifically about the use of reason, this was the reason of Scholastic philosophy. Worse still, some imagine that the apostle Paul attacked reason. This is false. Paul writes to the Thessalonians that they should have a right *mind* (Gk. *nous*; 1 Thess. 5:12, 14; 2 Thess. 3:15); and to the Galatians that they should not be bewitched by *failing to use their reason* (Gal. 3:1-2). He prays that the Philippians will use their minds (Phil. 4:7), and prays that his churches will

7. Charles Hodge, *Systematic Theology*, 3 vols. (Grand Rapids: Eerdmans, 1946; orig. 1871), 2:96.

8. Aquinas, *Summa* I, qu. 93, art. 9, reply to obj. 1.

9. Aquinas, *Summa* I, qu. 93, arts. 1-9, esp. 9.

10. Aquinas, *Summa* I, qu. 93, art. 2, reply; cf. arts. 1-3.

11. Calvin, *Institutes* 1.15.3; trans. Henry Beveridge, 2 vols. (Grand Rapids: Eerdmans, 1989), 1:165.

12. Calvin, *Institutes*, 1.15.4; 1:165.

13. Calvin, *Institutes*, 1.15.4; 1:165.

experience a *renewal of the mind* (Rom. 12:2; cf. Eph. 4:23). A powerful and convincing case is set out by S. K. Stowers, as well as earlier by G. Bornkamm and Robert Jewett.[14] Like Calvin, Paul does not stress reason alone, but also the human heart and will, and wisdom as well as reason.

Today secular interviewers often ask in the media, "How do you *feel* about *x?*" They used to ask about thought and judgment. By contrast Pannenberg declares, "In trusting the Spirit, *Paul in no way spared himself thinking and arguing.*"[15] Most post-Reformation theologians would embrace John Locke's plea for "reasonableness," including today Plantinga and Wolterstorff. Rahner holds together "mystery" and "reason." Mysteries, he says, are truths "communicated by divine revelation," not by "natural reason," but they are addressed to *"ratio"; they* "have come within the scope of reason," even if they also exceed it.[16]

In the history of Christian theology, reason has not been the only element of human nature to be identified with the image of God. Traditionally, especially in Psalm 8:6-8, in Hebrews 2:8-9, and in Aquinas, the exercise of *dominion* over the animal kingdom has been stressed as a distinctive quality of humankind derived from the image of God. "Dominion" reflects the *kingly rule,* or kingdom, of God. In Psalm 8:6-7, the psalmist writes,

> You have given them (humans) dominion over the works of your hands;
> you have put all things under their feet . . .
> the beasts of the field.

In Hebrews 2:8 God subjects "all things under their feet," but at present we see this entirely fulfilled *only in Jesus Christ.* But *"dominion"* does not mean brute mastery of nature. As Moltmann, Niebuhr, and many others point out, dominion (Heb. *rādāh* in Gen. 1:26, and *māshal* in Ps. 8:7) does not always involve "mastery" and exploitation of the earth, but sharing with God the *stewardship* of the world. Moltmann regards "the crisis of domination" as part of "the ecological crisis."[17]

"Dominion" constitutes one aspect of the image of God in humankind, because if humans are to represent God, they must somehow *participate in*

---

14. Stanley K. Stowers, "Paul on the Use and Abuse of Reason," in *Greeks, Romans, Christians,* ed. D. L. Balch and others (Minneapolis: Fortress, 1990), 253-86.

15. Pannenberg, *BQT* 2:35, italics mine; cf. 28-64.

16. Karl Rahner, *Theological Investigations,* vol. 4 (London: DLT, 1973), 37-47.

17. Jürgen Moltmann, *God in Creation: A New Theology of Creation and the Spirit of God* (London: SCM, 1985), 20 and 23.

his kingly qualities. But the kingdom or the reign of God is not one of brute force, but of loving fatherhood. Moltmann writes: "The creation of God's image on earth means that in his work God finds, as it were, the mirror in which he recognises his own countenance — a correspondence which resembles him."[18] He endorses the theme in Barth of christological and covenantal creation. It is a stewardship of care and concern for welfare. Reinhold Niebuhr, as we noted, is another among many theologians who make this point. In his words, "Man's pride and will-to-power disturb the harmony of creation" in an "effort to usurp the place of God."[19]

Nevertheless, we must not be seduced, like some older textbooks, into regarding the image of God as a string of particular qualities. It certainly *includes rationality, sovereignty* or stewardship, *freedom,* and *above all relationality.* But it is, beyond all this, *a vocation to represent God to the world,* to present those qualities that characterize God in a *visible* way. That is why *Christ alone* is so clearly the perfect image of God, and thereby expresses human potentiality. Human beings in the present may reason, order, choose, and enter into relationships, albeit imperfectly. But human destiny is to reflect and to represent *God* in all these ways. Meanwhile, Jesus Christ is the model and standard of the visible image of God, whose visibility in the world makes God (in Jüngel's memorable phrase) "thinkable" and "conceivable." We shall observe, when we discuss Christology, that so many ask: "Was the incarnate Christ *truly human?*" — but the question ought to be: "In the light of Christ, *are we 'humans' truly human?*" As Lossky stresses many times, the image of God lies *ahead,* and is given to human beings by God's *grace,* not by nature.

2. The Unity of Human Nature, in Contrast to Mind-Body Dualism

In the second century, Athenagoras argued that it would be mistaken to speak of the resurrection only of the soul, because "the soul" did not constitute the whole human person. On the other hand, Tertullian saw the matter in different terms, arguing that without the soul *(anima)* a human being is a mere carcass.[20] In the third century, Origen agreed with him that the "soul"

18. Moltmann, *God in Creation,* 77.
19. Reinhold Niebuhr, *The Nature and Destiny of Man: A Christian Interpretation,* 2 vols. (London: Nisbet, 1941), 1:191.
20. Tertullian, *Against Praxeas* 5; *On the Flesh of Christ* 12.

cannot be part of the natural world along the lines of Plato's view of human nature.

The biblical tradition presupposes what we should truly call an *integrated psychosomatic relation of mind and body.* W. Pannenberg writes of the unity of the body and soul, and "the biblical idea of psychosomatic unity."[21] The Hebrew word for soul, *nephesh,* can even denote a dead body, and NT scholars generally agree that the Greek *psychē* is a theologically colorless word, which may often be translated as "life" or "human life."[22] Jewett concludes, "It can bear the sense of one's earthly life as it is publicly observable in behaviour."[23]

Certainly, by contrast, and in opposition to the Gnostics, the early Christians *never disparaged* the body. John Macquarrie speaks of "body" as the essential nature of humanity, and points to its role as the seat of taste, art, and music in Jewish thought, as well as of the more negative experiences of suffering and disease.[24] He adds, "A case for man's material well-being is therefore built into this tradition."[25]

The biblical witness to the unity of the human being has special importance in view of the huge influence of the *dualism* of body and mind or soul in Plato, Descartes, and modern popular thought. The philosopher Gilbert Ryle has mercilessly attacked Descartes's dualism in what he has called "the myth of the ghost in the machine." Descartes (1596-1650) inherited from Plato (428-348 B.C.) the notion of "the liberation of the soul from . . . the body of death."[26] Ryle goes so far as to call this "the official doctrine," in which "every human being has both a body and a mind . . . harnessed together" with "two collateral histories."[27] But this dualism, he argues, rests on "a category mistake."[28] Mind and body "exist" in quite different ways, like "rising" in "the tide is rising," and "rising" in "hopes are rising."[29] Mind is not a "ghostly happening, but . . . a disposition, or complex of dispositions."[30]

21. Pannenberg, *ST* 2:181-202.

22. Robert Jewett, *Paul's Anthropological Terms: A Study of Their Use in Conflict Settings* (Leiden: Brill, 1971), 334-57, 448-49.

23. Jewett, *Paul's Anthropological Terms,* 448.

24. John Macquarrie, *In Search of Humanity: A Theological and Philosophical Approach* (London: SCM, 1982), 55; cf. 47-58.

25. Macquarrie, *In Search of Humanity,* 52.

26. Plato, *Republic* 611E.

27. Gilbert Ryle, *The Concept of the Mind* (London: Penguin, 1949, 1963), 13.

28. Ryle, *Concept of the Mind,* 17.

29. Ryle, *Concept of the Mind,* 24.

30. Ryle, *Concept of the Mind,* 33.

It is as misleading as the literary zeugma, "She came in a flood of tears and a sedan chair."[31]

Pauline theology implies the unity of human nature without question. J. D. G. Dunn points out that Paul used *psychē* ("soul" or "life") only thirteen times, and in Hebrew "Nephesh denotes the whole person."[32] D. E. H. Whiteley goes even further, and regards "body" and "soul" in Paul as "aspective" terms, not "partitive" ones.[33] N. T. Wright expresses this the other way round carefully: "The human body, *sōma* (the word *denotes* the entire human being and *connotes* the public, visible, and tangible physical presence in . . . the world), is God's creation."[34] To compare the force of 1 Thessalonians 5:23, "body, soul, and spirit" could not support a "trichotomous" view of human beings; here the words simply mean "wholly" or "through and through." They no more refer to "parts" of humans than Mary refers to "parts" in

"My soul magnifies the Lord,
    and my spirit rejoices in God." (Luke 1:46-47)

They are an example of Hebrew synonymous parallelism, even when rendered into Greek.

This is the point to introduce Paul's distinctive use of the term "body." Clearly it is a *positive* term, as in "Glorify God in your body" (1 Cor. 6:20). This is an especially informative verse in English translation, because the English KJV/AV chose to render it "in your body and in your spirit." But this reflects only poor manuscript readings in Greek, namely, C^3, D^2, and 1739 margin, as against the authentic text (i.e., without "spirit"), which includes p^{46}, A, B, C*, D*, F, 33, 1739*, Coptic, Irenaeus, Tertullian, Origen, and Cyprian. The later manuscripts betray a misunderstanding of Paul's view of man. The AV/KJV follows only the misnamed Textus Receptus, which Bruce Metzger calls "a gloss with no claim to be original."[35] Here probably a pious scribe sought to "correct" Paul in the light of the prevailing myth of the day.

Ernst Käsemann pinpoints Paul's distinctive concept of *body* probably

31. Ryle, *Concept of the Mind,* 23.
32. James D. G. Dunn, *The Theology of Paul the Apostle* (Edinburgh: T. & T. Clark, 1998), 76.
33. D. E. H. Whiteley, *The Theology of St. Paul* (Oxford: Blackwell, 1964, 1971), 34-39.
34. N. T. Wright, *Paul and the Faithfulness of God,* 2 vols. (London: SPCK, 2013), 1:491.
35. Bruce M. Metzger, *A Textual Commentary on the Greek New Testament,* 2nd ed. (New York: United Bible Societies, 1994), 488.

better than anyone else. He points out that it is a positive gift of God, and denotes

> that piece of the *world,* which we ourselves are and for which we bear responsibility, because it was the earliest gift of our Creator to us. "Body" is not primarily to be regarded . . . from the standpoint of the individual. For the apostle it signifies man in his worldliness [i.e., as part of the world] and therefore in his *ability to communicate.* . . . In the *bodily* obedience of the Christian . . . in the world of everyday, the *lordship of Christ finds visible expression,* and only when this visible expression takes personal shape in us does the whole thing become *credible* as Gospel message.[36]

The main points of Käsemann's quotation are that: (i) the contrast between "body" and "mind" is not primarily "material versus immaterial" but *visible* versus *invisible;* (ii) it therefore places *discipleship* in the *public visible world;* (iii) the special quality of being "embodied" is *communication* through the five senses; and (iv) it is both a *corporate and an individual* term.

J. A. T. Robinson has demonstrated the corporate aspect in his book *The Body,* especially in connection with the church as the body of Christ. But this meaning should not be identified with constitution of the human being. In his critique of Robinson, Whiteley comments, "The subject has been both complicated and illuminated by J. A. T. Robinson."[37] However, Robinson rightly distinguishes "body" (Gk. *sōma*) from "flesh" (Gk. *sarx*) in Paul. He declares, "While *sarx* stands for man in the solidarity of creation in his distance from God, *sōma* stands for man, in the solidarity of creation, as made for God."[38] "Flesh," he says, represents "man in his weakness and mortality."[39] This is true, but there are also more "theological" uses of *sarx,* which denote hostility to God, as in "the mind of the flesh" (cf. Rom. 8:6). We shall explore these uses further when we discuss what Bultmann calls "man under sin." According to Bultmann, "flesh" comes to mean "the self-reliant attitude of the man who puts his trust in his own strength."[40]

36. Ernst Käsemann, *New Testament Questions of Today* (London: SCM, 1969), 135, italics mine.

37. Whiteley, *Theology of St. Paul,* 192.

38. J. A. T. Robinson, *The Body: A Study in Pauline Theology,* SBT 5 (London: SCM, 1952; Philadelphia: Westminster John Knox, 1977), 31.

39. Robinson, *The Body,* 19.

40. Rudolf Bultmann, *Theology of the New Testament,* vol. 1 (London: SCM, 1952), 240.

3. The Diversity of Human Capacities

After "body" and "flesh," we next consider "heart" (Gk. *kardia;* Heb. *lēbh*). This plays a crucial role in biblical vocabulary and theology. Calvin also stresses the role of "heart" in God's relation to human beings, when it can denote the core of a person's being. Paul and other writers do not regard human beings *only* as embodied *thinkers;* they also regard them as having *deep feelings,* and able to make *decisions and resolutions,* even to the point of *obstinacy.* The Bible uses "heart" in all these ways. In the nineteenth century "heart" was taken to denote especially the *inner man,* as H. Lüdemann and C. Holsten argue. In the early twentieth century, A. Schlatter regarded it as almost equivalent to "person," and in effect he underlines Calvin's emphasis.

The *TDNT* showed that a whole range of meanings was applicable. Friedrich Baumgärtel showed that in the OT *lēbh* could denote inner man (1 Sam. 16:7); bravery and courage (2 Chron. 17:6); rationality (Judg. 5:16); will and purpose (1 Sam. 2:35); and commitment.[41]

The *heart* is the seat of deep feeling: grief (Gen. 6:6), fear and anxiety (Gen. 45:26; 1 Sam. 4:13), joy or merriment (1 Sam 2:1). A *heart* may be hardened repeatedly in Exodus (Exod. 7:13, 14, 22, 23, etc., of Pharaoh); or it may be pure (Matt. 5:8). It may be the sphere of reflection or pondering (Luke 2:19, 51), or of belief (Rom. 10:9). It occurs more than 700 times in the LXX, and almost 600 times in the Hebrew OT. In Isaiah 40:2 God "comforts" Israel by speaking "tenderly to the heart" (NIV; Heb. *d-b-r 'al lēbh*).[42] Johannes Behm sums up the NT uses: "The NT use of the term agrees with the OT use. . . . Even more strongly than the LXX it concentrates on the heart as the main organ of psychic and spiritual life . . . the central organ of the body . . . the centre of the inner life."[43]

Jewett pays careful attention to specific contexts and uses of *kardia* in Paul. In 1 Thessalonians 2:17, for example, it refers to "the centre of Paul's will and emotion."[44] In Galatians 4:6, the Holy Spirit works in the deepest place within humans. In Philippians 4:7 it functions in parallel with *nous,* "mind." In 2 Corinthians 1:22, "heart" "is used as a climax of the defence of Paul's apostolicity."[45]

---

41. Friedrich Baumgärtel, "*Kardia* in the OT," in *TDNT* 3:606-7.
42. Alex Luc, "*Lēbh,*" in *NIDOTTE* 2:749-54; BDB 523-26; BDAG 508-9.
43. Johannes Behm, "*Kardia* in the NT," in *TDNT* 3:611.
44. Jewett, *Paul's Anthropological Terms,* 315.
45. Jewett, *Paul's Anthropological Terms,* 331.

Perhaps the most distinctive and also important approach is found in the work of Gerd Theissen, briefly hinted at by Bultmann. In his *Psychological Aspects of Pauline Theology,* Theissen pays special attention to "the secrets of the heart" in 1 Corinthians 14:20-25 and less attention to "the purposes of the heart" in 1 Corinthians 4:5 (cf. 2 Cor. 5:10-11).[46] Bultmann had earlier commented, "The strivings *(boulai)* of hearts (1 Cor. 4:5) are purposes that need not be actualised in the conscious will."[47] In other words, long before Freud, Paul uses *kardia* to denote the *unconscious* or *preconscious.* Theissen provides a lengthy and constructive exposition of the relevant passages in Paul. Even in Romans 8:26-27 Paul declares, "We do not know how to pray as we ought," but the Holy Spirit prompts prayer within our hearts, at first with "inexpressible sighs." Theissen adds, "The constantly recurring theme of ignorance permits the conjecture that unconscious contents break through in ecstasy."[48] In fact, like Stendahl, he attributes *glossolalia,* or speaking in tongues, to the work of the Holy Spirit in the depths of the *unconscious.* Frank Macchia, from a Pentecostalist perspective, regards Romans 8:26-27 as alluding to speaking in tongues.[49] This does not prevent Theissen from also regarding tongues in Paul as "learned conduct" in a social environment. He also explores 1 Corinthians 2:6-16 with its reference to wisdom and the "depths of God" as promoting a new lifeworld "through regions that were previously unconscious."[50]

A third significant term is "conscience" (Gk. *syneidēsis*). The OT has no special term for this, but usually uses *lēbh,* "heart." A passage that comes close to "conscience" is: "David was stricken to the heart because he had cut off a corner of Saul's cloak" (1 Sam. 24:5). *Syneidēsis* is usually translated as "conscience," but sometimes, especially in 1 Corinthians 8–10, as "self-awareness." In the nineteenth century, some argued that Paul had borrowed from Greek Stoics. But most today accept decisive differences, although Bultmann and Dupont also note affinities with Stoic uses.

A new era began with C. A. Peirce, *Conscience in the New Testament* (1955), and J. N. Sevenster, *Paul and Seneca* (1961). The key point here is that *conscience* has nothing to do with "a divine voice" in Paul or the NT.

46. Gerd Theissen, *Psychological Aspects of Pauline Theology* (Edinburgh: T. & T. Clark, 1987), 96-114, 267-341.

47. Bultmann, *Theology of the New Testament,* 1:224.

48. Theissen, *Psychological Aspects,* 287.

49. Frank D. Macchia, "Groans Too Deep for Words," *Asian Journal of Pentecostal Studies* 1 (1998): 149-73.

50. Theissen, *Psychological Aspects,* 392; cf. 345-93.

Peirce defines conscience as "the pain consequent upon the inception of an act believed to be wrong."[51] In 1 Corinthians 8:7-12 the "strong" suffer little pain from a bad conscience, because they are secure, overconfident, and undersensitive. The "weak" are oversensitive and need protection from an overactive conscience, he claims, like the "little ones" of Matthew 18:3-4. Conscience, according to Peirce, is *retrospective,* following some act.

In 1967 Margaret Thrall proposed some modifications to Peirce's conclusion. She pointed out that conscience was not always negative in Paul. She argued that there were even some prospective, forward-looking passages.[52] In the fourth and latest stage of research, R. A. Horsley (1978) and P. W. Gooch (1987) argued that *"self-awareness"* was the actual meaning in 1 Corinthians 8-10. Alongside Gooch, H. J. Eckstein and Paul Gardner have added further insights in continuity with this.[53]

Outside 1 Corinthians, several passages witness to "a good conscience" (Acts 23:1; 24:16; Rom. 9:1; 2 Cor. 1:12; 1 Pet. 3:16). While some other passages are neutral, others still witness to a distorted conscience (Titus 1:15; Heb. 10:22). Conscience may thus *be fallible,* and *rather than teaching stable criteria of good or bad actions,* has to be *trained and instructed,* at least in the NT.

Thomas Aquinas includes a section on conscience in his *Summa Theologiae.*[54] He asserts, "*Syneidēsis* is said to incite to good, and to murmur at evil. . . . Conscience is a certain pronouncement of the mind . . . the habit of first principles."[55] The Quakers associated conscience with "the inner light," while Samuel Clarke expounded the Thomist notion of conscience as reason, just as Joseph Butler saw it as a faculty of the mind, or as a natural common sense, and a God-given intuitive gift. In modern times, Pope Benedict XVI (Joseph Ratzinger) made much of John Henry Newman's teaching on conscience as "an important basis for his theological personalism": integrity,

---

51. C. A. Peirce, *Conscience in the New Testament* (London: SCM, 1955), 22; cf. 13-22 and 111-30; and J. N. Sevenster, *Paul and Seneca* (Leiden: Brill, 1961), 84-102.

52. Margaret Thrall, "The Pauline Use of *Syneidēsis,*" *NTS* 14 (1967): 118-25.

53. P. W. Gooch, "'Conscience' in 1 Cor. 8 and 10," *NTS* 33 (1987): 244-54; Paul D. Gardner, *The Gifts of God* (Lanham, Md.: University Press of America, 1994), 42-54; H. J. Eckstein, *Der Begriff Syneidēsis bei Paulus* (Tübingen: Mohr, 1983); Anthony C. Thiselton, *The First Epistle to the Corinthians: A Commentary on the Greek Text,* NIGTC (Grand Rapids: Eerdmans, 2000), 607-61.

54. Aquinas, *Summa* I, qu. 79, arts. 12-13.

55. Aquinas, *Summa* I, qu. 79, reply to arts. 12 and 13.

courage, and inner calm. Conscience, he claimed, spurs us to know the truth. He stressed common ground between Paul and the Greek philosophers, including their love of freedom.

This brings us to *nous* (mind) and other terms. We discussed reason in Paul and the rest of the NT in the section on the unity of body and mind, or human nature. We also considered *psychē*, "soul" or "life." We concluded that *psychē* has a weak theological profile, and that neither *nous* nor *sōma* can be taken to imply a dualism of body and soul or body and mind in Paul. We noted Pannenberg's comments that in trusting the Holy Spirit, Paul in no way spared himself thinking and arguing. Paul often appealed to rational thinking, as when he remonstrated with the Galatians, to bring them to their senses by simple rational inference and deduction (Gal. 3:1-5). It is simply "foolish" to begin with the Spirit and return to the Law and flesh. Their minds have clearly been "bewitched" to begin in the Spirit and then to return to "works" of the law (3:1). "Reason" in no way undercuts devotion: "I will pray with the spirit, but I will pray with the mind also" (1 Cor. 14:15). The Holy Spirit brings "the mind of Christ" (1 Cor. 2:16). In Thessalonians, Paul's converts must be "put in the right mind" (*nouthetein;* cf. 1 Thess. 5:12, 14; 2 Thess. 2:2; 3:15). Jewett comments, "*Nous* is the agent of rationality."[56] He also discusses *mind* in Romans and 2 Corinthians. He concludes that *nous* or rationality features in every Pauline epistle.

Before we leave this subject, we must reinforce the place of *Jesus Christ* as the perfect example or *paradigm case of what constitutes being human.* Jerome Murphy-O'Connor writes, "Paul's anthropology has a Christological basis. In order to find the true and essential nature of humanity he did not look to the current time to find the nature of humanity; he looks not to his *contemporaries,* but *to Christ, for he alone embodied the authenticity of humanity.*"[57] In the case of Jesus Christ, the capacity to form *relationships* is crucial to the image of God. As Zizioulas asserts, "There is no true being without communion."[58] Thus the capacity to experience *reconciliation, fellowship, and love* characterizes human nature, and these have been renewed in Christ. Christ is the image of God, which is the goal of humanity by God's grace.

56. Jewett, *Paul's Anthropological Terms,* 379.

57. Jerome Murphy-O'Connor, *Becoming Human Together: The Pastoral Anthropology of St. Paul* (Wilmington, Del.: Glazier, 1984), 45, italics mine.

58. John D. Zizioulas, *Being as Communion: Studies in Personhood and the Church* (New York: St. Vladimir's Seminary Press, 1985, 1997), 18.

4. The Intervention of Sin and Alienation: Biblical Vocabulary

Misdirected will or human sin must *not* be seen primarily as an individual act. Too many family services in churches depict "sin" in this way. Sin or misdirected desire certainly *includes* an act. But the biblical writings place their main emphasis on *the effects* sin brings, especially *alienation from God* and *alienation from fellow humans.* If the goal of creation as a human being is that of *fellowship* with God, to turn away from God in self-sufficiency con-stitutes the heart of what theologians and biblical writers call sin. In popular thought today, people readily speak of "wrongdoing" but seldom, if ever, of sin or alienation.

"Wrongdoing," however, says nothing about *attitude, stance, habit, con-dition, mind-set, or state.* Paul declares, "To set the mind on the flesh is death" (Rom. 8:6). He adds, "For this reason the mind that is set on the flesh (Gk. *to phronēma tēs sarkos*) is hostile to God" (Gk. *echthra eis Theon;* 8:7). It cannot please God (v. 8). Cranfield rightly explains the "mind of the flesh" as "fallen nature's . . . outlook, assumptions, values, desires, and purposes."[59]

We shall shortly consider questions about the fall of humankind. First, we shall examine the biblical vocabulary that relates to godlessness, wick-edness, "wrongdoing," and sin. The OT has at least three major words for *sin;* the NT, especially Paul, uses a number of words. Hebrew mainly uses *chātā', pāsha',* and *'āwôn,* although it has up to a dozen related and relevant words altogether.

The Hebrew *chātā'* is probably the most congenial to the modern world. It means to fall short, to commit a mistake or an error, to miss a goal or tar-get, or to miss the way. The cognate noun, *chattā'th,* generally denotes an error or sin of omission (although occasionally it may mean sin offering). In the modern world, many people are happy to acknowledge their "failures." This does not sound too bad. Both BDB (the Hebrew lexicon) and Koch in *TDOT* agree that the verb means to "go wrong, sin, . . . commit a mis-take or an error, . . . miss the way . . . miss the path of duty," although Koch rejects the notion of any "basic meaning."[60] But in addition to the more characteristic "miss the way" (Judg. 20:16), the term may also sometimes denote rebellion (Gen. 40:1), or offenses against a king or a brother (Gen.

---

59. C. E. B. Cranfield, *The Epistle to the Romans,* 2 vols., ICC (Edinburgh: T. & T. Clark, 1975, 1979), 1:386.

60. BDB 306-10; K. Koch, *"Chātā',"* in *TDOT* 4:309-19; cf. Alex Luc, *"Chātā',"* and R. E. Averbeck, *"Chattāh',"* in *NIDOTTE* 2:87-103.

42:22; 50:17), or even murder (2 Kings 21:17). The reference in Judges 20:16 concerns a soldier who slings a stone without missing the target, but see Job 5:24, Proverbs 8:26, 19:2. In Leviticus 4:2 the phrase "When anyone sins *(chāṭā')* unintentionally" is used, as in Leviticus 4:13, 22, 27; 5:15, 18; 22:14; and Numbers 15:22. On the other hand, the word "unintentionally" can mean "in error." It occurs up to 200 times in the OT with varying translations.

The verb *pāsha'* means primarily "to rebel" or "to revolt," as in 1 Kings 12:19 and Isaiah 1:2.[61] First Kings 12:12-33 refers to Israel's rebellion against "the house of David." Isaiah 1:4-6 refers to Israel's rebellion against God. It involves *the breaking of a relationship* by self-assertion, or an act of independence. Isaiah expounds God's lawsuit against Israel for rebellion. Other Hebrew words can mean "rebel," including *mārad* and *pārāh*. Rebellion against God *(pāsha')* occurs in Jeremiah 2:8, 29; 3:13; 33:8; Lamentations 3:42; Ezekiel 2:3; Hosea 7:13; and Zephaniah 3:11. Other words are sometimes used. There are some uses of *mā'al* (2 Chron. 26:16). The word is theologically serious because it concerns the *rejection of a personal relationship* of loyalty to God. BDB translates *pāsha'* as "rebel" and "transgress," with the noun *pesha'*, "transgression." This word offers a special challenge to Christian confession and discipleship.

The third main Hebrew word is *'āwôn,* which is sometimes translated "iniquity" (in the KJV/AV over 200 times) or "sin" (verb, *'āwen*). BDB also translates *'āwôn* as "trouble," "sorrow," or "wickedness." But the meaning "sorrow" or "misery" can denote the *effects* of *sin,* just as "wickedness" can denote its *state* or *orientation.* In Proverbs 22:8, "Whoever sows injustice will reap calamity *('āwen)*" (cf. Deut. 26:14; Prov. 12:21; Amos 5:5). It may also mean "idolatry," which the OT regards as an effect of sin. It often means "wickedness" (Job 22:15).

The word *'āwen* occurs seventy-four times, mostly in Psalms, Proverbs, and Job, and mainly in poetic passages. It ranges in meaning from a general word for calamity or sorrow to an *attitude or state that brings harm and destruction.* It is not a spontaneous or accidental act. It may denote a heart that plots wicked schemes (Ps. 36:4; Isa. 59:7).[62] H. Wildberger regards it as a "power which is at work with a destructive power . . . that comes out of an evil heart, and that leads to hatching a plot to bring about disaster (Prov. 6:18)."[63]

61. BDB 833-34; and E. Carpenter and M. A. Grisanti, *"Pāsha' and pesha'*," in *NIDOTTE* 3:706-10.

62. BDB 19-20; E. Carpenter and M. A. Grisanti, *"'Āwen and 'āwôn*," in *NIDOTTE* 1:309-15; and Alex Luc, *"'Āwon*," in *NIDOTTE* 3:351; and *TDOT* 1:140-46.

63. Hans Wildberger, *Isaiah 1–12,* Hermeneia/Continental Commentary (Philadelphia: Fortress, 1991), 45.

Pannenberg carefully considers the combined force of these three or more words. In contrast to *chaṭṭā'th,* which suggests missing the mark or even carelessness, he writes, "The term *'āwôn* itself means wilful and therefore culpable failure to hit the mark."[64] This applies even more sharply in the case of *pāsha'.* This "has the character of a revolt against the norm itself, i.e., against an underlying authority. . . . In Isa. 1:2 all of God's people are in a state of apostasy and revolt against their God."[65] He continues, "Wickedness of the heart" points beyond an individual act.

This is clearly the case in the NT and especially in Augustine. The NT Greek words for *misdirected desire* or *sin* do not fall under these groups. Paul usually speaks of *sin* (singular) rather than *sins* (plural). The Synoptic Gospels begin with a call to *repent* (Matt. 3:2; Mark 1:4; *metanoeō*). This presupposes the problem of sin by the need to turn and to change. It is unfortunate that many preachers refer to the term's etymology in Greek as "having an after-mind." In the NT it reflects the Hebrew *shūbh,* "to turn," "to turn around," or "to return." It implies a new sense of direction and change. Thereby it lifts the network of concepts above the popular notion of "doing or not doing." John the Baptist and Jesus allude to judgment, which at minimum suggests *accountability.* In Paul Ricoeur's thought, accountability is a key element in the constitution of a stable "self" or person.[66]

The varied terms for misdirected desire underline its complex nature. The words include *parabasis,* "transgression" or "deviation from a norm" (Rom. 2:23; 4:15; 5:14; Gal. 3:19; Heb. 2:2). This may include "overstepping" the mark.[67] In Romans 2:23 it consists in "dishonoring, or failing to honor, God." This would constitute a much more challenging account of sin than those that often occur in all-age worship in churches. Another Greek term is *paraptōma* (Matt. 6:14-15; Mark 11:25-26; Rom. 4:25; 5:15-18, 20; 11:11-12; 2 Cor. 5:19; Gal. 6:1; Eph. 1:7; 2:1, 5; Col. 2:13). The word *paraptōma* denotes "offense, wrongdoing, sin," especially *sin against God.*[68] In Romans 5:15, 17, 18, Paul used it of the sin of Adam, as it is used in Wisdom 10:1. In Galatians 6:1, Paul wrote of "anyone . . . detected in a transgression."

The verb *hamartanō,* the nouns *hamartēma* and *hamartia,* and the adjective *hamartōlos* are the most general and perhaps most frequent words

64. Pannenberg, *ST* 2:239.

65. Pannenberg, *ST* 2:239.

66. Paul Ricoeur, *Oneself as Another* (Chicago: University of Chicago Press, 1992), 169-296.

67. BDAG 758.

68. BDAG 770.

for *sin* (Matt. 18:15, 21; 27:4; Luke 15:18, 21; 17:3-4; John 5:14; 9:2-3; Acts 25:8; Rom. 2:12; 3:23; 5:12, 14, 16; 6:15; 1 Cor. 6:18; 7:28, 36; 8:12; 15:34; Heb. 3:17; 10:26; 1 Pet. 2:20; 1 John 1:10; 2:1; 3:6; and others). Danker translates the verb "to commit a wrong"; the noun, "transgression" and "sin"; and the adjective, "sinner."[69] Other words include *planē,* "deceit, deception, error, wandering from the path" (Matt. 27:64; 1 Thess. 2:3; 2 Thess. 2:11); *asebeia,* "dishonoring God" or "impiety" (Rom. 1:18; Jude 18); and *adikia,* "unrighteousness," "injustice," or "wickedness" (Luke 13:27; 16:8-9; Rom. 2:8; 6:13; 2 Thess. 2:10). It is used in 1 Maccabees 3:6. Matthew and Paul also use *anomia,* "lawlessness" (Matt. 23:28; Rom. 6:19; 2 Cor. 6:14).[70] These provide seven or eight additional words, and occasional words might be added.

The upshot of this study of biblical vocabulary is to confirm the view that sin is *not* primarily a matter of *individual acts* that *fall short* of God's norm. It more fundamentally denotes an *attitude toward God,* which is *other than worship, trust, obedience, and fellowship.* Pannenberg emphasizes this. It is primarily a *state of godlessness.* It is *not* chiefly "doing no harm to anyone," as many (outside regular, instructed churchgoers) today often suggest. A more important aspect concerns the *destructive effect of sin.* It damages the image of God. If such sin provokes God to wrath, it is like the provocation of the parent or grandparent who sees the child in the process of destroying his or her life. However, sin is not *one thing.* We shall compare in the next chapter twenty or more ways in which theologians have interpreted sin. Most explicate *hermeneutical insights* into the concept; a few seem to view it in purely moralistic terms.

5. Understandings of the Universal Nature of Sin and the Fall, Notably in Paul

Paul, as we have seen, speaks not only of individual sin but also of *corporate, communal,* and *structural* sin. Whiteley calls three passages in Paul his version, so to speak, of the fall in Genesis.[71] He argues in Romans 1:18-32 that both Jew and Gentile share the same *universal* condemnation. This passage undoubtedly reflects overtones of a standard synagogue sermon. The overriding point is that "God gave them up" (Rom. 1:24 and 26). Sin, as Stählin

---

69. BDAG 49-52.
70. BDAG, respectively, 822, 141, 20, and 85.
71. Whiteley, *Theology of St. Paul,* 50-53.

and others have expressed it, is itself an *effect* of sin. For example, if sin brings blindness or bondage, this adds to the constraints of further action. Romans 2:1 begins, "Therefore you have no excuse, whoever you are." The Gentiles may be condemned for their idolatry and immoral practices, as the writer of Wisdom of Solomon 13:8-9 and 14:8-14 also insisted. But the Jew has no more excuse, for "in passing judgment on another, you condemn yourself." Dunn comments, "Lurking behind this [Wis. 13] we should probably see the figure of Adam, the archetypal human who deliberately refused to give God his due, by refusing to obey God's one command (Gen. 2.17). But in Rom. 1.22 the echo becomes stronger."[72]

Whiteley's second example addresses Romans 5:12, which he calls "Paul's fundamental teaching": it was through one man that sin came into the world, "and death came through sin, and so death spread to all because all have sinned." Augustine translated the Greek *eph' hō* not as "because," but, following the Latin Vulgate, as "in whom." Today scholars virtually unanimously accept that the Latin is not a faithful translation of the Greek. Further, Dunn understands "Adam" in Romans 5:12-21 to denote probably *humankind*. He comments, "Whether Paul thought of Adam as a historical individual . . . is less clear."[73] In Romans 7:7-11, Dunn argues, Paul is so like *2 Baruch* 54:19, which may well be using "Adam" as the archetype of everyman.

Certainly the intertestamental Jewish tradition with which Paul would have been familiar debated the significance of "Adam" for later generations. Fourth Ezra 7:118 laments: "O Adam, what have you done? For it was you who sinned; the fall was not yours alone, but ours also who are your descendants" (cf. 3:7-10). However, in *2 Baruch* 54:18-19 we read, "Though Adam sinned first, and has brought death in all . . . each of us has become *our own* Adam." There is some uncertainty and ambiguity, therefore, about the role of Adam. Nevertheless, in terms of *origin,* Paul stresses, "Sin came into the world through one man, and death came through sin, and so death spread to all because all sinned" (Rom. 5:12). Paul repeats: "Sin exercised dominion in death, so grace might also exercise dominion" (5:21).

Whiteley's third passage is Romans 7:7-13. This speaks of wrong desire, or covetousness, as the *root of sin,* as Augustine would also do. *Apocalypse of Moses* 19:3 asserts, "Desire (Gk. *epithymia*) is the origin of every sin." Dunn

72. Dunn, *The Theology of Paul,* 91; cf. James D. G. Dunn, *Romans,* 2 vols., WBC (Dallas: Word, 1988), 1:60.

73. Dunn, *The Theology of Paul,* 94.

declares, "The use of the Adam story once again to speak of the general condition of humankind seems clear beyond dispute."[74] In this passage, "If it had not been for the law, I would not have known sin" (Rom. 7:7). "The law is holy" (v. 12), but incapable of bringing life (v. 13). The following verses — for example, "I do not do what I want" (v. 15) — should not possibly be interpreted as Paul's autobiography; they should probably refer to the corporate experiences of Israel.[75] On the other hand, competent exegetes take different views of this passage.

The fallenness of humankind and the universality of sin, however, are not restricted in Paul to these three passages. In Romans 3:9 he declares, "All, both Jews and Greeks, are under the power of sin." He adds, "As it is written, 'There is no one who is righteous, not even one'" (3:10). He speaks of *alienation* from God in Romans 5:10: "While we were enemies, we were reconciled to God." In the Gospels, too, the universality of sin is a presupposition of the call of John the Baptist and of Jesus to repent (Matt. 3:2; Mark 1:4, 15; Luke 3:7-9). Other epistles add their voices: "You were dead [in] trespasses and sins" (Eph. 2:1); "If we say that we have no sin, we deceive ourselves" (1 John 1:8).

The biblical vocabulary, especially the theology of Paul and some other biblical authors, provides rich and complex concepts of sin, which stand both in continuity and in contrast with many concepts today. *Sin is not "doing no one any harm," but a self-destructive breach of fellowship with God and consequent alienation from God.* This principle is relevant to some churches and especially to popular thought. We cannot complete the full picture, however, until we compare the strengths and weaknesses of sometimes divergent notions of misdirected desire, alienation, and sin in historical theology. Our account in the next chapter is not simply to provide historical facts. It is to offer warnings of inadequate or mistaken views, and more especially to explore hermeneutics: to seek where many may offer greater understanding or explication of biblical themes, and contribute helpful hermeneutical bridges to the world of the day, or to the modern world.

74. Dunn, *The Theology of Paul*, 99.
75. See a balanced discussion in Cranfield, *Epistle to the Romans*, 1:354-61; N. T. Wright, *Paul and the Faithfulness of God*, 2:10, 16-21; Dunn, *The Theology of Paul*, 472-77; and Joseph A. Fitzmyer, *Romans*, AB 33 (New York: Doubleday, 1992), 472-79.

CHAPTER VII

Misdirected Desire and Alienation:
A Hermeneutical Comparison of Historical Thinkers

As we shall also comment in chapter 9, our purpose in this chapter is two-fold. First, a comparison between historical thinkers reveals how differently interpreters have viewed "sin," often reflecting biblical insights, but sometimes undervaluing significant points. Second, many explore aspects of the biblical material that either facilitate our understanding of these concepts or provide hermeneutical bridges to the modern world, as well as to that of their day. This is not simply a historical report. Both factors relate to hermeneutics. This concerns, first, deeper understanding; second, intelligibility; and third, more ready communication with others today.

1. The Ante-Nicene Church Fathers

(i) *Irenaeus* (c. 130–c. 200). Perhaps his most distinctive contribution was to view misdirected desire, selfishness, or sin primarily as a *hindrance to human growth and maturity.* Irenaeus had roots in both the Eastern and the Western Church, and wrote not long after the close of the NT writings. He especially attacked Gnosticism, which tended to associate evil and sin with the physical body and the physical world. This Gnostic view was entirely at variance with biblical teaching.

The teaching of Irenaeus about Adam and the "fall" of humankind remains controversial, and even questionable in certain respects. He regarded "Adam" as having been *like an immature child:* "Humankind was little, but a child. It had to grow and reach full maturity.... Its mind was not yet fully mature, and thus humanity was easily led astray by the de-

154

ceiver."[1] He was on firmer ground when he compared the contrasting figure of Christ. Christ, he wrote, through his growth and maturity, "showed forth the image [of God] truly."[2] Christ represents God to the fullest degree. As in Hebrews 5:8, Christ "learned obedience through what he suffered." Irenaeus also implied, on the other hand, that initially Adam must have had little knowledge of God.

John Hick cites this aspect of Irenaeus in his *Evil and the God of Love.* Encountering evil, Hick argues, can produce maturity of character. This is necessary if we are to reach the goal God set for us. As in many Church Fathers and modern thinkers, this does not reach the very heart of biblical passages, but shows an important secondary feature of sin. Sin prevents the *full purpose of God* coming *to fruition within us.* As Bonhoeffer and others warn us, *even Christian behavior can show childish traits,* for example, that of severe overdependence on other people, which simply constitutes sin.

(ii) *Tertullian* (c. 150–c. 225). This Father was out of step with many of his compeers. The problem with Tertullian is paradoxical, because while he attacked the notion of any decisive philosophical influence, his borrowing from the Stoics' view of the "soul" dominated his anthropology and view of sin. He argued: "Everything which exists is a bodily existence. . . . Nothing lacks bodily existence . . . the soul has an invisible body."[3] To be fair to him, he was attempting to argue that the humanity of Jesus Christ entailed Christ's bodily existence. But he then goes further than this. He regards *sin as a taint,* which is transmitted from Adam, and from parent to child. Thereby he formulated a theory of "*hereditary* sinful taint," which in due course provided the basis for Augustine's notion of original sin.[4] This theory of physical transmission is known technically as *Traducianism* in theology.

At first sight, it is perhaps difficult to see how this contributes anything positive to biblical accounts of sin. The biblical writers repudiate any connection between sin and the body. But on further reflection, we see from the *corporate* emphasis of the Bible in many passages and writers, that a *hereditary* dimension is not unimportant. In the Bible, however, this is not

1. Irenaeus, *Demonstration of the Apostolic Teaching* 12, in M. Froidevaux, ed., Sources chrétiennes 62 (Paris: Cerf, 1965), 52; cf. also 13-14; and *Against Heresies* 4.64.1.

2. Irenaeus, *Against Heresies* 5.16.2; cf. 3.32.1.

3. Tertullian, *On the Flesh of Christ* 11; ANF 3:531.

4. Cf. Reginald S. Moxon, *The Doctrine of Sin* (London: Allen and Unwin, 1922), 41-43; Norman P. Williams, *The Ideas of the Fall and of Original Sin* (London: Longmans, Green, 1929), 233-45.

necessarily "physical," but certainly includes the *environmental*. We may cite, for example, "Punishing children for the iniquity of parents, to the third and the fourth generation of those who reject me" (Exod. 20:5). Whether we think of unbelief in the home, or of drugs or immorality, tragically this often passes on to children. *Sin is not merely an individual affair.*

A supposedly individual sin may actually affect families and social environments. Tertullian had a neat phrase that paralleled the transmission of the soul and transmission of sin, namely: *"Tradux animae, tradux peccati,"* that is, the transmission of the soul (is) the transmission of sin.[5] Williams argues, " 'Traducianism,' 'seminal identity,' and 'original guilt,' constitute an apparently necessary sequence of ideas."[6] On the other hand, the notion of sin as a *"taint"* is without biblical foundation, and may mislead people today.

(iii) *Origen* (c. 185–c. 254) and *Clement* (c. 150–c. 215). Origen stressed the freedom of the human will. He interpreted the "Adam" account in Genesis as allegorical, not as literal or historical.[7] He wrote, "Every rational creature is capable of earning praise and censure."[8] Part of the reason for this is his strenuous opposition to Gnostic notions of determinism. Clement, like Socrates, had regarded sin primarily as a matter of ignorance and irrationality. In the case of Adam, he wrote, *ignorance and weakness* gave rise to sin.[9] *Refusal to learn* is a cause of sin.[10] Certainly, today, it also readily *leads to* sin. Williams calls the two approaches of Clement and Origen "far different," especially on Adam and the Fall.[11] Origen perhaps more readily appreciated the diversity of human experience.[12]

Origen therefore argued that the "Fall," such as it was, occurred *before time and creation:* the consequent *inequalities* of life implied sin in some *prior* existence, or previous life. Origen appears in fact to be the only Church Father to have speculated on "reincarnation," in order to exempt a just creator from causing the inequalities. His view of sin is essentially *moral.* He substituted, in effect, prenatal wrongdoing for "original sin." Nevertheless, he associated infant baptism with deliverance from original sin. He wrote,

5. Cf. Tertullian, *On the Soul* 36.
6. Williams, *Ideas of the Fall*, 237.
7. Origen, *De principiis* 4.1.16; *ANF* 4:365.
8. Origen, *De principiis* 1.5.2; *ANF* 4:256.
9. Clement, *Stromata* 2.14.
10. Clement, *Stromata* 7.16; *ANF* 2:553.
11. Williams, *Ideas of the Fall*, 208.
12. Origen, *De principiis* 2.9.

"If there is nothing in infants that requires remission . . . the grace of baptism would be unnecessary."[13] He appealed to such biblical passages as Genesis 3 and Psalm 51:5:

> I was born guilty,
>   a sinner when my mother conceived me.

But there are *other* ways of construing the origins of evil, as we shall note in the next section.

2. The Post-Nicene Church Fathers

(i) *Athanasius* (c. 296-373). This Church Father explicitly rejected Irenaeus's picture of Adam as like a child before the "Fall." He was, after all, *in constant fellowship and intercourse with God,* and bore his image.[14] He verges on teaching a later doctrine of "original righteousness," but is not fully explicit on this. Sin and the Fall bring *corruption or disintegration* (Gk. *phthora*).[15] Anticipating Lossky, Athanasius saw the effect of the Fall and sin as a *return to nature,* and fall from grace. Sin is essentially *putting the self in the place of God,* and choosing the way of corruption.[16] In *The Incarnation of the Word,* the context is that restoration from the Fall is *integrally* related with the work of Christ. Sin, to Athanasius, is a *collective* phenomenon involving "wickedness," "corruption," and social evil. He quotes Wisdom 2:23-24 and Romans 1:26-27. It brings "monstrous ruin of the work which God has created."[17] Above all, sin is *the breach of fellowship with God* and the *corruption of his image* in humankind. *Christian teaching today could well gain much by stressing that sin involves putting the self in place of God, and damaging or destroying our relationship with God.*

---

13. Origen, *Against Celsus* 7.50; *ANF* 4:631; cf. Tatha Wiley, *Original Sin* (New York: Paulist, 2002), 46.

14. Athanasius, *Against the Heathen* 2; *NPNF,* ser. 2, 4:4-5.

15. Athanasius, *Against the Heathen* 3-5; *NPNF,* ser. 2, 4:5-6; and *Against the Arians* 2.49-50; *NPNF,* ser. 2, 4:375.

16. Athanasius, *The Incarnation of the Word* 1.3-5; *NPNF,* ser. 2, 4:38; and *St. Athanasius on the Incarnation* (London: Mowbray, 1953), 29-30; and Edward R. Hardy, ed., *Christology of the Latin Fathers: On the Incarnation of the Word,* LCC (Philadelphia: Westminster, 1964), 58-60.

17. Athanasius, *The Incarnation of the Word* 6.

Athanasius also, secondarily, recognized the moral dimension of sin. But it was above all a personal affront *against God* and his goodness. This is what today most separates both him and the biblical tradition from *popular* notions of "not doing my neighbor harm." Sin and misdirected desire are not simply a matter of ethics and morality. This aspect of *"godlessness"* needs to be rehabilitated today.

(ii) *Ambrose* (c. 339-397). Ambrose constituted a crucial stepping-stone to Augustine in the Western or Latin Church. Most of all, he regarded human sin *"as a state rather than an act."*[18] Like Athanasius, he stressed that it means the loss, or at least corruption, of the divine image in humanity.

Ambrose is best known for his emphasis on the *corporate* nature of the fall of Adam. He discussed Romans 5:12, arguing that while "Adam first existed [before we were born, nevertheless] we all existed in him; Adam perished, and all perished in him."[19] He suggested what has become a difficult notion for today, that humankind in later generations participated in the sin of Adam. It is easier for many to see, however, that Adam's breach of fellowship and rebellion characterize sin *through the generations,* and that its effect is loss of "paradise," and alienation from God.

In terms of a remaining "taint," Ambrose seems to form a link in the Latin Church between Tertullian and Augustine. He was the first of the Latin Fathers explicitly to teach the "original righteousness," or perfection, of Adam.[20] He calls Adam in paradise "a heavenly being," "like an angel" and "accustomed to speak face to face with God." By contrast, in the present era, "We men are all born under sin, and our very origin is evil."[21] Nevertheless, Ambrose alone used Paul's language of "exchange" in relation to Christ. He quoted Romans 5:19: "As by one man's disobedience many were made sinners, so by the obedience of one shall many be made righteous."[22] He stated, "Death is alike to all . . . through the sin of one alone."[23] Free will is weakened by the Fall, the effects of which are progressive.

(iii) *Augustine of Hippo* (354-430). Augustine believed that humankind lost any equipoise of choice between good and evil at the Fall. In his *Confessions,* he declared, "The enemy held me, and thence made a chain for me,

---

18. Moxon, *The Doctrine of Sin,* 44, italics mine.

19. Ambrose, *On Original Sin* 41, and *On the Belief in the Resurrection* 2.1.6 (*NPNF,* ser. 2, 10:174-75).

20. Williams, *Ideas of the Fall,* 300.

21. Ambrose, *Concerning Repentance* 1.3.13; *NPNF,* ser. 2, 10:331.

22. Ambrose, *On the Christian Faith* 5.8.109; *NPNF,* ser. 2, 10:298.

23. Ambrose, *On the Belief in the Resurrection* 2.6; *NPNF,* ser. 2, 10:175.

and bound me."[24] We must stress, however, that, like Paul, his overriding concern was with the person and work of Christ and the nature of grace and redemption.

This section majors on historical and hermeneutical views of sin rather than the Fall as such, but in Augustine's case these two can scarcely be separated. He relied heavily on Paul's words in Romans 7:18-20: "I know that nothing good dwells within me. . . . I can will what is right, but I cannot do it. For I do not do the good I want, but the evil I do not want is what I do. . . . It is no longer I that do it, but sin that dwells within me."[25] This is not to deny that Augustine distinguished between *"the chain of original sin,"* by which "all die in Adam" (1 Cor. 15:22), and "all the evils I have committed against myself and against others," that is, personal sin.[26] Henry Chadwick tells us that this is probably the first reference (c. 398) to "original sin."[27] However, Augustine acknowledges, "My instructor is Cyprian . . . my instructor is Ambrose, whose books I have read and whose words I have heard from his own lips."[28]

Both Ambrose and Augustine were misled by the Latin Vulgate translation of the Greek *eph' hō pantes hēmarton* in Romans 5:12, which should be translated "because all have sinned," as in the NRSV. The Latin read *in quo,* "in *whom* all have sinned." Augustine discussed the exegesis of this verse in his *Against Two Letters of the Pelagians.*[29] Cranfield sets out six possible interpretations of this complex passage.[30] Like Ambrose and Ambrosiaster, Augustine saw the verse as implying the inclusion of all human nature in Adam. Paul is probably asserting, however, that it was through Adam that sin entered the world. On the other hand, Paul also affirms the *corporate solidarity of grace* in Christ, which, by parity of reasoning, more than cancels out this solidarity in sin. Undeniably, for Augustine *sin is both corporate and individual.*

Cyprian and Ambrose are not the only influences upon Augustine. Many of his writings show the depth of his concern in his opposition against Pelagius, and also against the Donatists. In the North African church, the Do-

---

24. Augustine, *Confessions* 8.10.11.

25. Augustine, *On Free Will* 3.51; cf. Wiley, *Original Sin,* 57.

26. Augustine, *Confessions* 5.9.16.

27. Augustine, *Confessions: A New Translation by Henry Chadwick* (Oxford: OUP, 1992), 82 n. 13.

28. Cited by Eugene TeSelle, *Augustine the Theologian* (New York: Herder, 1970), 265.

29. Augustine, *Against Two Letters of the Pelagians* 4.4.7; *NPNF,* ser. 1, 5:419.

30. C. E. B. Cranfield, *The Epistle to the Romans,* 2 vols., ICC (Edinburgh: T. & T. Clark, 1975, 1979), 1:274-81.

natists had at this time reached virtually a majority. Those who had fallen away during a time of persecution often came to regret their lapse, and to seek to be restored to the church. The Donatists opposed such restoration, arguing for a "pure" church. To Augustine a "perfectionist" account of human nature, even redeemed human nature, was contrary to the biblical writings. His doctrine of sin affirmed that all human beings, whether Christians or not, were fallible and inclined to sin. He believed in the "fallibility" of the church. Hence his stress on the reality of sin and the fall of Adam became part of a repertoire of resources in his fight against Donatism (c. 406). Today, people often forget that there is a pastorally positive side to exposing the full seriousness of sin, as is the case in Augustine and Calvin, since often it prevents unrealistic expectations of Christians, and disillusion when Christians fail.

Augustine was equally firm in his belief that Pelagius's emphasis on human free will undermined the radical nature of *grace* and of redemption in Jesus Christ. He was deeply concerned about such passages as 1 John 1:8: "If we say that we have no sin, we deceive ourselves, and the truth is not in us." Like Cyprian, he argued that infant baptism was necessary, because no human being could be without sin. Although he admired the British monk Pelagius for his piety and morality, from about 415 to the death of Pelagius in 420, Augustine attacked what he perceived as Pelagius's undermining of the work of grace. God was everything, and Christ was everything, for Augustine; Pelagius, in effect, saw moral and social evil as in principle reversible by *discipline and human effort.* Augustine regarded it as reversible *only by Christ and God's grace.* He insisted that the incapacity of the law to rescue humankind was precisely Paul's argument.

Pelagius, for his part, rejected any "inherited" view of sin. Sin was simply due to following Adam's example by free choice. He rejected the notion held by Augustine that human beings were incapable of doing good. By contrast, Augustine pointed to the universality of ignorance, concupiscence, weakness, suffering, and *indifference to God, and the inevitability of death.* The work of Jesus Christ and of the Holy Spirit, through the sheer unmerited grace of God, could overcome what human beings alone could not overcome.

Pannenberg comments positively on Augustine's theology of humankind and sin, as we shall note. But three more speculative elements remain open to question. First, Augustine connects *infant baptism* with the fall of humankind, often with the suggestion of removing the "taint" of sin. In the more neutral sense of *social contamination or influence,* this might be more acceptable. Both heredity and environment may communicate this. But this term too often implies *physical contamination* in the sense apparently used by Tertullian, Cyprian, and Ambrose. Some would regard their view as primarily genetic or biological. Many regard this view as more speculative, and related more to the *physical* mode of hereditary sin.

Second, Augustine explicitly teaches the "original righteousness" of Adam. This may be defended because of "Adam's" original intimacy with God. But many modern theologians are reluctant to speculate about "original righteousness." Augustine argues that when Adam enjoyed fellowship with God, he had the ability not to sin *(posse non peccare)*.[31] He had "a good will," and God "made him upright. . . . He did not need grace to receive good, because he had not yet lost it; but he needed grace to continue in it."[32] This stands in contrast with Adam's subsequent suffering, death, weakness, ignorance, and disobedience, after the Fall. He passed these penalties to his offspring since we were physically "in Adam" (Lat. *in lumbis Adam fuimus*). Williams states, "Augustine's beliefs . . . represent the culminating point of that tendency to exalt (the paradisal state) to the highest pitch of 'original righteousness.' "[33] The subject is controversial, although many regard it as perhaps implicit, not explicit, in the Genesis narrative. After all, "Adam" enjoyed uninterrupted fellowship with God before the Fall. N. P. Williams attacks these ideas, while Charles Hodge defends "original righteousness."[34]

The third and most seriously questioned element in Augustine is his association of sin with *sexual* activity. He regularly speaks of "concupiscence." He makes it clear that the natural good of marriage is not undermined by condemning lust.[35] Marriage is sinless.[36] But lust is part of "the body of death" (Rom. 7:24), which followed humanity's fall.[37] Sadly, Augustine must be held responsible for the mistaken but widespread thinking through the centuries that Christians are too often obsessed with sin and sexual immorality. On the other hand, some may wonder whether a possible counter-reaction has gone too far today.

As we shall see, a number of modern scholars accept the *idea* of original sin and sin's universality, but seek to replace the *term* because of its mislead-

---

31. Augustine, *On Rebuke and Grace* 12.33; *NPNF*, ser. 1, 5:485.
32. Augustine, *On Rebuke and Grace* 11.32; *NPNF*, ser. 1, 5:484-85.
33. Williams, *Ideas of the Fall*, 360.
34. Charles Hodge, *Systematic Theology*, 3 vols. (New York: Scribner, 1871), 2:99-102.
35. Augustine, *On Marriage and Concupiscence* 1.5.6.
36. Augustine, *On Marriage and Concupiscence* 1.16.18.
37. Augustine, *On Marriage and Concupiscence* 1.21.35.

ing associations. Karl Rahner provides one example. Even N. P. Williams, who attacks most of Augustine's ideas, and is sympathetic with Pelagius, nevertheless recognizes that some account must be given of original sin and the Fall, even if we settle for something like the universal experience of "weakness of will."[38]

Augustine's view of the *nature and universality* of sin was virtually endorsed by Leo I (d. 461) and Gregory I of Rome (c. 540-604). Bede of Jarrow and Alcuin of York also endorsed it in the medieval period. One of the few to retain Augustine's most uncompromising emphasis on predestination was Gottschalk (c. 804–c. 869), who was a Benedictine monk, and devoted student of Augustine. He even anticipated a doctrine of "double predestination." Scotus Erigena (c. 810–c. 877) and several others, however, opposed Gottschalk.

3. The Medieval and Reformation Periods

(i) *Anselm* (c. 1033-1109). The two outstanding theological minds of the medieval period were Anselm and Aquinas. Anselm carefully and rightly related human sin to our attitude toward God. In his *Why God Became Man,* he wrote, "Sin is the same thing as *not to render what is due to God*."[39] He added, "Everyone who sins must repay to God the honour he has taken away, and this is the satisfaction that every sinner ought to make to God."[40] Anselm's genius was to show the integral relation between sin and redemption, and between the person and work of Christ.[41] In due course he showed that only *Christ as God* can pay the *infinite* debt of human sin, and only *Christ as man* can offer it on *humankind's behalf.* Sin toward God cannot be equated with mere "injustice," as if, like evil, it is only a *negative* privation.[42]

Anselm included a separate argument about original sin. Human beings ought not to be "punished" for Adam's sin, as if "they had committed it personally, as Adam did"; yet it is even more serious, in that through it "death

38. Williams, *Ideas of the Fall,* 460; cf. 395-486; Moxon, *The Doctrine of Sin,* 78-108; and Wiley, *Original Sin,* 56-75.

39. Anselm, *Why God Became Man* 1.11, in *A Scholastic Miscellany: Anselm to Ockham,* ed. Eugene R. Fairweather, LCC (London: SCM; Philadelphia: Westminster, 1956), 119, italics mine.

40. Anselm, *Why God Became Man* 1.11.

41. Anselm, *Why God Became Man* 1.5; 1.9; and 25; also 2.67.

42. Anselm, *The Virgin Conception and Original Sin* 5.

reigned from Adam to Moses" (Rom. 5:14).[43] Original sin is "equal in all," and in some way "descends to infants."[44] Anselm utterly rejected any notion of "freedom" as "the power of sinning or not sinning." Since sin is universal, this implies necessity. *Humankind has become the servant of sin.* Yet this is also the result of the self's decision. In his stress on the *seriousness and bondage of sin,* with certain modification, he stands, in effect, with Augustine and Luther. Again, today, the notion of sin as not giving to God his full due is much more healthy and biblical than some vague moralism about "not harming anyone." We shall look further at this in discussion of the atonement in chapter 8.

(ii) *Thomas Aquinas* (1225-1274). In his *Summa Theologiae* Aquinas considered sin in part II/I, questions 71-80; original sin in II/I, questions 81-84; and the effects of sin in II/I, questions 85-89. Aquinas argues, following Cicero, that sin "is a habit or *affection of the self,* discordant and inconsistent with itself through life."[45] It involves *conflict within the self* and *weakness.* Sin may include "the sin of omission . . . omitting to act."[46] Anticipating Kant, he sees the cause of sin in the human will.[47]

In *Summa* II/I, question 81, Thomas considers sin as involving the *whole nature* of humankind. He examines Romans 5:12, and argues: "The sin of the first man was transmitted to his descendants, by way of origin."[48] He draws from Ambrose and Augustine the notion that human nature bears "the stain that infects it."[49] He also draws from Augustine that "Original sin is called concupiscence rather than ignorance."[50]

Aquinas sets out *the effects of sin* from question 85 onward. These include death, the loss of happiness, and corruption.[51] Most seriously of all, he argues that *sin can also be the punishment of sin.* For example, he states, "One sin can be the cause of another," as it is in Romans 1:24: "God gave them up to the desires of their heart." Second, sin can cause hurt, pain, and damage. Third, sin may further constitute punishment for sin.[52] Thomas appeals to Gregory of Rome for this concept. Moreover, he says, "Sin incurs everlasting punish-

43. Anselm, *The Virgin Conception and Original Sin* 22.
44. Anselm, *The Virgin Conception and Original Sin* 23 and 27.
45. Aquinas, *Summa* II/I, qu. 71, art. 1, reply, italics mine.
46. Aquinas, *Summa* II/I, qu. 71, art. 5, reply.
47. Aquinas, *Summa* II/I, qu. 71, art. 6, reply to obj. 2.
48. Aquinas, *Summa* II/I, qu. 81, art. 1, reply; cf. also art. 3.
49. Aquinas, *Summa* II/I, qu. 81, art. 1, reply to obj. 2.
50. Aquinas, *Summa* II/I, qu. 82, art. 3, reply.
51. Aquinas, *Summa* II/I, qu. 85, arts. 5 and 6.
52. Aquinas, *Summa* II/I, qu. 87, art. 2, reply.

ment."[53] He certainly traces "the slippery slope" of bondage to sin. He writes, "The soul, through sinning once, is more readily inclined to sin again."[54]

N. P. Williams and others examine the relation of Aquinas to Augustine.[55] Williams concludes that Thomas is almost a replication of the earlier thinker, except for a softening at certain points. The Augustinian tradition was then partially reversed by Duns Scotus (c. 1266-1308), who was Franciscan Regent Master in Paris. Williams perceives this as "a near return to the Irenaean view of the fall."[56] The Council of Trent (1545-1563) formalized the phrase "original sin." Nevertheless, in terms of a *hermeneutic for today,* the notion that sin can constitute one punishment for sin is sorely needed, and can be expounded also philosophically as "internal" consequences of sin, as seen also in Paul (Rom. 1:18-32 and 7:14-25).

(iii) *Martin Luther* (1483-1546). From among numerous scattered writings, Luther's *Preface to the Letter of St. Paul to the Romans* (1522) provides classic material and an excellent starting point for understanding his view of sin. It is readily accessible in English in the Christian Classics Ethereal Library.[57] Luther regarded Romans as "purest gospel," which ought to be "daily bread for the soul." We soon reach a key statement: "God judges what is in the depths of the heart." For Luther asserts, "*Sin* in the Scriptures means not only external works of the body, but also all those movements within us which . . . move us to do external works, namely the depth of the heart with all the powers" (5). If we speak of our inability to fulfill the law, this would include, "To do its work eagerly, lovingly and freely, without the constraint of the law."

Jesus Christ explicitly calls *unbelief* "sin" in John 16:9. This harmonizes with the NT promise to justify those who believe. Faith is not just assent to the gospel, but "a loving unshakeable confidence in God's grace" that a person would die for, and makes him "joyful, confident and happy" (6). In Romans 3, Luther wrote, "Paul lumps both secret and public sinners together. . . . They are all sinners, unable to glory in God" (7-8). Under the bondage of sin, "Paul proves . . . that a person cannot help himself by his works to get from sin to justice" (9). This becomes clear from his contrast between Adam and Christ. He concludes, "Sin is his very nature; of himself

53. Aquinas, *Summa* II/I, qu. 87, art. 5, reply to obj. 2.

54. Aquinas, *Summa* II/I, qu. 87, art. 3, reply.

55. Williams, *Ideas of the Fall,* 400-408; cf. Wiley, *Original Sin,* 83-88; and Moxon, *The Doctrine of Sin,* 156-61.

56. Williams, *Ideas of the Fall,* 409.

57. Martin Luther, *Preface to the Letter of St. Paul to the Romans* (Christian Classics Ethereal Library, online). Page references have been placed in the text.

he can't do otherwise" (10). Romans 1–8 also records a constant struggle against sin. There is no "sinless perfection" for believers, who are "righteous" only in the sight of God.

In his *Lectures on Romans* (1515-1516) Luther offers the analogy of a sick man under the doctor's promise of health. In that situation, "As a matter of man, he is ill; but he is healthy on account of the healthy promise of the doctor . . . because he is sure that he will cure him." Luther's *On the Bondage of the Will* provides a further important source for his doctrine of sin. Erasmus's notion of an equipoised "freedom," Luther urges, is undermined by the universality of sin.[58] All Jews and Gentiles are "under sin," in Paul's language: "Both Jews and Gentiles are under the power of sin" (Rom. 3:9; *Bondage,* 278). Paul adds, "There is none righteous. . . . There is none that does good, no not one" (Rom. 3:10-12). Luther adds, "It is no small thing when a man is said to be ignorant of God, and to despise him; for this is the fountain-head of all iniquities . . . a hell of evil. . . . Here is unbelief, disobedience, sacrilege, blasphemy towards God, cruelty and mercilessness" (282). Sin entails "senseless obstinacy of our hearts" (283). In Romans 8:6 Paul sums up this attitude as "the mind of the flesh" (cf. Rom. 8:9; *Bondage,* 299).

In 1530 the Augsburg Confession was edited by Philipp Melanchthon, and was part of the *Book of Concord,* which was intended as a joint declaration of Luther and Melanchthon. It has remained a major confession of the Lutheran church. Article 2 concerned original sin. It declares, "Since the fall of Adam all men . . . are born with sin, that is, without the fear of God, without trust in God, and with concupiscence." Article 19 considers the cause of sin and declares, "The cause of sin is the will of the wicked, that is, of the devil and ungodly men."

Clearly Luther is heavily influenced by Paul and Augustine. His view of sin, like Anselm's, is integrally related to his view of salvation and the work of Christ, and in Luther's case justification by grace. Sin is essentially *godlessness,* and is *universal.* His emphasis on the *heart* fully harmonizes with a central theme in Calvin. His stress on the Christian's struggle against sin also accords with Augustine. His *Disputation against Scholastic Theology* sums it up: "The natural man cannot want God to be God. Rather, he wants himself to be God, and God not to be God."[59] Again, *for hermeneutics today,* the

---

58. Luther, *On the Bondage of the Will* (London: James Clarke, 1957), 278-84. Page references have been placed in the text.

59. Luther, *Disputation against Scholastic Theology,* in *Luther: Early Theological Works,* ed. James Atkinson, LCC 16 (London: SCM, 1962), 267.

notion of sin as *lack of fear of God, lack of trust in his promises,* and sheer *godlessness,* as well as *inviting daily bondage,* constitutes necessary but often neglected themes.

(iv) *John Calvin* (1509-1564). Calvin also underlined Augustine's doctrine. He wrote, sin "is the hereditary corruption to which early Christian writers gave the name Original Sin, meaning by the term the depravation of a nature formerly good and pure."[60] He noted that this term was controversial, even in his day. Calvin devotes the first five or six chapters of the *Institutes* book 2 to this subject. The notion that Adam sinned "only to his own hurt" is called "a profane fiction," devised by Pelagius. Calvin cites Psalm 51:5,

> I was born guilty,
>> a sinner when my mother conceived me.

Humankind is therefore "a seed-bed of sin, and cannot but be odious and abominable to God" (2.1.8). Yet Calvin would never have denied "God so loved the world . . ." (John 3:16). He holds the two ideas together by grace in Christ bringing about a new creation. Meanwhile, "All the parts of the soul were possessed by sin, ever since Adam revolted from the fountain of righteousness" (2.1.9).

Like Luther and Paul, Calvin regarded humankind as under "the dominion of sin. . . . Man has no remaining good in himself" (2.2.1). His use of the term "total depravity" meant *"depraved in all parts,"* not "depraved in every action." He traced views of "freedom" through Origen, Bernard, Anselm, Peter Lombard, and Aquinas, and pointed to Paul's use of the word "slave" to underline Luther's view. He argued that man's natural gifts were corrupted by sin. Yet he insisted that human *reason* remains still intact and active (2.2.17). Again, however, like Luther, he saw only corrupt acts proceeding from a corrupt nature. He wrote, "When the will is enchained as the slave of sin, it cannot make a movement towards goodness. . . . To will ill (is) part of corrupt nature" (2.3.5). On the other hand, "Everything good in the will is entirely the result of grace" (2.3.6). Humankind has no ground for "boasting."

As in Luther, this dark picture serves to show the *generosity of God's grace.* All Augustine does, Calvin claimed, "is to mark the multiplication of

60. John Calvin, *The Institutes of the Christian Religion* 2.1.5; trans. Henry Beveridge, 2 vols. (Grand Rapids: Eerdmans, 1989), 1:214. References to the *Institutes* have been placed in the text; the English quotations can be found in the Beveridge translation.

grace. . . . Nothing is left for the will to arrogate as its own" (2.3.12). Goodness is "by the Spirit of God acting within" (2.5.5).

Among numerous evaluations of Calvin, A. Dakin seems to convey well his views on sin in the wider context of his theology of salvation. Salvation by faith, Dakin comments, "implies not merely distrust of good works . . . but distrust of all human ability."[61] Like Paul, he writes, "Calvin puts the emphasis not on sins but on sin. . . . He uses such terms as 'taint,' 'corruption,' 'vitiated.' "[62] He does not exclusively rely on Paul. In the Gospels, "Every good tree bears good fruit, but the bad tree bears bad fruit" (Matt. 7:17). We noted that "heart" was as important for Calvin as it was for Luther. As the Reformed theologians G. C. Berkouwer and Herman Bavinck stress, the main concern was the universality of human guilt and humanity's need for grace.[63]

As we saw in Luther, Calvin's emphasis on the seriousness and bondage of sin is not an end in itself, but shows the *generosity of God's grace,* and *realistic expectations* even of redeemed Christians, who are still in the process of discarding the old Adam. As we observed about Luther, these hermeneutical themes merit recovery today.

4. The Early Modern Period

(i) *Friedrich Schleiermacher* (1768-1834). Schleiermacher is often characterized as the father of modern theology. He regarded sin as the inadequacy of consciousness of God. In a theologically positive sense, he did not reduce sin to moralism and did relate it to *consciousness of God.* But he moved away from the tradition of Paul, Augustine, Aquinas, Luther, and Calvin. He regarded sin as basically *arrested development.* Pannenberg with justice regrets his "oversimplifying" of the problem and condition of sin.[64] One of the greatest problems in Schleiermacher on this subject is his overready assimilation of the *evolutionary* mood of the nineteenth century. He wrote,

61. A. Dakin, *Calvinism* (London: Duckworth, 1940), 30.

62. Dakin, *Calvinism,* 32 and 33.

63. G. C. Berkouwer, *Studies in Dogmatics,* vol. 10, *Sin,* 14 vols. (Grand Rapids: Eerdmans, 1971), and Herman Bavinck, *Reformed Dogmatics,* vol. 3, *Sin and Salvation in Christ* (Grand Rapids: Baker Academic, 2006).

64. Wolfhart Pannenberg, *Anthropology in Theological Perspective* (London and New York: T. & T. Clark, 1985), 352-53.

"Sin . . . has arrested the free development of the God-consciousness."[65] He spoke of "the principles of progressive development."

Rather than speculate about original righteousness before the Fall, Schleiermacher writes of "a time when the disposition to the God-consciousness had not yet actively emerged in us."[66] Against the Reformed view, he argues, "Sin in general exists only in so far as there is consciousness of it. . . . Sin . . . manifests itself only in connexion with, and by means of, already existent good."[67] This statement about *consciousness* is more than debatable. Dispositions lie beneath the fully conscious realm. The Holy Spirit sanctifies the heart. Not surprisingly, John Hick associates Schleiermacher with Irenaeus. Emil Brunner explicitly calls his view "idealistic evolutionism."[68] Original sin, Schleiermacher argues, is only "the personal guilt of every individual who shares in it."[69]

(ii) *Albrecht Ritschl* (1822-1889). Ritschl sought to reinstate the corporate and *communal* character of sin. This was especially in danger of being lost against the background of nineteenth-century individualism. The kingdom of God, Ritschl urged, "cannot be completely represented . . . within the framework of individual life."[70] All the same, Ritschl belongs broadly to the classic liberal school, and it is a matter of debate among interpreters whether this leads to a "Pelagian" view of sin. Moxon comments, "Ritschl repudiates the old doctrine of Original Sin, and seeks to explain sinfulness by a development of the Pelagian idea of the 'influence of example,' and finds its origin entirely in man's environment."[71] On the other hand, James Richmond has written a reappraisal of Ritschl, which aims to counteract Barth's "uncompromising hostility towards . . . Ritschl," and "to throw off new-orthodox preconceptions . . . and distorting stereotypes."[72] Many have accused him of putting "consciousness" in the place of God or Christ. At least, however, his view of sin concerns *humankind's relation to God* more than mere morality.

65. Friedrich Schleiermacher, *The Christian Faith* (Edinburgh: T. & T. Clark, 1989), 171.

66. Schleiermacher, *The Christian Faith*, 273.

67. Schleiermacher, *The Christian Faith*, 277.

68. Emil Brunner, *Man in Revolt: A Christian Anthropology* (London: Lutterworth, 1941; Louisville: Westminster John Knox, 1979), 123-24.

69. Schleiermacher, *The Christian Faith*, 285.

70. Albrecht Ritschl, *The Christian Doctrine of Justification and Reconciliation*, 3 vols. (Clifton, N.J.: Reference Book Publishers, 1966; orig. 1870-1874), 10-11.

71. Moxon, *The Doctrine of Sin*, 200.

72. James Richmond, *Ritschl: A Reappraisal* (New York: Collins, 1978), 35, 38, and 39.

(iii) *Frederick R. Tennant* (1866-1957). By contrast, Tennant tends to view sin in *moralistic terms.* He attempts to provide a philosophical, empirical, and individualistic account of sin, but is unduly influenced by naturalistic theories of evolution. "Adam" becomes a wholly mythological or symbolic figure. His rejection of the hereditary significance of "Adam" is made clear by his insistence that sin cannot include anything of which we are unconscious. "Sin will be imperfect compliance . . . with the moral ideal in so far as this is in the sight of God, capable of apprehension by an agent at the moment of the activity in question."[73] Although the ethical dimension of sin takes the center of the stage, he explicitly asserts, "Sin as it is used in theology . . . is not exclusively an ethical conception."[74]

Sin gains its significance, Tennant argues, in contrast with the light of God's nature. Jesus taught that it emerges from "the heart." On the other hand, he reduces the teaching of Jesus mainly to "offences" or "occasions of stumbling," even though he sometimes adds, "in the sight of God."[75] E. J. Bicknell makes a relevant point when he observes that Tennant writes as a philosopher, not as a theologian.[76] Although his view of sin is not *exclusively* moralistic, he comes near to this, not least because much of his argument is *psychological and empirical.*

(iv) *Karl Barth* (1886-1968). Barth defines sin in the light of his appreciation of *divine grace* and the righteousness of *Christ.* Jesus Christ is "man as God willed and created him."[77] He then offers a reasonably comprehensive account of the nature of sin. When seen in the light of Christ, he writes, sin is revealed as "a personal act and guilt, [humankind's] *alienation* from the grace of God and his command, his refusal of the gratitude he owes to God . . . his *arrogant attempt to be his own master, provider, and comforter,* his unhallowed lust for what is not his own, the falsehood, hatred, and pride in which he is enmeshed in relation to his neighbour, the stupidity to which he is self-condemned."[78]

As this quotation indicates, sin is fundamentally *pride in the sense of self-sufficiency.* But it also involves *ingratitude, alienation, falsehood, and stupid-*

---

73. F. R. Tennant, *The Concept of Sin* (Cambridge: CUP, 1912), 245, and F. R. Tennant, *The Origin and Propagation of Sin* (Cambridge: CUP, 1903).

74. Tennant, *The Concept of Sin,* 19.

75. Tennant, *The Concept of Sin,* 24 and 28.

76. E. J. Bicknell, *The Christian Idea of Sin and Original Sin: In the Light of Modern Knowledge* (London: Longmans Green, 1923), 32-34.

77. Barth, *CD* III/2, 50.

78. Barth, *CD* III/3, 305, italics mine.

ity. Under sin humans become "servants of nothingness . . . alien and enemy . . . general contrariety of creaturely existence."[79] This does not justify I. D. Campbell's claim that Barth is "open to the charge of an inherent Gnosticism . . . that all matter is evil."[80] Barth explicitly states, "The essence of sin (is) the pride of man," and *gnosis* brings pride (1 Cor. 8:1).[81] Campbell suggests further criticisms of Barth's interpretation of Adam and the Fall, but Barth mainly describes it as humankind's entry into a *state of corruption.* In relation to the atonement, following Anselm, Barth asserts, "He (the sinner) is a debtor who cannot pay."[82] Barth adds, "To show that man is inexcusably guilty of any one of his individual acts of pride is enough."[83]

(v) *Rudolf Bultmann* (1884-1976). At first, when we consult Bultmann's *Theology of the New Testament,* it seems difficult to disentangle his descriptive account of Paul's view of sin from his own view. But he has many other publications, and in all of them his view comes close to that of the earlier Barth. Admittedly in Paul, sin expresses "the mind of the flesh" (Rom. 8:8), which is essentially "trust in one's self as being able to procure life . . . through one's own strength," and to be "at war with God" (Rom. 8:7).[84] It is "boasting."[85] But we find the same assessment in *Faith and Understanding* and in *Essays Philosophical and Theological,* which are the English translations of the first and second volumes of *Glauben und Verstehen.* In the former, Bultmann declares: "*The real sin of man* is that he 'takes his will into and his life into his own hands, makes himself secure, and so has his self-confidence, his "boast." '"[86] In his *Essays* he comments that under sin, "*He (man) lives on the basis of his works.*"[87] In *hermeneutical* terms, this demonstrates a close link with justification by grace through faith.

(vi) *Emil Brunner* (1889-1966). Brunner holds a position close to Barth's. He writes, "Through sin man has lost . . . his God given nature."[88] Like Barth, he perceives sin as "the assertion of *human independence over against God*

79. Barth, *CD* III/3, 306.
80. I. D. Campbell, *The Doctrine of Sin: In Reformed and Neo-Orthodox Thought* (Fearn, Scotland: Mentor, 1999), 150.
81. Barth, *CD* IV/1, 478.
82. Barth, *CD* IV/1, 484.
83. Barth, *CD* IV/1, 489.
84. Rudolf Bultmann, *Theology of the New Testament,* vol. 1 (London: SCM, 1952), 236 and 239.
85. Bultmann, *Theology of the New Testament,* 1:242-43.
86. Rudolf Bultmann, *Faith and Understanding* (London: SCM, 1969), 228.
87. Rudolf Bultmann, *Essays Philosophical and Theological* (London: SCM, 1955), 81.
88. Brunner, *Man in Revolt,* 94.

... as independent of God's will."[89] "Presumption, arrogance," he says, is the "primal sin."[90] He also urges the corporate nature of sin: "We are a unity bound together in solidarity. . . . Sin is the destruction of communion with God."[91]

(vii) *Paul Tillich* (1886-1965). Tillich specifically calls sin *"hubris."* In volume 2 of his *Systematic Theology,* he writes, "*Hubris* is the self-elevation of man into the sphere of the divine. . . . One should not translate *hubris* as 'pride.' Pride is a moral quality. . . . *Hubris* is not the special quality of man's moral character. It is universally human."[92] Tillich, like many others, regards sin as *narcissism, when a person "is the centre of himself."* Not surprisingly, this involves "also tragic *self-destruction.* . . . Man identifies his cultural creativity with divine creativity. He attributes infinite significance to his finite cultural creations, making idols of them" (2:58, italics mine).

Tillich considers the Augustinian notion of "concupiscence." He asks whether Freud's concept of the libido would constitute an adequate reinterpretation, but rejects this, if it denotes primarily a discharge of tension (2:61-62). Nietzsche's "will to power" might be more adequate, but it, too, suffers from limitations. Tillich prefers a summary such as *"the universal* destiny of *estrangement,"* which is actualized by free acts (2:64, italics mine). Estrangement must be understood both individually and collectively. There is inner conflict in estrangement that leads both to "destruction" and to "disruption" (2:70-71). In the end, "estrangement, suffering, and loneliness" are part of the effects of sin. Ultimately one reaches "estrangement, doubt, and meaninglessness" (2:80-85). The person under sin also faces "the symbol of 'the wrath of God.'" Tillich asserts, "When man turns away from God . . . [he] turns towards himself," separated from "the will of God" (2:54).

Much of Tillich's analysis is *rich in hermeneutical insights. Estrangement, self-destruction, and self-centered narcissism are powerful images.* Yet often these remain on the level of psychological and existential insights. As a phenomenological approach it is suggestive and useful. Many, however, would require the more explicitly theological orientation of Barth, Nietzsche, Pannenberg, Rahner, or Küng.

(viii) *Reinhold Niebuhr* (1892-1971). Niebuhr shares the view of Barth, Bultmann, and Brunner that regards sin as *pride.* In his small book *Moral Man and Immoral Society* he shows further its essentially *communal* char-

89. Brunner, *Man in Revolt,* 129, italics mine.
90. Brunner, *Man in Revolt,* 130.
91. Brunner, *Man in Revolt,* 139, 141.
92. Paul Tillich, *Systematic Theology,* 3 vols. (London: Nisbet, 1953, 1957, 1963), 2:57. Page references have been placed in the text.

acter, largely in terms of its disruptive and socially *destructive effects.* For example, when someone casts others aside in the scramble for promotion, allegedly for the sake of the family, "The family may become a means of self-aggrandisement."[93] The interests of the self creep into the most universal endeavor. Napoleon, Niebuhr argues, could "bathe Europe in blood" as a device for "French patriotism" (17). In this connection he writes, "*The self-ishness of nations is proverbial.* It was a dictum of George Washington that nations were not to be trusted beyond their own interest" (84, italics mine). Most, if not all, nations are "held together much more by force and emotion, than by mind" (88).

On the role of social "class" to encourage sin, Niebuhr attacks the respective interests of the elite, the middle classes, and the proletariat. Even America, he insists, is not exempt from this, even if class barriers are less pronounced than in Europe. He writes, "The moral cynicism of Marxism and proletarianism . . . is particularly apparent in its estimate of the democratic state" (148). This is similar to nationalism, with its disguised power claims. Niebuhr speaks of "the exaltation of class loyalty" (152).

Niebuhr adopted a broader approach in his two-volume work *The Nature and Destiny of Man.* We need to relate "finiteness" to the problem of sin. He wrote, "Man's pride and will-to-power disturb the harmony of creation. . . . The religious dimension of sin is man's *rebellion against God,* his effort to *usurp the place of God.*"[94] This will to power seeks this sense of insecurity, which he seeks in himself, not in God. His pride leads him to seek to overcome natural limitations. Sin is manifested partly in "sensuality" and "inordinate love for all creaturely . . . values."[95] But it is also rooted in humankind's attempt *to replace God by the self.* Niebuhr opposed Pelagianism, but insisted on human responsibility. Paul asserts that humankind is "without excuse" (Rom. 1:20-21).[96] Niebuhr combined serious theological reflection with astute empirical and social observation. One of my Ph.D. graduates, Mark Lovatt, has published an excellent study of Niebuhr's theology and discussion of will to power in Nietzsche.[97] Once again, this is suggestive in

93. Reinhold Niebuhr, *Moral Man and Immoral Society* (New York: Scribner, 1932; London: SCM, 1963), 47. Page references have been placed in the text.

94. Reinhold Niebuhr, *The Nature and Destiny of Man: A Christian Interpretation,* 2 vols. (London: Nisbet, 1941), 1:191, italics mine.

95. Niebuhr, *Nature and Destiny,* 1:247; cf. 242-55.

96. Niebuhr, *Nature and Destiny,* 1:256; cf. 256-80.

97. Mark F. W. Lovatt, *Confronting the Will-to-Power: A Reconciliation of the Theology of Reinhold Niebuhr* (Carlisle: Paternoster, 2001; Eugene, Ore.: Wipf and Stock, 2006).

hermeneutical terms. To see the self-centeredness of what we often do in the name of our family, our country, or even our peer network of friends, is often salutary and revealing.

5. The Twentieth Century Onward

(i) *Karl Rahner* (1904-1984). Rahner was one of the most distinguished Catholic theologians of the twentieth century. He rightly saw the essence of sin as *"rejection of God."*[98] He did not reject the term "original sin" as such, but sought to retain the *idea* without what he regarded as the misleading language inherited from Ambrose, Augustine, and others. He had hesitations both about biological heredity and about judicial imputation of "Adam's" sin. He asserted, "Original Sin expresses nothing else but the *historical origin* of the present, universal, and ineradicable situation of our freedom as co-determined by guilt." He continued, "God's self-communication in grace comes not from 'Adam' . . . but from the goal of their history, from the God-Man Jesus Christ."[99] In Rahner, the Adam story is not to be understood as a historical eyewitness account.

Rahner also argued that sin should *not be restricted to the private sphere.* This would restrict it to individual moralism, whereas sin includes *social institutions.* He argued that we do not have to decide "how many people suffer eternal loss," because biblical statements concern the present and the present viewpoint; "God does not say what is going to come later."[100] He called this part of "the hermeneutic of eschatological statements"; even not all theologians would perhaps agree with this assessment. He also wrote, "The Church should be one which defends morality boldly and unambiguously, without moralising."[101] Rahner is entirely comfortable with Augustine's anti-Donatist emphasis: "The Church of God and of his Christ is a Church of sinners."[102] *Sinners, he wrote, are members of the church.* Indeed, Rahner comes close to the Lutheran and Protestant view that Christian believers are justified and sinners at the same time.

98. Karl Rahner, *Foundations of Christian Faith: An Introduction to the Idea of Christianity* (New York: Crossroad, 1978, 2004), 115, italics mine.

99. Rahner, *Foundations,* 114, italics mine.

100. Rahner, *Foundations,* 103.

101. Karl Rahner, *The Shape of the Church to Come* (London: SPCK, 1974), 64.

102. Rahner, *Theological Investigations,* vols. 1-18 (New York: Seabury Press and Crossroad; London: DLT, 1966-1983), 6:256.

Justice or righteousness, however, is not "a purely static possession. . . . The grace of justification must always be accepted and exercised anew again"; nevertheless, such a view is "under attack."[103] "Man remains a pilgrim . . . 'on the road,' we are all just and sinners at the same time."[104]

(ii) *Valerie Saiving* (1921-1992) and *Judith Plaskow* (b. 1947). These two are among several feminist writers who have criticized the emphasis on sin as pride in Barth, Bultmann, Brunner, and Niebuhr, on the ground that this represents only a distinctively "masculine" sin. Saiving suggested that distraction and triviality were more distinctive characteristics of sin for women.[105] Barth, Bultmann, Brunner, Niebuhr, and Tillich, however, presupposed that sin entailed human self-sufficiency, which characterized an attitude toward *God*. It is difficult to see how Saiving has fully engaged with the heart of the problem. Some might regard her largely empirical or phenomenological analysis of sin as perhaps itself a "distraction and triviality" away from a focus on *God*. Her younger contemporary, Judith Plaskow, who collaborated with her in feminist projects, also wrote on Niebuhr and Tillich, but related her work more closely to sin and grace.[106] She regards sin for women as "wanting to be rid of oneself," in contrast to the more male sin of competitiveness. Once again, however, this appears to be a more empirical, psychological, and phenomenological approach than a theological one in terms of human relationships to God. In terms of *hermeneutics,* this does provide pause for thought about gender-related concepts of sin.

(iii) *Wolfhart Pannenberg* (1928-2014). In his *Systematic Theology* Pannenberg devotes a hundred pages to the sin of humankind. Sinful humankind has lost engagement and communication with the source of all that is good in life. Hence he realistically prefers to characterize sinful humanity as in bondage to *misery*, rather than simply being *lost,* or some other term. He writes, "The term *'misery'* sums up our detachment from God. . . . The term *'alienation'* has a similar breadth."[107] He continues, "Misery, then, is the lot of those who are deprived of the fellowship with God that is the destiny of human life" (2:178). This is also described as the "ec-centric" character of humankind, regarded as sinner. We have ceased to regard ourselves, as we should, as being "there for others as well as [for ourselves]" (2:194).

103. Rahner, *Theological Investigations,* 6:227.

104. Rahner, *Theological Investigations,* 6:229 and 230.

105. Valerie Saiving, "The Human Situation: A Feminine View," *JR* 40 (1960): 100-112.

106. Judith Plaskow, *Sex, Sin, and Grace: Women's Experience and the Theologies of Reinhold Niebuhr and Paul Tillich* (Washington, D.C.: University Press of America, 1979).

107. Pannenberg, *ST* 2:179, italics mine. Page references have been placed in the text.

Pannenberg regrets that "Little is left of the transitional dogma of the first estate before the fall," and that "Through sin there was an increasing distortion in individuals" (2:214, 216). The misery of sin means that "we are caught fast in the self" (2:251). He writes, "Absolute self-willing... alienates us from God" (2:261). He adds, "We achieve liberation from sin and death only where the image of the Son takes shape in human life through the operation of the Spirit of God" (2:275).

One of Pannenberg's most important and relevant statements is his comment: "The decay of the doctrine of original sin led to the anchoring of the concept of sin in *acts* of sin, and finally *the concept was reduced to the individual act*" (2:234, italics mine). Our inability to master sin manifests itself in its severe and *destructive effects*. Alongside this first important statement lies another biblical and historical observation. Pannenberg writes, "The classical significance of *Augustine* for the Christian doctrine of sin consists in the fact that he viewed and analysed *the Pauline link between sin and desire more deeply* than Christian theology had hitherto managed to do. The many aspects of this teaching that call for criticism should not blind us to this extraordinary development" (2:241, italics mine). A third statement rivals the first two in importance: "In the nonobservance of the orders of nature, *Augustine found* an *autonomy of the will that puts the self in the centre,* and uses everything else as a *means* to the self as an *end*" (2:243, italics mine).

It is difficult not to regard Pannenberg's analysis as the most outstanding and climactic exposition of the doctrine of sin to date. As we noted, it rests heavily on biblical vocabulary and historical analysis. It is sorely needed in the face of popular moralistic notions of sin as an *act* today, including their relation to God. Even many church confessions of sin show that a true appreciation of alienation from God and self-destruction still persists. That is perhaps why many theologians and others appreciate the "General Confession" of the 1662 Book of Common Prayer, in contrast to several "contemporary" formulations. In terms of hermeneutical insights, much can be gained by focusing on such terms as "lostness," "alienation," "self-destruction," and corporate or societal "state," rather than *individual act*.

(iv) *Hans Küng* (b. 1928). Even as many would describe Pannenberg as our leading contemporary Protestant theologian, many would also regard Küng as our leading contemporary Catholic thinker, perhaps second only to Rahner. Much of his work on the doctrine of sin is set out in his earlier book *Justification*. In the light of the work of Christ, sin has "no absolute dominion" over the world.[108] But Küng examines many OT passages and some NT passages to indicate the seriousness of sin in bringing death (e.g., Pss. 55:23; 102:24-25; Isa. 38:10; Deut. 7:1-2; 20:13-14). He writes, "Sin is a fall from the covenant, a fall from God. Sin is *separation from God; that is its* essence. Man, whose whole existence depends on God's love, *turns away in sin from the foundation of his existence,* and thus this foundation is for him — lost" (146, italics mine).

Any account of sin, however, must also take account of *Christ.* Hence Küng underlines "the *wretchedness* of sin," but also declares that it stands under the *greater* dominance of salvation in Christ "from the beginning" (164). He tends to follow Barth's universalism, and quotes Isaiah 48:9,

> For my name's sake I defer my anger,
>   for the sake of my praise I restrain it for you.

Grace, he insists, has the last word. In that context he also cites Athanasius and Gregory. All this leads to "the sinner's inability to achieve any self-justification" (171).

Küng affirms, "Lost freedom is restored to the sinner in justification" (174). The *grace* (Heb. *chēn*) of God intervenes. He comments, following Barth, "In grace it is not in the first instance I who 'have' God, but God who 'has' me" (190). Like Barth, he sees grace as a *promise* or guarantee. He cites Aquinas, Peter Lombard, and Rahner in support of this. He tries to offer reconciliation between Catholic and Protestant accounts of justification and sin. We have in Küng a treasury of hermeneutics: separation from God, loss of our foundation, wretchedness, and rejecting God's hold on us.

(v) *John Zizioulas* (b. 1931). This thinker represents contemporary theology in the Greek Orthodox Church. He writes, "The fall consists in the *refusal to make being dependent on communion* [i.e., with God and others] in a rupture between truth and communion."[109] Communion with God is the standard from which the sinner falls, to make himself the center of Being. Thereby the sinner creates for himself "a fragmented existence."[110] He continues: "Adam died because he fell by making himself into God — i.e. the

---

108. Hans Küng, *Justification: The Doctrine of Karl Barth and a Catholic Reflection* (London: Burns and Oates; New York: Nelson, 1964), 141. Page references have been placed in the text.

109. John D. Zizioulas, *Being as Communion: Studies in Personhood and the Church* (New York: St. Vladimir's Seminary Press, 1985, 1997), 102.

110. Zizioulas, *Being as Communion,* 103.

ultimate reference-point of existence."[111] Rebellion against relationships or relationality changes God and "persons" into "objects," who have no material relation with the subject. As we saw in the discussion of the image of God, this is precisely the distinction expounded by the Russian Orthodox theologian Vladimir Lossky. Both Lossky and Zizioulas draw extensively on the Eastern Fathers. Although there are differences from Augustine, Luther, and Pannenberg, their common ground remains more significant. Whether we consider Athanasius or Augustine, Zizioulas or Pannenberg, sin is essentially a rejection of God, for whom the self is substituted. In Zizioulas relationship with God and others becomes a hermeneutical key.

Among all these twenty-three accounts of sin (except perhaps those of Tennant and Pelagius), concepts of sin stand far apart from popular notions of alienation or misdirected desire in today's secular world, and sometimes even in the church. A rapid survey of many liturgies, prayers of confession, and sermons in today's churches shows how frequently today's world and neoliberalism have diluted the root understanding bequeathed by the Bible, and also many historical theologians. The most serious problems of life are often left virtually untouched by such accommodation, and thereby the gospel has become seemingly *less credible.* In England this can be seen by comparing the Book of Common Prayer (1662) with the *Alternative Service Book* (1980). Happily *Common Worship* (2000) has begun to reverse this trend, and parallels may be cited in the prayers of other churches.

111. Zizioulas, *Being as Communion*, 105.

CHAPTER VIII

Jesus Christ the Mediator

Many scholars have argued that we should no longer consider theological anthropology, misdirected desire, and alienation *before* we have expounded the person and work of Jesus Christ. These are nowadays understandable reactions to the traditional sequence, in the light of the "new look" on Paul. Dietrich Bonhoeffer also attacked the sometimes "cheap" way of making people first feel guilty and inadequate, and only then expounding the good news of Jesus Christ. More seriously, E. P. Sanders has been highly influential in regarding Paul as perceiving "the solution as preceding the problem."[1] Whereas Bultmann, Conzelmann, and Bornkamm begin with Paul's exposition of the plight of humankind, and then present Christ's salvation, Sanders comments, "It seems likely that Paul's thought did not run from plight to solution, but rather from solution to plight."[2] Paul, Sanders argues, first expounded the gospel of Christ; he preached about God, not about men. He then moved on to discuss anthropology and sin as an implication of the gospel.

Expressed in those terms, this seems to ask us to think again. Peter's first sermon, according to Acts, begins: "Everyone who calls on the name of the Lord shall be saved," and Peter proceeds to preach "Jesus of Nazareth, a man attested to you by God" (Acts 2:21-22). Paul declares, "We proclaim Christ crucified. . . . I decided to know nothing among you except Jesus Christ, and him crucified" (1 Cor. 1:23; 2:2).

Further, Sanders rightly argues, what God has done and is doing through

---

1. E. P. Sanders, *Paul and Palestinian Judaism: A Comparison of Patterns of Religion* (London: SCM, 1977), 442-47.

2. Sanders, *Paul and Palestinian Judaism*, 443.

Jesus Christ constitutes a cosmic event. It constitutes a turning point in history, of greater concern than whether we respond in faith. We cannot claim that Sanders is wrong, or that this method would be wrong in a systematic theology.

Hermeneutical reflection, however, suggests that in the first place most or many of the first readers were Jews, who already knew the OT teaching about misdirected desire and alienation from God. The situation is different today. In the second place, we need to compare the existential and practical hunger for salvation in many readers in the first century with much indifference in today's secular world. Today, instead we find a more casual or passive attitude toward misdirected desire and alienation, even at times among some churches and some Christians. Non-Jews would not at all feel the same excitement as most first-century Jews at hearing the message, "The New Age has dawned." We must ask ourselves: Can the proclamation of Christ carry the same weight, excitement, and joy in the *absence* of a careful exposition of *alienation* from God, as proclamation can in the light of it? For this reason we have adhered to the traditional sequence, but accept that many others may perceive this differently.

1. The Gospel Defined in Terms of the Cross, and the Cross Defined in Terms of God's Grace

Paul defined his gospel as "the message about the cross" (1 Cor. 1:18). In 1 Corinthians 2:2, Paul "decided to know nothing among you except Jesus Christ, and him crucified." He also asserts, "If we or an angel from heaven should proclaim to you a gospel contrary to what we proclaimed to you, let that one be [*anathema*]," or an outcast (Gal. 1:8-9). In Galatians 1:4 Paul interrupts his usual greeting: "Grace to you and peace . . . from the Lord Jesus Christ" to insert: "who gave himself for our sins to set us free from the present evil age." All four major epistles of Paul agree. In Romans 8:3, "God has done what the law . . . could not do: by sending his own Son in the likeness of sinful flesh, and to deal with sin, he condemned sin in the flesh." He also writes, "For our sake he (God) made him (Christ) to be sin who knew no sin, so that in him we might become the righteousness of God" (2 Cor. 5:21).

In Moltmann's words, "The death of Jesus on the cross is the *centre* of all Christian theology."[3] This emphasis is not restricted to the Pauline Epistles

---

3. Jürgen Moltmann, *The Crucified God: The Cross as the Foundation and Criticism of Christian Theology* (London: SCM, 1974), 204.

in the NT. Jesus taught: "The Son of Man came not to be served but to serve, and to give his life a ransom for (Gk. *lytron anti*) many" (Mark 10:45). In John 3:16, "God so loved the world that he gave his only Son, so that everyone who believes in him . . . may have eternal life." John adds, "Whoever believes in the Son has eternal life" (3:36). In Acts 2:21 Peter quotes from the OT: "Everyone who calls on the name of the Lord shall be saved." In Hebrews 9:12 Christ entered "once for all" (Gk. *ephapax*) into "the Holy Place . . . with his own blood, thus obtaining eternal redemption (Gk. *lytrōsin*)." We read in 1 Peter, another important writing, "You were ransomed . . . with the precious blood of Christ, like that of a lamb without defect or blemish" (1 Pet. 1:18-19). In 1 John, "the blood of Jesus his Son cleanses us from all sin" (1:7). Finally, according to Revelation 5:9, "You are worthy . . . for you were slaughtered and by your blood you ransomed for God saints from every . . . people."

It is no accident that all these major sources from the NT use the words "the cross" or "his blood" rather than "death." Vincent Taylor observed, "To explain the allusions to 'blood' as synonymous for 'death' is mistaken. One can hardly fail to be conscious of a loss of meaning if, instead of 'being justified *by his blood*' (Rom. 5:9) we read, 'Being justified in Christ crucified.' "[4] Martin Hengel has also reminded us of the shameful, ignominious form of death that the cross signified in the first century.[5]

The second starting point in Paul and other NT writers was that the cross of Christ is essentially an act of *God* (not only of Christ), in particular, of *God's grace*. There is no sense in which God the Father simply "sent" his Son to undertake a costly task that he would not be prepared to undertake himself. Donald Baillie argued this fully in his book *God Was in Christ*. He wrote that the cross is "not simply about the love of Jesus, but about the love of God."[6] Jesus came not primarily to proclaim *himself*, but to proclaim the *grace and kingdom of God*. In Romans 5:8 Paul asserts: "*God* proves *his* love for us in that while we still were sinners Christ died for us." The classic verse, from which Baillie drew his title, is "God was in Christ reconciling the world to himself" (2 Cor. 5:19). A well-worn slogan tells us that the work of Christ constitutes the *fruit* of God's grace, not the *root* of God's grace.

The importance of this point can be illustrated from one of the most

---

4. Vincent Taylor, *The Atonement in New Testament Teaching* (London: Epworth, 1940), 92.

5. Martin Hengel, *The Cross of the Son of God* (London: SCM, 1986), 93-180.

6. Donald M. Baillie, *God Was in Christ* (London: Faber and Faber, 1948), 184.

conservative NT specialists and theologians of the mid–twentieth century. Leon Morris commented, "Sometimes in their anxiety to give due emphasis to what Christ has done for us, evangelicals have unwillingly introduced a division into the Godhead. . . . Emphatically this is not the position taken up in the Bible."[7]

Probably the most influential Protestant theologian in the late twentieth century to stress God the Father's involvement in the atonement was Jürgen Moltmann. He writes more than once, *"What does Christ's cross really mean for God himself?"*[8] He asks, "Was not God present in Jesus' sufferings seriously? God the Father does not stand in remote distance from Jesus Christ on the cross and in the world, like a father 'sending' his son to do a painful task in his place. He is not 'A God who is in love with himself' like the God sometimes postulated in 'theism.'"[9]

Moltmann cites Paul Althaus as declaring, "Jesus died for God before he died for us." Hence, Moltmann asks, "How can the death of Jesus be a *statement about God?*"[10] He declares, "The significance of the death of Jesus for God himself . . . enter(s) into the inner-Trinitarian tensions and relationships of God. . . . The more one understands the whole event of the cross as an event of God, the more any simple concept of God falls apart."[11] It requires, Moltmann asserts, a *revolution* in our concept of God.

Moltmann does not stand alone in exploring this approach. We have noted the work of Donald Baillie. More radical is the work of the two eminent modern Catholic theologians Hans Urs von Balthasar and Hans Küng, and the two eminent Protestant theologians Karl Barth and Eberhard Jüngel. It is not surprising that Küng should speak of the humility of God, when we recall that his major book, *The Incarnation of God,* involves a close study of Hegel. For Hegel did not conceive of God as abstract or static, but as entering history in Jesus Christ. He paid careful attention to the Johannine prologue (John 1:1-14), as a way of understanding "God in Jesus."[12] John shows that

7. Leon Morris, *Glory in the Cross: A Study in Atonement* (London: Hodder and Stoughton, 1966), 46 and 47.

8. Moltmann, *The Crucified God,* 201; Jürgen Moltmann, *Experiences in Theology: Ways and Forms of Christian Theology* (London: SCM, 2000), 15 and 16; also in Jürgen Moltmann, *History and the Triune God: Contributions to Trinitarian Theology* (London: SCM, 1991), 172.

9. Moltmann, *The Crucified God,* 200-278.

10. Moltmann, *The Crucified God,* 200.

11. Moltmann, *The Crucified God,* 204.

12. Hans Küng, *The Incarnation of God: An Introduction to Hegel's Thought* (Edinburgh: T. & T. Clark, 1987), 125-27. Page references have been placed in the text.

the connection between God and the world is not "lifeless." These verses also show us the deep and interpenetrating connection between *God* and the *Logos,* or Jesus. It is "a living relation of living beings. . . . Father and Son are simply modifications of the same life . . . not a plurality. . . . The divine takes shape in the form of a human life" (127).

The "holy mystery" that emerges is that "there is no separation between infinite and finite, divine and human" (127). We should expect that in God there would be movement, for all movement comes from God's Spirit. Küng writes, "Hegel's point of departure in this 'doctrine of salvation' of his was above all the Bible" (161). Hence he explicitly speaks of "the Incarnation of God" (162). Hence we must ponder what becomes possible "in the event that God were to empty himself . . . into history, into humanity . . . a death and resurrection of God" (169). But if there is any measure of reality in this possibility, *the self-giving of God is the grace of God.* We cannot conceive of Christ's atonement without regarding it as also an act of God in grace, humility, and generosity. Hegel explicitly speaks of "the career (Ger. *Lebenslauf*) of God" (181-86). This involves his life-giving grace and sacrifice. Küng's use of Hegel is positive and suggestive, even if it veers to the edge, sometimes, of speculative language.

Karl Barth is easier to understand, at least on this specific point. He explains that "the act of God" in the incarnation is "His entry into the state of *humility* . . . the divine humiliation as it took place in Jesus Christ. . . . God did this without ceasing to be God. . . . He is not a prisoner of His own exalted status, but can also be lowly."[13] This act of grace "includes an inconceivable humiliation and condescension and self-abasement of God. . . . It is the secret of grace — God does this for our sake . . . the secret of the incarnation."[14] Barth is aware that through the incarnation and cross God acts "in His mode of being as the Son," but Jesus Christ "does not do this without the Father . . . with whom He is one."[15]

Just as some accuse Küng of overdependence on Hegel's philosophy, others may accuse Barth of grazing "modalism," as if the three persons of the Holy Trinity were only three "modes of Being." This is a well-known criticism of Barth. But he is well aware of this danger. Like Küng, he cites John as stressing the oneness of Jesus with his Father. Elsewhere he writes of the will of God in the mission of Christ, which is also "His will to give

13. Barth, *CD* IV/2, 42, italics mine.
14. Barth, *CD* IV/2, 42.
15. Barth, *CD* IV/2, 43.

Himself for the sake of man. . . . God's self-giving is His eternal purpose. . . . He gave Himself . . . He hazarded Himself."[16] *The grace of this humility includes also "his hiddenness" in the incarnation.* Barth writes, "The Almighty exists and acts and speaks here in the form of One who is weak and impotent, the eternal as One who is temporal and perishing, the Most High in the deepest humility."[17]

Moltmann goes so far as to say that God the Father experienced even Jesus' agony of desolation and dereliction. He quotes the words of Elie Wiesel: "God himself hung on the gallows." He continues: "Like the cross of Christ, even Auschwitz is in God Himself . . . taken up with the grief of the Father; the surrender of the Son, and the power of the Spirit."[18] Elsewhere he writes, "A God who cannot suffer cannot love either."[19] Like Küng and Barth, Moltmann has been accused of extending the boundaries too far, this time with the danger of Patripassianism, the belief that God the Father suffered literally on the cross. But Moltmann means that the Father was *present* and *involved:* not that he was physically placed on the cross.

Thus *all the initiative for the work of Christ* came from *the grace of God,* who gave *himself* in giving Christ. This embraces the incarnation, the cross, and the resurrection of Christ. Indeed, on this last point, Paul explicitly speaks of "the Spirit of him (God) who raised Jesus from the dead" (Rom. 8:11).

2. The Transparent Meanings of Redemption and Salvation

(i) *Redemption.* "Redemption" and its related verb, "to redeem," translate one of two Hebrew words, namely, *pādāh* or *pᵉdûth* and *gā'al* or *gō'ēl.* Both are translated in the LXX and NT by the Greek *agorazō,* and occasionally by *rhuomai;* but also by *lytroō* and *lytron.* Hebrew *pādāh* generally means "to ransom" or "to redeem," "to free," or "to rescue," while *gā'al* means all this, together with "to act as kinsman" or "to fulfill the duties of a relationship," as we shall explain.[20] The Greek *agorazō* denotes "to buy," "to purchase,"

16. Barth, *CD* IV/2, 161.
17. Barth, *CD* IV/1, 176.
18. Moltmann, *The Crucified God,* 278.
19. Jürgen Moltmann, *The Trinity and the Kingdom of God: The Doctrine of God* (London: SCM, 1981), 38.
20. BDB 145 and 804; *TDOT* 2:344-50; G. V. Smith and V. P. Hamilton, *"Gō'ēl,"* in *NIDOTTE* 1:786-89; *TDNT* 4:330-34 and 6:998-1003; and R. L. Hubbard, *NIDOTTE* 3:578-82.

or "to exchange goods or services in exchange for money." Greek *rhuomai* occasionally translates the Hebrew but is also used in the NT for "rescue," "deliver," or "save."[21] The Greek *lytron*, "ransom," *lytroō*, "redeem" or "free," and *lytrōsis*, "redemption" or "release," are used frequently.

The words "redeem" and "redemption" provide virtually a three-point sermon in appropriate biblical contexts. Usually they denote redemption *from* bondage, peril, or jeopardy; *by* an agent such as a redeemer; *to* a state of freedom, security, new life, or new ownership. The monetary aspect may be metaphorical. Gregory of Nyssa and others were misled away from biblical concerns when they asked, "To whom is the price paid?" To ask this is to press too far the image or metaphor of the costly act of procuring freedom.

The classic paradigm of redemption is the *exodus* event in which God delivered and freed Israel *from* bondage in Egypt, *by* his saving acts, *to* a new life as his own people under Moses, and eventually to the Promised Land under Joshua. God said, "I have also heard the groaning of the Israelites. . . . I have remembered my covenant. . . . I am the LORD, and I will free you . . . and deliver you from slavery. . . . I will redeem you with an outstretched arm. . . . I will take you as my people, and I will be your God" (Exod. 6:5-7; cf. 15:13; Pss. 74:2; 77:15).

The second classic event that springs from this is the institution and celebration of the *Passover*. God delivered Israel *from* the death of the firstborn sons, *by* the agency of God's angel, and splashing blood on the lintel of the door, *to* the safe journey to the Promised Land as God's covenant people (Exod. 12:1-14, 17). Israel was to keep it as "a day of remembrance. . . . You shall celebrate it . . . throughout your generations you shall observe it as a perpetual ordinance" (12:14). Under the new covenant, redemption at the Passover prefigures the cross and Lord's Supper (see chap. 13).

The Hebrew *gā'al* and *gō'ēl* are used throughout Exodus 6, with God as the subject. But the word is also used in Isaiah 40–66 (e.g., 41:14-16: "I will help you, says the LORD; / your redeemer is the Holy One of Israel"). Here "redeemer" becomes virtually a title for Israel's God. In 43:14 God is

> your redeemer *(gō'ēl)*, the Holy one of Israel:
> For your sake I will send to Babylon
>   and break down all the bars [i.e., prison bars].

---

21. BDAG 14, 605-6, and 907-8; *TDNT* 1:124-28; F. Büchsel and others, *TDNT* 4:330-56 and 6:998-1003.

Isaiah 48:17 speaks of "your Redeemer" in similar terms. In 54:5, 8, the aspect of "my deliverance" is used. Isaiah 49:26 speaks of rescue from oppression. Isaiah regards this redemption from Babylon as a second version of the exodus redemption. The Lord "makes a way in the sea, a path in the mighty waters," which makes sense only as a parallel with the exodus event through the Red Sea. "In his love and in his pity he redeemed them" in 63:9 may well refer to the homecoming of Israel after the exile.

The psalmist pleads for redemption in the sense of *protection* (Ps. 19:14). Many passages follow "redeem" with Hebrew *min*, "from" (Gen. 48:16; Pss. 106:10; 107:2-3). In Proverbs 23:11 we read, in a legal context,

> Their redeemer *(gō'ēl)* is strong;
> he will plead their cause against you.

In a well-known verse Job exclaims, "I know that my Redeemer lives . . . in my flesh I shall see God" (Job 19:25-26).

This brings us near to the distinctive aspect of *gā'al* in contrast to *pādāh*. This concerns the *gō'ēl haddām,* the avenger of blood. If a close relative is murdered, the *gō'ēl haddām* may have the duty of killing the murderer in place of the dead victim and relative. He thereby "redeems" his dead relative's blood. But if the killing is accidental, the killer may escape the avenger by fleeing to "a city of refuge." Numbers 35:12 explains, "The cities shall be for you a refuge from the avenger" (cf. Num. 35:22-25 and Deut. 19:4-7, for a fuller explanation). In Ruth 2:20 Naomi explains to Ruth, "The man (Boaz) is a relative of ours, one of our nearest kin." *Gā'al* comes to mean "to do the part of a kinsman" on behalf of a victim or a person who is unable to help himself or herself. A *gō'ēl* might pay a price to redeem family property (Lev. 25:25-28). Leviticus 25:25 reads, "If anyone of your kin falls into difficulty and sells a piece of property, then the next of kin shall come and redeem what the relative has sold."

It is a short step to see how readily God may redeem those who are regarded as his family, and are unable to help themselves. In fact, there is little excuse for complaining that redeeming and *redemption* are concepts in theology that are unintelligible to the modern world. The three events of the exodus and the Passover, the threat of Assyria, and the return from exile provide transparent narratives or word pictures of what redemption is and involves. Even the aspect of "doing the work of a kinsman" by performing an act of redemption adds piquancy to the already clear act and process.

Pannenberg uses blunt words about *intelligibility or hermeneutics*. He writes, "The fact that a later age may find it hard to understand traditional ideas is *not sufficient reason for replacing them*. It simply shows how necessary it is *to open up their ideas to later generations* . . . and then *to keep their meaning alive*."[22] His immediate concern is the words "expiation" and "representation" or "substitution," but this equally applies to "redemption," "salvation," and "mediation." He adds, we must "explain their content with sufficient forcefulness or clarity."[23] *This is the task of exegesis and hermeneutics.*

The NT writings, as we should expect, build on the OT's transparent presuppositions. The idea is represented by at least three Greek words, as noted above, also with compounds. In our earliest Gospel Jesus tells the disciples, "The Son of Man came . . . to serve, and to give his life a ransom for many" (Gk. *dounai tēn psychēn autou lytron anti pollōn,* Mark 10:45). The Greek *lytron* usually translates Hebrew *gā'al.* The saying in Mark 10:45 has an exact parallel in Matthew 20:28. Whereas *agorazō* readily has an everyday use in commercial buying (Matt. 13:44, 46, and Gk. *agora,* "marketplace"), *lytron* more usually means "ransom," and *rhuomai* denotes "rescue" (Rom 7:24; Col. 1:13; 1 Thess. 1:10). The OT use is taken over in Luke 1:68: "He has looked favorably on his people and redeemed them" (cf. 2:38).

The word group is more typical of the OT and LXX, however, than of the NT, although Paul uses the word several times in the context of Christ's redeeming us from slavery and bondage. One classic reference occurs in Galatians 3:13, "Christ redeemed us from the curse of the law" (Gk. *exagorazō*). Similarly, in Hebrews 9:12 the writer says, "Obtaining eternal redemption *(lytrōsis)*" by his own blood. First Peter 1:18 reads, "You were ransomed from the futile ways inherited from your ancestors." Revelation uses *agorazō* three times:

"You were slaughtered and by your blood you ransomed for God
  saints from every tribe and language and people." (Rev. 5:9)

The one hundred forty-four thousand who have been redeemed from the earth. (Rev. 14:3)

They have been redeemed from humankind as first fruits for God and the Lamb. (Rev. 14:4)

22. Pannenberg, *ST* 2:422, italics mine.
23. Pannenberg, *ST* 2:422.

Often in the NT the word group may denote the less theological idea of redemption from earthly or social slavery, although 1 Corinthians 7:23, "You were bought with a price," has a double meaning, as human slaves, and as freed for God. We may compare 1 Corinthians 6:19-20, which is fully theological: "You are not your own. For you were bought with a price; therefore glorify God in your body."

Adolf Deissmann used a misleading, but much quoted, analogy when he cited the purchase of slaves to freedom or manumission by a fictitious act on the part of Greco-Roman deities. Dale B. Martin, in his significant book *Slavery as Salvation,* comments, "Most scholars have agreed that Deissmann's explanation of *buy (agorazein)* to mean redemption *from* slavery by way of sacral manumission must be rejected. . . . When Christ buys a person, the salvific element of the metaphor is . . . to a higher level of slavery (as the slave of Christ)."[24] Deissmann had drawn on nearly a thousand inscriptions at Delphi and elsewhere to show, for example, "Apollo bought a slave named X from Y at a price of Z," and to argue that Paul borrowed his theology of purchase and redemption from this pagan practice.[25] Martin and others have shown on historical, lexicographical, and theological grounds that this view is a distraction. All that emerges from it is how widespread in the Greco-Roman world was the notion of buying, selling, and redeeming.

Hence, to recapitulate, our lesson from the OT suggests that the term "redemption" is utterly transparent and clear in meaning, provided that we consider its background with sufficient care. Our *hermeneutical* task is performed primarily by expounding these *historical* events, and explaining their significance for today.

(ii) *Salvation.* "Salvation" shares the same transparency of meaning, especially when we consider the example of the judges and others in the OT. The Hebrew verb *yāshaʿ* and the Hebrew noun *shālōm* denote, respectively, "to save," "to deliver from oppression," and "to provide peace and prosperity"; and "salvation," "completeness," "peace," or "well-being." The verb *shālam* means "to be whole, uninjured, sound, peaceful," and the Hebrew Piel form (a term of Hebrew grammar denoting action) *shillēm* means "to restore," "to complete," "to secure."[26] Gerhard von Rad writes, "Seldom do

---

24. Dale B. Martin, *Slavery as Salvation: The Metaphor of Slavery in Pauline Christianity* (New Haven: Yale University Press, 1990), 63.

25. Adolf Deissmann, *Light from the Ancient East,* rev. ed. (London: Hodder and Stoughton, 1927), 323; cf. 319-32.

26. BDB 1022-23; Philip J. Niel, *"Sh-l-m,"* in *NIDOTTE* 4:130-35; and Gerhard von Rad, *"Shālōm,"* in *TDNT* 2:402-6.

we find in the OT a word which to the same degree as *shālōm* can bear a common use and yet can also be filled with a concentrated religious content for the level of the average conception."²⁷ It is "very comprehensive." Strictly, he argues, it means "peace" or "well-being." Hence it may convey good fortune or well-being in everyday situations. But it is also closely associated with Israel's God, and the blessings of the covenant. God promises, "I will make with them a covenant of peace" (Ezek. 34:25, *shālōm;* repeated in 37:26). Here it means "peace with God," not just well-being. But when it does denote well-being or salvation, it is the gift of God. The Lord gives salvation, restoration, peace, and what is good (Ps. 85:4, 7, 8, 12).

The most transparent meaning of the term is conveyed by the book of Judges. The narratives of Judges recount a repeated cycle of events in which God raises up "saviors" to deliver Israel. The cycle is as follows: (1) Israel sins against the Lord; (2) God sells Israel into the hands of the Philistines; (3) Israel cries to the Lord in its distress; (4) God *delivers Israel into a state of security, peace, and freedom* by raising up a *savior* (usually a judge); (5) Israel again dwells in safety, peace, and prosperity, until once again they fall into sin and oppression. This occurs, for example, in Judges 3:7-11. In this passage: (1) "Israel did what was evil in the sight of the LORD" (v. 7); (2) "the anger of the LORD was kindled . . . he sold them into the hand of King Cushan-rishathaim of Aram-naharaim . . . eight years" (v. 8); (3) "the Israelites cried out to the LORD" (v. 9); (4) "the LORD raised up a deliverer . . . Othniel" (v. 9); (5) "the land had rest forty years" (v. 11).

This cycle of events was then repeated, when "the LORD raised up for them a deliverer, Ehud" (3:15). A third cycle is recounted in 4:1-23, when God raised up Deborah and Barak. Judges 5 recounts Deborah's Song of Victory; Judges 6:1–8:35 recounts God's raising up of Gideon. Judges 9 concerns Abimelech, who is followed by Tola (10:1-2), Jair (10:3-18), Jephthah (11:1–12:7), and eventually Samson (13:24–16:31).

This cycle, then, provides a very clear picture of the meaning of "salvation" and "savior," with at least half a dozen parallels and repetitions. Each act of deliverance or saving event involves an agent through whom God brings salvation, which makes the role of the "savior" also transparent. In Judges they are largely military, although not in the sense of self-sufficient power. Each "judge" has a *perceived weakness* according to the expectations of the day. Ehud is left-handed (3:15); Deborah is a woman (4:4); Gideon has to reduce his army to a minimum (7:2) and doubts God (6:36-37); Abi-

27. Von Rad, *"Shālōm,"* 2:402.

melech is the target of humor (9:27-28); Jephthah makes a rash and foolish vow (11:30-31); and Samson is easily seduced and sometimes plays the fool (16:16-17). In each case the power comes by the hand of *God,* in spite of imperfections in the human agents. But as the drama of Israel's history unfolds, there arise *kings,* with Saul, David, and Solomon; *prophets,* with Aaron, Balaam, Elijah, Amos, Hosea, and others; and *priests,* when Moses and Aaron fulfilled a priestly function. John Calvin saw the three offices of prophet, priest, and king fulfilled above all in Jesus Christ. Hebrews compares the adequacy of Aaronic priests with the perfection of the priesthood of Jesus (Heb. 7:17-28; 8:1-7).

The OT has laid down a transparent picture of the meaning of salvation. The Greek *sōtēria,* "deliverance," "salvation," and *sōtēr* and *sōtērios,* "savior," "deliverer," "preserver," occur nearly 250 times in the LXX, and some 64 times in the NT.[28] The verb *sōzō,* "to save," occurs nearly 100 times. The Greek *sōtēr* generally translates Hebrew *yēsha'; sōtēria* usually translates *yēsha'* or *y^{e}shû'āh.*

Foerster and Fohrer show that there was hardly any aspect of life in the Greco-Roman world that was not touched by notions of *a savior or salvation.* "Saviors" sprang up with ideas of a "golden age" in the Roman imperial period, an age that would bring peace and security. To Hellenistic or Greek-speaking Jews, God kept Israel from dangers, and was *pantōn sōtēr,* "savior of all," and the author of deliverance (Wis. 16:7; cf. 1 Macc. 4:30; 3 Macc. 6:29, 32; 7:16). In Josephus the word is used of human deliverers. Foerster argues, "In the Hellenistic ruler cult the official designation of rulers [is] *sōtēres* . . . ; *sōzō* is the special task of the ruler."[29] The term could also be applied to philosophers, statesmen, physicians, and pagan deities. Foerster cites sources in *TDNT,* volume 7. Later Judaism, however, applies the term only to God.

At the beginning of the Gospels, the angel Gabriel told the shepherds, "To you is born this day . . . a Savior, who is the Messiah" (Luke 2:11); and Mary exulted, "My spirit rejoices in God my Savior" (Luke 1:47). Here the term would chiefly be understood as helper or deliverer. In Acts Peter declares, "God exalted him (Christ) . . . as Leader and Savior" (Acts 5:31). In one of his earlier speeches in Acts, Paul states, "God has brought to Israel a Savior, Jesus, as he promised" (Acts 13:23). In John Samaritans are portrayed

---

28. BDAG 985-86; Hatch-Redpath 2:1331-32; Werner Foerster and Georg Fohrer, *"Sōzō, sōtēria, sōtēr, sōtērios,"* in *TDNT* 7:965-1024.

29. Foerster and Fohrer, *"Sōzō, sōtēria, sōtēr, sōtērios,"* 7:1009; cf. 1012-14.

as saying, "We know that this is truly the Savior of the world" (John 4:42). These utterances are all credible in the sense of "deliverer." Notably, Paul rarely uses the term *sōtēr*. It occurs only in Ephesians 5:23, Philippians 3:20, and the Pastoral Epistles.[30]

It is otherwise with *sōtēria*. It is used eleven times in the Gospels and Acts (mainly in Luke-Acts) and sixteen times in the generally recognized epistles of Paul. Romans 1:16 carries the fuller sense of the term: "I am not ashamed of the gospel; it is the power of God for salvation *(eis sōtērian).*" Similarly in Romans 10:1, "My . . . prayer to God for them is that they may be saved" (Gk. *deēsis . . . hyper autōn eis sōtērian*). Romans 10:10 is similar. Paul's statements are noteworthy: "Salvation has come to the Gentiles" (Rom. 11:11), and "Salvation is nearer to us now than when we became believers" (Rom. 13:11). Second Corinthians 1:6 refers to "your consolation and salvation," and 7:10 speaks of "repentance that leads to salvation."

The verb *sōzō* is different, yet again. There are over fifty occurrences of the word in all four Gospels, nearly a dozen in Acts, and some twenty in Paul, excluding seven in the Pastorals. However, the word "save" occurs in so many different contexts that we cannot generalize about its meaning. What is clear is that "salvation" becomes so obviously a technical theological term in Paul that C. Anderson Scott and George B. Caird can speak of "the three tenses of salvation" in Paul.[31]

The upshot of all this is to repeat our comment on the *hermeneutical transparency* of the terms "save," "salvation," and "savior" on the basis of their distinctive use in Judges and elsewhere in the OT. The NT built on this. But such was its widespread use in other non-Jewish or pagan contexts that it may less frequently be used by Paul, Hebrews, and John than it would have been otherwise. Nevertheless, in Paul it remains an important theological term. The three-tense approach of Scott and Caird can readily *be illustrated from ordinary life today.* In the face of being on board a sinking ship, it may be said that the people in jeopardy *were* saved or *had been* saved from the sinking ship as a *past event;* that as the lifeboat took them to safety, they *were being saved* as a *present continuous process;* but, further, that they *would* or *will be* saved, as they land on *terra firma* as their *future* destiny.

---

30. Moulton-Geden 931.

31. C. Anderson Scott, *Christianity according to St. Paul* (Cambridge: CUP, 1927; 2nd ed. 1961); George B. Caird, with L. D. Hurst, *New Testament Theology* (Oxford: Clarendon, 1995), 118-35.

3. Two Further Transparent Presuppositions: Mediation and Sacrifice

(i) *Mediator, Mediation.* The Greek word *mesitēs*, "mediator," is linguistically already transparent. It means *one who stands between two parties,* derived from *mesos*, "middle," or "middle position." There is a verbal form in Greek, namely, *mesiteuō,* but this occurs only in Hebrews in the NT. The Hebrew seems to have no exact equivalent, even if *biyn* partly overlaps with it but usually means "perceive, discern, consider."[32] This does not imply that the *concept* is unimportant in the OT. It illustrates James Barr's work on the crucial distinction between *word* and *concept.* Many languages convey a specific *concept* by a series of *different words.* In the OT "to plead on behalf of" and "to declare on behalf of," and other phrases, serve as ways of expressing mediation. Moses is only one of many who mediate between Israel and God.

If we want a crystal-clear or transparent word picture of this, Moses provides an excellent example. C. Ryder Smith explains on one side "Moses' *unity with his people,*" especially by praying for them, and on the other his *representation of God,* especially by teaching them God's commands. Smith writes, "When he climbed the mount . . . *he was as a man torn in two.* His unity with his people was so vital that he was ready to die for them, yet he could not forsake Jehovah with them. It is the *tension* between these two passions that is the hall-mark of saviours [or *mediators*]."[33] Could there be a more transparent picture of mediation? The key text is Exodus 32:31-32: "Moses . . . said, 'Alas, this people has sinned a great sin; they have made for themselves gods of gold. But now, if you will only forgive their sin — but if not, blot me out of the book that you have written.'" Smith cites several other examples, including Elijah. He writes, "On Horeb Elijah was, as it were, *two men in one,* and the two struggled with each other."[34]

Just as Moses and Elijah are supreme examples of mediation in the OT, so Jesus and Paul constitute key examples in the NT. Paul explicitly states, "I have great sorrow and unceasing anguish in my heart. For I could wish that *I myself were accursed* (Gk. *anathema*) and *cut off from Christ* for the sake of *my own people,* my kindred according to the flesh" (Rom. 9:2-3).

32. A. Oepke, *"Mesitēs, mesiteuō,"* in *TDNT* 4:598-624; BDAG 634; BDB 106-8; G. Abbott-Smith, *Manual Greek Lexicon of the New Testament* (Edinburgh: T. & T. Clark, 1937), 285.

33. C. Ryder Smith, *The Bible Doctrine of Salvation: A Study of the Atonement* (London: Epworth, 1946), 32-33, italics mine.

34. Smith, *Bible Doctrine of Salvation,* 33, italics mine.

Paul stands in solidarity with Israel and in solidarity as an apostle with God. He, too, is *"torn in two"* as he seeks "to stand between" each side, God and the people of Israel.

This is another reason why we have tried to expound the situation of humankind under sin and alienation before moving on to the atonement. Oepke comments, "The theologically significant point is that *God cannot be approached at our pleasure, but only when He offers Himself for fellowship.* . . . The mediator, commissioned by God . . . stands over against God on the side of the community," but also as an agent on behalf of God.[35]

In Hebrews it is clear that humans have no natural right to enter the presence of God. The call, "Let us therefore approach the throne of grace with boldness" (Heb. 4:16), is due entirely to the high priestly mediation of Christ. The author of Hebrews uses Greek *mesitēs* three times: "Jesus . . . is the mediator of a better covenant" (8:6); "for this reason he (Christ) is the mediator of a new covenant" (9:15); and "Jesus, the mediator of a new covenant" (12:24). Each occurs in the context of Christ's high priesthood, sacrifice, and shed blood. Paul uses the word twice: in Galatians 3:19, of the mediation of the law by angels, and in 3:20, by way of explanation: "Now a mediator involves more than one party." Some uses in the biblical writings do not reach this high theological concept. Job pleads for a mediator in the sense of an arbitrator:

> There is no umpire (Gk. *mesitēs,* in LXX) between us,
>   who might lay his hand on us both. (Job 9:33)

Some have suggested that the absence of the word *mesitēs* from the Gospels suggests its lack of importance. But once again, this is to confuse *word* and *concept,* as Barr has argued.[36] We have only to elucidate the respective roles of "ascending" and "descending" mediators to see that Jesus fulfilled both roles. The *ascending* mediator stands between God and humankind in a *priestly* role, to plead to God on behalf of the people. Hebrews calls Jesus "a merciful and faithful high priest" (Heb. 2:17; cf. 3:1; 4:14-15; 5:5, 10); "a high priest forever" (6:20); and "a high priest, holy, blameless, undefiled" (7:26; cf. 7:27-28; 8:1, 3; 9:7, 11, 25). In 1 Peter 2:9, the people of God are "a chosen race, a royal priesthood," and in 1 Peter 2:5, "a holy priesthood, to offer spiritual sacrifices."

35. Oepke, *"Mesitēs, mesiteuō,"* 4:614, italics mine.
36. James Barr, *The Semantics of Biblical Language* (Oxford: OUP, 1961), 206-58.

A *"descending mediator"* stands between God and humankind in a *prophetic* role. Moses, Elijah, Amos, Hosea, Isaiah, and others spoke on behalf of God to the people. In the NT, this role was fulfilled mainly by apostles, but also by many others. Apostles and prophets are linked in Luke 11:49, "I will send them prophets and apostles." In Hebrews 3:1-2 we read, "Consider that Jesus, the apostle and high priest of our confession, was faithful to the one who appointed him." Whether we consider Moses, Peter, Paul, or the Twelve, they passed on the Word of God as descending mediators from God.

Nicholas Wolterstorff has written at length on the Word of God spoken both by God and by his mediating deputies. This is a concept made familiar today by secretaries and others who write and sign letters on someone's behalf.[37] In fact, this concept of mediation is full of *hermeneutical* possibilities for modern life, some of which are seldom fully explored. Wolterstorff's deputizing or secretarial example provides a hint of other possibilities.

(ii) *Sacrifice.* This term is also applied directly to Jesus Christ, by Paul, who writes, "Our paschal lamb, Christ, has been sacrificed" (Gk. *etythē Christos,* 1 Cor. 5:7), and by the author of Hebrews: "He (Christ) has appeared once for all at the end of the age to remove sin by the sacrifice of himself" (Gk. *hapax . . . dia tēs thysias autou,* Heb. 9:26), and "Christ . . . offered for all time a single sacrifice for sins" (Gk. *mian hyper hamartiōn . . . thysian,* Heb. 10:12).

The concept in the OT may not be quite as transparent as that of redemption, salvation, or mediation. The OT has at least five types of sacrifice. But those that relate to expiation or propitiation are almost as clear when they indicate *substitution* of the guilty by a sacrifice, or at least *solidarity* or *participation* between the sacrifice and the guilty.

First, the *minchāh,* or "meal offering," denoted simply a *gift* offered to God, usually in *thanksgiving.* Only in this broadest, weakest sense was the sacrifice of Christ an offering to God. The *minchāh,* in any case, was a bloodless gift. Second, the *shᵉlāmîm* were "peace offerings," which expressed *communion with God.* Normally the priest would take a part, the worshiper would take a part, and part would be offered to God. These were eaten in the sanctuary in the presence of God, as a symbol of *fellowship* with him. Third, the *'ōlāh,* or "burnt offering," expressed *dedication and devotion.* It was part of the *regular* morning and evening sacrifices of each day. Fourth, the enactment of five sacrifices formed a large part of the

37. Nicholas Wolterstorff, *Divine Discourse: Philosophical Reflections on the Claim That God Speaks* (Cambridge: CUP, 1995), 38-51.

ritual of the Day of Atonement (Heb. *yōm kippōrīm*). They constitute a special category, which includes the scapegoat (Lev. 16:21). A young bull is regarded as a sin offering, and a ram as a burnt offering. This bull is offered for the high priest (16:6), and one of the two goats is a *sin offering* for the people, and the other the *scapegoat* (16:8). Aaron (or his successors) is to lay his hand on the head of the live goat and confess over it all the sins of the people (16:20-22). This act is widely understood as one of *substitution* of the death of the sacrificial animal for the sins of the people. The act is also a *powerful visual aid or word picture of atonement.* Hebrews applies it to the sacrifice of Christ in 9:1-5, 6, 9. Equally striking as a word picture is the fifth category of sacrifice, the *'āshām,* or "guilt offering." Many scholars date it later on the ground that it features only in the so-called P texts, or Priestly strata of the OT. It arguably denotes *compensation, substitution,* and *expiation* or *propitiation.*

The fourth and fifth categories do present a relatively transparent picture of atonement. But many writers question and even attack the notion of *substitution* in these categories. The first objection is based on a misunderstanding. It is sometimes argued, as Whiteley does, that *substitution undermines* the notions of *participation* and *identification.* Whiteley insists that the atonement of Christ operates only on the basis "of our solidarity with him (Christ)."[38] He criticizes the three classic interpretations of substitution in Paul: Romans 8:3, 2 Corinthians 5:21, and Galatians 3:13-14, but his exegesis remains open to question. A second objection is also based on a misunderstanding. Supposedly it is said to look like an ancient version of child abuse, as if God the Father "sent" the Son to do a humiliating job in his place.[39] But we noted this objection when we discussed the *grace* of God as the *root* of the atonement, *not* its *fruit.* Further, we have noted how Barth, Moltmann, and Küng expound the humiliation of the incarnation and cross as profoundly involving the *humiliation of God.* Third, John Piper, Wayne Grudem, and others have written blistering criticisms of Chalke's work, saying that he has poured scorn on one of the most precious truths of the atonement. Grudem claims that Chalke is denying the heart of the gospel. This has given rise to much debate on the Internet, including the Atonement Debate sponsored by the London School of Theology.[40] N. T.

38. D. E. H. Whiteley, *The Theology of St. Paul* (Oxford: Blackwell, 1964, 1971), 130.

39. Steve Chalke, with Alan Mann, *The Lost Message of Jesus* (Grand Rapids: Zondervan, 2004).

40. Steve Chalke et al., *The Atonement Debate* (London: London School of Theology; Grand Rapids: Zondervan, 2008).

Wright argues that he is attacking only the "penal" aspect of "penal substitution." But some of his language does seem at the very least unguarded and one-sided. The fourth difficulty is that some try to make the concept of substitution an *exclusive* key to sacrifice and atonement. We should prefer to say that it is one of several *complementary* models, even if it remains an essential one. We discuss this further below, especially with reference to J. K. S. Reid.

To sum up this point, the reason why "sacrifice" seems less hermeneutically transparent than "redemption," "salvation," or "mediation" is that so many different effects are conveyed by the term. Some aspects clarify peace and reconciliation with God; others illustrate the logic of atonement. All are instructive but not utterly perfect representations of what they exemplify. That is why Hebrews looks to the one perfect sacrifice, which the OT simply prefigures.

Meanwhile *substitution* remains part of one of the more transparent word pictures of atonement. *Substitution and solidarity* are key notions today in many sports, especially football. There are four reasons to retain the idea. (1) Among the three *Greek prepositions* in this context, the word *anti,* "instead of," occurs in Mark 10:45 and Matthew 20:28.[41] The preposition *hyper* is broader, but usually also means "for the benefit of," "on behalf of," or "in the interest of" (John 11:50-52; 18:14; Rom. 5:7; 1 Cor. 5:7; 2 Cor. 1:11; 5:20; Gal. 2:20; 1 Thess. 5:10; Heb. 6:20; 1 Pet. 2:21).[42] (2) As J. K. S. Reid observes, in Paul and the NT there is "a rule of correspondence," for example, "because he lives, we shall live also"; and also "a *rule of contrariety:* Christ wins those benefits for us *who had himself no need of them.*"[43] (3) Substitution provides an *assurance* of salvation that is stronger even than identification, as Luther and Calvin argue. (4) Substitution does not offer an *alternative* to identification or participation. It undoubtedly involves active solidarity with Christ also.

All this suggests that "redemption," "salvation," "mediation," and "sacrifice" are either already virtually transparent terms for modern understanding, or at least readily explicable in hermeneutical terms with a little understanding of the OT. These transparent terms constitute the key *presuppositions* for understanding the atonement in the NT.

---

41. On *anti,* see BDAG 87-88.
42. BDAG 1030-31.
43. J. K. S. Reid, *Our Life in Christ* (London: SCM, 1963), 89-91, italics mine.

4. Complementary Models of the Atonement

The NT writers, especially Paul, state that Christ gave himself "for me" (Gal. 2:20), "for us," or "for our sins" (1 Cor. 15:3). Jeremias observes, "By an increasing number of comparisons and images, he (Paul) tries to make his hearers and readers understand the meaning of this 'for us,' i.e. the idea of Christ's vicarious death."[44] In addition to the four great transparent OT presuppositions of the atonement, Jeremias selects *four more explicit examples.* The first is the *sacrifice* of the Passover Lamb (1 Cor. 5:7), with which he couples new life on Easter morning, and the Day of Atonement and sin offering (Rom. 8:3).

A second theme is drawn from *criminal law.* "A second theme is used by Paul to illustrate how Christ took our place. It is borrowed from criminal law"; Jeremias cites the Suffering Servant in Isaiah 53, who bears "the punishment inflicted because of our transgressions" (Rom. 4:25; Col. 2:14).[45] In Colossians 2:14 Christ cancels the statement of debt that the criminal carried around his neck, on his way to execution.

A third theme is borrowed from the institution of *slavery.* The key words, Jeremias observes, are "to buy" (1 Cor. 6:20; 7:23), "to redeem" (Gal. 3:13; 4:5), and "with a price" (1 Cor. 6:20; 7:23). Christ redeemed us from slavery through his death.[46] We have noted the transparency of the word "redemption" above. Sacrifice, he adds, includes self-sacrifice out of love (1 Cor. 13:3). Slavery is associated with sin (Rom. 3:9), the law (Gal. 4:5), and God's curse (Gal. 3:13). We need to imagine the horror of life in bondage to appreciate "the wonderful ring of the word 'Redemption.'"[47]

A fourth theme, according to Jeremias, is "the ethical substitution consisting in Christ's *vicarious obedience*" (Rom. 5:18-19 and Gal. 4:4-5).[48] Christ's act of obedience ("the obedience of this one man") is offered in our place, and has contrasting effects with the disobedience of Adam. He concludes: the images may be different, but one and the same intention underlies these four themes: Paul wants to illustrate "the 'for us,' the sinless one taking the place of the sinners. He takes the very place of the ungodly (Rom. 5:6), of the enemies of God (5:10), of the world opposed to God (2 Cor. 5:19)."[49]

44. Joachim Jeremias, *The Central Message of the New Testament* (London: SCM, 1965), 36.
45. Jeremias, *Central Message,* 36-37.
46. Jeremias, *Central Message,* 37.
47. Jeremias, *Central Message,* 38.
48. Jeremias, *Central Message,* 38.
49. Jeremias, *Central Message,* 38-39.

Paul, in the first place, ransacks imagery from the *OT,* also from *criminal law, debt and finance, the sociological realities of slavery and liberation,* and the threefold meaning of redemption. He includes temple sacrifice, moral sacrifice, substitution, and "transference language" from one sphere of existence to another. How can anyone claim that all these images are foreign to the modern world? *Slavery, debt, the world of commerce, the world of sport,* and other contemporary examples suggest that only ignorance and lack of reading or understanding can render these terms other than *transparent.* Paul put as much energy and thought into *hermeneutics* as he did into theology.

We need simply add one further set of comments about his *distinctive* and original theme of *reconciliation,* and his more traditional theme of either *expiation* or *propitiation,* depending on how we translate the Greek word *hilastērion.* Since these themes are complex, we return to them in section 5, after we have looked at John and Hebrews.

Although he is also eager to transpose a purely *Jewish* terminology into one intelligible to the *Gentiles, John* appears to construct a very different world of terms and concepts. He begins his prologue with a Christ-centered exposition of the *logos.* Christ is the vehicle of the rational communication of the invisible God in language and action. "In the beginning was the Word (Gk. *ho logos*), and the Word was with God *(pros ton theon),* and the Word was God *(theos ēn ho logos)*" (John 1:1). Like Paul and the author of Hebrews, John uses whatever conceptual tools he can to render the gospel fully intelligible to Greek-speaking Jews and to Gentiles, whether they are Christian or not. In the Greco-Roman world, *Logos* speculation was closely parallel with Wisdom speculation, which would have been familiar, for example, to Philo, Josephus, Sirach, and the author of Wisdom of Solomon, as well as to many Hellenistic-speaking readers. Yet any links with Hellenistic concepts and language should not be exaggerated. Philo, for example, could never have said "the Word became flesh." A balanced introduction to the Gospel and its prologue is offered by George Beasley-Murray.[50] In the nineteenth and early twentieth century, Harnack had argued that the purpose of the prologue was to provide "intelligibility to Gentiles," and that it was not originally part of the main Gospel. But most scholars today see it as a key to the main body of the Gospel, with its themes of life, light, glory, and truth.

50. George R. Beasley-Murray, *John,* WBC (Nashville: Nelson, 1999), xliv-lxvi and 1-17; cf. Raymond E. Brown, *The Gospel according to St. John,* 2 vols. (London: Chapman; New York: Doubleday, 1966), 1:lii-lxxix and 4-37; and R. Alan Culpepper, "The Pivot of John's Prologue," *NTS* 27 (1980-1981): 1-31.

For Greek-speaking readers beyond the Holy Land, the *logos* remained a *revelatory* concept, which also underlined that the enfleshment of the Word was as much an act of *God* as an act of Jesus Christ. After all, "the Word was *God*" (John 1:1). What the Wisdom of God meant for many Jews, the *Logos* of God meant for many Greeks. In Philo, the *Logos* is a mediating agency, as Barrett and Sanders underline. In Philo, this can be an "idea" of God, and may also become God's agent in creation. The *Logos* is even called "High Priest," "Paraclete," image of God, and the firstborn of God, who controls the angelic world. T. W. Manson reminds us that John introduced the term *logos* without any prior explanation. He thereby confirms its familiarity to readers.[51]

What does this add to *complementary images of the atonement in Paul?* First, it underlines our first point: the atonement is in the first place an act of *God* and of God's *grace,* even if this is also *through Christ.* Second, the atonement and Christ bring *life* as well as light and truth. These themes occur not only in the prologue, but also throughout the Gospel (John 1:4; 3:15, 36; 4:14, 36; 5:24-29, 39, 40; 6:33, 35, 40, 47-48, 51-54, 63, 68; 8:12; 10:10, 28; 11:25; 12:25; 14:6; 17:2-3; 20:31; Gk. *zōē*). Light and truth involve judgment and self-knowledge. In contrast to popular interpretations of "lighten" or "shed light," *phōtizō* normally means "to shed light upon," in the sense of *expose,* or *judge* (1:9). Third, as in Paul, John portrays *Christ as Mediator,* who intercedes with God on behalf of his disciples, and reveals God's Word to them (14:8-9; 17:6-8 on revelation; and 17:9-24 on intercession, as well as 1:14, 14:6, and 18:37). Fourth, as is well known, in contrast to Paul's emphasis on Christ-union in his death and resurrection, John speaks of new birth, or birth from above (Gk. *gennēthē anōthen,* 3:3), in 3:3-10. Union with Christ, however, remains implicit in the image of the vine (15:1-11) and in eating the Bread of Life (6:35-58). John's imagery is also transformative. All these examples constitute transparent images to everyone, not only to Jews, often on the basis of the OT.

The Epistle to the Hebrews, likewise, uses words and concepts familiar especially to residents of Alexandria, as well as to Greek-speaking Jews and readers of the OT. Christ is "the exact imprint of God's very being" (Heb. 1:3). The theology of mediation, high priesthood, apostleship, prophecy, and sacrifice is carefully explained at length (4:14–10:18). This letter may require more concentration and reflection than Paul and John, but a patient thinker

---

51. T. W. Manson, *On Paul and John* (1963; reprint, London: SCM, 2012), 138, and C. K. Barrett, *The Prologue of St. John's Gospel* (London: Athlone, 1971).

will see the clear logic and structure of its argument about the *final and definitive work of Christ.* Like the Aaronic priests, Christ is duly appointed to his task; but unlike them, he is never replaced by successors, and does not need to make offerings for his own sins (5:1–8:7). He is one *in solidarity with sinners,* and one *in solidarity with God.* He is the definitive Mediator, the perfect Offering and perfect High Priest. He does not even mediate as a contingent "copy" (in Platonic language), but as a "heavenly" reality (9:11-14).

5. Expiation and/or Propitiation?
Paul's Distinctive Idea of Reconciliation

(i) *The Expiation-Propitiation Controversy.* Paul uses a rare word in the NT, which has one reference in Hebrews, namely, the Greek word *hilastērion.* It is usually translated as "expiation" in most modern versions, but was translated as "propitiation" in the KJV/AV and 1662 Book of Common Prayer (Rom. 3:25). The NRSV and NIV evade the controversy by translating the word "a sacrifice of atonement," and the NJB avoids it by translating "a sacrifice for reconciliation." But the REB and NEB have "the means of expiating sin," and the RSV has "expiation." The Greek of the LXX translates or represents Hebrew *kappōreth* from the verb *k-pp-r* in the Hebrew OT. The common meaning in everyday Greek is "to propitiate," but Barrett argues that it can only mean "expiate" in relation to God. In purely lexicographical terms, F. Danker favors "means of expiation" (or "sacrifice of atonement") in Romans 3:25, but accepts "place of propitiation" in Hebrews 9:5 and many OT passages. But he quotes T. W. Manson and others as defending "propitiation" in Romans 3:25.[52] Grimm-Thayer (1901) is only a little different.[53]

What is the difference in meaning, and what is at stake here? There is no doubt that "expiation" denotes "means of dealing with sin." C. H. Dodd compares it rather crudely with disinfecting a stain. David Hill points out, however, that while the two terms can often be interchangeable, "Propitiation is primarily and directly orientated towards a deity or offended person."[54] In others words, *it is a personal term.* In pagan religions it clearly means to render a deity favorable or to appease the deity. But the meaning, as Hill asserts,

52. BDAG 474; on the verb *hilaskomai,* cf. 473-74.
53. Grimm-Thayer 301. This translates the Greek as "relating to appeasing or expiating, having placating or expiatory force."
54. David Hill, *Greek Words and Hebrew Meanings* (Cambridge: CUP, 1967), 23.

depends on *context*. He translates the word in Hebrews 9:5 as "mercy seat," where Hebrew *kappōreth* denotes the lid of the ark, or mercy seat. Clearly in Romans 3:25 God is *already* gracious, and propitiation therefore cannot mean *to appease* or to *make* gracious. But Hill makes the key point that the presupposition of *hilastērion* is that of a *personal relationship*. It concerns "the personal nature of the breach with God caused by sin."[55] Moreover, as well as grace, the themes of judgment and even wrath feature in the context of Romans 3.

We shall conclude shortly that each translation has different advantages. Meanwhile, we note briefly the terms suggested in no fewer than seven standard commentaries of Romans. (1) Barrett translates the word as "bloody sacrificial death," rejects "propitiate," and sympathizes with "expiate."[56] Dodd rejects "propitiate" even more forcefully. (2) Anders Nygren seeks to avoid the controversy by translating the term as "mercy seat," as in Hebrews 9:5.[57] (3) Ernst Käsemann rejects this view, since the community in Rome is largely Gentile, and would not have recognized the OT allusion, and because the place of offering is not the offering itself. It denotes *expiation for forgiveness,* which maintains the *personal* dimension.[58] (4) F. J. Leenhardt insists on the Pauline appeal to Levitical sacrifice, and (later, also like Nygren) refers to the *covering of the ark,* in spite of Käsemann's criticism.[59] (5) Cranfield argues that in the LXX twenty-one of twenty-seven occurrences refer to the mercy seat, as in Hebrews 9:5. But in Romans 3:25 it does not mean this "unambiguously." The purpose is *propitiatory,* through Christ as both priest and victim. He cites the work of Leon Morris, and rejects that of Dodd. The material "would still indicate that a propitiatory sacrifice is in mind." He also cites 2 Maccabees 7:30-38 and 4 Maccabees 6:27-29 and 17:20-22.[60] (6) Dunn argues rightly that it is "a complex of ideas," a public display of Christ's shameful death. It is certainly *a sacrifice* or *blood of sacrifice:* "the sinner's sin was transferred to the spotless sacrifice."[61] (7) Joseph Fitzmyer sympathizes both with "means of expiation" and with "propitiate" (in the light of arguments from Morris

55. Hill, *Greek Words,* 37.

56. C. K. Barrett, *The Epistle to the Romans* (London: Black, 1962), 77-78.

57. Anders Nygren, *Commentary on Romans* (London: SCM, 1952), 156-60.

58. Ernst Käsemann, *Commentary on Romans* (London: SCM, 1980), 97-98.

59. Franz J. Leenhardt, *The Epistle to the Romans* (London: Lutterworth, 1961), 102-6.

60. C. E. B. Cranfield, *The Epistle to the Romans,* 2 vols., ICC (Edinburgh: T. & T. Clark, 1975, 1979), 1:214-18.

61. James D. G. Dunn, *Romans,* 2 vols., WBC (Dallas: Word, 1988), 170-74.

and Lohse). But later, like Käsemann, he doubts whether readers at Rome would appreciate the LXX meanings.[62]

In the end, the answer to these claims may be fairly straightforward. On one side, we cannot dispense with "propitiation," because as Hill, Morris, and Cranfield point out, the word concerns *a personal relationship,* unlike "expiation." "Expiation" is too impersonal and can seem mechanistic. On the other side, the translation "expiation" guards against any quasi-pagan notion of appeasement, and against any undermining of the *grace of God in initiating* the atonement. It does not seek to "change" a reluctant God. God caused and purposed it!

(ii) *Reconciliation.* It was part of Paul's genius to introduce "reconciliation with God" to denote *the reversal of sinners' situation of alienation* from God, or even hostility toward him. The Greek noun is *katallagē,* "reconciliation," or "reestablishment of an interrupted or broken relationship," while the verb *katallassō* denotes "the exchange of hostility for a friendly relationship," or "to reconcile."[63] Paul uses the word in Romans 5:10-11, 11:15, 1 Corinthians 7:11 (of husband and wife), and 2 Corinthians 5:18-19. *"Reconciliation" is fully transparent in meaning today:* it is used of conflicts within the family when they are solved; of industrial relations between employer and employee or trades unions; of nations that have been at war; and in many areas of everyday life. Romans 5:10 constitutes a classic example from Paul: "If while we were enemies, we were reconciled to God through the death of his Son, much more surely, having been reconciled, will we be saved by his life."

In 2 Corinthians 5:18-19 Paul states that God has "reconciled us to himself through Christ," and calls the gospel "the ministry of reconciliation." The message in 5:20 is, "Be reconciled to God." Outside the four major epistles, Paul states that "God was pleased to reconcile to himself all things." Although the readers were "once estranged and hostile in mind," God has now "reconciled" them (Col. 1:20-22).

At the beginning of the twentieth century, James Denney insisted that reconciliation "is a work which is finished . . . a work outside of us, in which God so deals in Christ with the sin of the world that it shall no longer be a barrier between himself and man."[64] Denney is right to emphasize its finished nature in terms of the atonement, but through the Holy Spirit it is also

---

62. Joseph A. Fitzmyer, *Romans,* AB 33 (New York: Doubleday, 1992), 348-50; cf. Leon Morris, *The Apostolic Preaching of the Cross,* 3rd ed. (Grand Rapids: Eerdmans, 1965), 155-57.

63. BDAG 521.

64. James Denney, *The Death of Christ: Its Place and Interpretation in the New Testament* (London: Hodder and Stoughton, 1922), 145.

to be appropriated in life. Hence Paul urges, "We entreat you on behalf of Christ, be reconciled to God" (2 Cor. 5:20).[65]

We have yet to consider historical interpretations of the atonement. But in terms of biblical vocabulary, the presuppositions and expositions of what was at stake and its meaning are virtually all transparent, and need little additional hermeneutical reflection. Certainly when the historical, linguistic, and theological background has been explained, only the most obtuse may still claim that this language is unintelligible to the modern world. We have tried to show that each major theme is potentially transparent in hermeneutical terms, especially when we approach the subject in the light of humankind's prior alienation and misdirected desire.

One other general application, at least, arises from all this. On one side stand theological acts that are entirely actions of *God:* redemption, salvation, substitution, grace, and atonement. If they were not entirely God's work, they would not be pure gifts, which originate from God's grace. On the other side, this does not make them any the less gifts that are actualized and made effective as we appropriate them, and respond to them in faith and obedience. Hence they involve *identification with Christ,* participation in Christ's work, and response to Christ as Mediator. Too often in theology these have been regarded as exclusively alternative emphases. We emphasize *both* their complete character as sheer *gift,* which gives us assurance and recognizes God's grace, *and* the need for daily practical, existential *response.*

65. Cf. Murray Harris, *The Second Epistle to the Corinthians,* NIGTC (Grand Rapids: Eerdmans, 2005), 434-52.

CHAPTER IX

Why Consider Historical Theologies of the Atonement? Historical Thought and Hermeneutics

Historical theology is part of systematic theology, but it comprises not merely dusty records of the past. For one thing, explorations by thinkers through the centuries often explicate biblical material with interpretations that speak to their time, and even to our time. Second, they are part of the corporate witness of the church. Third, in the best examples these become *hermeneutical resources* for better *understanding, communicating, applying,* and *illustrating* the biblical material that has been examined. Finally, Christians do not *exclusively* draw on the Bible. As Richard Hooker and others have insisted, our sources should first and foremost be *Scripture;* but they include the *corporate witness* of fellow Christians in the *church;* and they sometimes provide an assessment and judgment, over time, of what may count as *reasonable* and valid belief.

This gives us perspective, context, and space to distinguish *the true from the false.* This is important both for our own belief system and for debate with others, especially with those who may not share our beliefs. Christians are not, or should not be, gullible individualists. If one example of this is required, Anselm showed how the person and work of Christ constitute an integral whole, and how the atonement is bound up with God's governance of the world. Rightly or wrongly, he also borrows analogies of the honor of God from the feudal customs in his own day, which constitute a possible hermeneutical bridge to the concerns of this era. This analogy may also partly form a bridge to our own age.

1. The Atonement in the Early Church

(i) *The Subapostolic Writings. 1 Clement* (c. 96) is mainly concerned about church unity and order. But its author, Clement, bishop of Rome, also had other concerns, not least the moral implications of his readers' redemption. Hence he writes, "Let us look steadfastly to the blood of Christ, and see how precious that blood is to his Father, because it is poured out for our salvation."[1] Similarly, after quoting part of Paul's poem on love in 1 Corinthians 13, he adds, "For the sake of the love that He (God) had towards us, Jesus Christ our Lord gave his blood (Gk. *to haima autou edōken*) by the will of God for us, his flesh for (Gk. *hyper*) *our flesh, and his life for our lives."*[2] Then Clement confirmed our first point in the previous chapter, that *God's grace* initiated the cross, and he provided more than a hint about sacrificial death and substitution.

Ignatius (c. 35–c. 108), bishop of Antioch, wrote similarly fewer than ten years later, on his way to martyrdom in Rome. He wrote of identification with Christ in his death and resurrection. He opened his epistle *To the Smyrnaeans:* "You are established in immovable faith, as if nailed to the cross of the Lord Jesus Christ in flesh and spirit, and confirmed in love by the blood of Christ."[3] Ignatius interpreted Christ's work as being "carried up to the heights by the engine of Jesus Christ, that is, the cross, using the Holy Spirit as a rope."[4] He offered a summary of the atonement: Christ died "for our sake (Gk. *di' hēmas*) so that believing in his death you may escape death."[5]

Polycarp (c. 69–c. 155), bishop of Smyrna, frequently quoted NT passages, and provided a direct line of continuity between John, Irenaeus, and other leaders in Asia and probably Rome. For example, he quoted 1 Peter 2:21 and 24: "Christ Jesus, 'who bore our own sins in his own body on the tree . . . ,' endured all things for our sake that we might live in him."[6] He began this letter with a reference to the faith of the Philippians, which bore "fruit unto our Lord Jesus Christ, who endured for our sins, even to the suffering

1. *1 Clement* 7.4; *ANF* 1:7; also in Kirsopp Lake, *The Apostolic Fathers,* 2 vols. (London: Heinemann; Cambridge: Harvard University Press, 1965), 1:18-21; the manuscripts differ slightly.
2. *1 Clement* 49.6; *ANF* 1:18; Lake, *The Apostolic Fathers,* 1:93-95.
3. Ignatius, *To the Smyrnaeans* 1.1; *ANF* 1:86; Lake, *The Apostolic Fathers,* 1:252-53.
4. Ignatius, *To the Ephesians* 9.1; *ANF* 1:53; Lake, *The Apostolic Fathers,* 1:182-83.
5. Ignatius, *To the Trallians* 2.2; *ANF* 1:66; Lake, *The Apostolic Fathers,* 1:212-15.
6. Polycarp, *Epistle to the Philippians* 8.1; Lake, *The Apostolic Fathers,* 1:293.

of death, whom God raised up."[7] We noted that *life* constituted a Johannine theme.

The dating of the *Epistle of Barnabas* remains uncertain, but most date it between 70 and 150. "Barnabas" attacked the sacrificial system of Judaism, and regarded Jesus Christ as its fulfillment. The letter placed Isaiah 53:5-7 in the context of the *substitutionary* death of Christ. Alluding to Isaiah, Barnabas asserted, "The Lord endured to deliver up his flesh to corruption . . . for the remission of sins, that is, by his sprinkled blood."[8] In the next verse (5.2) he quoted Isaiah 53:5, 7 word for word, adding, "The Scripture relates partly to Israel, partly to us." Later he added, "The Lord endured to suffer for our life."[9] In chapter 7 he regarded the sacrifice of Isaac as a type *(typos)* of the sacrifice of Christ.[10]

Justin Martyr (c. 100–c. 165) belongs broadly to the period of the early apologists. He wrestled with Paul's statement in Galatians 3:13, about Christ's redeeming us from "the curse of the law by becoming a curse for us." He considered the passage in Deuteronomy to which Paul appealed: "Cursed is everyone who hangs on a tree" (Deut. 21:23), and compared it to Deuteronomy 27:26. He wrote, "The whole human race will be found to be under a curse" (Gk. *hypo kataran*), and then cited Deuteronomy 27:26. His argument was that Christ took upon himself the curse that was due to us. In spite of Whiteley's exegesis, Justin clearly regarded this as *substitutionary.*[11]

Justin also took up the theme of "the tree" as a metaphor or image for various approaches to the atonement. The Scriptures, he said, declare the work of Christ in many ways: "the tree of life" in Genesis; the event when Moses "cast a tree into the waters of Marah, which were bitter, [but] he made sweet" (Exod. 15:23); and God's appearing "from a tree to Abraham . . . near the oak in Mamre . . . even as our Christ was crucified on the tree."[12] At other times, however, he made a nonmetaphorical statement: "By his blood Christ cleanses those who believe in him."[13]

For the first seventy years after the NT era, then, *precisely the same gospel of the atonement was written about, preached, and taught* as that of the apostles themselves. The earliest writings emphasized especially substitu-

7. Polycarp, *Epistle to the Philippians* 8.1; Lake, *The Apostolic Fathers,* 1:293.
8. *Barnabas* 5.1; Lake, *The Apostolic Fathers,* 1:355.
9. *Barnabas* 5.5.
10. *Barnabas* 7.3; Lake, *The Apostolic Fathers,* 1:365; cf. Gen. 22:1-14.
11. Justin, *Dialogue with Trypho* 95.1; cf. 94; ANF 1:246-47.
12. Justin, *Dialogue with Trypho* 86; ANF 1:242.
13. Justin, *1 Apology* 32; ANF 1:173; cf. *Dialogue with Trypho* 74.

tion. Christian tradition had its roots firmly in the soil of the NT from the very beginning. It is irrelevant to cite the writings of proto-Gnosticism. The Church Fathers, especially Irenaeus and Tertullian, utterly repudiated this as falsifying the NT, and as outside mainstream Christian churches.

The *Epistle to Diognetus* is anonymous, and is of very uncertain date (although probably from the late second century). It emphasizes the death of Jesus Christ on the cross. This was clearly for the forgiveness of sins (5.1-3). In a justly famous passage, the writer asks, "For what else could cover our sins except his (Christ's) righteousness? In whom was it possible for us sinners to be justified (Gk. *dikaiōthēnai*), except in the Son of God alone? *O sweet exchange* and unexpected benefits! — *that the wickedness of many should be hidden in One who was righteous, and the righteousness of one justify many wicked!*"[14]

(ii) *The Ante-Nicene Church Fathers. Irenaeus of Lyons* (c. 130–c. 200) studied in Rome, and became the church's outstanding theologian of the second century. He continued the apostolic tradition, but also had other things to teach, which remain relevant to the present day. He had roots in both the Eastern and Western Churches, and confidently defended the apostolic tradition, which he called "the rule of faith." He also defended the belief that the apostolic faith was founded on revelation from God to the apostles. He expounded the Johannine theme that God made himself visible in Christ.

Irenaeus added a distinctive aspect, which he also regarded as true to apostolic teaching. He declared, "The Son of God . . . when he was incarnate, and was made man, commenced afresh (Lat. *in scipso recapitulavit*) the long line of human beings, and furnished us . . . with salvation, so that what we had lost in Adam — namely to be according to the image and likeness of God — *we might recover in Christ*."[15] (The translation "commenced afresh" comes from the Syriac.) More distinctively, this theme is even more explicit elsewhere. Irenaeus wrote: "In Him (Christ) dwells all the fullness of the Godhead," and again, "All things are gathered together by God in Christ."[16] Clearly the whole chapter is quoting biblical texts, and this quotation comes, respectively, from Colossians 2:9 and Ephesians 1:10. In Ephesians 1:10, "To gather up all things in him" (in Christ) translates the Greek *anakephalaiō-sasthai ta panta en tō Christō*.

14. *Epistle to Diognetus* 9.2-6, italics mine.
15. Irenaeus, *Against Heresies* 3.18.1; *ANF* 1:446.
16. Irenaeus, *Against Heresies* 1.3.4; *ANF* 1:320.

Recapitulation, or *anakephalaiōsis,* then, is *based on biblical and Pauline thought.* Danker translates the verb *anakephalaioō* as "to sum up, to recapitulate, to bring everything together," with particular reference to Ephesians 1:10. On Romans 13:9, he suggests "a commercial frame of reference for the understanding of a 'ledger entry.' "[17] Where the NRSV has "to gather up all things in him," RSV and NEB have "unite all things in him"; J. B. Phillips translates "should be consummated in him," and C. L. Mitton suggests "sum up" or "bring separate items into a single whole."[18] According to Irenaeus, the reference to Adam supports the notion of *recapitulating our bad fate in Adam by a new creation in Christ.* This lies at the root of the Eastern Orthodox theme of *deification.* Christ *reverses the effects of Adam's fall.* Irenaeus seems to have made explicit a theme that is genuinely implicit in Pauline ideas of the atonement. He has four references to Ephesians 1:10, and gives careful consideration to the image of God. He also depicts the atonement as victory over evil powers.

Tertullian (c. 150–c. 225) shares Irenaeus's concern for adherence to apostolic tradition.[19] In accordance with our argument above, Tertullian speaks of Jesus Christ as Mediator. He begins a distinctive "Latin" type of theology, which is also represented by Cyprian in the third century, by Hilary of Poitiers and Ambrose of Milan in the fourth century, and finally by Augustine in the fourth and fifth centuries. Christ is called the Mediator in *On the Resurrection.* In the final chapter of this work Tertullian writes that human identity "is in safe keeping in God's presence," through that "most faithful Mediator between God and man, and man to God."[20] He not only underlines the theme of mediation, but also supports those scholars who argue that reconciliation is two-sided rather than simply one-sided. This is partly due to his serious view of sin, which will reappear in Anselm and Calvin. In the same passage, following Irenaeus, he says Christ will "restore" (Lat. *reddet*) God to man.

In practice, Tertullian did not add much more of substance than Irenaeus on the subject of the atonement. R. S. Franks observes, "Tertullian has indeed no definitely formulated doctrine of the work of Christ beyond that of Irenaeus."[21] He did, however, also regard Christ's work as bringing in a new

17. BDAG 65.
18. C. Leslie Mitton, *Ephesians,* NCB (London: Oliphants, 1976), 55-56.
19. Tertullian, *Prescription against Heretics* 16-19.
20. Tertullian, *On the Resurrection* 63; *ANF* 3:593.
21. Robert S. Franks, *The Work of Christ: A Historical Study of Christian Doctrine* (London and New York: Nelson, 1962), 76-77.

moral law, and introduced the terms "merit" *(meritum)* and "satisfaction" *(satisfactio)* from Roman law.[22] Anselm will take up these terms, together with Tertullian's view of God as Lawgiver.

Origen (c. 185–c. 254). Clement of Alexandria, Origen's predecessor, had relatively little distinctive material on the atonement, apart from stressing the revelation of God through the *Logos,* Jesus Christ. Origen, by contrast, expounded systems of doctrine in *First Principles* (Lat. *De principiis;* Gk. *Peri archōn*), and also expounded the atonement in his commentaries and in his work *Against Celsus.* Two of the more distinctive themes include (following Clement) the *rationality* of the death of Christ for us, and the atonement as a *victory,* notably over evil powers. Origen wrote: Christ, the eternal Word and Wisdom, "suffered as one who was wise and perfect, whatever it behoved them to suffer, who did all for the good of the human race. . . . There is nothing absurd in a man having died . . . for the sake of piety . . . to overthrow the power of that evil spirit, the devil, who had obtained dominion over the whole world."[23]

In *De principiis* Origen regarded Christ as "the Word and the Wisdom of the Father" who shared "glory with the Father," and asserted that "the Author and Creator Himself was required to restore . . . obedience, which had been corrupted and profaned."[24] In *Against Celsus* Jesus Christ is Mediator, speaking God's Word, and also as one who would "pray and make intercessions, and offer thanksgivings and supplications to Him (God)."[25] Christ, Origen declared, is one with the Father (John 10:30; 17:22).[26] He explicitly cited Paul in 1 Corinthians 2:6-8: "We speak wisdom . . . not of the rulers of this age, who are doomed to perish"; if they had understood, "they would not have crucified the Lord of glory."[27]

A distinction must be made, however, between Origen's early and late writings. The early years show more of Plato's influence, and probably the teaching of Clement, his predecessor. The early works centered on Christ as Wisdom and *Logos.*[28] The *Logos* tended to be impassable, or incapable of suffering. Like Clement, he called Christ a physician to sinners. But in his late writings he used more biblical material. Redemption was expounded in

22. Tertullian, *Of Patience* 10; *ANF* 3:713.
23. Origen, *Against Celsus* 7.17; *ANF* 4:617.
24. Origen, *De principiis* 3.5.6; *ANF* 4:343.
25. Origen, *Against Celsus* 5.4; *ANF* 4:544.
26. Origen, *Against Celsus* 8.12; *ANF* 4:643.
27. Origen, *De principiis* 3.3.1-2; *ANF* 4:334, and 4.1.13; *ANF* 4:361.
28. Origen, *Commentary on John* 2.29, 33, and 6.15-16, 28.

terms of "buying back," and the theme of sacrifice became prominent.[29] He argued for the universality of redemption, citing Colossians 1:20. He stated that Christ's death wards off evil demons: "He was crucified . . . underwent his death voluntarily on behalf of the human race . . . the means of removing wicked spirits."[30] The ransom and victory motifs emerged, which Aulén later took up in the twentieth century. In spite of a few departures from it, Origen maintained the apostolic tradition of the NT, which is virtually unbroken until at least 250. The later ante-Nicene thinkers, Cyprian, Hippolytus, Novatian, and Lactantius, in the main had other concerns.

2. The Post-Nicene Period

To avoid merely providing a historical record of the past, and to stress hermeneutical relevance of the past for today, we shall focus only on those writers who remain of particular relevance to today. In effect, the most distinctive of the post-Nicene Fathers include Athanasius, Gregory of Nyssa, and Gregory of Nazianzus in the Eastern Church, and Hilary, Ambrose, and Augustine in the West.

(i) *Athanasius* (c. 296-373). Athanasius wrote *On the Incarnation of the Word of God,* a theological classic, when he was around twenty years of age. One major theme of this book is the *victory and triumph* of Christ over evil. He followed the Genesis account of the Fall, concluding that, as an effect, we were "not just to die only, but remain in the state of death and of corruption. . . . The law of death, which followed from the Transgression, prevailed upon us, and from it there was no escape."[31] If death did not hold dominion, God would not have been true to himself and his word.

Athanasius wrote that Jesus Christ, "Taking a body like our own . . . surrendered His body to death in place of all, and offered it to the Father. This He did out of sheer love for us" (2.8). He continued, "The Word perceived that corruption could not be got rid of otherwise than through death. . . . It was by surrendering to the death . . . as an offering and sacrifice free from every stain, that He forthwith abolished death for His human brethren by the offering of the equivalent" (2.9). This was worthy of God and God's honor,

29. Origen, *Homily on Luke* 14.4; *Homily on Exodus* 6.9.
30. Origen, *Against Celsus* 1.31; *ANF* 4:409.
31. *St. Athanasius on the Incarnation* (London: Mowbray, 1953), chap. 2, sects. 3 and 6 (29 and 32). References to this work, to chapter number followed by section number, have been placed in the text.

and put an end to the law of death. God knew the limitations of humankind, but "What was God to do in the face of this dehumanising of mankind," and loss of knowledge of himself (3.13)? Hence, in Christ Godhead is vested in human nature, though he is the Power and Word of God.

In chapter 4 Athanasius expounded the death of Christ, "to settle man's account with death, and free him from the primal transgression" (4.20). He died to ransom all. Athanasius continued, "He had come to bear the curse that lay on us . . . by accepting the accursed death (Gal. 3:13) . . . the ransom of all." This is "death on behalf of all" (4.25). Athanasius finished by expounding the resurrection (5.26-32). The resurrection constitutes "a very strong proof of the destruction of death and its conquest by the cross" (5.27). Death is like a tyrant who has been conquered. Those who disbelieve in the resurrection have "no support in facts." Athanasius added a postscript in refutation of the Jews and of the Gentiles.

Athanasius has argued that *the atonement fully follows* both the creation and the Fall, which introduced the dominion over death. Hence our sequence of topics in this book is not only "Lutheran"; Athanasius also fully stressed God's grace and kindness, and Christ's substitutionary sacrifice. He emphasized the integral relation of the incarnation of the *Logos* and the death of Christ. During his argument he appealed to biblical sources, including 2 Corinthians 5:14, Hebrews 2:9-10, and 1 Corinthians 15:21-22. He also took up the Johannine themes of knowledge of God, life, and revelation. As in Irenaeus and the Eastern Church, the image of God also played a part. In 6 he appealed to OT passages against the Jews, and in 7–8 to rational proofs against the Gentiles.

In a memorable sentence, used regularly to explain "deification" in the Eastern Orthodox Church, Athanasius wrote, "He, indeed, assumed humanity that we might become God (Gk. *autos enēnthrōpēsen, hina hēmeis theopoiēthōmen*), and He manifested Himself by a body that we might receive the idea of the unseen Father" (8.54). Franks described this work of Athanasius as "epoch-making" for its clarity and theology.[32] He gave, Franks urged, "fresh Pauline points of view" on the subject; he was systematic in his account, and had "gathered up and woven together the threads of doctrine which before him were floating loosely apart," and he also avoided a notion of "price paid to the devil," in favor of the doctrine of satisfaction to God.[33]

---

32. Franks, *The Work of Christ*, 49.
33. Franks, *The Work of Christ*, 51.

In addition to his great work *On the Incarnation,* Athanasius included comments on the atonement in *Four Discourses against the Arians* (c. 356-60). J. K. Mozley, however, insisted that his doctrine changed, and we should attend to the later writings, while P. J. Leithart gives his comments more careful consideration.[34] Mozley's impression may be exaggerated. Athanasius increasingly spoke of the *Logos* and used Johannine passages, but he still regarded Christ's death as a redemptive power over evil forces.[35] He wrote, "Being Word and Son of God, (he) bore a body and became Son of Man, that having become Mediator between God and man, he might minister the things of God to us, and ours to God."[36] Christ "took our infirmities, not being infirm, and hunger, not hungering," for our sake.[37] Leithart well argues for his use of a "double lens," where his Christology is well related to the atonement.

(ii) *Gregory of Nyssa* (c. 330-395). This Eastern Father is best known for his notorious analogy of redemption with a baited fishhook, in his *Great Catechism.* Allegedly its biblical foundation was 1 Corinthians 2:8, in which Paul spoke of "the rulers of this age" who failed to understand God's wisdom and purpose in the death of Christ, "for if they had, they would not have crucified the Lord of glory." Gregory writes, "In order to secure that the ransom on our behalf might be easily accepted by him who required it, the Deity was hidden under the veil of our nature, that so, as with ravenous fish, the hook of the Deity might be gulped down along with the bait of the flesh, and thus . . . light might vanish."[38] God's purpose was that Christ was "transfused throughout our nature, in order that our nature might . . . become itself divine, rescued as it was from death."[39]

Gregory's starting point was that corrupted humankind needed a physician. This emerged from the Gospels and from Clement of Alexandria. But to the pagan Greeks of the day, the biggest stumbling block to Christian faith was the incarnation. Hence Gregory discusses Christ's "being born and nurtured as a man, and even . . . tasting death." Why could not "the medical man" simply cure "the diseased part"?[40] Gregory regards humankind as

---

34. Peter J. Leithart, *Athanasius* (Grand Rapids: Baker Academic, 2011), 120-46, and J. K. Mozley, *The Doctrine of the Atonement* (London: Duckworth, 1915), 105-6.

35. Athanasius *Discourse* 1.42 and 43; *NPNF,* ser. 2, 4:331.

36. Athanasius *Discourse* 4.6; *NPNF,* ser. 2, 4:435.

37. Athanasius *Discourse* 4.7.

38. Gregory of Nyssa, *The Great Catechism* 24; *NPNF,* ser. 2, 5:494.

39. Gregory of Nyssa, *The Great Catechism* 25; *NPNF,* ser. 2, 5:495.

40. Gregory of Nyssa, *The Great Catechism* 17; *NPNF,* ser. 2, 5:489.

"legally purchased as a slave."[41] On this basis Gregory questionably infers that the ransom price must be "paid" by Christ to the devil, while the devil sought Christ's divine power. Franks comments: "Therefore God needed to hide it beneath the veil of flesh."[42] Hence Gregory formulated what Cave calls "a metaphor which to modern readers seems grotesque," namely, that of a greedy fish.[43] The devil had deceived humankind; so God deceived the devil. But Scripture does not imply that the "ransom" is "paid" to anyone: costliness is part of the metaphor, but *"payment to"* is *not*. The ransom is *from* bondage *by* the blood of Christ *to* new creation and life in Christ.

(iii) *Gregory of Nazianzus* (c. 330-390). Gregory rightly protested against the notion of the devil having any "right" over humankind. In his *Second Oration on Easter,* he explicitly asked, "To whom was the blood offered that was shed for us, and why was it shed . . . the precious . . . Blood of our God and High-priest and sacrifice? . . . If to the Evil One, fie [Old English expression of disgust] upon the outrage (Gk. *pheu tēs hybreōs*)!"[44] Ransom could neither be owed to the robber, nor owed to the Father, for "it was not by him that we were being oppressed." Nevertheless, "Humanity must be sanctified by the Humanity of God, that He might draw us to Himself by the mediation of His Son . . . to the honour of the Father."[45] Gregory therefore stresses mediation and redemption, but some of his sayings may seem to suggest that the primary means of the atonement is the incarnation, for example: "He assumed the worst that he might sanctify it by his incarnation."[46] Yet he also spoke of Christ's "sacrifice and priesthood . . . sacrificed to God."[47] At Easter he referred to the slain Lamb.[48] Finally, in his *Fourth Theological Oration* he quoted Galatians 3:13, in which Christ became a "curse"; and thereby took away "the sin of the world; and became a new Adam to take the place of the old."[49]

The lesson for today is that Gregory of Nazianzus returns to the language of sacrifice, redemption, and incarnation, duly purged of all misunderstand-

41. Gregory of Nyssa, *The Great Catechism* 22; *NPNF*, ser. 2, 5:493.

42. Franks, *The Work of Christ*, 55.

43. Sydney Cave, *The Doctrine of the Work of Christ* (London: University of London Press and Hodder and Stoughton, 1937), 106.

44. Gregory of Nazianzus, *Second Oration* 22 (*Orations* 45); also *NPNF*, ser. 2, 7:431.

45. Gregory of Nazianzus, *Second Oration* 22.

46. Gregory of Nazianzus, *Letter 101 to Cledonius; NPNF*, ser. 2, 7:439.

47. Gregory of Nazianzus, *In Defence of His Flight* 95; *NPNF*, ser. 2, 7:223.

48. Gregory of Nazianzus, *Oration* 1.1.

49. Gregory of Nazianzus, *Oration* 30.5 (*Fourth Oration); NPNF*, ser. 2, 7:311.

ing and exaggeration. He fully understood the need for the renewal of humankind through Christ.

(iv) *Ambrose* (c. 339-397). In the West, Hilary of Poitiers (c. 315-368) and Ambrose of Milan added relatively little to this doctrine beyond what was in Athanasius, and in effect their work was absorbed by Augustine. But Ambrose nevertheless did make some bold advances. He wrote, for example, "He (Christ) was made sin and a curse, not on his own account but on ours . . . for 'Cursed is everyone that hangs on a tree.' "[50] Franks went so far as to write: "Everywhere it is the death of Christ which is made central. In no Western theologian before or after . . . is there greater emphasis on the cross."[51] Through the flesh, Christ became "one with us. . . . Through . . . the death of the body did he loose the chains of death, and for the undertaking of death Christ became the death of death" (1 Cor. 15:54-55).[52] In *On the Christian Faith*, book 2, Ambrose expounded the death of Christ at length. He quoted Philippians 2:7-8, "Christ became obedient to the point of death — even the death on a cross," and asserted that in the passion "the power of the Trinity is one . . . both in and after the Passion itself."[53] Redemption, Ambrose wrote, came not with God's naked power but with the temptations, poverty, and humility of Christ: "O excellent remedy, healing our wounds and sins!"[54] He cited Galatians 3:13 at least twice: Christ, "who broke our curses became a curse."[55] Merit becomes transferable in Ambrose's thought.

(v) *Augustine* (354-430). Augustine, in the words of Franks, which Kelly endorses, not only "sums up in himself what has gone before, but also incorporates with it new and original elements."[56] This is all transmitted to Western medieval theology, and much to Luther and Calvin. The *grace of God* is seen as the root of the whole work of Christ. Augustine wrote, "For what good work could a lost soul perform, except in so far as he has been delivered from his lostness?"[57] Like other Church Fathers, he regarded Jesus Christ as "the One and true Mediator, reconciling us to God by the sacrifice

50. Ambrose, *On the Christian Faith* 5.14.178; *NPNF*, ser. 2, 10:306.

51. Franks, *The Work of Christ*, 82.

52. Ambrose, *On the Christian Faith* 3.11.84; *NPNF*, ser. 2, 10:255.

53. Ambrose, *On the Christian Faith* 2.10.84 and 85; *NPNF*, ser. 2, 10:235.

54. Ambrose, *On the Christian Faith* 2.11.92 and 93; *NPNF*, ser. 2, 10:235-36.

55. Ambrose, *On the Christian Faith* 2.11.94; *NPNF*, ser. 2, 10:236.

56. Franks, *The Work of Christ*, 87, and J. N. D. Kelly, *Early Christian Doctrines*, 3rd ed. (London: Black, 1977), 390.

57. Augustine, *Enchiridion* 8.30, in Augustine, *Confessions and Enchiridion*, ed. Albert Cook Outler, LCC 7 (Philadelphia: Westminster, 1955), 356; also *NPNF*, ser. 1, 3:247.

of peace . . . one with Him to whom He offered [Himself]."[58] He repeated the same theme in the *Confessions.*[59] Augustine used a variety of images to describe the atonement, including reconciliation and release from bondage.[60] In his discussion of predestination, he regarded the atonement as bringing new creation and new life.

Virtually all the images found in the NT can be found in Augustine. As in John 15:13, Augustine wrote, "Our Redeemer says, 'Greater love has no man than this, that a man lay down his life for his friends.'"[61] In the same passage he wrote, "By his death the one and most real sacrifice was offered up for us . . . whence principalities and powers held us fast . . . to pay for its penalty." In his *Reply to Faustus the Manichaean,* Augustine attacked Faustus for finding strange "the curse pronounced on sin, on death, and on human mortality, which Christ had on account of man's sin, though He Himself was sinless."[62] In the *Enchiridion* he repeated that Christ was "the one Mediator between God and man"; he fully discussed Christ and Adam; and he argued that Christ's life and ministry "provided an example of obedience by the God-Man, that the fount of grace might be opened up."[63]

It would be tedious and repetitive to gather together the numerous citations of biblical language about the atonement. We may conclude that, as Kelly comments, "Augustine adopts several avenues of approach."[64] We have tried to adopt this approach in speaking of complementary models, together with the initiating emphasis on the grace of God in Christ. We may now note how strongly Augustine has influenced medieval and Reformation thought.

3. Anselm and Abelard

Augustine's theology dominated the Western medieval church up to around 1100. Anselm and Abelard emphasized, respectively, the "objective satisfaction" and subjective "moral influence" aspects of the atonement, rather than the variety of images Augustine had stressed.

58. Augustine, *On the Trinity* 4.14.19; *NPNF,* ser. 1, 3:79.

59. Augustine, *Confessions* 10.68.

60. Augustine, *Epistles* 187.20, and *On the Trinity* 13.15.19; *NPNF,* ser. 1, 3:177.

61. Augustine, *On the Trinity* 4.13.17; *NPNF,* ser. 1, 3:78.

62. Augustine, *Reply to Faustus the Manichaean* 14.4; *NPNF,* ser. 1, 4:208.

63. Augustine, *Enchiridion* 18.108, in *Confessions and Enchiridion,* 404; *NPNF,* ser. 1, 3:272.

64. Kelly, *Early Christian Doctrines,* 191.

(i) *Anselm* (1033-1109). Anselm rightly understood the atonement as not simply an expression of God's love in Christ for humankind, but he saw how closely the *atonement was bound up with Christology,* or the person of Christ, and also with *God's governance of the world.* Only Christ, who was *both man and God,* could atone for the sin of the world. To dismiss Anselm because he also drew on the feudal imagery would be a mistake: every theologian has to consider hermeneutical bridges to the readers of the day.

Anselm's major work on the atonement was *Why God Became Man.* It is available in various editions.[65] We considered this work above, under the doctrine of sin. Anselm had rejected as inadequate the "recapitulation" approach of Irenaeus, the approach of "redemption from the devil" of Gregory of Nyssa, and an account of the atonement as *only* an expression of the love of God. The *reason* for the incarnation and death of Christ is deeper, involving *God's governance* of the world, and *Christ's person.* Mozley commented, "If any one Christian work, outside the canon of the NT, may be described as 'epoch-making,' it is the *Cur Deus Homo* of Anselm."[66] Denney called it "the truest and greatest book on the atonement that has ever been written."[67] It is only fair, however, to admit that not everyone shares these verdicts. Adolf Harnack dismissed the work as "ecclesiastical," and G. B. Stevens accused it of holding an unethical view of sin.

Anselm seeks to combine a stress on God's grace with an equal stress on God's justice. God cannot let an offense against his honor go unpunished without reparation, but in his grace he also provided for this. Anselm argues that only God can put right the damage that sin has done. If someone other than God were to try to redeem humankind, Anselm writes, "In that case man would in no sense have been restored to the dignity he would have had, if he had not sinned."[68] He cites Paul as saying that humankind is sold as "slaves of sin" (Rom. 6:20) or "sold into slavery under sin" (Rom. 7:14). But there are at least two reasons why Christ alone can redeem us: because it is God's will, and God loves us; and because Christ is one with God, just as he was one with humankind. Anselm calls him *the God-man.* He cites John 6:38, "I came not to do my own will, but the will of him who sent me," and Romans 8:32, the Father "spared not his only Son but delivered him up for us all" (111).

65. Anselm, *Why God Became Man,* in *A Scholastic Miscellany: Anselm to Ockham,* ed. Eugene R. Fairweather, LCC (London: SCM; Philadelphia: Westminster, 1956), 100-193.

66. Mozley, *Doctrine of the Atonement,* 125.

67. James Denney, *The Atonement and the Modern Mind* (London: Hodder and Stoughton, 1903), 116.

68. Anselm, *Why God Became Man,* 106. Page references have been placed in the text.

Anselm stresses that Christ freely underwent death: "God did not compel Christ to die, when there was no sin in him, but Christ himself freely underwent death" (113). In christological terms, the atonement depends on Christ's being both God and man, being sinless, and dying voluntarily for the sake of others.

In chapter 11 Anselm introduces his key concept of sin. He writes, "To *sin is the same thing as not to render his due to God*" (119, italics mine). Then he draws mostly from feudal law the following principle: "It is not enough for someone who violates another's honour to restore the honour, unless he makes some kind of restitution that will please him who was dishonoured, according to the extent of the injuring and dishonour" (119). Hence sinners need to make "satisfaction" to God.

It is at this point that Anselm introduces the phrase "it is *fitting*." He writes, "If it is not fitting for God to do anything unjustly or without due order, it does not belong to his freedom or kindness to forgive unpunished the sinner who does not repay to God what he took away" (121). This arguably is the lynchpin of most "objective" theories that causes such controversy. Often traditional or conservative Christians may be heard to say, "God *'must'* punish sin." Those who follow the "subjective" approach to the atonement respond, "Why?" Anselm offers an answer. It is because God "must" (*logical* "must") remain consistent with his own nature, his own promise, and his governance of the world. "Must" does not denote external compulsion. It is internal and logical, like the statement "God cannot lie." The phrase "it is fitting" excludes any idea of external compulsion. God remains sovereign, but he also remains faithful to his Word and his character.

Hence from chapters 19 to 25 (which end part 1), the words "must" and "cannot" constantly recur. Anselm argues that there "must be satisfaction" for sin (136-38). He declares, "God requires satisfaction according to the greatness of the sin" (139). The satisfaction can "necessarily be done through Christ" (145).

This sets the stage for book 2 of Anselm's work. Again, he stresses in chapter 5 that necessity is not compulsion. But chapter 6 is the keystone: "No-one but *God* can make this satisfaction. . . . No one ought to make it except *man*. . . . *It is necessary for a God-Man to make it*" (151, italics mine). Jesus Christ is this God-man. Jesus Christ as Man took his place in Adam's race, but born from a virgin (152-53). Yet Anselm insists on "the unity of person of God and man" as a single person (154-55). He is sinless, and therefore "not obliged to die," but does so voluntarily "for God's honour, freely . . . to make satisfaction for man's sin" (158, 160). His death outweighs all sins. The death of Christ "effected to benefit not only those who were alive at the time, but others as well" (167). Anselm has "shown a sure way by which God might have taken manhood" (175). Finally, Anselm explained, "If the Son willed to give to another what is owing to himself, could the Father rightly forbid him?" (180). Thus *the work of Christ presupposes orthodox Christology.*

As we might expect, the paradigmatic liberal theologian, Adolf Harnack, saw this as akin to Tertullian's view of placating an injured and angry God. Others argued that the whole notion of "satisfaction" for offending a person of high honor comes simply from feudal Europe or from Roman law. It even matched, they claimed, a medieval doctrine of *penance,* rather than the NT and Luther on *repentance.* Expressed in crude terms, it might suggest a numerical quantification of human sin and divine honor.

On the other hand, Anselm highlighted *God's* place in the work of Christ, and in the governance of the world. His careful analysis of "must" or "necessity" rejects the notion of *external* compulsion. Further, Anselm's approach found respect among the Protestant Reformers, as well as in the Catholic Church. Like so many approaches to the atonement, it adds insight and hermeneutical riches to the NT, as long as it is not treated as an *exclusive* and *comprehensive* model. It remains one of the most important expositions of the subject in historical theology. Colin Gunton comments, "Anselm's is one of the first essays in systematic theology of the atonement attempting to bring intellectual shape to an area where there had been much disorder."[69] The Catholic theologian Balthasar rigorously defends Anselm's notion of "ontological union" with God in Christ, as opposed to some one-sided obsession with "justice" or "delight in . . . the blood of the innocent."[70]

(ii) *Abelard* (1079-1142). Abelard represents a virtually opposite approach to that of Anselm, whose work he criticized. He is often regarded as the main representative of the *"subjective,"* exemplarist, or *"moral influence"* view of the atonement. He was later followed, with some modifications, by Faustus Socinus (1539-1604), Friedrich Schleiermacher (1768-1834), and Albrecht Ritschl (1822-1889). Franks argues: "He has reduced the whole process of redemption to one single clear principle, viz. the manifestation of *God's love* to us in Christ, which awakens an answering love in us. Out of this principle Abelard endeavours to explain all other points of view."[71] In Wayne

69. Colin E. Gunton, *The Actuality of Atonement: A Study in Metaphor, Rationality, and the Christian Tradition* (Edinburgh: T. & T. Clark, 1988), 87.

70. Hans Urs von Balthasar, *The Glory of the Lord: A Theological Aesthetics,* vol. 2 (Edinburgh: T. & T. Clark, 1984), 249.

71. Franks, *The Work of Christ,* 146, italics mine.

Grudem's words, "It robs the atonement of its objective character, because it holds that the atonement had no effect on God himself."[72]

On the other hand, Abelard was a sophisticated philosopher and theologian who wrote on the Trinity, undertook exegesis of biblical passages, and expounded ethics, as well as the atonement. Further, his work on the atonement was largely confined to short comments in his *Commentary on Romans,* especially on Romans 3:19-26, and it is inconceivable that this short passage conveys his comprehensive view of the subject. He had been a pupil of the nominalist Roscelin and of the realist William of Champeaux, and also of Anselm of Laon. Bernard also criticized him for putting reason in the place of faith.

Abelard's preoccupation with *love* probably relates to his tragic love affair with Heloise, as his work on ethics seems to suggest. Excerpts from three of his works are conveniently collected in English in Fairweather's *Scholastic Miscellany.*[73] In his exposition of Romans 3:19-26 he is certainly correct to say that (1) "justified" means "not having any previous merits"; (2) "God . . . first loved us"; (3) "grace" is "a free and spiritual gift of God"; and (4) "his blood" means "his death."[74] But his fifth definition is more questionable: namely, that "the showing of his justice" means "his love"; even if everything flows from God's love. Similarly he is right to question how far we should press "the price of blood paid for our redemption," but his description of the "demand" for "the blood of an innocent person" as "cruel and wicked"[75] remains open to question.

Again, Abelard is right to say: "He has more fully bound us to himself by love; with the result that our hearts should be re-kindled by such a gift of divine grace"; but this is open to question when he seems to imply that this is all we need to say about the atonement.[76] This is why Morris and others, rather than dismissing his approach, quote the well-known saying, *"Theories of the atonement are right in what they affirm, but wrong in what they deny."*[77] It is, however, impossible to consider Abelard's comprehensive thought on the basis of short and scattered writings, although he certainly reacted against Anselm's approach. Nevertheless, he is generally regarded

72. Wayne Grudem, *Systematic Theology* (Nottingham: IVP, 1994), 581-612.

73. Fairweather, *A Scholastic Miscellany,* 276-99; in Latin, Migne, PL 178.

74. Abelard, "Exposition of Romans," in *A Scholastic Miscellany,* 279.

75. Abelard, "Exposition of Romans," 183.

76. Abelard, "Exposition of Romans," 183-87.

77. Leon Morris, *The Cross in the New Testament* (Exeter: Paternoster; Grand Rapids: Eerdmans, 1969), 399, italics mine.

as the father figure of the "moral influence" or "subjective" approach, which forms one important, if not comprehensive, approach to the atonement. In Ritschl and his school, this became more pronounced, as Ritschl attacked the relevance of priesthood and sacrifice in Hebrews.

4. The Reformation: Luther and Calvin

(i) *Martin Luther* (1483-1546). Luther has written such a huge quantity of material relating to the cross that it is difficult to offer a coherent interpretation. The overriding factor, however, is his adherence throughout to the biblical writings. This especially marks his early writings from 1517-1518, namely, his *Commentary on Hebrews* and the *Heidelberg Disputation*. These are collected conveniently in English in the volume edited by James Atkinson, *Luther: Early Theological Works.*[78]

On Hebrews 5:1 Luther writes, "When Christ cried out for us on the cross, it was then in that atoning work where all human values are reversed, that his priesthood reached its moment of highest perfection" (102). On 8:3 he interprets "the offering" of Christ as for "expiation of sins" (149). On 9:14, "dead works" defile the conscience, but from these "a man is cleansed through the blood of Christ" (171). Luther asserts, "This sacrifice of the NT has been perfected and absolutely ended. . . . Christ has died but once. . . . A body is offered in some unique way" (185, 187, and 191, on Heb. 9:27 and 10:4).

Admittedly, we expect Luther to follow biblical passages in a commentary. But the *Heidelberg Disputation* reflects the same character. On the "reversal of values" exhibited in 1 Corinthians 1:18-25, Luther comments, "The theologian of *glory* says bad is good and good is bad. The theologian of *the cross* calls them by their proper name" (292; art. 23 of the *Heidelberg Disputation,* italics mine). In other words, the work of Christ on the cross *turns merely human values upside down,* with the result that the sinner is placed in a right relationship with God. In Luther, the work of Christ is always intimately bound up with justification by grace through faith. Luther then quotes Galatians 3:13 on the same page: "Christ has freed us from the curse of the law." In article 28 he asserts that *grace is not a response of love, but a*

---

78. *Luther: Early Theological Works,* ed. James Atkinson, LCC 16 (London: SCM; Philadelphia: Westminster, 1962), 19-250 and 274-307. Page references have been placed in the text.

cause of it: "The love of God . . . creates the object of its love" (295). Thus Luther anticipates our first main point in the previous chapter that the grace of God *initiated* the atoning work of Christ. Again it is related to justification by grace: "I have come to call not the righteous but sinners" (Matt. 9:13).

In his later writings Luther fills out the details of this biblical beginning in the light of other writers. He writes in the *Large Catechism* (1530), which includes a reflection on the creeds, "As Redeemer . . . he . . . brought us from Satan to God, from death to life, from sin to righteousness. . . . He suffered, died, and was buried that He might make satisfaction for me and pay what I owe (Lat. *culpa*) not with silver and gold, but with His own precious blood . . . in order to become my Lord."[79] This was intended to be an explanation, not least for children and "simple" readers, of the reference in the creeds to the suffering, death, and resurrection of Christ.

This exposition recalls a number of biblical passages, including 1 Peter 1:18-19, "You were ransomed . . . not with . . . silver or gold, but with the precious blood of Christ, like that of a lamb . . . without defect or blemish." But it also reflects the theology of Anselm, without perhaps its explicitly legal character. Gustav Aulén, whom we consider below, was right to urge that Luther emphasized victory and defeat in his theology of the atonement, but possibly wrong in underrating Luther's emphasis on sacrifice, expiation, and substitution. Indeed, in Luther's sermon for Good Friday on Luke 24:36-47, he wrote, "If God's wrath is to be taken away, and I am to obtain grace and forgiveness, someone must merit this, for God . . . cannot remit the punishment and wrath, unless payment and sacrifice is made . . . [by] the Son of God Himself."[80] In Harnack's words, Luther treated all the schemata of traditional theology.

(ii) *John Calvin* (1509-1564). The main difference between Luther and Calvin was not one of substance, but one of coherence and system. Chapters 12 to 17 of book 2 of the *Institutes* expound Christ's work as Mediator: as prophet, priest, and king, and his participation in human nature. Calvin stressed the necessity of the incarnation clearly, and clearly taught "penal substitution." He wrote, "Man, who by his disobedience had become lost should . . . pay the penalties for sin. Accordingly our Lord came forth as true man and took the person and the name of Adam, in order to take Adam's

79. Luther, *The Large Catechism* (St. Louis: Concordia, 1921), X, part II of the Creed, art. 2.

80. Luther, "Second Sermon in Luke 24:36-47," in *Luther: Sermons of Martin Luther,* vol. 2 (St. Louis: Concordia, 1983), 344.

place in obeying the Father, to present our flesh as the price of satisfaction to God's righteous judgement, and, in the same flesh, to pay the penalty that we had deserved."[81] In the same section he argued that, since "neither as God alone could he feel death, nor as man alone could he overcome it, he coupled human nature with the divine . . . to atone for sin." Jesus Christ was the God-man, as Anselm calls him.

Calvin discussed the offices of prophet, priest, and king in separate sections, but always in relation to Christ's atonement. As priest, Jesus Christ opens *access to God,* because God's righteous curse draws our access to him, but Christ, to perform this office, had to come forward with a sacrifice. By this sacrifice, he argued in the same section, "He wiped away our guilt and made satisfaction for our sins" (2.15.6). Elsewhere he wrote, "The guilt that made us liable for punishment has been transferred to the head of the Son of God. We must, above all, remember his substitution, lest we tremble and remain anxious throughout life" (2.16.5).

Among Calvin's reasons for expounding "penal substitution" lies the *wonderful assurance of reconciliation with God,* which this doctrine brings. He repeats: "If the effect of his shedding of blood is that our sins are not imputed to us, it follows that God's judgement was satisfied by that price" (2.17.4). There is no contradiction, for Calvin, between God's mercy and his justice. Christ "took the punishment upon himself . . . and with his own blood expiated the sins which rendered them (humankind) hateful to God . . . and duly propitiated God the Father. . . . On this basis [Christ] founded peace between God and man" (2.16.2). But the phrase "hateful to God" is virtually hypothetical. For Calvin, following Paul, stresses that God's *grace and love initiated* the process of redemption and atonement. In other words, humankind *would have been* hateful had not God's grace intervened. A few lines of summary cannot do justice to the numerous biblical passages Calvin cites. These include Galatians 4:4-5; "a ransom for many" in Matthew 20:28; the famous (Greek) *hilastērion* (propitiation/ expiation) verse in Romans 3:25; and especially "For our sake God made him (Christ) to be sin . . ." in 2 Corinthians 5:21 (2.16.5; 3.16.5; 2.16.6; and many others). In Christ, he writes, we see "the whole sum of our salvation" (2.16.19).

It is not surprising that many have misunderstood and caricatured Calvin's doctrine. One writer, Cave, argued that "the penal theory . . . has tended

81. John Calvin, *The Institutes of the Christian Religion,* trans. Henry Beveridge, 2 vols. (Grand Rapids: Eerdmans, 1989), 2.12.3. References have been placed in the text.

to make God appear not loving, but vindictive."[82] In more popular theology today, as we have noted, Steve Chalke has berated evangelicals for holding to this doctrine. But this ignores the careful emphasis of Calvin, J. K. S. Reid, and most others, in regarding the grace of God as *initiating the whole process.* God the Father, moreover, as Moltmann urges, is utterly involved in the cost of the atonement. We discussed these issues in the previous chapter. Anselm, Luther, and Calvin may have relied on this model of the atonement, but hardly exclusively or without qualification. We cannot dispense with it, as long as we recognize that there are complementary models of the atonement. Above all, as Calvin demonstrates, no other model provides such full *assurance* of reconciliation and faith.

In the immediate *post-Reformation period, Socinus* (1539-1604) rejected the approaches of Augustine, Anselm, Luther, and Calvin, and looked back to Duns Scotus. *Jacob Arminius* (1560-1609) was loyal to Reformed theology more clearly than many realize, but he did attack Calvin for his view of human freedom and predestination. *Hugo Grotius* (1583-1645), a Dutch jurist, tended to follow Arminius, adding ideas of his own.

5. Varied Approaches in the Modern Period

In the modern period perhaps the greatest classics include Gustaf Aulén's *Christus Victor;* Colin Gunton's *The Actuality of Atonement;* several works, including *The Crucified God,* by Jürgen Moltmann; and Wolfhart Pannenberg's *Systematic Theology,* among others. From the earliest modern period, we need briefly to summarize Schleiermacher and Ritschl. But others deserve note also. These include Dorner, Thomasius, Coleridge, Maurice, Dale, Westcott, Moberly, and Denney. Virtually all these thinkers are discussed in R. S. Franks, *The Work of Christ,* and some are considered in John Macquarrie's *Jesus Christ in Modern Thought.* More recently Leon Morris (1914-2006) produced books on the atonement in *The Apostolic Preaching of the Cross* (1955) and *The Cross in the New Testament* (1965), in which he defends a conservative, "objective" view. Other works also deserve careful consideration as major studies of the atonement, including Jürgen Moltmann's work *The Way of Jesus Christ* (Eng. 1990). Further, Barth, Brunner, Pannenberg, Küng, and Rahner have written outstanding systematic theologies or broader studies that include the work of Christ.

82. Cave, *Doctrine of the Work,* 167.

(i) *Friedrich Schleiermacher* (1768-1834). Schleiermacher had accepted an orthodox view of the atonement in his youth, as a pietist. Later he combined a liberal interpretation of orthodox faith with an appreciation of Kant and Romanticism. He tried to hold together the person and work of Christ. He wrote, "The peculiar activity and exclusive activity of the Redeemer imply each other, and we are inseparably one in the self-consciousness of believers."[83] Because Schleiermacher emphasized Christ's solidarity with humankind, many argue that he regarded him as different from humankind *only in degree,* although Macquarrie and McGrath differ in their assessment of this question. Schleiermacher wrote, "The Redeemer, then, is like all men in virtue of the identity of human nature, but is distinguished from them all by the constant potency of his God-consciousness, which was a veritable existence of God in him."[84] In general, he rejected notions of substitution and expiation, and held an exemplarist or "moral influence" view, roughly in effect following Abelard. Christ's suffering was "an absolutely self-denying love."[85]

(ii) *Albrecht Ritschl* (1822-1889). Ritschl has traditionally been regarded as a typical nineteenth-century liberal theologian. But more recently James Richmond has sought to establish a more balanced picture.[86] Ritschl takes closer account of biblical material than Schleiermacher, but in the end he tends to offer an account of the atonement that has perhaps more in common with Abelard than with Anselm. He seeks to stress the *interrelatedness of Christ's person and work,* seeing the establishment of the kingdom of God in mainly ethical terms, but primarily through his work as prophet, priest, and king.[87] This threefold vocation entails his sufferings.[88] But Christ is *not the bearer of vicarious punishment.* He represents, as priest, the *community of the kingdom,* and as prophet and king conveys God's exemplary *love.*

(iii) *Horace Bushnell* (1802-1876), *Robert Dale* (1829-1895), and *James Denney* (1856-1917). These thinkers represent utterly different theologies, but all tended to adopt a particular stance in the context of the controversy between the "objective" and "subjective" interpretations of the atonement.

83. Friedrich Schleiermacher, *The Christian Faith* (Edinburgh: T. & T. Clark, 1989; orig. 1821), sect. 92, 374.

84. Schleiermacher, *The Christian Faith,* sect. 94, 385.

85. Schleiermacher, *The Christian Faith,* sect. 104, 458.

86. James Richmond, *Ritschl: A Reappraisal* (New York: Collins, 1978).

87. Albrecht Ritschl, *The Christian Doctrine of Justification and Reconciliation,* 3 vols. (Clifton, N.J.: Reference Book Publishers, 1966; orig. 1870-1874), especially 3:428-29.

88. Ritschl, *Justification,* 3:448-49.

Bushnell stood in the *liberal tradition,* although he called it "progressive orthodoxy." He stressed the role of *metaphor and analogy* in expounding the atonement: for example, the analogy of a mother who vicariously suffered for her child. In reaction against Anselm's and Calvin's view, he asked, "To what, on the transaction of the cross, can God's abhorrence, by any possibility fasten itself?"[89] He was heavily influenced by Schleiermacher and Coleridge, and argued that the biblical sacrificial system offers no more than *symbols or analogies* of atonement. It could be argued that Charles Hodge's emphasis on "literal" meaning arose partly as an overreaction against Bushnell, his liberal rival.

By contrast with Bushnell, Dale and the firmly conservative Denney expounded an "objective" account of the atonement. Denney expounded biblical material in the Gospels, Acts, and Epistles, and concluded, "Something is done which enables God *to justify the ungodly* . . . and at the same time to appear signally and conspicuously *a righteous God.*"[90] He insisted that on the one hand the death of Christ is related essentially to sin; but on the other, it springs entirely from the love of God.

(iv) *Gustaf Aulén* (1879-1977). This Swedish theologian of note wrote the classic work *Christus Victor.*[91] He subtitled it "An Historical Study of the Three Main Types of the Idea of the Atonement." He wanted to move away from the well-worn debate, "objective" view versus "subjective" view, by introducing a *third* approach to the atonement, which regarded it as *Christ's victory over evil forces,* or "the Atonement as a Divine conflict and victory" (20). Aulén called this the "classic" and "dramatic" view of the NT and Church Fathers. He approved of the Eastern Orthodox formulation of *"deification":* "Christ became man that we might be made divine" (34).

Aulén appealed for this view especially to *Irenaeus.* Irenaeus had declared: Christ came "that he might destroy sin, overcome death, and give life to men" (35; Irenaeus, *Against Heresies* 3.18.7). He did not regard the main issue as "any infringement of justice," but at the cross to "overcome tyrants which hold man in bondage" (43, 50). He did not underrate the place of sacrifice, but he did stress *"restoration,"* like Irenaeus.

Aulén appealed to most of the Fathers, including Origen, Athanasius,

89. Horace Bushnell, *The Vicarious Sacrifice* (New York: Scribner, 1871), 399.

90. James Denney, *The Death of Christ: Its Place and Interpretation in the New Testament* (London: Hodder and Stoughton, 1922), 167, italics mine.

91. Gustaf Aulén, *Christus Victor: An Historical Study of the Three Main Types of the Idea of the Atonement* (London: SPCK; New York: Macmillan, 1931). Page references have been placed in the text.

the Cappadocian Fathers, Chrysostom, Ambrose, Augustine, and Leo. He also appealed to all NT passages that mention "ransom" or evil power, for example, Mark 10:45, 1 Corinthians 2:6, and Colossians 2:15. His most controversial argument is that "Luther returns to the classic type" (160). Some regard this as an exaggeration. The truth is that Luther appealed to a wide *variety* of approaches. But Aulén himself did not dismiss other models. He merely dismissed a tendency to rely on one of the other two exclusively. His exegesis may also occasionally seem strained. His appeal to Origen, Athanasius, and the Cappadocian Fathers seems to reflect firmer ground.

   (v) *Colin Gunton* (1941-2003). Gunton also contributed a classic modern study in his *The Actuality of Atonement* (1988), which he subtitled "A Study in Metaphor, Rationality, and the Christian Tradition."[92] He had two aims. One was to show that interpretations of, and approaches to, atonement were *complementary, not alternatives.* The other was to exhibit the *value and power of metaphors* among images of atonement. He regarded Kant, Schleiermacher, and Hegel as indirectly responsible for the "intellectual and cultural poverty" that characterizes much of our age. He singled out especially Hegel's devaluation of "images" *(Vorstellungen)* in religion, as against the critical "concept" *(Begriff)* in philosophy. Metaphor, Gunton argued, was "an indispensable means for the advance of cognitive knowledge and understanding" (17). Janet Martin Soskice and Paul Avis also argued this convincingly. Metaphor and discovery occur together "with metaphor serving as the *vehicle* of discovery" (31). He appealed for this explicitly to Paul Ricoeur, Eberhard Jüngel, and Janet Martin Soskice, as well as to Coleridge.

   In the course of more detailed theological argument, Gunton challenged the comprehensiveness of Aulén's approach, and showed concern that he advocated "too triumphalist a view of the atonement" (58). He valued the victory motif as a metaphor, rather than "the laws for a *theory* of the atonement" (61). This approach also tended too readily to personify the devil, which seems to happen in Gregory of Nyssa. "Evil powers" may include "political, social, economic, and religious structures of power," as George Caird, Oscar Cullmann, and others have maintained (65).

   In his chapter 4 Gunton considered the justice of God, and corrected misunderstandings of Anselm. God governs the universe in a way analogous to the duty of the feudal ruler "to maintain the order of rights and obligations

---

92. Colin E. Gunton, *The Actuality of Atonement: A Study in Metaphor, Rationality, and the Christian Tradition* (Edinburgh: T. & T. Clark, 1988). Page references have been placed in the text.

without which society would collapse" (89). He affirmed the grace and love of God, but insisted on "some objective righting of the balance" in the governance of the universe (91). Here he appealed to P. T. Forsyth, Balthasar, and Barth, as well as to Anselm and Luther. This governance is "the central metaphor" (112).

In chapter 5 Gunton sought to rescue the concept of "sacrifice" from being regarded as an outworn, "dead" metaphor. He carefully examined sacrifice in the OT, together with work by Mary Douglas and Frances Young. In this respect, he argued, Calvin was faithful to priesthood and sacrifice in Hebrews, and to the passage about "correct exchange" that we noted in the early *Epistle to Diognetus.* He concluded, "There are in Calvin elements of a substitutionary understanding of the atonement; indeed it seems unlikely that any conception that remains true to the Bible can avoid it" (130). The two final chapters return to Gunton's regular theme of the Holy Trinity, and to the need to reconcile the various approaches to the atonement. He concluded: *Jesus is "our substitute because he does for us what we cannot do for ourselves"* (165, italics mine).

Among Gunton's eighteen or so books, this book is a masterpiece. It seems to address a central nerve in the debate, and should not be underestimated.

(vi) *The Major Theologies of Barth and Balthasar.* We have tried to keep each chapter of this book to a comparable length. Hence we cannot embark on serious discussion or survey of six late-twentieth-century theologians we cite as very important. They deserve detailed consideration, but their works are too massive to be squeezed into a few lines. Nevertheless, we should select certain features that broadly indicate this approach.

Karl Barth (1886-1968) spoke of "the Judge judged in our place" and insisted upon a robustly orthodox exposition of the "for us" of Christ's work.[93] Jesus Christ, he declared, is "our Representative and Substitute. . . . Jesus Christ was and is 'for us' in that He took our place."[94] The incarnation, as well as the cross, is an act of God in Christ, which showed his "self-humiliation."

Hans Urs von Balthasar (1905-1988) matched the quantitative output of Barth, and also, while being a Catholic writer, greatly respected Barth's theology. He agreed with Barth's emphasis on prevenient grace and divine sovereignty, and with his critique of the Enlightenment. He defended Anselm, writing, "Anselm's Benedictine, contemplative reason is aesthetic in a

93. Barth, *CD* IV/1, 211 and 214.
94. Barth, *CD* IV/1, 230 and 231.

new and original way," in the "glorious form of order."[95] He shared Anselm's concern for *God, the Trinity, and his relation to the world,* in his exposition of the atonement.

(vii) *Jürgen Moltmann* (b. 1926). Moltmann writes extensively on the atonement, but especially in *The Crucified God, The Trinity and the Kingdom of God,* and *The Way of Jesus Christ.* One of his most distinctive contributions is to ask: *"What does the cross of Jesus mean for God himself?"*[96] Moltmann regards "the outcast and forsaken Christ" as "the visible revelation of God's being for man."[97] In this respect he follows Luther. In a later work, he argues, *"A God who cannot suffer cannot love either,"* and God's love is what *initiates* the whole Christ event of Calvary.[98]

The mythological language of liberalism, Moltmann argues, is anthropocentric; the NT proclaims in narrative the relationship of the Father, the Son, and the Holy Spirit. This applies, for example, to the account of the baptism of Jesus. The "cup" of the cross implies "horror in the face of 'the death of God.' . . . Abandonment by God is the 'cup.' . . . God is silent."[99] In *The Way of Jesus Christ* he rejects "Jesusology," and traces the vocation of Christ in solidarity with "the poor, the hungry, the unemployed, the sick . . . oppressed and humiliated people."[100] His work is more profound and subtle than can be indicated by a few quotations, but these suggest his general angle of approach.

(viii) *Wolfhart Pannenberg* (1928-2014). Pannenberg rightly interweaves the person and work of Christ, to which he devotes three extensive chapters, or nearly two hundred pages, in the second volume of his *Systematic Theology* (Ger. 1991; Eng. 1994).[101] He begins with the starting point: "Only God himself could be behind this event, i.e. by sending his Son into the world (Gal. 4:4; Rom. 8:3)."[102] But Pannenberg does not restrict his treatment of the atonement only to volume 2 of his *Systematic Theology.* He provides an

---

95. Balthasar, *Glory of the Lord,* 18, 211-59.

96. Jürgen Moltmann, *The Crucified God: The Cross as the Foundation and Criticism of Christian Theology* (London: SCM, 1974), 201.

97. Moltmann, *The Crucified God,* 208.

98. Jürgen Moltmann, *The Trinity and the Kingdom of God: The Doctrine of God* (London: SCM, 1981), 38, italics mine.

99. Moltmann, *Trinity,* 64, 76, and 77.

100. Jürgen Moltmann, *The Way of Jesus Christ: Christology in Messianic Dimensions* (London: SCM, 1990), 55 and 99.

101. Pannenberg, *ST* 2:277-404.

102. Pannenberg, *ST* 2:277.

extensive discussion in his earlier *Jesus — God and Man,* especially in part 2.[103] He expounds here Jesus' fulfillment of the human destiny to become one with God; in his office as King he brings "the nearness of God's Kingdom" and "the nearness of God himself expressed in addressing God as 'Father.' "[104] On the cross, he declares, Jesus died a vicarious death: "It could only be understood as dying for us, for our sins."[105] The substitutionary nature of his death is seen not only in Mark 10:45 ("a ransom for many") but also in 2 Corinthians 5:21 ("that in him we might become the righteousness of God") and Galatians 3:13 ("Christ redeemed us from the curse of the law by becoming a curse for us").

Pannenberg includes a section entitled "Theories of the Saving Significance of Jesus' Death," where he considers, first, his death as a ransom from sin and the devil; second, the satisfaction theory of Anselm; and third, the penal suffering of Christ.[106] He points out that the "satisfaction" theory lost favor after the Enlightenment, but that Gottlob Storr of Tübingen seems to have replaced it with an emphasis on penal suffering in the nineteenth century, while Tholuck renewed the "satisfaction" emphasis in 1823. After the work of Barth, the notion of vicarious suffering was widely rehabilitated.

In his *Systematic Theology* Pannenberg insists, "We cannot regard a Christology from below [i.e., one that begins with the historical ministry of Jesus] as ruling out completely the classical Christology of the incarnation."[107] Jesus Christ is "the new Man . . . the eschatological Adam" (2:315). But Christ is also the self-revelation of God, seen fully in the light of the resurrection. His death was an expiation for human sins, which removes "the offence, the guilt, and the consequences" of sin (Rom. 3:25; *ST* 2:411). Indeed, Pannenberg carefully discusses the relation between expiation (or propitiation) and reconciliation with God (2:403-16). Representation, Pannenberg concludes in characteristic hermeneutical fashion, may embrace *"something done for others."* In this section he discusses a multitude of biblical passages in the light of careful, sober exegesis (2:416-21 and 421-37). He writes, "The innocent suffered the penalty of death. . . . This vicarious, penal suffering . . . the vicarious suffering of the wrath of God at sin, rests on the fellowship that Jesus Christ accepted with all of us as sinners and with our fate as such" (2:427).

103. Pannenberg, *JGM* 191-282.
104. Pannenberg, *JGM* 229.
105. Pannenberg, *JGM* 247.
106. Pannenberg, *JGM* 274-80.
107. Pannenberg, *ST* 2:288. Page references have been placed in the text.

It may be that Colin Gunton and Jürgen Moltmann have offered especially distinctive approaches to the atonement, but Wolfhart Pannenberg's work deserves to rank at least as highly as these, not least for his exegetical and historical accuracy, and for his breathtaking thoroughness. His approach also constitutes a classic modern study.

(ix) *Karl Rahner* (1904-1984). Rahner stands with Balthasar, Küng, and Congar among the leading and most influential Catholic theologians of the later twentieth century. He was a shaping influence on Vatican II (1962-1965). He was professor at Münster from 1967 to 1971. On divine grace he followed Henri de Lubac in regarding grace as both supernatural and part of being human. Yet grace is also free and gratuitous. Mighty deeds, signs, and wonders were part of the ministry of Jesus in history. But Jesus was more: he was an "eschatological prophet" with a unique mission.[108] Rahner vehemently attacked Docetism, the view that Jesus was not fully human.[109] His main argument was to retain a Chalcedonian Christology *within the frame of transcendental philosophy*. In contrast to Bultmann, he argued that the *"ontological,"* that is, what Christ is in himself, the God-man, *is the foundation of the "existential,"* that is, what Christ means to us.[110] Rahner wrote, "We shall find . . . proximity of God in no other place but in Jesus of Nazareth."[111] The atonement, he argued, brings not only expiation but also God's involvement in the world.

(x) *Hans Küng* (b. 1928). Küng was influenced by Congar, Balthasar, and other "progressive" Catholic theologians, as well as by Barth, especially on justification by grace. He was professor at Tübingen, and an adviser for Vatican II, together with Joseph Ratzinger and Rahner. His work *The Incarnation of God* (Ger. 1970; Eng. 1987) paid very close and detailed attention to Hegel's work. In the light of Hegel he aimed to move away from a "static" account of the person and work of Christ. He quoted Hegel with approval: "The divine in a particular shape appears as a man. The connection of the infinite and finite is of course a 'holy mystery,' because this connection is life itself."[112] For Hegel the "pivotal statement of the Prologue (was) 'And

---

108. Karl Rahner, *Foundations of Christian Faith: An Introduction to the Idea of Christianity* (New York: Crossroad, 1978), 245-46.

109. Rahner, *Foundations of Christian Faith*, 177.

110. Rahner, *Foundations of Christian Faith*, 204.

111. Karl Rahner and W. Thüsing, *A New Christology* (London: Burns and Oates, 1980), 17.

112. Hans Küng, *The Incarnation of God: An Introduction to Hegel's Thought* (Edinburgh: T. & T. Clark, 1987), 111. Page references have been placed in the text.

the Word was made flesh' (John 1:14). . . . There is no separation between infinite and finite" (126-27).

This is interpreted theologically in terms of "Alienated Men," who cannot be restored by "moralism"; "what is lacking is love" (112-13). Küng further considers the "absolute suffering" of Good Friday as "the death of God" (162-74). He appeals for this to biblical passages, to the nature of God, and even to Karl Barth. The atonement makes space for God to be himself; it is "simply God's act and God's grace" (287).

A simpler approach to the atonement is expounded in Küng's small book *Credo*.[113] Jesus, he writes here, is "the servant of God who suffered innocently and vicariously for the sins of many; the sacrificial lamb who symbolically takes away the sins of humankind" (87). The one who dies "is not God himself . . . the Father, . . . but God's Messiah and Christ, God's Image, Word and Son" (87). Nevertheless, the Son is accepted "unto God's eternal life," and God show[s] himself to be near in solidarity with believers" (88). Küng adds, "God is . . . hiddenly present" (92).

This very short sketch of Küng is bound to oversimplify his complexity, and even to risk seeming confusing. The same is true of these sketches of Barth, Balthasar, Moltmann, Pannenberg, and Rahner. But the purpose of this historical discussion is limited: to explore what hermeneutical bridges, or ways of understanding, have been made more explicit. In modern times Aulén has underlined the cross as a redemptive act of *liberation and victory;* Gunton has explored the power of *metaphor* in the traditional *complementary* imagery; Moltmann has asked us to consider what *atonement means, not only to us, but also to God.* Pannenberg has shown that none of the biblical imagery is dispensable or optional, and that Christ's work must be seen *as a whole, together with his sacrifice and resurrection.* Rahner and Küng have shown that the cross impinges on *cosmic realities,* with some suggestive comments from Hegel about the finite becoming subsumed in the infinite. All these serve not to *add* in substance to biblical material, but *to draw out* some of its hermeneutical implications. The net result is to demonstrate the immense and varied potential impact on everyday life generated by reflection on the atoning work of Christ.

---

113. Hans Küng, *Credo: The Apostles' Creed Explained for Today* (London: SCM, 1993), 62-94. Page references have been placed in the text.

CHAPTER X

A Concise Christology

If we were to expound biblical passages and historical thinkers as fully as we should like, this topic would occupy at least two large chapters, if not more. But this would expand the present volume beyond agreed limits. Hence we entitle this chapter "A Concise Christology."

One theme has received affirmation from thinkers of every point of view. Whether we consider Robert Funk, John Dominic Crossan, and the Jesus Seminar (founded in 1985), or Geza Vermes, Anthony Harvey, and M. Borg, or at the more conservative end of the spectrum, James Dunn, N. T. Wright, Richard Bauckham, and Ben Witherington, all agree that the *historical context* of Jesus is of primary importance.[1] How this historical and sociological context should best be described, however, remains controversial. Almost all agree that we should not denigrate the context of *Judaism,* even if the Jesus Seminar also stresses the context of a rural peasant sage, who pronounced "wisdom" aphorisms. From a multitude of voices, from Oscar Cullmann to Jürgen Moltmann, or Karl Rahner and Edward Schillebeeckx to Wolfhart Pannenberg, very many agree that the *prophetic* context, and its relations to the *OT and Judaism,* remains extremely important, and cannot be overrated.

---

1. See James D. G. Dunn, *Jesus Remembered,* vol. 1 of *Christianity in the Making* (Grand Rapids: Eerdmans, 2003), 255-326, and N. T. Wright, *Jesus and the Victory of God* (London: SPCK, 2004), 3-144.

1. The Historical Context: The Prophetic and Apocalyptic Expectations of the Old Testament and Judaism

Two different streams of hope characterized parts of the OT and Judaism. The Jews expected a *human figure who would be empowered and anointed by the Holy Spirit to an unprecedented extent.* He would be the *anointed one* (Heb. *māshîach;* Aram. *mᵉshia';* Gk. *ho Christos*). Sometimes he would be identified with the eschatological prophet "like Moses" (Deut. 18:15).[2] Side by side with this prophetic stream of promise and hope was that of *apocalyptic.* The apocalyptists believed that *human* leaders had always failed to bring in the promised kingdom; hence *God alone* would one day intervene to do what a merely human leader could not do, even when anointed by God. An act of divine intervention would bring, not reformation, but *new creation* and the *new age.* D. S. Russell writes, "The triumph of God's predetermined purpose will provide the key to all life's mysteries and problems."[3] More recently the pivotal significance of apocalyptic for Christian origins has been affirmed by Klaus Koch, Ernst Käsemann, Wolfhart Pannenberg, and many others. We expand this apocalyptic background further in our chapter on the return of Christ, or his future parousia.

The significance of these two streams of hope for Christology is the *fulfillment through and in the person of Jesus Christ, both of a human person, anointed by the Holy Spirit, and of the embodiment in Christ of God himself.*

On the prophetic aspect, Moltmann writes, "Jesus' history as the Christ does not begin with Jesus himself. It begins with the *ruach/*the Holy Spirit. It is the Coming of the Spirit, the creative breath of God: in this Jesus comes forward as 'the anointed one' *(masiah, christos),* and proclaims the gospel of the kingdom with power, and convinces many with the signs of the new creation."[4] The Holy Spirit "descended upon" Jesus at his baptism (Mark 1:10; Matt. 3:16; Luke 3:22), and "drove him" (Mark 1:12), or led him (Matt. 4:1; Luke 4:1), into the wilderness to be tempted or tested for his messianic vocation. The messianic "history of promise" constitutes "the presupposition of every Christology . . . out of Jewish contours."[5]

2. Oscar Cullmann, *The Christology of the New Testament* (London: SCM, 1963), 16; cf. 14-50.

3. D. S. Russell, *The Method and Message of Jewish Apocalyptic, 200 B.C.–A.D. 100* (London: SCM, 1964), 106.

4. Jürgen Moltmann, *The Way of Jesus Christ: Christology in Messianic Dimensions* (London: SCM, 1990), 73.

5. Moltmann, *Way of Jesus Christ,* 73-74.

Cullmann traced the level of expectation in Judaism for some such es-chatological climax in history as the return of Elijah (Mal. 4:5), who will prepare the way of the Lord.[6] This expectation finds expression in Ben Sirach (Ecclus. 48:10-11) and in rabbinic texts. Occasionally Enoch is mentioned, sometimes to return as a prophet with Elijah (*1 En.* 90:31), or also occasion-ally Baruch is mentioned. In the Dead Sea Scrolls in the *Commentary on Ha-bakkuk,* the Teacher of Righteousness may receive the role of eschatological prophet, and there is some parallel with the prophet and the two Messiahs of Aaron and Israel in the *Manual of Discipline* (1QS 9:11).[7] The *Testament of Levi* also refers to the "Prophet of the Highest" (*T. Levi* 8:15). Cullmann wrote, "The eschatological Prophet of Jewish expectation originally pre-pares the way for Yahweh himself . . . at the end of days."[8]

The NT seems to accord to Jesus the role of prophet and also com-plete humanness. This does not exclude the role of eschatological prophet accorded to John the Baptist (Mark 9:11-13; Matt. 17:10-13), at least in the Synoptic Gospels. The popular view of Jesus was that "A great prophet has risen among us" (Luke 7:16). This is confirmed by the frustrated desires of the priests and Pharisees to arrest Jesus, which failed "because they [the crowd] regarded him as a prophet" (Matt. 21:46; cf. Mark 6:4). Dunn concedes that in this tradition "different strands of expectation were often woven together as various prophecies provided fresh insights or confir-mation."[9] Dunn also cites Luke 13:31-33 (Jesus' reply to Herod) on Jesus' acceptance of the term "prophet," as well as the prophetic declaration of Isaiah 61:1-3, and such utterances as "I was sent" and "I came to" (Mark 2:17; 10:45; Matt. 10:34).

Dunn also recognizes that Jesus is "more than a prophet."[10] This opens the way to consider two other designations embodied in earliest Christian tradition. John Calvin believed that he was reflecting the earliest tradition in his three "offices" of prophet, king, and priest.[11] Psalm 89:35, 37, which speaks of the Davidic "throne," is applied to Christ, together with Peter's

6. Cullmann, *Christology,* 15-23, and Dunn, *Jesus Remembered,* 655.

7. Dunn, *Jesus Remembered,* 656.

8. Cullmann, *Christology,* 23.

9. Dunn, *Jesus Remembered,* 657; cf. J. J. Collins, *The Sceptre and the Star: The Messiahs of the Dead Sea Scrolls and Other Ancient Literature* (New York: Doubleday, 1995), 74-75 and 112-22, on the background in Judaism and the Dead Sea Scrolls.

10. Dunn, *Jesus Remembered,* 664-66.

11. John Calvin, *The Institutes of the Christian Religion* 2.15.1-6; in English, 2 vols. (Lon-don: James Clarke, 1957), 1:425-32.

sermon in Acts 2:25 and 34-35, taken from Psalm 110:1. Christ's priesthood is implied in John 17:11-26, and becomes explicit in Hebrews 5:5-10 and 7:1–8:/. Pannenberg sees significance in the work of A. Osiander (1530), who regarded the threefold office of Christ in fulfilling expectations of the OT. But Pannenberg warns us not to confuse Christ's heavenly status with that of the incarnation.[12]

At all events, this tradition understands Jesus as *fully human*, even if also anointed by the Holy Spirit for the task. J. A. T. Robinson contended that this aspect has been grossly undervalued in his book *The Human Face of God*.[13] He caricatured the prevalent understanding of Jesus Christ as "God in disguise," which has "removed him from the likes of us."[14] Robinson especially censured the one-sided emphasis of Alexandrian Christology among the Church Fathers. For example, Clement of Alexandria wrote, "It would be ridiculous to imagine the body of the Redeemer . . . having the usual needs of a man."[15] Even Athanasius claimed, "The Word disguised himself by appearing in a body. . . . He showed himself to be not man but God."[16] Cyril of Alexandria believed that Jesus Christ was "incapable of grief."[17] Robinson, by contrast, argued that Christ is portrayed by too many "as an unreal figure with the static perfection of flawless porcelain, rather than a man of flesh and blood."[18] He attacked the popular notion of "the all-rounder of whom it could be said, 'You name it; he's got it.' "[19] Jesus, Robinson said, "was fully a man like ourselves."[20]

The *prophetic tradition* in general leads us to establish this full humanity of the anointed man Jesus Christ. By contrast, the *apocalyptic tradition* leads to the expectation that *God himself* will intervene in human history, even if in and through the person of Jesus Christ, who *acts in God's stead*. The importance of apocalyptic tradition and expectation was one-sidedly stressed by A. Schweitzer near the beginning of the twentieth century, and, after it was relatively neglected, it was decisively reintroduced by Klaus Koch and many others, especially by Pannenberg. In the 1960s Koch wrote, "Unexpectedly

12. Pannenberg, *ST* 2:448.

13. J. A. T. Robinson, *The Human Face of God* (London: SCM, 1973).

14. Robinson, *Human Face of God*, 3.

15. Clement of Alexandria, *Stromata* 6.9.

16. Athanasius, *On the Incarnation* 16.18.

17. Cyril of Alexandria, *Commentary on John* 7.

18. Robinson, *Human Face of God*, 68.

19. Robinson, *Human Face of God*, 70.

20. Robinson, *Human Face of God*, 85.

... the term apocalyptic re-emerged from the depths, and became a hotly disputed slogan."[21] But before the end of the decade, Ernst Käsemann had called it "the mother of Christian theology."[22] O. Plöger and D. Rossler argued for its importance, and the intervention of Pannenberg was decisive. In one of his very early studies, "The Revelation of God in Jesus of Nazareth," Pannenberg wrote, "Jesus . . . stood in a tradition that expected the coming of God, the coming of his reign. . . . Jesus did not demand trust in his person without giving reasons for it."[23]

It was characteristic of apocalyptic that the eschatological nearness of God was revealed, in Pannenberg's words, "only in the light of the End."[24] We should reckon with both "the intertwining . . . of prophetic words and of events" and "a whole connected history" that proceeded under "the God of history" as suggested by apocalyptic.[25] This context of apocalyptic was not confined to the early writings. In *Jesus — God and Man* Pannenberg asserts, "With Jesus, the end is not only — as in apocalyptic writings — seen in advance, but it has happened in advance."[26] God is not only near; he is present in Jesus. Apocalyptic includes notions of "the coming of a new aeon."[27]

Just as the *prophetic tradition* provided a horizon of understanding for the full *humanity* of Jesus, so the *apocalyptic horizon* provided a context for his proclamation of the kingdom of God, the new era, his resurrection, and even by implication, the *Godhood of Jesus Christ.*

Pannenberg certainly insists that the deity of Christ is seen most clearly in his *resurrection* as an "event which took place in this world, namely in the tomb of Jesus in Jerusalem."[28] Nevertheless, taking up Ritschl's terms of a contrast between "Christology from below" and "Christology from above," he also insists that this confession can be inferred from a historical "Christology from below"; especially if we look at "the total character of the com-

---

21. Klaus Koch, *The Rediscovery of Apocalyptic: A Polemical Work on a Neglected Area of Biblical Studies and Its Damaging Effects on Theology and Philosophy* (London: SCM, 1972), 13.

22. Ernst Käsemann, *New Testament Questions of Today* (London: SCM, 1969), 137.

23. Wolfhart Pannenberg, "The Revelation of God in Jesus of Nazareth," in *New Frontiers in Theology*, vol. 3, *Theology as History*, ed. James M. Robinson and John B. Cobb (New York: Harper and Row, 1967), 102-3.

24. Pannenberg, "Revelation," 113.

25. Pannenberg, "Revelation," 120, 121, 122, and 132.

26. Pannenberg, *JGM* 61.

27. Pannenberg, *ST* 2:326; cf. Wright, *Jesus*, 217-18.

28. Pannenberg, *ST* 2:360.

ing of Jesus."[29] He continues, "The history of Jesus" includes "the primitive Christian witness to the resurrection of Jesus . . . that legitimates his pre-Easter work."[30] The Easter message *follows* the Easter event. In effect, against Bultmann, Pannenberg argues, "We *cannot* regard a Christology from below as ruling out completely the classical Christology of the incarnation."[31] The classical Christology is, he insists, "presupposed" within a fully adequate historical approach. He concludes, "Material primacy belongs to the eternal Son, who has become man by his incarnation in Jesus of Nazareth."[32] In *Jesus — God and Man* Pannenberg insists that "the true divinity and true humanity of Jesus" are "indispensable"; nevertheless, this does not at all mean that we are fully committed to the Chalcedonian formulation of two *"substances."*[33] The outworking of this background material comes to full expression in the epistles of Paul and the Epistle to the Hebrews, which we consider in section 4 of this chapter.

2. Jesus' Proclamation of the Kingdom of God: Pointers to Christology

All four Gospels record the descent of the Holy Spirit at the baptism of Jesus as a pivotal and decisive event (Matt. 3:13-17; Mark 1:9-11; Luke 3:21-22; John 1:32-34). Jeremias strongly argues for the authenticity of this event. In addition to its multiple attestation, he points out, for the early church, these accounts might have risked appearing to make Jesus subordinate to John the Baptist, and to suggest that he had need of repentance and forgiveness: "Such a scandalizing piece of information cannot have been invented."[34] Its true meaning, as C. K. Barrett suggests, is to underline that in his baptism Jesus "became one of the prepared people of God, able to await the coming judgment without fear."[35]

The anointing of the Holy Spirit, the approval of the Father, and the Spirit's "driving" (Mark 1:12-13) or "leading" (Matt. 4:1; Luke 4:1) Jesus to his messianic temptations or testing confirm the pivotal nature of the event. As

---

29. Pannenberg, *ST* 2:278-97, especially 280.
30. Pannenberg, *ST* 2:283.
31. Pannenberg, *ST* 2:288, italics mine.
32. Pannenberg, *ST* 2:289.
33. Pannenberg, *JGM* 284-85.
34. Joachim Jeremias, *New Testament Theology* (London: SCM, 1971), 45.
35. C. K. Barrett, *The Holy Spirit and the Gospel Tradition* (London: SPCK, 1958), 33.

Moltmann and Eugene Rogers argue, from the beginning the ministry and person of Jesus are seen as a narrative of the Holy Trinity.[36] Although it indeed has a place in the Gospels, as Moltmann acknowledges, the virgin birth "is not one of the pillars that sustains the New Testament faith in Christ."[37]

Interestingly, the fourth-century phrase "Mary, the Mother of God" was regarded by the Fathers as a statement not about Mary but about the true humanness or *humanity of Jesus*. Again, in Moltmann's words, the virgin birth served to underline "that God alone is the Father of Jesus Christ."[38]

It is probably otherwise with the temptation narratives (Matt. 4:1-11; Luke 4:1-13). All three narrated messianic temptations invite Jesus to pursue an easier and more comfortable shortcut to the fulfillment of God's will. But they did not indicate *God's way;* this way involved the cross and *Calvary,* not spectacular miracles or underhanded methods to win approval from the crowd. Fitzmyer has doubts about the strong historical evidence for the temptations as such, but the Epistle to the Hebrews shows the importance of the "testing" or temptations (Heb. 2:17-18; 4:15; 5:7-10). The main lessons of the temptation narrative are the solidarity of Jesus with Israel or humankind, his acceptance of his messianic vocation, and his acceptance of the constraints and everyday limitations inherent in the human condition.

Jesus then at once began his public ministry in Galilee by proclaiming the kingdom of God (or, in Matthew's reverential terms, the kingdom of heaven, Matt. 4:17) and "the year of the Lord's favor" (Luke 4:19; cf. Matt. 4:23; 5:3, 19-20; 6:10, 33; 7:21; 9:35; 12:26; 13:52; 18:3; 19:23; 25:34; Mark 1:15; 3:24; 4:26). Dunn regards "The kingdom of God has drawn near" (Mark 1:14) as "a kind of summary statement or headline."[39] Especially in Mark, this is the "gospel" of Jesus. Jesus commissioned his disciples likewise to proclaim: "The kingdom of God has drawn near" (cf. Matt. 10:7; Luke 10:9). Dunn

36. Jürgen Moltmann, *The Trinity and the Kingdom of God: The Doctrine of God* (London: SCM, 1981), 65-75; Eugene F. Rogers Jr., *After the Spirit: A Constructive Pneumatology from Resources outside the Modern West* (London: SCM, 2005; Grand Rapids: Eerdmans, 2006), 136-68.

37. Jürgen Moltmann, *The Way of Jesus Christ: Christology in Messianic Dimensions* (London: SCM, 1990), 79. For a conservative view, see J. Gresham Machen, *The Virgin Birth of Christ* (London: Clarke, 1930, 1958), and Wayne Grudem, *Systematic Theology* (Nottingham: IVP, 1994), 529-32.

38. Moltmann, *Way of Jesus Christ,* 82.

39. Dunn, *Jesus Remembered,* 383; cf. also J. Becker, *Jesus of Nazareth* (Berlin: De Gruyter, 1998), 100-102.

counts thirteen occurrences of the phrase in Mark, and an additional nine in both Matthew and Luke. He concludes, "In short, the evidence we have points to only one clear conclusion: that Jesus was remembered as preaching about the Kingdom of God and that this was central to his message and his mission."[40]

The Greek *basileia* and Aramaic *malkûth* denoted "reign," exercise of kingship, or "kingly rule."[41] Admittedly the concept or image has blurred edges. Norman Perrin argues convincingly that "kingdom" constitutes a "tensive symbol."[42] Crossan follows this view. But much of the fundamental force of the term remains. The message of Jesus pointed primarily to God, but Jesus also spoke and acted in the name of God. The "mighty works" Jesus did also constituted "signs of the kingdom of God." These mighty deeds, Wright explains, represented "signs which were intended as, and would have been perceived as, the physical inauguration of the kingdom of Israel's God. . . . They were an integral part of the entire ministry."[43] Under the same heading we might include Jesus' "mighty word" (Wright's term), and his call to decision, as well as his call to discipleship. Even Bultmann conceded that his call to decision "implies a Christology."[44]

As Wright and others argue, in the precritical era, most readers regarded the mighty works as primary evidence for the deity of Jesus. Then after the eighteenth century, liberal interpreters often regarded them as fictitious events that had never happened. Wright concludes, "More thoroughgoing recent history has been coming to the conclusion that we can explain the evidence before us only if we reckon that Jesus did indeed perform deeds for which there was . . . no 'naturalist' explanation."[45] This does not imply that he wholly approves of the word "miracle," with its often implied two-story "natural" and "supernatural" dualism. He associates these deeds with Jesus' prophetic role and with his proclamation of the kingdom of God.

Similarly, the parables of Jesus were mainly parables of the kingdom of God, as was his saying about the temple. Wright comments, "It is hard to see

40. Dunn, *Jesus Remembered*, 387.

41. Gustav Dalman, *The Words of Jesus* (Edinburgh: T. & T. Clark, 1902), 91-96; Dunn, *Jesus Remembered*, 33-92; BDAG 168-69.

42. Norman Perrin, *Jesus and the Language of the Kingdom: Symbol and Metaphor in New Testament Interpretation* (Philadelphia: Fortress; London: SCM, 1976), 22-23, 29-32, and 56.

43. Wright, *Jesus*, 196.

44. Rudolf Bultmann, *Theology of the New Testament*, vol. 1 (London: SCM, 1952), 43.

45. Wright, *Jesus*, 186.

how the symbols and *praxis* associated with the Temple, Torah, Land, and Jewish identity, sustained and re-enforced the narrative of hope."[46]

Jesus' teaching on prayer especially shows his closeness to God the Father. All four Gospels witness to Jesus' concern for prayer, and Dunn comments, "When we 'listen in' on Jesus' prayers the distinctive word we hear is 'Abba.' "[47] Although he concedes that Jeremias may have pressed the argument too far, Dunn argues, "Jesus said 'Abba' to God for precisely the same reason as (most of) his contemporaries refrained from its use in prayer — viz. because it expressed his attitude to God as Father . . . as one of unusual intimacy. . . . *Jesus experienced an intimate relation of sonship in prayer.*"[48] This corroborates the use of the title Son of God for Jesus. Cullmann writes, "While 'Son of God' does indeed point to the divine majesty of Jesus and his ultimate oneness with God, it also essentially implies his obedience to the Father."[49] He continues that, in contrast to Greek understandings of the term, "The most important passages in the Synoptic Gospels in which Jesus appears as Son of God show him precisely not as a miracle-worker and saviour like many others, but as one radically and uniquely distinguished from all other men."[50]

Jesus' self-designation of the term "Son of Man" has a controversial meaning. Maurice Casey and others believe that it simply denotes *a man.*[51] The Greek *ho huios tou anthrōpou* could simply mean "the son of the human being." No firm consensus has been reached on this matter, as Dunn, among others, observes.[52] However, two other suggestions have traditionally commanded wide support. One appeals to the Aramaic term in Daniel 7:13-14, in which the Son of Man will come with the clouds of heaven at the end of history, to receive dominion and kingship (cf. Dan. 7:24-27). This seems to correspond with Mark 14:62: "I am; and 'you will see the Son of Man seated at the right hand of the Power,' and 'coming with clouds of heaven.' " In a similar vein, Mark 2:10 records, "The Son of Man has authority on earth to forgive sins," which seems to imply a unique position of power. In Mark 2:28,

46. Wright, *Jesus,* 206.
47. James D. G. Dunn, *Jesus and the Spirit: A Study of the Religious and Charismatic Experience of Jesus and the First Christians* (London: SCM, 1975), 21.
48. Dunn, *Jesus and the Spirit,* 23 and 26.
49. Cullmann, *Christology,* 270.
50. Cullmann, *Christology,* 276.
51. Maurice Casey, *The Solution to the "Son of Man" Problem* (New York and London: T. & T. Clark, 2007).
52. Dunn, *Jesus Remembered,* 724-62.

"The Son of Man is lord even of the sabbath." This also occurs in *1 Enoch* 61:8-9 and 62:9-11. But some hold the different view that "Son of Man" denotes the representative man, or the last Adam, who brings corporate Israel to a focus. Here humanness stands in contrast with the beasts of Daniel's vision.

T. W. Manson insisted that Jesus wished that he and his followers "together should be the Son of Man, the Remnant that saves by service and self-sacrifice."[53] Morna Hooker regarded such a corporate "last Adam" as compatible with the Daniel 7 references, where, as we have noted, "human" stands in contrast with other creatures.[54]

Normally a section about the person of Christ in the Gospels would discuss his suffering, rejection, death and resurrection, and self-identification with the Servant of the Lord in Isaiah 40–55. But we have discussed aspects of this in chapter 8, on the work of Christ. The biblical passages in which Jesus is most unambiguously called "God" are John 1:1, "and the Word was God"; John 20:28, "Thomas answered him, 'My Lord and my God!'"; Hebrews 1:8-9, "Your throne, O God, is forever and ever"; and Hebrews 1:3, "He is . . . the exact imprint of God's very being."[55] Romans 9:5, "The Messiah, who is over all, God blessed forever," is perhaps ambiguous in meaning and in its precise textual authenticity. Raymond Brown insists that Jesus did not apply this title to himself; Pannenberg explains that this would not be surprising prior to the resurrection. Larry Hurtado has shown that this would not have compromised Jewish monotheism; rather, it was refigured to include Christ.[56]

We shall later argue that John and Hebrews are unique in emphasizing simultaneously the humanness of Jesus and his deity. The former shows itself in Jesus' being weary (John 4:6), being thirsty (4:7), being troubled (11:33) and weeping (11:35), while there are outright statements of his divinity. Hebrews provides several parallels: "Jesus is not ashamed to call them brothers and sisters" (Heb. 2:11); Jesus said, "I will put my trust in (God)" (2:13); Jesus was "in every respect . . . tested as we are, yet without sin" (4:15). These writings protest against much British Christology of the later 1960s and early

53. T. W. Manson, *The Teaching of Jesus: Studies of Its Form and Content,* 2nd ed. (Cambridge: CUP, 1935), 231.

54. Morna Hooker, *The Son of Man in Mark* (London: SPCK, 1967), 71.

55. See Raymond E. Brown, *Jesus — God and Man* (London: Chapman, 1968), especially 23-38.

56. Larry W. Hurtado, *Lord Jesus Christ: Devotion to Jesus in Earliest Christianity* (Grand Rapids: Eerdmans, 2003), throughout, but especially 64.

1970s, which claimed that both of these assertions simultaneously stood in logical contradiction. *But there is no hint of such internal tension in John or in Hebrews.*

3. The Three So-Called Quests and the Need for Historical Research

Pressure of space, as we have explained, constrains us to present only a "concise" Christology. But it would be a mistake to bypass questions of accurate historical research. From well before 1906 to the present day there have been various historical approaches, of which it is conventional to distinguish between Schweitzer's *Quest of the Historical Jesus* (Ger. 1906; Eng. 1910); the so-called *New Quest* of Käsemann, Bornkamm, Fuchs, and others in the 1950s and 1960s; and the so-called *Third Quest,* mainly in the late 1980s and 1990s, and also up until today.[57] We may distinguish, in addition, although overlapping with the Third Quest, fourth, the Jesus Seminar of the SBL, founded by Robert Funk in 1985 and closely associated with J. D. Crossan. The latest approach places history within a more rounded and comprehensive frame. This fifth approach began with Pannenberg, and is reflected in various degrees in the work of Dunn, Wright, Bauckham, and others.

The irony of speaking seriously of "three quests" is that the term "quest" was invented by a translator or publisher who believed that Schweitzer's German title, *Von Reimarus zu Wrede. Eine Geschichte der Leben Jesus Forschung,* would not sell books as readily in England as the title *The Quest of the Historical Jesus.* (Colin Brown of Fuller first suggested this to me.)

(i) *The Original Quest.* Schweitzer surveyed the "lives of Jesus" that were written after H. J. Reimarus's claim that Jesus proclaimed the kingdom of God "according to Jewish ways of thought." Reimarus was a rationalist and a Deist who excluded all mysteries and miracles from Jesus' life, and argued that Jesus would return in the lifetime of the disciples. He overlaid the life with so much of his own thought that Schweitzer concluded, "Reimarus hung a mill-stone about the neck of the rising theological science of his time" (26).

Schweitzer next surveyed an era of "fictitious lives of Jesus," which included those suggested by Bahrdt and Venturini, and then further rationalist

---

57. Albert Schweitzer, *The Quest of the Historical Jesus,* 3rd ed. (London: SCM, 1954), 16. Page references have been placed in the text.

lives. These included one by Paulus. He also examined the work of David F. Strauss, whose final edition Schweitzer called "a dead book . . . bankrupt" (76). He examined criticisms of other editions, and then surveyed the work of Bruno Bauer (1809-1882). He concluded that "his purpose was really only to continue the work of Strauss" (145). Yet Bauer tartly observed, "There never was any historical Jesus" (147). Ernest Renan (1823-1892) reconstructed the life of Jesus "with artistic imagination" (181). Finally, W. Wrede (1859-1906) focused on Mark's prohibition of speaking about Jesus' messiahship, to expound his theological hypothesis of "the messianic secret" (328, 337-38, and 351). Schweitzer's assessment of the net effect of these writers is as follows: "The historical foundation of Christianity as built up . . . by modern theology *no longer exists,* although this does not mean that Christianity has lost its historical foundation" (397, italics mine). Jesus *"comes to us as one unknown"* (401, italics mine).

Although this nineteenth-century quest clearly failed, Bultmann seems to follow both Wrede's theory of the "messianic secret" and Schweitzer's conclusion about our supposed ignorance of historical foundations. He wrote, "Interest in the personality of Jesus is excluded. . . . We can now know almost nothing concerning the life and personality of Jesus, since the early Christian sources show no interest in either, and other sources . . . do not exist."[58]

(ii) *The New Quest.* It is little wonder that Bultmann's former pupils began what was called a "new quest." In 1954 Käsemann (1906-1998) delivered a lecture entitled "The Problem of the Historical Jesus," in which he defended the identity of the exalted Lord and that of the earthly Jesus. Another former pupil of Bultmann, alongside Käsemann and Hans Conzelmann, Günther Bornkamm (1905-1990) championed, as part of the New Quest, a closer relation between Jesus and the theology of the early church, while admitting that this seemed often to be "a misty country."[59] A third exponent of the New Quest was Ernst Fuchs (1903-1983). He saw "God's presence in the presence of Jesus' person," and argued that God's presence can be seen in the *actions* of Jesus. But he also followed Bultmann in his drawing on Heidegger's existentialism and theory of language. Hence, he argued that "language event" *(Sprachereignis)* was *"reality";* reality and the resurrection constituted "linguistic" events. God's *speaking* links Jesus with the early community. Fuchs also undertook a distinctive hermeneutical ap-

---

58. Rudolf Bultmann, *Jesus and the Word* (London and New York: Collins, 1958), 13.
59. Günther Bornkamm, *Jesus of Nazareth* (Minneapolis: Fortress, 1959).

proach to the parables of Jesus, in the so-called new hermeneutic, which he shared with Gerhard Ebeling.[60]

Meanwhile, several writers in Britain followed a more conservative path. These included C. H. Dodd (1884-1973), T. W. Manson (1893-1958), Vincent Taylor (1887-1968), and G. B. Caird (1917-1984). Perhaps the most decisive work at this time was Graham N. Stanton, *Jesus of Nazareth in New Testament Preaching*.[61] He showed that the assumption that the earliest sources showed no interest in the person and character of Jesus was frankly incredible. Would recent Christian converts really have had no desire to find out factual details concerning the Founder of their faith?

(iii) *The So-Called Third Quest.* This has at its heart an emphatic concern for both the Jewish roots of the ministry of Jesus and its historical context. James Dunn and N. T. Wright both rightly underline these two themes.[62] However, although he sees enough that is distinctive to earn this broad title, Wright recognizes that the Third Quest can be defined so widely as to leave little that is genuinely distinctive, other than its concern for history and most often Jewish roots. In practice Wright selects twenty widely differing characteristics or themes that represent the Third Quest, from Hengel, Caird, and Witherington on one side, to Vermes, Sanders, and Theissen on the other.[63] In the end he allows that we can define this movement no better by the questions they ask than by the conclusions they reach. They all use "serious historical method, as opposed to the pseudo-historical use of home-made 'criteria.' . . . The much-vaunted 'normal critical tools,' particularly form-criticism, are being tacitly (and . . . rightly) bypassed in the search for Jesus."[64]

Wright's proposed questions include: (1) How does Jesus fit into Judaism? (2) What were Jesus' aims? (3) Why did Jesus die? (4) How and why did the early church begin? and (5) Why are the Gospels what they are?[65] Wright calls these questions "the basic starting-point of this book."[66] But he also acknowledges that these broad questions overlap with other

---

60. Ernst Fuchs, *Studies of the Historical Jesus* (London: SCM, 1964); cf. Anthony C. Thiselton, "The Parables as Language-Event: Some Comments on Fuchs' Hermeneutics in the Light of Linguistic Philosophy," *SJT* 23 (1970).

61. Graham N. Stanton, *Jesus of Nazareth in New Testament Preaching* (Cambridge: CUP, 1974).

62. Dunn, *Jesus Remembered*, 85-92, and Wright, *Jesus*, 83-124.

63. Wright, *Jesus*, 84.

64. Wright, *Jesus*, 87.

65. Wright, *Jesus*, 89-116.

66. Wright, *Jesus*, 123.

categories. For example, Dunn broadly follows these questions, but also warns us against too ready a tendency to accept what is less convincing in postmodernism.[67]

(iv) *The Jesus Seminar.* The Jesus Seminar of the SBL, founded by Robert Funk, is also closely associated with John Dominic Crossan. In Wright's taxonomy it also overlaps with the Third Quest, but in Dunn's survey Crossan substantially overlaps with postmodernism and the flight from history.[68] Crossan (b. 1934) is a distinguished Irish American NT scholar who has increasingly moved in a postmodernist direction since the mid-1970s, in major books and in articles in *Semeia*.

In his later work Crossan portrays Jesus as a onetime follower of John the Baptist, who came from a rural peasant background, practiced healing and ate common meals, and uttered pithy "wisdom" aphorisms. This is reflected, he argues, especially in "Q," or in passages common to Matthew and Luke.[69] His book *The Historical Jesus* is only one of a dozen books, beginning with *In Parables* (1973), a most useful book, which develop in increasingly postmodern and speculative directions. Crossan regards many of the Gospel narratives as fiction, and as depicting Jesus as a magician and a sage. He regards the resurrection as a "vision" experience. Crossan is always willing to engage in dialogue, as he did with William Craig in *The Jesus Controversy* (1999). Ben Witherington rightly shows that the ascription of gnomic or "wisdom" aphorisms to Jesus is not wrong, although he does assess other aspects of Crossan's work differently.[70] Crossan's sociological study of rural village life is significant, although Wright argues that this kind of study is still in relative infancy. Crossan also uses extracanonical sources.

(v) *More Moderate or More Conservative Specialists.* Our last group is that of Dunn, Bauckham, and Wright, who also are said to overlap with the Third Quest, if this is defined broadly in terms of its concerns for Jewish history and Wright's five questions. Dunn (b. 1939) agrees that "Any historical study of Jesus has to take seriously the character of the Judaism of the time and the social and political circumstances in which Jesus undertook his mission."[71] The early tradition, Dunn concludes, "goes back *to the consistent*

---

67. Dunn, *Jesus Remembered*, 85-97.

68. Dunn, *Jesus Remembered*, 59-65, 83, and 99.

69. John Dominic Crossan, *The Historical Jesus: The Life of a Mediterranean Jewish Peasant* (San Francisco: HarperCollins; Edinburgh: T. & T. Clark, 1991).

70. Ben Witherington III, *Jesus the Sage: The Pilgrimage of Wisdom* (Edinburgh: T. & T. Clark, 1994).

71. Dunn, *Jesus Remembered*, 882.

and distinctive character made by Jesus himself."[72] This verdict stands utterly in contrast to the pessimism of the first and even the second quest. Too many older works insist on excluding theology from history, and thereby exclude what Pannenberg has called "the whole Christ."

Richard Bauckham (b. 1946) has produced especially creative and distinctive work in *Jesus and the Eyewitnesses* (2006) and *The Testimony of the Beloved Disciple* (2007).[73] He observes, "At the beginning of the twenty-first century the quest of the historical Jesus flourishes as never before, especially in North America."[74] Nevertheless, he argues, the key role of *eyewitnesses* has often been unduly neglected. By contrast, he refers to the Swedish scholar Samuel Byrskog, and includes the tradition of Greek and Roman historians on "ideal eyewitnesses" as participants rather than "dispassionate observers."[75] In the same vein, Bauckham discusses Papias's "preference for the 'living voice' over written sources."[76] Thus Eusebius refers to his use of the testimony of Peter (*Ecclesiastical History* 3.39.9). Bauckham follows this theme through, examining records of names, traditions about the Twelve, Peter in Mark, and so on. The Twelve, for example, is not a fiction of Luke. Graham Stanton, formerly professor of NT at London and Cambridge, commented that Bauckham's book "shakes the foundations of a century of scholarly study of the Gospels," with "a wealth of new insights."

We have already indicated the direction of approach adopted by N. T. Wright (b. 1948). On the teaching of Jesus and Christology he argues that this is "not to be squashed down into witty or proverbial aphorisms. . . . He (Jesus) spoke as he acted, as a prophet through whose work YHWH was doing a new thing, indeed *the* new theory for which Israel had waited so long."[77] At times he constructively builds on the work of G. B. Caird. For example, Caird and Wright rightly reject the view that Mark 9:1, "Some standing here . . . will not taste death until they see that the kingdom of God has come with power," must necessarily refer to the parousia or end time (cf. Luke 9:27). Wright comments, "To read this saying as though it was a prediction

---

72. Dunn, *Jesus Remembered*, 884.

73. Richard Bauckham, *Jesus and the Eyewitnesses: The Gospels as Eyewitness Testimony* (Grand Rapids: Eerdmans, 2006), and Richard Bauckham, *The Testimony of the Beloved Disciple: Narrative, History, and Theology in the Gospel of John* (Grand Rapids: Baker Academic, 2007).

74. Bauckham, *Jesus and the Eyewitnesses*, 1.

75. Bauckham, *Jesus and the Eyewitnesses*, 9.

76. Bauckham, *Jesus and the Eyewitnesses*, 21.

77. Wright, *Jesus*, 367.

of Jesus' return, or of the *Parousia* . . . is simply to fail to think historically."[78]
Years earlier, before 1980, Caird had argued that questions about the end of
Israel, or fall of Jerusalem, had become hopelessly entangled with questions
about the end of the world, because Jesus used end-of-the-world language
to describe the fall of Jerusalem.[79] In the first and second parts of his book,
Wright discusses the foundation for the messiahship and crucifixion of Jesus,
and turns to his vindication in part 3. The positive side of all this research
for the Christian is not only that it confirms aspects of *historical* inquiry and
continuity with the OT, but also that it underlines the *full humanness of Jesus*
of Nazareth.

4. The Christology of the Epistles and Acts:
Lord, Last Adam, One with God

(i) *Paul and Acts.* In the pre-Pauline confessions transmitted from common
apostolic doctrine, Paul uses the word "Lord" of Jesus Christ, as in "you proclaim the Lord's death" (1 Cor. 11:26). Peter in his early preaching declared,
"God has made him both Lord and Messiah, this Jesus whom you crucified"
(Acts 2:36). Paul states that "Jesus Christ our Lord" was declared "Son of
God . . . by resurrection from the dead" (Rom. 1:4). He proclaims that salvation is received "if you confess with your lips that Jesus is Lord and believe
. . . that God raised him from the dead" (Rom. 10:9). First Corinthians 12:3,
"No one can say 'Jesus is Lord' except by the Holy Spirit," probably reflects
another pre-Pauline tradition.

In assessing controversies within the NT, A. M. Hunter argues that
"there is no evidence that they (Paul's predecessors) ever disagreed on the
capital issue of Christology."[80] Bultmann insists, "For Paul, Lord, and not
Christ, is Jesus' title."[81] Hunter and Vincent Taylor call it "clearly his (Paul's)
favourite title."[82] Taylor counts over 220 uses of the term in Paul. This term
occurs in a variety of contexts, for it not only denotes the theological belief
that God *enthroned Christ as Lord* at the resurrection (ontologically, or in
reality, Lord), but also *signifies trust, surrender, devotion, freedom, and obe-*

78. Wright, *Jesus,* 470.
79. George B. Caird, *The Language and Imagery of the Bible* (London: Duckworth,
1980), 265.
80. A. M. Hunter, *Paul and His Predecessors,* 2nd ed. (London, SCM, 1961), 79.
81. Bultmann, *Theology of the New Testament,* 80.
82. Hunter, *Paul and His Predecessors,* 142.

dience (existentially Lord in *experience*). It is used in all these contexts. Jeremias holds that it carries a close relationship to Paul's *conversion experience*. Since the confession of Christ as Lord is bound up with receiving salvation, clearly it involves *more* than a *theological belief,* but it does not imply less than this. In the words of the pre-Pauline hymn that Paul adopts, "God gave him (Christ) the name that is above every name . . . that at the name of Jesus every knee should bend . . . and every tongue should confess that Jesus Christ is Lord" (Phil. 2:9-11). Cerfaux thinks of Christ's Lordship in Paul as his *enthronement* as messianic King, and links it to judgment and the parousia.[83]

By contrast, Deissmann regarded the *Kyrios* confession as intelligible "only by the simplicity of *silent devotion.*"[84] Werner Kramer regarded it as typical in the context of *ethical instruction.*[85] Cullmann viewed the term as characteristically an expression of worship, as in *maranatha* (1 Cor. 16:22).[86] All these five views can be defended. To the five contexts we add a sixth, which is well identified by Bultmann. To *belong to* Christ as Lord, he writes, is a glorious experience of Christian *freedom.* He explains: "This freedom arises from the fact that the believer, as one 'ransomed,' *no longer 'belongs to himself'* (1 Cor. 6:19). He no longer bears the care for himself, his own life, but lets this care go, yielding himself entirely to the grace of God; he recognizes himself to be the property of God . . . and lives for him."[87]

Bultmann's moving words are corroborated by recent research on the relationship between lord and slave in ancient Rome and the provinces. Admittedly, to a thoughtless, unethical slave owner a menial slave was usually a mere "thing" (Lat. *res*), over whom he could determine rights of marriage, property, and so on. But to a high-minded, ethically sensitive slave owner, especially in the case of a literate or managerial slave, the relationship could be entirely different. The slave might manage his estate or his accounts, could enjoy his full protection, probably provision for his family in the event of death, and sufficient income (or "pocket money") to enable him to save up to buy his freedom, often by the age of thirty. Dale Martin, in his book on the subject, attributes to slavery "meanings not of humility, but of authority and power."[88]

83. L. Cerfaux, *Christ in the Theology of St. Paul* (New York: Herder, 1959), 465 and 469.

84. Adolf Deissmann, *Paul: A Study in Social and Religious History* (London: Hodder and Stoughton, 1912), 194.

85. Werner Kramer, *Christ, Lord, and Son of God* (London: SCM, 1966), 181.

86. Cullmann, *Christology,* 207-11.

87. Bultmann, *Theology of the New Testament,* 331.

88. Dale B. Martin, *Slavery as Salvation: The Metaphor of Slavery in Pauline Christianity* (New Haven: Yale University Press, 1990), 56.

Martin also attributes some authority to Paul's self-definition as "a slave of Christ" (Rom. 1:1; 1 Cor. 4:1; Phil. 1:1). Some have argued that Martin over-states the case, but clearly he convincingly shows that what slavery consists of depends entirely on the attitude and stance of the slave's master or lord. When Christ is his Lord, this is not drudgery, but loyalty and freedom. As Bultmann states, "He no longer bears the care for himself."

This brings us to the earlier comments of J. Weiss, who was one of Bult-mann's teachers. He wrote, "What appears in the Greek as ignoble or servile appears rather in the Semitic as a proud title. We can understand how Paul, now and then . . . designated slavery as a mark of liberty."[89] He declared, "What it [the *Kyrios* confession of Christ as Lord] means in a practical religious sense will best be made clear through the correlative concept of 'servant' or 'slave' of Christ (Rom. 1:1; 1 Cor. 7:22-23; Gal. 1:10; Phil. 1:1; Col. 4:12)."[90]

Yet we must be firm in holding *together* the *ontological* and *existential* aspects of Lordship, which Bultmann fails to do. It is because *God made and declared* Jesus to be Lord (his ontological status) that Christians can *confess* him as their Lord (their existential experience). Kuschel, Cerfaux, Pannenberg, and many others affirm this. This is part of what follows from examining the many *contexts* in which "Lordship" has a special application. This reaches a climax in Philippians 2:9-11. Whether he composed this pas-sage or adopted it as his own, Paul states that because God "highly exalted him" (v. 9), "every tongue should confess that Jesus Christ is Lord" (v. 11).

As N. T. Wright points out, like many before him, it is commonplace to note that Paul regularly used biblical quotations in which the LXX uses the Greek word *Kyrios* where it translates the Hebrew *YHWH*. This especially applies, he argues, to Philippians 2:10-11 and 1 Corinthians 8:6. Wright re-marks, "He (Paul) clearly intends in these passages that the *Kyrios,* which in the original stands for *YHWH,* should now be understood to refer to Jesus himself."[91] In both Romans 14:11 and Philippians 2:10-11 Paul quotes Isaiah 45:23. Wright concludes that probably Jesus couples his messianic identity "with his embodiment of the returning YHWH himself."[92] Paul, he adds, also cites Joel 2:32: "All who call on the name of the Lord shall be saved," where the context makes it clear that it refers to Jesus. He suggests, "This is not

89. Johannes Weiss, *Earliest Christianity: A History of the Period A.D. 30-150,* 2 vols. (New York: Harper, 1959; orig. 1937), 2:460.

90. Weiss, *Earliest Christianity,* 2:452.

91. N. T. Wright, *Paul and the Faithfulness of God,* 2 vols. (London: SPCK, 2013), pt. 3, 702.

92. Wright, *Paul and the Faithfulness,* 702.

simply a happy linguistic accident. . . . It opens up a possible 'incarnational' reading of Romans 10:6."[93]

We have yet to note the further dimension in Paul of *the cosmic Christ.* In Romans 5:14 Paul refers to Christ as the one of whom Adam is a "type" (Gk. *typos*). In 1 Corinthians 15:45 Paul declares, "'The first man, Adam, became a living being'; the last Adam [Christ] became a life-giving spirit." Paul adds in verse 49, "Just as we have borne the image of the man of dust [Adam], we will also bear the image of the man of heaven [Christ]." Such terms as "the image of God" (2 Cor. 4:4; Col. 1:15), "the firstborn" (Rom. 8:29; Col. 1:15, 18), the "wisdom" of God (1 Cor. 1:24, 30; Col. 2:3), as well as "last Adam," witness to the cosmic scope of Paul's thought. He refers to Christ as "Savior" in Philippians 3:20 and Ephesians 5:23.

Paul uses the term "Son of God" four times (Rom. 1:4; 2 Cor. 1:19; Gal. 2:20; Eph. 4:13). But the term "the Son" occurs once (1 Cor. 15:28), and the phrase "his Son" eleven times (Rom. 1:3, 9; 5:10; 8:3, 29, 32; 1 Cor. 1:9; Gal. 1:16; 4:6; Col. 1:13; 1 Thess. 1:10). In Romans 1:4, for example, Jesus Christ was declared to be Son of God with power according to the spirit (or Spirit) of holiness by the resurrection from the dead.

The cosmic dimension of Christ's status is expressed also in other terms. For example, in 1 Corinthians 8:6, Paul states: "For us there is one God, the Father, from whom (Gk. *ek hou*) are all things and for whom we exist, and one Lord, Jesus Christ, through whom (Gk. *di' hou*) are all things and through whom we exist (Gk. *hēmeis di' autou*)." Taylor rightly notes that here the Father "is the ultimate ground of the existence of the universe." Hence Paul uses *ek* of God the Father, whereas the Son "is the mediate cause of the universe of man," and hence he uses *dia*.[94] Taylor also observes that this Pauline passage has "strong affinities" with the doctrine of the *Logos* in John.

A second passage of cosmic significance is Romans 11:36: "For from him and through him and to him are all things. To him be the glory forever. Amen" (Gk. *ex autou kai di' autou kai eis auton ta panta*). The different choice of prepositions is significant. The origin of all things is God the Father. Their mediate Creator is God the Son, or Jesus Christ, whose mediating work actualizes creation.

A third cosmic passage is Colossians 1:16-17: "For in him (Christ; Gk. *en autō*) all things in heaven and on earth were created, things visible and

---

93. Wright, *Paul and the Faithfulness,* 703 and 704.

94. Vincent Taylor, *The Person of Christ in New Testament Teaching* (New York: Macmillan, 1958), 51.

invisible, whether thrones or dominions or rulers or powers — all things have been created through him and for him (Gk. *di' autou kai eis auton ektistai*). He himself is before all things (Gk. *pro pantōn*), and in him all things hold together (Gk. *en autō synestēken*)." This seems to go even beyond Romans 11:36.

Larry Hurtado has paid particular attention to this passage in Colossians. He examines its cadences and vocabulary, especially in the light of work by C. Stettler (2000). He believes it was written by the author of Colossians; it "lyrically proclaims Christ as the unique divine agent of creation and redemption. . . . In 1:15-17 the focus is on Christ and creation . . . the one through whom everything was created . . . 1:17 asserts his chronological priority."[95] C. F. D. Moule, similarly, describes this passage as "the startling statement . . . that Christ is . . . the goal or purpose towards which the created world is destined to move."[96] P. T. O'Brien also regards these passages as giving a *unique cosmic place* to Christ, in which "firstborn" (v. 15) denotes the Father's love: "Christ is unique. . . . He is both prior to and supreme over . . . creation."[97] Clearly the Colossian passage uses language drawn from the Jewish Wisdom tradition.

In Romans 9:5 Paul uses the phrase: "the Messiah, who is over all, God blessed forever." But the earliest Greek Uncial manuscripts contained no punctuation. Hence Cranfield lists at least five possible ways of understanding the phrase: (1) "To understand the whole as referring to Christ," that is, "who is God over all, blessed forever"; (2) to understand the phrase as referring to Christ, but separating the *theos* clause, that is, "who is over all, God blessed forever"; (3) to understand *ho ōn epi pantōn* as referring to Christ, and the rest as an independent doxology, that is, "who is over all. God blessed forever"; (4) to understand the phrase as an independent doxology having *Theos* as its subject, that is, "God who is over all, be blessed forever"; and (5) "to understand the whole as an independent doxology" with "who is over all" as its subject and *theos* in apposition to it, that is, "He who is over all, God, be blessed forever."[98]

Cranfield concludes that "the only serious argument" against (1) and (2) is that Paul appears explicitly to call Christ God only in 2 Thessalonians

95. Hurtado, *Lord Jesus Christ,* 507-8.
96. C. F. D. Moule, *The Epistles to the Colossians and to Philemon,* CGTC (Cambridge: CUP, 1962), 59.
97. Peter T. O'Brien, *Colossians, Philemon,* WBC (Nashville: Nelson, 1982), 45; cf. 44-47.
98. C. E. B. Cranfield, *The Epistle to the Romans,* 2 vols., ICC (Edinburgh: T. & T. Clark, 1975, 1979), 2:465.

1:12 and Titus 2:13, of which the Pauline authorship is often disputed. But, he adds, "*To conclude that he cannot have done so here seems to us quite unjustified,* in view of the stylistic considerations," which *favor* (1) or (2).[99] The verse, he concludes, "affirms first Christ's lordship over all things . . . and *secondly His divine nature.*"[100] Cranfield finally quotes Calvin's forthright comments: "To separate this clause from the rest of the context for the purpose of depriving Christ of this clear witness to his divinity is an audacious attempt to create darkness where there is full light."[101]

Joseph Fitzmyer is fully aware of the complexities of the interpretation of this verse and its punctuation, but similarly concludes, "The use of *theos* to refer to Christ is compatible with Paul's teaching, even though the appellation is not found elsewhere, save possibly in Gal. 2:20."[102] But this conclusion remains controversial. With Cranfield and Fitzmyer stand Wright, Bruce, Leenhardt, Nygren, and Metzger (Metzger in 1973). Against this view stand (broadly) Dodd, Dunn, Käsemann, and O. Kuss. In 1994 Metzger reported that a majority of the United Bible Committee was in favor of the more cautious reading, but a minority favored his 1973 reading.[103]

Larry Hurtado well sums up the net impact of all this for the practice of early Christian devotion to Christ. He writes, "Jesus is reverenced in a constellation of actions that resemble the ways in which a god is reverenced in the Roman-era religious scene. . . . Jesus is not reverenced as another, second, god. . . . Jesus is regularly defined with reference to the one God in Pauline christological statements."[104]

(ii) *The Epistle to the Hebrews.* Hebrews remains especially important since many modern theologians have argued that an emphasis on the deity of Christ is *logically incompatible* with his full humanity. But Hebrews bears early testimony to an outright assertion of Christ's divinity side by side with a moving and fully explicit account of his manhood. *This twofold emphasis is essential for expounding his role as the Mediator, or God-man, and his high priesthood.* It has even been called "The Epistle of Priesthood."[105] It is es-

99. Cranfield, *Romans,* 2:468, italics mine.
100. Cranfield, *Romans,* 2:469, italics mine.
101. Cranfield, *Romans,* 2:470.
102. Joseph A. Fitzmyer, *Romans,* AB 33 (New York: Doubleday, 1992), 549.
103. Bruce M. Metzger, *A Textual Commentary on the Greek New Testament,* 2nd ed. (New York: United Bible Societies, 1994), 460.
104. Hurtado, *Lord Jesus Christ,* 151.
105. Alexander Nairne, *The Epistle of Priesthood: Studies in the Epistle to the Hebrews* (Edinburgh: T. & T. Clark, 1913).

sential for Hebrews that Christ *represents God* to humanity, and *represents humanity* to God.

Hence, in his humanity, Christ belonged to the tribe of Judah (Heb. 7:14); endured the contradiction of sinners (12:3); suffered outside Jerusalem (13:12); was faithful to him who appointed him (3:2); "in every respect has been tested as we are, yet without sin" (4:15); put his trust in God (2:13); and "In the days of his flesh, . . . offered up prayers and supplications, with loud cries and tears, to the one who was able to save him from death" (5:7). In an older book, Mackintosh rightly wrote, "Nowhere in the NT is the humanity of Christ set forth so movingly."[106] Christ even "learned obedience through what he suffered" (Heb. 5:8).

This clearly establishes Christ's high-priestly role as a true representative of humankind to God, that is, "ascending mediator." Thus "Christ . . . entered into heaven itself [not a mere human sanctuary] . . . to remove sin by the sacrifice of himself" (Heb. 9:24-26). Hence the Lord declared, " 'You are a priest forever' — accordingly Jesus has also become the guarantee of a better covenant. . . . He always lives to make intercession for [us]" (7:21-25), and is "the mediator of a better covenant" (8:6).

Side by side with all this, God says of the Son, "Your throne, *O God,* is forever and ever" (1:8, italics mine). Hugh Montefiore comments on this quotation from Psalm 45:6-7 (44:7-8 LXX), "The author must have been *accustomed to the outright ascription of divinity to the Son,* for he shows here not the slightest embarrassment. This is the only place in the NT where the Son is described simply as *ho theos* (God)."[107] Similarly, Harold Attridge considers the Jewish tradition of interpreting the Psalms, and concludes, "For our author, then, Christ as divine is seen to have eternal reign, unlike the transitory angels."[108] William Lane argues similarly: "He (Christ) is addressed as God" in the application of Psalm 45.[109] Hurtado refers to the "impressive and distinctive exposition . . . of traditional and exalted claims for Jesus."[110]

To the exposition of Hebrews 1:8 can be added the equally impressive

106. H. R. Mackintosh, *The Doctrine of the Person of Christ* (Edinburgh: T. & T. Clark, 1913).

107. Hugh W. Montefiore, *A Commentary on the Epistle to the Hebrews* (London: Black, 1964), 47, italics mine.

108. Harold W. Attridge, *The Epistle to the Hebrews,* Hermeneia (Philadelphia: Fortress, 1989), 59.

109. William L. Lane, *Hebrews 1–8,* WBC 47A (Dallas: Word, 1991), 29.

110. Hurtado, *Lord Jesus Christ,* 499.

introduction of Hebrews 1:1-4, especially verses 3-4. Christ is "the reflec-tion of God's glory and the exact imprint of God's very being" (Gk. *hos ōn apaugasma tēs doxēs kai charaktēr tēs hypostaseōs autou,* v. 3). In the words of Montefiore, Christ is "the *exact imprint, die-stamp, or engraving (charaktēr)* of God's very being." He does not simply reflect God "in certain respects."[111] Lane takes this to mean "the exact representation of God's nature," where the author reflects on Psalm 2, Psalm 110, and contemporary currents of Jewish Wisdom theology.[112] To Attridge, verse 3 includes Christ's "pre-existence, incarnation, and exaltation, the unique images of 'effulgence' and 'imprint.'"[113] The Greek *apaugasma,* he continues, may denote active "radiance" of God, or passive "reflection" of God. God intervened in human history in the person of Christ. Christ exactly and precisely *represents God* to humankind.

(iii) *John.* If this were not a "concise" Christology, we should include a large section on John. Clearly in John, Christology constitutes a central and transparent theme. The culmination of rising confessions of Jesus Christ is the climactic confession of Thomas: "My Lord and my God!" (John 20:28).

The beginning of this Gospel sets out the *logos* theme, in which the Greek is *theos ēn ho logos* (John 1:1). This may better be rendered by the En-glish emphasis, "The Word was *God*" (Gk. emphatic word-order) than the more popular "the Word *was* God" (where there is no emphasis in Greek). The phrase "was with God" (Gk. *ēn pros ton theon,* John 1:1) means strictly "face to face with God." Danker calls it a "marker of closeness of relation or proximity."[114] The prologue also stresses, as Paul does, Christ's role as mediate Creator: "All things came into being through him, and without him not one thing came into being" (1:3). The NRSV punctuation is supported by most manuscript readings.[115] The ending of the prologue, "and the Word became flesh and lived among us," establishes Christ's humanity, as well as its witness to Christ (1:14; cf. 1:7, 11).

There are several different verdicts on the relation of the prologue to the main body of the Gospel, but most writers conclude that the thematic links with the rest of the Gospel are too numerous to allow us to think of the prologue as an independent composition.[116] The theme of *testimony or*

111. Montefiore, *Hebrews,* 35.

112. Lane, *Hebrews 1–8,* 9.

113. Attridge, *Hebrews,* 41.

114. BDAG 874.

115. Metzger, *A Textual Commentary,* 167-68.

116. Cf. Catrin H. Williams and Christopher Rowland, eds., *John's Gospel and Intima-*

witness recurs regularly (1:19; 2:25; 4:39; 5:39; 15:26; 21:24); as do *life,* with twenty-two references (1:4; 3:15, 36; 4:14; and at least eighteen further references); *light,* with fourteen (1:4, 5, 7, 8-9; 3:19-21; and at least seven further references); and *belief or believing* with seventy-one references (1:7, 12, 50; 2:11, 22, 23; 3:12, 15-16, 18, 36; and at least sixty further references).

We have already noted many allusions to the humanity of Jesus in John. We see his role as *Mediator* in John 1:51: "You will see heaven opened and the angels of God ascending and descending upon the Son of Man." He is the unique Son of God (3:16), who "speaks the words of God" (3:34), and must receive honor "just as they honor the Father" (5:23). Just as in the Synoptic Gospels, only God can forgive sin, so in John only God is the ultimate source of life (6:27, 35, 54; 14:6). W. L. Knox argued long ago that life and light, glory and truth, revelation and Word recur repeatedly in the Gospel, to which the prologue is an overture, and Cullmann endorses this. T. W. Manson argued that the *Logos* idea was "the hallmark of John himself."[117]

Only John applies *monogenēs* in the NT to Jesus (John 1:14, 18; 3:16, 18; cf. 1 John 4:9). Other "sons of God" are different in kind. Belief in God is associated with belief in Christ (John 14:1, 19). Jesus declared, "The Father and I are one" (10:30), and "I am in the Father and the Father is in me" (14:11). He loves, wills, and acts as God the Father loves, wills, and acts. Christ's preexistence is implied not only by the more ambitious "I was sent" (which can apply to prophets) but also by "I came from God" (8:42). Further, Jesus "comes from above [and] is above all" (3:31), and "comes down from heaven" (6:33, 41). John 16:28 begins, "I came from the Father and have come into the world." In 17:5 Jesus speaks of "the glory that I had in your presence before the world existed." In spite of the comments of Dunn and others, which tend to deny or reinterpret the "preexistence" of Jesus, it is difficult to see how else this cumulative list of passages could be understood.[118] The ascending witnesses of Jesus, as we have noted, reach their climax in 20:28, when Thomas exclaimed, *"My Lord and my God!"*

---

tions of Apocalyptic (London: Bloomsbury, 2013), especially essays by Rowland and Ashton; R. Alan Culpepper, "The Pivot of John's Prologue," *NTS* 27 (1980-1981): 1-31; and C. K. Barrett, *The Prologue of St. John's Gospel* (London: Athlone, 1971).

117. T. W. Manson, *On Paul and John: Some Selected Theological Themes* (1963; reprint, London: SCM, 2012), 138.

118. Cf., for example, E. K. Lee, *The Religious Thought of St. John* (London: SPCK, 1950), 56-73.

5. Radical Contrasts between Ancient and Modern Christologies

Curiously, as we noted, from the Enlightenment to the late twentieth century, a host of writers on Christology have argued that the full humanity and deity of Jesus Christ are *logically incompatible with each other,* in spite of the early witness to the *contrary in Hebrews, John, probably Paul, and certainly most of the Church Fathers* up to Chalcedon. A number of British theologians, including J. A. T. Robinson in *The Human Face of God* (1973), Maurice Wiles in Sykes and Clayton (eds.), *Christ, Faith, and History* (1972), and contributors to the John Hick–edited volume *The Myth of God Incarnate* (1977) focus on the alleged logical incompatibility of the divine and human.[119] In German Christology, at least according to McGrath, from Reimarus and Lessing to the Bultmann school, the *"Christ of faith"* has been split off from "the *Jesus of history."*[120] Only with Pannenberg, Moltmann, Rahner, and Kuschel in Germany, and Wright, Dunn, Hurtado, and Bauckham in Britain, and Joel Green and Ben Witherington, among others, in America, has this dualism become overcome and resolved.[121]

(i) *The Ancient Church.* Immediately after the close of the NT canon, Clement of Rome (c. 96) testified to the humanity of Jesus, who "came not with pomp or arrogance, for all his power" (*1 Clement* 16.1-2). Ignatius (c. 110-112) wrote, "He (Jesus) was truly born, ate and drank . . . truly crucified and truly died" (*To the Trallians* 9.1-2), but also "in union with God" (*To the Smyrnaeans* 1.1-2). *Irenaeus* (c. 130–c. 200) expounded both the deity and humanity of Christ. He opposed the Gnostic notion of Jesus "without body" (*Against Heresies* 1.24.2), and affirmed his birth as "Son of David, born of the Virgin Mary" (3.16.2, 3). But, he stated, Christ is also "God with us" (3.19.3), and "Son of God, our Lord, Word of the Father" (3.19.3).

Tertullian (c. 150–c. 225) insisted, "The Father is God, the Son is God,

119. Robinson, *The Human Face of God;* Maurice F. Wiles, "Does Christology Rest on a Mistake?" in *Christ, Faith, and History,* ed. Stephen W. Sykes and J. P. Clayton (Cambridge: CUP, 1972), 11, cf. 1-12; and John Hick, ed., *The Myth of God Incarnate* (London: SCM, 1977), including Wiles (1-19 and 148-66), Goulder (48-86), and Cupitt (133-47).

120. Alister E. McGrath, *The Making of Modern German Christology, 1750-1990* (Oxford: Blackwell, 1986), especially 9-31 (from Lessing and Reimarus), 53-68 (from Ritschl to Harnack), and 127-60 (from Bultmann to Ebeling).

121. Pannenberg, *Jesus — God and Man* (London: SCM, 1968); Moltmann, *The Way of Jesus Christ;* Karl Rahner, *Foundations of Christian Faith: An Introduction to the Idea of Christianity* (New York: Crossroad, 1978, 2004), 178-321; Karl-Josef Kuschel, *Born before All Time? The Dispute over Christ's Origin* (London: SCM, 1992); Wright, *Jesus and the Victory of God;* and Dunn, *Jesus Remembered.*

and the Holy Spirit is God, and each is God" (*Against Praxeas* 13). Christ took upon himself "a twofold state, which is not confused, but co joined in one person — Jesus, God and man" (*Against Praxeas* 27). Tertullian rejected a hybrid figure of Christ, almost anticipating Robinson's extreme language about "a bat-centaur."

Origen (c. 185–c. 254) went even further, explaining that the Father and the Son were one in essence or being (Gk. *homoousios*). Christ's generation, he asserted, is eternal (*De principiis* 1.2.4). He came "in the glory of God the Father" (2.6.3). Perhaps one of the places in which Origen overstretched language was his allusion to Christ as "a second God" (*Against Celsus* 5.39), and perhaps to his receiving honor "second only to that given to the Most High God" (7.57).

The most notorious exception to the corporate mind of the Church Fathers was probably *Arius* (c. 250-336). Although Rowan Williams defends him against more extreme criticisms, Arius argued that "The Son did not always exist. . . . He had a beginning." But *Eusebius, Athanasius,* and the *Cappadocian Fathers* asserted, in the words of the Nicene Creed (325), "We believe in one Lord, Jesus Christ . . . God from God, Light from Light . . . the Only Begotten Son." Athanasius explicated the theme: "Christ is not a creature, for Christians worship and pray to Jesus Christ." Jesus Christ was "of the same being" as the Father. He wrote, "Being God, he became as a human being. . . . As a human being he felt thirst and tiredness, he suffered pain. . . . As God he said, 'I am in the Father and the Father in me'" (*Epistle to Serapion* 14).

In the West, *Hilary* and *Ambrose* endorsed the work of Athanasius, and this was consolidated further by Basil, Gregory of Nyssa, and Gregory of Nazianzus. Admittedly there were differences of emphasis between the School of Alexandria (including Cyril, 378-444) and the School of Antioch (including Theodore of Mopsuestia, 350-428). Nevertheless, Gregory of Nazianzus represented the mainstream when he wrote, "We do not separate the humanity from the divinity. . . . We assert . . . the unity and the identity of the person . . . the only Son. . . . Both natures are one by combination" (*Letter* 101).

For reasons of space, we shall not trace the complex twists and turns of the patristic debate that followed Apollinarius (c. 310-390), the interpretation of whom is complex, and Nestorius (d. c. 451), who was condemned at the Council of Ephesus (431). Allegedly Apollinarius regarded the body and soul of Jesus as fully human, while Nestorius construed the relation between the divine and human "natures" differently. The church saw the need to insist that these are integrally combined in one person, Jesus Christ. In very broad terms, Apollinarius appeared to separate the divine and human from the Alexandrian or "divine" side, while Nestorius appeared to separate them from the Antiochene or "human" side. Modern theologians repudiate both, whatever their genuine intentions.

In these debates the term *theotokos,* as applied to the Virgin Mary, served not to elevate her but to clarify the *status of Christ.* The Council of Chalcedon (451) stressed that Christ was one-in-being *(homoousios)* with God the Father. It is a pity that the creeds use a Latinized version, "of the same substance" *(substantia)* as the Father. It was then equivalent to *ousia,* "being," in Greek. But today "substance" may suggest more philosophical difficulties.

This formulation held sway until modern times. After the Enlightenment, however, several complicating factors emerged. To attempt some working clarity, we shall broadly and selectively distinguish between three groups of modern thinkers, although these may overlap in particular respects.

(ii) *The Modern Era.* (1) *Very Broadly "Liberal" Protestant Approaches.* (a) *G. E. Lessing* (1729-1781) published and probably edited the *Fragments* of H. S. Reimarus. His most famous (or infamous) aphorism was: "The accidental truths of history can never become the proof of necessary truths of reason."[122] He argued that between history and reason there lay "an ugly broad ditch *(garstige, breite Graben)."*[123] This paved the way for a thoroughly *rationalist* view of Christ, which also matched the "age of reason" in the eighteenth century.

(b) *Friedrich D. E. Schleiermacher* (1768-1834), as a Lutheran, did regard Christ as Redeemer and "last Adam"; but he also argued, "The Redeemer . . . is like all men in virtue of the identity of human nature, but distinguished from these by the constant potency of his God-consciousness, which was a veritable existence of God in him."[124] J. Macquarrie understands Christ's person to be different only in degree, not in kind, although A. McGrath dissents from this, as we noted in chapter 9.[125] Macquarrie calls this "humanistic Christology."

122. G. E. Lessing, "On the Proof of the Spirit and of Power," in *Lessing's Theological Writings,* ed. Henry Chadwick (Stanford: Stanford University Press, 1956), 53.

123. Lessing, "On the Proof," 55.

124. Friedrich D. E. Schleiermacher, *The Christian Faith* (Edinburgh: T. & T. Clark, 1989; orig. 1821), sect. 94, 385.

125. John Macquarrie, *Jesus Christ in Modern Thought* (London: SCM, 1990), 204-7.

(c) *David Strauss* (1808-1874) published the first edition of his *Life of Jesus* in 1835 at a very early age, and denied a "supernatural" foundation of events in the Gospels. To describe such past events he used the term "myth," which he defined as *ideas* presented in the form of *narrative.* A myth did not recount a "fact." He regarded Schleiermacher's Christology as the last "churchly" account of Christology. His *Life of Jesus* passed through five editions, the last becoming a polemical attack against traditional Christian faith.

(d) *Albrecht Ritschl* (1822-1889) also rejected the "two natures" Chalcedonian Christology. He sought a "scientific" approach, which rejected "mysteries" but looked to the historical Jesus as a teacher of ethics and facilitator of community. Yet he regarded Christ as God's final revelation. His Lutheranism, we noted, has been defended by James Richmond, who also questions his popular title as the father of the liberal theology that characterized Harnack.

(e) *Rudolf Bultmann* (1884-1976) argued that Heidegger's philosophy had provided him with conceptual tools to formulate his NT Christology. We have noted his pessimistic assessment of the "Quest" in Schweitzer. His major concern was not for an ontological assessment of the status of Jesus in himself in reality, but for his *existential* or practical impact on the earliest communities (and hence on "me" today). He borrowed Strauss's notion of "myth," complicated it, and set about "demythologizing" the mythical elements of the NT, in order to expose only its *kerygmatic* (or proclamatory) language. Almost single-handedly he was responsible for a mid-twentieth-century swing toward the *existential dimension of Christology.* It was against this background that Pannenberg in Protestant theology and Kuschel in Catholic theology have made loud protests. Whereas Bultmann attacks "objectification," Pannenberg regards event and meaning as "intertwined." "Fact" and "value" are not separate, as in the neo-Kantian tradition.

(f) *J. A. T. Robinson, Maurice Wiles,* and *John Hick.* These represent a British movement in the 1970s, which argued that the Chalcedonian formula committed a "category mistake." Wiles argued that we should reject the notion of "two storys" (as in a building) in favor of "two different kinds of story . . . a frankly mythological story" and a historical one; he added, "But we don't try to bind the two stories together."[126] Robinson derided the notion that "Jesus was a hybrid . . . a God-man . . . a sort of bat-man or centaur," seen in "two natured terms."[127] John Hick insisted, "Incarnation in

126. Wiles, "Does Christology Rest?" 8.
127. J. A. T. Robinson, "Need Jesus Have Been Perfect?" in *Christ, Faith, and History,* 39.

its proper sense is not . . . directly presented in Scripture"; we must seek "a pictorial way of expressing these truths."[128]

(2) *The Catholic Reaction.* (a) *Karl Rahner* (1904-1984). In general terms, many, if not most, traditional Catholic theologians continued the tradition of Chalcedon and Aquinas. In contrast to Bultmann, Rahner sees the origin of Christology in the faith of *Jesus himself.* God's self-communication "reaches its goal and climax in Jesus Christ."[129] Jesus, he says, was conscious of "a radical and unique closeness to God."[130] Karen Kilby writes, "Rahner affirms, with the Christian tradition, the full divinity, as the full humanity of Jesus Christ."[131] Nevertheless, Rahner also departs from the "two natures" Christology of Chalcedon at the same time. He explicates the Chalcedonian formula in terms of a *transcendental* philosophy. He writes, "Today, an *a priori* doctrine of the God-Man must be developed in a transcendental theology," that is, exploring conditions of *possibility.*[132] This allows for an *"ascending"* Christology as well as a "descending" one. The lynchpin of his theology, in explicit contrast to Bultmann, is that he allows for an "ontological" Christology (what Christ is in himself and in reality) as well as an "existential" one (what he means to me in practice).[133]

(b) *Hans Urs von Balthasar* (1905-1988). Balthasar's most important study of Christology comes in the second part of volume 3 of his *Theo-Drama.* Mission, he states, stands "at the centre of John's Christology and expresses both the Trinitarian and soteriological dimension of the mind of Jesus."[134] The identity of Jesus is "given along with his mission"; the two are indissolubly tied together. The activity of the Holy Spirit, and his prayer to, and closeness with, God the Father, are essential to the person and work.[135] This is both "Christology from below" *and* "Christology from above."[136]

(c) *Edward Schillebeeckx* (1914-2009) could be called one of the most "daring" or "progressive" Catholic theologians in Christology. But by the same token, many regard him as too liberal. He was born in Antwerp, studied

---

128. Hick, *Myth of God Incarnate,* 3 and 9.

129. Rahner, *Foundations of Christian Faith,* 176.

130. Rahner, *Foundations of Christian Faith,* 249.

131. Karen Kilby, *Karl Rahner: Theology and Philosophy* (London: Routledge, 2004), 16.

132. Rahner, *Foundations of Christian Faith,* 177.

133. Rahner, *Foundations of Christian Faith,* 204.

134. Hans Urs von Balthasar, *Theo-Drama: Theological Dramatic Theory,* 5 vols. (San Francisco: Ignatius; Edinburgh: T. & T. Clark, 1973-1992), 3:151.

135. Balthasar, *Theo-Drama,* 3:155.

136. Balthasar, *Theo-Drama,* 3:150; cf. 170-227.

theology at Louvain and the Sorbonne, and was professor at Nijmegen. By 1976 Rome had become concerned about his christological views, although he was active in Vatican II (1962-1965). In 1974 he published *Jesus: An Experiment in Christology*. He was influenced by Robinson, and wrote of the need to explore "the intelligibility for man of Christological belief . . . (and) what it can signify for people today."[137]

(d) *Hans Küng* (b. 1928) published *The Incarnation of God: An Introduction to Hegel's Thought* (1970). He insists, "The divine in a particular shape appears as man."[138] He comments, "This is the Word made flesh."[139] In the first chapter he shows the limitations of post-Enlightenment theologians, and in the second chapter the limitations of the "lives of Jesus." Chapter 3 focuses on the God-man. On the cross we see *"the true nature of God."*[140] Hegel, he suggests, understood "the reality of . . . the God-Man." Post-Enlightenment theology is "one-sided." He concedes that conceptual formulations may change, but only as "changing; yet the same."[141] A *transcendental* approach allows for a wider vision of God and the whole world, and the manifestation of the infinite in history: "the teaching of Christ was accordingly . . . backed up by his life and death."[142]

(e) *Karl-Josef Kuschel* (b. 1948) published *Born before All Time?* (1990). He considers the first "Quest" from Harnack to Bultmann under the informative and pithy heading: "Failed Conversations of Yesterday."[143] This part includes the dispute over history and myth. Kuschel rightly identifies as "Bultmann's weak point" an "imprecise concept of myth."[144] Bultmann had even reversed Harnack's claim that "there can be no Christianity without the specific historical Jesus."[145] Kuschel takes more seriously "the Word became flesh" (John 1:14), not only in relation to Bultmann, but also in Barth and Brunner.

Kuschel's second and third parts become more complex. Part 2 con-

137. Edward Schillebeeckx, *Jesus: An Experiment in Christology* (London: Collins, 1979), 37.

138. Hans Küng, *The Incarnation of God: An Introduction to Hegel's Thought* (Edinburgh: T. & T. Clark, 1987), 111.

139. Küng, *The Incarnation of God,* 126.

140. Küng, *The Incarnation of God,* 209.

141. Küng, *The Incarnation of God,* 143.

142. Küng, *The Incarnation of God,* 369; cf. 312-412.

143. Karl-Josef Kuschel, *Born before All Time? The Dispute over Christ's Origin* (London: SCM, 1992), 35-176.

144. Kuschel, *Born before All Time?* 161-63.

145. Kuschel, *Born before All Time?* 174.

siders biblical material exegetically. He insists, for example, that the hymn in Philippians 2:6-11 does not speak of Jesus Christ's preexistence and incarnation, only of Christ's high status. Similarly he regards Galatians 4:4 as implying no more than Christ's unique relation to God. Appealing to the exegesis of K. Berger, James Dunn, and others, he insists, "There is no sign of any unambiguous and explicit statement about pre-existence outlined by Paul."[146] However, Kuschel does not let the matter rest there in his third part. Although, he insists, neither Paul nor Hebrews nor John teaches the preexistence of the incarnate *man* Jesus Christ, the raised Christ's oneness with God suggests more than a beginning in time. Some Protestants may see a tension between exegesis and doctrine (as in some other Catholic works). But Kuschel is well aware of the dangers of such a divorce. That is precisely why his work becomes highly complex.

(iii) *Pannenberg and Moltmann.* A schematic grouping of three different approaches can be misleading, if pressed too far, but in contrast to liberal Protestant theology and Catholic theology, Pannenberg and Moltmann stand apart as representing a distinctive approach.

(a) *Wolfhart Pannenberg* (1928-2014). From the first, Pannenberg stressed the importance of the *apocalyptic background* to the person and ministry of Christ. Although this was emphasized in his earliest writings, he applies it directly to Christology in *Jesus — God and Man.* He stresses *history,* as against Kähler: "Only on the basis of what happened in the past, not because of present experience, do we know that he (Jesus) lives as the exalted Lord."[147] He also regards as inadequate Barth's "Christology from above" (33-37). Jesus' unity with God "is substantiated in most cases by the claim to authority in his proclamation" (53). In his acts of authority, Jesus "put himself in God's place" (67). Further, Pannenberg argues that the *resurrection* of Jesus Christ is crucial to this: "Thereby the end of the world has begun. . . . God is ultimately in Jesus" (69).

This was not an unintelligible event. To return to our point about apocalyptic, Pannenberg observes, "The basis of the knowledge of Jesus' significance remains bound to the original apocalyptic horizon of Jesus' history, which has also been modified by this history. If this horizon is lost, then Christology becomes mythology" (83). The resurrection appearances to Peter and the Twelve are to be taken seriously. Pannenberg also regards *the tradition of the empty tomb* as "historical fact" (100).

146. Kuschel, *Born before All Time?* 303; cf. 250-54 and 274.
147. Pannenberg, *JGM* 28. Page references have been placed in the text.

As Mediator, Jesus represents both God to humankind and humankind to God (109 and 123-24). The Holy Spirit mediates "God's presence in Jesus" (116). Against many NT specialists, he rightly insists, "Paul presupposed the pre-existence of the Son of God (Gal. 4:4; Rom, 8:3)," even if Kuschel understands this as referring only to the *heavenly figure* of Christ, not to the *man* Jesus (151). Kuschel also ascribes this distinction to Pannenberg, which may be debated.[148]

Pannenberg is equally emphatic that what it means to be *truly human* is shown in Jesus Christ: Jesus was pleasing to God, and took "the risk of trust" (*JGM* 203). The nearness of God found expression in Jesus' address to God as "Father," which sets in train the consequences of obedience and love (229). He died a vicarious death "for us, for our sins" (247).

In the third part of *Jesus — God and Man,* Pannenberg concedes that the Chalcedonian formula of two "substances" brings its own difficulties, as even two "natures" does, but he nevertheless affirms "the true divinity and true humanity of Jesus . . . as indispensable" (284-85). The terminology of "two natures" ensured conceptual inflexibility on both the Alexandrian and Antiochene side of the patristic debate. A better term was the "mutual interpenetration" *(perichōrēsis)* of the two natures, a term that had already featured in the Cappadocian Fathers.

In his *Systematic Theology* Pannenberg endorses much of his earlier work. Against a Christology exclusively "from above" or "from below," he insists that we "go back instead to the total character of the coming of Jesus."[149] Yet, as before, "The foundation is the history of Jesus" (2:282). It is "the resurrection of Jesus . . . that legitimates his pre-Easter work" (2:283). The Easter message, he insists, against Bultmann, *"follows* the Easter event; it does not constitute it" (2:288). No NT exegesis excludes "the classical Christology of the incarnation" (2:288). He adds: *"The first Christian could not have successfully preached the resurrection of Jesus, if his body had been intact in the tomb. . . . We must assume that [the] tomb was in fact empty"* (2:358-59, italics mine). In Pannenberg's view, "The event took place *in this world,* namely in the tomb of Jesus in Jerusalem before the visit of the women" (2:360, italics mine).

On the preexistence of Jesus Christ, Pannenberg asserts, "The origin of the divine Sonship of Jesus can lie, then, only in the eternity of God himself. Though pre-existence statements in the New Testament might be rather

---

148. Kuschel, *Born before All Time?* 403-6.
149. Pannenberg, *ST* 2:280. Page references have been placed in the text.

vaguely formulated for the most part, this is their true point" (2:371). Finally, "Jesus Christ is the paradigm of all humanity in its relation to God . . . as we are to be" (2:430).

(b) *Jürgen Moltmann* (b. 1926). Moltmann, like Pannenberg, argues that Jesus should be regarded in terms of the messianic expectation of the OT, Israel's history, and Judaism. The Messiah is "a historical figure of hope, with a background in Isaiah 7, 9, and 11, Zechariah, 9, and Micah 4:5."[150] The pivotal point is "Emmanuel," or "God with us," as Barth has argued, and also the coming of *God.* Moltmann, like Pannenberg, rejects a value-neutral, or supposedly exclusively "historical," Christology. He writes, "Every Christology presupposes belief. . . . Believing and thinking inevitably belong together" (39). Pannenberg described a value-neutral approach as "anthropocentric."

There are limits, Moltmann argues, to how far a "Christology from below" can take us. He calls "anthropological" Christology simply "Jesusology, and nothing else" (55). He then offers his criticism of the liberal "lives of Jesus." Together with Zizioulas, he regards the messianic mission as beginning with the Holy Spirit. The narrative of the baptism of Jesus is fully Trinitarian in character. Jesus is anointed and empowered by the Holy Spirit to please his Father, who pronounces this. Jesus now begins to call men and women to conversion and discipleship, and initiates them into a "way of life" (116-19). At the end of his life Jesus experiences "the frightening eclipse of God" (Mark 14:32-42) and "God-forsakenness at Golgotha" (166-67). He concludes, like Pannenberg, that "God's raising of Christ was the foundation for faith in Christ" (213). A pathway now opens, leading us ultimately to "the cosmic Christ" and to "the renewal of creation" (275-87). This, once again, falls "within the special horizon of prophetic and apocalyptic expectations."[151]

The genius of Moltmann and Pannenberg has been to expound a convincing Christology, which is firmly anchored both in the NT and in history, and also theologically to present the person of Christ and Christ's resurrection in their full theological depth and dimensions.

150. Moltmann, *Way of Jesus Christ,* 5-13. Page references have been placed in the text.
151. Jürgen Moltmann, *Theology of Hope* (London: SCM, 1967), 191.

CHAPTER XI

The Holy Spirit: (I) Biblical Doctrine

This subject needs a slightly different format from most of the others. We must first note reasons for the traditional neglect of the doctrine, both in the formation of the great creeds and in the modern era of theology until relatively recently. We must also set out some fundamental conclusions, and distinguish these from more controversial issues. In addition, we must take special account of the Pentecostal movement and charismatic churches. Our conclusions will be summarized at the end. These will contain such themes as the personhood and otherness of the Holy Spirit, in contrast to looser and non-Pauline popular uses of such terms as "spirituality" to denote religious aspirations from below, rather than what relates to the Holy Spirit from above. These will also include the Trinitarian context of the person and work of the Holy Spirit, his presence and gifts to all Christian people, his holiness, and the relevance of hermeneutics to some key biblical passages.

We can surmise two reasons for the relative neglect of this doctrine until recently. First, J. E. Fison and others have rightly drawn attention to "the *self-effacement*" of the Holy Spirit.[1] In the words of Jesus, the Spirit does not speak of himself, but throws the spotlight *onto Christ*. The Spirit operates within a christological (and corporate and eschatological) frame of reference. In the words of Jesus and John: "He (the Spirit) will not speak on his own (Gk. *aph' heautou*). . . . He shall glorify me" (John 16:13-14). This suggests that to put the Spirit in the spotlight would only with difficulty be seen as due to the prompting of the Holy Spirit.

1. Joseph E. Fison, *The Blessing of the Holy Spirit* (London and New York: Longman, Green, 1950), 11, 22, 27, 72, 93, 107, 138, 140, 175, 177, and 199.

Second, a number of references both to the Hebrew word for "Spirit," *rûach,* and to the Greek word for "Spirit," *pneuma,* seem ambiguous in meaning, and can even refer to the human spirit. Indeed, the NRSV renders the term "spirit" (with a lowercase *s*), when in most responsible exegesis the word denotes "Spirit" (uppercase *S*). A typical ambiguity arises in Romans 12:11, where the Greek is *tō pneumati zeontes.* The KJV/AV renders it, "fervent in spirit"; the RSV renders it, "be aglow with the Spirit"; the NEB and NRSV have "ardour of spirit"; the NJB translates, "an eager spirit"; and the NIV has "spiritual fervor," skillfully leaving both options open. Personally I have no doubt that C. E. B. Cranfield captures what is most characteristic of Paul. He writes, "The Christian is to allow himself to be set on fire . . . by the Holy Spirit"; there should be "nothing languid, nothing lukewarm in us, but [we] should do all things with the Spirit's fervour."[2]

Only one more example of acknowledged ambiguity is needed. In Genesis 1:2 the NRSV translates the Hebrew, "A wind *(rûach)* from God swept over the face of the waters." But of the 387 times the OT uses *rûach,* the LXX translates it as *pneuma* 264 times, and as *anemos* (wind) only 49 times, of which none appear in Genesis, including in Genesis 1:2.[3] No doubt *rûach* denotes "wind" on a number of occasions.[4] But C. K. Barrett and many others render the word in Genesis 1:2 as denoting the creative Spirit of God, and compare Psalm 104:30: "When you send forth your Spirit, they are created."[5] Here, however, the difference is not so great. As Wheeler Robinson long ago commented, in the wind there is transcendent mysterious power, and as C. Ryder Smith observed, "In the wind there is God . . . for men cannot make the winds blow."[6]

1. Foundations and Themes in the Old Testament and Judaism

The OT provides the major presuppositions behind all the NT writings. One is that *the Spirit is transcendent and "Other,"* in relation to humans and creatures. The Spirit represents *God* in *action.* But there are also two widespread overgeneralizations here. First, many claim that the Spirit is given to *indi-*

---

2. C. E. B. Cranfield, *The Epistle to the Romans,* 2 vols., ICC (Edinburgh: T. & T. Clark, 1975, 1979), 2:634.

3. Hatch-Redpath 1:86 and 2:1151.

4. BDB 924-26; M. V. Van Pelt and W. C. Kaiser, *"Rûach,"* in *NIDOTTE* 3:1073-78.

5. C. K. Barrett, *The Holy Spirit and the Gospel Tradition* (London: SPCK, 1958), 17-18.

6. C. Ryder Smith, *The Bible Doctrine of Man* (London: Epworth, 1951), 9.

viduals in the OT, as against the community in the NT. This is only partially true. Second, many claim that the Spirit is *hardly, if at all, a person.* Long ago Paul Feine argued that the Hebrews had no concept of *person,* purely on the basis of Hebrew *vocabulary.* But as James Barr has shown, this argument is misleading. Words do not have one-to-one relationships to concepts. We shall address these points sequentially.

(i) *Transcendent and "Other."* In Ezekiel 37:7-14 God pours out his Spirit onto dead Israel. The dead bones can contribute nothing of themselves, but God says, "I will put my spirit within you, and you shall live" (v. 14). This stands in contrast with the popular idea that *"spirituality"* sometimes comes from *within.* Cyril Powell comments on the Spirit, "It does not belong to him whose native sphere is that of *bāśār* (flesh)."[7] Ezekiel mentions the Spirit some forty-two times. Four "living creatures" carry the throne of God ahead with speed, and wherever the Spirit would go, they went (Ezek. 1:12). The Spirit "lifted up" the prophet and bore him away (3:14), just as the Spirit bore Elijah (3:12, 14; 8:3; 11:1, 24; 37:1).

Even more pointed is this notion:

By the word of the LORD the heavens were made,
    and all their host by the *rûach* of his mouth. (Ps. 33:6)

Job echoes this:

"The spirit of God has made me,
    and the breath of the Almighty gives me life." (Job 33:4: cf. Ps. 104:30)

One classic passage reads:

The Egyptians are human, and not God;
    their horses are flesh, and not spirit *(rûach).* (Isa. 31:3)

That is, the Egyptians are weak and human, but the Spirit of God powerful and "Other."

(ii) *Given to Individuals within the Context of Community.* The second popular generalization is that the Spirit is given only to *individuals, not to the community.* There is much truth in this, except that it often applies to individuals only *within the context of community.* The Spirit is given to indi-

7. Cyril H. Powell, *The Biblical Concept of Power* (London: Epworth, 1963), 26.

viduals for tasks that concern the welfare of the community. In Luke 4:18-19 Jesus applies to himself the prophecy of Isaiah 11:2:

"The Spirit of the Lord is upon me,
    because he has anointed me to bring good news to the poor.
He has sent me to proclaim release to the captives. . . ."

In the OT the Spirit is *often given to chosen individuals* to perform specific tasks for the benefit of *the whole community.* In one of the earliest writings of the OT, the Lord raised up the judges as individuals. These included Othniel (Judg. 3:9-10), Ehud (3:15), Deborah (4:4-23), Gideon (6:34; cf. 8:35), probably Abimelech (9:1–10:2), Jephthah (11:29; cf. 11:1–12:7), and Samson (13:25; cf. 13:2–16:31). Although these were examples of an individual anointing for a task, the task was to deliver the *corporate community* from bondage and oppression within God's purposes for Israel.

Although Bezalel received the Spirit as an individual for the gift of craftsmanship (Exod. 31:3), the gift was given to enhance the worship of God by Israel (31:2-11). In the prophecies of Isaiah the Spirit of the Lord is to rest on the One who emerges from the "stump of Jesse" for the blessing of the remnant of Israel (Isa. 11:2; cf. 11:1-16). The same is true of the figure of the Servant of the Lord (Isa. 42:1; cf. 44:3; 48:16). Joel 2:28, famously quoted by Peter in Acts 2, is clearly a reference to the eschatological gift of the Spirit to the whole *community of God's people:* "I will pour out my spirit on all flesh." Many passages are not restricted either to an individual or the community, for example, "Not by might, nor by power, but by my spirit" (Zech. 4:6); while others are more clearly communal (Hag. 2:5). Floyd Filson stressed the overlap of conceptual schemes in the OT and NT. Of the NT he observed, "It is likewise true that chosen individuals are given the Spirit for special tasks, but this does not mean that some are left without the Spirit."[8]

(iii) *Personal or Suprapersonal.* A third main characteristic of the Spirit of God in the OT is that the Spirit often constitutes an *extension of God himself.* But to regard the Spirit as *impersonal* or subpersonal seems to contradict the notion that *God is personal.* This theme is emphasized especially by Gordon Fee. Often the Spirit is mentioned in synonymous parallelism with God. In the familiar Psalm 51, the first part of the verse "Do not cast

8. Floyd V. Filson, *The New Testament against Its Environment: The Gospel of Christ, the Risen Lord* (London: SCM, 1950), 78.

me away from your presence" is parallel with "and do not take your Holy Spirit from me" (Ps. 51:11 NRSV, where term is lowercase). The Spirit of God is clearly a mode of God's activity. Statements about God's Word, Eichrodt argues, often "overlap with those about the Spirit."[9] Fee especially but not exclusively associates this aspect with Paul, in his book *God's Empowering Presence.*[10] To seek the Spirit of God is to seek God.

This suggests the *developing* theme that *the Spirit of God is* personal or *suprapersonal.* If the Spirit is truly an extension of God, *we would not dream of calling the Spirit "it," as so often occurs in popular parlance.* But, as in the case of God himself, this does not mean that God or his Spirit is "personal" *in the same sense that human beings are personal* (see chap. 1, sect. 1).

The same cannot be said of the three *creatures* of God, the Angel of the Lord, the Wisdom of God, and the Word of God. God *created* these as his servants or instruments. In the fourth century, as we shall see, Athanasius had to rescue and emphasize this point by using Scripture. Admittedly Gerhard von Rad, followed by Knight and by Charles Talbert, asserts: we are often "not really able to distinguish between Jahweh himself and his angel *(Heb. Mal'āk)*. . . . The angel is Jahweh himself, appearing to human beings in a human form."[11] Talbert and Knight cite the appearance of angels to Abraham (Gen. 19:1, 13; 22:11-18); and Proverbs 8:22-36 speaks of the heavenly Wisdom who existed before creation (8:25-29), and who calls to people not unlike how a person would call (8:1, 3-10).[12] But Wisdom also declares, "the Lord *created* me . . . I was set up" (8:22-23). Talbert insists that this "speaks of the descent of wisdom from the heavens with saving intent."[13] He cites parallels in Sirach 24; Baruch 3:27–4:4; and Wisdom of Solomon 6:18-20; 8:13, 17; 9:10; and by implication *2 Baruch* 48:36 and *1 Enoch* 42:1-2. But to explain differences from Proverbs 8, Talbert does not resort to "a common myth," as Pannenberg similarly insists that we do not. To be sure, the functions of the Angel, Wisdom, and the Word of God are

9. Walther Eichrodt, *Theology of the Old Testament,* 2 vols. (London: SCM, 1961, 1964), 2:79.

10. Gordon Fee, *God's Empowering Presence: The Holy Spirit in the Letters of Paul* (Peabody, Mass.: Hendrickson, 1994; Milton Keynes: Paternoster, 1995), especially 6-9.

11. Gerhard von Rad, *Old Testament Theology,* 2 vols. (Edinburgh: Oliver and Boyd, 1962, 1965), 1:287.

12. G. A. F. Knight, *A Biblical Approach to the Doctrine of the Trinity* (Edinburgh: Oliver and Boyd, 1953), and Charles H. Talbert, *The Development of Christology during the First Hundred Years and Other Essays on Early Christian Christology* (Leiden: Brill, 2011), 86-89.

13. Talbert, *Development of Christology,* 86-87.

redemptive; but in a this-worldly context, they *belong to the world order of what God has created.*

The Spirit, however, as Athanasius and Basil stressed, does *not* belong to this created order. In the words of Edmond Jacob, *"The spirit is God himself in creative and saving activity . . . the creative breath of life."*[14] He is "the means *par excellence* by which God asserts his presence," and "being of the very essence of God was brought into relation with the holiness which constituted his principal attribute."[15]

(iv) *Themes in Postbiblical Judaism.* In *postbiblical Judaism,* three themes stand out, in addition to the points about the Spirit we have already made. There is a distinction between Aramaic-speaking or rabbinic Judaism rooted in the Holy Land, and Greek-speaking Judaism rooted in the Diaspora, and expressed in such sources as the LXX, Philo, and Hellenistic Jewish writings. This remains the case, even if Martin Hengel, Howard Marshall, and others have rightly shown us that this contrast has blurred edges.

Three dominant features remain. First, the role of the Spirit in inspiring the *prophets* and encouraging the study of the *Law* is clearly seen, especially in the Dead Sea Scrolls, for example, 1QS 8:15-16, and in *Jubilees* 31:12. Second, the Holy Spirit is associated with *holiness* and *purification.* Whether this is an *effect* or a *cause* of the gift of the Spirit is not as clear-cut as in the NT. Third, *the community* emphasis becomes a clear focus of the Spirit's activity (e.g., 1QS 3:7-8). Simultaneously, Greek-speaking Judaism expresses a more *immanent* emphasis on the Spirit.

The Wisdom of Solomon, Philo, and 4 Maccabees are heavily indebted to Greek concepts and influences. By contrast, the Qumran scrolls (discovered from 1948 onward) and most apocalyptic literature represent Aramaic-speaking Judaism. These include the *Psalms of Solomon,* which looks forward to Jewish victory "over Latin men," and parts of *1 Enoch* and of the *Testament of the Twelve Patriarchs.* Ben Sirach (Ecclesiasticus) comes from the second century B.C., and often, like Proverbs, reflects a positive or optimistic view of Providence, and regards Wisdom and the Spirit as agents of God. Wisdom of Solomon belongs to the first century B.C., and represents the more cautious views of Ecclesiastes and Job. It denounces idolatry and any compromise with Greek values. In Wisdom 1:7, "The spirit of the LORD . . . holds all things together," as Christ does in Colossians 1:17. The use of "spirit"

---

14. Edmond Jacob, *Theology of the Old Testament* (London: Hodder and Stoughton, 1958), 124 and 127, italics mine.

15. Jacob, *Theology of the Old Testament,* 127.

becomes more anthropological. Montague argues, "Man holds his life-breath precariously as a gift from God (Psalm 104:29)."[16]

Erik Sjöberg associates the Spirit with *obedience* in the rabbinic writings.[17] He quotes Rabbi Nehemiah as saying, "He who undertakes a commandment in faith is worthy that the Holy Spirit should rest on him."[18] Similarly Rabbi Acha declared, "He who sacrifices himself for Israel shall receive . . . the Holy Spirit."[19] This is emphatically not Paul's view. Paul sees the Spirit as *cause,* and righteousness as *effect* (Gal. 3:1-5). In the Dead Sea Scrolls the holiness of the Spirit appears in the *Thanksgiving Hymns* (1QH 7:6; 9:32; 12:1; 13:19; 14:15; 16:11-12; 17:17). In the *Manual of Discipline* the Spirit will cleanse the community (1QS 3:13-40, 26). By contrast, Philo sees the Spirit as immanental and all-pervasive (Philo, *Allegorical Interpretation* 1.31-42). The Spirit is "diffused in its fullness in everything" (*On Giants* 27). The Spirit in humankind is "a particle of ethereal substance" (*On Planting* 18).[20] John Levison argues that Platonism is pivotal for Philo.[21] In Seneca the Spirit's immanental character is even more pronounced. He writes, "God is in you . . . a holy spirit is resident in us . . . a guardian of both what is good and evil in us" (*Epistle* 41.1).

The LXX goes even further than the Hebrew OT in stressing God's *creative* activity. This especially appears in *Targum Pseudo-Jonathan; 1 Enoch* 9:1; 4 Ezra 14:22; *Jubilees* 31:12; 1QS 8:16; and CD 2:12.[22]

In brief, the OT lays a foundation on which the NT writers build: the Spirit of God is transcendent and "other"; he is given to individuals, but only for tasks that serve the whole community; the Spirit constitutes an extension of God himself; and we have the beginnings of a personal understanding of the Spirit. In contrast to two widespread misunderstandings today, all this affirms that *the Spirit is not an "it"; and "spirituality" is not a matter of religious aspiration from within, but of being open to the Spirit as "other" and creative.*

16. George Montague, *The Holy Spirit: The Growth of Biblical Tradition* (Eugene, Ore.: Wipf and Stock, 1976), 102.

17. Erik Sjoberg, "*Rûach* in Palestine Judaism," in *TDNT* 6:383; cf. 375-89.

18. *Mekilta Exodus* 15:1.

19. *Numbers Rabbah* 15:20.

20. John R. Levison, *The Spirit in First-Century Judaism* (Boston and Leiden: Brill, 2002), 148.

21. Levison, *Spirit in First-Century Judaism,* 155.

22. Max Turner, *Power from on High: The Spirit in Israel's Restoration and Witness in Luke-Acts* (Sheffield: Sheffield Academic, 1996), especially 62-66, 86-104, and 107.

2. The Holy Spirit in the Synoptic Gospels and Acts

(i) *The Synoptic Gospels.* All four Gospels agree in marking the baptism of Jesus as an important event, in which God the Father, Jesus the Son, and the Holy Spirit are integrally involved. Moltmann, Pannenberg, and Rogers call it a Trinitarian event, recounted as a Trinitarian narrative. Mark 1:10-11 reads, "As he was coming up out of the water, he saw . . . the Spirit descending like a dove on him. And a voice came from heaven, 'You are my Son, the Beloved; with you I am well pleased.'" Luke 3:16, 21-22, and Matthew 3:16-17 add further details. Moltmann comments, "The NT talks about God by proclaiming in narrative the relationships of the Father, the Son, and the Spirit."[23]

C. K. Barrett comments further, "It is essentially the solemn appointment of the Messiah to his office, the installation of the Son of God."[24] This is confirmed by the next verse in Mark: "And the Spirit immediately drove him (Jesus) out into the wilderness . . . [for] forty days [to be] tempted by Satan" (Mark 1:12-13). Matthew and Luke provide parallels with minor variants (Matt. 4:1-2; Luke 4:1-2). Jesus was prepared for his messianic work by a time of struggle, just as the Holy Spirit will provoke conflict and testing in the life of Christians (Rom. 8:18-29). Max Turner describes Luke's "full of the Holy Spirit" (Luke 4:1) as typical of Luke, and marking "the person concerned as one in whose life the Spirit was regularly and powerfully felt."[25]

Mark, Matthew, and Luke also have the well-attested passage, "Whoever blasphemes against the Holy Spirit can never have forgiveness" (Mark 3:29; cf. Matt. 12:31; Luke 12:10). This verse causes perplexity and anxiety to many. But the context makes the meaning clear. Jewish authorities had argued that Jesus cast out demons by the prince of demons. Hence the reply of Jesus concerns calling good (as inspired by the Spirit) bad (as inspired by demons). If people become so distorted and corrupted that they reverse "good" and "bad," how could they even repent and be converted? The saying constitutes a warning against a stubborn and obstinate attempt to twist the truth. Those who worry about whether they have ever "blasphemed against," or spoken ill of, the Holy Spirit may be reassured that this very anxiety is a sign of the Spirit's working within them, and in no way a sign of his departure.

---

23. Jürgen Moltmann, *The Trinity and the Kingdom of God: The Doctrine of God* (London: SCM, 1981), 64.

24. Barrett, *The Holy Spirit*, 115.

25. Turner, *Power from on High*, 202.

At the end of the forty days the tempter departed only "until an opportune time" (Gk. *achri kairou,* Luke 4:13). On Hebrews 4:15, which says Jesus "has been tested as we are, yet without sin," Westcott comments that only "One who is sinless has experienced the greatest intensity of temptation, for only such a person has not yielded before the last and greatest strain."[26]

Only Matthew and Luke refer to the Holy Spirit at the conception and birth of Jesus. Matthew asserts, "She (Mary) was found to be with child from (Gk. *ek*) the Holy Spirit" (Matt. 1:18); Luke has more detail: "The Holy Spirit will come upon you (Mary)" (Luke 1:35). Ulrich Luz comments on Matthew 1:20, "The reference to the Holy Spirit, already familiar from v. 18, is repeated. This refers to the creative intervention of God through the Holy Spirit, and not the Spirit as a second partner for Mary."[27] In spite of those who have reservations about these birth narratives, this is a logical explanation in full accord with other biblical writings.

Luke includes more material about the Holy Spirit than Mark and Matthew. In Luke 4:18-19 he quotes Jesus as citing part of Isaiah 42:1 and of Isaiah 61:1: "The Spirit of the Lord is upon me, because he has anointed me to bring ... the year of the Lord's favor." G. W. H. Lampe regards this as one of "two great discourses" on the Spirit in Luke-Acts, the other being Peter's sermon at Pentecost (Acts 2:14-36).[28] Both discourses link the Spirit, he comments, with prayer and the word of God. Dunn regards Luke 4:18-19 as the introduction in Luke to Jesus as a charismatic figure.[29] Barrett, however, is more cautious about this. He writes that in Jesus' ministry prior to Easter, "Lack of glory and a cup of suffering were his (Jesus') Messianic vocation, and part of his poverty was the absence of all the signs of the Spirit of God. These would have been inconsistent with the office of a humiliated Messiah."[30] This is part of the reason, he suggests, that the Synoptic Gospels, especially Mark and Matthew, say so little about the Spirit. Dunn, however, rightly stresses the need for Jesus to trust God for his ministry and signs of the kingdom. We may also recall Fison's insistence on the "self-effacement" of the Holy Spirit, especially prior to Easter.

26. B. F. Westcott, *The Epistle to the Hebrews: The Greek Text* (New York and London: Macmillan, 1903), in 4:15.

27. Ulrich Luz, *Matthew 1–7: A Commentary* (Edinburgh: T. & T. Clark, 1990), 120.

28. G. W. H. Lampe, "The Holy Spirit in the Writings of St. Luke," in *Studies in the Gospels: In Memory of R. H. Lightfoot,* ed. D. E. Nineham (Oxford: Blackwell, 1967), 159-200.

29. James D. G. Dunn, *Jesus and the Spirit: A Study of the Religious and Charismatic Experience of Jesus and the First Christians* (London: SCM, 1975), 54-55 and 68-92.

30. Barrett, *The Holy Spirit,* 158; cf. 140-62.

We see in the Synoptic Gospels what may be clearer in the Epistles and in the Gospel of John. The Holy Spirit is an eschatological gift, a gift of the New Age. "Miracles" and exorcisms are a *sign of the in-breaking of the kingdom of God.* In one sense, the kingdom has arrived in the person of Jesus; but in another sense, it is only *"near"* (Gk. *engizō,* Mark 1:15). Hence there is some ambiguity today about "miracles." They do occur, but they are to be *expected* only if the kingdom of God has *arrived.* It is, in fact, still *in the process of* arriving.

The Synoptic Gospels do carry other allusions to the Holy Spirit. For example, the Spirit will guide the disciples of Jesus in moments of crisis (Mark 13:11; Matt. 10:19-20; Luke 12:12), although R. T. France warns us that this is not a resort for "lazy preachers."[31] Finally, Luke 24:49 looks forward to the Father's promise of "power from on high." In sum, (1) the writers of the Synoptic Gospels understand the Holy Spirit as anointing Jesus for his messianic task, as we might expect from the OT. (2) There are various reasons for relative restraint of language about the Holy Spirit in the Synoptic Gospels. (3) Whether Jesus could be called "charismatic" probably depends on how we define the term, and what we wish to emphasize. (4) Moltmann and Rogers are correct to describe the baptism of Jesus Christ as a "Trinitarian" narrative. The Holy Spirit never works on his own, but always in cooperation with the Father and with Jesus. Paul, John, and the Church Fathers make this clear.

(ii) *Acts.* It is often said that Pentecostals appeal primarily to Acts rather than to Paul and perhaps the Gospels. For one thing, Acts recounts the pouring out of the Holy Spirit on the Day of Pentecost (Acts 2:1-13; cf. 2:14-20). However, one major question remains: Was the purpose of the narrative in Acts to provide a model to be *replicated* in the future *for all time,* or to describe *once-for-all* happenings in the *earliest* church? As soon as we encounter narrative theory, the *varied functions of narratives* become clearer, and this will be addressed when we consider Pentecostalism and hermeneutics.

Clearly God remains active through the Holy Spirit in Acts at every critical juncture of the church's early history. This process began with the birth of the church at Pentecost. Luke showed interest in the *phenomena* that accompany the "pouring out" of the Holy Spirit. Some signs are audible, as with the sound of a rushing wind (2:2). Luke's use of the Greek *ēchos* rather

---

31. Richard T. France, *The Gospel of Mark: A Commentary on the Greek Text,* NIGTC (Grand Rapids: Eerdmans, 2002), 517.

than *phōnē* for "sound" recalls theophanies in the LXX (Exod. 19:16; 1 Sam. 4:5). Signs are also *visible:* "tongues, as of fire, appeared among them, and a tongue rested on each of them" (Acts 2:3). Fire is often an image denoting judgment (Isa. 66:16; *1 En.* 14:8-13; Luke 3:16). In 1 Kings 19:11-12 and Ezekiel 1:4 wind and fire accompany a theophany.

Luke next recounts, "All of them were filled (Gk. *eplēsthēsan pantes*) with the Holy Spirit and began to speak in other (Gk. *heterais*) languages, as the Spirit gave them ability" (Acts 2:4). There has long been debate about whether these were unintelligible sounds. The view that they were can be perhaps supported (1) by appealing to Paul's understanding of "tongues" in 1 Corinthians 14; (2) the subsequent charge of the Christians "being drunk" (Acts 2:13); and (3) whether Swete was correct to declare that Jews of the Diaspora were from rural areas and would need to hear a language other than Greek.[32] Max Turner argues that the purpose of "other tongues" was not evangelistic; it was "Peter's preaching that communicates the gospel."[33] F. F. Bruce regards "tongues" here as "beyond . . . conscious control."[34] Even in the *Journal of Pentecostal Theology,* Janet E. Powers argues that there is "no biblical evidence" for regarding these tongues as a missionary gift; in Acts they "preach in the vernacular, not tongues."[35]

The more traditional view of tongues as foreign languages goes back not later than John Chrysostom.[36] Among modern writers, J. H. E. Hull declares: "Luke appears to wish us to conclude that it was . . . foreign languages that were spoken at Pentecost."[37] Donald Carson emphatically takes this view: "We are dealing with *xenoglossia:* real, human languages, never learned by the speakers."[38] A body of scholars from K. Lake to more recent writers endorses this.

Many, however, stress that if this was miraculous, it was a miracle of *hearing* rather than of speaking. Most writers also regard the event as a reversal of the Babel story in Genesis. Dewar understands "filled with the Holy

32. H. B. Swete, *The Holy Spirit in the New Testament* (London: Macmillan, 1909), 73.

33. Max Turner, *The Holy Spirit and Spiritual Gifts: Then and Now* (Carlisle: Paternoster, 1996), 223.

34. F. F. Bruce, *The Book of Acts* (Grand Rapids: Eerdmans, 1965), 57.

35. Janet E. Powers, "Missionary Tongues," *JPT* 17 (2000): 40; cf. 39-55.

36. Chrysostom, *Commentary on Acts,* Homily 4; *NPNF,* ser. 1, 11:28-29.

37. J. H. E. Hull, *The Holy Spirit in the Acts of the Apostles* (London: Lutterworth, 1967), 61.

38. Donald A. Carson, *Showing the Spirit: A Theological Exposition of 1 Corinthians 12–14* (Grand Rapids: Baker, 1987), 138.

Spirit" as a variant of "to be baptized" or "saturated in the Spirit."[39] The vast majority of NT scholars regard the event as *initiatory for the whole church.* Dunn judiciously observes, "In one sense . . . Pentecost can *never be repeated* — the new age is here, and cannot be ushered in again. But in another sense . . . the experience of Pentecost *can and must* be repeated in the experience of all who would become Christians."[40] Arie Zwiep goes still further. He rightly sees Pentecost as a "barrier-breaking event," as the gift of the Holy Spirit to Cornelius and the Samaritans also was.[41] Zwiep also stresses the apocalyptic context ("the sun shall be turned to darkness and the moon to blood," in Acts 2:19-20).

We shall discuss Pentecostal interpretations in a separate subheading, but we may follow Hans von Baer in regarding the event of Pentecost as empowerment for witness to Christ, and perhaps also as an inspiration of prophecy. Many Pentecostals also interpret this experience as *subsequent* to that of becoming a Christian. Edward Irving, Charles Parham, William Seymour, and Robert Menzies adopt this view. But Luke seems to profile it as a *corporate* event, which founded the church and inaugurated a new era. This also sheds light on the experiences recounted in Acts 8, Acts 10, and Acts 19.

The passages just mentioned are notoriously controversial. In Samaria (Acts 8:17), in the case of Cornelius the Roman centurion (Acts 10:44-46), and in that of some of the Ephesians who were disciples of John the Baptist, the Holy Spirit came to them with unusual phenomena, such as speaking in tongues. Each event has multiple interpretations. Dunn calls the first of the three events "the riddle of Samaria."[42] Frank Macchia comments, "The Samaritans are filled with the Holy Spirit at the laying on of hands by the representatives of the Jerusalem Church."[43] It is not surprising, then, that both Pentecostals and Catholics appeal to this passage, some of the latter

39. Lindsay Dewar, *The Holy Spirit and Modern Thought: An Inquiry into the Historical, Theological, and Psychological Aspects of the Christian Doctrine of the Holy Spirit* (London: Mowbray, 1959), 43.

40. James D. G. Dunn, *Baptism in the Holy Spirit: A Re-examination of the New Testament Teaching on the Gift of the Spirit in Relation to Pentecostalism Today* (London: SCM, 1970), 53, italics mine.

41. Arie W. Zwiep, *Christ, the Spirit, and the Community of God,* WUNT, ser. 2, 293 (Tübingen: Mohr, 2010), 116.

42. Dunn, *Baptism in the Holy Spirit,* 55-72; cf. 35 and 131-86.

43. Frank D. Macchia, *Baptized in the Spirit: A Global Pentecostal Theology* (Grand Rapids: Zondervan, 2006), 166.

even comparing confirmation with it. Dunn distinguishes between four or five views of this passage.[44]

Lampe and Dunn both describe this event rightly as "a turning point in the missionary enterprise."[45] The Samaritans were in a unique position, and Luke-Acts aims at stressing the unity and catholicity of the church. Bruner and Zwiep rightly emphasize that this event constitutes a key transition in the missionary expansion of the church. In this respect it precisely corresponds with Pentecost. In Bruner's words, it was a "bridge to be crossed . . . a base to be occupied."[46]

This, in turn, is closely parallel with the Cornelius event (Acts 11:15, 17). There is no mention here, however, of baptism or the laying on of hands. The event is a milestone. The Gentiles "catch up" with what Christian Jews have experienced. Each decisive step in the expansion of the church is to be publicly perceived as initiated by the Holy Spirit. Peter is a witness to this, as he informs the council of Jerusalem (Acts 10:19, 44; 11:12, 18; 15:7-11).

Acts 19:1-7 constitutes another "foundational" passage for Pentecostals. But the "disciples" did not belong to a Christian group, knowing only the baptism of John. The gift of the Holy Spirit was the *cause of their becoming Christians.* In Acts 9:17 the prayer of Ananias for the Spirit to be given to Paul appears at first sight to be *subsequent* to his conversion and encounter with Christ. But Dunn, Turner, and others regard it as "the completion" of a process of conversion that Paul experiences. They insist: "The emphasis lies on the commissioning."[47]

About the Spirit in Acts, the main emphasis is well conveyed by Zwiep: the gift of the Holy Spirit is a *corporate* gift, which makes a person a *Christian.* The Spirit is also the Spirit of empowerment, prophecy, and mission.

3. The Pauline Epistles and Gifts of the Spirit

(i) *Christ-Centered and Corporate.* The first major theme we can trace in Paul is that the Holy Spirit is Christ-centered and corporate, that is, for *all*

---

44. Dunn, *Baptism in the Holy Spirit,* 56-62.

45. Dunn, *Baptism in the Holy Spirit,* 62, and Geoffrey W. H. Lampe, *The Seal of the Spirit: A Study in the Doctrine of Baptism and Confirmation in the New Testament and the Fathers* (London and New York: Longmans, Green, 1951), 70-72.

46. F. Dale Bruner, *A Theology of the Holy Spirit: The Pentecostal Experience and the New Testament Witness* (Grand Rapids: Eerdmans, 1970), 175.

47. Dunn, *Jesus and the Spirit,* 110; Turner, *Power from on High,* 375.

Christians, not simply for some. Paul declares, "Anyone who does not have the Spirit of Christ does not belong to him. But if Christ is in you . . . the Spirit is life. . . . If the Spirit of him who raised Jesus from the dead dwells in you, he who raised Christ . . . will give life to your mortal bodies also through his Spirit that dwells in you" (Rom. 8:9-11). Dunn comments, "Rom. 8:9 rules out the possibility *both* of a non-Christian possessing the Spirit and of a Christian *not* possessing the Spirit."[48] Elsewhere Dunn declares, "The Spirit is thus to be seen as the defining mark of the Christian. . . . In Rom. 8:9 . . . Paul provides the nearest thing to a definition of a Christian . . . who is 'of Christ.' "[49]

Like becoming a son, "being in Christ" is the foundation and cause of receiving the Holy Spirit. In this sense Hamilton calls Christology "the key to pneumatology."[50] Yet Paul also expresses the converse: "No one can say 'Jesus is Lord' except by the Holy Spirit" (1 Cor. 12:3). Do the two concern cause or effect? Or is each different? In *theological* terms, Romans 8:9-10 appears to express the *causal* priority of being-in-Christ. Christians can share Christ's anointing by the Spirit, because they are "in Christ." But 1 Corinthians 12:3 appears to express the converse in *experiential* or chronological terms. The Holy Spirit causes or makes possible the Christian's public confession of Christ's Lordship. Then he enables the Christian to acknowledge Jesus as Lord. The Spirit prompts and actualizes the filial consciousness of belonging to Jesus Christ as Lord.[51] Schweitzer called the Spirit "the life-principle of his personality."[52]

In Galatians 5:25 Paul regards the Holy Spirit not only as the initial cause of Christian faith and existence, but also its daily actualization and sustaining power: "If we live by the Spirit, let us also be guided by the Spirit" (NRSV); or NEB, "If the Spirit is the source of our life, let the Spirit direct our course."

Initiation in Christ is often articulated as Christian baptism. Hence Paul declares, "In one Spirit we were all baptized into one body — Jews or Greeks, slaves or free — and we were all made to drink of one Spirit" (1 Cor. 12:13). This is the only NT passage that speaks explicitly of "being baptized in the Spirit" (Gk. *en heni pneumati hēmeis pantes eis sōma ebaptisthēmen*).

48. Dunn, *Baptism in the Holy Spirit,* 95; cf. Dunn, *Jesus and the Spirit,* 310-16.

49. James D. G. Dunn, *The Theology of Paul the Apostle* (Edinburgh: T. & T. Clark, 1998), 423; cf. 413-41.

50. Neil Q. Hamilton, *The Holy Spirit and Eschatology in Paul,* SJT Occasional Papers 6 (Edinburgh: Oliver and Boyd, 1957), 3.

51. Swete, *The Holy Spirit,* 204-6.

52. Albert Schweitzer, *The Mysticism of Paul the Apostle* (London: Black, 1931), 165.

Schnackenburg argues that *en* may mean "in," "by," or "with" here.[53] I have discussed in my more lengthy commentary on the Greek text whether this presupposition is locative (NRSV, JB, Collins), instrumental (AV/KJV, ASV, NASB, NIV, Moffatt), or simply indicates "one Spirit" (REB, Barrett). I have also included a note on "Spirit baptism" in relation to 12:13 and Pentecostal traditions.[54] The term here clearly denotes entry into the new world of Christ's body. I have also argued for this conclusion in *The Holy Spirit in Biblical Teaching, through the Centuries, and Today*.[55] We shall return to this verse when we look especially at Pentecostalism.

(ii) *The Eschatological Nature of the Gift of the Spirit*. Paul declares: "Not only the creation, but we ourselves, who have the first fruits of the Spirit (Gk. *aparchēn tou pneumatos*), groan inwardly while we wait (Gk. *apekdechomenoi*) for adoption, the redemption of our bodies" (Rom. 8:23). "First fruits" *(aparchē)* denotes "the first portion" or a pledge of "what is to come."[56] It is parallel with Paul's use of Greek *arrabōn,* a deposit or guarantee of something in the future, or first installment, as in 2 Corinthians 5:5, God "has given us the Spirit as a guarantee," that is, that of which more, or better, is to come. Two good modern examples are the commercial one of a *deposit* and the industrial one of a *prototype* off the production line. A deposit constitutes the *down payment,* which guarantees the full and larger payment in due course.[57] A prototype denotes a model of many more productions to come. The word is often translated as "first installment" in 2 Corinthians 1:22. Cullmann writes, "The Holy Spirit is nothing else than the anticipation of the end in the present."[58]

For Christian behavior and discipleship, there are three practical applications. First, as Hamilton argues, the center of gravity of the experience of the Holy Spirit "lies in the future."[59] We have seen only a *little* or *some* of what the Holy Spirit can do in transforming a life or community; one day

---

53. Rudolf Schnackenburg, *Baptism in the Thought of St. Paul: A Study in Pauline Theology* (Oxford: Blackwell, 1964), 22-24 and 83-86.

54. Anthony C. Thiselton, *The First Epistle to the Corinthians: A Commentary on the Greek Text,* NIGTC (Grand Rapids: Eerdmans, 2000), 997-1001.

55. Anthony C. Thiselton, *The Holy Spirit in Biblical Teaching, through the Centuries, and Today* (Grand Rapids: Eerdmans; London: SPCK, 2013), 129-30, 337-38, 423, 456-60, and 490-92.

56. BDAG 98.

57. BDAG 134.

58. Oscar Cullmann, *Christ and Time: The Primitive Christian Conception of Time and History* (London: SCM, 1951), 72.

59. Hamilton, *Holy Spirit,* 79.

we shall see in heaven the *full extent* of the Spirit's power and presence. Second, the less-than-perfect transformation of Christians in the present brings God's *guarantee* of the full *completion* of his work within us and within the church in the future. Third, the present remains a time of *tension and struggle*. Hamilton, again, heads a chapter "The Spirit and Eschatological Tension."[60] The climax of this *process* (not simply "event") is the spiritual body of the resurrection (1 Cor. 15:44), by which Paul means a mode of existence characterized by the power and transformation of the *Holy Spirit*, as we shall argue further when we discuss resurrection. As we shall note, Pannenberg and Wright expound this view of a future life "wholly permeated by the divine Creator Spirit."[61]

This is confirmed by the use of "you were sealed," or you "were marked with the seal of the promised Holy Spirit (Gk. *esphragisthēte*); this is the pledge (Gk. *arrabōn*) of our inheritance toward redemption" (Eph. 1:13-14). The seal was a mark of recognition, given to Christian believers in the present life, so they could not be lost in the Great Ordeal of the future (cf. Ezek. 9:4, "Put a mark on the foreheads of those who sigh and groan"). In terms of the history of theology, the Holy Spirit provokes conflict and struggle, as Luther stressed. There is no "sinless perfection" in this world. Nevertheless, the Holy Spirit "lives" or "dwells" in the church and in believers, even now in the present (1 Cor. 3:16; 6:19; Eph. 2:22).

(iii) *Gifts of the Spirit.* Paul stresses especially *the gifts of the Holy Spirit.* The classic long passage that illustrates this is 1 Corinthians 12:4-14:40. Paul explains, "There are varieties of gifts, but the same Spirit. . . . To each is given the manifestation of the Spirit for the common good (Gk. *pros to sympheron*)" (1 Cor. 12:4, 7). Paul shows that the gifts are given to chosen individuals for the benefit of the whole church. The list in 1 Corinthians 12:4-11 contains a number of gifts the meaning of which remains controversial.

(1) The *"utterance of wisdom"* (Gk. *logos sophias*) and the *"utterance of knowledge" (logos gnōseōs)* in 12:8 cannot readily be distinguished from each other. *Logos* may denote a discourse or a stretch of language or *revelation*. But *sophia* and *logos* may have negative overtones of manipulation.[62] Paul probably borrowed these terms from the church in Corinth, since "wisdom" occurs sixteen times in 1 Corinthians, in comparison with eleven in all the

---

60. Hamilton, *Holy Spirit*, 26-40.

61. Pannenberg, *ST* 3:622; N. T. Wright, *The Resurrection of the Son of God* (London: SPCK; Minneapolis: Fortress, 2003), 254.

62. Stephen M. Pogoloff, *Logos and Sophia: The Rhetorical Situation in 1 Corinthians* (Atlanta: Scholars Press, 1992), 99-196.

other epistles, and *gnōsis* is discussed in 8:1-3, 7, 10 and 11: "Knowledge inflates; love builds . . ." Yet these are gifts *from the Holy Spirit.* Hence where *sophia* is used positively, it refers to the wisdom *of God* in the proclamation of the *gospel through the cross* (1:18-25; 2:1-10). W. Schrage, S. Schatzmann, James Dunn, and many other NT exegetes agree that these utterances are likely to relate to the message of the cross.[63]

If there is any difference between "word of wisdom" and "word of knowledge," the former must refer to the gospel and the cross; the latter could refer to "basic Christian truths," as I have allowed in my book *The Holy Spirit.*

(2) The *charisma,* or free gift, of *faith* cannot be the saving faith given to *every* Christian, and through which Christians are justified by grace. By contrast, Paul uses *heterō,* "to another," in 12:9. Paul uses "faith" in *no single* way, but in a *variety* of ways. It is sometimes related to trust, at other times to obedience. Here it is likely to denote a buoyant confidence in God's love, sovereignty, and power, which can lift up a discouraged congregation and reenergize it. As Bornkamm asserts, "The nature of faith is given in the object to which faith is directed."[64]

(3) *Gifts of healing* (Gk. *charismata iamatōn,* 12:9) must not be restricted to "supernatural" healings as if in a two-story universe, although it may well include what many people *mean* by this term. A minority who are called "cessationalists" believe that all these "gifts" ceased at the close of the apostolic age, but most writers believe that such a cutoff point could be arbitrary. One problem, as we have noted, is that signs of the kingdom of God were bound up with eschatological timing, and the promised future is not yet here. If this is so, "supernatural" interventions *can neither be excluded nor regularly "expected."* The evangelical pietist and NT exegete J. A. Bengel observed that the gift of healing then and today includes "natural remedies" (Lat. *naturalia remedia*).[65]

(4) In 1 Corinthians 12:10 the NRSV translation reads: "the *working of miracles* . . . prophecy . . . discernment of spirits . . . kinds of tongues . . . interpretation of tongues." But the Greek term for "working of miracles" is *energēmata dynameōn,* and I have elsewhere translated this as "effective deeds of power."[66] Karl Barth argues that in 1 Corinthians "power" denotes what

63. Thiselton, *The Holy Spirit,* 85-89.

64. Günther Bornkamm, *Paul* (London: Hodder and Stoughton, 1972), 141; cf. Thiselton, *The Holy Spirit,* 89-91.

65. J. A. Bengel, *Gnomon Novi Testamenti* (Stuttgart: Steinkopf, 1866), 652.

66. Both in Thiselton, *First Epistle to the Corinthians,* 952, and in *The Holy Spirit,* 105.

is *effective* against obstacles.[67] John Calvin also prefers "power" *(virtutem)*, rather than miracles, and W. Hollenweger also warns us against what has been called "a God of the gaps" dualism. On the other hand, Craig Keener, in an exhaustive study of miracles, concludes, "Paul anticipated noticeable miraculous phenomena in the Christian communities (1 Cor. 12:9-10, 28-30; Gal. 3:5)."[68]

(5) *"Prophecy"* constitutes no less controversial a term. The noun (Gk. *prophēteia*) occurs not only in 1 Corinthians 12:10, but also in Romans 12:6, 1 Corinthians 13:2, 14:6, and 1 Thessalonians 5:20. The verb *(prophēteuō)* occurs in 1 Corinthians 11:4-5; 13:9; 14:1-5, 24, 31, and 39. Its primary purpose is to "build up" (Gk. *oikodomeō*) the church. *Prophētēs* usually denotes one who proclaims inspired revelation. The verb also often means to encourage or to bring comfort.

Controversy, however, surrounds the vexed question of *spontaneity*. Many argue that since these are "charismatic" gifts in 12:8-10, prophecy is "charismatic" in the popular sense used in the Renewal Movement and usually in Pentecostalism, of nonreflective speech, as if this meant "deliberately generated by the self." Max Turner, Christopher Forbes, and James Dunn seem broadly to support this "charismatic" stress on spontaneity. Dunn states: "It (prophecy) does not denote a previously prepared sermon. . . . It is a spontaneous utterance"; he cites 14:30: "A revelation is made to someone else sitting nearby."[69]

On the other hand, there are at least three convincing arguments for the opposite view. First, K. O. Sandnes and Philipp Vielhauer associate Paul's apostolic commission to build up the church with his call and commission to be a *prophet* (Gal. 1:15-16; 1 Cor. 3:6, 10).[70] Yet Paul's epistles use *argument and reflection,* not "revelation speech," as Bornkamm and Pannenberg both stress. Second, David Hill, Ulrich Müller, and Thomas Gillespie have carefully argued that prophecy in the NT denotes *"applied pastoral preaching."*[71] Hill stresses

---

67. Karl Barth, *The Resurrection of the Dead* (London: Hodder and Stoughton, 1933), 18.

68. Craig S. Keener, *Miracles: The Credibility of the New Testament Accounts,* 2 vols. (Grand Rapids: Baker Academic, 2011), 1:30-31.

69. Dunn, *Jesus and the Spirit,* 228; cf. 205-300; and Dunn, *Theology of Paul,* 552-64 and 580-98; Christopher Forbes, *Prophecy and Inspired Speech in Early Christianity and Its Hellenistic Environment,* WUNT, ser. 2, 75 (Tübingen: Mohr, 1995), 229 and 236.

70. K. O. Sandnes, *Paul — One of the Prophets?* WUNT, ser. 2, 43 (Tübingen: Mohr, 1991), and Philipp Vielhauer, *Oikodomē: Das Bild vom Bau in der christlichen Literatur vom Neuen Testament bis Klement* (Karlsruhe: Harrassowitz, 1940), 77-98.

71. David Hill, *New Testament Prophecy* (London: Marshall, 1979), especially 110-40 and

that it may involve "sustained utterance."[72] Müller insists that it includes "re-pentance speech" *(Bussrede),* and is "ordered."[73] All three appeal to numerous passages, including 1 Corinthians 14:3, 13-19. Third, the "charismatic" view indeed gives hostage to a "two story" worldview, to suggest that the Holy Spirit does not work *through reflection, thought,* and *rational* processes. This is not to deny that the Spirit may *sometimes* provide "spontaneous" flashes of insight; it asserts that this is *not* the *usual* way in which the Spirit works.

(6) *Tongues and interpretation of tongues* are of various *kinds.* Paul states this in 1 Corinthians 12:10 (Gk. *genē glōssōn*). This may partly explain the difference from Luke's account of Pentecost in Acts 2. One common feature, as Paul stresses, is that "Those who speak in a tongue do not speak to other people but to God" (1 Cor. 14:2). Thus, unlike prophecy, tongues do not "build up" the church. Many stress that Paul appears to add, "unless ['someone'] (but there is no equivalent Greek word for this) interprets" (14:5). Since the Greek has no word here for "someone," this may well be part of Paul's plea for intelligible utterance, that is, "Tongues-speakers, learn to express your revelation (in due course) in intelligible speech."

In my commentary on the Greek text of 1 Corinthians, I distinguish at least six views of tongues taken by NT scholars. The following are the main possibilities: tongues are angelic speech (E. Ellis and G. Dautzenberg); tongues are the miraculous power to speak other languages (Origen, Chrysostom, Aquinas, Calvin, Robert Gundry, Forbes); tongues are liturgical, archaic, or rhythmic phrases (Bleek, Heinrici); tongues are ecstatic speech (Tertullian, S. D. Currie, M. E. Boring, L. T. Johnson, C. G. Williams); tongues are a welling up from the unconscious (Gerd Theissen and, in effect, Krister Stendahl); and tongues are "sighs too deep for words," as in Romans 8:26 (Frank D. Macchia, E. Käsemann). The sixth view is not incompatible with the fifth: release from the inhibiting censors of the conscious mind may be a release provided by the Holy Spirit, or analogy with Romans 8:26.[74]

The most convincing work of all comes from Gerd Theissen, which overlaps at times with that of Käsemann, Stendahl, and Macchia. Stendahl recognizes that tongues-speech can be a genuine gift of the Holy Spirit, but adds, "Few human beings can live healthily with high voltage religious ex-

---

193-213, and Thomas W. Gillespie, *The First Theologians: A Study in Early Christian Prophecy* (Grand Rapids: Eerdmans, 1994), throughout, especially 25.

72. Hill, *New Testament Prophecy,* 123.

73. Ulrich B. Müller, *Prophetie und Predigt im Neuen Testament* (Gütersloh: Mohr, 1975), 26.

74. Cf. Thiselton, *First Epistle to the Corinthians,* 970-88 and 1062-64.

perience over a long period of time."[75] Theissen and Käsemann show how the Holy Spirit can give liberty and release from the constraints of conscious inhibition and repression, but warn us that tongues can be divisive for the church, as they were for the church in Corinth.[76]

4. Further Major Themes in Paul

First Corinthians 12:28-31 largely recapitulates 12:8-10. But some gifts are different. The NRSV translates *antilēmpseis* as "forms of assistance, forms of leadership" in 12:28. While this may seem safe, it is too bland for the Greek terms *antilēmpseis* and *kybernēseis*. The first word probably refers to *administration. Administration is equally part of the Spirit's gifts,* and cannot possibly be "spontaneous"! Admittedly Danker translates it as "helpful deeds."[77] The verb from which this noun is derived, *antilambanō,* can mean "to help by coming to the aid of," as Danker admits. But in today's world, to give support to a ministry generally involves *infrastructure,* or secretarial or *administrative support.* Grimm-Thayer declares, "It does not have a miraculous character, and this leads to those [gifts] that follow."[78]

Even more stark is the word coupled with this term, *kybernēsis.* I have suggested that this should, or may, be translated "ability to formulate strategies."[79] The verb and noun associated with it denote "the steering of a ship," or "being a pilot." This time Danker translates it "administration."[80] But most scholars recognize that it is a strongly nautical metaphor: the word *kybernētēs* denotes a "steersman" or "shipmaster," and by extension, Danker agrees also that it denotes "one who directs the destiny of humans."[81] Often a church

---

75. Krister Stendahl, "Glossolalia — the New Testament Evidence," in Stendahl, *Paul among Jesus and the Gentiles* (London: SCM, 1977), 123; cf. 109-24; cf. Ernst Käsemann, "The Cry for Liberty in the Church's Worship," in Käsemann, *Perspectives on Paul* (London: SCM, 1973), 122-37.

76. Gerd Theissen, *Psychological Aspects of Pauline Theology* (Edinburgh: T. & T. Clark, 1987), 59-80 and 267-342.

77. BDAG 89.

78. Grimm-Thayer 50; cf. W. F. Moulton and G. Milligan, *The Vocabulary of the Greek Testament Illustrated from the Papyri and Other Non-Literary Sources* (London: Hodder and Stoughton, 1952), 47-48, and H. G. Liddell, R. Scott, and H. S. Jones, with R. McKenzie, *A Greek-English Lexicon* (Oxford: Clarendon, 1996), 144.

79. Thiselton, *First Epistle to the Corinthians,* 1021-22.

80. BDAG 573.

81. BDAG 574.

needs advice or vision about its priorities, or the direction it should progress. This gift would fit such a task.

Romans 12:6-8 also lists gifts that largely follow those mentioned in 1 Corinthians, and Ephesians 4:11-13 also underlines that the aim of such gifts is to build up the church — it mentions pastors and teachers also. Nevertheless, this passage also overlaps with "the fruit of the Spirit." Ephesians 4:12-13 declares that the gifts of the Spirit are "to equip the saints . . . for building up the body of Christ, until all of us come to the unity of the faith . . . to maturity, to the measure of the full stature of Christ."

(i) *Christlikeness, Love, and Holiness Constitute a Fourth Major Theme in Paul.* While "gifts" often relate to given tasks, what Paul calls *the "fruit" of the Spirit* in Galatians 5:22-23, and *"a still more excellent way"* in 1 Corinthians 12:31, constitute more *general* or widespread characteristics of the Spirit-filled or Spirit-led Christian life. As a word denoting a *habit* and *character* of life, Paul urges that the Holy Spirit produces Christ-like-ness, love, holiness, and all the virtues listed in Galatians 5:22-23.

To become like Christ reflects the very first of our major themes: "being-in-Christ," and the Christ-centered nature of the Holy Spirit. We have already noted this. This also in practice entails *sanctification* or *holiness,* which constitutes a major theme in the history of the doctrine of the Spirit; and *love,* which constitutes a kindred theme. Paul has plenty of material on sanctification. He prays: "May the God of peace himself sanctify you entirely" (1 Thess. 5:23). There are possibly fewer passages in Paul than we might imagine that associate holiness *explicitly* with the Holy Spirit. Yet implications remain frequently, and Luther, Martin Bucer, Calvin, and many others are not wrong in regarding the fruit of a holy life as one of the main themes of Paul. The one point that has attracted some controversy is whether sanctification constitutes *a process, not completed until after death,* or a *single event.* In the sense of "holy" as *belonging to God,* it perhaps constitutes an *event;* but in the more usual sense of *growth in holiness of life,* it is a *process,* in which both Paul and Luther underline the role of conflict and struggle (Rom. 7:22-25; 8:18-30).

The fruit of *love* has been studied in depth, although Galatians 5:22-23 adds joy, peace, patience, kindness, generosity, faithfulness, gentleness, and self-control to it. Of very many studies on love in 1 Corinthians 13 and in Paul, those by James Moffatt, C. Spicq, and Anders Nygren clearly remain classics worth consulting.[82]

---

82. James Moffatt, *Love in the New Testament* (London: Hodder and Stoughton, 1929;

(ii) *The Implicit Trinitarian Framework of the Spirit in Paul.* This subject deserves a long essay or a book. Here we may point to 1 Corinthians 12:4-6 and other passages. Paul declares, "There are varieties of gifts, but the same Spirit; and there are varieties of services, but the same Lord; and there are varieties of activities, but it is the same God who activates all of them in everyone." The Holy Spirit, Paul stresses, does not act in isolation from the Father and the Son. He works *through Christ* to fulfill the will and *purpose of God the Father.* A variety of passages support this perspective in Paul, just as we saw with reference to the Trinitarian narratives of the Gospels.

It is clear that in Paul God the Father sends the Holy Spirit, just as he did in the Gospels. Paul writes: "*God* has sent the Spirit of his Son into our hearts" (Gal. 4:6); "God's love has been poured into our hearts through the Holy Spirit" (Rom. 5:5); and "No one comprehends what is truly God's except the Spirit of God" (1 Cor. 2:11). In Romans 8:11, Paul coordinates the work of God the Father, the Son, and the Holy Spirit, in Christ's resurrection. In Galatians 3:13-14, Paul writes: "Christ redeemed us . . . so that we might receive the promise of the Spirit." But J. Christiaan Beker rightly insists, "Paul has only an incipient doctrine of the Trinity."[83] Similarly Pannenberg speaks of "the beginnings of the doctrine of the Trinity in the NT."[84]

One practical application for Christians is what Fiddes calls the tension "between integrity of the self and openness to the other."[85] God the Father has never been "self-contained." He has always been "open to the other," in the sense of his relationship to the Son as Jesus Christ, and to the Holy Spirit. To be restored in the image of God, human beings need both the integrity of the self, and simultaneously openness to the other.

5. John and the Rest of the New Testament

(i) *Gospel of John.* We return to J. E. Fison's theme concerning the Paraclete discourses. The Spirit, he says "effaces himself, and advertises Jesus: 'He will

---

New York: Richard Smith, 1930), 168-93; C. Spicq, *Agape in the New Testament,* 3 vols. (London and St. Louis: Herder, 1963), especially vol. 2; Anders Nygren, *Agape and Eros* (London: SPCK, 1957), especially 61-145.

83. J. Christiaan Beker, *Paul the Apostle: The Triumph of God in Life and Thought* (Edinburgh: T. & T. Clark, 1980), 200.

84. Pannenberg, *ST* 1:259.

85. Paul S. Fiddes, *Participating in God: A Pastoral Doctrine of the Trinity* (Louisville: Westminster John Knox, 2000), 23.

not speak of his own (Gk. *aph' heautou*) . . . He will glorify me' (John 16:13-14)."[86] In John 14:3 Jesus declares concerning the Paraclete, "I will come to you" (cf. 14:18). Essentially he is the Revealer of God and of Jesus.

In the main body of the Gospel, John recounts the baptism of Jesus, asserting that the Spirit "descends and remains" on Jesus (John 1:32-34). First John also uses the word "anoint" of Christians who belong to Christ (1 John 2:20, 27). In John 3 Jesus speaks of the new birth by water and the Spirit from above (*anōthen,* John 3:3-7). Moltmann insists on this translation of *anōthen,* following Swete.[87] The Spirit in John also reflects the OT notion of his transcendence and otherness. The Spirit, like the wind, Jesus says, "blows where it chooses, and you hear the sound of it, but do not know where it comes from or where it goes" (John 3:8). God gives the Spirit to Jesus "without measure" (John 3:34-35). Both C. H. Dodd and J. Moltmann insist that the translation "God is *a* spirit" in John 4:24 is wrong, and both insist on "God is Spirit." The emphasis in this chapter on "living waters" (4:10, 13-14) coheres with the notion of the Spirit as ongoing, dynamic, and ever-fresh, like running water. Indeed, in John 7:37-39 "living water" explicitly refers to the Spirit. This may also allude to Isaiah 55:1 and Isaiah 12:3, among other passages.

The Paraclete passages come in John 14:15-17, 26; 15:26-27; and 16:5-15. In John 14:16-17 the Paraclete (Gk. *paraklētos*) is explicitly identified with the Holy Spirit. Hans Windisch argued in 1926 that these passages are secondary to John, partly because they reflect a distinctive vocabulary, and partly because John 14–16 remains coherent even if the passages are removed. But his view is generally rejected. The verb *parakaleō* means "to call alongside (to help)," and Danker gives the first meaning of the noun *paraklētos* as "helper," "intercessor," or "one who appears on another's behalf."[88] In about 1950 J. Behm proposed a legal content, suggesting "advocate" or "defending counsel."[89] Kenneth Grayston and G. R. Beasley-Murray doubt the legal context, but Swete and Turner accept it, and C. K. Barrett even considers the meaning "prosecuting" counsel.[90]

86. Fison, *Blessing of the Holy Spirit,* 137.

87. Jürgen Moltmann, *The Spirit of Life: A Universal Affirmation* (London: SCM, 1992), 145; Swete, *The Holy Spirit,* 133.

88. BDAG 766.

89. Johannes Behm, "Paraklētos," in *TDNT* 5:809; cf. 800-814.

90. Kenneth Grayston, "Paraclete," *JSNT* 13 (1981): 67-82; George R. Beasley-Murray, *John,* WBC (Nashville: Nelson, 1999), 256; Turner, *The Holy Spirit,* 77; C. K. Barrett, *The Gospel according to St. John,* 2nd ed. (London: SPCK; Louisville: Westminster John Knox, 1978).

Most of these suggested meanings fit the context. The words of Jesus "I will not leave you orphaned; I am coming to you" (John 14:18) imply that the Paraclete "appears on another's behalf." "He will prove the world wrong about sin and righteousness and judgment" in 16:8 (Gk. *ekeinos elenxei ton kosmon peri hamartias*); this indeed seems to suggest "prosecuting counsel." But the verses "He will testify on my behalf" (15:26) and "He will give you another Advocate" (14:16) seem to suggest "defending counsel" or "comforter."[91] Dunn comments, "The Spirit . . . continues the presence of Jesus. . . . Both come forth from the Father."[92] The Spirit reminds the disciples of "all that I have said to you" (14:26), which implies both Johannine teaching and indirectly the witness of Scripture, for this includes the words: "many things to say to you, but you cannot bear them now" (16:12). Turner declares, "John insists on this historical anchor. The Paraclete's task is *not to bring independent revelation.*"[93]

A comment from E. F. Scott may suggest an explanation of the remarkably effective preaching of Billy Graham, who broadly repeated what many less remarkable preachers also said. Scott commented on John 16:8-11: "Confronted by the holy community in which the divine power is manifestly working, the world will be brought to a sense of its wickedness and unbelief."[94] Perhaps the committed crowds added power and conviction to the preacher's words.

We offer one other comment on these Paraclete chapters. As we have said, God, including God as the Holy Spirit, is *beyond gender.* The Hebrew *rûach* may be grammatically feminine, while *pneuma* is neuter; but in these chapters *ekeinos,* which refers to the Spirit, is masculine. As James Barr long ago demonstrated, *grammatical* gender is arbitrary and conventional, and cannot constitute "gender" in a deeper way. Finally, John 20:22, Jesus "breathed on them and said to them, 'Receive the Holy Spirit,'" underlines the christocentric character of the Holy Spirit. This verse is not a rival version of Pentecost in Acts 2.

(ii) *First John.* First John emphasizes that God gives the gift of the Holy Spirit to *all* Christians: "You have been anointed by the Holy One, and all of you have knowledge" (1 John 2:20). In 4:1-6 there are six references to

91. Cf. G. E. Ladd, *A Theology of the New Testament* (Grand Rapids: Eerdmans 1974; rev. 1993), 322, for an extensive bibliography.

92. Dunn, *Jesus and the Spirit,* 350.

93. Turner, *The Holy Spirit,* 83, italics mine.

94. E. F. Scott, *The Spirit in the New Testament* (London: Hodder and Stoughton, 1924), 201.

"spirit" or "Spirit," which include "testing" (4:1); the confession of Jesus Christ as Lord (4:2; cf. 1 Cor. 12:3); the coming of Jesus in the flesh (1 John 4:2-3); and the Spirit's opposition to "worldliness" (4:4-6). Some verses may imply a reference to later true and false prophecy.[95] First John 5:6 takes up the Johannine theme of truth and witness.[96]

(iii) *First Peter.* In 1 Peter the new community has been "sanctified by the Spirit" (Gk. *en hagiasmo pneumatos,* 1 Pet. 1:2). The Spirit testifies to Christ and to his sufferings. He is also the Agent or Vehicle of "good news . . . sent from heaven — things into which angels long to look" (1:12). In 3:18, "made alive in the spirit" may well refer to the resurrection of Christ, in parallel with Romans 1:4 and 8:11. Some, like Swete, ascribe the phrase to the human spirit of the lord, but this is less convincing.[97] Kelly more convincingly ascribes the phrase to the Holy Spirit.[98] A complex and controversial passage is 1 Peter 3:19. We cannot review all interpretations here, but Kelly focuses on Christ's resurrection within the framework of the Holy Spirit, the Giver of Life.[99] Finally 1 Peter 4:14 refers to "the Spirit of God . . . resting on you," which may offer a parallel with John 1:32. The Spirit, at all events, is associated with Christ, Christians, and glory.

(iv) *The Epistle to the Hebrews.* This book constitutes a powerful piece of theology. But Westcott comments, "The action of the Holy Spirit falls into the background."[100] Nevertheless, Hebrews 2:4 does speak of "gifts of the Holy Spirit," in the context of warning those who received such gifts not to drift in the Christian life with passive inertia. A second clear reference to the Holy Spirit comes in 6:4, where those who "have tasted the heavenly gift, and have shared in the Holy Spirit," are urged not to fall back, but rather to move ahead. All commentators agree that this passage stresses the *ongoing* character of Christian life. Any debate relates to whether "falling away" could be a genuine possibility for an authentic Christian. F. F. Bruce writes, "Continuance is the test of reality. . . . He (the writer) is not questioning the perseverance of the saints."[101] Hugh Montefiore likewise declares, "Apart from apostasy, no retrogression is possible in the Christian life. . . . The only

95. Stephen S. Smalley, *1, 2, and 3 John* (Waco: Word, 1984), 218; cf. 214-32.
96. Swete, *The Holy Spirit,* 269.
97. Swete, *The Holy Spirit,* 262.
98. J. N. D. Kelly, *The Epistles of Peter and Jude* (London: Black, 1969), 151.
99. Kelly, *Epistles,* 153.
100. B. F. Westcott, *The Epistle to the Hebrews: The Greek Text* (New York and London: Macmillan, 1903), 331.
101. F. F. Bruce, *The Epistle to the Hebrews* (Grand Rapids: Eerdmans, 1964), 118.

way of recovering lost ground is to forge ahead."[102] W. L. Lane and H. W. Attridge compare the "once-for-all" (Gk. *ephapax*) of Christ's sacrifice and the once-for-all of becoming a Christian.[103]

The third reference to the Spirit concerns the Holy Spirit's inspiring Scripture: "The Holy Spirit testifies . . ." (10:15-16; cf. 3:7). The fourth reference in 10:29 parallels 6:4 regarding the *hubris* of apostasy. The exegesis of "Spirit" or "spirit" in 9:14 is disputed.

(v) *The Revelation of John.* Many associate "the seven spirits" in Revelation 1:4, 3:1, 4:5, and 5:6 with the Holy Spirit, since often *seven* represents the number of perfection or fullness. Caird regards *seven* here as "a symbol of completeness."[104] The seer describes his own prophetic condition as "in the Spirit" (1:10; 4:2; 17:3; 21:10). Swete describes this as "mental exultation," and Montague as "caught up in the prophetic state."[105] In many ways it is reminiscent of the experience of Ezekiel. Similarly Revelation 11:11, "After the three and a half days, the breath of life (Gk. *pneuma zōēs*) from God entered them," reflects Ezekiel 37:5, 9, 14, where the Spirit of life raises the dry bones of dead Israel into a living community. Revelation 14:13 and 19:10 regard the Holy Spirit as giving witness or testimony, as in John. In Revelation 22:17 the Spirit implants the longing for the Christian's heavenly home, as Paul also does.

102. Hugh Montefiore, *A Commentary on the Epistle to the Hebrews* (London: Black, 1964), 104.

103. William L. Lane, *Hebrews 1–8*, WBC 47A (Dallas: Word, 1991), 141-42, and Harold W. Attridge, *The Epistle to the Hebrews*, Hermeneia (Philadelphia: Fortress, 1989), 168-70.

104. George B. Caird, *The Revelation of St. John* (London: Black, 1966), 14.

105. Montague, *The Holy Spirit*, 323.

CHAPTER XII

The Holy Spirit: (II) Historical Insights

1. The Rise of the Pentecostal Movement

In the history of the church, the first eighteen centuries represented a relatively uniform conception of the Holy Spirit. Admittedly there were exceptions. The Montanists stood out as a distinctive movement in the early church, and some see them as partly anticipating classical Pentecostalism. Similarly, the "radical" or "left-wing" Reformers, or "enthusiasts," were distinctive in their approach to the Spirit. They included Thomas Müntzer and Andreas Carlstadt; Martin Luther called them "the fanatics" *(Schwärmer)*, and accused them of undermining his doctrine of justification by faith. He argued that their spiritual "perfectionism" and appeal to "experience" put the law in the place of the gospel, and experience in place of the Bible. He regarded them as a major threat to the heart of the gospel of Christ, comparable in danger to the Catholic establishment of that time. There have been several such movements. These included George Fox (1624-1691) and the early Quakers, and movements led by Edward Irving (1792-1834), probably Benjamin Irwin (c. 1854-1900), and Albert B. Simpson (1843-1919) with his "fourfold gospel."

(i) *Origins.* Classical Pentecostalism, however, originated with *Charles Fox Parham* (1873-1929) and *William Joseph Seymour* (1870-1922), although many regard the selection of these two as arguably "Eurocentric." Parham founded a Bible school at Topeka, Kansas, in which he taught the "full" gospel, or "fivefold gospel" of justification, sanctification, baptism in the Spirit, divine healing, and the imminence of the end-time, or the return of Christ.[1]

---

1. For a detailed account, see Anthony C. Thiselton, *The Holy Spirit in Biblical Teaching,*

These five themes developed into a "full gospel" of *four:* salvation, baptism in the Spirit, healing, and the expectation of the imminent return of Christ. Parham first heard reports of speaking in tongues from his friend Frank Sandford in the Holiness Movement.

Parham identified this phenomenon with the "latter rain" of the Spirit, to which Joel 2:23 alludes:

> He (God) has poured down for you abundant rain,
> the early and the later rain.

This allegedly referred to Pentecost and the descent of the Spirit today. In 1901 speaking in tongues emerged among students at Topeka Bible School. Healings would also come after the "dryness" of previous centuries. Parham held a "premillennialist" view of the return of Christ, that is, that the parousia would usher in a thousand-year reign of Christ on earth (see chap. 14). He also insisted on a "Restorationist" (or replicatory) view of Acts. Tongues-speech constituted a sign of the new Pentecost before the imminent return of Christ. A revival in Kansas followed his proclamation of this "full" gospel. Parham then carried this gospel to Houston, Texas, where William Seymour became a convert in about 1905. By 1906 Parham had nearly ten thousand followers in Los Angeles.

Seymour became pastor of the Apostolic Faith Mission in Azusa Street, Los Angeles, and sparked off "the Azusa Street Revival" of 1906-1909. His parents had been Afro-American slaves. He learned of "baptism in the Spirit" from Parham. He drew on the classic biblical texts of Pentecostalism, such as "The Spirit of the Lord is upon me" (Luke 4:18-19) and "All of them . . . began to speak in other languages" (Acts 2:4). It appears surprising that when Parham visited Azusa Street in 1906, he was appalled at "animalism . . . trances . . . shaking, jabbering; chattering . . . meaningless sounds and noises."[2]

Parham, in fact, attempted to take over Seymour's church, but Seymour's followers resisted him, and he set up a rival church five blocks away. Thus began power play, division, and fragmentation, which has plagued Pen-

---

through the Centuries, and Today (Grand Rapids: Eerdmans; London: SPCK, 2013), 327-39, 373-79, and elsewhere; and Yongnan Jeon Ahn, *Interpretation of Tongues and Prophecy in 1 Corinthians 12–14*, JPTSS 41 (Blandford Forum: Deo, 2013), 14-39.

2. C. M. Robert, "Seymour, William Joseph," in *The New International Dictionary of Pentecostal and Charismatic Movements,* ed. Stanley M. Burgess and Eduard M. van der Maas, rev. ed. (Grand Rapids: Zondervan, 2002-2003), 1053-58.

tecostalism from the very first. Where, we may ask, was the "unity of Spirit" at that time, and through to the late 1920s? Most Pentecostals also look back with dismay at what was undoubtedly Parham's "racist" outlook.

Seymour, it is said, was modest and gentle, yet when he traveled to Alabama, Illinois, and other states, he soon came into conflict with William Durham, another Pentecostal leader. Seymour died of a heart attack in 1922. Meanwhile "Pentecostal roots" had emerged elsewhere in the world, including in Africa, Korea, Latin America, and perhaps Wales, by the end of the first decade or so of the movement.[3] In Korea the Great Revival of 1907 took place in Pyongyang, and the church grew "like wildfire," according to R. E. Shearer. Juan Sepúlveda traces an independent movement in Chile before 1910.[4] Mark Cartledge recounts the Pyongyang Revival, the Welsh Revival of 1904-1905, and activity at other centers of growth.[5]

(ii) *The Second Phase.* A second phase of Pentecostalism emerged with Alfred G. Garr (1874-1944), Frank J. Ewart (1876-1947), Eudorus N. Bell (1866-1923), Aimee Semple McPherson (1890-1944), and Ivan Quay Spencer (1888-1970). Garr agreed with Parham that tongues-speech constitutes *"initial evidence"* of baptism in the Spirit, but differed from him in not seeing tongues-speech as a *missionary* gift. Garr found that "tongues" could not help with the Bengali and Tibetan languages, when he attempted evangelism there. Ewart, with Durham, announced the *"Oneness" movement,* which stressed the oneness of God, and thereby divided the Pentecostal movement further. Bell founded the Assemblies of God in 1913. Aimee Semple McPherson was a pastor in the Assemblies of God, and proclaimed "the *foursquare gospel."* In 1923 she founded "the Lighthouse for International Foursquare Evangelism" Bible College, and later broadcasted to large audiences. Jesus, she taught, was, first, Savior; second, Baptizer in the Spirit; third, Healer; and, fourth, Coming King. She influenced perhaps several million people. Spencer founded the Elim Fellowship in 1933.

On the negative side, these might appear as *divisive* subsects, even *splinter groups.* More positively they might also be seen as a *diversity of theological beliefs,* no less fragmented than Lutheranism, Reformed theology, and Anglicanism, at the Reformation. Yet the divisions do seem surprising in the

3. A. H. Anderson and W. J. Hollenweger, *Pentecostals after a Century: Global Perspectives,* JPTSS 15 (Sheffield: Sheffield Academic, 1999).

4. Juan Sepúlveda, "Indigenous Pentecostalism and the Chilean Experience," in *Pentecostals after a Century,* 111-35.

5. Mark J. Cartledge, *Testimony in the Spirit: Rescripting Ordinary Pentecostal Theology* (Farnham, UK, and Burlington, Vt.: Ashgate, 2010), 2-3.

face of the claim to be immediately directed by the Holy Spirit in the light of "the unity of the Spirit" (Eph. 4:3).

To sum up, early Pentecostalism included the following four central themes or doctrines: (1) what Frank Macchia calls in *Baptized in the Spirit* "a powerful experience with, or at a moment distinctive from Christian initiation," and also "an organising principle of a Pentecostal theology."[6] Veli-Matti Kärkkäinen comments similarly that Spirit baptism stands at the forefront of the theological agenda of Pentecostalism today.[7] Macchia and Kärkkäinen are arguably two of the major Pentecostal theologians today. (2) *Restorationalism* constitutes an attempt to replicate today what is recounted in the narrative genre of Acts and in other biblical material. (3) *Premillennialism* and the *"rapture"* regard the parousia, or return of Christ, as immediately imminent, and as ushering in a thousand years of the earthly rule of Christ. The rapture is supposedly based on 1 Thessalonians 4:17. (4) *Speaking in tongues* is regarded in "classical Pentecostalism" as *initial evidence* of Spirit baptism, although some Pentecostals today question this.

Over the last twenty or so years, what began as a degree of indifference to doctrine and hermeneutics has changed. Gordon Fee (b. 1934) writes as a respected NT scholar from the Assemblies of God, although he has questioned the Assemblies' teaching on baptism in the Spirit (their Article 7). His book *God's Empowering Presence* constitutes a generally classic guide to Paul on the Holy Spirit, with a helpful section on "different kinds of tongues."[8] He rejects the normal Pentecostal understanding of 1 Corinthians 12:13, "In the one Spirit we were all baptized into one body." Other Pentecostal NT exegetes include Roger Stronstad and Yongnan Jeon Ahn, and Max Turner is a respected NT charismatic in the mainline churches.[9]

Yet each of the four themes identified above remains controversial in other churches. Admittedly the frequent *thirst for the living God* and *dynamic*

---

6. Frank D. Macchia, *Baptized in the Spirit: A Global Pentecostal Theology* (Grand Rapids: Zondervan, 2006), respectively, 153 and 17.

7. Veli-Matti Kärkkäinen, *Spiritus Ubi Vult Spirat: Pneumatology in Roman Catholic–Pentecostal Dialogue (1972-1989)* (Helsinki: Luther Agricola Society, 1998), 198.

8. Gordon Fee, *God's Empowering Presence: The Holy Spirit in the Letters of Paul* (Peabody, Mass.: Hendrickson, 1994; Milton Keynes: Paternoster, 1995).

9. Roger Stronstad, *The Charismatic Theology of St. Luke* (Peabody, Mass.: Hendrickson, 1984) and *The Prophethood of All Believers: A Study in Luke's Charismatic Theology*, JPTSS 16 (Sheffield: Sheffield Academic, 1999); Ahn, *Interpretation of Tongues and Prophecy in 1 Corinthians 12–14;* Max Turner, *Power from on High: The Spirit in Israel's Restoration and Witness in Luke-Acts* (Sheffield: Sheffield Academic, 1996).

worship of Pentecostals are approved by such theologians as the Catholics Yves Congar and Cardinal Suenens and the Protestant Jürgen Moltmann. In spite of this, (1) *Restorationism* fails to take account of the *multiple functions* and purposes of biblical *narrative;* (2) *premillennialism* includes a one-sided emphasis on the *imminence* of the end-time. (3) We have noted several different approaches to *tongues-speech* in Acts and Paul. (4) *"Baptism in the Spirit"* cannot be defended as an experience *subsequent to* that of becoming a Christian.[10] Finally, (5) *prophecy* may well include *pastoral preaching,* as noted above. In addition to these five exegetical and doctrinal problems, we may suggest that (6) Pentecostal and "charismatic" patterns of worship may not be suitable for everyone, as Congar, Smail, and others recognize.[11] In addition to these points, (7) many Pentecostals acknowledge that the movement may owe too much to the "high-voltage" or "revivalist" experience of the Holiness revivals of earlier years.

On the other hand, Pentecostalism has many enviable features. Many acknowledge that they were first drawn into the movement by the warmth of its *social fellowship,* and the intensity of its longing for a *genuine encounter with God.* It has also recently achieved a level of self-scrutiny and self-criticism that goes far beyond any self-criticism in the charismatic movement of the "mainline" churches. Yet both the Pentecostals and the charismatics remain young movements. Time will allow us to see positive and negative factors more clearly.

In the history of the doctrine of the Holy Spirit, we may distinguish between four eras and approaches for convenience. The first phase of the earliest writings tended to repeat apostolic doctrine and tradition. After Nicaea, the post-Nicene Fathers, especially Athanasius, Hilary, and Basil, concentrated on defending the personhood of the Holy Spirit. The Holy Spirit was no mere creature, thing, or "it." The Reformation and post-Reformation writers stressed the Spirit's work in revelation and sanctification. The fourth period, from the nineteenth century until the present, has witnessed a more radical parting of the ways, in several directions.

10. See James D. G. Dunn, *Baptism in the Holy Spirit: A Re-examination of the New Testament Teaching on the Gift of the Spirit in Relation to Pentecostalism Today* (London: SCM, 1970), throughout.
11. Yves Congar, *I Believe in the Holy Spirit,* 3 vols. (New York: Seabury Press, 1983), 156-57; Thomas Smail and others, *The Love of Power, or, the Power of Love: A Careful Assessment of the Problems within the Charismatic and Word-of-Faith Movements* (Minneapolis: Bethany House, 1994), 96-98.

2. The Holy Spirit before Nicaea

(i) *The Apostolic Fathers, the Early Apologists, and the Ante-Nicene Church Fathers.* We do not have space for a comprehensive survey. We select some typical contributions. (1) Among the apostolic Fathers or subapostolic writings, *1 Clement* is probably the earliest (c. 96). Clement attributed the inspiration of the Old and New Testaments to the Spirit, and other very early writings do the same, including Ignatius, the *Didachē,* and the *Epistle of Barnabas.*[12] They also associated the Holy Spirit with repentance, revelation, illumination, and unity.[13] Ignatius regarded the Spirit as the agent of the virginal conception of Jesus, and used the possible crude analogy of Jesus Christ as the engine of salvation "using the rope of the Holy Spirit" in its appropriation.[14] Polycarp anticipated the threefold Gloria to the Father, the Son, and the Holy Spirit, according to Eusebius.[15]

Among the *early Christian apologists,* Aristides (c. 140) asserted that Jesus came from heaven in the Holy Spirit.[16] Justin Martyr (c. 100–c. 165) declared that the Spirit brought revelation, and abode in Jesus.[17] He quoted Joel 2:28 and Acts 2:17, and referred to the gifts of the Spirit. He linked Spirit-prophecy with rationality.[18] Theophilus of Antioch (d. 180) saw the Spirit as the hand of God.[19] The earliest Christian writings may seem uneventful, but nevertheless they reflected apostolic teaching.

(2) *Montanism* constituted virtually a unique phenomenon in the second and third centuries. Montanus began to "prophesy" in about 160-170. He proclaimed the imminence of the End and the new Jerusalem. With his disciples Prisca and Maximilla, Montanus expected a speedy outpouring of the Holy Spirit. The Montanist movement was at first located in Phrygia. Typical sayings of Montanist "prophets" included: "The human person sleeps, and I remain awake"; and "After me shall be no prophets anymore," but the End.[20]

---

12. *1 Clement* 16.2-3; 45.2; Ignatius, *To the Philadelphians,* preface; *Didachē* 1.3-5; *Barnabas* 10.2; 14.2.

13. *1 Clement* 8.1; 21.2; 46.6; Ignatius, *To the Philadelphians* 7.1; *Didachē* 13.8.

14. Ignatius, *To the Ephesians* 18.2 and 9.1, respectively.

15. Eusebius, *Ecclesiastical History* 5.15.

16. Aristides, *Apology* 15.

17. Justin, *Dialogue with Trypho* 4; *ANF* 1:196; *Dialogue with Trypho* 87; *ANF* 1:243.

18. Justin, *Dialogue with Trypho* 88; *ANF* 1:214; *1 Apology* 13 and 44.

19. Theophilus, *To Autolycus* 1.5; cf. 1.7 and 2.13.

20. R. E. Heine, *The Montanist Oracles and Testimonies* (Macon, Ga.: Mercer University Press, 1989), 163-69, and Christine Trewett, *Montanism: Gender, Authority, and the New People Prophecy* (Cambridge: CUP, 1996), for a positive and feminist verdict.

There were understandable tensions with the mainline church. H. M. Gwatkin, the church historian, suggested that Montanists set back preaching for a thousand years. Yet on the positive side, Tertullian and others admired their ethical and ascetic lifestyle.

Indeed, by about 206, Tertullian, in spite of earlier misgivings, became converted to Montanism. Many centuries later, even John Wesley had second thoughts about the movement. Most of the church, however, shared Eusebius's retrospective evaluation that they were elated, puffed up, and estranged from the true faith: "They talked wildly, unreasonably. . . . The arrogant spirit taught them to revile the entire universal Church."[21] Some have argued that they were forerunners of the Donatists, left-wing Reformers, and the stricter Puritans in their doctrine of the church, aiming at a "pure" visible church. In some respects they anticipated more extreme Pentecostals in their doctrine of the Holy Spirit.

(3) *The Ante-Nicene Church Fathers. Irenaeus* became bishop of Lyons in 180, and is sometimes called "the first theologian of the church." His main writing, *Against Heresies,* is chiefly directed against the Gnostics. In positive terms he defended the "rule of faith" as representing biblical, apostolic, and church teaching, especially in his shorter work *The Demonstration of the Apostolic Preaching.* He emphasized the work of the Holy Spirit in *revelation* and *tradition,* but above all in *public, testable tradition,* not the "private" revelation of the Gnostics. He specifically attacked Valentinus, Basilides, and Marcion.

Specifically on the Holy Spirit, Irenaeus declared that Christ and the Holy Spirit are of the same order of being as God. Indeed, the Son and the Spirit are the "two hands of God" through whom he created humans and the world.[22] The Holy Spirit, he urged, descended upon Jesus Christ to anoint him for his ministry.[23] The revelation of truth through the Spirit is not only through biblical and apostolic *public tradition,* but is also *rational.*[24] To claim to receive private revelation is "presumptuous."[25] Even the apostle Paul, he writes, concedes that we know "in part" and prophesy "in part" (1 Cor. 13:9).[26] Irenaeus even grasped what today is called the eschatological nature of the gift of the Holy Spirit. Paul called this "an earnest" of the Spirit, with

21. Eusebius, *Ecclesiastical History* 5.16; *NPNF,* ser. 2, 1:231-32.
22. Irenaeus, *Against Heresies* 4.20.1; *ANF* 1:487-88.
23. Irenaeus, *Against Heresies* 3.17.1 and 3; *ANF* 1:445; and 3.18.3 and 3.9.3; *ANF* 1:423.
24. Irenaeus, *Against Heresies* 2.18.1; *ANF* 1:399.
25. Irenaeus, *Against Heresies* 2.18.6; *ANF* 1:401.
26. Irenaeus, *Against Heresies* 2.18.7; *ANF* 1:401.

more to come.[27] Irenaeus thus had a firm grasp of the NT themes that relate to the Holy Spirit in the late second century.

Tertullian (c. 150–c. 225) was converted to the Christian faith in his late thirties, and wrote prodigiously in Latin. His work falls into pre-Montanist and post-Montanist periods. In *On Baptism,* written before his conversion to Montanism, he spoke of the creative Spirit "hovering over the waters" (Gen. 1:2) and over the water of baptism.[28] The baptized, he urged, are cleansed by the Spirit.[29] During the same period, in *On Prescription against Heretics,* he expounded the "rule of faith," in which he stated that the Son was "brought down by the Holy Spirit and power of the Father into the Virgin Mary . . . was made flesh . . . and crucified."[30] Christ sent the Spirit after his glorification.

In his Montanist period Tertullian made much of the Paraclete passages in John 14–16. In this period he also made a momentous statement that the Western (Latin) Church adopted, but not the Eastern: "I believe the Spirit to proceed from no other source than from the Father and through the Son."[31] However, in his treatise *On Monogamy* he radically departed from Paul in favor of Montanism. He wrote: "The psychics [ordinary Christians] . . . receive not the Spirit," and cited Galatians 5:17 on the works of the flesh in supposed confirmation of this.[32] The context explains his point: those who fail in ethical standards are not "of the Spirit"; but there is a danger of falling into the Donatist heresy of demanding a "pure" church. As we might expect, he also stressed the "gifts of the Spirit" in Paul.[33] He advocated "ecstasy in which the sensuous stands out of itself."[34] He defended utterances of "the new prophecy," which others criticized, and from which Cyprian and Hilary distanced themselves.

Origen (c. 185–c. 254) insisted, "The Spirit and the Son are worthy of equal honour, and are equally far above creation."[35] Thereby he both reflected biblical testimony and built a bridge to Athanasius and Basil. Indeed, he devoted two chapters of *De principiis* to the Holy Spirit, namely, book 1, chapter 3, and book 2, chapter 7. He also paved the way for Calvin, declaring:

27. Irenaeus, *Against Heresies* 5.8.1; *ANF* 1:533.
28. Tertullian, *On Baptism* 4; *ANF* 3:670.
29. Tertullian, *On Baptism* 6.
30. Tertullian, *On Prescription against Heretics* 13.
31. Tertullian, *Against Praxeas* 4; *ANF* 3:599.
32. Tertullian, *On Monogamy* 1; *ANF* 4:59.
33. Tertullian, *On the Soul* 9; *ANF* 3:188.
34. Tertullian, *On the Soul* 45; *ANF* 3:223.
35. Origen, *De principiis* 1.3.2; *ANF* 4:252.

"All knowledge of the Father is obtained by revelation of the Son through the Holy Spirit," noting the effect of a careful consideration of 1 Corinthians 2:10.[36] He examined Paul's teaching in the *charismata* on the Holy Spirit on the basis of 1 Corinthians 12:7-10. Calling attention to Christ's resurrection and glorification, he noted Peter's use of Joel's prophecy that God would pour out the Spirit on all flesh, and stressed Romans 8:26, "The Spirit intercedes for us," commenting, "Our minds cannot pray unless the Spirit prays." Clement of Alexandria, Hippolytus, Novatian, Cyprian, and Lactantius do not appear to add much that is distinctive alongside Irenaeus, Tertullian, and Origen.

3. The Holy Spirit in the Post-Nicene Fathers

The post-Nicene Fathers Athanasius, Basil, Hilary, Ambrose, and Augustine represent the second of our four broad periods "through the centuries." With these thinkers we move from a general affirmation of apostolic tradition and orthodoxy to a more nuanced and careful emphasis on *the personhood of the Holy Spirit,* initially provoked by claims to the contrary by the *"Pneumatomachi."*

(i) *Athanasius* (c. 296-373). The post-Nicene Fathers explored especially the status of the Holy Spirit as being *not* part of the *created* order, but of the *same being as God.* The breakthrough occurred in Athanasius's *Epistle to Serapion* (358-359). Serapion had written to him about the *Pneumatomachi* (Eng.: fighters against the Spirit). Athanasius replied less in the vein of a polemic, and more in the vein of pastoral guidance. In sections 3-14 he discussed *biblical* passages to which these opponents appealed. Then in 15-21 he expounded relations between the persons of the Godhead. The Godhead is indivisible, as Paul stressed in 1 Corinthians 12:4-7. In sections 21-27 Athanasius scrutinized their arguments further. He pressed the point: "Why do they say that the Holy Spirit is a creature (Gk. *ktisma* and *ktisis*) [when he] has the same oneness with the Son as with the Father? . . . By dividing the Spirit from the Word *(logos)* they no longer ensure that the Godhead in the Triad is One."[37]

Athanasius also appealed to 1 Corinthians 2:11: "Who among men knows

---

36. Origen, *De principiis* 1.3.5.

37. Athanasius, *Epistle to Serapion* 1.2; in English, C. R. B. Shapland, *The Letters of St. Athanasius concerning the Holy Spirit* (London: Epworth, 1951), 77.

the thoughts of God, except the Spirit of God?" and urged, "If he (the Spirit) were a creature, he would not be ranked with the Triad. The whole Triad is One God."[38] Athanasius insisted, "When the Holy Spirit is given to us . . . God is in us."[39] Created beings include angels, human beings, and animals. The popular tendency *to call the Spirit "it" demotes the Spirit and reduces him to the order of mere "things"* — the lowest in the order of creation! To Athanasius he is no less transcendent than God the Father. In Paul's words, "We have received not the spirit of the world, but the Spirit that is from God" (Gk. *to pneuma to ek tou theou,* 1 Cor. 2:12).[40] Lastly, Athanasius appealed to the tradition of the apostles and the church.[41] The Spirit gives life, as God does; he anointed Jesus for his work; he dwells in all Christians. Athanasius repeated his arguments in the second, third, and fourth letters. The Spirit is the fountain of life, and is indivisible from the Son.[42] Michael Haykin rightly argues that Athanasius draws all this prematurely from Scripture.[43]

(ii) *Hilary of Poitiers* (c. 315-368). Meanwhile in the Western Church, Hilary's major work, only a few years later than that of Athanasius, reflected a similar teaching. In *On the Trinity* (362) he argued that the Holy Spirit "is joined with the Father and the Son" (Gal. 4:6; 1 Cor. 2:12; Rom. 8:9).[44] He wrote, "The Paraclete Spirit comes from the Father or from the Son. . . . He is both sent by him (Christ) and proceeds from the Father. . . . Such a unity admits no difference."[45] If either the Son or the Spirit is part of creation, to serve or to worship one or the other would be idolatry. Predictably he appeals also to 1 Corinthians 12:4-7: "the same Spirit . . . the same Lord . . . the same God." Hilary wrote as an excellent exegete of the NT. On "gifts of the Spirit," he insisted that the gift of healing should not exclude medical means, while "prophecy" denoted an understanding of doctrine.[46]

(iii) *Basil of Caesarea* (c. 330-379). Basil explicitly wrote a treatise on the Holy Spirit in about 373. In this he insisted on the triple Gloria: "Glory to the Father, to the Son, and to the Holy Spirit." He appealed primarily

38. Athanasius, *Epistle to Serapion* 1.17; Shapland, *Letters,* 103.
39. Athanasius, *Epistle to Serapion* 1.19; Shapland, *Letters,* 113.
40. Athanasius, *Epistle to Serapion* 1.22; Shapland, *Letters,* 121.
41. Athanasius, *Epistle to Serapion* 1.28-31; Shapland, *Letters,* 130-41.
42. Athanasius, *Epistle to Serapion* 2.2; 3.5; Shapland, *Letters,* 160-89.
43. Michael A. G. Haykin, *The Spirit of God: The Exegesis of 1 and 2 Corinthians in the Pneumatomachian Controversy of the Fourth Century* (Leiden: Brill, 1994), 21-24 and 63-98.
44. Hilary, *On the Trinity* 2.29; *NPNF,* ser. 2, 9:60.
45. Hilary, *On the Trinity* 8.20; *NPNF,* ser. 2, 9:143; cf. also 1.3.
46. Hilary, *On the Trinity* 8.29; *NPNF,* ser. 2, 9:145.

to Scripture and to the apostolic church.[47] He stressed the individuality or inseparability of the Father, the Son, and the Spirit, citing especially 1 Corinthians 12:3, "No one can say 'Jesus is Lord' except by the Holy Spirit."[48] He appealed to 1 Corinthians 2:10, on the Spirit's relation with God, and on the deity of the Holy Spirit. He discussed the *charismata* of the Holy Spirit (1 Cor. 12:4-11 and Rom. 12:5-6), stressing mutual dependence and the unity of the Spirit.[49] Basil's work was complemented by Gregory of Nazianzus and Gregory of Nyssa, the other two Cappadocian Fathers. They also stressed that the "oneness of being" of the Trinity is especially a oneness of *activity.*

(iv) *Ambrose of Milan* (c. 339-397). In the Western Church, Ambrose produced three books on the Holy Spirit. He insisted that "The Holy Spirit is not among, but above all things."[50] Thus he is certainly not a "thing" or created being.[51] The Spirit, he argued, spoke through the prophets and apostles in Scripture, and anointed Jesus for his work. He declared, "Who can dare say that the Holy Spirit is separated from the Father and Christ *(audit dicere discretum a deo patre et Christo esse)?*"[52] In book 2 he added, "The Holy Spirit is of one will and operation with God the Father."[53]

(v) *Augustine of Hippo* (354-430). Augustine assimilated most of the work of Hilary and Ambrose, as well as drawing much from Basil and Gregory of Nazianzus. Much of his thought on the Spirit comes in his treatises *On Christian Doctrine* (397) and *On the Trinity* (399–c. 423). The Holy Spirit, he argued, constitutes *the bond of love between the Father and the Son,* sharing the same equality *(et aequalitate consistit).*[54] This communion is "consubstantial and *co-eternal,*" and is "more aptly called love *(caritas). . . .* God is love *(caritas).*"[55] Finally, Augustine was explicit on the Western *filioque* clause: "the Spirit proceeds from the Father *and the Son.*" Between them, these five Church Fathers, but especially Augustine, laid the foundations for all Western medieval writing about the Holy Spirit.

47. Basil, *On the Holy Spirit* 9.22–10.26; *NPNF,* ser. 2, 8:15-17; and Haykin, *The Spirit of God,* 104-69.

48. Basil, *On the Holy Spirit* 16.38; *NPNF,* ser. 2, 8:24.

49. Basil, *On the Holy Spirit* 16.61; *NPNF,* ser. 2, 8:38.

50. Ambrose, *On the Holy Spirit* 1.1.19; "non inter omnia, sed super omnia spiritus sanctus est; *NPNF,* ser. 2, 10:96.

51. Ambrose, *On the Holy Spirit* 1.1.26; "non esse socium creaturae"; *NPNF,* ser. 2, 10:97.

52. Ambrose, *On the Holy Spirit* 1.6.80; *NPNF,* ser. 2, 10:103.

53. Ambrose, *On the Holy Spirit* 2.12.142.

54. Augustine, *On the Trinity* 6.5.7; Migne, PL 42:928; *NPNF,* ser. 1, 3:100.

55. Augustine, *On the Trinity* 6.5.7.

4. The Holy Spirit in the Reformation and Post-Reformation Periods

Luther, Calvin, and the post-Reformation period constitute the third of our four eras, each with its distinctive trends. Whereas the post-Nicene Fathers, especially Athanasius, Hilary, and Basil, focused on the *personhood* of the Holy Spirit, the Reformers and their successors tended to stress his power to reveal truth, or *to communicate revelation*. Second to this, they also regarded his work as especially that of *sanctification*.

(i) *Martin Luther* (1483-1546). Luther brought a new perspective to teaching about the work of the Holy Spirit. The medieval church had assimilated much of Augustine's teaching, but tended, in general, especially among medieval mystics, to think of the Spirit as enabling an *ascent* through spiritual journeying to God. Luther saw the Holy Spirit as primarily a *descent from the gracious God* to humankind under bondage, bringing grace, new creation, and renewal. He found himself forced to fight on two fronts: against the institutional powers and traditions of the papacy; and against the "fanatics" *(Schwärmer),* who included Nicolaus Storch, Thomas Müntzer, and Andreas Carlstadt. These were the "enthusiasts": the "radical" or so-called left-wing Reformers. Today, Regin Prenter has done much to emphasize Luther's hitherto neglected emphasis on the Holy Spirit.[56]

Luther stressed that I cannot come to Christ by "my own reason or strength," but through the Holy Spirit, who "sanctifies me by bringing me to faith in Christ": the Holy Spirit is "the Sanctifier, the One who makes us holy."[57] Just as Paul had alluded to conflict in Romans 7 and 8, so Luther spoke of *Anfechtung,* or inner struggle, through which the Holy Spirit achieves this goal. Some translate the term as "trial," "temptation," or "testing."

Andreas Carlstadt denounced images, infant baptism, monastic vows, the Mass, and clerical robes, claiming the authority of the Spirit for this. By contrast, Luther looked to the Word, or Scripture, and often to early tradition. In 1521 he preached against the *Schwärmer,* urging a different approach to society and the state. He regarded the "new prophets" as satanic, and argued that they even undermined biblical teaching on justification by grace, by an emphasis on a "pure" church. In Prenter's words, "enthusiasm" leads to the "terrible end of the way of legislative pietism."[58] Luther's at-

---

56. Regin Prenter, *Spiritus Creator: Luther's Concept of the Holy Spirit* (Philadelphia: Muhlenberg, 1953).

57. Martin Luther, *The Large Catechism* (St. Louis: Concordia, 1921), pt. 1, art. 3, pars. 34-37.

58. Prenter, *Spiritus Creator,* 219.

tack is uncompromising.[59] Luther's collaborator Philipp Melanchthon was less confrontational against the enthusiasts than Luther, but Ulrich Zwingli shared Luther's strong criticisms. They represented a different view of the Holy Spirit, with Luther reflecting perhaps that of Paul, and the *Schwärmer* perhaps that of Paul's opponents at Corinth. Martin Bucer also urged that it is through the word that the Holy Spirit works, and like Luther, held a higher view of the pastors, teachers, and ministers than the *Schwärmer.* The Holy Spirit equips ministers to minister.

(ii) *John Calvin* (1509-1564). Like the Church Fathers, Calvin asserted "the divinity of the Holy Spirit."[60] He urged that the Father, the Son, and the Holy Spirit are coeternal (1.13.18). The operations of the Holy Spirit, he argued in part 3 of the *Institutes,* make available the "benefits of Christ" (3.1.1). Calvin wrote: "His secret irrigation . . . makes us bud forth and produce the fruits of righteousness," providing the waters of life and the oil of anointing (3.1.3). The Spirit provides "confirmation of the heart . . . sealing upon the hearts the very promises [of God]" (3.2.36). In part 4 Calvin discussed faith and the sacraments. He declared, "Faith is the proper and entire work of the Holy Spirit . . . by whom we recognise God and the treasures of his grace" (4.14.8). The Spirit "must penetrate our hearts" to perform this (1.7.8).

This short summary cannot do justice to Calvin's teaching in depth and scope, but it conveys his concerns. He further wrote, "By means of Him (the Holy Spirit) we become partakers of the Divine nature, so as . . . to feel his quickening energy within us. . . . From him is power, sanctification, truth, grace, and every good thought, since it is from the Spirit alone that all these good gifts proceed" (1.13.14). Calvin amplified much of this in his commentaries. For example, "The spirit alone is the faithful and sure witness to each person of his election."[61]

(iii) *John Owen* (1616-1683). Owen wrote a lengthy book called *The Holy Spirit* (1674). He began with general principles, including an examination of 1 Corinthians 12:4-11 and spiritual gifts. In book 1, chapter 3, he considered the Spirit's deity and personhood. Recipients of the "gifts" remain of the same status as *all* Christians. He warned readers against the possible deceits of false prophecy. The Holy Spirit must be understood in terms of God

---

59. Martin Luther, *Against the Heavenly Prophets,* in *Luther's Works,* vol. 40 (St. Louis: Concordia, 1958), e.g., 142.

60. John Calvin, *The Institutes of the Christian Religion,* 2 vols. (London: James Clarke, 1957), 1.13.14. References have been placed in the text.

61. John Calvin, *The First Epistle to the Corinthians* (Edinburgh: St. Andrew's Press, 1960), 23.

himself.[62] He is "a distinct, living, powerful, intelligent person."[63] He works *through* works of nature, and does not bypass them. *Sanctification* constitutes his primary gift, and this remains *progressive, not instant.*[64] There may even be "delays" in growth in holiness.[65]

(iv) *George Fox and the Earliest Quakers.* Although he belongs to this post-Reformation period, Fox (1624-1691) anticipated the Pentecostal stress on "experience." As well as "the inner light," he stressed the manifestation of religious and emotional fervor, of waiting and silence, of informal worship, and of absence of a priest or minister. In his *Journals* Fox recounted various private "revelations," from 1647 onward. By 1655 "Quakerism," or the Society of Friends, had spread from the English East Midlands to Bristol. Fox recalled, "The Lord's power was so great that the house seemed to be shaken. . . . It was now as in the days of the apostles."[66] His near contempt for mainline churches, which he called "steeple houses," led to various periods of imprisonment in Derby and elsewhere.

(v) *John Wesley* (1703-1791). Wesley never renounced his allegiance to the Church of England, even if his lay preachers became ordained clergy in the Methodist Church. He was more sympathetic to "phenomena" that he regarded as of the Holy Spirit. His attitude toward "sinless perfection" is highly controversial, but it may be doubted whether he held this view fully. The Holy Spirit, he insisted, is at work in ordinary Christians, and he defended Luther's view of the law and grace.[67] Yet he was more sympathetic to what would later be called "Pentecostal leanings" than were mainline churches. Bishop Joseph Butler is said to have exclaimed to him, "Sir, pretending to extraordinary revelations and gifts of the Holy Ghost is a horrid thing, a very horrid thing!" He did also come eventually to regard the Montanists with more favor than previously. But the eighteenth century in general was also the "age of reason," when, as Newman expressed it, "love grew cold," and his emphasis was understandable in the context of his times. He never went as far in this direction as his successor, John Fletcher.

(vi) *Jonathan Edwards* (1703-1758). Edwards took a leading role in the

---

62. John Owen, *The Holy Spirit* (Grand Rapids: Kregel, 1954), 39-40.

63. Owen, *The Holy Spirit,* 41.

64. John Owen, *The Holy Spirit: Longer Version* (Rio, Wis.: Ages Software, 2004), 461.

65. Owen, *The Holy Spirit: Longer Version,* 468.

66. *The Journal of George Fox* (New York: Cosimo, 2007), 13, and (Leeds: Pickard, 1836), 102.

67. John Wesley, "On the Holy Spirit: Sermon 141" (1736), ed. George Lyons, in Christian Classics Ethereal Library.

First Great Awakening in America in the 1730s and 1740s. He wrote *A Faithful Narrative of the Surprising Works of God* in 1737. But he followed this with *A Treatise concerning Religious Affections* (1746), in which he defended some *genuine* professions of faith and expression of emotions, but also urged the need for *self-criticism* and critical intellectual inquiry.[68] Some (or even many) examples of "awakening," he argued, were not genuine at all. Every claim to "experience" of the Spirit called for discernment. Here Edwards's philosophical gifts and background complemented his Christian theology and devotion. "True" affections are "opinions," and must also, he concluded, be "reasonable, solid."[69] They must witness to Christ, and must lead to the fruit of the Spirit.

5. The Holy Spirit from the Nineteenth Century until the Present

The fourth era of our historical sketch witnessed a parting of the ways on the subject of the Holy Spirit. It would not be possible to trace all the twists and turns of the modern debate since Schleiermacher and at the same time to limit this to a medium-length one-volume work. So we must hit the high points.

(i) *Schleiermacher and Hegel.* In the first part of the nineteenth century, Friedrich Schleiermacher (1768-1834) and Georg W. F. Hegel (1770-1831) sharply diverged from each other. To some extent Schleiermacher retained the Pietist emphasis on the *experience* of the Holy Spirit, but he also introduced Kantian and post-Enlightenment concerns. Gerrish characterizes him as a "liberal evangelical."[70] In his *Speeches,* Schleiermacher rejected undue concern with the "trappings" of religion.[71] He likewise rejected preoccupation with "metaphysical and ethical crumbs."[72] In his *Hermeneutics,* he recognized the Spirit's role in biblical inspiration.[73] In *The Christian Faith,*

---

68. Jonathan Edwards, *A Treatise concerning Religious Affections,* in *Select Works of Jonathan Edwards,* vol. 3 (London: Banner of Truth, 1959), and *Works of Jonathan Edwards,* vol. 2 (New Haven: Yale University Press, 2009).

69. Edwards, *Religious Affections,* 5.1.

70. B. A. Gerrish, *A Prince of the Church: Schleiermacher and the Beginning of Modern Theology* (London: SCM, 1984), 18-20.

71. Friedrich D. E. Schleiermacher, *On Religion: Speeches to Its Cultured Despisers* (London: Kegan Paul, Trench and Trübner, 1893), 1.

72. Schleiermacher, *On Religion,* 31 and 36.

73. Friedrich D. E. Schleiermacher, *Hermeneutics: The Handwritten Manuscripts* (Missoula, Mont.: Scholars Press, 1977) 67.

he regarded the Holy Spirit as the source and origin of the church.[74] He declared, "The Holy Spirit is the union of the Divine Essence with human nature in . . . animating the life in common of believers."[75] On the other hand, critics of Schleiermacher argue that he tended to reduce human consciousness of the Spirit to that of consciousness itself, in spite of assertions to the contrary. Undoubtedly there was the danger of reducing theology to a phenomenology of religion.

Hegel began from a different starting point. Spirit *(Geist)* became a key concept for his philosophical theology. God as Spirit actualizes himself in history. He wrote, the "divine Idea unfolds itself . . . in divine history, the process of self-differentiation."[76] God unfolds himself, first, by creation; second, in his "death" in the crucifixion of the Son; and third, in the exaltation and gift of the Spirit, who raises the church. He argued that Roman Catholicism remained at the second stage, with a static crucifix, rather than becoming a religion of the Spirit. The Holy Spirit gives "the formation of the Spiritual Community."[77] Here, he wrote, "All men are called to salvation" through God as Spirit.[78] In speculative terms, this represents a brilliant account of the Holy Trinity, and Pannenberg develops his notion of God's self-differentiation. However, whether this owes more to the dictates of Hegel's system of logic or to biblical and theological tradition is far from clear.

(ii) *Hodge, Smeaton, and Kuyper.* These three theologians followed the path of *Reformed theology.* Charles Hodge (1797-1878) championed Calvinism at Princeton. In his *Systematic Theology* he expounded the nature, personality, divinity, and office of the Holy Spirit, focusing especially on regeneration and sanctification.[79] He argued that the Holy Spirit is personal, but not in the way that human beings are personal. We earlier suggested the term "suprapersonal." Jesus, he urged, was full of the Spirit. The Spirit is "involved in the religious experience of all Christians."[80] He did not endorse perfectionism.

74. Friedrich D. E. Schleiermacher, *The Christian Faith* (Edinburgh: T. & T. Clark, 1989; orig. 1821), 533 and 560-81.

75. Schleiermacher, *The Christian Faith,* 569.

76. Georg W. F. Hegel, *Lectures on the Philosophy of Religion,* 3 vols. (London: Kegan Paul, Trench and Trübner, 1895), 3:2-3.

77. Hegel, *Philosophy of Religion,* 3:104.

78. Hegel, *Philosophy of Religion,* 3:108.

79. Charles Hodge, *Systematic Theology,* 3 vols. (New York: Scribner, 1871), 1:376-80, 522-34; 2:710-32; and 3:31-40, 213-32.

80. Hodge, *Systematic Theology,* 1:532.

George Smeaton (1814-1889) belonged to the Church of Scotland, and his book *The Doctrine of the Holy Spirit* appeared in 1892. In it he addressed a number of relevant issues, including the personality and procession of the Spirit; his anointing of Christ; and his work in revelation and sanctification. On gifts of the Spirit, as recounted in 1 Corinthians 12:8-10, he warned his readers: "These extraordinary gifts of the Spirit were no longer needed when the canon of Scripture was closed."[81] This so-called cessationist view is associated with Benjamin Warfield. Smeaton reaffirmed that the Holy Spirit is given to all Christians (Rom. 8:9) as part of union with Christ.[82]

Abraham Kuyper (1837-1920), a Dutch Calvinist, produced his book of some 650 pages, *The Work of the Holy Spirit,* in 1888. Kuyper anchored his account of the Holy Spirit in the doctrine of the Holy Trinity. He ascribed creation to the Spirit, and natural talents. He held no "dualist" view of natural and "supernatural."[83] Kuyper expounded much of the material also covered by Hodge and Smeaton, especially the Christ-centered character of the work of the Holy Spirit. He also examined his empowerment of those called to ministry.

(iii) *Irving, Irwin, and Simpson.* These theologians anticipated some aspects of Pentecostalism. In 1828 and 1831 there were outbreaks of speaking in tongues in western Scotland, and in the London church pastored by Edward Irving (1792-1834). His presbytery excommunicated him for unorthodox views both of Christology and of the Holy Spirit. Together with Henry Drummond, he formed the Catholic Apostolic Church, a revivalist group, who held to an imminent eschatology. By 1835 this group had appointed twelve *"apostles,"* while they gave the name "angels" to those who had been appointed as bishops. Irving was appointed bishop in the Catholic Apostolic Church. Warfield explicitly attacked Irving's theology in his *Counterfeit Miracles.*

The American Benjamin H. Irwin (b. 1854) received a "sanctification experience" in 1891. He was influenced by the Iowa Holiness Association, and by John Fletcher's "baptism of burning love." He worked among American Methodists, teaching the need for a "third blessing." But in 1900 he confessed to "open and great sin," and fell from leadership.

81. George Smeaton, *The Doctrine of the Holy Spirit* (London: Banner of Truth Trust, 1958), 140.

82. Smeaton, *Doctrine of the Holy Spirit,* 204-29, especially 208, 211, and 221.

83. Abraham Kuyper, *The Work of the Holy Spirit* (New York and London: Funk and Wagnalls, 1900), 39-43.

Albert B. Simpson (1843-1919) urged the "fourfold gospel," which became the forerunner of the Pentecostal "Foursquare Gospel." He taught that Christ was Savior, Sanctifier, Healer, and Coming King. He espoused a Restorationist hermeneutic of Scripture.

(iv) *John Henry Newman* (1801-1890). We have observed three directions of the doctrine of the Holy Spirit. A fourth direction comes from the "progressive" and creative Catholic thinker John Henry Newman. He was originally one of the "High Church" Anglican Tractarians, who also included E. B. Pusey and John Keble. Together they held a high view of the church, and protested against liberal tendencies in it. In 1833 they protested against the spirit of the age, and defended the ancient traditions of the church in the *Tracts for the Times* series. Newman later wrote: "Dogma has been the fundamental principle of my religion."[84] He even anticipated Barth by stating that evangelical Pietism is both too subjective and "idolatrous in worshipping religion rather than God."[85] In 1843 he resigned from his Anglican office, and preached the sermon "The Parting of Friends." His view of the Holy Spirit is colored by his conviction that doctrine develops, rightly, as a bud develops into a flower. Doctrine includes continuity, assimilation, and logical sequence.[86] Newman called attention especially to the Spirit's indwelling, and that the Holy Spirit works in and through human actions. He distanced himself alike from the barren dryness of liberalism and from the "rash, irreverent, and self-exalting" movements of ecstatic religion. I have examined these nineteenth-century thinkers in detail in my book *The Holy Spirit in Biblical Teaching, through the Centuries, and Today* (2013).

This brings us to the twentieth century. Similar differences of direction may also be ascribed to thinkers in the *twentieth and twenty-first centuries,* to whom we devote 150 pages of the above book.[87]

(v) *Henry B. Swete* (1835-1917). Swete made the first classic attempt to cover comprehensively the biblical and patristic writings in an impartial and scholarly way (1909 and 1912).[88]

(vi) *Karl Barth* (1896-1968). Barth wrote *The Holy Spirit and the Chris-*

84. John Henry Newman, *Apologia pro Vita Sua* (Boston: Houghton Mifflin, 1956; orig. 1864), 127.

85. Newman, *Apologia,* 231.

86. John Henry Newman, *An Essay on the Development of Doctrine* (London: Penguin, 1974), 122-47.

87. Thiselton, *The Holy Spirit,* 316-467.

88. Henry B. Swete, *The Holy Spirit in the New Testament* (London: Macmillan, 1909), and *The Holy Spirit in the Ancient Church* (London: Macmillan, 1912).

tian Life (1929), and from 1932 onward his *Church Dogmatics.*[89] New creation by the Holy Spirit stands in contrast to human "spirituality" or "religion" (in the sense of human religious aspiration). The work of the Spirit is not a matter of feelings and urges, but the voice of the living God. Thus in *The Resurrection of the Dead* he commented on 1 Corinthians 12–14: "What we are really concerned with is *not phenomena in themselves,* but with their *whence?* and *whither?* To what do they point?"[90] Barth also declared, "The Holy Spirit cannot be separated from the Word. . . . His power . . . lives in and by the Word."[91] The Holy Spirit facilitates the appropriation of this Word. He is "the 'yes' to God's Word."[92]

(vii) *Lampe and Dunn.* We have already outlined the rise of the Pentecostal movement from about 1905. Theologians since then have also made notable contributions. G. W. H. Lampe (1912-1980) carefully compared the work of the Spirit in baptism and confirmation. He attacked the work of A. J. Mason and Gregory Dix, who he thought presupposed an anachronous reading of confirmation into the NT and especially Acts. He asserted a strong theology of baptism, and his work did much to check the advance of Anglo-Catholic tendencies in the Church of England.[93] Lampe also published the Bampton Lectures, *God as Spirit,* in which he traced the Spirit acting at decisive stages in the development of the church.[94] He also rejected an immanental understanding of the Spirit.

James D. G. Dunn (b. 1939) has written two books on the Holy Spirit, both of which engage with Pentecostal experience. In his *Baptism in the Holy Spirit,* Dunn shows decisively that "baptism in the Spirit" in 1 Corinthians 12:13 cannot possibly refer to some subsequent experience to that of becoming a Christian: "The Pentecostal arguments fall to the ground."[95] He also appeals to Romans 8:9 for the view that every Christian receives the Holy Spirit. Yet he shows respect for the Pentecostal emphasis on living experi-

89. Karl Barth, *The Holy Spirit and the Christian Life* (Louisville: Westminster John Knox, 1993).

90. Karl Barth, *The Resurrection of the Dead* (London: Hodder and Stoughton, 1933), 80.

91. Barth, *CD* I/1, 150.

92. Barth, *CD* I/1, 453.

93. Geoffrey W. H. Lampe, *The Seal of the Spirit: A Study in the Doctrine of Baptism and Confirmation in the New Testament and the Fathers* (London and New York: Longmans, Green, 1951).

94. Geoffrey W. H. Lampe, *God as Spirit* (Oxford: Clarendon, 1977), 67.

95. James D. G. Dunn, *Baptism in the Holy Spirit* (London: SCM, 1970), 129.

ence. His later book, *Jesus and the Spirit,* works out fundamental exegetical issues of the NT.

Five significant theologians also receive special attention in my book, and limits of space limit my comments here. These are Jürgen Moltmann, Yves Congar, Wolfhart Pannenberg, John Zizioulas, and Vladimir Lossky. Among these, Moltmann and Congar express sympathies with the charismatic renewal movement in the mainline churches.

(viii) *Jürgen Moltmann* (b. 1926). Moltmann also focuses on the Trinitarian framework of the person and work of the Holy Spirit, and his role as dynamic life-giver. He urges that we must not lose "the qualitative difference between God and humans."[96] The Spirit, he insists, "has a wholly unique personhood" (12). Like Zizioulas, he argues that the Spirit is always "being-in-relationship" (14). Moltmann writes, "The other side of Jesus' death is also presented as his experience of the Spirit" through the resurrection (65).

Moltmann urges that the Holy Spirit brings especially liberation from bondage and oppression. Through the Spirit, being a Christian "means continually beginning afresh" (155). Satisfaction remains a *process through the Spirit,* although he sanctifies "what God has already sanctified" (175). The Holy Spirit "gives himself" in the corporate experience of *koinōnia* (217-20). He is indeed, as our creed states, "the Lord and Giver of life" (270). Moltmann's writing often lifts and refreshes the spirits of readers. For example: "Where light, water, and warmth come together, the meadows become green, and trees blossom and bear fruit" (283).

(ix) *Yves Congar* (1904-1995). Congar wrote *I Believe in the Holy Spirit* (3 vols., Eng. 1983). In the first volume he explored biblical and historical material. He argued that the Spirit is known from his *effects.* The Spirit empties himself to become the bond of love between the Father and the Son, and between God and humankind. In his second volume Congar was eager to strike a balance between the institutional and the "charismatic." He wrote, "The Church is made by the Spirit."[97] Christ and the Holy Spirit are the two missions of God, like the Father's two hands in Irenaeus. He warmed to charismatic renewal, but recognized that it may not be for everyone, because of its style of worship.

(x) *Wolfhart Pannenberg* (1928-2014). Pannenberg emphasized the role of the Holy Spirit in the resurrection of Christ and in that of believers. He

96. Jürgen Moltmann, *The Spirit of Life: A Universal Affirmation* (London: SCM, 1992), 5. Page numbers have been placed in the text.

97. Congar, *I Believe in the Holy Spirit,* 2:5.

also regarded the event of creation as a Trinitarian event. He wrote: "The Spirit is at work already in creation as God's mighty breath, the origin of all movement and life."[98] He stressed the work of the Holy Spirit in sanctification and "transfiguring power."[99] The Holy Spirit therefore anointed Jesus for his messianic work. Christ "imparts" the Spirit to his disciples (John 20:22). Like Moltmann and Rogers, he saw a narrative of the Holy Trinity in the Gospels.

(xi) *Zizioulas and Lossky.* John D. Zizioulas (b. 1931) writes as Greek Orthodox metropolitan of Pergamon, and shares many themes with the Russian Orthodox thinker Vladimir Lossky (1903-1958). One of his most distinctive themes is that the Holy Spirit constitutes the very identity of Christ. He writes, "There is . . . *no Christ until the Spirit is at work* . . . as the one who *constitutes his very identity as Christ.*"[100] Zizioulas thus expounds the Holy Spirit in the double context of Christ and the Holy Trinity, and also stresses the Spirit's transcendence or "otherness."

Other theological studies have recently come from Michael Welker (b. 1947), Amos Yong (b. 1965), and many others. But we have once again run up against the limitations of space for our "affordable" one-volume work.

98. Pannenberg, *ST* 3:1.
99. Pannenberg, *ST* 3:4.
100. John Zizioulas, *Being as Communion: Studies in Personhood and the Church* (New York: St. Vladimir's Seminary Press, 1985, 1997), 127.

CHAPTER XIII

Why the Church? Why Ministry? Why Sacraments?

1. Foundations: The Call of God's People and Modern Individualism

Many Christians come to faith as individuals, and may even be tempted to ask, *"Why the church?"* Yet baptism is the "normal" or formal way of entering the corporate community of the church and of being initiated in principle as Christians. More specifically, God called to himself *a people,* not a random collection of individuals. This is admirably illustrated in the question-and-answer that takes place in Jewish Passover. When the son asks, "What do these testimonials mean?" the reply should be: "*We* were Pharaoh's slaves in Egypt, and the Lord brought *us* out of Egypt" (Deut. 6:20-24). In Deuteronomy 26:5-9 the confession of faith begins in the singular: "An Aramaean ready to perish was *my* father," but continues in the plural: "The Lord brought *us* forth from Egypt."

From a *biblical* perspective, today's commonly used phrase "go to church" could seem to verge on the ridiculous. If a person was not part of the *community of God's people "in Christ,"* that individual would hardly be "Christian"! The modern and popular phrase "go to church" arises from the regrettable (but well-established) custom of using the word "church" to denote a *church building,* a location, where a body of Christians assembles. This use of the term is *not wrong, but remains entirely secondary and unbiblical.* For the Greek term *ekklēsia,* "church," is usually used to denote an *assembly* (Heb. *qāhāl*). Nevertheless, the related doctrines of the church, the ministry, and the sacraments have to contend with a massive hermeneutical switch: from the *communal* horizons of biblical, Jewish, and Christian faith to the *individualism* that arose especially in our industrial and marketplace consumerist economy from the nineteenth century onward, and also even earlier in terms of a philosophical legacy.

Many argue that modern individualism took its rise from Descartes (1596-1650). He sought "certain" knowledge, and chose to shut himself away to work out his own "absolutely certain" and "self-evident knowledge," namely, his *cogito, ergo sum*.[1] William Temple attacked this solitary Cartesian individualism; he called it, even if with some exaggeration, "The most disastrous moment in the history of Europe," and "a faux-pas of monumental proportions."[2] In the wake of Descartes, philosophical rationalists (including Leibniz) and empiricists (including Locke, Berkeley, and Hume) all conceived of knowledge as a fundamentally *individualistic* enterprise, whether through an individual *mind* (with the rationalists) or through *the senses* (with the empiricists). Even Immanuel Kant, in his critical or transcendental philosophy, understood the "Enlightenment" to represent, above all, *thinking for oneself*, which he regarded as throwing off second-hand authorities, and thereby corporate tradition. "Thinking for oneself" may at first sound courageous and admirable, but not on reflection if this is taken to mean ignoring or bypassing the corporate witness and findings of previous generations. From one side it may seem bold and creative; from the other side it looks like pitting a single individual consciousness (as Descartes did) or judgment (as Kant did) against that of *thousands* from previous generations.

The witness of the biblical writings and of "the rule of faith," as Irenaeus called it, points in a different direction. J. A. T. Robinson expressed this contrast between biblical and modern perspectives sharply and vividly in his book *The Body*. Body (Gk. *sōma*) stands in contrast with *flesh* (Gk. *sarx*) in Paul. Following Bultmann, Robinson sees *flesh* as representing "human self-sufficiency" (2 Cor. 3:5-6; 1:12; Col. 2:18).[3] By contrast, Robinson urged, "The Body is that which joins all people, irrespective of individual differences, in life's bundle together."[4] His case becomes most vivid and memorable when he speaks the language of "membership" of a body such as a club, which has now become "trite."[5]

When Paul says that we are members of the body of Christ, or of the

1. René Descartes, *Discourse on Method* (Cambridge: CUP, 1984-1991), pt. 4, 53-54.

2. William Temple, *Nature, Man, and God* (London: Macmillan, 1940), 57.

3. John A. T. Robinson, *The Body: A Study in Pauline Theology*, SBT 5 (London: SCM, 1952; Philadelphia: Westminster John Knox, 1977), 25.

4. Robinson, *The Body*, 29.

5. Robinson, *The Body*, 51.

church, Robinson explains, this is *not* like being a "member" of a golf club or of an association. It is more akin to being a "limb" or "membrane" of Christ's body. Paul declares: "Just as the body is one and has many members, . . . all the members of the body, though many, are one" (1 Cor. 12:12). He adds: "The body does not consist of one member but of many. . . . If the whole body were an eye, where would the hearing be? . . . If all were a single member, where would the body be?" (12:14, 17, 19). The whole body is bound together in corporate solidarity: "If one member suffers, all suffer together with it; if one member is honored, all rejoice together with it" (12:26).

Another striking advocate of this communal and corporate perspective is Lionel S. Thornton, especially in his book *The Common Life in the Body of Christ.* In it he traces the corporate identity of the people of God, which culminates in the image of the vine in John 15 and the body of Christ in Paul. Thornton traces the history of how corporate Israel failed, but could be restored in Christ. "The hope of Israel went down into the grave, and their hopes went too. . . . There is no Israel apart from the Messiah. So also, finally when he (Christ) rose from the tomb, they rose. . . . *When Christ rose, the Church rose from the dead.*"[6]

Thornton traces the buildup of the Christian church from the corporate common life in Acts 2–4, when the community shared "all things common," through their sharing in Christ's sufferings, resurrection, and life, and their sharing also in the gift of the Holy Spirit. The expression "the *koinōnia* of the Holy Spirit" (Phil. 2:1) is translated by Thornton as *"that in which we share,"* or "in which we *participate,"* as involving "common and mutual interest, and participation in a common object."[7] Paul's image of "grafting" onto the olive tree of Israel in Romans 9–11 implies that "we have become united by growth."[8] Thornton develops his theme by portraying the church as "partakers of God's love," "partakers of Christ's victory," "partakers of Christ's Sonship," and so on. For Thornton the notion of a solitary Christian, isolated from the church, has become a contradiction in terms. "Christian fellowship" does *not* mean simply having social relations with other people in a shared building, but common participation as one who holds a *joint share in the body of Christ.*

Some critics, especially many evangelicals, show understandable con-

---

6. Lionel S. Thornton, *The Common Life in the Body of Christ,* 3rd ed. (London: Dacre Press, 1950), 282, italics mine.

7. Thornton, *Common Life,* 74; cf. 70-75.

8. Thornton, *Common Life,* 62-63.

cern lest this catchphrase, "body of Christ," be used to suggest that to join the visible church is necessarily and in itself to be joined to Christ. There is some truth in this expression of concern; yet it is also true that Jesus addressed Paul on the road to Damascus with the words: "Why do you persecute me?" (Acts 9:4), when he was on his way to persecute *the church*. Robinson makes this point.[9] Jesus Christ stood in solidarity with God's people, although Whiteley comments, "The subject has been both complicated and illuminated by J. A. T. Robinson."[10]

Like Moltmann, Ricoeur, Lossky, and Zizioulas, Stanley Grenz has emphasized that the self is "relational-with-others."[11] These five writers, especially Lossky, stress that an isolated, individual, narcissistic self is not genuinely a "person" in the fullest sense of the word. In his book *In the Image and Likeness of God*, Lossky declares, "Personal existence supposes a relationship to the other. . . . A person can be fully personal only in so far as he has nothing that he seeks to possess for himself to the exclusion of others. . . . Otherwise we are in the presence of *individuals*."[12] He also insists, *"Individual and person mean opposite things."*[13] An individual, he argues, becomes a person when the self opens itself up to other selves and to God.

Ricoeur, Zizioulas, and Moltmann are no less emphatic. Ricoeur writes: "Otherness is not added on to selfhood from outside as though to prevent its solipsistic drift. . . . It belongs instead . . . to the ontological constitution of selfhood."[14] Zizioulas likewise regards "fragmented existence" a result of human fallenness, and comments, "There is no being without communion. Nothing exists as an 'individual,' conceivable in itself."[15] He argues that through the Holy Spirit "Christ is not just an individual," but a "corporate personality."[16] This, he concludes, has profound consequences for the church both local and universal, in which *koinōnia* is a more significant "ontologi-

---

9. Robinson, *The Body*, 58.

10. D. E. H. Whiteley, *The Theology of St. Paul* (Oxford: Blackwell, 1964, 1971), 192.

11. Stanley J. Grenz, *The Social God and the Relational Self: A Trinitarian Theology of the Imago Dei* (Louisville: Westminster John Knox, 2001), 69-97; Paul Ricoeur, *Oneself as Another* (Chicago: University of Chicago Press, 1992), throughout.

12. Vladimir Lossky, *In the Image and Likeness of God* (London and Oxford: Mowbray, 1974), 106.

13. Vladimir Lossky, *The Mystical Theology of the Eastern Church* (New York: St. Vladimir's Seminary Press, 1976; Cambridge: Clarke, 1991), 121, italics mine.

14. Ricoeur, *Oneself as Another*, 317.

15. John D. Zizioulas, *Being as Communion: Studies in Personhood and the Church* (New York: St. Vladimir's Seminary Press, 1985, 1997), 103 and 18.

16. Zizioulas, *Being as Communion*, 130.

cal category" than being or substance.[17] Moltmann likewise declares, "The modern culture of subjectivity has long since been in danger of turning into a 'culture of narcissism,' which makes the self its own prisoner."[18] In his work on the church, he urges fellowship and participation.[19] Karl Rahner also speaks of the church as "the community of pilgrims."[20]

In the NT the term *koinōnia* mostly stands emphatically in contrast with "narcissism." Danker lists for this term a range of meanings from "communion," "fellowship," and "close relationship" (1 Cor. 1:9; Phil. 2:1; 1 John 1:3, 6; Rom. 15:26) to "participation" and "sharing" (Phil. 3:10; 1 Cor. 1:9; 10:16; Philem. 6).[21] *Koinōnos* denotes "partner" or "sharer" and may even denote "shareholder," as Thornton understands it to mean in 2 Corinthians 13:13.[22] In Wainwright's words, it grounds in the world the corporate dimension of God's own mission to the world through his people.[23] As we have noted, in Johannine theology this finds expression in images such as the vine and the branches (John 15:1-11) that represent both Christ and his people (the church and, in the OT, Israel), and the Good Shepherd and his flock (John 10:1-18). In Paul it finds expression in the remnant (Rom. 9:27; 11:5); the wild olive shoot (Rom. 11:17-24); God's field, God's building, and God's temple (1 Cor. 3:9-17); the church of God (1 Cor. 11:22); the body of Christ (1 Cor. 12:12-26; Eph. 1:23; 2:16; 4:4, 12; Col. 1:18); and the bride of Christ (Eph. 5:25-26, 32; cf. Rev. 21:2).

2. Theological Debates about the Doctrine of the Church

(i) *Corporate Foundations and Nature of Christian Faith.* Regarding the corporate foundations and nature of Christian faith, writers such as Newton Flew fought boldly and in one sense rightly to insist that Jesus founded the church, in spite of many criticisms at the time. But today, as N. T. Wright and

---

17. Zizioulas, *Being as Communion*, 334; cf. 332-42.

18. Jürgen Moltmann, *The Trinity and the Kingdom of God: The Doctrine of God* (London: SCM, 1981), 5.

19. Jürgen Moltmann, *The Church in the Power of the Spirit* (London: SCM; Philadelphia: Fortress, 1977).

20. Karl Rahner, *Theological Investigations*, vol. 6 (London: DLT, 1969), 298; cf. 295-312.

21. BDAG 352-54.

22. Thornton, *Common Life*, 71-77.

23. Geoffrey Wainwright, *Doxology: A Systematic Theology* (London: Epworth, 1980), 122-46.

others have shown, such a question is seen as virtually "anachronistic; individualism is a comparatively modern, and a largely western phenomenon." He continues: "Jesus did not intend to 'found' a church because there already was one, namely the people of Israel itself. Jesus' intention was therefore to reform Israel, not to found a different community altogether."[24] Language about the people of God, the kingdom of God, the vine, and the flock was *already at hand.* So this old-fashioned question should not arise again today.

(ii) *Church: A Local or Universal Concept?* Of more practical interest is the issue raised by Rahner, Pannenberg, Jenson, and others, concerning whether *church (ekklēsia)* was primarily a local concept or a universal one. Vatican II, under Rahner's influence, regarded the church as "a sacrament, as it were" (Lat. *uti sacramentum*); it is "the universal sacrifice of salvation" in the sense of an outward and visible sign of God's indwelling his people.[25] Pannenberg rightly distinguishes between the kingdom of God and the church, while the church is simply "an anticipatory sign of God's coming rule."[26] He points out that the "local church" is much more complex than we realize. "What precisely is the meaning of the term 'local church' for the primary units of the church's life? Are we speaking of the congregation assembled locally for the preaching of the Word and the Eucharist, or is 'local church' a term for the diocese subject to a bishop?"[27] Pannenberg endorses the definition of Vatican II: the church is "a sacrament of salvation."

This specific concept of the church goes back to Cyprian. As Schnackenburg points out, like the kingdom, the church is not built up by human persons, but by God, even if the church, unlike the kingdom of God, has blemishes and fallibility in the world.[28]

(iii) *Mission, Not Maintenance.* Moltmann and others rightly emphasize that the task of the church is mission, not just maintenance. Yet many churches spend proportionately more time and energy on questions of maintaining structure and fabric than on reaching out to others and to the world. Nevertheless, "structure" remains important. As Bonhoeffer has argued, the

24. N. T. Wright, *Jesus and the Victory of God* (London: SPCK, 1996), 275.

25. Vatican II, *Lumen Gentium* (21 November 1964), 1:1, "The Mystery of the Church," in *Documents of Vatican II,* ed. Austin P. Flannery (Grand Rapids: Eerdmans, 1975), 350; cf. Robert W. Jenson, "The Church and the Sacraments," in *Cambridge Companion to Christian Doctrine,* ed. Colin Gunton (Cambridge: CUP, 1997), 207-25.

26. Pannenberg, *ST* 3:30 and 32.

27. Pannenberg, *ST* 3:109.

28. Rudolf Schnackenburg, *God's Rule and Kingdom* (London: Nelson, 1963), 23-34; cf. Cyprian, *Epistle* 69, sect. 6; and *On the Unity of the Church* 4.

visible church is a *sociological reality of the church in this world,* as well as a spiritual work of God. Bonhoeffer expounded this in his book *Sanctorum Communio,* which was his dissertation of 1927, first published in 1930. Like Lossky and Zizioulas, he believed: "The individual exists only in relation to an 'other'; individual does not mean solitary. On the contrary, for the individual to exist, 'others' must necessarily be there."[29] He added, "There would be no self-consciousness without community."[30] Bonhoeffer is realistic about the present church and its fallibility and sin. Thus he wrote, "Genuine life arises only in the conflict of wills; strength unfolds only in strife."[31] Yet for Bonhoeffer the church is also theologically grounded in the cross of Christ.

Sociologists have regularly observed the changing balance between vision and structure as time elapses. Often an *initial vision* or calling drives the church into action, with a minimal infrastructure. Gradually the infrastructure becomes more complex as differing situations emerge. Perhaps the earliest example was the need to arbitrate between Aramaic-speaking widows and Greek-speaking widows in Acts 6:1-6. After this we reach a third stage when the vision is served by a *growing* but still generally proportionate sociological *infrastructure.* Finally, however, attention seems to be given increasingly to the structure itself, until it finally becomes an end in itself, with hardly any, or none, of the vision or call it was meant to serve.

Bonhoeffer was keen for the church to avoid this fate. If Jesus, in his words, was "the Man for others," the church must be "for others." The church, he declared, is her true self "only when she exists for humanity." Similarly Moltmann asserts, "Ecclesiology can only be developed from Christology."[32] Commenting on its empowerment by the Spirit of God, Moltmann declares: "It is not the *church* that has a mission of salvation to fulfil to the world: it is the mission of the Son and the Spirit through the Father that includes the church, *creating a church as it goes on its way.*"[33] On the same page he insists: "It is not the church that administers the Spirit. . . . The Spirit administers the church with the events of word and faith, sacrament and grace, offices and traditions." The "true" church is "the church under the cross."[34]

The Catholic theologian Avery Dulles attempts to achieve a propor-

29. Dietrich Bonhoeffer, *Sanctorum Communio: A Theological Study of the Sociology of the Church* (Philadelphia: Fortress, 1998), 50-51.
30. Bonhoeffer, *Sanctorum Communio,* 70.
31. Bonhoeffer, *Sanctorum Communio,* 85.
32. Moltmann, *The Church,* 66.
33. Moltmann, *The Church,* 64, italics mine.
34. Moltmann, *The Church,* 65.

tionate balance between call and vision, on one side, and institution and office on the other, as Congar also does. Like Rahner, Dulles stresses that the "institutional" model of the church values the *traditions, corporate identity, and continuity* of the church, but risks falling into clericalism and legalism. Rahner writes, "The life-style especially of the higher clergy even today sometimes conforms too much to that of 'managers' in secular society."[35] It is well known that today Pope Francis is often outspoken on this matter. Dulles also explores the church's role in worship and in looking toward the end. The church cannot "dig in" as part of the world, for it is always a pilgrim church, traveling ever onward until the final end and goal are reached.

Yet the public visibility of the church remains part of its necessary role, as Luke-Acts makes clear. This reminds us of what Käsemann has said about the body. It is this that makes confessions of faith testable *in the public domain,* and therefore *credible.* The church's handling of money is only one of many such criteria offered to public scrutiny. The whole range of loving, ethical conduct is another. Käsemann's research on "body," therefore, gives added point to Paul's language about the church as the body of Christ.

(iv) *Government and Constitution of the Church.* Debates continue about the government of the church and its constitution. These also inevitably relate to the *ministry* of the church, and to our earlier discussion of the "local" church. Over the years three basic patterns have emerged, with secondary variations. These may be described broadly as the *episcopal,* the *presbyterian,* and the *congregational.* Each group used regularly to insist that it *alone* represented *the* "biblical" view. However, many today recognize that earliest Christianity had *no firmly fixed pattern,* even if a pattern had begun to emerge by the early second century.

Although it also urges continuity of faith, the *episcopal* view tends to stress the need for both *institutional and doctrinal continuity.* It also stresses the need for presbyters to be accountable, and to maintain unity, under a bishop. Controversy begins over the *nature* of episcopacy, and especially over whether the term for, or office of, an *episkopos,* "bishop" or "overseer," was originally interchangeable with the term for, or office of, a *presbyteros,* "elder" or "presbyter." In both the Roman Catholic and Eastern Orthodox Churches they are regarded as distinct offices that perform distinct functions. The so-called High Churchmen of the Oxford Movement in Anglicanism tended toward this view, while J. B. Lightfoot, G. W. H. Lampe, and the

---

35. Karl Rahner, *The Shape of the Church to Come* (London: SPCK, 1974), 58; cf. Avery Dulles, *Models of the Church* (Dublin: Gill and Macmillan, 1988), 39-46.

majority of Anglican evangelicals regard the difference as originally more fluid, but still useful in indicating a distinct and valuable "order" of ministry. This became a more pragmatic argument. Episcopacy, for example, came to be regarded not as the *"esse"* of the church, but in the view of some, as the *"bene esse."* This seemed to become so, as the church faced threats to its unity and continuity. Even many Presbyterians, Methodists, and those Lutherans who do not formally appoint "bishops" may argue that some presbyters can perform a valid "episcopal" oversight.

The English translation of *episkopos* in the NT is hotly debated. In 1 Timothy 3:1-2, for example, there are various translations of *episkopos* and *episkopē*. The NRSV translates the word as "bishop"; NJB as "presiding elder" and as "president" in verse 2. The REB suggests "leadership"; the NEB, "leader" or "bishop"; and the NIV, "overseer." Danker gives six columns to these words, suggesting, first, "One who has responsibility of safeguarding, or seeing to it, that something is done in the correct way, a guardian," and also citing Titus 1:7 and 1 Peter 2:25. In the Greco-Roman world, Danker continues, the term denotes "guardianship."[36] This accords well with the notion of a bishop's "guarding" against disunity or heresy. Lampe devotes some five columns to *episkopos* in his work *A Patristic Greek Lexicon,* as well as more to *episkopē*. He suggests "pertaining to a bishop's office, having the oversight, overseer, or superintendent."[37]

Controversy begins historically with the special regard for bishops found in *Ignatius* and in later years. Around 112 Ignatius wrote to the church at Ephesus: "It is fitting that you should live in harmony with the will of the bishop *(tē tou episkopou gnōmē)*. . . . Your . . . presbytery *(presbyterion)* . . . is attuned to the bishop, as the strings to a harp."[38] He continues, "Join in the common meeting . . . in one faith . . . so that you may obey the bishop *(tō episkopō)* and the presbytery *(tō presbyteriō)* . . . breaking one bread."[39] Similarly in his *Letter to the Magnesians,* he speaks of "some who recognise the bishop in their words, but disregard him in their actions."[40]

With certain exceptions, this approach prevailed in the Christian church

---

36. BDAG 379-80.

37. Lampe 531-34; cf. Grimm-Thayer's proposal of "overseer, guardian, or superintendent"; Grimm-Thayer 243.

38. Ignatius, *To the Ephesians* 4.1; Gk. and Eng. from Kirsopp Lake, *The Apostolic Fathers,* 2 vols. (London: Heinemann; Cambridge: Harvard University Press, 1965), 1:176 and 177.

39. Ignatius, *To the Ephesians* 20.2; Lake, *The Apostolic Fathers,* 1:194 and 195.

40. Ignatius, *To the Magnesians* 4.1; Lake, *The Apostolic Fathers,* 1:201.

until the Reformation.[41] *Calvin* discussed the place of bishops in the earliest churches in *Institutes* 4.4. He wrote, "All to whom the office of teaching was committed they called presbyters, and in each city these presbyters selected one . . . to whom they gave the title of 'bishop,' lest from equality dissension should arise. The bishop, however, was not superior in honour and dignity."[42] He is to advise, consult, collect opinions, and preside, but not command.

Richard Hooker (c. 1554-1600) laid the theological foundation for the Elizabethan Settlement in his *Laws of Ecclesiastical Polity* (1593-1597, and then posthumously in 1648-1662). He rejected the Puritan notion that the church could follow *only* patterns that were *explicit* in Scripture; but maintained that newer patterns must *not* be *against* Scripture. He preferred the term "presbyter" to "priest" because ancient sacrifices had been abolished.[43] But since the church grew and developed, the three orders of bishops, presbyters, and deacons came to serve the church in a pragmatic way. J. B. Lightfoot (1828-1889) produced his well-known essay "The Christian Ministry" in his commentary on Philippians, in which he argued for a similar understanding. G. W. H. Lampe followed him in advocating this view in the twentieth century. Thus bishops continue to be appointed in the Anglican Communion, in Lutheran churches in Scandinavia and in some German provinces, and in many American and African Methodist churches. By contrast, Presbyterian churches, especially in Scotland, formally reject the title, but insist that they exercise an episcopal *function*. Congregational and Baptist churches would not, or do not, usually make this claim. Hence there is broad but not universal agreement about episcopal function, but a strong minority oppose episcopal office or status. The Eastern Orthodox Church broadly shares the Roman Catholic view, with minor modifications.

(v) *Apostolic Succession.* This term denotes an unbroken continuity of doctrine, tradition, and church order, supposedly with the original apostles. The Catholic and Orthodox churches trace this through an unbroken succession of bishops. Catholics trace the papacy to the primacy of Peter, according to the Catholic interpretation of Matthew 16:18: "On this rock I will build my church." By contrast, in Reformed theology the continuity is not institutional, but that of the church's *doctrine, preaching, and* adminis-

41. One of the more careful studies of differences between Luther, Calvin, and Hooker is offered by Paul Avis, *The Church in the Theology of the Reformers* (London: Marshall, 1981), especially 95-150.

42. Calvin, *Institutes of the Christian Religion* 4.4.2, from the edition translated by Henry Beveridge, 2 vols. (Grand Rapids: Eerdmans, 1989), 2:328.

43. *Hooker's Works*, ed. J. Keble, 7th ed., 3 vols. (Oxford: Clarendon, 1885), 2:471-72.

tration of *the sacraments*. Recent Catholic formulations insist that these are not exclusive alternatives. Vatican II softens the notion to allow *degrees* of apostolicity, granting that Lutheran and Anglican churches possess "some degree" of apostolicity.

(vi) *Marks of the Church.* The "marks of the church" are traditionally defined as that the church is one, holy, catholic, and apostolic. These are not in themselves matters of debate, provided that they are regarded as characteristics, not requirements. Holiness, for example, was misunderstood by Donatists, some more extreme radical Reformers, and some more extreme Puritans, in an exclusivist way, to demand a doctrinally and morally "pure" church. By contrast, most follow Augustine and many of the Church Fathers in *rejecting* this view as untenable for the *visible* church. The oneness and catholicity of the church connote "one body and one Spirit . . . one Lord, one faith, one baptism" (Eph. 4:4-5), and also that this should be lived out, and fragmentation avoided. The church is to be "united by growth" (Col. 2:19).

Geoffrey Paul, formerly bishop of Bradford, England, made a humorous but utterly realistic comment about the marks of the church in his "enthronement" sermon as bishop. He declared: "There is no way of belonging to Christ except by belonging gladly and irrevocably to all that marvellous ragbag of saints and fatheads who make up the one, holy, catholic, and apostolic church."

3. Theological Principles Relating to Ministry

The most profound of a number of principles concerns the *mutuality or reciprocity* of the church and the ministry, *as against self-sufficient individualism and autonomy.* We have already identified this as a key principle in relation to the church. Whatever the seductions of post-Enlightenment secularism about a self-contained, self-sufficient individual, no Christian individual possesses *all* the gifts of the Holy Spirit. For a healthy Christian life we depend on others, especially the teaching and guidance of Christian ministers, as Paul stressed in 1 Corinthians, and Calvin in his *Institutes*.

Yet ministers must be *accountable* not only to God, but also to others. They, like the people of God, are not autonomous. They depend upon superintendents or bishops for unity, arbitration, and consultation. They are also mutually dependent on other Christians, and most churches express suspicion of any local "pope." One of the most significant advances in the Christian church since the 1960s has been the agreement among most Catholics (especially since Vatican II) and many Pentecostals, that ministry is a *collegiate* and *collaborative* activity. Catholics and Anglicans now stress the importance of the "college" of bishops. Bishops should not act alone in isolation from fellow bishops.

This is supported by biblical scholarship. Even Paul the apostle was far from a *lone* missionary-pastor. He worked *collaboratively* with a host of colleagues, including Barnabas, Silvanus, Apollos, Timothy, Titus, Epaphras, Mark, Luke, Priscilla, Aquila, and Philemon. Some nine of these, including the woman Junia, are named among the plurality of apostles (Rom. 16:3, 9, 21; 1 Cor. 3:9; 2 Cor. 8:23; Phil. 2:25; 4:3; Col. 4:11; 1 Thess. 3:2; Philem. 1, 24).[44] In his book *The Pioneer Ministry,* Anthony Hanson argues that rather than consider general abstract principles, we should focus on how ministry was actually carried out in the NT.[45]

Paul often compares the responsibility of a minister with that of the *managers* of a household or an estate. Admittedly there are widespread criticisms of importing a "management" culture into the church, lest this perpetuate an unlimited notion of "line management." Paul simply states, however, that ministers are *stewards* or *managers (oikonomoi)* of what has been committed to them (1 Cor. 4:1-2). Danker gives as the first meaning of *oikonomia,* "responsibility of management, management of a household" (cf. also 1 Cor. 9:17). It also can be translated as "order." He proposes for *oikonomos:* "managers of a household or estate, steward, managers."[46]

We have already discussed the term *episkopos* and the debates about whether it is interchangeable with *presbyteros.* Whatever our conclusions, a ministry of bishops, overseers, or superintendents is implied in Acts 20:28; Philippians 1:1; 1 Timothy 3:1-7; and 1 Peter 2:12, 15. The qualities expected of a bishop or of an overseer are enumerated in 1 Timothy 3:1-7, and are

44. D. J. Harrington, "Paul and Collaborative Ministry," *New Theological Review* 3 (1990): 62-71; Bengt Holmberg, *Paul and Power: The Structure of Authority in the Primitive Church,* ConBNT 11 (Lund: Gleerup, 1978), especially 204-7; Ernst Käsemann, "Ministry and Community in the New Testament," in *Essays on New Testament Themes* (London: SCM, 1969), 217-35; Ernest Best, "Paul's Apostolic Authority," *JSNT* 27 (1986): 3-25; Jeffrey A. Crafton, *The Agency of the Apostle: A Dramatistic Analysis of Paul's Responses to Conflict in 2 Corinthians* (Sheffield: Sheffield Academic, 1991), 53-103; Wolf-Henning Ollrog, *Paulus und seine Mitarbeiter* (Neukirchen-Vluyn: Neukirchen, 1979); Eldon Jay Epp, *Junia: The First Woman Apostle* (Minneapolis: Fortress, 2005); C. K. Barrett, *The Signs of an Apostle* (London: Epworth, 1970), 39-73; Anthony Hanson, *Church, Sacraments, and Ministry* (London: Mowbray, 1975), 99-119.

45. Anthony Hanson, *The Pioneer Ministry* (London: SCM, 1961), 46.

46. BDAG 697-98.

carefully explored by W. D. Mounce, Danker, and others. These include at least the following seven: (i) *being skilled in teaching* (Gk. *didaktikos*); (ii) *being level-headed* or *avoiding extremes (nēphalios);* (iii) *disliking conflict* (and so constituting a focus of unity, *amachos*), or, in other words, managing conflict-resolution; (iv) *being self-disciplined,* or *prudent (sōphrōn);* (v) *being gracious, tolerant, and courteous (epïeikēs);* (vi) *being able to win people's approval* or *being dignified,* in the sense of having *gravitas* or weight *(kosmios);* and (vii) having *ability to manage (proïstanai),* whether a household or a church. Other passages also suggest (viii) *being a leader in mission* (Matt. 28:19), and (ix) *having a pastoral heart* (John 21:15-17). To be a *"shepherd"* implies not only "feeding" but also protecting the flock against enemies and marauders.

Mounce shows that the qualities expected of *elders* overlap with this, but are not identical. In both cases, Mounce proposes (x) being "a one-woman man" and (xi) "being above reproach" *(anepilēmptos).* Both imply teaching "health-giving doctrine."[47]

Paul and other writers in the NT also use *diakonos* (2 Cor. 6:4; 1 Thess. 3:2; cf. 2 Cor. 3:6; 11:15; Col. 1:25; Eph. 6:21; Rom. 16:1). Traditionally the church has understood this to represent the third order among bishops, priests or presbyters, and deacons, or a second order of presbyters and deacons. But clearly Danker follows recent work by John Collins. Following Collins, he translates the Greek term as "one who serves as an intermediary, an agent or an assistant."[48] Collins argues that a *diakonos* serves as a deputy or assistant to a bishop or presbyter, and not explicitly as a social worker or agent for the relief of the poor. He proposes "go-between" or "deputy," rather than a menial servant or financial administrator. This fits 2 Corinthians 3:7-9, but the verb *diakoneō* remains ambiguous in Acts 6:2, where "serving tables" *(trapezais)* may include a financial sense. Danker calls this a "special problem."[49]

Paul applies the term *architektōn* to himself in 1 Corinthians 3:10. It could be significant for the work of oversight, for in the Greco-Roman first-century world this figure would oversee and coordinate the workforce of builders, implement building contracts, and coordinate projects. He would collaborate with the other builders. This may suggest three particular fea-

---

47. William D. Mounce, *Pastoral Epistles,* WBC 46 (Nashville: Nelson, 2000), 168-90.
48. John N. Collins, *Diakonia: Re-interpreting the Sources* (Oxford: OUP, 1990).
49. BDAG 229-31; cf. Stephen Croft, *Ministry in Three Dimensions: Ordination and Leadership in the Local Church* (London: DLT, 1999).

tures about the work of bishops or overseers. First, they work *collaboratively;* second, they perhaps have a *translocal* ministry; third, they ensure a *unity of purpose* among the builders. We recall Pannenberg's caution about defining a "local church."

In historical thought, John Calvin is clear about the need for ministers or presbyters in general. In his view, "Pastors (except that each has the government of a particular church assigned to him) have the same function as apostles."[50] They serve "as watchmen in the Church," and preach the gospel.[51] *Ordination* is necessary (Titus 1:5). Calvin stressed that all things should be done "decently and in order" (1 Cor. 14:40); the *public call by the church* is vital, "lest restless and turbulent men should presumptuously push themselves forward to teach or rule (an event which actually was to happen). . . . No one should assume a public office in the Church without a call (Heb. 5:4; Jer. 17:16)."[52]

Calvin continued, "To all who discharge the ministry of the word it (Scripture) gives the name of bishops."[53] He added, "The care of the poor was committed to deacons," which had been the traditional view until Collins (1990).[54] Calvin then discussed whether "the whole church" or "colleagues and elders" should choose and appoint presbyters. He considered that in Titus 1:5 and 1 Timothy 5:22 "one man" seems to be implied, but he also points to Acts 14:23 and to Cyprian's claim of choosing ministers "in the presence of the people."[55] Calvin did not follow the Episcopalian tradition.

By stark contrast, Thomas Aquinas, traditionally followed by the Roman Catholic Church, had argued concerning Peter's key: "Priests alone have this key. . . . The key reaches to heaven . . . by excommunication or absolution."[56] The laity cannot use this "key," which was given to Peter and his successors. In spite of some changes, Vatican II still uses the term "priesthood," and differentiates priests as a church order from the laity. The joint Lutheran–Roman Catholic International Commission (1981) stated that in the postapostolic church a special office proved to be necessary for the sake of leadership and unity. In Catholic, Lutheran, Anglican, and Calvinist tradition, ministers elected for public office do not simply teach and preach in

---

50. Calvin, *Institutes* 4.3.5.
51. Calvin, *Institutes* 4.3.6.
52. Calvin, *Institutes* 4.3.10.
53. Calvin, *Institutes* 4.3.8.
54. Calvin, *Institutes* 4.3.9.
55. Calvin, *Institutes* 4.3.11.
56. Aquinas, *Summa* III, qu. 19, art. 3.

their own name.[57] But whereas Catholics regard ordination as a sacrament, Anglicans and Lutherans restrict the name to the two dominical sacraments.

The recent emphasis on the collegial or collaborative nature of the ministry, including the episcopate, underlines the principle about the church that we established above. Everything rests on *mutual dependency and lack of self-sufficiency.* In 1 Corinthians 3 Paul explains to the church in Corinth that either by rejecting specific ministers or by limiting themselves to the ministry of choice favorites, they are *depriving themselves* of what God wills to give them. Paul writes, "Do not deceive yourselves. . . . All things are yours, whether Paul or Apollos or Cephas . . . all belong to you" (1 Cor. 3:18, 21-22).

4. The Sacrament of Baptism

A few comments on the term "sacrament" are needed before we examine baptism and the Lord's Supper. We also have the more distinctive aim of exploring the relevance of speech-act theory or performative utterances to the sacraments. The term "sacrament" does not occur in the NT, as C. K. Barrett insists.[58] But although this is argued on all sides, Barrett suggests that its significance is often overlooked.

(i) *The Sacraments.* The word first enters Christian currency circa 200, the approximate date of Tertullian's treatise *On Baptism.* He begins the treatise, "Here is our sacrament of water."[59] Elsewhere he urges that all presbyters must be ready to undertake the duties of baptism at all times.[60] The Greek counterpart to the Latin term *sacramentum* is *mystērion,* which first appears in Eusebius.

The term "sacrament" may denote one of three concepts, depending on its context. First, traditionally most Protestants speak of the *two* "dominical" sacraments of baptism and the Lord's Supper. Second, Catholic and Eastern Orthodox speak traditionally of the *seven* sacraments that emerged in the medieval period. These include not only baptism and the Eucharist, but also confirmation, marriage, ordination, penance, and traditionally extreme unction. Third, "sacrament" may also denote an *unlimited number* of examples less formally. Virtually any action or object through which *invisible grace* is

---

57. Cf. Pannenberg, *ST* 3:349.
58. Barrett, *Church, Ministry, and the Sacraments,* 55-57.
59. Tertullian, *On Baptism* 1.1.
60. Tertullian, *An Exhortation to Charity* 7.

conveyed through *visible signs* may be called a "sacrament" in the broadest sense of the term. But in this third category "sacrament" has become virtually reduced to *symbol* or *sign*. In devotional literature of all church traditions, acts of washing on rising in the morning may be thought of as symbolically conveying cleansing, or using fire may suggest purification or illumination.

It is not usually relevant to ask what might be the "right" use of the term "sacrament," except in a particular context. What is required is that it should be clear to speaker and hearer in what sense and in what context the word is used. What is right or wrong is the doctrine of sacramental grace and its implications, which may vary between Catholic and Protestant traditions. The heart of the earliest meaning is that sacraments constitute *promises*. Luther, Tyndale, Calvin, and most of the Reformers regarded them as *effective signs* of divine promise. Promise was important to Tyndale and Melanchthon. The latter wrote: "The gospel is the promise of grace. This section on signs is very closely related to the promises. The Scriptures add these signs to the promises as seals which remind us of the promises, and definitely testify of the divine will toward us."[61] Calvin defined a sacrament as "an eternal sign by which the Lord *seals* in our consciences his *promise* of good will towards us, in order to sustain the weakness of our faith, and we in turn testify our piety towards him."[62] He added, "There never is a sacrament without an antecedent promise."[63]

One main reason for any sacrament is our *weakness of faith*. Sacraments also contain parallels with OT signs, and are associated with the covenant. They are "symbols of the covenant" and a "pledge of His (God's) grace."[64] Martin Bucer and Peter Martyr underlined that they are also "visible words," which "offer what they show." They may involve more of the senses than sight, but hardly less. Most writers stress that they are part of the "not yet" of the Christian life.[65] They are also related to the community of the church, not only to the individual. When Christ returns, we shall no longer need symbols or sacraments, because we shall encounter that to which they now point. This is expounded in chapter 15, in the section on the new Jerusalem.

(ii) *The Theology of Baptism*. Rudolf Schnackenburg has correctly distin-

61. Philipp Melanchthon, *Loci Communes Rerum Theologicarum*, in *Melanchthon and Bucer*, ed. Wilhelm Pauck (London: SCM; Philadelphia: Westminster, 1969), 133.

62. Calvin, *Institutes* 4.14.1; Beveridge ed., 2:491-92, italics mine.

63. Calvin, *Institutes* 4.14.3; 2:492.

64. Calvin, *Institutes* 4.14.6 and 7; 2:494.

65. Pannenberg, *ST* 3:353; Gerhard Ebeling, *Word of God and Tradition: Historical Studies Interpreting the Divisions of Christianity* (London: Collins, 1968), 225-35.

guished between *three emphases or themes of baptism in Paul.*[66] (1) Probably the least important, yet most popular today, is the theme of *cleansing.* Although Paul uses *apolouesthai,* "to wash," in 1 Corinthians 6:11, we cannot be certain that this is genuinely a so-called baptismal aorist, or refers to baptism rather than to what Dunn has called a *conversion-initiation event.*[67] Ephesians 5:26 represents a parallel case: Is the reference to water and word explicitly to baptism? Titus 3:5 uses *loutron,* but an allusion to baptism is no more than probable.

(2) *Baptism as allegiance to Christ, as "assignment to Christ,"* and as incorporation in Christ "are indeed major themes in Paul, for which he often uses the phrase *baptizein eis Christon.*"[68] Schnackenburg traces the context to "You belong to Christ" in 1 Corinthians 3:23, 6:19, 2 Corinthians 10:7, and elsewhere. One example is "baptism in the name of Christ" (1 Cor. 1:13). Hence he discusses the debated expression *baptizein eis Christon* (Gal. 3:27; Rom. 6:3). One view is that *eis* here indicates the goal, as with all verbs of movement, but Schnackenburg suggests that this should not be given significance in *every* passage. Others propose that it describes *effect,* like baptism to Christ. Danker has shown how variable the meaning of the preposition *eis* can be. It may, he writes, indicate any of four meanings: *goal,* as in *toward;* or *direction toward;* or it may act as a marker of degree; or function with respect to the name of someone. Thus Schnackenburg concludes that it can suggest "direction of faith" *without* movement, and must "always be viewed in the light of the context in which it occurs."[69] It frequently means incorporation into the body of Christ, as in 1 Corinthians 12:13 and Galatians 3:27. It can thus be parallel with *pisteuein eis,* "to believe in," that is, the *direction* of faith.

(3) Paul's third theme, according to Schnackenburg, is *"baptism as salvation event,"* as in the classic passage Romans 6:1-11. This expounds "a dying and rising [Greek] *syn Christō,*" with Christ.[70] This involves "dying to the ruin wrought by the power of sin, with the goal of walking in a new life for God." It relates to the concept of *being crucified with Christ* (Gal. 2:20; 3:13-14), and being raised with him. It entails dying to the law (Rom. 7:4-6). This in turn belongs to the concept of "putting off" and "putting on" Christ.

---

66. Rudolf Schnackenburg, *Baptism in the Thought of St. Paul: A Study in Pauline Theology* (Oxford: Blackwell, 1964), 3-61.

67. James D. G. Dunn, *Baptism in the Holy Spirit: A Re-examination of the New Testament Teaching on the Gift of the Spirit in Relation to Pentecostalism Today* (London: SCM, 1970), 104; cf. 120-23.

68. Schnackenburg, *Baptism,* 18-29.

69. Schnackenburg, *Baptism,* 26; cf. 23.

70. Schnackenburg, *Baptism,* 30; cf. 30-82.

To Schnackenburg's three themes in Paul, C. F. D. Moule and Alan Richardson helpfully expound a fourth. (4) This is the *eschatological* dimension of understanding baptism in relation to the Last Judgment as a *"pleading guilty" before the judgment.* Moule writes, "If Baptism is voluntary death, it is also a pleading guilty, an acceptance of the sentence."[71] Similarly Richardson writes: "To be baptised is to accept God's verdict of guilty, and so to be brought past the great assize and the final judgement of the last day into the life of the Age to come."[72] We may compare Colossians 2:14, Mark 10:38, and Luke 12:50. This also coheres with the view of Luther, Calvin, and many others, that baptism is an *interim* institution, which looks forward to the future, in a present situation when faith may be weak.

(5) Tom Holland also stresses the *corporate* nature of baptism, which becomes important when we consider debates about infant baptism.[73] He argues that baptism is modeled on Israel's entry into a *covenant relationship* with God (Rom. 6:1-11; 1 Cor. 12–13; Gal. 3:5-29; Eph. 4:6; 5:25-27). He concludes, "Paul has stayed within the corporate categories of the OT . . . in the same terms as Israel's inauguration, when she was brought out of Egypt."[74]

(6) *In the Gospels* baptism has an eschatological flavor from John the Baptist onward. John the Baptist baptized the people of God, to prepare them for the Last Judgment (Matt. 3:1-12; Mark 1:8-11; Luke 3:18-22; John 1:29-36). Oscar Cullmann spoke rightly of "the anchorage of baptism in the work of Christ. . . . Jesus is baptised in view of his death. . . . Jesus must unite himself in solidarity with his whole people."[75] The baptism of Jesus, he said, "points forward to the cross." Hence he asks the disciples, "Are you able to . . . be baptized with the baptism that I am baptized with?" (Mark 10:38), alluding to his death. The baptism of Jesus cannot be for cleansing from sin, for Jesus has none. In Barrett's words, in baptism Jesus becomes "one of the prepared people of God."

(7) The well-known debate about *infant baptism* and *believer's baptism* relates directly to the *theology of baptism,* rather than depending on an in-

71. C. F. D. Moule, "Judgement Theme in the Sacraments," in *The Background to the New Testament and Its Eschatology: In Honour of C. H. Dodd,* ed. W. D. Davies and David Daube (Cambridge: CUP, 1956), 465; cf. 464-81.

72. Alan Richardson, *An Introduction to the Theology of the New Testament* (London: SCM, 1958), 341.

73. Tom Holland, *Contours of Pauline Theology: A Radical New Survey of the Influences on Paul's Biblical Writings* (Fearn, Scotland: Mentor, 2004), 141-56.

74. Holland, *Contours of Pauline Theology,* 153.

75. Oscar Cullmann, *Baptism in the New Testament* (London: SCM, 1950), 14 and 18.

conclusive debate about the date and evidence for infant baptism. To deal with the second point first, the exhaustive debate between Kurt Aland and Joachim Jeremias set out the arguments on both sides. Jeremias attempted a defense of infant baptism in historical terms. He appealed to "household baptisms," which included those of Lydia (Acts 16:15), the Philippian jailor (Acts 16:31-33), and Stephanas (1 Cor. 1:16; cf. 16:15), as well as other examples.[76]

Kurt Aland responded to Jeremias by defending believer's baptism. He argued that "households" (the *oikos* formula) might just as well include childless couples or adult children, with slaves or servants; full-scale infant baptism, he argued, appeared only later, around 200-203.[77] Jeremias replied to Aland in a second book, challenging the latter's assumptions about baptismal policy around 200, and further discussing Jewish proselyte baptism.[78] In addition to these studies, Pierre-Charles Marcel argued theologically on the basis of grace and justification, but also partly historically on the basis of the covenant and Jewish rites of circumcision and baptism.[79]

This debate on historical origins does no more than touch the surface of the debate as a symptom, not the cause, of the fundamentally different views of the *purpose of baptism.* If baptism is understood as admission to the *corporate community of the church,* or as entry into the covenant, or as a rite of initiation, the case against infant baptism seems to collapse. If, however, it is regarded primarily as a *confession of individual faith,* the case seems to stand. Arguments about "cleansing" may favor either side, depending on whether sin and alienation is viewed, with Paul, Augustine, Luther, and Calvin, as characterizing fallen humanity, or whether it is viewed with Pelagius and some modern liberals as merely an individual and conscious act. Strangely, against Augustine, Aland argued: "Because children are innocent, they do not need baptism."[80] Thus, on the Baptist side, Wheeler Robinson argued, "Believers' Baptism emphasises . . . the necessity and individuality of *conversion;* it is a conscious acceptance of his (Christ's) authority."[81] Karl Barth, perhaps surprisingly, also stressed the issue of consciousness.

76. Joachim Jeremias, *Infant Baptism in the First Four Centuries* (London: SCM, 1960).

77. Kurt Aland, *Did the Early Church Baptise Infants?* (London: SCM, 1962).

78. Joachim Jeremias, *The Origins of Infant Baptism: A Further Study in Reply to Kurt Aland* (London: SCM, 1963).

79. Pierre-Charles Marcel, *The Biblical Doctrine of Infant Baptism: Sacrament of the Covenant of Grace* (London: Clarke, 1953, 2002), especially 34-98.

80. Aland, *Did the Early Church Baptise Infants?* 106.

81. H. Wheeler Robinson, *Baptist Principles,* 4th ed. (London: Carey Kingsgate, 1960), 17 and 23; cf. Stephen R. Holmes, *Baptist Theology* (London: T. & T. Clark, 2012).

On the opposite side of the debate, Cullmann urged that baptism is *initiatory,* stressing that divine *grace* comes *before* human response, and that baptism is *corporate, not primarily or exclusively individual,* involving entry into the covenant and invoking the faith of the congregation. He regarded infant baptism as "normal," commenting: "Those who dispute the biblical character of infant baptism have to reckon with the fact that *adult baptism for sons and daughters of Christian parents* is even worse attested by the NT than infant baptism."[82] He also explicitly states, "It is of the essence [of divine grace] that faith must *follow* as an answer to the divine act," or grace would not be grace.[83] Much more fundamental than the well-worn debate about "NT evidence" is the respective understanding of the nature of human sin, the nature of divine grace, and corporate or individual dimensions.

(8) We suggest that on top of all these arguments we may also take account of the importance of *speech-act theory and performative utterances.* We noted that in Luther, Tyndale, and the other Reformers, the Bible, or the Word of God, does not merely *inform,* but also *does* something. It typically comes to people as *promise,* but also as *appointment, call, liberation, forgiveness, commission,* or a range of communications that *changes* a person's status or work in life. If baptism is "making a profession of faith," this seems to reduce it to a merely *informative* or "locutionary" act. But in the light of speech-act theory, it can be a communicative act that involves *more* than this. Catholics may be more ready to regard it as a transfer of grace. Most Lutherans, Anglicans, and Presbyterians would regard baptism not exactly in these terms, but nevertheless as in some sense an *act.* Hence the Reformation language speaks about its constituting an *effective* sign from God to humankind. This principle, we shall see, also applies to the sacrament of the Lord's Supper.

5. The Eucharist, Holy Communion, or the Lord's Supper

The three terms "Eucharist," "Holy Communion," and "Lord's Supper" can all be defended from biblical usage. The Greek *eucharistēsas* means "having given thanks" in 1 Corinthians 11:24; "Communion" reflects *koinōnia,* "sharing in" the blood of Christ, in 1 Corinthians 10:16; and the "Lord's supper" is Paul's term for the rite in 1 Corinthians 11:20 (Gk. *kuriakon deipnon,*

82. Cullman, *Baptism in the New Testament,* 26, italics mine.
83. Cullman, *Baptism in the New Testament,* 33.

probably the main meal of the day regardless of chronological timing). It is a secondary consideration that Roman Catholic and "High Church" traditions tend to use "Eucharist" while evangelicals and others use "Lord's Supper" or "Holy Communion." "Mass" may have become, or is becoming, a little dated, since it reflects a popularization of the last words of the Latin rite.

(i) *Biblical Material.* In the Synoptic Gospels and in Paul the *context* of the administration of the Last Supper and Lord's Supper is crucial to its understanding. Jesus was observing the *Jewish Passover meal,* the liturgy of which is known as the *Sēder* in Judaism. This takes the form of *reliving the narrative world of participants* in the Passover (Exod. 12:1-51). In effect, participants "relive" the Passover events of the deliverance from their bondage in Egypt, and the beginning of a new life as the redeemed people of God.

Exodus 12 and the Jewish Mishnah make it clear that this is a *dramatic event,* as Balthasar and Vanhoozer describe doctrine. Exodus 12:25-27 declares, "When you come to the land that the LORD will give you, as he has promised, you shall keep this observance. And when your children ask you, 'What do you mean by this observance?' you shall say, 'It is the passover sacrifice to the LORD.'" The Mishnah adds: "In every generation a man must *so regard himself as if he came forth himself out of Egypt*" (*m. Pesaḥim* 10:5).[84] In the Synoptic Gospels the preparation for the meal as a preparation for the Passover is explicit (Mark 14:14; Matt. 26:17-19; Luke 22:7-13, 15).

J. Jeremias and F. J. Leenhardt show convincingly that the Last Supper dovetails with observance of the Passover, and that there are close parallels between the *Sēder* or Jewish Haggadah and the words of institution of the Lord's Supper. Roth's edition of the Haggadah begins with the doxology: "Blessed art Thou, O Lord, our God, King of the Universe, Creator of the produce of the vine."[85] Jeremias and Leenhardt link Jesus' blessings of God for the bread and the wine with this.[86] (The KJV/AV version, "blessed it," is a mistake; God is the object of the blessing: there is no thought of "consecrating" the bread. Even the NRSV inserts "it," when this word is not in the earliest Greek.) In the earliest manuscript the Haggadah then reads: "This is the bread of affliction that our forefathers ate in the land of Egypt." Leen-

---

84. The text of the Mishnah can be found in Herbert Danby, ed., *The Mishnah: Translated from the Hebrew* (Oxford: OUP, 1933), italics mine. Tractate *Pesahim* 10:6 is on 151.

85. Cecil Roth, ed., *The Haggadah: New Edition with Notes* (London: Soncino Press, 1934), 8.

86. Joachim Jeremias, *The Eucharistic Words of Jesus* (London: SCM, 1966), 41-49; F. J. Leenhardt, "This Is My Body," in Oscar Cullmann and F. J. Leenhardt, *Essays on the Lord's Supper* (London: Lutterworth, 1958), 39-40.

hardt notes the sudden departure from the expected words as a "surprise" to the disciples, when Jesus pronounced, "This is my body" (Matt. 26:26-27; 1 Cor. 11:24).

This sheds a flood of light on the meaning of "This is my body." Historical theology has entertained endless debate about whether the sentence is literal (as Aquinas thought), fully and effectively symbolic (as Luther and Calvin thought), or metaphorical (as Zwingli thought). In the light of the use of the "dramatic" by Balthasar, Vanhoozer, and Ricoeur, it is probable that "dramatic" would be a more appropriate word.[87] An examination of "remembrance" (Gk. *anamnēsis;* Heb. *zēker*) confirms this. First Corinthians 11:24-25 and Luke 22:19 read "Do this in remembrance of me" *(touto poieite eis tēn emēn anamnēsin).* The Greek and Hebrew verb does not just mean "to call to mind" in the sense of purely intellectual recollection. A generation ago the "objective" force of the Hebrew was probably overstated, as if it were an objective, virtual *repetition* of a past event. Today most or probably all traditions recognize that the work of Christ on the cross remains in principle *"once for all"* (Gk. *ephapax*). The Hebrew and Greek usage implies both this and also a middle course: that of *dramatic participation.* When believers pray to God: "Remember the distress of your servants" (cf. Lam. 5:1; Exod. 32:13; Deut. 9:27; Ps. 20:3), they ask God to act as a *participant* in their woe.

The purpose of dramatic symbolism is to create a *narrative world* in which participants almost (but not literally) "relive" their part. It is well summed up by the black spiritual, "Were you there when they crucified my Lord?"

(ii) *Two Misleading Accounts.* Before we turn to the historical debate, we must note two erroneous theories, which are now thoroughly dated. One was Hans Lietzmann's theory of "two primitive types" of observance of the Lord's Supper. Lietzmann expounded this in successive editions of *Mass and Lord's Supper,* first published in 1926.[88] Lietzmann distinguished between a joyous "Jerusalem" tradition, which celebrated fellowship with Christ and with fellow Christians, and a more solemn "Pauline" one, which was centered on remembering the Lord's death. Lietzmann also speculated about

---

87. Hans Urs von Balthasar, *Theo-Drama: Theological Dramatic Theory,* 5 vols. (San Francisco: Ignatius; Edinburgh: T. & T. Clark, 1973-1992), vol. 1, especially prolegomena, 25-50, 125-257; Kevin Vanhoozer, *The Drama of Doctrine: A Canonical-Linguistic Approach to Christian Theology* (Louisville: Westminster John Knox, 2005); Paul Ricoeur, *Time and Narrative,* 3 vols. (Chicago: University of Chicago Press, 1984-1988); and Anthony C. Thiselton, *The Hermeneutics of Doctrine* (Grand Rapids: Eerdmans, 2007), 65-80, 103-6, and 527-28.

88. Hans Lietzmann, *Mass and Lord's Supper: A Study in the History of Liturgy,* with further enquiry by R. D. Richardson (Leiden: Brill, 1979), especially 172-86 and 193-209.

the *Chaburah,* or common meal. A. J. B. Higgins and Gregory Dix promoted modified versions of this theory, while Ernst Lohmeyer proposed a dualism between a Pauline and a "Galilean" version. Nevertheless, the whole theory, including speculation about the *Chaburah,* has received convincing criticism from Jeremias, I. Howard Marshall, O. Hofius, C. F. D. Moule, and others.[89] Jeremias argued that *every* meal was sacred, and that the whole theory was no more than conjecture.

A related blind alley was that of S. Mowinckel, A. Bentzen, and S. H. Hooke, with their outdated "Myth and Ritual" approach. In effect they make *anamnēsis* a virtual "reenactment" of the atonement, on the basis of a theory of myth and ritual in the OT, especially in the Psalms.[90] Although this may resonate with some older Catholic views, virtually all traditions now agree that the *once-for-all (ephapax)* character of the one sacrifice of Christ is paramount (Rom. 6:10; Heb. 7:27; 9:12; 10:10).

Some convergence of approaches is perhaps suggested by more recent ecumenical documents, for example, the agreed statement by the Anglican–Roman Catholic International Commission (ARCIC) or the "Windsor" Statement of 1971. Here Anglicans and Catholics agree that "Christ's redeeming death and resurrection took place once for all in history . . . one, perfect, and sufficient sacrifice for the sins of the world."[91] There can be "no repetition" of it, although in the Communion there is indeed a "making effective of an event in the past."[92] Regrettably there appears to remain some inconsistency in Roman views; Vatican II still adheres to Aquinas's doctrine of transubstantiation.[93]

(iii) *The Five Main Historical Theories: A Brief Account.* In the history of thought, four main theologians stand out for attention above most others: Thomas Aquinas, Martin Luther, John Calvin, and Ulrich Zwingli. To these we may add Cranmer and Anglicanism as a fifth, although Anglican traditions tend to move between Luther (at the more "High Church" end of the spectrum) and Calvin (at the more evangelical end).

(1) *Thomas Aquinas* (1225-1274), followed by the Council of Trent (1545-

---

89. Jeremias, *Eucharistic Words of Jesus,* 16-36; I. Howard Marshall, *Last Supper and Lord's Supper* (Grand Rapids: Eerdmans, 1980), 108-23.

90. A. Bentzen, *King and Messiah,* 2nd ed. (Oxford: Blackwell, 1970), 12 and 72-80.

91. Anglican–Roman Catholic International Commission (ARCIC), *Agreed Statement* (London: Anglican Consultative Council; Rome: Pontifical Council for Promoting Christian Unity, 1971), 2:5.

92. ARCIC, *Agreed Statement,* 2:5; cf. 3:6 and 10.

93. Flannery, *Documents of Vatican II,* 104 (*Sacred Liturgy: Eucharistic Mystery,* 3).

1563), formulated a formal doctrine of *transubstantiation.* This largely depended on appropriating Aristotle's categories of substance and accidents. Aquinas fully acknowledged this. On that basis he argued: "The complete *substance* of the bread and wine is converted into the complete *substance* of Christ's body *(tota substantia panis convertitus in totam substantiam corporis Christi);* and likewise the complete *substance* of the wine is converted into the complete *substance* of Christ's blood."[94] But Aquinas admits although the *substance* or underlying content *changes,* the superficial "accidents" *(accidentia)* of the bread and wine, or their *form,* does *not change:* "There is no deception."[95] The "accidents," according to Aristotle and Aquinas, are the *secondary* qualities that lie open to sight. In the case of bread and wine, "accidents" denote color, shape, taste, smell, texture, and so on. But Aquinas claims that the underlying essence or "substance" beneath the visible accidents can and does change.

(2) *Martin Luther* (1483-1546) opposed transubstantiation not because it was necessarily untrue, but on the ground that it was *without biblical warrant, and drew on secular philosophy.* In contrast to Calvin and Zwingli, Luther insisted that in Holy Communion bread and wine become "the real flesh and blood of Christ" even if they *also* remain "real bread and real wine."[96] In today's language, Luther affirmed "the real presence" of Christ. In addition to opposing Zwingli for denying this, he also attacked "the fanatics" for regarding the elements as no more than "memorial signs."

(3) *John Calvin* (1509-1564) most strongly insisted on *the parity of word and sacrament.* The word must accompany the sacrament for it to be effective. The function of the Lord's Supper is that it "present[s] Christ the *more clearly* to us. . . . The Supper . . . testifies that we are redeemed."[97] He avoided any crude, localized notion that the presence of Christ is tied to the location of the elements. But he regarded the presence of *Christ* as *directly* mediated, and not mediated exclusively through the presence of the Holy Spirit. He strenuously attacked transubstantiation as a "mask" and "fictitious."[98] In the Genevan Confession (1536), Calvin maintains that the Lord's Supper brings "spiritual communion," while "the mass of the Pope" is "a reprobate and

94. Aquinas, *Summa* III, qu. 75, art. 4; Eng. and Lat., Blackfriars ed., 58:73.
95. Aquinas, *Summa* III, qu. 75, art. 5.
96. Martin Luther, *On the Babylonian Captivity of the Church,* in *Luther's Primary Works,* ed. Henry Wace and Carl Buchheim (London: Murray, 1883; London: Hodder, 1896), 147-48.
97. Calvin, *Institutes* 4.14.22; Beveridge ed., 2:507, italics mine.
98. Calvin, *Institutes* 4.17.13-14; 2:565-66.

diabolical ordinance, subverting the mystery of the Holy Supper . . . , an idolatry, condemned by God."[99]

(4) *Ulrich Zwingli* (1484-1531) argued that a "literal" interpretation of "This is my body" has *no scriptural support*. He believed that all gifts and blessings from God come through the Holy Spirit, and that this includes the Lord's Supper. In 1525, the Roman Mass was abolished in Zurich. Zwingli rejected the three views of Aquinas, Luther, and even Calvin as "falsehoods," which "go beyond Scripture." The sentence "This is my body" is *metaphorical*, like "I am the vine."[100] A sacrament, he insisted, is a sign, not that to which the sign points.[101] He continued to comment that while John 6:52 speaks of "eating the flesh" of Jesus, Christ declared, "The flesh profits nothing" (John 6:63). In John, "the Lamb of God" is also metaphorical.

(5) *Thomas Cranmer* presided over two editions of the Book of Common Prayer. The first edition, of 1549, was close to Luther's view; his view in the second edition (1552) was influenced by Peter Martyr and Martin Bucer, and was close to that of Calvin. Evangelical Anglicans, like Calvin, insist on the *parity of word and sacrament,* notably by insisting on wearing the same robes for both. The 1552 Prayer Book (as in 1662) stressed the *once-for-all* character of Christ's sacrifice. The sacrifice is "a sacrifice of praise," not of Jesus Christ. After the nineteenth-century Oxford Movement, "High Church" Anglicans returned to the 1549 rite, which was near to Luther's view, while the "Low Church" and other Anglicans followed Calvin, with a small minority following Zwingli. In the Elizabethan Settlement Richard Hooker asserted "the real presence of Christ's most blessed body and blood," but also declared that this was not in the *sacrament* or *elements,* but "in the *worthy receiving* of the sacrament."[102] Blessing is received in the *appropriation* of the *promissory* word. The liturgical revision's *Common Worship* (2000) combines the 1662 Prayer Book with this pattern. "Remembrance" *(anamnēsis)* means, once again, *active and dramatic participation.*

A significant degree of controversy still attaches to the amount of ceremonial that surrounds the Lord's Supper. The "Catholic" side tends to regard this as "honoring" the Eucharist. The opposite side tends to argue that elaborate ceremony obscures, rather than "makes clear," as Calvin emphasized,

99. John Calvin, *The Genevan Confession of Faith* (1536), in *Calvin: Theological Treatises,* ed. J. K. S. Reid, LCC 22 (London: SCM, 1954), art. 16, 30.

100. Ulrich Zwingli, *The Genevan Confession of Faith* (1536), in *Calvin: Theological Treatises,* ed. J. K. S. Reid, LCC 22 (London: SCM, 1954), art. 1, 190.

101. Zwingli, *On the Lord's Supper,* art. 3.

102. *Hooker's Works,* 2:361.

the gospel. It too readily becomes an end in itself, and destroys the parity of word and sacrament.

(6) *A Tailpiece on Speech-Act Theory and Summary.* Do the *words* of the Holy Communion merely *recollect* the events of Calvary, as Zwingli thought, or do they actively perform *actions* of grace, as Aquinas, Luther, and even Calvin urged? Most theorists of speech acts agree that *promising* is a paradigm case of performative language. A promise *commits* the speaker to perform the promise. Hence Calvin calls the actions of the Lord's Supper *effective* signs, *pledges,* and *promises.* In a promise the speaker signs away alternative possibilities of *action,* in order to do *only* what has been promised. Hence Calvin views this as God's *acting* in such a way as to provide *assurance* to any who are weak in faith. This does not detract from the fact that God's Word also often functions as promise. Both word and sacrament promise the blessings and grace of Christ's life, death, and resurrection; commission obedience; and celebrate mutual fellowship as communion. In 1 Corinthians 10–11 Paul emphasizes the bonding of fellowship in a church that in some respects is divided.

The Lord's Supper becomes, in fact, a two-way speech act. In the Lord's Supper God gives visible pledges in the form of bread and wine, which can be seen, felt, and tasted. The Reformers often called them "visible words," which is a true description, as long as we also realize that they are tasted, and appreciated through other senses. In the case of wafers, the "fraction," or breaking of bread, is heard and seen, and all the human senses are employed. But in the Lord's Supper a two-way pledge is made. God pledges grace and assurance; Christian believers pledge trust, loyalty, and obedience.

In the pre-Pauline and Pauline tradition (1 Cor. 11:23-32), "You proclaim the Lord's death until he comes." In other words, the whole congregation is invited as participants to preach a sermon on what Christ means "to me." The visible, physical, and tangible nature of the elements helps to provide concrete assurance of God's presence and grace to those who (in Calvin's phrase) are *weak* in faith. *Reception* of the elements constitutes a *public testimony* to "my" dependence on the work of Christ. Believers also pledge themselves in *fellowship* to one another. Remembrance, or *anamnēsis,* ensures that salvation is rooted in Jesus Christ, and *anchored in his death and resurrection.* Insofar as it reflects the events of the passion and Calvary, it constitutes, first, *an acted-out* sermon in which we all share; second, a *remembrance or "making contemporary"* of Christ's death and resurrection; third, a bond of *union and fellowship;* and fourth, *an assurance* to the weakhearted before the End. On both sides, it constitutes a speech act with visible and tangible objects, and is instituted for an assurance until Christ comes.

CHAPTER XIV

The Return of Christ, the Resurrection, and Related Issues

1. Death and Debated Claims about Purgatory and the Millennium

Traditionally, eschatology denotes the parousia (the return of Christ), the Last Judgment, and the resurrection of the dead. These constitute the three "last events" with which the biblical material is most concerned. Yet, over the years, death, heaven and hell, and personal destiny assumed greater popular importance than they seem to hold in biblical passages, and some studies of eschatology also include claims about purgatory and the millennium.

The following treatment includes these more secondary concerns, even if in a less detailed way. Two warnings should be made here. First, discussions about both purgatory and the millennium may appear to be negative to some, but, more important, there is less here than we aim normally to provide of any inspiration for Christian discipleship. The first part of this chapter serves purely to inform readers theologically. Those whose interests lie elsewhere may prefer to omit this! Sections 3-5, if not 2, will certainly provide inspiration for Christian discipleship. Second, it is inevitable that some small overlap may occur with my earlier book *Life after Death: A New Approach to the Last Things* (also called *The Last Things* in the UK).

(i) *Death and Mourning.* Where the Bible does speak about death, this is usually seen as a *phenomenon in this human world at the end of a human life.* It enjoins honesty, as we all face death, whether near or far. The psalmist writes,

> "LORD, let me know my end; . . .
> let me know how fleeting my life is." (Ps. 39:4)

> So teach us to count our days
>> that we may gain a wise heart. (Ps. 90:12)

Today, this attitude is remote, at least in the West. Thoughts and expectations of death are pushed away and often suppressed, even though its inevitability for all is known full well. As Moltmann observes, "To push away every thought of death and to live as if we had an infinite amount of time ahead of us makes us superficial and indifferent . . . to live an illusion."[1]

(1) Today, even to grieve for the death of relatives and friends is often minimized, at least in the West. In the ancient world the process of mourning and grieving was experienced in fuller length and detail. Moltmann again notes that whereas the churchyard used to be situated in the center of the village or town, today cemeteries are often situated on the periphery of towns and cities. "Dying and death are privatized. . . . There is an unconscious oppressive taboo on dying, death and mourning."[2] The biblical passages, however, imply the healthiness of mourning and grieving, as well as of facing up to one's own death.

This does *not* mean that the biblical writers regard death as anything other than a tragedy. Jesus shared the grief of Martha and Mary of Bethany at the death of their brother Lazarus, when, John recounts, "Jesus began to weep" (John 11:35). Paul described death as "the last *enemy* to be destroyed" (1 Cor. 15:26). Death constitutes an unwelcome intrusion into the daily life of men and women.

(2) This raises the problematic notion of the causal *link between sin and death*. When he expounds the difference between unearned grace and "wages" or rewards, Paul declares, "The wages of sin is death," in contrast to "the free gift of God," which is "eternal life" (Rom. 6:23). Humankind's earliest temptation was to doubt whether God had instituted death as a consequence of human self-affirmation and disobedience (Gen. 3:3-4). Moses declared to Israel, "See, I have set before you today life and prosperity, death and adversity. If you obey . . . the LORD your God . . . God will bless you. . . . But if your heart turns away . . . you shall perish" (Deut. 30:15-18). To cite Paul again, "Sin came into the world through one man, and death came through sin, and so death spread to all because all have sinned. . . . Death exercised dominion from Adam to Moses" (Rom. 5:12-14).

---

1. Jürgen Moltmann, *The Coming of God: Christian Eschatology* (London: SCM, 1996), 50.

2. Moltmann, *The Coming of God*, 56.

In the light of modern biological sciences, Bultmann regarded this simply as ancient mythology. How, he asked, could we today regard death as a "punishment," when it is clearly a natural, biological process? If, however, we interpret death as lack of vital life and of eternal futurity, Paul describes in Romans 7:2-25 "the pervasive human striving that pursues life and yet only garners death."[3] Absence of God entails absence of life, which comes from God alone. Alienation from God entails alienation from life.

Whether the relation between sin and death is immediate and physical, or involves biological processes, which also affect the animal and vegetable kingdom, is a complex issue and not always clear-cut. However, Pannenberg makes the basic theological point. He writes, "The inner logic between sin and death, as Paul stated it, arises on the presupposition that all life comes from God. . . . Death is not just a penalty . . . but its severity lies in 'separation from God' as source of all life."[4] On this basis, Pannenberg points out, Athanasius regarded mortality as natural to us, but distinguished it from "the actual entry of death."[5] Athanasius wrote: "Men, having turned from the contemplation of God to evil of their own devising, had come inevitably under the law of death. Instead of remaining in the state in which God had created them, they were in process of becoming corrupted entirely, and death had them completely under its dominion."[6] God called humankind into existence from nonbeing, but humans "were now on the way to returning, through corruption, to non-existence again." This does not imply that the animal kingdom is necessarily estranged from God, but that animals do not, as far as we know, enjoy *intimate fellowship* with God, who is the giver of life. Hence: "Creation was subjected to futility, not of its own will but by the will of the one who subjected it, in hope that the creation itself will be set free from its bondage to decay" (Rom. 8:20-21). We considered animals more broadly and in more detail in chapter 5.

Christians, as the new creation, are still partly embodied in the old creation. Hence, in Cullmann's words, "Christians still sin and still die"; nevertheless, he adds: "Death *as such* is the enemy of God. For God is Life and the Creator of life. It is not by the will of God that there are withering and decay, dying and sickness, the by-products of death working in our life."[7] By

---

3. Rudolf Bultmann, *Theology of the New Testament,* vol. 1 (London: SCM, 1952), 247.
4. Pannenberg, *ST* 2:266.
5. Pannenberg, *ST* 2:267.
6. Athanasius, *On the Incarnation* 4.
7. Oscar Cullmann, *Immortality of the Soul or Resurrection of the Dead?* (London: Ep-

the time of Augustine, a distinction was made between "a death of the soul resulting from sin, and physical death . . . Yet the death of the body . . . , too, results from sin."[8]

(ii) *Purgatory*. Purgatory has traditionally been defended by Catholics but vehemently opposed by Protestants, in its traditional sense. Pope Benedict XII declared in the fourteenth century: "There is a Purgatory, that is, a state of punishment and purification, in which the souls which are still burdened by venial sins . . . are purified."[9] A little earlier Thomas Aquinas wrote, "The punishment of purgatory is extended to supplement the satisfaction which was not fully completed in the body."[10] All but a few Protestants would regard this view as compromising the all-sufficient and once-for-all nature of Christ's work to cover sin.

Today some Catholics and some Anglo-Catholics share these reservations about "punishment" but adhere to the notion of purgatory as a process of purification. Karl Rahner, for example, among Catholic theologians, understands purgatory as allowing for postmortal growth, development, or "ripening."[11] Geoffrey Rowell represents an Anglo-Catholic view that is not dissimilar; he stresses the need to complete the process of sanctification, even after death.[12] Luther denounced the doctrine of Aquinas and Benedict XII as an "ungodly doctrine," which led to the notion of indulgences;[13] such have been offered recently and perhaps surprisingly by Pope Francis. This practice was connected not only with Luther's condemnation of indulgences, but also with medieval misunderstanding of *penance*. Luther insisted that the term was a corruption of the NT term "repentance," or "turning" (Heb. *shûbh*) away from sin to God.

In terms of NT exegesis, there is no passage that can justify the concept, and certainly not 1 Corinthians 3:13-15, where "only as through fire" (v. 15) serves as a metaphor meaning "only just" or "narrowly." Moltmann urges,

worth, 1958), 29; cf. Oscar Cullmann, *Christ and Time: The Primitive Christian Conception of Time and History* (London: SCM, 1951), 75-76 and 154-55.

8. Pannenberg, *ST* 2:267, and Augustine, *City of God* 13.6; cf. 13.2.

9. Pope Benedict XII, *Benedictus Deus* (1336), in *Papal Encyclicals Online* (2008).

10. Aquinas, *Summa* II/II, qu. 71, art. 6.

11. Karl Rahner, "Purgatory," in *Theological Investigations,* vol. 19 (London: DLT, 1984), 181-93; cf. also *Theological Investigations*, vol. 7 (London: DLT, 1971), 287-91.

12. Geoffrey Rowell, *Hell and the Victorians: A Study of the Nineteenth-Century Theological Controversies concerning Eternal Punishment and the Future Life* (Oxford: Clarendon, 1974), 90-115 and 153-79.

13. Martin Luther, "Letter to Justus Jonas" (1530), in his *Letters of Spiritual Counsel,* ed. Theodore G. Tappert, LCC 18 (London: SCM, 1965), 153.

"The idea of purgatory seems to be incompatible with the experience of the unconditional love with which God in Christ finds us, accepts us, reconciles us, and glorifies us."[14] Clearly the main ground of objection is the gift of *justification by grace* through faith. But we add an important tailpiece, especially to the "softer" view of purification or sanctification. If, as we shall argue in the last chapter, the "body," or mode of being, of the resurrection is "spiritual" (Gk. *sōma pneumatikon,* 1 Cor. 15:44), that is, empowered and transformed by the Holy Spirit, this state of being will be "raised in incorruption" (Gk. *egeiretai en aphtharsia;* cf. 15:42); "raised in glory" (*egeiretai en doxē,* 15:43); and "raised in power" or effectiveness (*egeiretai en dynamei,* 15:43).

I have argued in *Life after Death* that, especially if holiness is rightly understood as a *disposition* rather than a quality, the Holy Spirit completes the process of sanctification or holiness *instantaneously in the resurrection body.*[15] This takes place, not least, in the context of face-to-face communion with God, and in a whole new environment and new world. As a well-known hymn expresses it, "When I see Thee as Thou art, I'll praise Thee as I ought." The two approaches to the doctrine of purgatory are countered respectively by these two objections to it. Luther and Calvin would add that purgatory also undermines a Christian doctrine of *assurance.*

(iii) *Claims and Arguments about the Millennium.* The claims that a millennium will take place in the future are far more familiar in America than in Britain and Europe, except perhaps in classical Pentecostalism. It is not surprising, then, to find one of the clearest definitions of three or more main approaches to the millennium from an American scholar, Wayne Grudem. Thus Grudem clearly defines *amillennialism, postmillennialism,* and *premillennialism* in his *Systematic Theology.*[16] After defining these three views, he urges a premillennialist approach. Grudem points out that the word "millennium" denotes "one thousand years," which comes from Revelation 20:4-6. Here the martyrs who have been beheaded for their testimony to Christ "reigned with Christ a thousand years" (Gk. *chilia etē,* v. 4), while the rest of the dead did not "come to life (Gk. *ezēsan*) until the thousand years were ended" (v. 5).

(1) According to *amillennialism,* Grudem continues, "Rev. 20:1-10 de-

14. Moltmann, *The Coming of God,* 98.
15. Anthony C. Thiselton, *Life after Death: A New Approach to the Last Things* (Grand Rapids: Eerdmans, 2012), 132-36; in the UK, entitled *The Last Things* (London: SPCK, 2012).
16. Wayne Grudem, *Systematic Theology: An Introduction to Biblical Doctrine* (Nottingham: IVP, 1994), 1108-14 (definitions); cf. also 1114-35. Page references have been placed in the text.

scribes the present church age . . . in which Satan's influence over the nations has greatly reduced so that the gospel can be preached to the whole world" (1110). Although probably Revelation 20:4-5 is the only place in the Bible to speak explicitly of the millennium, Grudem argues strongly that to ignore a biblical passage because it occurs *only once* would have negative consequences in many directions (1116-17). He regards "the binding of Satan" as more extensive than amillennialists allow.

(2) By contrast, *postmillenialists,* Grudem explains, believe that "Christ will return *after* the millennium . . . ; a larger and larger proportion of the world's population will be Christians . . . and gradually a 'millennial age' of peace and righteousness will occur on earth" (1110-11). But, he insists, this is a very different kind of millennium from that which "premillennialists" expect. Moreover, it ignores the biblical passages that predict a time of tribulation and suffering before the return of Christ. Indeed, 2 Timothy 3:1-5 foresees a time of apostasy, and Matthew 24:15-31 speaks of the "great tribulation."

(3) *Premillennialism,* again by contrast, is the belief that, in Grudem's words, "Christ will come back *before* the millennium," and is sometimes called *chiliasm: "Christ will return to earth to establish a millennial kingdom . . . believers will reign with Christ on earth for one thousand years"* (1111-12). But Grudem distinguishes between two versions of this belief: between "classic or historic" premillennialism and "pretribulational" premillennialism, in which the parousia, or return of Christ, occurs before the great tribulation. This is often associated with the so-called rapture, which many find in 1 Thessalonians 4:16-17: "The Lord himself, with a cry of command, . . . will descend from heaven, and the dead in Christ will rise first. Then we who are alive, who are left, will be caught up (Gk. *harpagēsometha*) in the clouds together with them to meet the Lord in the air; and so we will be with the Lord forever." Danker proposes "to seize suddenly" or "to snatch/take away" as the meaning of *harpazō,* in which he cites 1 Thessalonians 4:17.[17] This is what advocates of a premillennialist approach call "the rapture." This term came into prominence with J. N. Darby (1800-1882), who became well known as a "dispensationalist," and whose work was published in the influential Scofield Reference Bible in 1909. Bernard McGinn defined the rapture as "Christ's bodily rescue of the faithful by way of a collective physical ascent to heaven."[18] Darby, in effect, originated "dispensationalism," or the theory

17. BDAG 134.

18. Bernard McGinn, *Antichrist: Two Thousand Years of Human Fascination with Evil* (San Francisco: Harper, 1994), 253.

that God places humankind under different rulers or epochs. This approach, for example, is often associated with an era that began with the founding of the Jewish state in 1948. In popular thought premillennialism in its second form derives from dispensationalism.

Grudem's defense of this approach appeals to Revelation 3:10, "I will keep you from the hour of trial that is coming on the whole world." Furthermore, it allows for the expectation that Christ could come at any moment.[19]

One of the greatest difficulties of premillennialism, however, is the virtual assumption of a *chronological sequence* of events in the book of Revelation. Largely on this basis, one of the major commentators on Revelation, George Caird, argued that belief in a literal thousand-year millennium is "demonstrably false," at least in the assumption that John had no alternative but to borrow it from Jewish sources.[20] Among writers who would be closer to Grudem in general theological tradition, William Hendriksen insisted that Revelation is *not* a sequential historical account. In fact, a series of events constitute parallels: chapter 20 reflects Revelation 11–14; Revelation 12:5-11 is parallel with 20:1-3, 11:2-6; and Revelation 11:7 matches 20:7-10.[21] In addition, much of the book's language is clearly symbolic. He concludes, "The theory of the premillennialists is at variance with the facts here."[22] By contrast he writes: "The thousand years indicates that throughout this present gospel age, the devil's influence on the earth is curtailed. He is unable to prevent the expansion of the Church."[23]

Admittedly, in the ante-Nicene era many cite Justin, Irenaeus, Tertullian, Lactantius, and perhaps Hippolytus in favor of understanding the millennium of a thousand years.[24] But Origen, Tyconius, and especially Augustine opposed the idea, recognizing the symbolic character of the language of Revelation.[25] In the later history of the church, Luther opposed millenarianism. Only a minority of the "radical" Reformers held chiliasm in the Reformation period, such as Obbe Philips. In Caird's memorable language,

---

19. Grudem, *Systematic Theology*, 1132.

20. George B. Caird, *The Revelation of St. John* (London: Black, 1966), 250.

21. W. Hendrikson, *More Than Conquerors: An Interpretation of the Book of Revelation* (Grand Rapids: Baker; London: Tyndale Press, 1962), 182.

22. Hendrikson, *More Than Conquerors*, 185.

23. Hendrikson, *More Than Conquerors*, 188.

24. Justin, *Dialogue with Trypho* 80; Irenaeus, *Against Heresies* 3.23.7; Tertullian, *Against Marcion* 3.25; Lactantius, *Divine Institutes* 72.

25. Origen, *De principiis* 4.2; *Exhortation to Martyrdom* 30; Tyconius, *On Christian Doctrine* 3.6-9; Augustine, *City of God* 20.9; Augustine, *On Christian Doctrine* 3.10.14.

to treat the book of Revelation as a chronological sequence of events "is to unweave the rainbow. . . . John uses his allusions not as code . . . but for their evocative and emotive power."[26]

This is confirmed by a host of modern writers. Robert Gundry, for example, devotes an essay to the new Jerusalem in Revelation 21:1–22:5. This has "unheard of dimensions, having gates that consist of a single pearl, being paved with gold that can be seen through, and so on."[27] The new Jerusalem is not a "place," but the future people of God. Further, if Revelation (and other biblical books or passages) embodies prophecy as a prediction of sequential world-events, McGinn strikingly comments, "Prophecy took a holiday for almost two thousand years (the dispensation of the Gentiles) between the fall of the Second Temple of Jerusalem in 70 C.E. and the restoration of the Jewish state in 1948."[28] "Historical" interpretations of Revelation began in the modern era with Henry Drummond (1786-1860) and Edward Irving (1792-1834), in which some saw Napoleon II as the Antichrist figure; others later regarded Mussolini, Hitler, or Stalin as the Antichrist. More recently, John E. Walvoord, and at a popular level Hal Lindsey, have developed and dramatized these ideas, sometimes in terms of the invasion of Israel and Middle Eastern oil.[29] Many still follow Tim LaHaye in his Left Behind series (from 1995) of a fictional account of the rapture. But biblical scholars in general would reject these claims.

2. The Return of Christ, or the Parousia

The parousia, or the return of Christ, raises at least five issues. We need to discuss: (i) the *terms* used to denote it; (ii) the *validity* of the belief in the future and the public coming of Christ; (iii) the significance of its *apocalyp-*

26. Caird, *The Revelation of St. John,* 25.

27. Robert H. Gundry, "The New Jerusalem: People as Place, Not Place for People," in Gundry, *The Old Is Better: New Testament Essays in Support of Traditional Interpretations,* WUNT 178 (Tübingen: Mohr, 2005), 399; cf. 399-411.

28. McGinn, *Antichrist,* 153.

29. J. F. Walvoord, *Armageddon: Oil and the Middle East,* 2nd ed. (Grand Rapids: Zondervan, 1990); Hal Lindsey, *The Late Great Planet Earth* (Grand Rapids: Zondervan, 1970); cf. Anthony C. Thiselton, *1 and 2 Thessalonians through the Centuries* (London: Wiley-Blackwell, 2011), 115-20 and 143-45; Judith Kovacs and Christopher Rowland, *Revelation* (Oxford: Blackwell, 2004), 1-38; G. K. Beale, *The Book of Revelation: A Commentary on the Greek Text,* NIGTC (Grand Rapids: Eerdmans; Carlisle: Paternoster, 1999); and Robert H. Mounce, *The Book of Revelation* (Grand Rapids: Eerdmans, 1977).

tic context; (iv) claims about its *prediction* and possible *dating;* and (v) the *language* in which the event is described.

(i) *New Testament Terms.* Of the terms used in the NT, the most frequent is "parousia," not "return." Danker cites the use of the term to denote Christ's "Messianic Advent in glory to judge the world at the end of this age," for example, in Matthew 24:3, "the sign of your coming *(parousia)* and of the end of the age"; in a variant textual reading, 1 Corinthians 1:8, "the day of our Lord"; 1 Thessalonians 3:13, "at the coming of our Lord Jesus Christ with all his saints"; 5:23, "at the coming of our Lord"; 2 Thessalonians 2:8, "the manifestation of his coming"; 2 Peter 3:4, "Where is the promise of his coming?"; and 1 John 2:28, "not be put to shame before him at his coming," and other passages.[30] In all these passages "coming" translates *parousia.*

In the Greco-Roman world the term may denote the *coming* of a person of high rank. The same word, however, may also denote "the state of being present at a place, presence" (as in 1 Cor. 16:17; Phil. 2:12; and 2 Cor. 10:10); and sometimes it denotes "the arrival or the first stage in presence, or coming advent."[31] Funk has devoted an essay to Paul's apostolic parousia.[32] This double meaning may explain why many more conservative writers tend to avoid the term in favor of "the return." But the latter term is implied by "parousia," rather than making the event explicit.

The only single NT passage to speak of the "second coming" is Hebrews 9:28, where Christ "will appear a second time," in contrast to his once appearing "to bear the sins of many." But other terms are also used. The Greek for "revelation," *apokalypsis,* is used of Christ's final coming in 1 Corinthians 1:7; 2 Thessalonians 1:7; 1 Peter 1:7, 13; and probably elsewhere.[33] The noun *epiphaneia,* "appearance," is also used in Titus 2:13 and 2 Thessalonians 2:8, and may also mean "manifestation."[34]

(ii) *The Validity of Belief in the Parousia.* The validity of Christ's *public, future* coming cannot be doubted, although some have attempted to regard it only as a mythological remnant from Jewish messianic apocalyptic. In the teaching of Jesus, many of his parables look forward to a great "reversal" at the end of the world when the hidden will become manifest (Matt. 11:25); the

---

30. BDAG 781.

31. BDAG 780.

32. R. W. Funk, "The Apostolic Parousia: Form and Significance," in *Christian History and Interpretation: Studies Presented to John Knox,* ed. W. R. Farmer, C. F. D. Moule, and R. R. Niebuhr (Cambridge: CUP, 1967), 249-68.

33. BDAG 112.

34. BDAG 385-86.

poor will become rich (Luke 6:20); the hungry will be filled (Luke 6:21). Jeremias provides many more examples, such as the parables of the weeds sown among the wheat (Matt. 13:24-30) and the net that catches good and bad fish (Matt. 13:47-48).[35] The most explicit discourses of Jesus are the "apocalyptic" ones in Mark 13, Matthew 24, and Luke 21. Some language here needs to be examined carefully, because in these discourses Jesus usually responds to *two* distinct questions: (1) What are the signs of the future coming? and (2) What will it be like when the end of the temple and the Jewish "world" come? It is impossible to reduce the discourses to one question only. Jesus often uses cosmic language: "The sun will be darkened, . . . and the stars will be falling from heaven. . . . Then they will see 'the Son of Man coming in clouds' with great power and glory" (Mark 13:24-26).

Jesus also uses the analogy of a man going away on a long journey (Matt. 25:14-30; Mark 13:34; Luke 19:12-27). Other parables concern the man left in charge of a household (Matt. 24:45-51) and the return of a bridegroom (Matt. 25:1-13). Some argue that Matthew alone is concerned with the eschatological End, but Stephen Wilson finds both an "imminent expectation" strand and a "delay of the parousia" strand in Luke. Both address "practical pastoral problems. . . . By treading a deliberate path *via media,* he . . . corrected two false extremes."[36]

The earliest expression of expectation of the future parousia comes in 1 Thessalonians 4:16-17, where the language is pictorial but explicit: "The Lord himself . . . will descend from heaven." We consider Paul's language further later. In 1 Corinthians 15:49 Paul speaks of Jesus Christ as "the man of heaven" in the context of the resurrection of the dead. Paul also uses the idea in 1 Corinthians 15:23, 2 Thessalonians 2:8, 1 Timothy 6:14, 2 Timothy 1:10, 4:1, and Titus 2:13. C. H. Dodd appeared to give these passages a reduced future significance when he restricted hope of the future parousia to the earlier epistles and insisted that Paul moved toward a "realized eschatology."[37] But in a convincing article, John Lowe showed that Paul consistently maintained both a "future" and a "realized" eschatology throughout all periods of his writings.[38] The rel-

---

35. Joachim Jeremias, *The Parables of Jesus* (London: SCM, 1963), 221-22 and 224-27.

36. Stephen G. Wilson, *The Gentiles and the Gentile Mission in Luke-Acts,* SNTSMS 23 (Cambridge: CUP, 1973), 67-85; cf. John T. Carroll and Alexandra Brown, *The Return of Jesus in Early Christianity* (Peabody, Mass.: Hendrickson, 2000), 26-45.

37. Charles H. Dodd, "The Mind of Paul I" (1933) and "The Mind of Paul II" (1934), in Dodd, *New Testament Studies* (Manchester: Manchester University Press, 1953), 67-127.

38. John Lowe, "An Examination of Attempts to Detect Developments in St. Paul's Theology," *JTS* 42 (1941): 129-42.

atively late epistle to the Philippians, for example, speaks of pressing toward the goal (Phil. 3:12, 14), and of the future transformation of our bodies (3:21). Lowe provided extensive references by way of example. Further, as we shall observe, Käsemann and others have shown that *apocalyptic* made a permanent mark on Paul. Arthur L. Moore has contributed a detailed volume on the parousia in the NT, which includes Paul, and Joost Holleman has followed it with a similar book more recently.[39]

(iii) *The Significance of the Apocalyptic Context.* In the past, R. H. Charles and others have suggested that Paul felt obliged to borrow the notion of the Christian hope from Jewish apocalyptic. But this was to put the cart before the horse. Apocalyptic influenced the very structure of Pauline thought and content of his theology. Its themes stress the sovereignty of God, new creation, the two ages, and redemption as transference "from the present evil age" (Gal. 1:4); God has "rescued us (Gk. *rhuomai*) from the power of darkness and transferred us into the kingdom of his beloved Son, in whom we have redemption" (Col. 1:13-14). Galatians and Colossians represent respectively the early and late epistles.

Ernst Käsemann began a new era in the sixties, when he showed decisively the influence of apocalyptic in primitive Christianity and especially in Paul. Primitive Christian apocalyptic may have denoted the expectation of an imminent parousia, but it also denoted much else.[40] Käsemann's approach received massive support from Klaus Koch (1972), J. Christiaan Beker (1980 and 1982), J. L. Martyn (1967 and 1985), Alexandra Brown (1995 and 2000), and many others.[41] David Tracy describes apocalyptic, or "the genre most frequently employed to articulate the sense of expecting the *parousia*."[42]

---

39. Arthur L. Moore, *The Parousia in the New Testament*, NovTSupp 13 (Leiden: Brill, 1966); Joost Holleman, *Resurrection and Parousia: A Traditio-Historical Study of Paul's Eschatology in 1 Corinthians 15*, NovTSupp 84 (Leiden: Brill, 1996).

40. Ernst Käsemann, "Primitive Christian Apocalyptic," in Käsemann, *New Testament Questions of Today* (London: SCM, 1969), 109, 113, and 108-37.

41. Klaus Koch, *The Rediscovery of Apocalyptic: A Polemical Work on a Neglected Area of Biblical Studies and Its Damaging Effects on Theology and Philosophy* (London: SCM, 1972); J. Christiaan Beker, *Paul the Apostle: The Triumph of God in Life and Thought* (Edinburgh: T. & T. Clark, 1980); J. Christiaan Beker, *Paul's Apocalyptic Gospel: The Coming Triumph of God* (Philadelphia: Fortress, 1982); J. Louis Martyn, "Epistemology at the Turn of the Ages," in *Christian History and Interpretation;* Alexandria R. Brown, *The Cross and Human Transformation: Paul's Apocalyptic Word in 1 Corinthians* (Minneapolis: Fortress, 1995); Alexandra R. Brown, "Paul and the Parousia," in *The Return of Jesus in Early Christianity*, 47-76.

42. David Tracy, *The Analogical Imagination: Christian Theology and the Culture of Pluralism* (New York: Crossroad, 1981), 265.

Apocalyptic encourages concern for the history of the whole world, and the forward-moving direction of God's purposes. The first impetus toward such a rediscovery for Paul came perhaps from Johannes Weiss in 1914, but Weiss's work tended to be eclipsed by some of the more speculative suggestions found later in Albert Schweitzer.[43] The further massive influence in promoting the importance of apocalyptic was the so-called Pannenberg circle, with Rolf Rendtorff on the OT, Ulrich Wilckens and Dietrich Rössler on the NT, Trutz Rendtorff in systematic theology, and of course most of all, Klaus Koch and Wolfhart Pannenberg.[44]

(iv) *Predictions for the Parousia.* Although many have predicted dates for the parousia over the centuries, the predictions founder on the words of Jesus himself: "About that day or hour no one knows, neither the angels in heaven, nor the Son, but only the Father" (Mark 13:32). It is unthinkable that the early church could have imposed these words onto the lips of Jesus, not least because they imply a limitation of knowledge on the part of Jesus. Similarly, in Mark 13:35 Jesus says, "You do not know when the master of the house will come."

In spite of this, self-proclaimed prophets have repeatedly claimed to foretell the date of the end. Martin Luther underlined that "Christ can come at any hour," and said Michael Stiefel's desire to predict such a date was "mistaken," "false," and even inspired by Satan (letter of June 1533).[45] Luther regarded this as a heresy of the "radical" Reformers and "fanatics."

(v) *The Language Used to Describe the Parousia.* We turn, lastly, to the language with which the parousia is described. Jesus and Paul use *pictorial* language, which is usually described as *symbolic,* and sometimes as *metaphorical.* But this does *not* mean that it is *only* symbolic or metaphorical. In an entire book devoted to the language and imagery of the Bible, G. B. Caird declared, it "displays a curious interplay between the metaphorical and the literal. . . . We find Paul more than once using both forms of language in close contiguity, even in a single letter."[46]

Tom Wright, who stands prominently today among the more conservative or moderate NT specialists, has no doubt about the future coming of

43. Johannes Weiss, *Earliest Christianity: A History of the Period A.D. 30-150*, 2 vols. (New York: Harper, 1959; orig. 1937), 543-45.

44. Cf. James M. Robinson, "Revelation as Word and History," in *Theology as History*, ed. J. M. Robinson and J. B. Cobb (New York: Harper and Row, 1967), 10-13.

45. Luther, *Letters of Spiritual Counsel*, 301.

46. George B. Caird, *The Language and Imagery of the Bible* (London: Duckworth, 1980), 246 and 247.

Jesus. He compares it with "meeting face-to-face someone whom we have only ever known by letter, telephone or perhaps email."[47] He quotes the hymn: "And our eyes at last shall see him." Nevertheless, he also argues that some texts about the "the Son of God coming in the clouds" quote Daniel 7, and have more to do with Jesus' vindication after suffering than with a "second" coming.[48] Some stories about a "coming" refer to a first coming in the incarnation. The term "parousia," as we noted, often has a double meaning.

Wright then discusses *language* about the parousia, and observes that many verses (for example, 1 Thess. 4:16-17) are *"not* to be taken as a literal description of what Paul thinks will happen. They are simply a different way of saying what he is saying in 1 Corinthians 15:23-27 and 51-54 and in Phil. 3:20-21."[49] Whereas 1 Thessalonians 4:16-17 speaks of being "caught up in the clouds," 1 Corinthians 15 and Philippians 3:21 speak of transformation. First Thessalonians 4:16-17 is richly "metaphorical."[50] It is pictorial, like the woman who goes into labor, or the thief who comes in the night. He concludes, "When Paul speaks of 'meeting' the Lord 'in the air,' the point is precisely not — as in popular rapture theology — that the saved believers would then stay up in the air somewhere, away from the earth. The point is that, having gone out to meet their returning Lord, they will escort him royally into his domain. . . . The meaning is the same as the parallel in Phil. 3:20."[51] This view, Wright declares, is unanimous in the NT writings.

This comes close to Caird's comment that "Luke and Paul did not expect their language about life after death to be taken with flat-footed literalness."[52] We examine this more closely in the next section on imminence and expectation. Caird, however, does not say that this language is merely metaphorical or symbolic. Janet Martin Soskice and Paul Avis suggest that metaphor can make cognitive truth claims.[53] Caird regularly shows that eschatological language often allows for an "interweaving" of historical and symbolic language. Brevard Childs and George Caird both recognize that even if the language

---

47. N. T. Wright, *Surprised by Hope: Rethinking Heaven, the Resurrection, and the Mission of the Church* (London: SPCK, 2007), 135.

48. Wright, *Surprised by Hope,* 137.

49. Wright, *Surprised by Hope,* 143.

50. Wright, *Surprised by Hope,* 144.

51. Wright, *Surprised by Hope,* 145.

52. Caird, *Language and Imagery,* 248.

53. Janet Martin Soskice, *Metaphor and Religious Language* (Oxford: Clarendon, 1987), and Paul Avis, *God and the Creative Imagination: Metaphor, Symbol, and Myth in Religion and Theology* (New York: Routledge, 1999), 44-69, 82-99, and 120-38.

of eschatology borrows and uses what was *once* merely myth, it is no longer so, but is emphatically *"broken myth."*[54]

3. Claims about the Imminence of the Parousia and the Nature of Expectation

Paul describes Christians as "[waiting] for his Son from heaven" (Gk. *anamenō*, 1 Thess. 1:10). The English of the NRSV is similar in 1 Corinthians 1:7, "as you wait for the revealing of our Lord Jesus Christ," but the Greek uses a different verb: *apekdechomenous tēn apokalypsin tou kuriou hēmōn Iēsou Christou.* Galatians 5:5 speaks of waiting, not for the return of Christ, but for the hope of righteousness; Romans 8:19 concerns waiting for the revealing of the sons of God; and Romans 8:23 speaks of "[waiting] for adoption" (in Rom. 8:19 and 23, Gk. *apekdechomai*). Romans 8:19 uses a third verb, which is translated as "creation waits with eager longing for . . ." (Gk. *apokaradokia tēs ktiseōs*). In Philippians 1:20 the same Greek word is translated "my eager expectation" in the NRSV, and Danker agrees.[55] The part-compound *kara* denotes "head," and in Aquila's LXX it denotes "stretching the neck, craning forward," with *apo*-intensive, to denote imaginative, eager anticipation with intense longing, craning one's neck to see.[56] Hence, while *anamenō* may simply mean "wait for," other words mean very much more.

In everyday life in the modern world, *waiting* can suggest dull and *static* situations like sitting in a railway waiting room, or standing at a bus stop. But *eager expectation* or *craning one's neck* is different, like expecting a bride, or a world-famous concert soloist. The problem about Christian eschatological expectation is that some people interpret this as whipping oneself up into a state of joyous, frenzied expectation, sometimes through an infinite series of disappointments, or huge span of time. *To keep up emotional fervor for an interminable period is impossible and unhealthy, and, in the event of flagging zeal, even causes guilt.*

But Jesus, Paul, and Hebrews do not invite such a state. For *expectation constitutes a disposition, not an emotion.* Indeed, Paul invites the Thessalonians "to calm down" (Gk. *nouthetein*, 1 Thess. 5:14; 2 Thess. 3:15), just as

54. Brevard Childs, *Myth and Reality in the Old Testament,* 2nd ed. (London: SCM, 1962), 31-43; cf. Caird, *Language and Imagery,* 219.

55. BDAG 112.

56. C. E. B. Cranfield, *The Epistle to the Romans,* 2 vols., ICC (Edinburgh: T. & T. Clark, 1975, 1979), 1:410.

the Galatians needed to cast off "bewitchment" (Gal. 3:1). The Gospels use a less misleading word, "readiness," or "being ready," for the coming of the Lord Christ. In the parable of the five wise and five foolish bridesmaids, the bridegroom was met by those who were "ready" (Gk. *hetoimoi,* Matt. 25:1-10). The word denoted the *actions* of the bridesmaids. To ask, "Were they ready?" concerns *not* their conscious thoughts, and certainly *not their emotions,* but their state of *readiness.* What constitutes *"being ready"* depends on readiness for *what,* and how we prepare. Augustine and Luther regarded readiness for the coming of Christ as continuing in everyday Christian trust, work, and obedience in everyday tasks.

An illuminating answer to the question "What is it to expect?" comes from the philosopher Ludwig Wittgenstein. What should I do, he asks, if I "expect" my friend for tea? I put out cups, saucers, plates, jam, bread, cake, and so forth. I make sure that my room is tidy. He observes, " 'To expect' . . . certainly does not refer to one process or state of mind. . . . I prepare the tea for two," and so on.[57] The notion that expectation constitutes a mental act, he said, is "a curious superstition."[58] He concluded, "An expectation is embedded in a situation from which it arises."[59] In the *Zettel,* he substitutes for "expect" the phrase *"Be prepared for* this to happen."[60] This is why it is a *disposition.* It is a disposition *to respond* in an appropriate way when given *circumstances* bring it into play.

We may move now from the conceptual clarification of "to expect" to claims by, alas, the majority of NT specialists, that the earliest church, including Jesus and Paul, expected an *imminent parousia,* or *imminent return of Christ,* within the lifetime of the first generation of believers. The two most frequently cited passages for this are: "We who are alive [and] are left" (NRSV, 1 Thess. 4:15 and 17), and "There are some standing here who will not taste death until they see that the kingdom of God has come with power" (Mark 9:1). A further support for these passages comes from the apocalyptic discourse in the parallels Matthew 24 and Mark 13. Some passages appear to apply to a situation within a lifetime, such as "Flee to the mountains" (Mark 13:14; Matt. 24:16), or more especially, "This generation will not pass away until all these things have taken place" (Mark 13:30; Matt. 24:34). We shall

57. Ludwig Wittgenstein, *The Blue and Brown Books: Preliminary Studies for the "Philosophical Investigations,"* 2nd ed. (Oxford: Blackwell, 1969), 20.

58. Wittgenstein, *Blue and Brown Books,* 143.

59. Wittgenstein, *Philosophical Investigations,* 2nd ed. (Oxford: Blackwell, 1958), sect. 579.

60. Wittgenstein, *Zettel* (Oxford: Blackwell, 1967), sect. 65, italics mine.

consider these in turn, although we have already hinted that *two* questions, not one, lie behind these words.

(i) *First Thessalonians 4:15 and 17.* This passage speaks of "we who are left" (Gk. *perileipomenoi*) and invites the typical comment from Ernest Best: "This imminence is clear. . . . Judaism already had attached some importance to being in the generation of the End (Dan. 12:12-13; 4 Ezra 13:24; Ps. Sol. 17:50)." He continues, "Many attempts have been made to evade what appears to be the plain meaning of the phrase. We have to reject outright any attempt to allegorise the words (cf. Origen) or to weaken their meaning (cf. Calvin)."[61] The majority of writers today hold this view. Earl J. Richards, similarly, declares, "Paul includes himself within the group that will survive until the end. Paul believed in the imminent Parousia."[62]

Yet a significant minority dissent from this view, offering arguably a more careful and thoughtful exegesis of this verse. Among these were writers in the premodern church, including Chrysostom, Theodore of Mopsuestia, Rabanus Maurus, Aquinas, Calvin, and Bengel. Today, at the very least, seven reputable NT specialists, Arthur L. Moore, Béda Rigaux, George B. Caird, Joost Holleman, Ben Witherington, A. C. Thiselton, and N. T. Wright, belong to this solid minority.[63] First, we have simply to explore the well-known principle in philosophy and linguistics: meaning is *choice;* what *else* could Paul have said? If he had written "those who remain," this would have distanced him from the Thessalonians, with whom he wanted to stand in *solidarity.* Second, we may explore further P. F. Strawson's careful philosophical and conceptual distinction between *assertion* and *presupposition.*[64] A proposition, Strawson argues, has an explicit truth value; a presupposition

---

61. Ernest Best, *The First and Second Epistles to the Thessalonians* (London: Black, 1972), 195.

62. Earl J. Richards, *First and Second Thessalonians* (Collegeville, Minn.: Glazier/Liturgical Press, 1995, 2007), 241.

63. Arthur L. Moore, *1 and 2 Thessalonians,* NCB (London: Nelson, 1969), 69-71; Moore, *The Parousia in the New Testament,* 108-10; Béda Rigaux, *Saint Paul: Les Épitres aux Thessaloniciens* (Paris: Gabalda, 1956), 538-39; cf. also 195-234; Thiselton, *1 and 2 Thessalonians,* 117-19, cf. 120-43; Caird, *Language and Imagery,* 248; Ben Witherington III, *1 and 2 Thessalonians: A Socio-Rhetorical Commentary* (Grand Rapids: Eerdmans, 2006), 133-34; N. T. Wright, *The Resurrection of the Son of God* (London: SPCK; Minneapolis: Fortress, 2003), 214-16; and N. T. Wright, *Paul and the Faithfulness of God,* 2 vols. (London: SPCK, 2013), 2:1084 and 1234.

64. P. F. Strawson, *Individuals: An Essay in Descriptive Metaphysics* (London: Methuen, 1959), 190-92 and 199-204, and P. F. Strawson, *Introduction to Logical Theory* (London: Methuen, 1963), 175-79.

has only a *conditional* truth value. Paul's logic reflects his faithfulness to the principle expressed by Jesus: "Of that day and that hour knows no one, not even the Son, but only the Father" (cf. Matt. 24:36; Mark 13:32). Whether Paul's generation is alive at the parousia indeed remains a possibility, but *by no means a necessity.* Third, Moore argues that Paul does not define a specific group that he describes as "We who are alive" or "left." More recently, Joost Holleman endorses Moore's arguments.[65] Finally, Ben Witherington asserts, "Paul did not know in advance when he would die," and did not expect a specific time or date for the parousia.[66]

(ii) *Mark 9:1.* This verse is notoriously controversial. Once again, the majority of writers regard the verse as pointing to the imminence of the parousia. C. E. B. Cranfield admits that it is "one of the most puzzling sayings in the gospels."[67] But he offers seven distinct interpretations of this verse, of which the first three are "unlikely." The remaining four understand "the kingdom of God has come with power" as, first, the destruction of Jerusalem in A.D. 70; second, Pentecost and the spread of the gospel; third, "a visible manifestation of the Rule of God displayed in the life of an Elect Community" (Taylor); and fourth, the transfiguration, which Cranfield believes is most true to the context.[68] None of these seven approaches identifies the coming kingdom explicitly with the parousia, but Cranfield urges, "The Transfiguration points forward to, and is as it were a foretaste of, the Resurrection, which in turn points forward to, and is a foretaste of, the Parousia."[69]

Caird blamed J. Weiss and A. Schweitzer for the endlessly repetitive statement of the supposedly majority view. But he points out that Jesus repeatedly taught that the parousia would not come "unheralded," but after a "series of warnings — wars, famines, earthquakes, persecution, the ravaging of Judea. . . ."[70] He also acknowledged that other sayings appear to support the notion of an imminent End, such as "you will not have gone through all the towns of Israel before the Son of Man comes" (Matt. 10:23) and "the Lord is near" (Phil. 4:5). But such verses do not "necessarily" refer to the *future parousia,* any more than Mark 9:1 does.

(iii) *Mark 13:1-37 and Matthew 24:1-31.* This is also the case with the

65. Holleman, *Resurrection and Parousia,* 24.

66. Witherington, *1 and 2 Thessalonians,* 133-34.

67. C. E. B. Cranfield, *The Gospel according to St. Mark,* CGTC (Cambridge: CUP, 1959), 285.

68. Cranfield, *Mark,* 286-89.

69. Cranfield, *Mark,* 288.

70. Caird, *Language and Imagery,* 251.

double allusions of Mark 13:1-37 and Matthew 24:1-31. Each of the parallel discourses begins by considering *two* distinct questions. The question "When will this be?" (Mark 13:4) applies first to "Not one stone will be left here upon another" (13:2), which matches the historical setting of the fall of the temple, and only second to "the end is still to come . . . the beginning of the birth pangs . . . [when finally] 'the sun will be darkened'" (13:7, 8, 24). Caird commented, "To put it bluntly, the great day cannot happen for a long time yet, nevertheless the disciples had better be on the lookout for it now."[71]

R. T. France is clear and explicit: the first question invites a "clear, definite . . . straightforward statement" about historical events, the temple, and the fall of Jerusalem, especially in Mark 13:14-22.[72] The second question invites the answer, ultimately, "About that day or hour no one knows, neither the angels in heaven, nor the Son, but only the Father. Beware, keep alert; for you do not know when the time will come" (Mark 13:32-33). Caird also commented, "Mark 13 begins with Jesus predicting the destruction of the Temple. . . . Mark . . . has tacked on an answer to a completely different question: when is the world going to end?"[73]

The supposed eschatology of imminence is on this basis largely misleading. In place of "imminent" we should substitute "at any time." In place of "expectancy," we should substitute "readiness." Paul could not have written "those who are left," because to do so would have been to undermine the important themes set out above.

4. The Resurrection of Jesus Christ

Simultaneously with the return of Christ, the resurrection of the dead will take place. But the resurrection of the dead is theologically part of the event of the resurrection of Jesus Christ, which Paul describes as the "first fruits" of the general resurrection. Indeed, in Paul's classic exposition of the nature, credibility, and intelligibility of the resurrection, the first part of 1 Corinthians 15 concerns the resurrection of Christ as its basis and presupposition. Paul also alludes to the resurrection in Romans 4:16-25, 8:11, 2 Corinthians 1:9, 5:1-10, and 1 Thessalonians 4:14-17.

71. Caird, *Language and Imagery*, 252.
72. R. T. France, *The Gospel of Mark: A Commentary on the Greek Text*, NIGTC (Grand Rapids: Eerdmans, 2002), 538.
73. Caird, *Language and Imagery*, 266.

In all passages about the resurrection, *the sovereign power of God* is either stated or presupposed. Romans 4:17 speaks of God, "who gives life to the dead and calls into existence the things that do not exist"; Romans 8:11 speaks of God and God's Spirit raising Christ, and hence those in Christ; in 1 Corinthians 15:38, "God gives it (a bare seed) a body as he has chosen." It is the presupposition of the whole chapter. Barth declares, "This 'of God' is clearly the secret nerve of this whole."[74] On 1 Corinthians 15 I probably draw on several writers, as well as *The First Epistle to the Corinthians: A Commentary on the Greek Text, 1 Corinthians: A Shorter Exegetical and Pastoral Commentary,* and *Life after Death.*[75]

The hope of the resurrection constitutes not simply an individual event, but one made possible by a union with Christ. As Paul writes, "He who raised Christ from the dead will give life to your mortal bodies also through his Spirit that dwells in you" (Rom. 8:11b). As we earlier noted, Thornton writes, "Those who belong to the Messiah (Rom. 8:23) will one day share with him that risen state to which he has already attained. . . . The hope of Israel went down into the grave. . . . When he rose from the tomb . . . the Church rose from the dead."[76] Strictly he might or should have written "was raised" (passive) in place of "rose." Anticipating Barrett and Ortkemper, Dahl rightly asserts,

> *God* is practically always the subject of "resurrection" verbs in the NT. The only instances of explicit statements that Christ (*not* his resurrection) causes our resurrection are John 6:39, 40, and 54. . . . The vast majority of texts containing *egeirō* and *anistēmi* . . . in a transitive, active sense, have God as subject and Christ or man as object (Acts 3:15; 4:10; 5:30; 10:40; 13:30, 37; Rom. 8:11; 10:9; 1 Cor. 6:14; 15:15; 2 Cor. 4:14; Gal. 1:1; Col. 2:12; 1 Thess. 1:10 . . .).[77]

74. Karl Barth, *The Resurrection of the Dead* (London: Hodder and Stoughton, 1933), 18.

75. Anthony C. Thiselton, *The First Epistle to the Corinthians: A Commentary on the Greek Text,* NIGTC (Grand Rapids: Eerdmans, 2000), 1169-1313; Anthony C. Thiselton, *1 Corinthians: A Shorter Exegetical and Pastoral Commentary* (Grand Rapids: Eerdmans, 2006), 253-90; and Thiselton, *Life after Death,* 111-28, 132-36.

76. Lionel S. Thornton, *The Common Life in the Body of Christ,* 3rd ed. (London: Dacre Press, 1950), 266 and 282.

77. M. E. Dahl, *The Resurrection of the Body: A Study of I Corinthians 15* (London: SCM, 1962), 96-97; cf. 96-100; C. K. Barrett, *First Epistle to the Corinthians,* 2nd ed. (London: Black, 1971), 341; F. J. Ortkemper, *1 Korintherbrief* (Stuttgart: Verlag Katholisches Bibelwerk, 1993), 145.

In 1 Corinthians 15 Paul introduces the resurrection by reaffirming that he had communicated to the Corinthians the death, burial, and resurrection of Jesus Christ, as *common pre-Pauline apostolic doctrine or tradition,* which is of "first importance" (15:1-5). Paul constantly appeals here to the shared, common tradition of the apostles, which he did not originate.[78] This "tradition" was both "transmitted and received," which Eriksson, Cullmann, and others identify as technical terms for the faithful transmission of a doctrine or creed. "Died for our sins" (15:3) indicates the *saving efficacy of the cross* (cf. 1:18-25); "he was buried" (15:4) indicates *the reality of the death of Jesus;* "he was raised" (15:4) shows the *reality of the resurrection;* "in accordance with the scriptures, and that he appeared to Cephas, then to the twelve" indicates *its public visibility* in accordance with the act of *divine vindication of his Servant, as the OT expectation anticipates.*

Some writers would challenge this use of "public" and "visibility," but far from all. This controversy is largely based on the alleged ambiguity of the Greek word *ōphthē* (v. 5), which the NRSV, REB, NJB, RV, and NIV all translate as "he appeared." It is the aorist passive of *horaō*, "to see," and the KJV/AV renders it literally "was seen." H.-W. Bartsch insists that *ōphthē* characteristically denotes theophanies, or in effect, visionary experiences, and W. Marxsen and Hans Conzelmann insist that the Greek term is "ambiguous."[79] Marxsen insists with equal firmness, "The appearance to Peter is not *described,* it is simply mentioned."[80] In broad terms, Bultmann and Conzelmann similarly do not regard the resurrection of Jesus Christ as an "objective" event.[81] Bultmann also argues that an "objective" view would contradict "otherworldly language" in 15:20-22.

On the opposite side of the debate, however, Walter Künneth insists on the more traditional, "objective," or visible and public understanding. Like the creation of the world, the resurrection of Christ is "a new and final creation," which has a "qualitative difference" from ecstatic experiences, such as that of 2 Corinthians 12:2-3.[82] The real breakthrough in scholarly consensus, however, came with Pannenberg. In his *Systematic Theology* he argues: "The

78. Anders Eriksson, *Traditions as Rhetorical Proof: Pauline Argumentation in 1 Corinthians,* ConBNT (Stockholm: Almqvist & Wiksell, 1998), 241.

79. Willi Marxsen, *The Resurrection of Jesus of Nazareth* (Philadelphia: Fortress, 1970), 72.

80. Marxsen, *The Resurrection of Jesus,* 81.

81. Rudolf Bultmann, in *Kerygma and Myth,* ed. H.-W. Bartsch, 2 vols. (London: SPCK, 1962-1964), 1:38, 39, and 41.

82. Walter Künneth, *The Theology of the Resurrection* (London: SCM, 1965), 75 and 84.

event (of the resurrection) took place *in this world,* namely, in the tomb of Jesus in Jerusalem before the visit of the women on the Sunday morning after his death."[83] He comments, *"The first Christians could not have successfully preached the resurrection of Jesus if his body had been intact in the tomb. . . . We must assume that the tomb of Jesus was in fact empty."*[84] Against Bultmann, he declares, "The resurrection of Jesus . . . legitimates his pre-Easter work. . . . (The Easter message) *follows* the Easter event; it does not constitute it."[85] Pannenberg also rightly argues that the resurrection is not unintelligible. "The familiar experience of being *awakened and rising from sleep* serves as a parable for the completely unknown destiny expected for the dead."[86]

In addition to the transmitted tradition of the empty tomb, the common apostolic teaching included the appearances of Christ to Peter and to the Twelve (1 Cor. 15:5). Paul regularly uses "Cephas" for Peter (1 Cor. 1:12; 3:22; 9:5; Gal. 1:18; 2:9, 11, 14), and the majority of writers include verse 5 in the common apostolic transmission. Peter, Paul, and the Twelve all experience the "reversal" of grace that the resurrection brings. There are no solid grounds for excluding verse 6, "He appeared to more than five hundred brothers at one time, most of whom are still alive," although some do. Certainly Richard Hays regards this verse as recounting *not* "truth beyond history," but an event "for which historical eyewitness testimony was readily available."[87] Gordon Fee also understands "at one time" less as a time marker, than "as an attempt to indicate the reality and objectivity of the appearances."[88]

Outside the Epistles, all four Gospels recount the appearance of the raised Christ to the women at the tomb, or at least to Mary Magdalene (Matt. 28:1-8; Mark 16:1-8; Luke 24:1-12; John 20:1-18). Probably the earliest Gospel, Mark, recounts the visit of Mary Magdalene, Mary the mother of James, and Salome (Mark 16:1); Luke adds Joanna (Luke 24:10); John recounts only Mary Magdalene (John 20:1). They all witnessed that the tomb was empty. In Mark 16:5 "a young man" (Gk. *neaniskos*), and in Matthew 28:2-3 "an angel of the Lord . . . (whose) appearance was like lightning" (Gk. *angelos kuriou . . . hōs astrapē*), commissioned Mary (with the others) to send word to Peter

83. Pannenberg, *ST* 2:360, italics mine.
84. Pannenberg, *ST* 2:358 and 359, italics mine.
85. Pannenberg, *ST* 2:283 and 288.
86. Pannenberg, *JGM* 74, italics mine.
87. Richard B. Hays, *First Corinthians* (Louisville: John Knox, 1997), 257.
88. Gordon Fee, *The First Epistle to the Corinthians,* NICNT (Grand Rapids: Eerdmans, 1987), 730.

and the disciples. Luke records that, at first, the apostles did not believe the women — until they had witnessed further proof (Luke 24:11).

In a closely related episode, however (Matt. 28:9-10; Mark 16:9-11; Luke 24:10-11; John 20:14-18), Jesus himself encountered Mary Magdalene. In John 20:14-15 she at first supposed him to be the gardener, but recognized Jesus as soon as he spoke to her, using her name, "Mary!" (John 20:16). Like Jesus' command, "Do not hold on to me," this succession of events exemplified the double principles of *continuity* and *contrast*. The raised Christ was the *same person* (continuity of identity), but *different in form* (contrast). We shall expand this point when we look more clearly at the general resurrection of the dead, and what is meant by "the resurrection of the body."

Clearly in the Gospels the raised "body" (Gk. *sōma*) is *more than visible and perhaps "physical,"* but *not less* than this. The whole point of the word "body," as we saw when we looked at the doctrine of humankind, and especially Käsemann's definition of "body" in the NT, was its *visibility in the public sphere.* Its "physicality" might have been implied, but it remains *secondary.* Hence the two disciples on the way to Emmaus at first did not recognize Jesus, but when he took the bread, "then their eyes were opened, and they recognized him" (Gk. *diēnoichthēsan hoi ophthalmoi kai epegnōsan auton,* Luke 24:31). Similarly in the appearance of Jesus Christ to the disciples (Luke 24:36-43; John 20:19-23), Jesus declared, "It is I myself" (Luke 24:39), and he "showed them his hands and his side" (John 20:20). But he evidently passed through closed or locked doors, and was perceived at first as "a spirit" (Gk. *pneuma,* Luke 24:37; John 20:19). It was exactly the same continuity-and-contrast in Jesus Christ's appearance by the Sea of Tiberias (John 21:1-14). Jesus apparently could eat fish, but there was at first ambiguity about his identity (John 21:12).

All this will set the tone and the context for our discussion of the general resurrection of the dead, and the general resurrection of the body. The First Epistle of John tells us, "When he is revealed, we will be like him" (1 John 3:2).

5. The General Resurrection of the Dead

First Corinthians 15:1-11 focuses on the reality of Christ's resurrection; 15:12-19 then sets out what would follow if the very *concept* of *resurrection* were to be denied. If resurrection, as such, proved to be impossible, the effects would be devastating: Christ could not have been raised (15:12); the proclamation of the gospel would be hollow (15:14); the apostolic witness would be proved false (15:15); the faith of Paul's converts would be without effect; they would still be under sin (15:17); and Christians who have died would be lost (15:18). Thus Paul traces *six* fatal consequences of denying resurrection in general, in which case "we are of all people most to be pitied" (15:19). In *rhetorical* terms the Roman world would have called this the *refutatio*. Belief in the possibility of resurrection is so fundamental that even to hold a "confused" or superficial belief is inadequate (15:1).

First Corinthians 15:20-28 constitutes in *rhetorical* terms the *confirmatio;* in reality (Greek uses the adverb *nuni*, meaning here "but as a matter of fact"), "Christ *has* been raised from the dead, the first fruits of those who have died" (15:20). "First fruits" (Gk. *aparchē*) is derived from the OT, and denotes the first portion of the crop (or flock), which is offered to God, and *pledges that more of the same kind (the rest of the crop) will come.* There will be a full harvest. As Joost Holleman argues, the term embodies two ideas: a temporal one (more is *yet* to come) and a representative one (this is the first of the *same kind* of crop).[89] Both Holleman and De Boer understand the term as pivotal for Christianity and resurrection. Christ's resurrection is the "first installment" of the resurrection of the dead. Karl Barth regarded the term as linking "the order of things" between God's past actions and God's future actions, looking forward to verses 26-28. There is a *taxis* (order) because there will be *hypotaxis* (submission). Christ's resurrection is the *paradigm* for the resurrection of believers in solidarity with him. This representative character finds expression in 15:21-22: "Since death came through a human being . . . ; for as all die in Adam, so all will be made alive in Christ." Adam and Christ respectively represent the old and new humanity. Paul draws the same parallel in 1 Corinthians 15:45-48 and in Romans 5:12-21.

This underlines three points. (i) The resurrection of Christ constitutes an event of *cosmic significance,* not simply one event among others. For Christians it initiates the *new creation.*[90] (ii) Christ's resurrection is *not an isolated event,* but carries with it God's pledge of the resurrection *of believers.* Christians stand in corporate solidarity with the raised Christ. To first-century Jews and Christians, this would be self-evident. But today we have to think ourselves out of several centuries of Western individualism. (iii) The

89. Holleman, *Resurrection and Parousia,* 49-50; Neil Q. Hamilton, *The Holy Spirit and Eschatology in Paul,* SJT Occasional Papers 6 (Edinburgh: Oliver and Boyd, 1957), 19-25 and 31-33; BDAG 98; M. C. De Boer, *The Defeat of Death: Apocalyptic Imagery in 1 Corinthians 15 and Romans 5,* JSNTSup 22 (Sheffield: JSOT Press, 1988), 109.

90. Beker, *Paul the Apostle,* 168-70.

role of Jesus Christ also points to his *Lordship and enthronement.* Paul expounds this in 1 Corinthians 15:23-28.

15:23-28 shows that all will be made alive in Christ "each in his own order" (v. 23). Christ's resurrection comes first ("the first fruits"); then "at his coming those who belong to Christ" (v. 23). There is no distinction here between the timing of the parousia and the timing of the resurrection of the dead. Only God knows when that time will be. Meanwhile Christ must reign as Lord, until "he hands over the kingdom to God the Father, after he has destroyed every ruler and every authority and power" (v. 24b). He destroys "all his enemies" (v. 25), and finally "the *last* enemy to be destroyed is death" (v. 26). This will include the structured and corporate evil of injustice and oppression, false values, and regimes. Death will be no more. Jesus had consistently proclaimed the kingdom of *God.* Here Paul speaks of the final future, when "God may be all in all" (v. 28). God is the ultimate Source and Goal of all (cf. Rom. 11:36).[91]

Paul may appear to make a puzzling digression in 1 Corinthians 15:29-34. But it is not in fact a digression: it concerns the resurrection of the dead. For whatever our interpretation of 15:29 may be, it means, at the very least: baptism as such without belief in the resurrection of the dead would mean nothing. As I have argued elsewhere, "vicarious baptism" would not be true to Paul: baptism is not a cause-effect mechanism. It could just refer to those who were baptized to meet their loved ones again. But the most convincing view is that some became baptized because they witnessed the radiant testimony of the Christians on their deathbed. The Greek preposition *hyper* (v. 29) has a wide range of meanings, including "for the sake of."[92] 15:30-33 also sets out the pointlessness of life without the resurrection of the dead.

15:35-58 directly and explicitly addresses the subject of the resurrection of the body, beginning with the question: "How are the dead raised? With what kind of body do they come?" (v. 35). In 15:35-50 Paul addresses the *"conceivability"* of the resurrection: How can resurrection be both *credible* and *intelligible?* The passage begins with a second *refutatio,* in rhetorical terms. The skeptic cannot *conceive* of the resurrection.

First, Paul offers several analogies, as parallels or models, from *creation.* This provides a magnificent hermeneutical bridge for ready understanding.

91. Neil Richardson, *Paul's Language about God,* JSNTSup 99 (Sheffield: Sheffield Academic, 1994), 114-15. Moffatt has a useful note on "subordination" in 1 Corinthians; cf. James Moffatt, *The First Epistle to the Corinthians* (London: Hodder and Stoughton, 1938), 250.
92. Thiselton, *First Epistle,* 1240-49, and Thiselton, *1 Corinthians,* 274-75.

Like the this-worldly body, a seed ("what you sow," 15:36) "does not come to life unless it dies" (v. 36b), that is, comes to the end of its life *in that form.* But in the case of purely natural phenomena, "God gives it a body" (Gk. *ho de theos didōsin auto sōma,* 5:38) as he has willed; that is, God gives it a new form. If we saw a tulip bulb planted in the earth, we should not expect that same bulb to reappear at the end of a stalk, but a new creation — the tulip. Paul adds, "And to each kind of seed its own body" (i.e., a tulip from a tulip bulb, a daffodil from a daffodil bulb, and so on). What could be more *intelligible* than resurrection, once we reflect on "new creation" in nature? The old form *as such* comes to an end; God gives it a *new form of life.*

Second, the *same identity* or entity can live through the experience of *changing* forms of life. Even the infant, the middle aged, and the frail elderly person can retain the same identity, though the visible *form* may *radically* change. Alongside *contrast* there is *continuity.* Everyday phenomena such as pension rights confirm this, even when dementia occurs. God relishes the diversity of forms in creation: "Not all flesh is alike, but there is one flesh for human beings, another for animals, another for birds" (15:39). Each manifests its own "glory" (15:41). "So it is," Paul observes, in the case of "the resurrection of the dead" (15:42).

Now that the explanation has reached this critical point, Paul describes the "resurrection body" (Gk. *sōma*) in terms of *four specific contrasts* with the former earthly body (15:42-44). (i) The old *sōma* is "perishable," it is "raised imperishable" (NRSV, v. 42). (ii) The old is "sown in dishonor" (NRSV); it is raised "in glory" (v. 43). (iii) The old is "sown as weakness; it is raised in power" (v. 43b). (iv) It is sown "a physical body" (NRSV); it is raised a "spiritual body" (NRSV; Gk. *sōma pneumatikon,* v. 44). All these NRSV translations are reasonable, but arguably inadequate as accurately indicating Paul's thought. Paul aims to show *contrast, continuity,* and *transformation,* as in his earlier analogies.

With regard to (i), in 15:42, the NRSV, REB, NIV, and NJB all translate "perishable . . . imperishable," although the AV/KJV reads "in corruption . . . in incorruption." The contrast in Greek is expressed as *phthora* and *aphtharsia.* But whereas the English implies a *quality,* the Greek denotes a *process.* The word *phthora* denotes the process of *decreasing capacities, increasing weakness,* and *approaching exhaustion,* which are all too familiar to those of us in our seventies, eighties, or nineties. These finally reach stagnation and death. The term *aphtharsia* in *Paul's context* does not denote the static quality of "being immortal," but the *reversal* of decreasing capacities, that is, increasing ones.

Here we see the necessary limitation of a lexicon. Danker is quite correct to translate *aptharsiai* as "not being subject to decay . . . incorruptibility, immortality" in context-free or Hellenistic occurrences of the word. He can reasonably call it a "quality of the future life."[93] But *in this particular context*, it denotes the reversal of a *process*. We shall see that "spiritual body" (NRSV) in verse 44 confirms this. It is further confirmed when we recall that in LXX *phthora* means "spoiled," and *chebel* usually means "emptiness" or "fruitlessness." To him *aphtharsia* denotes the very opposite, especially when it is animated and sustained by the Holy Spirit (15:44).[94] The reversal of a *decrescendo to pianissimo* in music is not *fortissimo*, but *crescendo leading to fortissimo*.

With regard to (ii), the NRSV renders the second contrast (15:43) as "dishonor" and "glory." The Greek *atimia* does indeed regularly denote "dishonor," "disgrace," and "disrespect."[95] This is appropriate if Paul alludes to human fallenness; but his view of the earthly body as such is less negative, and the word can mean "humiliation" (Phil. 3:21). At all events, it rightly stands in contrast to the Greek *doxa*, "glory" or "splendor," which regularly translates the Hebrew *kābōd*.[96] The word *kābōd* usually means what makes someone weighty, impressive, or majestic, with the added suggestion of glory, radiance, light, or luminosity.[97] In this context *light* may be less relevant, but *radiance* is helpful. It suggests the joy of the bride, or of the child waking up on Christmas morning, or of lovers meeting after a long absence. The raised community will be meeting Jesus Christ!

With regard to (iii), the contrast "weakness . . . power" (NRSV) is also reasonable. The former body was subject to the ravages of time, disease, and the constraints of the physical body. Mistaken or sinful choices can further incapacitate it. By contrast, the power (Gk. *egeiretai en dynamei*) of the new "body" is determined by its future, its release from the past, and the Holy Spirit.

With regard to (iv), 1 Corinthians 15:44 reaches the climax of the argument. Here NRSV "sown a physical body . . . raised a spiritual body" is *very disappointing* for *speiretai sōma psychikon . . . egeiretai sōma pneumatikon*. First, *psychikos* does not primarily, if at all, denote "physical." The noun *psychē* means "life principle": normally "life," sometimes "soul"; not physical

---

93. BDAG 155.
94. Thiselton, *First Epistle*, 1271-72, and Thiselton, *1 Corinthians*, 281-82.
95. BDAG 149.
96. BDAG 256-58.
97. BDB 458-59.

"body." The adjective, according to Danker, denotes "pertinent to the life of the natural world" or "natural," and in 15:44 should be translated "ordinary or earthly body."[98] Christians who are *psychikoi* (2:14) are insufficiently influenced by the Holy Spirit. Hence "spiritual body" *(sōma pneumatikon)* means *here not "spiritual" in contrast to material or physical, but "a body constituted by the Holy Spirit"* or "a body from the realm of the Spirit" (Thiselton) or "a body possessing the Spirit," as in 15:46 (Danker).[99]

N. T. Wright correctly comments, "The four contrasts are mutually explanatory."[100] He rightly exclaims that *the NRSV translation of verse 44 is "brazen"!* He examines Paul's vocabulary in 1 Corinthians 2 and 12–14 and correctly speaks of "a jungle of misinterpretation." The *sōma pneumatikon*, he concludes, denotes *"a body animated by, enlivened by, the Spirit of the true God,* exactly as Paul has said more extensively in several other passages" (e.g., Rom. 8:9-11).[101] Pannenberg also shares this view, declaring, "The Holy Spirit is the creative source of the resurrection life."[102]

If the resurrection mode of existence is to be sustained, energized, and transformed by the Holy Spirit, the four contrasts leap to life. First, one subsidiary point is that no "purgatory" is needed for purification: the full experience of the Holy Spirit will *sanctify and purify* the raised people of God entirely. Second, and no less important, the resurrection mode of existence will be *ever fresh and ever ongoing, as is the Holy Spirit.* We shall return to this point when we examine "eternity." Third, this Holy Spirit binds us to God through Jesus Christ in utter *intimacy.* Finally, the relevance of "body" ensures some *counterpart to public recognition of identity,* and the possibility of communication.

First Corinthians 15:45-52 further establishes the intimate relation between raised believers and the raised, or risen, Christ, who is the last Adam, and that this transformation will occur in a flash. Paul declares, "Just as we have borne the image of the man of dust [the first Adam], we will also bear the image of the man of heaven [Jesus Christ]" (15:49); that is, *only God can bring about this transformation to glory by his Holy Spirit.* God will transform us instantaneously: "We will all be changed, in a moment, in the twinkling (or blink) of an eye" (15:51-52). The Greek *atomō,* literally "in an uncut unit,"

98. BDAG 1098-1100.
99. Thiselton, *1 Corinthians,* 279 and 283; Thiselton, *First Epistle,* 1275-80; BDAG 837; cf. Thiselton, *Life after Death,* 120-22.
100. Wright, *The Resurrection of the Son of God,* 347.
101. Wright, *The Resurrection of the Son of God,* 354, italics mine.
102. Pannenberg, *ST* 3:622.

is the smallest conceivable moment of time; *rhipē* is a rapid movement, and a rapid movement in the eyes is usually a blink. Paul uses one more analogy or metaphor. The trumpet blast (v. 52) is a command to an army that must instantly be obeyed: a sleeping army is awakened to stand on its feet in a flash.

First Corinthians 15:53-58 shows how thereby "Death has been swallowed up in victory" (v. 54), for the sting of death is sin, and Christ's victory over sin leaves only a *stingless transformation.* The victory is Christ's and God's; but with the generosity of grace, Paul concludes, God "gives *us* the victory through our Lord Jesus Christ" (v. 57). Hence the future certainty of the resurrection becomes the basis for every Christian "work of the Lord" (v. 58).

Other passages that look forward to the resurrection echo some of the same themes. Romans 4:17 speaks of "the God . . . who gives *life to the dead,*" and who enacts an act of *sovereign new creation.* The analogy of the dry bones in Ezekiel 37 establishes the principle that God creates resurrection life from nothing. "Dry bones" are dismembered skeletons, without any hint or prospect of life, except as a gracious gift of God. Resurrection is no harder for God than creation. Such a God merits trust without wavering (Rom. 4:20). In 2 Corinthians 5:2 we long "to be clothed with our heavenly dwelling," when death will be "swallowed up by life" (5:4). In 1 Thessalonians 4:16, "The dead in Christ will rise first," at the sound of the trumpet blast, to meet with all who have died and been raised in Christ. *The resurrection of the dead constitutes a consistent and coherent theme in Paul,* and is, apart from its timing, *one with the resurrection of Christ.* This in turn is based on God's promises in the OT, and common pre-Pauline doctrine and experience. In hermeneutical terms, several analogies and models make the concept and the event utterly understandable.

CHAPTER XV

The Last Judgment, Eternity, and the Restoration of All Things

1. The Purpose of the Last Judgment

Paul and the earliest Christians expected that the Last Judgment would be universal. Paul writes, "All of us must appear before the judgment seat of Christ, so that each may receive recompense for what has been done in the body, whether good or evil" (2 Cor. 5:10). Many Christians hesitate to believe that their "good" deeds could really be *good,* and are conscious of so much more that God might call "evil." Hence many view the prospect of judgment with some trepidation and anxiety.

Yet many biblical writers view the prospect of God's judgment with longing and joy. The psalmist exclaims,

> Then shall all the trees of the forest sing for joy
> before the LORD; . . .
> for he is coming to judge the earth. (Ps. 96:12-13)

Nowhere, however, does this soften the inevitability of judgment for all. In Hebrews 9:27 a writer different from Paul asserts, "It is appointed for mortals to die once, and after that the judgment."

The main explanation for this difference lies in the nature of the judgment we expect. Western individualists may construe judgment on the analogy of a headmaster dispensing punishments and rewards to school students or pupils. When the psalmist prays, "Judge me, O Lord, my God" (AV/KJV), the NRSV translates

> *Vindicate me,* O LORD my God,
>
> according to your righteousness (Ps 35:24)

Both English versions translate the Hebrew verb *shāphat*. BDB does give "judge" as the first meaning. But the word also means to act as lawgiver or governor, to discriminate or to *vindicate* (Ps. 10:18; 1 Sam. 24:15). It is used 202 times in the OT.[1] The corporate noun *mishpāt*, according to Peter Enns, "encompasses a variety of meanings," and occurs 425 times in the OT.[2] The AV/KJV uniformly translates *mishpāt* as "judgment," but Schultz argues that this is "untenable," because so often it denotes not only the vindication of the oppressed, the downtrodden, and the needy, but also in some contexts their rescue or deliverance.

Moreover, *sh-ph-t* is not the only verb for "to judge." The Hebrew word *dyn* often overlaps with it, sometimes occurring in poetic synonymous parallelism (Ps. 9:8; Prov. 31:9).[3] Both verbs can denote "establishing order," and *dyn* often means defending the weak and oppressed. It can apply to the work of the Davidic king (Jer. 21:12). When God is the subject, "judgment" *(mishpāt)* belongs to God (Zech. 7:9; 8:16); he executes his sovereign rule over creation (Job 36:31-32); and he *vindicates* Israel in battles against her enemies (Gen. 49:16).

Contrary to much popular misunderstanding, it is simply not true that judgment in the NT is "softer" or more "liberal" than the teaching of the OT. In the OT the concept of the judgment as vindication, even liberation from oppression, is prominent. In the NT John the Baptist speaks of "the wrath to come," and of unfruitful trees being "thrown into the fire" (Matt. 3:7, 10). In John 5:29 Jesus warns his hearers that "those who have done evil" await "the resurrection of condemnation." Paul declares, "Do you imagine, whoever you are, that . . . you will escape the judgment of God?" (Rom. 2:3). The seer of the Apocalypse observes, "The dead were judged according to their works" (Rev. 20:12).[4]

Yet the fact remains that *vindication* constitutes a significant part of judgment. In practice, four reasons give grounds for joy, rather than anxiety, at the prospect of the Last Judgment. First, God will *publicly and definitively vindicate the oppressed.* This includes all who have suffered injustice, or those

---

1. BDB 1047; and Richard Schultz, "*Sh-ph-t,*" in *NIDOTTE* 4:213-20.

2. "*Mishpāt,*" in *NIDOTTE* 2:1142; *TDOT* 3:194-97; and V. Heinrich, in *TDNT* 3:923-33.

3. BDB 192; *TDOT* 1:187-94; Richard Schultz, in *NIDOTTE* 1:938-42.

4. Friedrich Büchsel, "*Krinō, krisis, krima,*" in *TDNT* 3:933-54, gives many more examples.

whose motives have been misunderstood; all who have been falsely accused and persecuted; and all Christian martyrs. Psalm 98 declares,

> He has revealed his vindication in the sight of the nations. . . .
> Make a joyful noise to the LORD, . . .
> for he is coming to judge the earth. (Ps. 98:2, 4, 9)

Second, the revelation of God's righteousness in judgment *puts an end to all deception, ambiguity, seduction, and illusion.* What "success" amounts to will be definitively and publicly revealed, both in terms of supposed "worldly" success and in terms of the practice of ministry, when "God will bring to light the things now hidden in darkness and will disclose the purposes of the heart" (1 Cor. 4:5). Paul Tillich rightly expounded the *ambiguity* in this present era of the church and the world. Third, God is publicly revealed to all *as universal King of all creation and history, with Christ as Lord of the church and the world.* God will be seen in his glory and sovereignty; Christ will be seen in the saving light of the cross; doubters will be silenced. Fourth, Christians will appropriate the promised verdict of *justification by grace.* We shall no longer "*wait for* the hope of righteousness" (Gal. 5:5), for the future promise of righteousness will be performed. As we argued in the context of baptism, justification anticipates the verdict of the Last Judgment.

These are the deciding factors that place the Last Judgment in perspective. Admittedly there is much else to say. What do we genuinely mean by "the *wrath* of God"? Why, as James Martin implies, did interest in the Last Judgment appear to *decline* after the end of the seventeenth century and beginning of the eighteenth?[5] Is "judgment" a purely *internal process* of cause and effect, whereby every failure, sin, falling short, or alienation from God brings its own consequences during and even after this life? These questions can best be tackled by examining them individually, perhaps in reverse order.

To Charles H. Dodd must go the credit and also the notoriety for introducing the *question of "internal" consequences of acts or states of alienation* prominently into theology, in his commentary on Romans. Credit for the question is valid; notoriety is equally deserved, for Dodd understands "the wrath of God" more like a *cause-effect impersonal mechanism* than the disposition of "person." He argues that the actual phrase "the wrath of God" occurs only three times in Paul: Romans 1:18, Colossians 3:6, and Ephesians

---

5. James P. Martin, *The Last Judgement in Protestant Theology from Orthodoxy to Ritschl* (Edinburgh: Oliver and Boyd, 1963), 87 and throughout.

5:6.[6] It does not denote emotion or passion, but, Dodd argues, "Paul . . . retains it . . . to describe an inevitable process of cause and effect in a moral universe."[7] Dodd repeats impersonal and mechanical analogies, as when he compares "propitiation" or "expiation" (Gk. *hilastērion*) to "so to speak, a . . . disinfectant."[8]

Nevertheless, Dodd is correct to suggest that in *some* or in *many* cases human failures, sins, or states of alienation from God invite consequences from the very nature of the sin itself. A deliberate refusal to pray, for example, may erect a barrier to intimacy with God; just as refusing to practice a musical instrument may block any path to masterly performance. The judgment of God becomes manifest in such self-induced processes. But Dodd is surely wrong to suggest that this *always* exhausts what is implied in the phrase "the wrath of God." We shall consider this phrase in more detail later in this chapter.

Why did the reality of the Last Judgment play an *ever-decreasing role in theological thought after the beginning of the eighteenth century,* as James Martin maintains? Büchsel shows some concern about this in his long article on *krinō* in Kittel's *TDNT,* written in German before 1940. He writes: "The NT concept of judgement is confronted today by a rationalistic criticism which rejects the concept as mythical and unethical. In face of this we must stress the fact that in the NT judgement is not capricious or emotional, as so often in myths of judgement. It is an inwardly necessary consequence of the sin of man. All human acts are a sowing; God's judgement is the related and self-evident reaping (Gal. 6:7-8)."[9] He continues, "Disobedience to God's order inevitably means the restriction of life, and finally death. . . . The concept of judgement cannot be taken out of the NT gospel."[10] Bultmann notoriously regarded the Last Judgment as a myth. He even appealed to the fact that sometimes judgment is an act of God, while at other times it is an act of Christ, as a major reason why we cannot understand the event of judgment literally.[11] By contrast, Büchsel observed, "It makes no odds whether the

6. Charles H. Dodd, *The Epistle of Paul to the Romans* (London: Hodder and Stoughton, 1932), 21.

7. Dodd, *Romans,* 23.

8. Dodd, *Romans,* 54.

9. Büchsel, *"Krinō, krisis, krima,"* 3:940.

10. Büchsel, *"Krinō, krisis, krima,"* 3:940 and 941.

11. Rudolf Bultmann, *Jesus Christ and Mythology* (London: SCM, 1960), 33-34; Rudolf Bultmann, "New Testament Mythology," in *Kerygma and Myth,* vol. 1, ed. H.-W. Bartsch (London: SPCK, 1964), 210-11; and in *Essays Philosophical and Theological* (London: SCM,

judgement will be by God (Matt. 10:32-33) or by Jesus (Matt. 7:22-23; 16:27; 25:31-46; 26:64)."[12]

Büchsel notes a number of serious passages in the Gospels about the Last Judgment. On the basis of NT evidence he writes, "God's judgement hangs over every man . . . (in) the Sermon on the Mount, Matt. 5:22 . . . 7:1, 22-23. . . . The preaching of Jesus plumbs the very depths of the concept of judgement. . . . The preaching of Paul is dominated by expectation of the day of wrath and the righteous judgement of God . . . Rom. 2:1-11 . . . John 5:28 is a constant presupposition."[13]

James Martin declares that in Protestant orthodoxy, "The *parousia* and the Last Judgement were viewed as one event. . . . This followed the pattern of the Creeds."[14] But two factors, he continues, complicated this. First, some failed to give careful enough attention to passages in which the parousia was associated with the fall of Jerusalem; second, eschatology became isolated, and the importance of the apocalyptic for the NT writers became obscured. It is more than just a Jewish residue of obsolete imagery. In Calvin the doctrine of the Last Judgment indicated and encouraged respect for *God's righteousness;* in Francis Turretin it became an incentive for *good works;* in Luther it stood in contrast with the *hidden* nature of the church in the present era. In none of these writers did it undermine or contradict justification by grace or the centrality of the atonement. In the eighteenth century John Turretin related the Last Judgment especially to an honest and careful interpretation of Scripture and the "laws" of hermeneutics. Martin further surveys the doctrine in Richard Baxter and the Puritans, and through to J. A. Bengel and the Pietists.

These occupy Martin's first one hundred pages, after which he considers the impact of "rationalism." He explains: "The presupposition of rationalism led to the conviction that superstition, not unbelief, was the greatest enemy of faith," and to the elevation of "tolerance" (93). The ethic of virtue and righteousness tended to move from God to man in a greater degree of self-sufficiency. *From Kant onward "eschatological realism" became abandoned, and much came increasingly from within the universe* (106). Eschatology seemed to become "a *non sequitur*" in much prevailing thought, and

---

1955), 283; for a detailed critique, see Anthony C. Thiselton, *The Two Horizons: New Testament Hermeneutics and Philosophical Description* (Grand Rapids: Eerdmans; Carlisle: Paternoster, 1980), 252-92.

12. Büchsel, *"Krinō, krisis, krima,"* 3:936.

13. Büchsel, *"Krinō, krisis, krima,"* 3:936, 937, and 938.

14. Martin, *The Last Judgement,* 4. Page numbers have been placed in the text.

in "the anthropocentricity" of much nineteenth-century theology (136). A scapegoat was too often made of "literal exegesis" from Schleiermacher onward. Martin traces this trend only as far as Ritschl, in whose work "The Last Judgement does not even appear as a final vindication or confirmation of justification" (205). He might have traced the climax of thought to Bultmann.

2. Judgment, Verdicts, Wrath, and Justification by Grace

We have so far argued that the OT writers could often look forward to the Last Judgment with eagerness and joy, because for them it would primarily be a *public* event of *vindication,* especially of the oppressed and of the faithful. This attitude shapes the NT writers also. Nevertheless, we noted several other issues: whether judgment was primarily or exclusively an internal result of an action; whether it was a dominant doctrine only before the eighteenth and nineteenth centuries; and how it relates to the wrath of God, to justification by grace, and also to the verdictive utterances of speech-act theory.

(i) *Biblical Language about the Wrath of God.* Fundamentally "wrath" (Gk. *orgē*) is *neither an emotion nor the opposite of love. The opposite of love is not wrath but indifference.* We have only to imagine the attitude of loving parents or grandparents, when their child or grandchild is bent on self-destruction or foolish choices, to appreciate that *not* to experience some reaction of anger or wrath would simply indicate lack of concern or of love. I have argued this elsewhere.[15] An unloving parent may either remain indifferent or "spoil" the child with bribes and treats. Hebrews 12:6-11 reminds us, "The Lord disciplines those whom he loves, and chastises every child whom he accepts. . . . What child is there whom a parent does not discipline? . . . Discipline always seems painful."

Even so, the wrath of God is *not* a *permanent* quality or characteristic, like his love or righteousness. Hebrew uses at least five words for "wrath." These include *'aph* (Exod. 22:24; 32:10-12; Job 16:9; 19:11; Pss. 2:5, 12; 95:11), which occurs over 200 times; *chēmâ* (Deut. 29:23, 28; 2 Kings 22:13, 17; Job 21:20; Ezek. 13:15); and *chārôn,* *'ebrâ,* and *qetseph,* among others. These are potential *dispositions,* which require appropriate *situations* for them to come into play. The NT uses two terms, for which the Greek is *orgē* and

---

15. Anthony C. Thiselton, *Life after Death: A New Approach to the Last Things* (Grand Rapids: Eerdmans, 2012), 159; cf. 160-65.

thymos.[16] These are also contingent dispositions, when they are applied to God. Thus in the OT *chēmâ* can be "kindled" or "turned away" (2 Kings 22:13, 17; Prov. 15:1; 21:14). In the face of obstinate or recalcitrant self-will, it may even destroy (Deut. 9:19), but it may also be remedied (Num. 25:11; Ps. 106:23). Hence wrath is sometimes "provoked," for example, by idolatry, by oppression, by "despis[ing] the word of the Holy One" (Isa. 5:24), or by breaking the Sabbath (Exod. 20:8-11). Clearly it relates to alienation from God. Pannenberg, we noted, comments: "Self-willing . . . alienates from God by putting the self in the place that is God's alone."[17]

It is sometimes forgotten that while Paul refers to "the wrath to come," the context is usually or frequently that of God's providence for us to flee from or to escape it. In his earliest missionary preaching Paul recalls that he proclaimed Jesus, "who rescues us from the wrath that is coming" (1 Thess. 1:10). But a number of references do not concern "rescue." For example, in the face of stubborn sin, "God's wrath has overtaken them at last" (1 Thess. 2:16). Stephen Travis writes with great sensitivity on this subject. He argues that the wrath of God is very often "remedial," although not exclusively or uniformly.[18] He rightly recognizes the place of vindication and of "internal" consequences of actions, but equally urges that not every instance of "the wrath of God" can come under these headings. His exegesis is careful and judicious. Romans 1:18-32, he argues, avoids "retributive" wrath, but nevertheless shows "the fittingness of punishment."[19] In general, God's sovereign purpose, he concludes, is a positive one. Even "vessels of wrath" may become "vessels of mercy."[20]

(ii) *Judgment, Verdicts, and Justification by Grace.* At an everyday level many imagine that the Last Judgment somehow stands in tension with justification by grace through faith. But if we fully appreciate the nature of justification as *verdict,* we begin to see that the two events are of the same kind. When we considered Christian baptism in chapter 13, we noted that C. F. D. Moule and Alan Richardson stressed baptism as an anticipation of the Last Judgment. It involved "pleading guilty" in advance of the public judgment; it appropriated in the present the related verdict of "right with God," but only in *faith* or trust, *not yet demonstrably* as a *public pronouncement and verdict.*

---

16. Cf. Moulton-Geden 703 and 263-64.

17. Pannenberg, *ST* 2:243.

18. Stephen H. Travis, *Christ and the Judgement of God: The Limits of Divine Revelation in New Testament Thought* (Milton Keynes: Paternoster; Peabody, Mass.: Hendrickson, 2008), 53-73.

19. Travis, *Christ and the Judgement,* 60-62.

20. Travis, *Christ and the Judgement,* 65.

Much can be learned for theology from linguistics, linguistic philosophy, and the philosophy of language. Martin Luther's famous aphorism "righteous and yet a sinner" (Lat. *simul iustus et peccator*) would appear to constitute a *logical contradiction* if each half were a *proposition* or descriptive *statement*. But if the two halves are *verdicts,* they will not be contradictory, but will represent *verdicts from different vantage points.* A school report may pronounce "good in French; bad in mathematics." God pronounces the verdict: " 'Guilty' in terms of *cause-effect* attitudes and actions under the *law and in history,*" but "put right with God" in terms of *grace, faith, and eschatology.* Or these might be expressed in shorthand: "Guilty as past history"; "rightwised as future promise." I have explained this principle more fully in *The Two Horizons.*[21]

In this work of 1980, I made much of "seeing . . . as . . ." *within a system* (with special reference to Ludwig Wittgenstein), or in terms of *"onlooks"* (with reference to D. D. Evans). Each constitutes a verdict; but "guilty" is a valid verdict within the *system of law and history,* while "counted right with God" is valid within the *system of grace and eschatology.* In spite of confusions about "myth," Bultmann, following Luther, was right to appreciate the radical difference between history and eschatology, and between "works" and grace.

What has come to be known as *speech-act theory* clarifies the distinctive grammar of verdicts even further. J. L. Austin not only clarified the relation between proposition and verdicts (or what he called "verdictives"), but did so more accurately than most European theologians. He also clarified the difference between different kinds of verdicts. On one hand, verdicts imply a *different logic from propositions,* but on the other hand they usually *presuppose* propositions. Second, the verdict of condemnation or acquittal differs from formulating or declaring a sentence for the alleged crime. Austin writes, "*Verdictives* consist in the delivering of a finding . . . upon evidence or reasons as to value or fact. . . . An *exercitive* is the giving of a decision in favour of or against a certain course of action. . . . It is a decision that something *is to be so,* as distinct from a judgement that *it is so.* . . . It is an *award,* as opposed to an *assessment;* it is a *sentence,* as opposed to a *verdict.*"[22]

Both, however, are *"illocutions"* or true performatives; both perform an action *in* saying the utterance: "They confer powers, rights, names, etc., or change or eliminate them."[23] Searle, Briggs, and others add various qualifi-

21. Thiselton, *The Two Horizons,* 415-22.
22. John L. Austin, *How to Do Things with Words* (Oxford: Clarendon, 1962), 152 and 154, italics mine.
23. Austin, *How to Do Things,* 155.

cations and provisos, but the principle still stands.[24] Briggs includes a useful section on speech acts and truth, and discusses the example of forgiveness. But whereas forgiveness may be declared afresh and even repeatedly, justification by grace constitutes a *once-for-all, permanent* event of incorporation into Christ. If justification is an anticipation of the Last Judgment, it is an *appropriation through promise and faith* of what will be *declared and confirmed publicly at the Last Judgment.*

We recall that the Last Judgment ends all that is both secret and ambiguous. God's judgment is final and definitive and cannot be revised. Christians in this present life are often attacked by doubt. Even ministerial "success" is ambiguous and can be doubted (1 Cor. 4:1-5). But "God will disclose the purposes of the heart. Then each one will receive commendation from God" (4:5). The saints in heaven, the angels, the world, and the universal church will acknowledge,

> "Great and amazing are your deeds,
>   Lord God, the Almighty!
> Just and true are your ways,
>   King of the nations!" (Rev. 15:3)

The seer adds,

> "All nations will come
> and worship before you,
> for your judgments have been revealed." (Rev. 15:4)

Johannes Weiss calls justification by grace a "pre-dating of what will take place only on the day of divine judgement (Rom. 2:12, 13, 16 . . . Gal. 5:5)."[25] Kent Yinger also relates judgment and justification by grace. In his view, "Eschatological recompense . . . *confirms* . . . one's justification."[26] Stephen Travis also concurs.[27]

24. John R. Searle, *Expression and Meaning: Studies in the Theory of Speech Acts* (Cambridge: CUP, 1979), 8-29; Richard S. Briggs, *Words in Action: Speech Act Theory and Biblical Interpretation* (Edinburgh and New York: T. & T. Clark, 2001), 38-72, 217-55.

25. Johannes Weiss, *Earliest Christianity: A History of the Period A.D. 30–150*, 2 vols. (New York: Harper, 1959; orig. 1937), 2:502.

26. Kent L. Yinger, *Paul, Judaism, and Judgement according to Deeds*, SNTSMS 105 (Cambridge: CUP, 1999), 290.

27. Travis, *Christ and the Judgement*, 95.

3. Progression "after" Judgment? What Is "Eternal" Life?

In our chapters on God, we noted that "the living God" of the OT had an *ongoing* character, which stood in contrast to more static "theism." If God himself characterizes heaven, there we should expect to participate in his *dynamic, purposive, ongoing life*. This is precisely confirmed by the concept of "the resurrection body" *(sōma pneumatikon)*, which the Holy Spirit enlivens and sustains. It is frequently said that the authentic experience of the Holy Spirit is of One who is ever-fresh, *ever-new, and onward-going*. Thus there would be nothing static or "fixed" about life animated and sustained by the Holy Spirit, after death. "After" the resurrection of the dead, and "after" the Last Judgment, life (Gk. *zōē*) will be like a *flowing river*, rather than a static pool (Rev. 22:1-2). Raised believers will experience the purposive, progressive, new creation.

This, in turn, will be confirmed by a third factor. "Eternal life" does not mean a life consisting simply of everlasting duration. Such a mistaken idea was imported into theology by the philosophical view of Thomas Aquinas and others, that "perfection," once established, can allow for no further advance. If a condition is "perfect" now, it is argued, it cannot become *more than* perfect, because if it could, "perfection" would never have been *perfect* in the first instance. But we use "perfect" in *different ways*. A "perfect" baby would not retain baby-perfection when he or she became a "perfect" teenager, or a "perfect" adult. The qualities that make for perfection would be *different at different times* or stages.

This applies even more sharply to the equally mistaken notion that *eternity* means *timelessness*. Admittedly the strongest argument for this view is that God created time when he created the universe. When he puzzled about how it could make sense to speak of events or entities "before" or "after" time, Augustine wrote, "The world was made *with* time and not *in* time (Lat. *mundus non in tempore sed cum tempore factus est*)."[28] Dorner and others endorsed this view.[29] More recently Paul Helm has attempted to argue that God is "timeless" in his book *Eternal God*.[30] But William Craig has criticized his book, not least for a "timeless" theory of time as such.[31] Helm regards

28. Augustine, *City of God* 11.6.

29. J. A. Dorner, *System of Doctrine* (Edinburgh: T. & T. Clark, 1881), 2:30.

30. Paul Helm, *Eternal God: A Study of God without Time* (Oxford: Clarendon, 1988; 2nd ed. 2011), 37.

31. William L. Craig, review of *Eternal God: A Study of God without Time*, by Paul Helm, *JETS* 36 (1993): 254-55.

the contrast between past and future as analogous to the spatial contrast between before and behind; but Craig remains understandably unconvinced by Helm's explanation of God's knowledge of the future.

According to Brian Leftow, a "timeless" God would have no past or future, no plans or purposes. Richard Swinburne regards such a God as "a lifeless being"; God is "in continual interaction with men."[32] As we have already observed, the better translation of Exodus 3:14 is not, with the Greek LXX, "I am what I am," but, with the Hebrew indefinite or future imperfect, "I *will be* what I will be." The well-known verse "Jesus Christ is the same yesterday and today and forever" (Heb. 13:8) has nothing to do with timelessness or his supposedly immutable nature, but expresses Christ's *permanency* as High Priest, in contrast to an endless succession of Aramaic Jewish priests.

Most theologians today tend to favor the view that originated with Plotinus and Boethius, namely, that *eternity* denotes the gathering up of *all temporal moments simultaneously*. This view recognizes that God is *beyond* time, as well as acknowledging that time is real for God as well as for humankind.

Nevertheless, this still cannot do full justice to the dynamic, ongoing nature of God. It is widely recognized that time is not one single entity. In daily life chronological time is not "subjective" time, as Heidegger constantly emphasized. Clock time is only one way of calculating time. Humans also count "time for a walk," or "time for a sleep," and these may vary in chronological duration. Literary theorists and philosophers, especially Paul Ricoeur, frequently speak of "narrative time," in which slow motion, flashbacks, or other literary devices make time spans quite novel and different from clock time.[33] The Gospel of Mark shows this pattern in using narrative time, in which early events take place at a speed entirely different from the slow motion of the passion.[34]

This same lesson is confirmed through *post-Einsteinian philosophy of*

---

32. Richard Swinburne, *The Coherence of Theism* (Oxford: Clarendon, 1977), 214.

33. Seymour Chatman, *Story and Discourse: Narrative Structure in Fiction and Film* (Ithaca, N.Y.: Cornell University Press, 1978), 19-42; Gérard Genette, *Narrative and Discourse: An Essay in Method* (Ithaca, N.Y.: Cornell University Press, 1980), chaps. 4-6; Paul Ricoeur, *Time and Narrative,* 3 vols. (Chicago: University of Chicago Press, 1984-1988), throughout.

34. Wesley A. Kort, *Story, Text, and Scripture: Literary Interests in Biblical Narrative* (University Park: Pennsylvania State University Press, 1988), traces some thirty-two instances of *euthys,* "at once," before Peter's confession in Mark 8:29; and only six instances in the passion narrative.

science. In the theory of relativity, time dilation is an actual difference of elapsed time between two events as measured by observers either moving relative to each other or differently situated from gravitational masses. An accurate clock at rest with respect to one observer may be measured to tick at a different rate than a second observer's own equally accurate clock. For example, clocks on the Space Shuttle run slightly slower than reference clocks on Earth.[35]

In the light of this and similar considerations, we should be wise to distinguish between *time-as-we-know-it* in this world, and the dimension of *time that will be appropriate for the eschatological postresurrection mode of existence.* Käsemann and others contend that *body* entails visibility, communication, identification, and recognition. But after the resurrection of the "body" *(sōma),* this will *not* be by *physical* sight or sound or by recognition through the senses, but will be by some *hitherto unspecified counterpart* to what served for these purposes in the present life. Why should the nature of "time" be any different? If God through the Holy Spirit will open up a new future, which as yet is unimaginable, why should this not be through some *unspecified counterpart* of space and *time?*[36]

We need only be assured that the living God will not cast his people into static boredom or monotony, as if we were forever reciting the same well-known hymn or psalm, or repeating well-known phrases of worship. Perhaps this is part of what "a new song" will one day signify. When he expounds the infinite possibilities of what God can and will do at the resurrection, Paul reminds us of the infinite *variety and ingenuity* of God's creation already. Will the future hold anything less than this?

4. The New Jerusalem

The most explicit references to the new Jerusalem occur in Revelation 21:1–22:5, especially 21:1-7, 10, and 22:1-5. But John the seer did not invent this symbol. Moltmann succinctly sums up this point: "John expounds the Ezekiel vision with material from Isaiah, and takes up the apocalyptic ideas

35. Cf. George F. R. Ellis and Ruth M. Williams, *Flat and Curved Space-Times,* 2nd ed. (Oxford: OUP, 2000), 28-29.

36. Cf. David Wilkinson, *Christian Eschatology and the Physical Universe* (London: Continuum and T. & T. Clark, 2010), 121-26 and throughout, and E. M. Conradie, "Resurrection, Finitude, and Ecology," in *Assessments,* ed. Ted Peters (Grand Rapids: Eerdmans, 2012), 277-96.

about the New Jerusalem."[37] The most extensive OT source is Ezekiel 37–48. Ezekiel 48:35 makes the central statement about it: "The LORD is There" (Heb. *y-h-w-h* [Yahweh or Jehovah] *shāmmāh*).

John uses Ezekiel as a source not only for this imagery, although Ezekiel provided more detail about the new Jerusalem than any other book; he uses Ezekiel throughout his apocalypse. Zechariah uses the prophetic image of God as "a wall of fire," in place of material walls, around Jerusalem, when "I will be the glory within it" (Zech. 2:4-5). Isaiah 54:11-12 foresees a Jerusalem whose foundations God will lay with sapphires.

> I will make your pinnacles of rubies,
> > your gates of jewels,
> > and your wall of precious stones.

There "in righteousness you shall be established," and the city will be free "from terror" (54:14).

This vision was in the veins of the Jewish apocalyptic writers. *First Enoch* sees "a house, new and larger and loftier than the former" (90:29). The Dead Sea Scrolls envisage the new city with gates named after the sons of Jacob (4Q554). Although some Jewish sources may postdate the NT, a temple in heaven features in 2 Esdras or 4 Ezra; it also features in *2 Baruch,* which foresees God's new creation of paradise (4:3), while *3 Baruch* mentions the new Jerusalem, in which the temple is no longer necessary (1:3). There are further resonances in Isaiah 49:18; 60–62; and 65:17-25.

In Revelation the three key points are stressed: that God is there; that the city is the symbol for the church as the bride of Christ; and that the city is free from sin and from any fear. In one of his earliest and major epistles, Paul speaks of "the Jerusalem above; she is free, and she is our mother" (Gal. 4:26), in contrast to the earthly, historical, or "present Jerusalem (who) . . . is in slavery" (4:25). Robert H. Gundry argues that the new Jerusalem is symbolic, "stretching out and up to unheard-of dimensions, having gates which each consist of a single pearl," and that "The new Jerusalem *symbolises the saints.* . . . John is not describing the eternal dwelling place of the saints."[38]

Hebrews 12:22 also uses the "new Jerusalem" symbols, contrasting it

37. Jürgen Moltmann, *The Coming of God: Christian Eschatology* (London: SCM, 1996), 313.

38. Robert H. Gundry, "The New Jerusalem: People as Place, Not Place for People," in Gundry, *The Old Is Better: New Testament Essays in Support of Traditional Interpretations,* WUNT 178 (Tübingen: Mohr, 2005), 399 and 400; cf. 399-411.

with the terrifying "blazing fire, and darkness, and gloom" of the Mosaic Law (12:18-21). Christians, by contrast, "have come to Mount Zion and to the city of the living God, the heavenly Jerusalem, and to innumerable angels in festal gathering, and to the assembly of the firstborn who are enrolled in heaven, and to God the judge of all, and to the spirits of the righteous made perfect, and to Jesus, the mediator" (12:22-24). John also speaks of "the city of my God, the new Jerusalem that comes down from my God out of heaven" (Rev. 3:12), and elsewhere, using the same phrase, "the holy city, the new Jerusalem, coming down out of heaven from God, prepared as a bride adorned for her husband" (Rev. 21:2; cf. 21:10).

Before we look in detail at the relevant New Testament passages, one puzzle needs to be resolved. Moltmann argues that from Irenaeus onward, through Augustine and Gregory of Rome until Aquinas, the verdict in historical theology was that the old earthly creation is not destroyed, but undergoes "transformation." With this dominant view he contrasts "Lutheran orthodoxy," in which "annihilation, not transformation, is the ultimate destiny of the world."[39] In his commentary on Revelation, G. K. Beale insists that "John sees 'a new heaven and a new earth'" (Rev. 21:1a) because "the first earth passed away, and the sea was no more" (21:1b). The new creation, Beale argues, "has been established to replace it."[40] This implies annihilation.

Moltmann's solution to this tension is to argue that "the *form* of this world is going to be destroyed . . . the annihilation of godless powers and compulsions of 'this world.'"[41] This is especially poignant in the case of Jerusalem. In one sense it is the place of tragedy: of the rejection, suffering, and crucifixion of Jesus Christ, and the ultimate failure of Israel. Yet it features positively in so many ways. The OT is full of references to it, and it is God's "chosen" city in Deuteronomy. In the NT Paul makes a priority of the collection for the church in Jerusalem, and the church there is the "mother" church until Rome or Antioch emerges as a Gentile Christian center. In the new Jerusalem the tragic and sinful dimension is destroyed; the positive aspects become transformed.

(i) *God Will Dwell with Us.* Among several key themes, it is of first importance that God "will dwell with them" (Rev. 21:3). John writes: "I saw no temple in the city, for its temple is the Lord God the Almighty and the Lamb"

39. Moltmann, *The Coming of God*, 268.
40. G. K. Beale, *The Book of Revelation: A Commentary on the Greek Text*, NIGTC (Grand Rapids: Eerdmans; Carlisle: Paternoster, 1999), 1039.
41. Moltmann, *The Coming of God*, 269 and 270.

(21:22). Similarly, "The city has no need of sun or moon to shine on it, for the glory of God is its light, and its lamp is the Lamb" (21:23). As we observed in relation to Ezekiel: *"The LORD is There"* (Ezek. 48:35). The earthly temple was a symbol of God's presence, but we no longer need a symbol when the reality to which the symbol points is present! (That is one reason why the symbol of the Lord's Supper operates only "until he comes.") Caird observes that the earthly temple was necessarily amidst a polluted environment, but this is no longer applicable in the new Jerusalem.[42] Again, we must repeat a key point: it is not that in some remote heaven we find God; God *is* heaven, just as the new Jerusalem *is* his people. Revelation is also "Trinitarian": God himself is always coupled with the Lamb who was slain for our sin, and the vision of the future is conveyed "in the Spirit." There is no "new Jerusalem" without Calvary.

(ii) *Walls, Streets, Gates.* John gives careful attention to the walls, the streets, and to the twelve gates of the New Jerusalem. They denote *security, glory,* and *splendor:* "It has a great, high wall with twelve gates, and at the gates twelve angels" (Rev. 21:12). As in Ezekiel, the dimensions are measured, and the city is huge. "The city is pure gold, clear as glass" (Rev. 21:18). The twelve foundations are each adorned with a particular jewel (21:19-20). Allusions to Ezekiel 40 and 48 in Revelation 21:10-11 are unmistakable (especially Ezek. 40:5-6 and 48:31-34). Beale comments: "The 'great and high wall' represents the inviolable nature of fellowship with God, as implied by [Rev.] 21:27 and 22:14-15."[43] Similarly, in *2 Enoch* 65:10 the new paradise is guarded by such a wall. The number twelve is prominent, sometimes to represent the twelve tribes of Israel and the twelve apostles, sometimes perhaps as the square root of 144. Pure gold, clear glass, topaz, and amethyst are translated in the same way in the AV/KJV, NRSV, and NJB, but some translations of jewels are different: diamond instead of jasper (NJB); lapis lazuli (NJB) instead of sapphire (AV/KJV, NRSV); turquoise or agate instead of chalcedony; crystal (NJB) instead of emerald (NRSV, AV/KJV); and so on (Rev. 21:19-20). But the general theme of security, glory, and prosperity is clear. The glory of God is symbolized by "jasper and cornelian . . . emerald" in Revelation 4:3.

(iii) *Other Images.* Other complementary images concern *satisfaction, healing, and ever-fresh life.* Revelation 21:6 says, "To the thirsty I will give water as a gift from the spring of the water of life (Gk. *tō dispsānti dōsō ek*

---

42. George B. Caird, *The Revelation of St. John* (London: Black, 1966), 278-79.
43. Beale, *The Book of Revelation,* 1128-29.

tēs pēgēs tou hydatos tēs zōēs)." This may partly reflect "springs of water" in Isaiah 49:10 and "everyone who thirsts" in Isaiah 55:1. This promise to "those who conquer" includes not only the martyrs, but all who have not given in to demands to deny the faith. Furthermore, in Revelation 22:17, "Let everyone who is thirsty come" is offered to the whole redeemed community. As David Aune points out, "water of life" can mean *flowing, running water*, which is *ever-fresh*, in contrast to stale supplies, or "living water" in a more traditional religious sense. In the end there is little real difference.[44]

(iv) *The New Eden*. Revelation 22:1-2 resumes this theme: "The river of the water of life, bright as crystal, [flows] from the throne of God and of the Lamb. . . . On either side of the river is the tree of life . . . and the leaves of the tree are for *the healing of the nations*." Like so many of the visionary statements or promises of Revelation, this imagery also probably draws on several OT passages. "Living waters" flowing from Jerusalem appear in Ezekiel 47:1-9, Zechariah 14:8, and Joel 3:18. In the hot and often dry East, the cooling, life-giving, and refreshing quality of water, especially spring water, is well known. This language is also reminiscent of Eden, from which "a river flows" (Gen. 2:10) and where "the LORD God made to grow every tree that is pleasant to the sight and good for food, the tree of life . . . and the tree of the knowledge of good and evil" (Gen. 2:9). Ezekiel 47:12 says, "There will grow all kinds of trees for food. Their leaves will not wither nor their fruit fail. . . . Their fruit will be for food, and their *leaves for healing*."

(v) *Eden as Paradise*. This passage clearly reflects the new Eden and paradise. "Paradise" is a Persian loanword that came to denote a beautiful garden in Hebrew, Aramaic, Syrian, and Greek. In many ancient cultures it symbolized streams of crystal-clear water, which were full of healing properties, fruitful trees, and multicolored flowers. Peace and well-being replace sickness, and the climate is ideal, with no extremes of heat or cold. The OT writers compare the Garden of Eden with such a description, and Isaiah 58:11 speaks of a "watered garden," while Isaiah 51:3 compares Zion, Eden, and the Lord's garden. Ezekiel, again, compares God's garden, the trees of Eden, and trees of blessing by the waters (Ezek. 31:8-9). In Psalm 1:1-3 the righteous are like "trees planted by streams of water." Fourth Ezra speaks of a paradise of delight in 6:2, 7:36, and 7:123, where there is abundance of healing. It occurs in *2 Enoch* 42:3 and *Psalms of Solomon* 14.

Beale has an extended note on "the world-encompassing nature of the paradisal temple" with reference to Psalm 78:69, to other OT texts, and to

---

44. David E. Aune, *Revelation 17–22*, WBC (Nashville: Nelson, 1998), 1128-29.

Josephus and Philo.[45] Often it refers to a future time when "it would encompass the whole world," and Revelation 22:1-6 "appears to be aware of an earlier interpretation of Eden." The nations, he argues, will be healed because "there will no longer be any curse" (Zech. 14:11). He continues, "Those inhabiting the New Jerusalem will be immune from the destructive curse that God sends on humanity for its sins."[46]

(vi) *The Holiness of God's People.* A further characteristic of the new Jerusalem is that

"He (God) will wipe every tear from their eyes.
Death will be no more;
mourning and crying and pain will be no more." (Rev. 21:4)

"But as for the cowardly, the faithless, the polluted, the murderers, the fornicators, the sorcerers, the idolaters, and all liars, their place will be in the lake that burns with fire and sulfur, which is the second death." (Rev. 21:8)

The exclusion of sin and of habitual sinners implies the abolition of everything hurtful or destructive.

The people of God, represented by the image of new Jerusalem, will be holy. This is entirely compatible with the teaching of Paul about the spiritual body, that is, a mode of existence energized, sustained, and characterized by the Holy Spirit. Just as the qualities noted already of ever-fresh life and healing come from the Holy Spirit, so purity, righteousness, and holiness (and consequently lack of tears, mourning, and death) equally come from the Holy Spirit. When "the nations will walk by its light," that light comes directly from God and the Lamb. Calvary is never left behind; the new Jerusalem lives out its consequences through the Holy Spirit.

(vii) *The Bride of Christ.* Finally, for "The new Jerusalem (comes) down out of heaven from God, *prepared as a bride adorned for her husband*" (Rev. 21:2), Beale alludes to the marital imagery of Isaiah 52 and 62. "Adorned . . . with ornamentation as a bride" comes from Isaiah 62:5, as a metaphor for Israel. Revelation 21:2 looks back to Revelation 19:7-8:

"The marriage of the Lamb has come,
    and his bride has made herself ready;

45. Beale, *The Book of Revelation,* 1110.
46. Beale, *The Book of Revelation,* 1114.

> to her it has been granted to be clothed
>> with fine linen, bright and pure" —
> for the fine linen is the righteous deeds of the saints.

This image of "bride" is found in Hosea 2:5, Isaiah 1:21, Jeremiah 2:2, and Ephesians 5:31-32.

Since the bride is the people of God, this fully confirms the interpretation of Robert Gundry, noted above; "The new Jerusalem symbolises the saints.... We already know from [Rev.] 19:7-8 that the lamb's bride is the saints, arrayed in their righteous acts."[47] Thus "the new Jerusalem is holy.... Sheer happiness characterises the city, a happiness unadulterated by tears, pain or death."[48] Caird also comments, "The woman robed with the sun is the church, and the church members her children."[49] This new creation stands in contrast to the pain, suffering, and distress of persecution and oppression. Caird vividly portrays the situation of the persecuted church: "'If only we knew,' the martyrs have cried, 'where it is all going to end!'; and much of John's vision ... becomes intelligible, credible ... when we know the answer."[50] The "queenly splendour and enticements of Babylon," he concludes, are now "recognised as the seductive gauds of an old and raddled whore."[51] The new Jerusalem puts everything into perspective: God and the Lamb are there: he will dwell with them as their God (Rev. 21:3). The living water, the precious stones, and pure gold that is transparent remind us of the "more wonderful yet," which earthly analogies, for all their limitations, can suggest.

5. From Glory to Glory; the Restoration of All Things

The vision of John the seer is limited in the same way that a two-dimensional picture cannot be expected to indicate events or qualities beyond the world and in motion. John the seer provides a marvelous picture of glory, together with God's presence, holiness, and security. But with the exception of growing trees and flowing rivers, there is little more than a hint of the dynamic, moving-onward character of these images. The nearest nonanalogical or nonmetaphorical aspect is the continuing onward, ever-fresh work of the

47. Gundry, "The New Jerusalem," 400 and 401.
48. Gundry, "The New Jerusalem," 402 and 404.
49. Caird, *The Revelation of St. John,* 234.
50. Caird, *The Revelation of St. John,* 261-62.
51. Caird, *The Revelation of St. John,* 262.

Holy Spirit. This is even clearer in Paul. The raised people of God will be animated and sustained by the Holy Spirit (1 Cor. 15:44).

Rather than speaking simply of *glory,* then, the situation of the redeemed in heaven can perhaps better be described as *"from glory to glory."* The NRSV translates 2 Corinthians 3:18 as: "[We] are being transformed into the same image [of the Lord] from one degree of glory to another; for this comes from the Lord, the Spirit." Clearly this statement from Paul refers to *earthly* pilgrimage and satisfaction, and does *not* apply directly to the postresurrection life of heaven. Initial glory will entail *total* likeness to Christ, and *total* purity and holiness. But the very fact that Paul can speak of degrees of glory suggests the possibility of *ever-increasing glory,* even if initially it involves sinlessness and holiness.

Glory (Heb. *kābōd;* Gk. *doxa*) denotes what is weighty or impressive. In one sense, all glory belongs to God: "My glory I give to no other" (Isa. 42:8). Further, Christ is "the reflection of God's glory" (Heb. 1:3; Gk. *apaugasma tēs doxēs*). The glory of God is seen "in the face of Jesus Christ" (2 Cor. 4:6). As the Gospel of John stresses, what makes God so "impressive" is not only his sovereign majesty, but also his humility in the incarnation and the cross. Barth and Moltmann, with others, emphasize this. As Stauffer commented, "John conceived of Christ's passion as the last and decisive service to the glory of God. . . . Good Friday itself [is] the glorifying of the Son" (John 12:23).[52] This verse reads, "The hour has come for the Son of Man to be glorified." In heaven this glory is seen from the very first.

Nevertheless, in everyday life a person may appear weighty and impressive from the very first, but as subsequent features of the person's character are revealed, "fully impressive" may become "even more impressive." Here philosophical but secular notions of "perfection" may mislead us. God, Christ, and the Holy Spirit may be seen from the first as *perfectly glorious;* but as the inexhaustible God reveals more of his acts and purposes, who can say that we *exhaust our sense of wonder and glory on the basis of what God in Christ has already done?*

If God himself, as we believe, constitutes the focus of adoration and contemplation in heaven, will not the Holy Spirit deepen and expand our appreciation and understanding of his glory? Sometimes people experience anxiety about whether others will recollect all our misdeeds, mistakes, and sins; but shall we not become fully and totally absorbed in contemplating the wonders and glory of God himself and the slain Lamb? Shall we be distracted

52. Ethelbert Stauffer, *New Testament Theology* (London: SCM, 1955), 130.

by the mistakes or failures of those still on earth? Sometimes we are misled by the allusion in Hebrews to a "cloud of witnesses" (Heb. 12:1). But these are witnesses *to Christ,* not to us; they, too, are "looking to Jesus" (12:2), as the whole passage in Hebrews stresses and enjoins. This even appears to cast doubt on the Roman Catholic theology of saints who are preoccupied with helping us. If they are conscious at all (which, before the parousia, some may doubt), would not these "saints," too, be fully absorbed by God and his glory? Would the doings on earth distract them from Christ? In the visionary narrative of Revelation, it is God and the slain Lamb who occupy the center of the stage for the heavenly court, certainly after the parousia, Last Judgment, and resurrection of the dead.

This becomes all the more poignant in the light of *the restoration of all things.* The phrase "the restoration of all things" occurs only in Acts 3:21, which NRSV, NJB, and REB translate "universal restoration" (Gk. *apokataseōs pantōn;* NIV uses the verb "restore," and AV/KJV translates "restitution of all things"). Danker gives "restoration" as the primary meaning of the word.[53] Moltmann calls this "universal salvation," but admits that universalism remains "the most disputed question in Christian eschatology."[54] The RV more cautiously translates "establish," and the Greek verb *apokathistēmi* translates the Hebrew *shûbh,* "to turn or return." Hence the Greek verb can mean reestablish, reinstate, as in the restoring or reestablishment of Israel in the OT. The Persian conquest opened the way for the reestablishment of the southern kingdom, as recounted in Ezra, Haggai, and Zechariah 1–8. Many interpret Acts 3:21 in this light.

Only certain commentators on Acts understand this passage in Moltmann's way. William Neil takes the phrase to refer to Christ's "vindication beyond the cross," and "the ultimate triumph of God's cause," or "the OT Scriptures . . . in pictorial language."[55] C. S. Williams has a similar comment. H. A. W. Meyer takes it to mean "the universal renewal of the world into glory such as preceded the fall," on the basis of Malachi 4:6. It further denotes "the restoration of all moral relations to their original normal condition. . . . The moral corruption of God's people is removed . . . rendering obedience in all points to what the Messiah has . . . spoken."[56] Calvin comments, "Christ by his death has already restored all things . . . but the effect

53. BDAG 112.

54. Moltmann, *The Coming of God,* 237.

55. William Neil, *The Acts of the Apostles,* NCB (London: Oliphants, 1973), 86.

56. H. A. W. Meyer, *Critical and Exegetical Commentary: The Acts of the Apostles,* vol. 1 (Edinburgh: T. & T. Clark, 1877), 115.

of it is not yet fully seen, because that restoration is still in process of completion."[57] C. K. Barrett adopts a view similar to that of Meyer. He writes: "Luke suggests what is restoration of *creation* to the biblical state of Adam in Eden. . . . [It] is clear that he did not think in [Jewish] nationalistic terms."[58] The most emphatic is Emil Brunner. He writes: "The reference [Acts 3:21] is not to the salvation of all men."[59] Several of the Church Fathers refer to both the Greek word and Acts 3:21.[60]

With Acts 3:21 we may compare Colossians 1:20: "Through him (Christ) God was pleased to reconcile to himself all things, whether on earth or in heaven" (Gk. *apokatallaxai ta panta*). Moule comments that *to reconcile* "relates exclusively to persons; the idea of reconciling to God 'everything' — the animate and the inanimate alike is a difficult one. . . . But Colossians includes the 'cosmic' scene."[61] He compares with this verse Ephesians 2:15-16, and especially Romans 8:19-23, where "the creation waits with eager longing for the revealing of the children of God . . . creation itself will be set free from its bondage to decay." A number of commentators, however, interpret Colossians 1:20 differently. One of the clearest of these is F. F. Bruce. Bruce stresses that "ultimate reconciliation" involves peace. This does not imply "that every human being, irrespective of . . . his attitude to God, will at last enjoy celestial bliss." He continues, "When Paul speaks here of reconciliation in the widest scale, he includes in it what we should call *pacification*"; the hostile powers of Colossians 2:15 are not "gladly surrendering to His grace, but *submitting*, against their wills, to a power which they cannot resist."[62] Colossians 1:20 is one of the most difficult verses to interpret. See our open but tentative and inconclusive discussion of it in chapter 5.

If Colossians 1:20 is understood in Bruce's way, it avoids the problem of dualism. We may still conceive of the eternal survival of any part of creation

---

57. John Calvin, *The Acts of the Apostles*, vol. 1 (Edinburgh: St. Andrew's Press, 1965), 103.

58. C. K. Barrett, *The Acts of the Apostles*, 2 vols., ICC (Edinburgh: T. & T. Clark, 1994), 1:206, italics mine.

59. Emil Brunner, *The Christian Doctrine of God: Dogmatics*, vol. 1 (London: Lutterworth, 1949), 352; cf. C. F. D. Moule, *The Epistles to the Colossians and to Philemon*, CGTC (Cambridge: CUP, 1962), 71.

60. Lampe 195.

61. Moule, *Epistles to the Colossians and to Philemon*, 71.

62. F. F. Bruce and E. K. Simpson, *Commentary on the Epistles to the Ephesians and Colossians*, NICNT (Grand Rapids: Eerdmans, 1957), 210, italics mine.

that does not directly participate in salvation. On the other hand, belief in everlasting "punishment" should not be regarded as the *only "orthodox,"* or "biblical," view in Christian theology. Scripture does admittedly speak of "Gehenna," which occurs in the teaching of Jesus at least six times: three in the Sermon on the Mount (Matt. 5:22, 29, 30), and in Matthew 10:28; 23:15, 33. The NRSV translates it as "hell" or "hell of fire." Mark 9:43, 45, 47, and Luke 12:5 offer parallels. Mark adds, "Where their worm never dies, and the fire is never quenched." Cranfield, however, understands this as Mark's own comment on the image of burning rubbish.[63] The reference to "weeping and gnashing of teeth" (Matt. 8:12 and Luke 13:28) arises from the imagery of a parable. But there are other biblical passages that suggest destruction (perhaps Matt. 7:23), and David Powys declares, "Destruction is the most common way of depicting the fate of the unrighteous in the Synoptic Gospels."[64] A third group seems to hint at Paul's cosmic vision in Colossians 1:20 and the early apostolic preaching in Acts 3:21. *In truth, all three views find serious support* in the history of theology, and *none should be lightly or thoughtlessly dismissed.* Each makes a serious and thoughtful point.

(i) *Eternal Torment.* Augustine (354-430) championed the view that the unrepentant and wicked will suffer eternal torment. He wrote, "The soul . . . is tormented. For in that penal and everlasting punishment . . . the soul is justly said to die . . . ; [but] in the last damnation, man does not cease to feel . . . this feeling is painfully penal."[65] Elsewhere Augustine wrote: "This damnation is certain and eternal. . . . Pain perpetually afflicts but never destroys; corruption goes on endlessly."[66] Augustine's approach was endorsed by Aquinas, and in 1215 the Fourth Lateran Council spoke of "perpetual punishment." Among the Reformers, Calvin followed this path on the basis of biblical passages. He spoke of "wailing and gnashing of teeth, inextinguishable fire, (and) the ever-gnawing worm" on the basis of Matthew 8:12, 22:13, and Mark 9:43; and "everlasting destruction" in 2 Thessalonians 1:9.[67] Arminius also followed Calvin. Perhaps the most "ferocious" or outspoken was Thomas Vincent (1634-1678), who wrote, "Hell

63. C. E. B. Cranfield, *The Gospel according to St. Mark,* CGTC (Cambridge: CUP, 1959), 314; cf. Thiselton, *Life after Death,* 145-59.

64. David Powys, *"Hell": A Hard Look at a Hard Question* (Milton Keynes, and Waynesboro, Ga.: Paternoster, 1997), 284.

65. Augustine, *City of God* 13.2; *NPNF,* ser. 1, 2:245.

66. Augustine, *Enchiridion* 23.92; *Confessions and Enchiridion,* ed. Albert Cook Outler, LCC 7 (Philadelphia: Westminster, 1955), 393.

67. Calvin, *Institutes* 3.25.12.

shall burn the wicked eternally. . . . You will be ready to tear yourselves to pieces for madness."[68]

(ii) *"Conditional Immortality."* A second steady stream of thought began historically with Irenaeus. The basic argument is that to become separated from God is to become *separated from life,* and therefore to invite *destruction* or *extinction. Irenaeus* (c. 130–c. 200) asked, "How can man be immortal, who [if] in his mortal nature (he) did not obey his Maker?"[69] If a person is "deprived of God's gift, which is eternal life," he said, such a one cannot attain to "incorruptibility and immortality."[70] Only God is without beginning and without end. This avoids the problem of an eternal dualism, which appears to mark Augustine's view. It is understandable but unfortunate that Irenaeus's view is often called "conditional immortality," since most Christian theologians would prefer to speak of resurrection. But this view has always found a place in Christian theology and deserves respect.

(iii) *Universalism.* In the most comprehensive sense, universalism is especially associated in the patristic period with *Origen* (c. 185–c. 254). Origen understood *apokatastasis* to mean that all creatures, including even the devil, will be saved. Origen's teaching was officially condemned at the Council of Constantinople in 543. Many, however, emphasize the fragmentary character of Origen's writings, and argue that his teaching is not entirely clear. But he wrote, "The Creator Himself was required to restore the one . . . (who) had been corrupted and profaned . . . when all things shall be subdued unto Him (Christ)" (cf. 1 Cor. 15:28).[71] Earlier he wrote: "All things have become subject to Christ . . . in respect of spirits being rational natures. . . . All things which are seen pass away."[72] Elsewhere in *On First Principles,* Origen declared, "When God shall be all in all . . . the process of . . . correction will take place imperceptibly in individual instances. . . . We are to suppose that at the consummation and restoration of all things, those who will make a gradual advance . . . will arrive in due measure at that land."[73] Origen's homilies and commentaries repeat the point.[74] Some patristic specialists insist that Origen did not include the devil in this restoration, even if other Church Fathers

68. Thomas Vincent, *Fire and Brimstone in Hell;* reprinted for Gospel-Truth Forum, on CD, chaps. 1 and 5.

69. Irenaeus, *Against Heresies* 4.39; *ANF* 1:523.

70. Irenaeus, *Against Heresies* 3.19.1; *ANF* 1:448.

71. Origen, *De principiis* 3.5.6; *ANF* 4:343.

72. Origen, *De principiis* 2.3.7; *ANF* 4:275.

73. Origen, *De principiis* 3.6.6 and 9; *ANF* 4:347 and 348.

74. Origen, *Homily on Joshua* 1.16.9 and *Commentary on Romans* 8.9.

attributed this to him.[75] He appeals to God's sovereignty to ordinary and intelligent people, and to selected biblical passages.

Gregory of Nyssa (c. 330-395) also believed in "the restoration of all things" (Acts 3:21), and is only a little less sweeping. He argued, "It is the peculiar effect of light to make darkness vanish, and of life, to destroy death. . . . What is dead [is] restored to life."[76] If the Deity penetrates the universe, "Therefore all things are in him, and he in all things."[77] In *On the Making of Man,* he asserts, "Now the resurrection promises us nothing else than the restoration of the fallen to their ancient state . . . bringing back again to Paradise him who was cast out from it."[78]

Today Jürgen Moltmann is one of the most thoughtful advocates of this view. He carefully notes that the Pietists J. A. Bengel (1687-1752) and F. C. Oetinger (1702-1782) held that ultimately God is "All in all," even if both the Last Judgment and hell are realities. God purposes "to gather up all things in him, things in heaven and things on earth" (Eph. 1:10).[79] He also discusses Emil Brunner's famous accusation that Karl Barth had brought universalism into modern theology.[80] Brunner stresses the two ways of life and death, and the vital importance of preaching decision and responsibility. Yet Moltmann considers that universalism does not contradict judgment. He considers the verdict of Paul Althaus, that God's purpose for unbelievers remains a mystery. We must hold, he says, *to the fear of being lost; and yet even more to* apokatastasis, *and that God "will put everything to rights. . . . We must think both thoughts."*

Moltmann raises the issue that troubles so many ordinary people: "Why did God create human beings if he is going to damn most of them in the end?"[81] He also cites the conclusion of the hymn in Philippians 2:6-11: "every tongue should confess that Jesus Christ is Lord" (2:11), and 1 Corinthians 15:25, "All his enemies [will be] put under his feet."[82] But, like Althaus, he attempts to hold this together with the two ways that lead to life or destruction (Matt. 7:13-14), and the parable of the wise and foolish virgins (Matt.

75. Frederick W. Norris, in John A. McGuckin, *The SCM Press A-Z of Origen* (London: SCM, 2006), 61.

76. Gregory of Nyssa, *Catechism* 24; *NPNF,* ser. 2, 5:494.

77. Gregory of Nyssa, *Catechism* 25; *NPNF,* ser. 2, 5:495.

78. Gregory of Nyssa, *On the Making of Man* 17.2; *NPNF,* ser. 2, 5:407.

79. Moltmann, *The Coming of God,* 238.

80. Brunner, *Christian Doctrine of God,* 352-53.

81. Moltmann, *The Coming of God,* 239.

82. Moltmann, *The Coming of God,* 240.

25:1-13). In the end, however, the argument for Moltmann rests on the "even more" of divine grace; "grace abounded all the more" (Rom. 5:20).[83] It depends on "boundless confidence" in God's grace, and the all-sufficiency of Christ's work. He writes further, "*Christ's descent into hell* means, finally: hell and death have been gathered up and ended in God: 'Death is swallowed up in victory' (1 Cor. 15:54)."[84]

In the end, in several works Moltmann argues that anything less than this would be a defeat for the love of God. With Charles Wesley, he exclaims, "Christ hath burst the gates of hell." Psalm 139:8 declares: "If I make my bed in hell, thou art there"; he adds, "If there are any lost in hell, it would be a tragedy for Christ."[85] In a third book, he stresses that "the righteousness of God" has little or nothing to do with Aristotle's concept of equivalent justice, but expresses his "putting things right, which saves and heals."[86]

Tom Wright also shares a universal *hope,* but in a way that avoids the "double dogmatism . . . both of the person who knows exactly who is and who isn't 'going to hell,' and that of the universalist who is absolutely certain that there is no such place (as hell)."[87] God's love, he urges, is all-conquering and triumphant. It is hard to imagine self-absorption and narcissism choosing ultimately to resist God's love, but God's love invites and calls, without *forcing* consent: *God will be "all in all."*

83. Moltmann, *The Coming of God,* 243.

84. Moltmann, *The Coming of God,* 252.

85. Jürgen Moltmann, *In the End — the Beginning: The Life of Hope* (London: SCM, 2004), 148.

86. Jürgen Moltmann, *Sun of Righteousness, Arise! God's Future for Humanity and the Earth* (London: SCM, 2010), 130.

87. N. T. Wright, *Surprised by Hope: Rethinking Heaven, the Resurrection, and the Mission of the Church* (London: SPCK, 2007), 190.

Bibliography

Abbott-Smith, G. *Manual Greek Lexicon of the New Testament.* Edinburgh: T. & T. Clark, 1937.

Adams, Jim W. *The Performative Nature and Function of Isaiah 40–55.* New York and London: T. & T. Clark, 2006.

Ahn, Yongnan Jeon. *Interpretation of Tongues and Prophecy in 1 Corinthians 12–14.* JPTSS 41. Blandford Forum: Deo, 2013. Pp. 14-39.

Aland, Kurt. *Did the Early Church Baptise Infants?* London: SCM, 1962.

Alter, Robert. *The Art of Biblical Narrative.* New York: Basic Books, 1981.

Anderson, A. H., and W. J. Hollenweger. *Pentecostals after a Century: Global Perspectives.* JPTSS 15. Sheffield: Sheffield Academic, 1999.

Angel, Andrew. *Angels: Ancient Whispers of Another World.* Eugene, Ore.: Wipf and Stock, Cascade Books, 2012.

Anglican–Roman Catholic International Commission. *Agreed Statement.* London: Anglican Consultative Council; Rome: Pontifical Council for Promoting Christian Unity, 1971.

Anscombe, G. E. M. "Hume's Argument Exposed." *Analysis* 34 (1974); reprinted in her *Collected Philosophical Papers,* 3 vols. (Oxford: Blackwell, 1981).

Anselm. "An Address (Proslogion)." In *A Scholastic Miscellany: Anselm to Ockham,* edited by Eugene R. Fairweather, 69-93. LCC. London: SCM; Philadelphia: Westminster, 1956.

———. "An Excerpt from the Author's Reply to the Criticisms of Gaunilo." In *A Scholastic Miscellany: Anselm to Ockham,* edited by Eugene R. Fairweather, 94-96. LCC. London: SCM; Philadelphia: Westminster, 1956.

———. *Why God Became Man.* In *A Scholastic Miscellany: Anselm to Ockham,* edited by Eugene R. Fairweather, 100-183. LCC. London: SCM; Philadelphia: Westminster, 1956.

Apel, Karl-Otto. *Understanding and Explanation: A Transcendental-Pragmatic Perspective.* Cambridge: MIT Press, 1984.

Aquinas, Thomas. *Summa Theologiae.* Edited by Thomas Gilby et al. Blackfriars ed. 60 vols. New York: McGraw-Hill; London: Blackfriars, 1963-1973.

Athanasius. *Epistle to Serapion.* In *The Letters of St. Athanasius concerning the Holy Spirit,* edited and translated by C. R. B. Shapland. London: Epworth, 1951.

———. *St. Athanasius on the Incarnation.* London: Mowbray, 1953.

Attridge, Harold W. *The Epistle to the Hebrews.* Hermeneia. Philadelphia: Fortress, 1989.

Augustine. *City of God.* In *NPNF,* ser. 2, 2:1-511.

———. *Confessions and Enchiridion.* Edited by Albert Cook Outler. LCC 7. Philadelphia: Westminster, 1955.

———. *Confessions: A New Translation by Henry Chadwick.* Oxford: OUP, 1992.

Aulén, Gustaf. *Christus Victor: An Historical Study of the Three Main Types of the Idea of the Atonement.* London: SPCK; New York: Macmillan, 1931.

Aune, David E. *Revelation 17-22.* WBC. Nashville: Nelson, 1998.

Austin, John L. *How to Do Things with Words.* Oxford: Clarendon, 1962.

Avis, Paul. *The Church in the Theology of the Reformers.* London: Marshall, 1981.

———. *God and the Creative Imagination: Metaphor, Symbol, and Myth in Religion and Theology.* New York: Routledge, 1999.

Baillie, Donald M. *God Was in Christ.* London: Faber and Faber, 1948.

Bakhtin, M. *Problems of Dostoevsky's Poetics.* Minneapolis: University of Minnesota Press, 1984.

Balthasar, Hans Urs von. *Theo-Drama: Theological Dramatic Theory.* 5 vols. San Francisco: Ignatius; Edinburgh: T. & T. Clark, 1973-1992.

———. *The Glory of the Lord: A Theological Aesthetics.* Vol. 2. Edinburgh: T. & T. Clark, 1984.

Barbour, Ian G. *Religion and Science: Historical and Contemporary Issues.* London: SCM, 1998.

Barr, James. *The Semantics of Biblical Language.* Oxford: OUP, 1961.

———. *Old and New in Interpretation: A Study of the Two Testaments.* London: SCM, 1966.

Barrett, C. K. *The Holy Spirit and the Gospel Tradition.* London: SPCK, 1958.

———. *The Epistle to the Romans.* London: Black, 1962.

———. *The Signs of an Apostle.* London: Epworth, 1970. Pp. 39-73.

———. *First Epistle to the Corinthians.* 2nd ed. London: Black, 1971.

———. *The Prologue of St. John's Gospel.* London: Athlone, 1971.

———. *The Gospel according to St. John.* 2nd ed. London: SPCK; Louisville: Westminster John Knox, 1978.

———. *The Acts of the Apostles.* 2 vols. ICC. Edinburgh: T. & T. Clark, 1994.

Barth, Karl. *The Resurrection of the Dead.* London: Hodder and Stoughton, 1933.

———. *Church Dogmatics.* 14 vols. Edinburgh: T. & T. Clark, 1957-1975.

———. *Anselm: Fides Quaerens Intellectum.* London: SCM, 1931; Richmond, Va.: John Knox, 1960.

———. *Protestant Theology in the Nineteenth Century.* London: SCM, 1972.

———. *The Holy Spirit and the Christian Life.* Louisville: Westminster John Knox, 1993.

Bauckham, Richard. *Jesus and the Eyewitnesses: The Gospels as Eyewitness Testimony.* Grand Rapids: Eerdmans, 2006.

————. *The Testimony of the Beloved Disciple: Narrative, History, and Theology in the Gospel of John.* Grand Rapids: Baker Academic, 2007.

Bavinck, Herman. *Reformed Dogmatics.* Vol. 3, *Sin and Salvation in Christ.* Grand Rapids: Baker Academic, 2006.

Beale, G. K. *The Book of Revelation: A Commentary on the Greek Text.* NIGTC. Grand Rapids: Eerdmans; Carlisle: Paternoster, 1999.

Beasley-Murray, George R. *John.* WBC. Nashville: Nelson, 1999.

Becker, J. *Jesus of Nazareth.* Berlin: De Gruyter, 1998.

Behm, Johannes. "*Paraklētos.*" In *TDNT* 5:800-814.

Beker, J. Christiaan. *Paul the Apostle: The Triumph of God in Life and Thought.* Edinburgh: T. & T. Clark, 1980.

————. *Paul's Apocalyptic Gospel: The Coming Triumph of God.* Philadelphia: Fortress, 1982.

Benedict XII. *Benedictus Deus* (1336). In *Papal Encyclicals Online* (2008).

Bengel, J. A. *Gnomon Novi Testamenti.* Stuttgart: Steinkopf, 1866.

Bentzen, A. *King and Messiah.* 2nd ed. Oxford: Blackwell, 1970.

Berkouwer, G. C. *Studies in Dogmatics.* Vol. 10, *Sin.* 14 vols. Grand Rapids: Eerdmans, 1971.

Berman, David. *A History of Atheism in Britain from Hobbes to Russell.* London and New York: Routledge, 1990.

Best, Ernest. *The First and Second Epistles to the Thessalonians.* London: Black, 1972.

————. "Paul's Apostolic Authority." *JSNT* 27 (1986): 3-25.

Bicknell, E. J. *The Christian Idea of Sin and Original Sin: In the Light of Modern Knowledge.* London: Longmans Green, 1923.

Bonhoeffer, Dietrich. *Sanctorum Communio: A Theological Study of the Sociology of the Church.* Philadelphia: Fortress, 1998.

Bornkamm, Günther. *Jesus of Nazareth.* Minneapolis: Fortress, 1959.

————. "Faith and Reason in Paul." In *Early Christian Experience,* 29-46. London: SCM, 1968.

————. *Paul.* London: Hodder and Stoughton, 1972.

Briggs, Richard S. *Words in Action: Speech Act Theory and Biblical Interpretation.* Edinburgh and New York: T. & T. Clark, 2001.

Brightman, Edgar. *A Philosophy of Religion.* New York: Skeffington and Prentice-Hall, 1940.

Brown, Alexandra R. *The Cross and Human Transformation: Paul's Apocalyptic Word in 1 Corinthians.* Minneapolis: Fortress, 1995.

————. "Paul and the Parousia." In *The Return of Jesus in Early Christianity,* edited by John T. Carroll, 47-76. Peabody, Mass.: Hendrickson, 2000.

Brown, Raymond E. *The Gospel according to St. John.* 2 vols. London: Chapman; New York: Doubleday, 1966.

————. *Jesus — God and Man.* London: Chapman, 1968.

Bruce, F. F. *The Epistle to the Hebrews.* Grand Rapids: Eerdmans, 1964.

————. *The Book of Acts.* Grand Rapids: Eerdmans, 1965.

Bruce, F. F., and E. K. Simpson. *Commentary on the Epistles to the Ephesians and Colossians.* NICNT. Grand Rapids: Eerdmans, 1957.

Brümmer, Vincent. *The Model of Love: A Study in Philosophical Theology.* Cambridge: CUP, 1993.

Bruner, F. Dale. *A Theology of the Holy Spirit: The Pentecostal Experience and the New Testament Witness.* Grand Rapids: Eerdmans, 1970.

Brunner, Emil. *Man in Revolt: A Christian Anthropology.* London: Lutterworth, 1941; Louisville: Westminster John Knox, 1979.

———. *Revelation and Reason: The Christian Doctrine of Faith and Knowledge.* Philadelphia: Westminster, 1946.

———. *The Christian Doctrine of God: Dogmatics.* Vol. 1. London: Lutterworth, 1949.

Brunner, Emil, in dialogue with Karl Barth. *Natural Theology.* Eugene, Ore.: Wipf and Stock, 2002; orig. 1948.

Büchsel, Friedrich. "*Krinō, krisis, krima.*" In *TDNT* 3:933-54.

Bultmann, Rudolf. *Theology of the New Testament.* Vol. 1. London: SCM, 1952.

———. *Essays Philosophical and Theological.* London: SCM, 1955.

———. *Jesus and the Word.* London and New York: Collins, 1958.

———. *Jesus Christ and Mythology.* London: SCM, 1960.

———. "New Testament Mythology." In *Kerygma and Myth,* vol. 1, edited by H.-W. Bartsch. London: SPCK, 1964.

———. *Faith and Understanding.* London: SCM, 1969.

Bushnell, Horace. *The Vicarious Sacrifice.* New York: Scribner, 1871.

Caird, George B. *Principalities and Powers: A Study in Pauline Theology.* Oxford: Clarendon, 1956.

———. *The Revelation of St. John.* London: Black, 1966.

———. *The Language and Imagery of the Bible.* London: Duckworth, 1980.

Caird, George B., with L. D. Hurst. *New Testament Theology.* Oxford: Clarendon, 1995.

Calvin, John. *Commentaries on the First Book of Moses.* Vol. 1. Edinburgh: Calvin Translation Society, 1847.

———. *The Genevan Confession of Faith* (1536). In *Calvin: Theological Treatises,* edited by J. K. S. Reid. LCC 22. London: SCM, 1954.

———. *The Institutes of the Christian Religion.* 2 vols. London: James Clarke, 1957.

———. *The First Epistle to the Corinthians.* Edinburgh: St. Andrew's Press, 1960.

———. *The Acts of the Apostles.* Vol. 1. Edinburgh: St. Andrew's Press, 1965.

———. *Genesis.* Edinburgh: Banner of Truth Trust, 1965.

Campbell, C. A. *On Selfhood and Godhood.* New York: Macmillan; London: Allen and Unwin, 1957.

Campbell, I. D. *The Doctrine of Sin: In Reformed and Neo-Orthodox Thought.* Fearn, Scotland: Mentor, 1999.

Capps, Donald E. *Pastoral Care and Hermeneutics.* Philadelphia: Fortress, 1984; Eugene, Ore.: Wipf and Stock, 2012.

Carlyle, Thomas. *Sartor Resartus: The Life and Opinions of Herr Teufelsdrockh.* Project Gutenberg e-book, #1051.

Carr, Wesley. *Angels and Principalities: The Background and Meaning and Development of the Pauline Phrase* hai archai kai hai exousiai. SNTSMS 42. Cambridge: CUP, 1981.

Carroll, John T., and Alexandra Brown. *The Return of Jesus in Early Christianity.* Peabody, Mass.: Hendrickson, 2000.

Carson, Donald A. *Showing the Spirit: A Theological Exposition of 1 Corinthians 12–14.* Grand Rapids: Baker, 1987.

Cartledge, Mark J. *Testimony in the Spirit: Rescripting Ordinary Pentecostal Theology.* Farnham, UK, and Burlington, Vt.: Ashgate, 2010.

Casey, Maurice. *The Solution to the "Son of Man" Problem.* New York and London: T. & T. Clark, 2007.

Cave, Sidney. *The Doctrine of the Work of Christ.* London: University of London Press and Hodder and Stoughton, 1937.

Cerfaux, L. *Christ in the Theology of St. Paul.* New York: Herder, 1959.

Chadwick, Henry, ed. *Confessions of Augustine.* Oxford: OUP, 1992.

Chalke, Steve, with Alan Mann. *The Lost Message of Jesus.* Grand Rapids: Zondervan, 2004.

Chalke, Steve, Chris Wright, I. H. Marshall, Joel Green, and others. *The Atonement Debate.* London: London School of Theology; Grand Rapids: Zondervan, 2008.

Chatman, Seymour. *Story and Discourse: Narrative Structure in Fiction and Film.* Ithaca, N.Y.: Cornell University Press, 1978.

Childs, Brevard S. *Myth and Reality in the Old Testament.* 2nd ed. London: SCM, 1962.

———. *Exodus: A Commentary.* London: SCM, 1974.

Choisy, Eugène. "Calvin's Conception of Grace." In *The Doctrine of Grace,* edited by Thomas W. Whitley, 228-34. London, 1932.

Clines, David J. A. "The Image of God." *Tyndale Bulletin* 19 (1968): 53-103.

Clough, David L. *On Animals.* Vol. 1, *Systematic Theology.* London and New York: Bloomsbury, 2012.

Coakley, Sarah. *Powers and Submissions: Philosophy, Spirituality, and Gender.* Cambridge: CUP, 2002.

———. *God, Sexuality, and the Self: An Essay "On the Trinity."* Cambridge: CUP, 2013.

Collins, Anthony. *Discourse in Free Thinking.* London, 1713; also New York: Garland, 1978.

Collins, J. J. *The Sceptre and the Star: The Messiahs of the Dead Sea Scrolls and Other Ancient Literature.* New York: Doubleday, 1995.

Collins, John N. *Diakonia: Re-interpreting the Sources.* Oxford: OUP, 1990.

Congar, Yves. *The Meaning of Tradition.* San Francisco: Ignatius, 1964.

———. *I Believe in the Holy Spirit.* 3 vols. New York: Seabury Press, 1983.

Conradie, E. M. "Resurrection, Finitude, and Ecology." In *Assessments,* edited by Ted Peters, 277-96. Grand Rapids: Eerdmans, 2012.

Copleston, F. *A History of Philosophy.* Vol. 7. London: Burns and Oates, 1968.

Cotter, D. W. *Genesis.* Collegeville, Minn.: Liturgical Press, 2003.

Crafton, Jeffrey A. *The Agency of the Apostle: A Dramatistic Analysis of Paul's Responses to Conflict in 2 Corinthians.* Sheffield: Sheffield Academic, 1991.

Craig, William L. Review of *Eternal God: A Study of God without Time,* by Paul Helm. *JETS* 36 (1993): 254-55.

Cranfield, C. E. B. *The Gospel according to St. Mark.* CGTC. Cambridge: CUP, 1959.

———. *The Epistle to the Romans.* 2 vols. ICC. Edinburgh: T. & T. Clark, 1975, 1979.

Croft, Stephen. *Ministry in Three Dimensions: Ordination and Leadership in the Local Church.* London: DLT, 1999.

Crossan, John Dominic. *The Historical Jesus: The Life of a Mediterranean Jewish Peasant.* San Francisco: HarperCollins; Edinburgh: T. & T. Clark, 1991.

Cullmann, Oscar. *Baptism in the New Testament.* London: SCM, 1950.

———. *Christ and Time: The Primitive Christian Conception of Time and History.* London: SCM, 1951.

———. *Immortality of the Soul or Resurrection of the Dead?* London: Epworth, 1958.

———. *The Christology of the New Testament.* London: SCM, 1963.

———. *The State in the New Testament.* London: SCM, 1963.

Culpepper, R. Alan. "The Pivot of John's Prologue." *NTS* 27 (1980-1981): 1-31.

Dahl, M. E. *The Resurrection of the Body: A Study of I Corinthians 15.* London: SCM, 1962.

Dakin, A. *Calvinism.* London: Duckworth, 1940.

Dalman, Gustaf. *The Words of Jesus.* Edinburgh: T. & T. Clark, 1902.

Daly, Mary. *Beyond God the Father: Toward a Philosophy of Women's Liberation.* Boston: Beacon Press, 1974.

Danby, Herbert, ed. *The Mishnah: Translated from the Hebrew.* Oxford: OUP, 1933.

Davies, Oliver. *The Theology of Compassion: Metaphysics of Difference and the Renewal of Tradition.* London: SCM, 2001.

Deane-Drummond, Celia. *Eco-Theology.* Winona, Minn.: Anselm Academic, 2008.

De Boer, M. C. *The Defeat of Death: Apocalyptic Imagery in 1 Corinthians 15 and Romans 5.* JSNTSup 22. Sheffield: JSOT Press, 1988.

Deissmann, Adolf. *Paul: A Study in Social and Religious History.* London: Hodder and Stoughton, 1912.

———. *Light from the Ancient East.* Rev. ed. London: Hodder and Stoughton, 1927.

Denney, James. *The Atonement and the Modern Mind.* London: Hodder and Stoughton, 1903.

———. *The Death of Christ: Its Place and Interpretation in the New Testament.* London: Hodder and Stoughton, 1922.

Derrida, Jacques. *Margins of Philosophy.* London: Harvester, 1982.

Descartes, René. *Meditations 5* (1641). In *The Philosophical Works of Descartes,* edited by E. S. Haldane and G. R. T. Ross. Cambridge: CUP, 1911.

———. *Discourse on Method.* Cambridge: CUP, 1984-1991.

Dewar, Lindsay. *The Holy Spirit and Modern Thought: An Inquiry into the Historical, Theological, and Psychological Aspects of the Christian Doctrine of the Holy Spirit.* London: Mowbray, 1959.

Dodd, Charles H. *The Epistle of Paul to the Romans.* London: Hodder and Stoughton, 1932.

———. "The Mind of Paul I" (1933) and "The Mind of Paul II" (1934). In Dodd, *New Testament Studies,* 67-127. Manchester: Manchester University Press, 1953.

Dorner, J. A. *System of Doctrine.* Edinburgh: T. & T. Clark, 1881.

Downing, F. G. *Has Christianity a Revelation?* London: SCM, 1964.

Dulles, Avery. *Models of the Church.* Dublin: Gill and Macmillan, 1988.

Dunn, James D. G. *Baptism in the Holy Spirit: A Re-examination of the New Testament Teaching on the Gift of the Spirit in Relation to Pentecostalism Today.* London: SCM, 1970.

————. *Jesus and the Spirit: A Study of the Religious and Charismatic Experience of Jesus and the First Christians.* London: SCM, 1975.

————. *Romans.* 2 vols. WBC. Dallas: Word, 1988.

————. *The Epistles to the Colossians and to Philemon.* NIGTC. Grand Rapids: Eerdmans, 1996.

————. *The Theology of Paul the Apostle.* Edinburgh: T. & T. Clark, 1998.

————. *Jesus Remembered.* Vol. 1 of *Christianity in the Making.* Grand Rapids: Eerdmans, 2003.

Ebeling, Gerhard. *Word of God and Tradition: Historical Studies Interpreting the Divisions of Christianity.* London: Collins, 1968.

Eckstein, H. J. *Der Begriff Syneidēsis bei Paulus.* Tübingen: Mohr, 1983.

Edwards, Jonathan. *A Treatise concerning Religious Affections.* In *Select Works of Jonathan Edwards,* vol. 3. London: Banner of Truth, 1959.

————. *Works of Jonathan Edwards.* Vol. 2. New Haven: Yale University Press, 2009.

Edwards, M. J. *Origen against Plato.* Aldershot, UK, and Burlington, Vt.: Ashgate, 2002.

Eichrodt, Walther. *Theology of the Old Testament.* 2 vols. London: SCM, 1961, 1964.

Ellis, George F. R., and Ruth M. Williams. *Flat and Curved Space-Times.* 2nd ed. Oxford: OUP, 2000.

Epp, Eldon Jay. *Junia: The First Woman Apostle.* Minneapolis: Fortress, 2005.

Eriksson, Anders. *Traditions as Rhetorical Proof: Pauline Argumentation in 1 Corinthians.* ConBNT. Stockholm: Almqvist & Wiksell, 1998.

Evans, Donald D. *The Logic of Self-Involvement.* London: SCM, 1963.

Farkasfalvy, Denis O. *Inspiration and Interpretation: A Theological Introduction to Sacred Scripture.* Washington, D.C.: Catholic University of America Press, 2010.

Farrer, Austin. *Love Almighty and Ills Unlimited.* New York: Doubleday; London: Collins, 1962.

Fee, Gordon. *The First Epistle to the Corinthians.* NICNT. Grand Rapids: Eerdmans, 1987.

————. *God's Empowering Presence: The Holy Spirit in the Letters of Paul.* Peabody, Mass.: Hendrickson, 1994; Milton Keynes: Paternoster, 1995.

Feuerbach, Ludwig. *The Essence of Christianity.* New York: Harper, 1957.

————. *Thoughts on Death and Immortality: From the Papers of a Thinker.* Berkeley: University of California Press, 1980.

Fiddes, Paul S. *Participating in God: A Pastoral Doctrine of the Trinity.* Louisville: Westminster John Knox, 2000.

Filson, Floyd V. *The New Testament against Its Environment: The Gospel of Christ, the Risen Lord.* London: SCM, 1950.

Fison, Joseph E. *The Blessing of the Holy Spirit.* London and New York: Longman, Green, 1950.

Fitzmyer, Joseph A. *Romans.* AB 33. New York: Doubleday, 1992.

————, ed. *The Biblical Commission's Document "The Interpretation of the Bible in the Church."* Rome: Pontifical Biblical Institute, 1995.

Flannery, Austin P., ed. *Documents of Vatican II.* Grand Rapids: Eerdmans, 1975.

Foerster, Werner, and Georg Fohrer. "*Sōzō, sōtēria, sōtēr.*" In *TDNT* 7:965-1024.

Forbes, Christopher. *Prophecy and Inspired Speech in Early Christianity and Its Hellenistic Environment.* WUNT, ser. 2, 75. Tübingen: Mohr, 1995.

Fowler, Robert. *Loaves and Fishes: The Function of the Feeding Stories in the Gospel of Mark.* Chico, Calif.: Scholars Press, 1975.

Fox, George. *The Journal of George Fox.* New York: Cosimo, 2007; orig. Leeds: Pickard, 1836.

France, Richard T. *The Gospel of Mark: A Commentary on the Greek Text.* NIGTC. Grand Rapids: Eerdmans, 2002.

Franks, Robert S. *The Work of Christ: A Historical Study of Christian Doctrine.* London and New York: Nelson, 1962.

Freud, Sigmund. "An Autobiographical Study." In *Complete Psychological Works of Sigmund Freud,* edited by James Strachey. 1959. Reprint, London and Toronto: Hogarth Press, 1989.

———. *The Future of an Illusion.* New York: Norton, 1961.

———. *Totem and Taboo: Points of Agreement in Mental Life between Savages and Neurotics.* London and New York: Routledge, 2004; orig. 1913.

Fuchs, Ernst. *Studies of the Historical Jesus.* London: SCM, 1964.

Funk, R. W. "The Apostolic Parousia: Form and Significance." In *Christian History and Interpretation: Studies Presented to John Knox,* edited by W. R. Farmer, C. F. D. Moule, and R. R. Niebuhr, 249-68. Cambridge: CUP, 1967.

Gadamer, Hans-Georg. *Truth and Method.* 2nd ed. London: Sheed and Ward, 1989.

Gardner, Paul D. *The Gifts of God.* Lanham, Md.: University Press of America, 1994.

Gay, Volney P. *Reading Freud: Psychology, Neurosis, and Religion.* Chico, Calif.: Scholars Press, 1983.

Genette, Gérard. *Narrative and Discourse: An Essay in Method.* Ithaca, N.Y.: Cornell University Press, 1980.

Gerkin, Charles V. *The Living Human Document: Re-visioning Pastoral Counseling in a Hermeneutical Mode.* Nashville: Abingdon, 1984.

Gerrish, B. A. *A Prince of the Church: Schleiermacher and the Beginning of Modern Theology.* London: SCM, 1984.

Gillespie, Thomas W. *The First Theologians: A Study in Early Christian Prophecy.* Grand Rapids: Eerdmans, 1994.

Goldingay, John. "Poetry and Theology in Isaiah 56–66." In *Horizons in Hermeneutics: A Festschrift in Honor of A. C. Thiselton,* edited by S. E. Porter and M. R. Malcolm, 15-31. Grand Rapids: Eerdmans, 2013.

Gollwitzer, Helmut. *The Existence of God as Confessed by Faith.* London: SCM, 1965.

Gooch, P. W. " 'Conscience' in 1 Cor. 8 and 10." *NTS* 33 (1987): 244-54.

Grant, Robert M. *Greek Apologists of the Second Century.* London: SCM, 1988.

Grayston, Kenneth. "Paraclete." *JSNT* 13 (1981): 67-82.

Greenslade, S. L., ed. *Early Latin Theology.* LCC. London: SCM, 1956.

Grenz, Stanley J. *The Social God and the Relational Self: A Trinitarian Theology of the Imago Dei.* Louisville: Westminster John Knox, 2001.

Grudem, Wayne. *Systematic Theology: An Introduction to Biblical Doctrine.* Nottingham: IVP, 1994.

Gundry, Robert H. "The New Jerusalem: People as Place, Not Place for People." In Gundry, *The Old Is Better: New Testament Essays in Support of Traditional Interpretations,* 399-411. WUNT 178. Tübingen: Mohr, 2005.

Bibliography

Gunton, Colin E. *The Actuality of Atonement: A Study in Metaphor, Rationality, and the Christian Tradition.* Edinburgh: T. & T. Clark, 1988.

Habermas, Jürgen. *Knowledge and Human Interests.* London: Heinemann, 1978.

———. *The Theory of Communicative Action.* 2 vols. Cambridge: Polity Press, 1984, 1987.

Hamilton, Neil Q. *The Holy Spirit and Eschatology in Paul.* SJT Occasional Papers 6. Edinburgh: Oliver and Boyd, 1957.

Hanson, Anthony. *The Pioneer Ministry.* London: SCM, 1961.

———. *Church, Sacraments, and Ministry.* London: Mowbray, 1975.

Hardy, Edward R., ed. *Christology of the Latin Fathers.* LCC. Philadelphia: Westminster, 1964.

Harnack, Adolf von. *What Is Christianity?* London: Benn, 1958.

Harrington, D. J. "Paul and Collaborative Ministry." *New Theological Review* 3 (1990): 62-71.

Harris, Murray. *The Second Epistle to the Corinthians.* NIGTC. Grand Rapids: Eerdmans, 2005.

Haykin, Michael A. G. *The Spirit of God: The Exegesis of 1 and 2 Corinthians in the Pneumatomachian Controversy of the Fourth Century.* Leiden: Brill, 1994.

Hays, Richard B. *First Corinthians.* Louisville: John Knox, 1997.

Hegel, Georg W. F. *Lectures on the Philosophy of Religion.* 3 vols. London: Kegan Paul, Trench and Trübner, 1895.

Heine, R. E. *The Montanist Oracles and Testimonies.* Macon, Ga.: Mercer University Press, 1989.

Helm, Paul. *Eternal God: A Study of God without Time.* Oxford: Clarendon, 1988; 2nd ed. 2011.

Hendrikson, W. *More Than Conquerors: An Interpretation of the Book of Revelation.* Grand Rapids: Baker; London: Tyndale Press, 1962.

Hengel, Martin. *The Cross of the Son of God.* London: SCM, 1986.

Hermelink, Heinrich. "Grace in the Theology of the Reformers." In *The Doctrine of Grace,* edited by William Thomas Whitley, 176-227. Edinburgh and London: Oliver and Boyd, 1948.

Hick, John. *Evil and the God of Love.* London: Macmillan, 1966; 2nd ed. 1977.

———, ed. *The Myth of God Incarnate.* London: SCM, 1977.

Hill, David. *Greek Words and Hebrew Meanings.* Cambridge: CUP, 1967.

———. *New Testament Prophecy.* London: Marshall, 1979.

Hodge, Charles. *Systematic Theology.* 3 vols. New York: Scribner, 1871.

Holland, Tom. *Contours of Pauline Theology: A Radical New Survey of the Influences on Paul's Biblical Writings.* Fearn, Scotland: Mentor, 2004.

Holleman, Joost. *Resurrection and Parousia: A Traditio-Historical Study of Paul's Eschatology in 1 Corinthians 15.* NovTSupp 84. Leiden: Brill, 1996.

Holmberg, Bengt. *Paul and Power: The Structure of Authority in the Primitive Church.* ConBNT 11. Lund: Gleerup, 1978.

Holmes, Stephen R. *Baptist Theology.* London: T. & T. Clark, 2012.

Hooker, Morna. *The Son of Man in Mark.* London: SPCK, 1967.

Hooker, Richard. *Hooker's Works.* Edited by J. Keble. 7th ed. 3 vols. Oxford: Clarendon, 1885.

Howard-Snyder, Daniel, and John O'Leary-Hawthorne. "Transworld Sanctity and Plantinga's Free Will Defense." *International Journal for Philosophy of Religion* 44 (1998): 1-28.

Hull, J. H. E. *The Holy Spirit in the Acts of the Apostles.* London: Lutterworth, 1967.

Hume, David. *Dialogue concerning Natural Religion.* New York: Harper, 1948; orig. 1779.

———. *A Treatise of Human Nature.* Oxford: OUP, 1978; orig. 1739.

Hunter, A. M. *Paul and His Predecessors.* 2nd ed. London: SCM, 1961.

Hurtado, Larry W. *Lord Jesus Christ: Devotion to Jesus in Earliest Christianity.* Grand Rapids: Eerdmans, 2003.

Iser, Wolfgang. *The Act of Reading: A Theory of Aesthetic Response.* Baltimore: Johns Hopkins University Press, 1978, 1980.

Jacob, Edmond. *Theology of the Old Testament.* London: Hodder and Stoughton, 1958.

Jauss, H. R. *Towards an Aesthetics of Reception.* Minneapolis: University of Minnesota Press, 1982.

Jeeves, Malcolm, ed. *The Emergence of Personhood: A Quantum Leap.* Grand Rapids: Eerdmans, 2014.

Jenson, Robert W. *Systematic Theology.* 2 vols. Oxford: OUP, 1997-1999.

———. "The Church and the Sacraments." In *Cambridge Companion to Christian Doctrine,* edited by Colin Gunton. Cambridge: CUP, 1997.

Jeremias, Joachim. *Infant Baptism in the First Four Centuries.* London: SCM, 1960.

———. *The Origins of Infant Baptism: A Further Study in Reply to Kurt Aland.* London: SCM, 1963.

———. *The Parables of Jesus.* London: SCM, 1963.

———. *The Central Message of the New Testament.* London: SCM, 1965.

———. *The Eucharistic Words of Jesus.* London: SCM, 1966.

———. *New Testament Theology.* London: SCM, 1971.

Jewett, Robert. *Paul's Anthropological Terms: A Study of Their Use in Conflict Settings.* Leiden: Brill, 1971.

Jones, O. R. *The Concept of Holiness.* London: Allen and Unwin, 1961.

Jüngel, Eberhard. *God as the Mystery of the World.* Edinburgh: T. & T. Clark, 1983.

———. *Theological Essays.* 2 vols. Edinburgh: T. & T. Clark, 1989.

Kant, Immanuel. *Critique of Pure Reason.* 2nd ed. 1787. London: Macmillan, 1933.

Kärkkäinen, Veli-Matti. *Spiritus Ubi Vult Spirat: Pneumatology in Roman Catholic–Pentecostal Dialogue (1972-1989).* Helsinki: Luther Agricola Society, 1998.

Käsemann, Ernst. "Ministry and Community in the New Testament." In *Essays on New Testament Themes,* 217-35. London: SCM, 1969.

———. *New Testament Questions of Today.* London: SCM, 1969.

———. "Primitive Christian Apocalyptic." In Käsemann, *New Testament Questions of Today,* 108-37. London: SCM, 1969.

———. "The Cry for Liberty in the Church's Worship." In Käsemann, *Perspectives on Paul.* London: SCM, 1973.

———. *Commentary on Romans.* London: SCM, 1980.

Kasper, Walter. *The God of Jesus Christ.* New York: Crossroad, 1991; orig. 1982.

Keener, Craig S. *Miracles: The Credibility of the New Testament Accounts.* 2 vols. Grand Rapids: Baker Academic, 2011.

Kelly, J. N. D. *The Epistles of Peter and Jude.* London: Black, 1969.

―――. *Early Christian Doctrines.* 3rd ed. London: Black, 1977.

Kierkegaard, S. *Concluding Unscientific Postscript to the Philosophical Fragments.* Princeton: Princeton University Press, 1941.

Kilby, Karen. *Karl Rahner: Theology and Philosophy.* London: Routledge, 2004.

Knight, G. A. F. *A Biblical Approach to the Doctrine of the Trinity.* Edinburgh: Oliver and Boyd, 1953.

Koch, K. *"Chāṭā'."* In *TDOT* 4:309-19.

―――. *The Rediscovery of Apocalyptic: A Polemical Work on a Neglected Area of Biblical Studies and Its Damaging Effects on Theology and Philosophy.* London: SCM, 1972.

Kort, Wesley A. *Story, Text, and Scripture: Literary Interests in Biblical Narrative.* University Park: Pennsylvania State University Press, 1988.

Kovacs, Judith, and Christopher Rowland. *Revelation.* Oxford: Blackwell, 2004.

Kramer, Werner. *Christ, Lord, and Son of God.* London: SCM, 1966.

Küng, Hans. *Justification: The Doctrine of Karl Barth and a Catholic Reflection.* London: Burns and Oates; New York: Nelson, 1964.

―――. *Does God Exist? An Answer for Today.* New York and London: Collins, 1980.

―――. *The Incarnation of God: An Introduction to Hegel's Thought.* Edinburgh: T. & T. Clark, 1987.

―――. *Credo: The Apostles' Creed Explained for Today.* London: SCM, 1993.

Künneth, Walter. *The Theology of the Resurrection.* London: SCM, 1965.

Kuschel, Karl-Josef. *Born before All Time? The Dispute over Christ's Origin.* London: SCM, 1992.

Kuyper, Abraham. *The Work of the Holy Spirit.* New York and London: Funk and Wagnalls, 1900.

Ladd, G. E. *A Theology of the New Testament.* Grand Rapids: Eerdmans, 1974; rev. 1993.

Lake, Kirsopp. *The Apostolic Fathers.* Vol. 1. 2 vols. London: Heinemann; Cambridge: Harvard University Press, 1965.

Lampe, Geoffrey W. H. *The Seal of the Spirit: A Study in the Doctrine of Baptism and Confirmation in the New Testament and the Fathers.* London and New York: Longmans, Green, 1951.

―――. "The Holy Spirit in the Writings of St. Luke." In *Studies in the Gospels: In Memory of R. H. Lightfoot,* edited by D. E. Nineham. Oxford: Blackwell, 1967.

―――. *God as Spirit.* Oxford: Clarendon, 1977.

Lane, William L. *Hebrews 1–8.* WBC 47A. Dallas: Word, 1991.

Lee, E. K. *The Religious Thought of St. John.* London: SPCK, 1950.

Leenhardt, Franz J. "This Is My Body." In Oscar Cullmann and F. J. Leenhardt, *Essays on the Lord's Supper.* London: Lutterworth, 1958.

―――. *The Epistle to the Romans.* London: Lutterworth, 1961.

Leibniz, Gottfried W. *Theodicy: Essays on the Goodness of God, the Freedom of Man, and the Origin of Evil.* London: Routledge, Kegan Paul, 1952.

Leithart, Peter J. *Athanasius.* Grand Rapids: Baker Academic, 2011.

Lessing, G. E. "On the Proof of the Spirit and of Power." In *Lessing's Theological Writings,* edited by Henry Chadwick. Stanford: Stanford University Press, 1956.

Levison, John R. *The Spirit in First-Century Judaism.* Boston and Leiden: Brill, 2002.

Lietzmann, Hans. *Mass and Lord's Supper: A Study in the History of Liturgy.* With further enquiry by R. D. Richardson. Leiden: Brill, 1979.

Lindsey, Hal. *The Late Great Planet Earth*. Grand Rapids: Zondervan, 1970.
Linzey, Andrew. *Animal Theology*. Urbana and Chicago: University of Illinois Press, 1995.
———. *Animal Gospel*. Louisville: Westminster John Knox, 1998.
Livingstone, David N. *Darwin's Forgotten Defenders: The Encounter between Evangelical Theology and Evolutionary Thought*. Grand Rapids: Eerdmans, 1987.
Lochman, Jan Milič. *The Faith We Confess: An Ecumenical Dogmatics*. Edinburgh: T. & T. Clark, 1985.
Lossky, Vladimir. *In the Image and Likeness of God*. London and Oxford: Mowbray, 1974.
———. *The Mystical Theology of the Eastern Church*. New York: St. Vladimir's Seminary Press, 1976; Cambridge: Clarke, 1991.
Lovatt, Mark F. W. *Confronting the Will-to-Power: A Reconciliation of the Theology of Reinhold Niebuhr*. Carlisle: Paternoster, 2001; Eugene, Ore.: Wipf and Stock, 2006.
Lovejoy, Arthur. *The Great Chain of Being: A Study of the History of an Idea*. Cambridge: Harvard University Press, 1936.
Lowe, John. "An Examination of Attempts to Detect Developments in St. Paul's Theology." *JTS* 42 (1941): 129-42.
Luther, Martin, *On the Babylonian Captivity of the Church*. In *Luther's Primary Works*, edited by Henry Wace and Carl Buchheim. London: Murray, 1883; London: Hodder, 1896.
———. *The Large Catechism*. St. Louis: Concordia, 1921. Especially section "Of the Creed."
———. *On the Bondage of the Will*. London: James Clarke, 1957.
———. *Against the Heavenly Prophets*. In *Luther's Works*. St. Louis: Concordia, 1958.
———. *Disputation against Scholastic Theology*. In *Luther: Early Theological Works*, edited by James Atkinson, 266-73. LCC 16. London: SCM, 1962.
———. *Luther: Early Theological Works*. Edited by James Atkinson. LCC 16. London: SCM; Philadelphia: Westminster, 1962.
———. *Letters of Spiritual Counsel*. Edited by Theodore G. Tappert. LCC 18. London: SCM, 1965.
———. *Luther: Sermons of Martin Luther*. St. Louis: Concordia, 1983.
———. *Preface to the Letter of St. Paul to the Romans*. Christian Classics Ethereal Library, online.
Luz, Ulrich. *Matthew 1–7: A Commentary*. Edinburgh: T. & T. Clark, 1990.
Macchia, Frank D. "Groans Too Deep for Words." *Asian Journal of Pentecostal Studies* 1 (1998): 149-73.
———. *Baptized in the Spirit: A Global Pentecostal Theology*. Grand Rapids: Zondervan, 2006.
Machen, J. Gresham. *The Virgin Birth of Christ*. London: Clarke, 1930, 1958.
Mackie, J. L. *The Miracle of Theism: Arguments for and against the Existence of God*. Oxford: Clarendon, 1982.
Mackintosh, H. R. *The Doctrine of the Person of Christ*. Edinburgh: T. & T. Clark, 1913.
Macquarrie, John. *In Search of Humanity: A Theological and Philosophical Approach*. London: SCM, 1982.

Bibliography

————. *Jesus Christ in Modern Thought.* London: SCM, 1990.

Malcolm, Norman. "Anselm's Ontological Arguments." *Philosophical Review* 69 (1960): 41-62.

Manson, T. W. *The Teaching of Jesus: Studies of Its Form and Content.* 2nd ed. Cambridge: CUP, 1935.

————. *On Paul and John: Some Selected Theological Themes.* 1963. Reprint, London: SCM, 2012.

Marcel, Pierre-Charles. *The Biblical Doctrine of Infant Baptism: Sacrament of the Covenant of Grace.* London: Clarke, 1953, 2002.

Marshall, I. Howard. *Last Supper and Lord's Supper.* Grand Rapids: Eerdmans, 1980.

Marshall, Paul. *Thine Is the Kingdom.* London: Marshall, Morgan and Scott, 1984.

Martin, Dale B. *Slavery as Salvation: The Metaphor of Slavery in Pauline Christianity.* New Haven: Yale University Press, 1990.

Martin, James P. *The Last Judgement in Protestant Theology from Orthodoxy to Ritschl.* Edinburgh: Oliver and Boyd, 1963.

Martyn, J. Louis. "Epistemology at the Turn of the Ages." In *Christian History and Interpretation: Studies Presented to John Knox,* edited by W. R. Farmer, C. F. D. Moule, and R. R. Niebuhr. Cambridge: CUP, 1967.

Marx, Karl. *Economic and Philosophical Manuscripts.* Moscow: Progress Publisher, 1959; orig. 1832.

————. *Critique of Hegel's Philosophy of the Right.* Cambridge: CUP, 1970; orig. 1843.

————. "Eleventh Thesis on Feuerbach" (1845). In *Marx: Early Writings.* London: Pelican, 1975.

Marx, Karl, and Friedrich Engels. *Communist Manifesto.* London: Pluto Press, 2008.

Marxsen, Willi. *The Resurrection of Jesus of Nazareth.* Philadelphia: Fortress, 1970.

McDonald, H. D. *Ideas of Revelation, 1700-1860.* New York and London: Macmillan, 1959.

————. *Theories of Revelation, 1860-1960.* London: Allen and Unwin, 1963.

McFarland, Ian A., David A. S. Fergusson, Karen Kilby, and Iain E. Torrance, eds. *The Cambridge Dictionary of Christian Theology.* Cambridge: CUP, 2011.

McGinn, Bernard. *Antichrist: Two Thousand Years of Human Fascination with Evil.* San Francisco: Harper, 1994.

McGrath, Alister E. *The Making of Modern German Christology, 1750-1990.* Oxford: Blackwell, 1986.

McGuckin, John A. *The SCM Press A-Z of Origen.* London: SCM, 2006.

McLaughlin, Ryan Patrick. *Christian Theology and the Status of Animals: The Dominant Tradition and Its Alternatives.* New York: Macmillan/Palgrave, 2014.

Meister, Chad. *Introducing Philosophy of Religion.* New York and London: Routledge, 2009.

Melanchthon, Philipp. *Loci Communes Rerum Theologicarum.* In *Melanchthon and Bucer,* edited by Wilhelm Pauck. London: SCM; Philadelphia: Westminster, 1969.

Metzger, Bruce M. *A Textual Commentary on the Greek New Testament.* 2nd ed. New York: United Bible Societies, 1994.

Meyer, H. A. W. *Critical and Exegetical Commentary: The Acts of the Apostles.* Vol. 1. Edinburgh: T. & T. Clark, 1877.

Mill, John Stuart. *Three Essays on Religion.* London: Longman Green, 1875.

Mir, Jeong Kii. *Sin and Politics: Issues in Reformed Theology.* New York: Peter Lang, 2009.

Miranda, José P. *Marx and the Bible: A Critique of the Philosophy of Oppression.* London: SCM, 1977.

Mitton, C. Leslie. *Ephesians.* NCB. London: Oliphants, 1976.

Moberly, R. W. L. *Old Testament Theology.* Grand Rapids: Baker Academic, 2013.

Moffatt, James. *Love in the New Testament.* London: Hodder and Stoughton, 1929; New York: Richard Smith, 1930.

———. *The First Epistle to the Corinthians.* London: Hodder and Stoughton, 1938.

Moltmann, Jürgen. *Theology of Hope.* London: SCM, 1967.

———. *The Crucified God: The Cross as the Foundation and Criticism of Christian Theology.* London: SCM, 1974.

———. *The Church in the Power of the Spirit.* London: SCM; Philadelphia: Fortress, 1977.

———. *The Trinity and the Kingdom of God: The Doctrine of God.* London: SCM, 1981.

———. *God in Creation: A New Theology of Creation and the Spirit of God.* London: SCM, 1985.

———. *The Way of Jesus Christ: Christology in Messianic Dimensions.* London: SCM, 1990.

———. *History and the Triune God: Contributions to Trinitarian Theology.* London: SCM, 1991.

———. "My Theological Career." In *History and the Triune God: Contributions to Trinitarian Theology.* London: SCM, 1991.

———. *The Spirit of Life: A Universal Affirmation.* London: SCM, 1992.

———. *The Coming of God: Christian Eschatology.* London: SCM, 1996.

———. *Experiences in Theology: Ways and Forms of Christian Theology.* London: SCM, 2000.

———. *In the End — the Beginning: The Life of Hope.* London: SCM, 2004.

———. *A Broad Place: An Autobiography.* London: SCM, 2007.

———. *Sun of Righteousness, Arise! God's Future for Humanity and the Earth.* London: SCM, 2010.

Montague, George. *The Holy Spirit: The Growth of Biblical Tradition.* Eugene, Ore.: Wipf and Stock, 1976.

Montefiore, Hugh W. *A Commentary on the Epistle to the Hebrews.* London: Black, 1964.

Moore, Arthur L. *The Parousia in the New Testament.* NovTSupp 13. Leiden: Brill, 1966.

———. *1 and 2 Thessalonians.* NCB. London: Nelson, 1969.

Morris, Leon. *The Apostolic Preaching of the Cross.* 3rd ed. Grand Rapids: Eerdmans, 1965.

———. *Glory in the Cross: A Study in Atonement.* London: Hodder and Stoughton, 1966.

———. *The Cross in the New Testament.* Exeter: Paternoster; Grand Rapids: Eerdmans, 1969.

Moule, C. F. D. "Judgement Theme in the Sacraments." In *The Background to the New Testament and Its Eschatology: In Honour of C. H. Dodd,* edited by W. D. Davies and David Daube, 464-81. Cambridge: CUP, 1956.

———. *The Epistles to the Colossians and to Philemon.* CGTC. Cambridge: CUP, 1962.

Bibliography

Mounce, Robert H. *The Book of Revelation*. Grand Rapids: Eerdmans, 1977.
Mounce, William D. *Pastoral Epistles*. WBC 46. Nashville: Nelson, 2000.
Mouw, Richard. *Politics and the Biblical Drama*. Grand Rapids: Baker, 1983.
Moxon, Reginald S. *The Doctrine of Sin*. London: Allen and Unwin, 1922.
Mozley, J. K. *The Doctrine of the Atonement*. London: Duckworth, 1915.
Müller, Ulrich B. *Prophetie und Predigt im Neuen Testament*. Gütersloh: Mohr, 1975.
Murphy-O'Connor, Jerome. *Becoming Human Together: The Pastoral Anthropology of St. Paul*. Wilmington, Del.: Glazier, 1984.
Nairne, Alexander. *The Epistle of Priesthood: Studies in the Epistle to the Hebrews*. Edinburgh: T. & T. Clark, 1913.
Neil, William. *The Acts of the Apostles*. NCB. London: Oliphants, 1973.
Neufeld, Dieter. *Re-conceiving Texts as Speech-Acts: An Analysis of 1 John*. Leiden: Brill, 1994.
Newman, John Henry. *Apologia pro Vita Sua*. Boston: Houghton Mifflin, 1956; orig. 1864.
———. *An Essay on the Development of Doctrine*. London: Penguin, 1974.
Nichols, Aidan. *Yves Congar*. London: Chapman, 1989.
Niebuhr, Reinhold. *Moral Man and Immoral Society*. New York: Scribner, 1932; London: SCM, 1963.
———. *The Nature and Destiny of Man: A Christian Interpretation*. 2 vols. London: Nisbet, 1941.
Nietzsche, Friedrich. *The Complete Works of Friedrich Nietzsche*. 18 vols. London: Allen and Unwin, 1909-1913.
———. "On Truth and Lie." In *The Portable Nietzsche*, edited by W. Kaufmann. New York: Viking, 1968; orig. 1954.
———. *The Gay Science*. London: Vintage, 1974.
Nygren, Anders. *Commentary on Romans*. London: SCM, 1952.
———. *Agape and Eros*. London: SPCK, 1957.
O'Brien, Peter T. *Colossians, Philemon*. WBC. Nashville: Nelson, 1982.
O'Donovan, Oliver. *Resurrection and Moral Order: An Outline for Evangelical Ethics*. Grand Rapids: Eerdmans; Leicester: IVP, 1986.
———. *The Desire of Nations: Rediscovering the Roots of Political Theology*. Cambridge: CUP, 1996.
———. *The Ways of Judgment*. Grand Rapids: Eerdmans, 2005.
Oepke, A. "*Mesitēs, mesiteuō.*" In *TDNT* 4:598-624.
Ollrog, Wolf-Henning. *Paulus und seine Mitarbeiter*. Neukirchen-Vlvyn: Neukirchen, 1979.
Orr, James. *Revelation and Inspiration*. London: Duckworth, 1910.
Ortkemper, F. J. *1 Korintherbrief*. Stuttgart: Verlag Katholisches Bibelwerk, 1993.
Owen, John. *The Holy Spirit*. Grand Rapids: Kregel, 1954.
———. *The Holy Spirit: Longer Version*. Rio, Wis.: Ages Software, 2004.
Paley, William. *Natural Theology; or, Evidences of the Existence and Attributes of the Deity*. London: Rivington, 1802.
Pannenberg, Wolfhart. "The Revelation of God in Jesus of Nazareth." In *New Frontiers in Theology*, vol. 3, *Theology as History*, edited by James M. Robinson and John B. Cobb, 101-33. New York: Harper and Row, 1967.

————. *Jesus — God and Man.* London: SCM, 1968.

————. *Basic Questions in Theology.* 3 vols. London: SCM, 1970, 1971, 1973.

————. *Theology and the Philosophy of Science.* Philadelphia: Westminster, 1976.

————. *Anthropology in Theological Perspective.* London and New York: T. & T. Clark, 1985.

————. *Systematic Theology.* 3 vols. Edinburgh: T. & T. Clark; Grand Rapids: Eerdmans, 1991, 1994, 1998.

Peirce, C. A. *Conscience in the New Testament.* London: SCM, 1955. See p. 22; cf. 13-22 and 111-30.

Perrin, Norman. *Jesus and the Language of the Kingdom: Symbol and Metaphor in New Testament Interpretation.* Philadelphia: Fortress; London: SCM, 1976.

Plantinga, Alvin. "Free Will Defence." In *Philosophy in America,* edited by Max Black. Ithaca, N.Y.: Cornell University Press; London: Allen and Unwin, 1965.

————. *The Ontological Argument.* New York: Doubleday, 1965.

————. *God and Other Minds: A Study of the Rational Justification of Belief in God.* Ithaca, N.Y.: Cornell University Press, 1967, 1991.

————. *The Nature of Necessity.* Oxford: Clarendon, 1974.

————. *God, Freedom, and Evil.* Grand Rapids: Eerdmans, 1977.

Plaskow, Judith. *Sex, Sin, and Grace: Women's Experience and the Theologies of Reinhold Niebuhr and Paul Tillich.* Washington, D.C.: University Press of America, 1979.

Pogoloff, Stephen M. *Logos and Sophia: The Rhetorical Situation in 1 Corinthians.* Atlanta: Scholars Press, 1992.

Pojman, Louis. "The Ontological Argument." In his *Philosophy of Religion,* 3rd ed., 15-24. Belmont, Calif.: Wadsworth, 1998.

Polkinghorne, John. *One World: The Interaction of Science and Theology.* Princeton: Princeton University Press, 1987.

————. *Quarks, Chaos, and Christianity: Questions to Science and Religion.* London: SPCK, 2005.

Powell, Cyril H. *The Biblical Concept of Power.* London: Epworth, 1963.

Powers, Janet E. "Missionary Tongues." *JPT* 17 (2000): 39-55.

Powys, David. *"Hell": A Hard Look at a Hard Question.* Milton Keynes, and Waynesboro, Ga.: Paternoster, 1997.

Prenter, Regin. *Spiritus Creator: Luther's Concept of the Holy Spirit.* Philadelphia: Muhlenberg, 1953.

Price, H. H. *Belief.* New York: Humanities Press; London: Allen and Unwin, 1969.

Rahner, Karl. *Theological Investigations.* 23 vols. New York: Seabury Press and Crossroad; London: DLT, 1961-1992.

————. *The Shape of the Church to Come.* London: SPCK, 1974.

————. *Encyclopedia of Theology: A Concise Sacramentum Mundi.* London: Burns and Oates, 1975.

————. *Foundations of Christian Faith: An Introduction to the Idea of Christianity.* New York: Crossroad, 1978, 2004.

————. *Hearer of the Word.* London: Bloomsbury, 1994.

————. "The Angels: A Homily." At www.thevalueofsparrows.com.

Rahner, Karl, and W. Thüsing. *A New Christology.* London: Burns and Oates, 1980.

Ramsey, Ian T. *Religious Language: An Empirical Placing of Theological Phrases.* London: SCM, 1957.

Reid, J. K. S. *Our Life in Christ.* London: SCM, 1963.

Reno, R. R. *Genesis.* Grand Rapids: Brazos, 2010.

Reventlow, Henning Graf. *The Authority of the Bible and the Rise of the Modern World.* London: SCM, 1984.

Richards, Earl J. *First and Second Thessalonians.* Collegeville, Minn.: Glazier/Liturgical Press, 1995, 2007.

Richardson, Alan. *An Introduction to the Theology of the New Testament.* London: SCM, 1958.

Richardson, Neil. *Paul's Language about God.* JSNTSup 99. Sheffield: Sheffield Academic, 1994.

Richmond, James. *Ritschl: A Reappraisal.* New York: Collins, 1978.

Ricoeur, Paul. *Freud and Philosophy: An Essay in Interpretation.* New Haven: Yale University Press, 1970.

———. *Time and Narrative.* 3 vols. Chicago: University of Chicago Press, 1984-1988.

———. *Oneself as Another.* Chicago: University of Chicago Press, 1992.

Rigaux, Béda. *Saint Paul: Les Épitres aux Thessaloniciens.* Paris: Gabalda, 1956.

Ritschl, Albrecht. *The Christian Doctrine of Justification and Reconciliation.* 3 vols. Clifton, N.J.: Reference Book Publishers, 1966; orig. 1870-1874.

Robert, C. M. "Seymour, William Joseph." In *The New International Dictionary of Pentecostal and Charismatic Movements,* edited by Stanley M. Burgess and Eduard M. van der Maas, rev. ed., 1053-58. Grand Rapids: Zondervan, 2002-2003.

Robinson, H. Wheeler. *Baptist Principles.* 4th ed. London: Carey Kingsgate, 1960.

Robinson, J. A. T. *The Body: A Study in Pauline Theology.* SBT 5. London: SCM, 1952; Philadelphia: Westminster John Knox, 1977.

———. "Need Jesus Have Been Perfect?" In *Christ, Faith, and History,* edited by Stephen W. Sykes and J. P. Clayton. Cambridge: CUP, 1972.

———. *The Human Face of God.* London: SCM, 1973.

Robinson, James M. "Revelation as Word and History." In *Theology as History,* edited by J. M. Robinson and J. B. Cobb. New York: Harper and Row, 1967.

Rogers, Eugene F., Jr. *After the Spirit: A Constructive Pneumatology from Resources outside the Modern West.* London: SCM, 2005; Grand Rapids: Eerdmans, 2006.

Roth, Cecil, ed. *The Haggadah: New Edition with Notes.* London: Soncino Press, 1934.

Rowe, William. "An Examination of the Cosmological Argument." In *Philosophy of Religion: An Anthology,* edited by Louis Pojman, 16-25. Belmont, Calif.: Wadsworth, 1994.

Ruether, Rosemary Radford. *Sexism and God-Talk: Toward a Feminist Theology.* London: SCM, 1983.

Russell, D. S. *The Method and Message of Jewish Apocalyptic, 200 B.C.–A.D. 100.* London: SCM, 1964.

Ryle, Gilbert. *The Concept of the Mind.* London: Penguin, 1949, 1963.

———. *Dilemmas.* Cambridge: CUP, 1954.

Saiving, Valerie. "The Human Situation: A Feminine View." *JR* 40 (1960): 100-112.

Sanders, E. P. *Paul and Palestinian Judaism: A Comparison of Patterns of Religion.* London: SCM, 1977.

Sandnes, K. O. *Paul — One of the Prophets?* WUNT, ser. 2, 43. Tübingen: Mohr, 1991.

Schillebeeckx, Edward. *Jesus: An Experiment in Christology.* London: Collins, 1979.

Schleiermacher, Friedrich D. E. *On Religion: Speeches to Its Cultured Despisers.* London: Kegan Paul, Trench and Trübner, 1893.

———. *Hermeneutics: The Handwritten Manuscripts.* Missoula, Mont.: Scholars Press, 1977.

———. *The Christian Faith.* Edinburgh: T. & T. Clark, 1989; orig. 1821.

Schlier, Heinrich. *Principalities and Powers in the New Testament.* New York: Herder and Herder, 1961.

Schnackenburg, Rudolf. *God's Rule and Kingdom.* London: Nelson, 1963.

———. *Baptism in the Thought of St. Paul: A Study in Pauline Theology.* Oxford: Blackwell, 1964.

Schüssler-Fiorenza, Elizabeth. *In Memory of Her: A Feminist Theological Reconstruction of Christian Origins.* New York: Crossroad; London: SCM, 1983.

Schweitzer, Albert. *The Mysticism of Paul the Apostle.* London: Black, 1931.

———. *The Quest of the Historical Jesus.* 3rd ed. London: SCM, 1954.

Scott, C. Anderson. *Christianity according to St. Paul.* Cambridge: CUP, 1927; 2nd ed. 1961.

Scott, E. F. *The Spirit in the New Testament.* London: Hodder and Stoughton, 1924.

Searle, John R. *Expression and Meaning: Studies in the Theory of Speech Acts.* Cambridge: CUP, 1979.

Sennett, James E., ed. *The Analytic Theist: An Alvin Plantinga Reader.* Grand Rapids: Eerdmans, 1998.

Sepúlveda, Juan. "Indigenous Pentecostalism and the Chilean Experience." In *Pentecostals after a Century: Global Perspectives,* edited by A. H. Anderson and W. J. Hollenweger, 111-35. JPTSS 15. Sheffield: Sheffield Academic, 1999.

Sevenster, J. N. *Paul and Seneca.* Leiden: Brill, 1961. Pp. 84-102.

Shapland, C. R. B. *The Letters of St. Athanasius concerning the Holy Spirit.* London: Epworth, 1951.

Singer, Peter. *Animal Liberation.* Berkeley and Los Angeles: University of California Press, 1978.

———, ed. *In Defence of Animals.* New York: Blackwell, 1985.

Sjoberg, Erik. "*Rûach* in Palestine Judaism." In *TDNT* 6:375-89.

Smail, Thomas, and others. *The Love of Power, or, the Power of Love: A Careful Assessment of the Problems within the Charismatic and Word-of-Faith Movements.* Minneapolis: Bethany House, 1994.

Smalley, Stephen S. *1, 2, and 3 John.* Waco: Word, 1984.

Smeaton, George. *The Doctrine of the Holy Spirit.* London: Banner of Truth Trust, 1958.

Smith, C. Ryder. *The Bible Doctrine of Salvation: A Study of the Atonement.* London: Epworth, 1946.

———. *The Bible Doctrine of Man.* London: Epworth, 1951.

Soskice, Janet Martin. *Metaphor and Religious Language.* Oxford: Clarendon, 1987.

Spicq, C. *Agape in the New Testament.* 3 vols. London and St. Louis: Herder, 1963.

Spinoza, Benedict de. *Theological-Political Treatise.* Leiden: Brill, 1991.

Stanton, Graham N. *Jesus of Nazareth in New Testament Preaching.* Cambridge: CUP, 1974.

Stauffer, Ethelbert. *New Testament Theology.* London: SCM, 1955.

Stendahl, Krister. "Glossolalia — the New Testament Evidence." In Stendahl, *Paul among Jesus and the Gentiles,* 109-24. London: SCM, 1977.

Stowers, Stanley K. "Paul on the Use and Abuse of Reason." In *Greeks, Romans, Christians,* edited by D. L. Balch and others, 253-86. Minneapolis: Fortress, 1990.

Strawson, P. F. *Individuals: An Essay in Descriptive Metaphysics.* London: Methuen, 1959.

———. *Introduction to Logical Theory.* London: Methuen, 1963.

Strong, A. H. *Systematic Theology.* 3 vols. in one. London: Pickering and Inglis, 1907, 1965.

Stronstad, Roger. *The Charismatic Theology of St. Luke.* Peabody, Mass.: Hendrickson, 1984.

———. *The Prophethood of All Believers: A Study in Luke's Charismatic Theology.* JPTSS 16. Sheffield: Sheffield Academic, 1999.

Swete, Henry B. *The Holy Spirit in the New Testament.* London: Macmillan, 1909.

———. *The Holy Spirit in the Ancient Church.* London: Macmillan, 1912.

Swinburne, Richard. *The Coherence of Theism.* Oxford: Clarendon, 1977.

———. *The Existence of God.* Oxford: Clarendon, 1979.

Sykes, Stephen W., and J. P. Clayton, eds. *Christ, Faith, and History.* Cambridge: CUP, 1972.

Talbert, Charles H. *The Development of Christology during the First Hundred Years and Other Essays on Early Christian Christology.* Leiden: Brill, 2011.

Taylor, Richard. "The Cosmological Argument: A Defence." In Taylor, *Metaphysics,* 91-99. Englewood Cliffs, N.J.: Prentice-Hall, 1983.

Taylor, Vincent. *The Atonement in New Testament Teaching.* London: Epworth, 1940.

Temple, William. *Nature, Man, and God.* London: Macmillan, 1940.

Tennant, F. R. *The Origin and Propagation of Sin.* Cambridge: CUP, 1903.

———. *The Concept of Sin.* Cambridge: CUP, 1912.

———. *Philosophical Theology.* 2 vols. Cambridge: CUP, 1930.

TeSelle, Eugene. *Augustine the Theologian.* New York: Herder, 1970.

Theissen, Gerd. *Psychological Aspects of Pauline Theology.* Edinburgh: T. & T. Clark, 1987.

Thielicke, Helmut. *Theological Ethics.* Vol. 2, *Politics.* Grand Rapids: Eerdmans, 1979.

Thiselton, Anthony C. "The Parables as Language-Event: Some Comments on Fuchs' Hermeneutics in the Light of Linguistic Philosophy." *SJT* 23 (1970); reprinted in *Thiselton on Hermeneutics* (Grand Rapids: Eerdmans; Aldershot, UK: Ashgate, 2006), 417-40.

———. *The Two Horizons: New Testament Hermeneutics and Philosophical Description.* Grand Rapids: Eerdmans; Carlisle: Paternoster, 1980.

———. *New Horizons in Hermeneutics: The Theory and Practice of Transforming Biblical Reading.* London: Harper-Collins, 1992; Grand Rapids: Zondervan, 1992, 2012.

———. *The First Epistle to the Corinthians: A Commentary on the Greek Text.* NIGTC. Grand Rapids: Eerdmans, 2000.

———. *Thiselton on Hermeneutics.* Grand Rapids: Eerdmans; Aldershot, UK: Ashgate, 2006.

———. *The Hermeneutics of Doctrine.* Grand Rapids: Eerdmans, 2007.

————. *1 and 2 Thessalonians through the Centuries.* London: Wiley-Blackwell, 2011.

————. "Wisdom in the Jewish and Christian Scriptures." *Theology* 114 (2011): 163-72; and vol. 115 (2011): 1-9.

————. *Life after Death: A New Approach to the Last Things.* Grand Rapids: Eerdmans, 2012; otherwise entitled *The Last Things* (London: SPCK, 2012).

————. "Reception Theory, Jauss, and the Formative Power of Scripture." *SJT* 65 (2012): 289-308.

————. *The Holy Spirit in Biblical Teaching, through the Centuries, and Today.* Grand Rapids: Eerdmans; London: SPCK, 2013.

Thornton, Lionel S. *The Common Life in the Body of Christ.* 3rd ed. London: Dacre Press, 1950.

Thrall, Margaret. "The Pauline Use of *Syneidēsis*." *NTS* 14 (1967): 118-25.

Tilley, Terrence W. *The Evils of Theodicy.* Washington, D.C.: Georgetown University Press, 1991.

Tillich, Paul. *The Shaking of the Foundations.* New York: Scribner, 1948, 1962.

————. *Systematic Theology.* 3 vols. London: Nisbet, 1953, 1957, 1963.

Toland, John. *Christianity Not Mysterious.* New York: Garland, 1702.

Torrance, T. F. *The Trinitarian Faith.* Edinburgh: T. & T. Clark, 1995.

Towner, W. S. *Genesis.* Louisville: Westminster John Knox, 2001.

Tracy, David. *The Analogical Imagination: Christian Theology and the Culture of Pluralism.* New York: Crossroad, 1981.

Travis, Stephen H. *Christ and the Judgement of God: The Limits of Divine Revelation in New Testament Thought.* Milton Keynes: Paternoster; Peabody, Mass.: Hendrickson, 2008.

Trewett, Christine. *Montanism: Gender, Authority, and the New People Prophecy.* Cambridge: CUP, 1996.

Trible, Phyllis. *God and the Rhetoric of Sexuality.* Philadelphia: Fortress, 1978.

————. *Texts of Terror: Literary-Feminist Readings of Biblical Narratives.* Philadelphia: Fortress, 1984.

Trigg, J. W. *Origen: The Bible and Philosophy.* Atlanta: John Knox, 1983.

Turner, Max. *The Holy Spirit and Spiritual Gifts: Then and Now.* Carlisle: Paternoster, 1996.

————. *Power from on High: The Spirit in Israel's Restoration and Witness in Luke-Acts.* Sheffield: Sheffield Academic, 1996.

Tyndale, William. *A Pathway into the Holy Scripture.* Cambridge: CUP/Parker Society, 1848. Pp. 7-29.

Vanhoozer, Kevin. *Is There a Meaning in This Text? The Bible, the Reader, and the Morality of Literary Knowledge.* Grand Rapids: Zondervan, 1998.

————. *The Drama of Doctrine: A Canonical-Linguistic Approach to Christian Theology.* Louisville: Westminster John Knox, 2005.

Van Pelt, M. V., and W. C. Kaiser. "*Rûach.*" In *NIDOTTE* 3:1073-78.

Vanstone, W. H. *Love's Endeavour, Love's Expense: The Response of Being to the Love of God.* London: DLT, 2007; orig. 1977.

Vatican II. *Gaudium et Spes.* In *Documents of Vatican II,* edited by Austin P. Flannery. Grand Rapids: Eerdmans, 1975.

Bibliography

————. *Lumen Gentium* 1:1, "The Mystery of the Church." In *Documents of Vatican II,* edited by Austin P. Flannery. Grand Rapids: Eerdmans, 1975.

Vico, G. B. *On the Study Methods of Our Time.* Indianapolis: Bobbs-Merrill, 1965.

Vielhauer, Philipp. *Oikodomē: Das Bild vom Bau in der christlichen Literatur vom Neuen Testament bis Klement.* Karlsruhe: Harrassowitz, 1940.

Vincent, Thomas. *Fire and Brimstone in Hell.* 1670. Reprinted as e-book compiled by the Bible Truth Forum.

Volf, Miroslav. *Free of Charge: Giving and Forgiving in a Culture Stripped of Grace.* Grand Rapids: Zondervan, 2005.

Von Rad, Gerhard. *"Shālōm."* In *TDNT* 2:402-6.

————. *Genesis: A Commentary.* Philadelphia: Westminster, 1961.

————. *Old Testament Theology.* 2 vols. Edinburgh: Oliver and Boyd, 1962, 1965.

Vriezen, Th. C. *An Outline of Old Testament Theology.* Oxford: Blackwell, 1962.

Wainwright, Geoffrey. *Doxology: A Systematic Theology.* London: Epworth, 1980.

Waltke, Bruce K., with C. J. Fredericks. *Genesis: A Commentary.* Grand Rapids: Zondervan, 2001.

Walvoord, J. F. *Armageddon: Oil and the Middle East.* 2nd ed. Grand Rapids: Zondervan, 1990.

Webster, John. "Systematic Theology." In *The Oxford Handbook of Systematic Theology,* edited by John Webster, Kathryn Tanner, and Iain Torrance, 1-15. Oxford: OUP, 2007.

————. *Holy Scripture: A Dogmatic Sketch.* Cambridge: CUP, 2003.

————. *The Domain of the Word: Scripture and Theological Reason.* London and New York: Bloomsbury, 2012.

Webster, John, Kathryn Tanner, and Iain Torrance, eds. *The Oxford Handbook of Systematic Theology.* Oxford: OUP, 2007.

Weil, Simone. *Waiting for God.* London: Routledge, 1974; orig. 1939.

Weiss, Johannes. *Earliest Christianity: A History of the Period A.D. 30–150.* 2 vols. New York: Harper, 1959; orig. 1937.

Welborn, L. L. "On Discord in Corinth: 1 Cor. 1–4 and Ancient Politics." *JBL* 106 (1987): 85-111; also in Welborn, *Politics and Rhetoric in the Corinthian Epistles* (Macon, Ga.: Mercer University Press, 1997), 1-42.

Wenham, Gordon. *Genesis 1–15.* Waco: Word, 1987.

Wennberg, Robert N. *God, Humans, and Animals: An Invitation to Enlarge Our Moral Universe.* Grand Rapids: Eerdmans, 2003.

Wesley, John. "On the Holy Spirit: Sermon 141." 1736. Edited by George Lyons. Christian Classics Ethereal Library.

Westcott, B. F. *The Epistle to the Hebrews: The Greek Text.* New York and London: Macmillan, 1903.

Westermann, Claus. *Genesis 1–11: A Commentary.* Minneapolis: Augsburg, 1984.

Whiteley, D. E. H. *The Theology of St. Paul.* Oxford: Blackwell, 1964, 1971.

Wiesel, Elie. *Night.* New York: Hill and Wang, 1960, 1969.

Wildberger, Hans. *Isaiah 1–12.* Hermeneia/Continental Commentary. Philadelphia: Fortress, 1991.

Wiles, Maurice F. "Does Christology Rest on a Mistake?" In *Christ, Faith, and History,* edited by Stephen W. Sykes and J. P. Clayton. Cambridge: CUP, 1972.

Wiley, Tatha. *Original Sin.* New York: Paulist, 2002.

Wilkinson, David. *Christian Eschatology and the Physical Universe.* London: Continuum and T. & T. Clark, 2010.

Williams, Catrin H., and Christopher Rowland, eds. *John's Gospel and Intimations of Apocalyptic.* London: Bloomsbury, 2013.

Williams, Norman P. *The Ideas of the Fall and of Original Sin.* London: Longmans, Green, 1929.

Williams, Rowan D. *Arius: Heresy and Tradition.* Grand Rapids: Eerdmans, 2001.

Wilson, Stephen G. *The Gentiles and the Gentile Mission in Luke-Acts.* SNTSMS 23. Cambridge: CUP, 1973.

Wink, Walter. *Naming the Powers: The Language of Power in the New Testament.* Philadelphia: Fortress, 1984.

———. *Unmasking the Powers: The Invisible Forces That Determine Human Existence.* Philadelphia: Fortress, 1986.

———. *Engaging the Powers: Discernment and Resistance in a World of Domination.* Philadelphia: Fortress, 1992.

Witherington, Ben, III. *Jesus the Sage: The Pilgrimage of Wisdom.* Edinburgh: T. & T. Clark, 1994.

———. *1 and 2 Thessalonians: A Socio-Rhetorical Commentary.* Grand Rapids: Eerdmans, 2006.

Wittgenstein, Ludwig. *Philosophical Investigations.* 2nd ed. Oxford: Blackwell, 1958.

———. *Zettel.* Oxford: Blackwell, 1967.

———. *The Blue and Brown Books: Preliminary Studies for the "Philosophical Investigations."* 2nd ed. Oxford: Blackwell, 1969.

Wolterstorff, Nicholas. "Contemporary Views of the State." *Christian Scholar's Review* 3 (1974).

———. *Divine Discourse: Philosophical Reflections on the Claim That God Speaks.* Cambridge: CUP, 1995.

———. *Justice, Rights, and Wrongs.* Princeton: Princeton University Press, 2008.

Wright, N. T. *Jesus and the Victory of God.* London: SPCK, 1996.

———. *The Resurrection of the Son of God.* London: SPCK; Minneapolis: Fortress, 2003.

———. *The Last Word: Scripture and the Authority of God — Getting beyond the Bible Wars.* New York: Harper One, 2005.

———. *Surprised by Hope: Rethinking Heaven, the Resurrection, and the Mission of the Church.* London: SPCK, 2007.

———. *Paul and the Faithfulness of God.* 2 vols. London: SPCK, 2013.

Yinger, Kent L. *Paul, Judaism, and Judgement according to Deeds.* SNTSMS 105. Cambridge: CUP, 1999.

Yoder, John Howard. *The Politics of Jesus.* Grand Rapids: Eerdmans, 1972; 2nd ed. 1994.

Zizioulas, John D. *Being as Communion: Studies in Personhood and the Church.* New York: St. Vladimir's Seminary Press, 1985, 1997.

Zwiep, Arie W. *Christ, the Spirit, and the Community of God.* WUNT, ser. 2, 293. Tübingen: Mohr, 2010.

Zwingli, Ulrich. *On the Lord's Supper.* In *Zwingli and Bullinger,* edited by G. W. Bromiley. LCC. Philadelphia: Westminster; London: SCM, 1953.

411

Index of Names

Index of Names

416

Index of Subjects

Bold italic page numbers indicate important pages; bold headings alone indicate headings introducing subheadings.

Apostolic Faith Mission, Azusa Street,
291
apostolic: parousia, 345; succession,
320-21; tradition, 100, 206-7
appeasement, 201
argumentation, 4-5, 6
art, artist, 56, 82
aseity, 66
aspective terms, 142
Assemblies of God, 292-93
assurance, 79, 221, 341
atheism, xii, 7, 40, *80-91*; avowed,
8; explicit, 80; and mechanistic
account, worldview, 82, 86
atonement, the, 75, *203-30*; centrality
of, 369; complementary models of,
195-202; comprehensive view of,
218; debate about, 194; exemplarist
or moral influence theory of, *217-19*,
223; triumphalist view of, 225; word
picture of, 194
Augsburg Confession, 165
Auschwitz, 78
authority, 261; of the will, 175
avenger of blood (Heb. *gō'el haddam*),
185

Babel, 274
Babylon, 382
baptism, *325-30*; anchored in work of
Christ, 328, 336; eschatological aspect of, 328; household, 329; infant,
160, *328-30*; as initiation event, 275,
327; into one body, 293; in Paul,
327-28; as pleading guilty, 371; as
salvation event, 327; and sons and
daughters of Christian parents, 330;
theology of, *326-30*
baptism in the Spirit, 275, 291, 293; initial evidence of, 292-93; subsequent
to becoming Christian, 308
baptism of Jesus: 34, 232, 236, 273; as
preparation of people of God, 236
"because/in whom" (Gk. *eph' hō*), 152
being-in-relationship, 309
believing as disposition, 17

Bible, authority of, 12, *93-95*; criticism
of, 95; reasoning of, 94
biological processes, 339. *See also*
Modern era
birth from above, 198
bishops or overseers, 318; as above
reproach, 323; as angels, 306; college
of, 322; collegial or collaborative, 325;
as guardians, 319; level-headed leaders, 323; managers of a household,
322; tolerant and courteous, 323
body (Gk. *sōma*), *142-43*; animated
by Holy Spirit, *361-63*; decreasing
capacities of, 361; obedience of, 143,
ordinary, 363; spiritual, 341
bond of union and fellowship, 336. *See
also* Holy Spirit
Book of Concord, 165
born from above, 286
Brahman, 99
Bread of Life, 198
bride of Christ, 315, 377, *381-82*
burnt offering *('olah)*, 193

call to discipleship, 238
Calvin, caricature of, 221
Cappadocian Fathers, 225
Cartesian individualism, 312
category mistake, 141, 258
Catholic Apostolic Church, 306
causal chain, causality, *61-71*, 80; contingent cause, 64; efficient cause, 64
cause and effect, internal process of,
367-68, 71; of law and history, 372
cemeteries, 338
certain knowledge, certainty, *72-73*, 312
cessationalists, 280
chance and necessity, 69
cherubim, 102, 108, 112
child abuse, 194
childish dependency, 85, 155
children and simple readers, 220
chosen individuals, 267
Christ: as agent of creation, 250;
all-sufficiency of work of, 340, 389;
blood of, 204, 218; Christ-centered

Index of Scripture and Other Ancient Sources

434